Mastering Dyalog APL
A Complete Introduction to Dyalog APL

Bernard Legrand

With most grateful acknowledgements to the contributors:

Kim S.	Andreasen
Daniel	Baronet
Gitte	Christensen
Peter	Donnelly
Morten	Kromberg
John	Scholes
Adrian	Smith
Tim JA.	Smith

Published by Dyalog Limited

First Edition November 2009

Dyalog Limited

http://www.dyalog.com

ISBN : 978-0-9564638-0-7

Contents

INTRODUCTION - WILL YOU PLAY APL WITH ME? 1

Will You Follow Us? 1

Our First Steps into APL's Magic World 4

Array Processing 5

More Symbols 7

Most Symbols Have a Double Meaning 8

Reduction Unifies Traditional Notations 9

Let's Write Our First Programs 10

Indexing 11

Calculating Without Writing Programs 12

Friendly Binary Data 14

A Touch of Modern Math 16

A Powerful Search Function 17

After Values, Let Us Process Shapes 20

Back to Primary School 22

There Is a Lot to Discover Yet 25

FAQ 28

CHAPTER A: GETTING STARTED 31

1 - Installing the Software **31**
1.1 Installation 31
1.2 First Contact 33
1.3 Demonstration Files 36

2 - Working with This Tutorial **40**

CHAPTER B: DATA AND VARIABLES 43

1 - Simple Numeric Values **43**
1.1 Our First Operations 43
1.2 Variables 44
1.3 Operations on Variables 46

2 - Arrays of Items **47**
2.1 Create a List or a Matrix 47
2.2 Special Cases with Reshape 48
2.3 Multi-dimensional Arrays 49

3 - Shape, Rank, and Vocabulary **50**
3.1 Shape and Rank 50
3.2 Scaling Down the Ranks 51
3.3 Vocabulary 51
3.4 Beware! 52

4 - Simple Character Values **53**
4.1 Character Vectors and Scalars 53
4.2 Character Arrays 55

5 - Indexing **56**
5.1 Traditional Vector Indexing 56
5.2 The Shape of the Result 57
5.3 Array Indexing 58
5.4 Convention 60
5.5 Warnings 61
5.6 The Index Function 62

6 - Mixed and Nested Arrays **63**
6.1 Mixed Arrays 63
6.2 Four Important Remarks 64
6.3 Nested Arrays 64
6.4 DISPLAY 66
6.5 Be Simple! 68
6.6 That's *Not* All, Folks! 70

7 - Empty Arrays **70**

8 - Workspaces and Commands **71**
8.1 The Active Workspace 72
8.2 The Libraries 73
8.3 Load a WS 74
8.4 File Extensions 75
8.5 Merge Workspaces 76
8.6 Exiting APL 78
8.7 Contents of a WS 78
8.8 Our First System Commands 79
Exercises 81

The Specialist's Section **83**
Spe-1 Variable Names 83
Spe-2 Representation of Numbers 83
Spe-3 The Shape of the Result of Indexing 84
Spe-4 Multiple Usage of an Index 86
Spe-5 A Problem With Using Reshape (⍴) 86
Spe-6 Monadic Index (⌷) 87

CHAPTER C: SOME PRIMITIVE FUNCTIONS **89**

1 - Definitions **89**

2 - Some Scalar Dyadic Functions **90**
2.1 Definition and Examples 90
2.2 Division By Zero 92
2.3 Power 92
2.4 Maximum & Minimum 92
2.5 Relationship 93
2.6 Residue 94

3 - Order of Evaluation **94**

4 - Monadic Scalar Functions **96**
4.1 The Four Basic Symbols 96
4.2 Other Scalar Monadic Functions 97

5 - Processing Binary Data **99**
5.1 Membership 99
5.2 Binary Algebra 100
5.3 Without 102

6 - Processing Nested Arrays **102**
6.1 Scalar *vs.* Non-scalar Functions 102
6.2 Be Careful With Shape/Type Compatibility 103

7 - Reduction **104**
7.1 Presentation 104
7.2 Definition 105
7.3 Reduction of Binary Data 106
7.4 Reduction of Nested Arrays 107
7.5 *Application 1* 107
7.6 *Application 2* 108

8 - Axis Specification **109**
8.1 Totals in an Array 109
8.2 The Shape of the Result 111
8.3 Special Notations 111

9 - Our First Program **112**

10 - Concatenation **113**
10.1 Concatenating Vectors 113
10.2 Concatenating Other Arrays 114
10.3 Concatenating Scalars 117
10.4 Special Notations 117

11 - Replication **118**
11.1 Basic Approach: Compression 118
11.2 Replication 120
11.3 Scalar Left Argument 120
11.4 Special Notations 121

12 - Position (*Index Of*) **121**
12.1 Discovery 121
12.2 *Application 3* 123

13 - Index Generator **125**
13.1 Basic Usage 125
13.2 *Application 4* 126
13.3 Comparison of *Membership* and *Index Of* 127
13.4 Idioms 130
13.5 *Application 5* 131
13.6 *Application 6* 132

14 - Ravel **132**

15 - Empty Vectors and Black Holes **134**
Exercises 136

The Specialist's Section **140**
Spe - 1 Division Control - ⎕DIV 140
Spe - 2 Derived Functions 141
Spe - 3 Nor & Nand 141
Spe - 4 Index Generator of Arrays 142
Spe - 5 Ravel With Axis 143
Spe - 6 Residue 145

CHAPTER D: USER DEFINED FUNCTIONS **147**

1 - Landmarks **147**
1.1 Some Definitions 147
1.2 Configure Your Environment 148

2 - Single-Line Direct Functions **152**
2.1 Definition 152
2.2 Unnamed D-Fns 153
2.3 Modifying The Code 153

3 - Procedural Functions **154**
3.1 A First Example 154
3.2 Local Names 156
3.3 Miscellaneous 159
3.4 Second Example 161
Exercises 164
3.5 Calls to Sub-Functions 166

4 - Flow Control **167**
4.1 Overview 167
4.2 Conditional Execution 169
4.3 Disparate Conditions 174
4.4 Predefined Loops 176
4.5 Conditional Loops 178
4.6 Exception Control 181
4.7 Endless Loops 182

5 - Traditional Flow Control **186**
5.1 Conditional Execution 186
5.2 Multiple Conditions 190
5.3 Modern and Traditional Controls Cooperate 192

6 - Input, Output, and Format **193**
6.1 Some Input and Output Methods 193
6.2 Format 194
6.3 Displaying Intermediate Results 196
6.4 Using Global Variables 197
6.5 Exchanging Data With an Excel Worksheet 198
6.6 Reading or Writing a Text File 199
6.7 Printing Results on a Printer 201
6.8 Using a Graphical User Interface 202
6.9 Requesting Values From the Keyboard 203

7 - Syntax Considerations **205**
7.1 Comments & Statement Separators 205
7.2 Why Should a Function Return a Result? 206
7.3 Different Types of Functions 207
7.4 Nested Argument and Result 211
7.5 Choice of Names 212

8 - Multi-Line Direct Functions **213**
8.1 Characteristics 213
8.2 Guards 215
8.3 Syntax Considerations 215

9 - Recursion **217**

10 - Synonyms **218**

11 - About the Text Editor **220**
- 11.1 What Can You Edit? 220
- 11.2 What Can You Do? 221
- 11.3 Undo, Redo, Replay 222
- 11.4 Miscellaneous 224

12 - SALT **225**
- Exercises 227

The Specialist's Section **230**
- Spe-1 Shadowed Names 230
- Spe-2 Loop Control 231
- Spe-3 Labels and the Branch Arrow 231
- Spe-4 Other Conditional Execution 233
- Spe-5 Name Category of Synonyms 234
- Spe-6 Bare Output 235
- Spe-7 :InEach 236

CHAPTER E: FIRST AID KIT 239

1 - When an Error Occurs **240**
- 1.1 Our First Error 240
- 1.2 Cascade of Errors 243
- 1.3 Information and Actions 249
- 1.4 Why Should You Reset Your State Indicator? 250

2 - Most Frequent Error Messages **252**
- 2.1 Execution Errors 252
- 2.2 Some Other Errors 257

3 - Trace Tools **258**
- 3.1 Invoke and Use the Tracer 258
- 3.2 Choose Your Configuration 261
- 3.3 Break-points and Trace-controls 262
- 3.4 System Functions 265
- Exercises 267

The Specialist's Section **268**
- Spe-1 Value Errors 268
- Spe-2)SINL 269
- Spe-3 Namespaces and Indicators 269

CHAPTER F: EXECUTE & FORMAT CONTROL 273

1 - Execute **273**
1.1 Definition 273
1.2 Some Typical Uses 274
1.3 Make Things Simple 276

2 - The Format Primitive **276**
2.1 Monadic Format 276
2.2 Dyadic Format 277

3 - The ⎕FMT System Function **280**
3.1 Monadic Use 280
3.2 Dyadic Use 281
3.3 Qualifiers and Affixtures 288

The Specialist's Section **292**
Spe-1 Execute 292
Spe-2 Formatting data 295

CHAPTER G: WORKING ON DATA SHAPE 299

1 - Take and Drop **299**
1.1 Take and Drop Applied to Vectors 299
1.2 Three Basic Applications 302
1.3 Take and Drop Applied to Arrays 303

2 - Laminate **305**
2.1 Application to Vectors and Scalars 307
2.2 Applications 308

3 - Expand **310**
3.1 Basic Use 310
3.2 Extended Definition 310
3.3 Expand Along First Axis 311

4 - Reverse and Transpose **312**

5 - Rotate **314**
5.1 Rotate Vectors 314
5.2 Rotate Higher-Rank Arrays 315

6 - Dyadic Transpose **316**
Exercises 319

The Specialist's Section **322**
Spe - 1 More About Laminate 322
Spe - 2 Dyadic Transpose 322

CHAPTER H: SPECIAL SYNTAX 325

1 - Modified Assignment **325**

2 - Multiple Assignment **326**

3 - Selective Assignment **327**
3.1 Quick Overview 327
3.2 Available Primitives 328

CHAPTER I: NESTED ARRAYS (CONTINUED) 331

1 - First Contact **331**
1.1 Definitions 331
1.2 Enclose & Disclose 332
1.3 More About DISPLAY 336

2 - Depth & Match **338**
2.1 Enclosing Scalars 338
2.2 Depth 339
2.3 Match & Natch 341

3 - Each **342**
3.1 Definition and Examples 342
3.2 Three Compressions! 345

4 - Processing Nested Arrays **346**
4.1 Scalar Dyadic Functions 346
4.2 Juxtaposition vs. Catenation 346
4.3 Characters and Numbers 348
4.4 Some More Operations 350
Exercises 353

5 - Split and Mix **354**
5.1 Basic Use 354
5.2 Axis Specification 355

6 - First & Type **357**

7 - Prototype, Fill Item **358**

8 - Pick **361**
8.1 - Definition 361
8.2 - Beware! 362
8.3 - Important 363
8.4 - Selective Assignment 364
8.5 - An Idiom 365

9 – Partition & Partitioned Enclose **365**
9.1 The Dyalog Definition 366
9.2 The IBM Definition 367

10 - Union & Intersection **369**

11 - Enlist **369**
Exercises 371

The Specialist's Section **372**
Spe-1 Compatibility and Migration Level 372
Spe-2 The IBM Partition on Matrices 375
Spe-3 Ambiguous Representation 376
Spe-4 Pick Inside a Scalar 376

CHAPTER J: OPERATORS 377

1 - Definitions **377**
1.1 Operators & Derived Functions 377
1.2 Sequences of Operators 378
1.3 List of Built-in Operators 379

2 - More About Some Operators You Already Know **379**
2.1 Reduce 379
2.2 *n*-Wise Reduce 380
2.3 Axis 382

3 - Scan **383**
3.1 Definition 383
3.2 Scan with Binary Values 384
3.3 Applications 385

4 - Outer Product **386**
4.1 Definition 386
4.2 Extensions 387
4.3 *Applications* 389
Exercise 393

5 - Inner Product **394**
5.1 A Concrete Situation 394
5.2 Definitions 396
5.3 Typical Uses of Inner Products 396
5.4 Other Uses of Inner Product 405
5.5 *Application* 406
Exercises 408

6 - Compose **410**
6.1 Form 1 411
6.2 Form 2 412
6.3 Form 3 412
6.4 Form 4 413

7 - Commute **414**

8 - Power Operator **415**
8.1 - Elementary Use (Form 1) 415
8.2 - Conditional Execution (Form 1) 416
8.3 - Left Argument (All Forms) 417
8.4 - Inverse Function 417
8.5 - Fixpoint, and Use with Defined Operators 418

9 - Spawn **418**
9.1 Main Features 418
9.2 Special Syntax 420

10 - User-Defined Operators **421**
10.1 Definition Modes 421
10.2 Some Basic Examples 422

The Specialist's Section **424**
Spe-1 Reduction Applied to Empty Vectors 424
Spe-2 Index Origin and Axis operator 426
Spe-3 The Power Operator 427
Spe-4 Defined Operators 429
Spe-5 The Result of an Inverse Function 429

CHAPTER K: MATHEMATICAL FUNCTIONS 431

1 - Sorting and Searching Data **431**
1.1 Sorting Numeric Data 431
1.2 Sorting Characters 433
1.3 Finding Values 435

2 - Encode and Decode **436**
2.1 Some Words of Theory 436
2.2 Using Decode & Encode 438
2.3 Applications 441

3 - Randomised Values **444**
3.1 Deal: Dyadic Usage 445
3.2 Roll: Monadic Use 445
3.3 Derived Uses 446

4 - Some More Maths **447**
4.1 Logarithms 447
4.2 Factorial & Binomial 448
4.3 Trigonometry 449
4.4 GCD and LCM 450
4.5 Set Union and Intersection 451

5 - Domino **452**
5.1 Some Definitions 452
5.2 Matrix Inverse 453
5.3 Matrix Division 455
5.4 Two or Three Steps in Geometry 455
5.5 Least Squares Fitting 457
Exercises 461

The Specialist's Section **463**
Spe - 1 Encode and Decode 463
Spe - 2 Random Link 466
Spe - 3 Gamma and Beta Functions 468
Spe - 4 Domino and Rectangular Matrices 468

CHAPTER L: SYSTEM INTERFACES 473

1 - Overview **473**
1.1 Commands, System Variables, and System Functions 473
1.2 Common Properties 474
1.3 Organisation 475

2 - Workspace Management **475**
2.1)WSID & ⎕WSID Workspace Identification 476
2.2 ⎕LX Startup Expression 477
2.3)LOAD,)XLOAD & ⎕LOAD Load a Workspace 478
2.4)COPY,)PCOPY & ⎕CY Import Objects 479
2.5)LIB Explore a Workspace Library 480
2.6)CLEAR & ⎕CLEAR Clear the Active Workspace 480
2.7)SAVE & ⎕SAVE Save a Workspace 481
2.8 ⎕WA Memory Space Available 482

3 - Object Management **482**
3.1)VARS,)FNS,)OPS,)OBS & ⎕NL Object Lists 482
3.2 ⎕NC Name Category 485
3.3)ERASE & ⎕EX Delete Objects 486
3.4 ⎕SIZE Object Size 487

4 - Environment Control & Information **488**
4.1 ⎕TS Current Date & Time 488
4.2 ⎕PP Print Precision 488
4.3 ⎕IO Index Origin 489
4.4 ⎕AI Account Information 490
4.5 ⎕PFKEY Programmable Function Keys 491

5 - Function Definition and Processing **493**
5.1)ED & ⎕ED Edit Objects 493
5.2 ⎕CR, ⎕NR, ⎕VR & ⎕OR Function Representations 493
5.3 ⎕FX Function Creation 496
5.4 ⎕SHADOW Name Shadowing 497
5.5 ⎕LOCK Locking a Function 497
5.6 ⎕REFS Internal References 498
5.7 ⎕AT Function Attributes 498

6 - Debugging and Event Trapping **500**

7 - Calculation Control **501**
7.1 Already Studied 501
7.2 ⎕CT Comparison Tolerance 501
7.3 ⎕DL Delay 503

8 - Character Processing, Input/Output **503**
8.1 ⎕AV & ⎕AVU Atomic Vectors 503
8.2 ⎕UCS Unicode Conversions 504
8.3 ⎕TC Terminal Control 504
8.4 ⎕A & ⎕D Alphabet & Digits 505
8.5 ⎕NULL Null Item 505

9 - Miscellaneous **507**
9.1 ⎕OFF &)OFF Quit APL 507
9.2 ⎕SH, ⎕CMD,)SH &)CMD Host System Commands 507
9.3 ⎕PW Page Width 508

The Specialist's Section **509**
Spe-1 Commands vs. System Functions 509
Spe-2 ⎕SAVE 510
Spe-3)CONTINUE Save & Continue 511
Spe-4 ⎕OR 511
Spe-5 ⎕VFI Verify and Fix Input 512
Spe-6 ⎕RTL Response Time Limit 513
Spe-7 ⎕MONITOR Execution Monitoring 514
Spe-8 System Variables vs. System Functions 516

CHAPTER M: EVENT HANDLING 517

1 - Diagnostic Tools **518**

2 - Event Trapping **518**
2.1 Event Numbers / Event Messages 519
2.2 `:Trap / :Else / :EndTrap` 520
2.3 `⎕TRAP` 522
2.4 Beware of These Errors 527
2.5 Neutralise the Traps 530

3 - Event Simulation **530**
3.1 `⎕SIGNAL` Example 532

CHAPTER N: FILE PROCESSING 535

1 - Component Files **536**
1.1 First Steps 536
1.2 Utility Functions 540
1.3 Shared Files 544
1.4 How to Queue File Operations 551

2 - Data Representation **554**
2.1 Representation of Values 554
2.2 Representation of Variables 557

3 - Native Files **559**
3.1 Similarities and Differences 559
3.2 Basic Operations 561

4 - External Variables **566**

The Specialist's Section **569**
Spe-1 Component Files 569
Spe-2 Native Files 572

CHAPTER O: NAMESPACES 577

1 - Simple Namespaces **577**
1.1 Introduction 577
1.2 Use the Contents of a Namespace 583

2 - More about References **588**
2.1 Namespace References 588
2.2 Display Form 591

3 - Arrays of Refs **592**
3.1 Create an Array 592
3.2 Indexing Arrays of Refs 594

4 - The Session Namespace **594**

The Specialist's Section **597**
Spe - 1 The Dot as a Syntactic Element 597
Spe - 2 State Indicators 598
Spe - 3 Evaluation of Statements 598
Spe - 4 The Dyalog Workspace Explorer 600
Spe - 5 Control of Exported Functions 601
Spe - 6 Retrieving a Namespace Source 602

CHAPTER P: GRAPHICAL USER INTERFACE **603**

1 - Guidelines **603**
1.1 Terminology and Options 603
1.2 Create a Simple Dialog Box 607
1.3 Get Information 610
1.4 Changing Properties 611
1.5 Make It Work 612

2 - Call-Back Functions **613**
2.1 Discovery 613
2.2 The Arguments of a Call-Back Function 618
2.3 The Result of a Call-Back Function 622
2.4 Improve It 625
2.5 Tracing Call-Back Functions 628

3 - Selection Tools **628**
3.1 List 628
3.2 Combo 631

4 - Colours, Fonts, and Root **633**
4.1 Colours 633
4.2 Fonts 633
4.3 Properties of the Root Object 636

5 - Improve Your User Interface **639**
5.1 Default Keys 639
5.2 Enqueuing Events and Using Methods 640
5.3 Activating Objects 641
5.4 Form Appearance 642

6 - Menus **644**

7 - The Grid Object **646**
7.1 Geometry & Titles 647
7.2 Cell Types 648
7.3 Interaction with a Grid 653
7.4 Example 654
7.5 Multi-Level Titles 658
7.6 Some Additional Properties 660

8 - Using Printers **661**
8.1 The Printer Object 661
8.2 Printer Management 664

9 - And Also ... **667**

The Specialist's Section **669**
Spe-1 Lists of Properties, Methods, Events 669
Spe-2 Different Syntaxes 671
Spe-3 Using Classes 672

CHAPTER Q: INTERFACES **675**

1 - Introduction **675**

2 - OLE Interface with Excel **676**
2.1 Introduction 676
2.2 Create, Fill, and Save a Workbook 677
2.3 Open and Process a Workbook 680
2.4 A Simple Example 683

3 - Name Association **686**
3.1 Introduction 686
3.2 Detailed Syntax 688
3.3 See How It Works 690

CHAPTER R: SALT 693

1 - Introduction **693**
1.1 Why a Source Code Management System? 693
1.2 Using Script Files 697
1.3 Updating a Script From the APL Session 700

2 - Version Management **702**
2.1 Creating and Using Versions 702
2.2 File Management 705
2.3 Comparing Scripts 707

3 - Settings **709**

The Specialist's Section **711**

CHAPTER S: PUBLISHING TOOLS 713

1 - NewLeaf **714**
1.1 Getting Started 714
1.2 Frames and Text 715
1.3 Fonts 720
1.4 Tables 722
1.5 The Page Designer 726
1.6 More Tools, Better Quality 735

2 - RainPro **738**
2.1 Getting started 738
2.2 Multiple Bar Chart 740
2.3 Scattered Points 744
2.4 Min-Max Vertical Lines 750
2.5 Polar Representations 753
2.6 Multiple Charts 754
2.7 There is Much More To Explore! 756

CHAPTER X: SOLUTIONS 757

Chapter B 757
Chapter C 758
Chapter D 761
Chapter G 765
Chapter I 767
Chapter J 768
Chapter K 771

APPENDICES 773

Appendix 1 : Scalar Functions 773

Appendix 2 : Invoking the Editor 774

Appendix 3 : Selective Assignment 775

Appendix 4 : Dyalog APL Operators 776

Appendix 5 : Identity Items 777

Appendix 6 : Event Numbers 778

Appendix 7 : System Variables and Functions 780

Appendix 8 : System Commands 783

Appendix 9 : Symbolic Index 784

INDEX M-789

Introduction - Will You Play APL With Me?

Will You Follow Us?

We would like to have you discover a new land, a land where people who may or may not be specialists in programming can process their data, build computerised applications, and take pleasure in using a programming language which is an extremely elegant and powerful tool of thought.

Beware: Dyalog APL is Addictive!

Among the hundreds of programming languages which have been created, most of them share the same fundamentals, the same basic instruction set, approximately the same functions, and by and large the same methods to control the logic of a program. This greatly influences the way people imagine and build solutions to computing problems. Because the languages are so similar, the solutions are similar. Does it mean that these are the only ways of solving problems? Of course not!

Dyalog APL is there to open doors, windows, and minds, prove that original new methods do exist, and that mathematics is not limited to four basic operations. Using APL will expand and extend the range of mental models that you use to solve problems, but beware:

Once you are hooked on APL, there is a real risk that you will no longer accept the limitations of "traditional" programming languages.

Installation and Keyboard

If you do not have access to a computer with Dyalog APL installed, you should still be able to gain an appreciation of the language from these pages and, we hope, enjoy the experience.

If you have installed Dyalog, not only can you read this book, but you can also experiment on your own computer using the examples below, and invent your own data and calculations.

If you have a copy of Dyalog APL, install it as explained in the User Guide. Just run the installation program and accept all the defaults; there is no need to change anything.

You might like to refer to section A-1 for additional installation hints.

As you will see in the following pages, APL uses special symbols, like ⍉, ⍴, and ↓, which you enter using a special keyboard layout.

You will not need all of the special symbols to read the following pages. The picture below illustrates a cut-down version of the UK keyboard layout, with only the APL symbols that are referred to in this introduction. They are shown on a grey background. The US keyboard is slightly different, but the symbols we need are positioned identically. The full keyboard layout is shown in the User Guide.

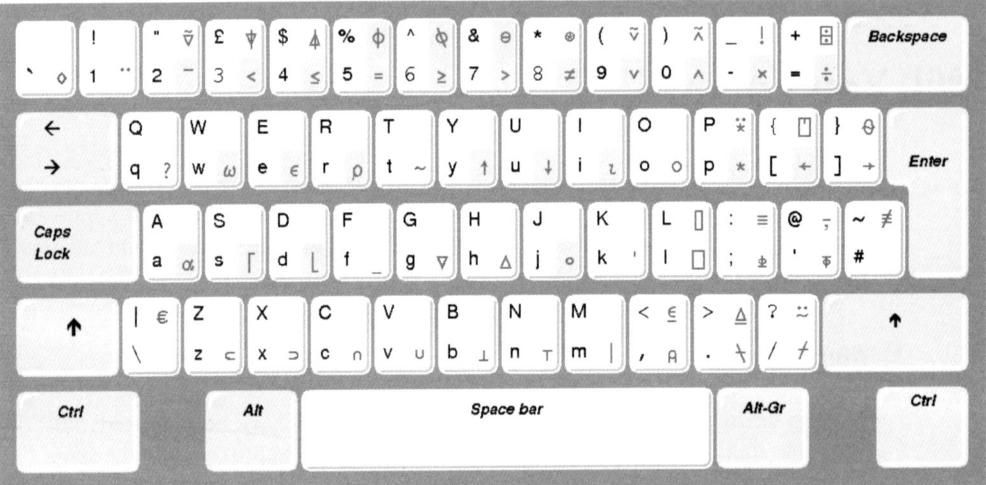

Here is how the keyboard is to be used:

- All the standard English letters, numerals and symbols are typed as usual.
- The majority of the APL symbols are obtained by pressing the "*Ctrl*" key, in conjunction with another key. For example, to obtain ⍴, you must press *Ctrl* and R. From now on, this keystroke will be identified as "*Ctrl*+R". On the keyboard layout illustrated above, the symbols that you enter this way are printed at the bottom-right corner of each key.
- Most other APL symbols are obtained by simultaneously pressing "*Ctrl*" and "*Shift*" and then the appropriate key. For example, to obtain ⍉, you must press *Ctrl* and *Shift* and 6. From now on, this keystroke will be identified as "*Ctrl*+*Shift*+6". On the keyboard layout illustrated above, the symbols that you enter this way are printed at the top-right corner of each key.
- A few APL symbols are obtained by pressing the "*Alt Gr*" key (or *Ctrl*+*Alt* if your keyboard does not have an "*Alt Gr*" key), simultaneously with another key, but you don't have to bother about them here: We won't be using them in the examples in this introduction.

- In case you initially have any difficulty with the keyboard, there is a "language bar" on top of the session screen, with all the APL symbols on it. When you need a symbol, you just have to click on it and the symbol will appear wherever your cursor is positioned.

You may notice that some symbols appear twice on the keyboard. This is the case for example for the symbols `< = >`. These symbols are all part of a normal keyboard (the black ones), but they have been repeated on the APL keyboard, mostly in order to group the symbols used for *comparison functions* together (the red ones). Do not worry: No matter which key you use to produce one of the duplicated symbols, you'll obtain the same result.

Utilities and Data

For most of the examples, you can just type what you read in the following pages, but sometimes you will need some data which we have prepared for you.

This data is contained in a special file (called a WorkSpace) named DyalogTutor_EN.dws which accompanies this book.

If you don't have the file, please refer to section A-1 for instructions on how to download it.

The file can only be opened by Dyalog APL. You can open it as follows:

- In Windows Explorer, double-click on the file's name. APL will be started, and it will then open the file.
- Or, start APL by double clicking on the Dyalog APL icon. Then, using the "File/Open" menu, search for the file and open it.

Once the workspace has been loaded, a welcome message is displayed, and you can check that the workspace contains the variables we shall be using in the following pages:

```
      )vars
Actual Ages AlphLower  AlphUpper  Area  Big  Category etc...
```

You can display the contents of any variable by hovering over its name with the mouse-pointer, by double-clicking on its name, or just by typing its name and pressing the *Enter* key, like this:

```
      Forecast
150 200 100  80  80  80
300 330 360 400 500 520
100 250 350 380 400 450
 50 120 220 300 320 350
```

Now, you are ready, fasten your seatbelts, we're off!

Our First Steps into APL's Magic World

Simple Operations

In APL, what you type starts 6 characters right from the left margin (we say it is "*indented*"), whereas the computer's response begins at the left margin. For additional clarity, in the following pages the characters typed by the user are printed in red, the response given by the computer being in black.

You will notice that in the examples given in the book we very often put a blank space between a symbol and the surrounding names or values. This is in most cases unnecessary; we only do so in order to improve readability. Later on, we will gradually cease to insert the blank spaces in expressions that you should become familiar with along the way.

An expression gets evaluated and the result shown in the session when you press the *Enter* key. Let's try some simple expressions:

```
      27 + 53
80
      1271 - 708
563
      86 ÷ 4                 The Divide sign is obtained using  Ctrl+ =
21.5
      59 × 8                 The Multiply sign is obtained using  Ctrl+ -
472
```

You can see that APL behaves like any hand-held calculator with, however, a small difference; multiplication is represented by the multiplication symbol (×) which is used in schools in many countries; likewise for division (÷).

In most other computer languages, a star * is used for Multiply and / for Divide. This is a legacy of the early days of computers, when the character set was limited to the one available on a typewriter. At the time it was decided to use * and / in place of × and ÷. But it is now possible to display any type of symbol on a screen and on a printer, and this transposition is no longer justifyable. The use of common symbols, which are taught all over the world, aids the understanding of APL by non programmers.

If you are familiar with other programming languages, you may occasionally and erroneously use * instead of ×. Let's see what might happen then:

```
      7 * 3                            ⇦ In APL the star means "Power"
343                                      so that 7*3 is equivalent to 7×7×7
```

Variables

As in any programming language, it is possible to create variables. Just choose a name and use the left arrow to assign it a value. In APL a numeric value can consist of a single number, or several numbers separated by at least one blank space. The arrow can be obtained using *Ctrl+* [

```
      VAT ← 19.6                    ⇦ Read it as: VAT gets 19.6
      Years ← 1952 1943 1986 2007
```

The names are "*case sensitive*". It means that three variables named respectively `VAT`, `Vat`, and `vat`, would be distinct, and may contain different values.

To ask for the contents of a variable, just type its name and press *Enter*, like this:

```
      VAT
19.6
      Years
1952 1943 1986 2007
```

Array Processing

APL is able to operate on two sets of numbers, provided those two sets have the same "shape". For the moment, understand this as "the same number of items". For example, suppose that you have a list of prices of 5 products, and the quantity bought of each:

Prices	5.20	11.50	3.60	4.00	8.45
Quantities	2	1	3	6	2

You can create two variables like this:

```
      Price ← 5.2 11.5 3.6 4 8.45
      Qty   ← 2 1 3 6 2
```

When multiplied together, the variables are multiplied item by item, and produce a result of the same length. That result can be assigned to a new variable.

```
      Costs ← Price × Qty
      Costs
10.4 11.5 10.8 24 16.9
```

This *array processing* capability eliminates most of the "loops" which are common to other programming languages. This remains true even if the data is not a simple list but a multi-dimensional array, of almost any size and number of dimensions.

To make it clear, imagine that a Sales Director makes forecasts for sales of 4 products over the coming 6 months, and assigns them to the variable `Forecast`. At the end of the 6 months, he assigns the real values to the variable `Actual`. Here they are:

```
      Forecast                                   Actual

150 200 100  80  80  80                  141 188 111  87  82  74
300 330 360 400 500 520                  321 306 352 403 497 507
100 250 350 380 400 450                  118 283 397 424 411 409
 50 120 220 300 320 350                   43  91 187 306 318 363
```

We have not yet explained how you can build such arrays of data, but if you have APL installed, these variables are provided in the Workspace file named "DyalogTutor_EN.dws". Refer to the "*Utilities and Data*" section above to see how you can load the workspace and access the data.

It is clear that the first idea of any Sales Director will be to ask for the differences between what he expected and what he has really got. This can be done easily by typing:

```
      Actual - Forecast
¯9 ¯12  11  7  2  ¯6
21 ¯24  ¯8  3 ¯3 ¯13
18  33  47 44 11 ¯41
¯7 ¯29 ¯33  6 ¯2  13
```

⇦ Note that to distinguish the sign attached to negative values from subtraction, negative values are shown with a high minus sign.

To enter negative values, this high minus sign can be obtained by pressing *Ctrl*+2.

In most traditional programming languages an operation like the one above requires two embedded loops. See what is needed in PASCAL:

```
DO UNTIL I=4
   DO UNTIL J=6
      DIFF(I,J):=ACTUAL(I,J)-FORECAST(I,J)
   END
END.
```

Even if this may seem obvious to a programmer, it is worth noting that most of the code has nothing to do with the user requirement. The only important thing (subtract forecasts from actual values) is hidden behind the detailed workings of the computer program.

To have a calculation done by a machine, one must translate our human wording into something that the computer can understand. With traditional languages, most of that effort is made by the man, to produce a program like the PASCAL example above. The great advantage of APL is that the man has generally much less effort to make, and the machine does the rest.

We have seen that APL will work on two variables of the same shape; it also works if one of the variables is a single item, which is called a *scalar*. If so, the other variable may be of any shape.

For example, if we want to calculate the amount of 19.6% VAT applied to the variable `Price` above, we can type `Price × VAT ÷ 100` (or `VAT × Price ÷ 100` as well), as shown here:

```
      Price × VAT ÷ 100
1.0192 2.254 0.7056 0.784 1.6562   ⇦ This result would require some rounding
                                     but this is not important for now
```

More Symbols

Most programming languages represent only a very small subset of the mathematical functions using symbols (typically +, -, * and /). The creator of APL, Kenneth E. Iverson, chose to include many traditional mathematical symbols in his language, and also added some new symbols to the set that we already know so well.

E.g.: Many functions which in other programming languages are library routines with names like "Maximum" have their own symbols in APL.

The function "*Maximum*" (⌈) returns the greater of two numbers, or of two arrays of numbers compared item by item.

There is also, as one might expect, a symbol for "*Minimum*" (⌊).

```
      75.6 ⌈ 87.3                   ⇦ Maximum (Ctrl+S)
87.3
      11 28 52 14 ⌈ 30 10 50 20     ⇦ Comparison item by item
30 28 52 20
      11 28 52 14 ⌊ 20              ⇦ Minimum (Ctrl+D)
11 20 20 14
```

APL supports about 70 symbols. Since some symbols have more than one meaning one could argue at length about the exact number.

This is nothing to worry about: Some of the symbols are familiar; such as × or > or again ÷ and -, but also ! and a good many others.

Most Symbols Have a Double Meaning

This is not a peculiarity of APL; in algebra we are familiar with the use of symbols as common as the minus sign being used in two different ways.

In the expression	$a = x - y$	the minus sign means subtract
Whereas in	$a = -y$	the minus sign indicates the negation of y, that's different

The first form is called the "*dyadic*" use of the symbol.
The second form is called the "*monadic*" use of the symbol.

It is the same in APL, where most of the symbols can have two meanings.

For example, to find the shape (the dimensions) of an array, one uses the Greek letter Rho (`⍴`), which can be read "*shape of*...", in its monadic use. It is produced using *Ctrl*+R.

```
      ⍴ Price                    ⇦ Monadic use
5                                  Price has 5 items
      ⍴ Forecast
4 6                                Forecast has 4 rows of 6 items
```

Used dyadically, the same symbol will organise items into a specified shape. For example, suppose that we want to create the matrix below:

```
25 60
33 47
11 44
53 28
```

We must give the computer two pieces of information:

- First the *shape* to give to the matrix: `4 2` (4 rows of 2 columns)
- Next the *contents* of the matrix: `25 60 33 47 11 44 53 28`

It is the symbol `⍴` (Rho) which makes the connection between the shape and the contents:

```
      Tab ← 4 2 ⍴ 25 60 33 47 11 44 53 28
      Tab
25 60
33 47
11 44
53 28
```

A new variable `Tab` is thereby created, and this is also how the variables `Forecast` and `Actual` above were made.

Conventions

In APL, we give special names to certain shapes of data:

- *Scalar* is used for a single value, a number like `456.18` or a single letter like `'Q'`.
- *Vector* is a plain list of values
  It may be composed of numbers like `Price` and `Qty`,
  or of letters like `'Once upon a time'` within single quotes
- *Matrix* is an array with two dimensions, like `Forecast` or `Tab`
- *Array* is a generic word for any set of values, whatever the number of its dimensions
- *Table* is a common word used for arrays with 2 dimensions (matrices)
- *Cube* is a common word used for arrays with 3 dimensions

Reduction Unifies Traditional Notations

Perhaps you remember the variable `Costs`: `10.4 11.5 10.8 24 16.9`

So what must we do to work out the total? Mathematicians are creative people who long ago devised the symbol ∑, always with a pretty collection of indices above and below, which make it complex to understand and to type on a typewriter.

In APL, the operation is written like this:

```
      +/ Costs
73.6
```

Simple isn't it? This gives the total of all the items of the array.

You can read this as "*Plus Reduction*" of the variable `Costs`.

To gain a better understanding of the process:

When we write an instruction such as `+/ 21 45 18 27 11`
- it works as if we had written `21 + 45 + 18 + 27 + 11`
- and we obtain the sum `122`

In fact, it works as if we had "inserted" the symbol `+` between the values.

But then, if we write `×/ 21 45 18 27 11`
- it is as if we had written `21 × 45 × 18 × 27 × 11`
- so, we get the product `5051970`

Similarly, if we write `⌈/ 21 45 18 27 11`
- it is as if we had written `21 ⌈ 45 ⌈ 18 ⌈ 27 ⌈ 11`
- so, we obtain the largest term `45`

Reduction, represented by the symbol `/`, belongs to a special category of symbols called *Operators*. All the other symbols (`+ - × ⌈ ρ ⍉` ...) are called *Functions* (addition, subtraction, multiplication, maximum, shape, etc.).

The arguments of a function are data (arrays): `Price × Qty`

Whereas at least one of the arguments of an operator is a function: `+/ Qty`

The left argument of *Reduction* can be one of many of the APL symbols, and it can also be the name of a user-defined program. This may give you an idea of the generality and power of the concept.

Dyalog APL contains 10 such powerful operators. If that is not enough, you can even write your own operators, just like you can write your own functions!

Let's Write Our First Programs

Imagine that we want to calculate the average of the following numbers:

```
Val ← 22 37 41 19 54 11 34
```

We must:

- first calculate the sum of the values: `+/ Val` giving `218`
- next calculate the number of values: `ρ Val` giving `7`
- and finally divide one result by the other

The calculation can be written as the single formula: `(+/Val) ÷ (ρVal)`

As it is quite likely that we shall often want to make this sort of calculation, it is preferable to store this expression in the form of a program.

In APL, we prefer the name *defined function* to the name "program".

Defined functions may be used in the same way as the built-in functions represented by special symbols like `+ - × — > ρ`..., which are called *primitive functions.*

To define a simple function like this one, here is the easiest way:

```
Average ← {(+/⍵)÷(ρ⍵)}
```

`Average` is the program name
`⍵` is a generic symbol which represents the array passed on the right.
`⍺` would be the generic symbol for the array passed on the left, if any

The definition of the function is delimited by a set of curly braces `{` and `}`. For more complex functions it is also possible to use a text editor, but this is beyond the scope of this short introduction.

Once defined, this function may be invoked in a very simple way:

```
      Average Val                    ⇦ For execution, ⍵ will get the values
31.1428571428                          contained in Val
      Average 12 74 56 23
41.25
```

Let us also write two little dyadic functions, the left argument of which is `⍺`, and the right is `⍵`:

```
      Plus ← {⍺+⍵}
      Times ← {⍺×⍵}
      (3 Plus 6) Times (5 Plus 2)
63
```

As you can see, these functions behave exactly as if we had written `(3+6) × (5+2)`

We said in the preceding section that a user-defined program could be used by the *Reduce* operator; let us try:

```
      Plus/ Val
218                                  ⇦ It works!
```

Indexing

Returning to our vector of numbers `Val`: `22 37 41 19 54 11 34`

In order to extract the 4th item, we just write: `Val[4]`

In many other programming languages one uses parentheses instead of brackets; this is not very different.

What is new is that one can extract several items in one instruction.

```
      Val
22 37 41 19 54 11 34
      Val[2 4 7 1 4]                 ⇦ One may extract the same item twice or more
37 19 34 22 19
```

And of course, in the same way, one may modify one or more items of `Val` using their indexes. Naturally, one must provide as many values as there are items to modify, or a single value for all:

```
      Val[3 5 1] ← 0
      Val
0 37 0 19 0 11 34
      Val[3 5 1] ← 300 77 111
      Val
111 37 300 19 77 11 34
```

⇦ You can check that the 3rd item is now 300, the 5th is 77, etc.

It is often necessary to extract the first few items from a list of values, for example the first 5. Nothing could be easier:

```
      Val[1 2 3 4 5]
111 37 300 19 77
```

But if one needs to extract the first 500 items from a long list, typing the integers from 1 to 500 would of course be very inconvenient.

This is why APL has been given the symbol ⍳ (*Iota*), which produces the set of the first *n* integers (⍳ can be obtained using *Ctrl*+I)

Thus, instead of writing `1 2 3 4 5 6 7 8`, it is sufficient to write `⍳8`.

And to extract the first 500 terms of a large vector, one may write: `Big[⍳500]`

We shall discover later an even simpler method.

Calculating Without Writing Programs

The employees of a company are divided into three hierarchical categories, denoted simply 1, 2, and 3. One assigns to two variables the salaries and the categories of these employees; as partly shown here:

```
Salaries   ← 4225 1619 3706 2240 2076 1389 3916 3918 4939 2735 ...
Categories ←    3    1    3    2    2    1    3    3    3    2 ...
```

Do they never want to increase these salaries? (what has our poor world come to!).

A rumour reaches us about their plans: They want a different percentage increase for each category, according to the following scale:

Category	Suggested increase
1	8%
2	5%
3	2%

How much is this going to cost the company?

We create a variable containing the above three rates:

```
      Rates ← 8 5 2 ÷ 100       ⇦ APL allows us to divide three numbers by a single one
      Rates
0.08 0.05 0.02
```

The first employee is in category 3, so the rate that applies to him is:

```
      Rates[3]
0.02
```

It follows that the first 5 employees, being in categories 3 1 3 2 2 respectively, are entitled to the following increases:

```
      Rates[3 1 3 2 2]
0.02 0.08 0.02 0.05 0.05
```

More generally, the rates applied to all of our employees could be obtained like this:

```
      Rates[Categories]
0.02 0.08 0.02 0.05 0.05 0.08 0.02 0.02 0.02 0.05 0.05 0.02 etc.
```

Having the rates, one has just to multiply by the salaries to obtain the individual increases:

```
      Salaries × Rates[Categories]
84.5 129.52 74.12 112 103.8 111.12 78.32 78.36 98.78 136.75 etc.
```

Finally, by adding them all, one will know how much it will cost the company:

```
      +/ Salaries × Rates[Categories]
2177.41
```

You may note that:

- The expression remains valid whatever the number of employees or categories,
- the result has been obtained without writing any program,
- and this expression can be read as the simplest possible English, like this:

Sum the Salaries multiplied by Rates according to Categories

Clever, no?

This illustrates how the expression of a solution in APL can be very close to the way that the solution could be phrased in everyday language. This also shows clearly that the ways of reasoning induced by traditional programming languages are not the only possible ones. This difference and originality, introduced by APL, are among the major features of the language.

Friendly Binary Data

APL makes much use of binary data. It is most often created by means of relational functions like = or >, which give the answer 1 or 0, depending whether the relation is true or not:

```
      Salaries > 3000
1 0 1 0 0 0 1 1 1 0 1 1 0 0 1 1 0 0 0 0
      Actual > Forecast
0 0 1 1 1 0
1 0 0 1 0 0                               ⇦ One can see the favourable results instantly
1 1 1 1 1 0
0 0 0 1 0 1
```

APL offers the conventional mathematical form of the 6 relational functions:

< ≤ = ≥ > ≠

Naturally one can operate on this binary data using all the functions of Boolean algebra, and moreover, the symbols used are those familiar to mathematicians of all nationalities around the world:

Function *AND*	is represented by the symbol	∧	(represented by the word AND in many programming languages)
Function *OR*	is represented by the symbol	∨	(represented by the word OR in these languages)

Thus, if I am looking for people in category 3 whose salary is less than 4000 euros, I can write:

```
      (Categories = 3) ∧ (Salaries < 4000)
0 0 1 0 0 0 1 1 0 0 0 0 0 0 0 1 0 0 0 1
```

In fact APL offers all the functions of Boolean algebra, including some perhaps less familiar functions like *NOR* and *NAND* (Not-OR and Not-AND), but they are very useful in finance and electronic automation.

There is, however, no special symbol for the function *Exclusive OR* (often called *XOR*). This is because it is not needed: The function *Not Equal* ≠ gives the same result as *Exclusive OR* when it is used with Boolean values, as you can see below:

```
      0 0 1 1 ≠ 0 1 0 1
0 1 1 0
```

Finally, not only can these binary vectors be used as we have described but also for novel purposes, such as counting and selecting.

Counting

Having found which salaries are less than 2500 euros by means of the following expression:

```
      Salaries < 2500
0 1 0 1 1 1 0 0 0 0 0 0 1 1 0 0 1 0 1 0
```

It is easy to add all the 1s and 0s to calculate how many people earn less than 2500 euros:

```
      +/ Salaries < 2500
8
```

Selection

One can also use the binary vector as a "mask" to select the items corresponding to the binary "1"s from another array:

```
      1 1 0 1 0 0 1 / 23 55 17 46 81 82 83
23 55 46 83
```

The procedure is identical for character data:

```
      1 0 1 0 0 0 0 1 1 / 'Drumstick'
Duck
```

This function, called *Compress*, is particularly useful for extracting the items conforming to a given criterion from a variable. For example, to display the salaries of people in Category 2, one writes:

```
      (Categories = 2) / Salaries
2240 2076 2735 3278 1339 3319        ⇦ Powerful, isn't it?
```

Discovery

To practise our skills some more, let us find in our variable `Val` the positions of numbers greater than 35. Here are the necessary steps:

```
Val        ←      22 37 41 19 54 11 34
Val>35     is      0  1  1  0  1  0  0
⍴Val       is     7
⍳⍴Val      is     1 2 3 4 5 6 7    ⇦ All possible positions
```

Let us compare two of these results

```
Val>35     ⇨      0 1 1 0 1 0 0
⍳⍴Val      ⇨      1 2 3 4 5 6 7
```

You can see that that if you eliminate (using *Compress*) the items which correspond to zeros in order to retain only those corresponding to 1, you easily get the positions required: 2 3 5

Thus the job may be done as follows:

```
      (Val>35) / ⍳⍴Val
2 3 5
```

This expression is applicable in many different situations.

Here is a similar use, but applied to character data: To find the positions of "a" within a phrase; the method is the same.

```
      Phrase ← 'Panama is a canal between Atlantic and Pacific'
      (Phrase = 'a') / ⍳⍴Phrase
2 4 6 11 14 16 30 36 41                    ⇦ You can check it!
```

A Touch of Modern Math

Proudly having found all the "a"s, we may wish to find all the vowels.

Alas, although we can write `Phrase = 'a'`, because a vector can be compared with a single value, one cannot write `Phrase = 'aeiouy'`(1), because that would require the item by item comparison of a phrase of 46 letters and "aeiouy" which has only 6.

In other words: You may compare 46 letters with 46 other letters, or compare them with one letter, but not with 6.

So we shall use a new function: ***Membership*** which is represented by the symbol `∊`, also used in mathematics.(`∊` can be obtained by pressing *Ctrl*+E)

The expression `A ∊ B` returns a Boolean result which indicates which items of the variable `A` appear in the variable `B`, wherever they may be. And it works no matter what are the shapes, the dimensions or the type (numeric or character) of `A` and `B`, a pure marvel!

For example:

```
      5 7 2 8 4 9 ∊ 3 4 5 6
1 0 0 0 1 0                     ⇦ Only 5 and 4 are found in 3 4 5 6
      'dandelion' ∊ 'garden'
1 1 1 1 1 0 0 0 1               ⇦ The letters "lio" do not appear in "garden"
```

---

[1] "Y" is considered to be a vowel in many European languages.

So in pursuit of our enquiry we shall write:

```
      (Phrase ∊ 'aeiouy') / ⍳⍴Phrase
2 4 6 8 11 14 16 20 23 24 30 33 36 41 43 45
```

One can also use membership between a vector and a matrix, as shown below, assuming that the list of towns is a variable created earlier.

We have represented side by side the variable itself and the result of using *Membership*:

```
      Towns                              Towns ∊ 'aeiouy'
Canberra                            0 1 0 0 1 0 0 1 0 0
Paris                               0 1 0 1 0 0 0 0 0 0
Washington                          0 1 0 0 1 0 0 0 1 0
Moscow                              0 1 0 0 1 0 0 0 0 0
Martigues                           0 1 0 0 1 0 1 1 0 0
Mexico                              0 1 0 1 0 1 0 0 0 0
```

We can reverse the expression, but the result has always the same shape as the left argument:

```
      'aeiouy' ∊ Towns
1 1 1 1 1 0                    ⇦ None of the town names contains a "y"
```

A Powerful Search Function

We have harnessed a very useful method to look for the positions of letters or numbers in a vector, but the answer obtained does not provide a one to one correspondence between the search values and the resultant positions:

```
      List ← 15 40 63 18 27 40 33 29 40 88     ⇦ Vector of values
      Where ← 29 63 40 33 50                   ⇦ We want to find these
      (List ∊ Where) / ⍳⍴List                  ⇦ Let's apply our method
2 3 6 7 8 9                                    ⇦ Positions found
```

The positions are correct, but 29 is not in position 2, and 40 is not in position 6.

The question we have answered using the expression above is: "In which positions in `List` do we find a number that also appears somewhere in `Where`?"

If we want to answer the slightly different question: "Where in `List` do we find each number in `Where`?" we need to use a different method.

This new method uses the dyadic form of the symbol ⍳ (*Iota*).

```
      List ← 15 40 63 18 27 40 33 29 40 88     ⇦ Same vector of values
      Where ← 29 63 40 33 50                   ⇦ Where are these?
      List ⍳ Where                             ⇦ New method using dyadic ⍳
8 3 2 7 11                                     ⇦ Positions found
```

It is true that 29, 63, 40 and 33, occur respectively in positions 8, 3, 2 and 7. It's much better!

But, first surprise: The value 40 occurs 3 times in `List`, but only the first one is reported in the result. This is because, by definition, dyadic *Iota* returns only the first occurrence of a given item. If the response for each value sought has to match a position; how may one, looking for 5 numbers, obtain 7 results?

Second surprise: The value 50 is reported as being found in position 11 in a vector comprising only 10 items! This is how the function *IndexOf* (dyadic `⍳`) reports that a value is absent.

At first sight this seems a bit surprising, but in fact it is a property which makes this function so generally powerful, as we shall soon see.

An Example

A car manufacturer decides that he will offer his customers a discount on the catalogue price (you can see how this example is imaginary!)

The country has been divided into 100 areas, and the discount rate will depend on the area according to the following table:

Area	Discount
17	9 %
50	8 %
59	6 %
84	5 %
89	4 %
Others	2 %

The problem is to calculate the discount rate that may be claimed for a potential customer who lives in given area `D`; for example `D ← 84`.

Let us begin by creating two variables:

```
      Area     ← 17 50 59 84 89
      Discount ←  9  8  6  5  4  2
```

Let us see if `84` is in the list of favoured areas:

```
      D ∊ Area
1                                  ⇦ Yes, it's there
      Area ⍳ D
4                                  ⇦ 84 is the 4th item in the list
```

Let us find the current rate of discount for this index position:

```
      Discount[4]
5
```
⇦ This customer can claim a 5% discount; good!

One may simply write: `Discount[Area⍳D]`

If a customer lives in any area such as 75, 45, or 93, the expression `Area⍳D` will in all cases give the result 6, because those values are absent in `Area`. Then `Discount[6]` will always find the rate 2%, as expected.

The importance of this approach is that it is vector-based. Suppose that publicity attracts crowds and that therefore `D` is no longer a single value but a vector, the solution is still valid:

```
      D ← 24 75 89 60 92 50 51 50 84 66 17 89
      Discount[Area⍳D]
2 2 4 2 2 8 2 8 5 2 9 4
```

All that without a program, neither "loop" nor "test", and whatever the number of areas. Readers who know other programming languages will have no difficulty in making the comparison.

Generalisation

In truth, the expression we just wrote is an example of an algorithm for "changing the frame of reference". Don't panic, the name may seem esoteric, but the concept is simple. A list of area numbers (the initial set) is translated into a list of discount rates (the final set).

Let us now imagine the initial set to be an alphabet composed of lower case and upper case letters, and the final set to be composed of only upper case letters (with a blank space in the middle):

```
      AlphLower
abcdefghijklmnopqrstuvwxyz ABCDEFGHIJKLMNOPQRSTUVWXYZ
      AlphUpper
ABCDEFGHIJKLMNOPQRSTUVWXYZ ABCDEFGHIJKLMNOPQRSTUVWXYZ*
```

Notice that `AlphUpper` is one character longer than `AlphLower`. We have added an asterisk at the end, and you will see why we did so:

Here is a little French sentence, with one accented letter.

```
      Tale ← 'Le Petit Chaperon-Rouge a bouffé le Loup'
```

The expression below converts from lower to upper case.

```
      AlphUpper[AlphLower⍳Tale]
LE PETIT CHAPERON*ROUGE A BOUFF* LE LOUP
```

As one might expect, the characters - and é, which are absent from the initial alphabetic set have been replaced by the * of the final set, but the conversion is acceptable. This solution can easily be improved.

Once more, the rational steps to be taken to create a solution are easily translated into a programming algorithm, and the programmer can thereby get a much more extensive insight into the problem itself.

After Values, Let Us Process Shapes

Many traditional programming languages do not really handle arrays of numbers or characters. They hold them in memory, but when the arrays are required for processing they can only be handled one item at a time. It is not surprising in these circumstances, that these languages have only limited means of controlling the shape of the data.

It is quite the opposite in APL, which offers many tools for working with the shape of the data. We shall only look at a few of them here.

Take and Drop

The functions *Take* (↑) and *Drop* (↓) serve, as their names suggest, to extract part of a set of values. Here we shall show only examples based on vectors, but all the other shapes of data can be treated in a similar way.

Recalling that `List` has values `15 40 63 18 27 40 33 29 40 88`

```
      4 ↑ List                  (Ctrl+Y)
15 40 63 18                  ⇦  Take the first 4 items of the vector
      5 ↓ List                  (Ctrl+U)
40 33 29 40 88               ⇦  Drop the first 5 items
```

If the left argument is negative, these same functions count from the end of the vector.

```
      ¯3 ↑ List
29 40 88                     ⇦  Take the last 3 items of the vector
      ¯7 ↓ List              ⇦  If one drops the last 7 items; it only leaves
15 40 63                        the first three ones
```

That last result is the same as obtained by `3 ↑ List`.

Some pages ago, we used `Big[⍳500]` to extract the first 500 items of `Big`. We can now see that we also could have used `500↑Big`.

Here again, using these new symbols, it is possible to create innovative solutions to classical problems.

Let us imagine a business with a turnover which has grown over 12 years.

The variable `Tome` is Turnover in millions of euros.

```
      Tome ← 56 59 67 64 60 61 68 73 78 75 81 84
```

We want to calculate the difference between each year and the year before; how can we do it?

`1 ↓ Tome`	would give	`59 67 64 60 61 68 73 78 75 81 84`
`¯1 ↓ Tome`	would give	`56 59 67 64 60 61 68 73 78 75 81`

In other words, in each position of the first result we have "this year's turnover", and in the same position in the second result we have "the previous year's turnover".

We see that all that remains is to subtract these results item by item:

```
      (1↓Tome) - (¯1↓Tome)
3 8 ¯3 ¯4 1 7 5 5 ¯3 6 3
```

⇦ Without a program or loops; all very simple!

In place of a subtraction, a division would calculate (with some obvious adjustments) the rates of growth instead of the differences:

```
      100 × ( (1↓Tome) ÷ (¯1↓Tome) )-1
```

Let us put that in a small defined function, and apply it:

```
      Growth ← {100×((1↓⍵)÷(¯1↓⍵))-1}
      Growth Tome
5.36 13.56 ¯4.48 ¯6.25 1.67 11.48 7.35 6.85 ¯3.85 8 3.70
```

This is **not** the real appearance of the result; it has been rounded just for printing purposes.

Mirrors and Transposition

APL is also well equipped with functions to pivot data about any axis, as suggested by the appearances of the symbols used. They apply to both numeric and character data; as we are going to show by applying these functions to the variable `Towns` that we used earlier.

The symbols used hereafter are obtained like this:

⌽	⇨	*Ctrl*+*Shift*+5
⊖	⇨	*Ctrl*+*Shift*+7
⍉	⇨	*Ctrl*+*Shift*+6

Initial Variable	Left-right reverse (Mirror)	Top-bottom reverse (Mirror)	Swap Rows & Columns (Transpose)
`Towns`	`⌽Towns`	`⊖Towns`	`⍉Towns`

`Canberra`
`Paris`
`Washington`
`Moscow`
`Martigues`
`Mexico`
	`arrebnaC`
	`siraP`
	`notgnihsaW`
	`wocsoM`
	`seugitraM`
	`ocixeM`
		`Mexico`
		`Martigues`
		`Moscow`
		`Washington`
		`Paris`
		`Canberra`
			`CPWMMM`
			`aaaoae`
			`nrssrx`
			`bihcti`
			`esioic`
			`r nwgo`
			`r g u`
			`a t e`
			`  o s`
			`  n`

The symbols used (⌽ ⊖ ⍉) are self-explanatory, no effort is required to remember any of them. They also have dyadic uses, but we shall not demonstrate them here.

Back to Primary School

Remember when we learned our multiplication tables? In that practically Palaeolithic era, to make sure that we knew all our tables, my teacher made us calculate the multiplication table for the integers 1 to 9:

×	1	2	3	4	5	6	7	8	9
1	1	2	3	4	5	6	7	8	9
2	2	4	6	8	10	12	14	16	18
3	3	6	9	12	15	18	21	24	27
4	4	8	12	16	20	24	28	32	36
etc.	etc.								

You see, I haven't forgotten!

Probably you have done all this just like me. And then we quickly forgot that very powerful tool, one which APL provides under the name *Outer Product*.

The task consists of taking all possible pairs of items of two vectors, (the column and row headings) and making them the left and right arguments of the function at the top left. For example, 3 times 7 gives 21 (in red here above).

Next we shall go on to see what we get if we change the values a little:

×	8	5	15	9	11	40
5	40	25	75	45	55	200
4	32	20	60	36	44	160
10	80	50	150	90	110	400
3	24	15	45	27	33	120

This operation is written as follows in APL:

```
      5 4 10 3 ∘.× 8 5 15 9 11 40
40 25  75 45  55 200
32 20  60 36  44 160
80 50 150 90 110 400
24 15  45 27  33 120
```

The *Outer Product* symbol is made of a small circle (*Ctrl*+J), a dot, and the function to be applied. It is an *operator*, as one of its arguments is a function (× in this case) rather than an array.

Despite of its name "*Outer Product*" this operator is by no means restricted to working with multiplication. We can replace the symbol for *Multiplication* by any other dyadic function (like = < ≥ or ⌈), or even functions which you have defined yourself (like Plus), and you will understand, as for *Reduce* which we saw earlier, that *Outer Product* is an operator of amazing power.

Let's have some fun with it:

(⍳5)∘.=(⍳5)	(⍳5)∘.<(⍳5)	(⍳5)∘.≥(⍳5)	(⍳5)∘.⌈(⍳5)	(⍳5)∘.Plus(⍳5)
1 0 0 0 0 0 1 0 0 0 0 0 1 0 0 0 0 0 1 0 0 0 0 0 1	0 1 1 1 1 0 0 1 1 1 0 0 0 1 1 0 0 0 0 1 0 0 0 0 0	1 0 0 0 0 1 1 0 0 0 1 1 1 0 0 1 1 1 1 0 1 1 1 1 1	1 2 3 4 5 2 2 3 4 5 3 3 3 4 5 4 4 4 4 5 5 5 5 5 5	2 3 4 5 6 3 4 5 6 7 4 5 6 7 8 5 6 7 8 9 6 7 8 9 10

A Useful Application

Suppose the vector `Ages` contains the ages of 400 respondents to an opinion poll. We want to establish how many people there are in each of the following categories:

0 - 25 - 30 - 35 - 45 - 50 - 55 - 65 or above.

Here is an extract of the data:

```
Ages       ⇨    32 19 50 33 23 65 46 26 31 58 51 23 51 36 28 42 ... etc
Category   ⇨    0 25 30 35 45 50 55 65
```

We are going to use the *Outer Product* `Category ∘.< Ages` , and here are the first items of the result:

<	32	19	50	33	23	65	46	26	31	58	51	23	51	36	28	42	34	... etc
0	1	1	1	1	1	1	1	1	1	1	1	1	1	1	1	1	1	
25	1	0	1	1	0	1	1	0	1	1	1	0	1	1	1	1	1	
30	1	0	1	1	0	1	1	0	1	1	1	0	1	1	0	1	1	
35	0	0	1	0	0	1	1	0	0	1	1	0	1	1	0	1	0	
45	0	0	1	0	0	1	1	0	0	1	1	0	1	0	0	0	0	
50	0	0	0	0	0	1	0	0	0	1	1	0	1	0	0	0	0	... etc.
etc.																		

If one adds up this Boolean matrix, one obtains for each row the number of people who are older than 0 years, older than 25 years, older than 30 years, etc. This is the expression:

```
cum ← +/ (Category ∘.< Ages)
```

With the cut-down extract shown above, the value of `cum` would be: `17 14 12 8 6 4`

In other words there are 12 people older than 30. But among them, 8 are older than 35. In order to know how many people are between 30 and 35, it is necessary to calculate 12-8 to obtain 4.

If one wants to reproduce this calculation for all categories, it is necessary to perform a series of subtractions as here:

```
     17 14 12 8 6 4     This is cum
-    14 12  8 6 4 0     This is cum without its first item and followed by zero
     --------------     Let us subtract
=     3  2  4 2 2 4     This result was obtained by the calculation cum-(1↓cum,0)
```

To append a zero to the right, we used a comma, which joins variables together. This is a function called *Catenate*.

If one no longer works with a small extract of data, but with the full list of 400 people, this is what one gets:

```
      cum ← +/ (Category ∘.< Ages)
      cum - (1↓cum,0)
56 32 56 104 63 38 37 14
```

All that without real programming, and it works whatever the number of people or categories. What luck!

Once again, APL allowed us to find straightforward and original solutions to traditional problems.

There Is a Lot to Discover Yet

In the course of these pages we have flown over APL country and glimpsed certain bold ideas which explain the attraction of the language. A thousand other things remain to be seen! If you are convinced that Dyalog APL is worth the effort, you can start studying APL in much more detail in the rest of this book.

Let us just discover some additional attractive features of APL.

Attractively Simple Syntax Rules

Most other programming languages contain rather complex rules to determine how an expression is evaluated; a concept called *operator precedence*. Very often it says that for example multiplication and division have higher precedence than addition and subtraction, meaning that an expression like 5 × 3 + 2 gives 17, because the multiplication is done first, and then the addition.

This sounds simple and familiar, but it quickly gets very complex and difficult to remember, especially in a language containing many functions, like APL. For example, which precedence should we give to ⍳ or ↓ or ⌈, for which we do not have an established tradition? And what about the functions we write ourselves?

The democratic solution adopted in APL is "*We hold these truths to be self-evident that all functions are created equal!*" The only and very simple rule is that any function works on the result of the entire expression to its right, and, if it is a dyadic function, the value immediately to the left of it. As usual, parentheses can be used to group parts of an expression.

So, let us see how this applies to the expression above:

```
      5 × 3 + 2
```

`×` works on 5 (the value immediate to the left of it) and the result of `3 + 2`, the entire expression to the right of it. Even though it is not strictly correct, many people say that APL evaluates from right to left. In any case, the result of the expression is 25 in APL!

Had we written `(5 × 3) + 2` instead the result would of course have been 17.

It may take a little while to get used to this slightly unfamiliar rule, but once it has been learned it is really a great advantage because you can direct your energy towards solving your problem and not have to remember complex rules just to satisfy the computer's need for guidance.

Use Many Other Calculating Tools

We have discovered some original functions, which are completely absent from most other programming languages, like `⍴`, `↑`, `⍒`, `∊`, and *Outer Product*. Those features lead to new methods and new algorithms to process data; this is one of the main advantages of APL.

Not only do you have a lot more functions: *Inner Product* (generalized matrix product), many built-in mathematical tools (trigonometry, matrix inverse, conversions to and from any numerical base, etc.), but you can also handle generalized (nested) arrays; arrays which contain arrays, which themselves contain arrays, and so on.

The scope of the possible solutions to a single problem is often so wide that it is probably the reason why people never get tired of using APL: They always have something new to discover and to invent.

Create User-friendly Applications with the GUI

Like all modern programming languages, Dyalog APL has a Graphic User Interface (GUI) under Microsoft Windows and Win32 emulators under Unix. It allows you to design pleasant user interfaces with all the items and features you are familiar with. Even a beginner can quickly create an interface and process the data with all the power of the language, whereas in traditional languages, the same operation would need days or weeks of programming. The Microsoft.Net interface supports the use of WinForms and Windows Presentation Foundation GUI elements as well.

Access Your Data

Of course, Dyalog APL has built-in instructions to access data files, and SQL databases like Oracle, SQL Server, or other popular databases. These interfaces allow you to visualise and process part or all of a data base as if it were an array, to which you can apply all the array processing functions available in APL. That saves you a lot of heavy programming tasks.

Dyalog APL has also its own powerful file system. These files are collections of arrays of any shapes or sizes, which can be processed with the full power of the language. Databases built with this special feature are extremely compact (2 to 3 times smaller than an equivalent relational database). They can be shared, and they offer much greater flexibility and superior performance compared to traditional database management systems.

Build an Efficient Partnership With Microsoft Excel

Microsoft Excel, probably the most popular spreadsheet manager, is used all over the world by millions of people. It appears that Excel is an easy way to enter data into a computer in a tabular form, and it is also an excellent product to produce everyday business reports and graphs.

While Excel is convenient for small business applications, it is too limited to process complex calculations, or when some operations involve data located in many workbooks.

Excel and APL can easily be combined in an efficient partnership. Excel is used to input data in a very flexible way into spreadsheets, which most users are familiar with. APL can then read dozens (and sometimes hundreds) of sheets, aggregate the data, and perform very complex calculations, which may be controlled and parameterized through the GUI interface. Of course, the results can be printed, but they can also be output to the users in the form of specially prepared Excel worksheets. In these worksheets, the users can proceed to additional operations for their particular needs, or produce graphs of their own.

And Also...

You can interface APL with Internet, write your own web server, use multithreading to process simultaneous tasks, use all the advantages of true *Object Oriented Programming*, and use many attractive features, which are beyond the scope of this quick survey.

FAQ

Perhaps you have found this language rather engaging, but before you decide to invest time and energy in developing APL applications, you would like to be sure of your choice. Let's give you some answers.

Is Dyalog APL A Professional Tool?

Among many others, here are some significant examples of important applications:

- Long term Board level financial planning for one of the world's five biggest petroleum companies, used over 12 years.
- The management of supplies required from 'today + 2 days' to 'today + 3 months', by the assembly lines of the 6 principal factories of a major international car manufacturer.
- Risk Management for an important insurance group.

These three examples have common characteristics, positioning them as major industrial applications:

- They are particularly crucial because considerable finances are at stake.
- They must be absolutely reliable. A major car manufacturer works must not be brought to a stop by a programming bug.
- The first two applications operate in a highly volatile business environment. As their requirements are always changing, the programs undergo constant mutation. These evolutions must be made with very short development cycles.

So we can answer: Yes, for a reasonable cost in labour, APL makes it possible to create, maintain, support, and further develop large, sensitive applications of the highest level of quality, reliability, and flexibility.

Can Dyalog APL Fit a Professional Developer's Needs?

The characteristics of APL make it easy to use, lead to quick development, and help to produce light and flexible code. Programs developed in APL can evolve quickly, to fit changing user requirements at will.

- Because APL uses symbols rather than words to represent operations, a programmer can use any word for his own data and program names; they will never be in conflict with the language structure and contents.

- Due to its array-processing capability, APL dramatically reduces the needs for programming loops. Because all such intricacies are removed, the code is much lighter, and the programmer can concentrate all his attention and skill on the true core of computing requirements.
- In most programming languages, a programmer would have to declare that each variable will be an array of such and such dimensions, containing values with a specific data type. There is nothing similar in APL. The size and the data type of a variable arise from the way in which the variable has been produced. If one extracts two rows and five columns from a matrix, the result will of course be a 2 by 5 matrix. And if we divide 486 into 7, the result will of course be a fractional value; there no need to specify it in advance.
- The extensive set of direct operations on data offered by APL leads to new approaches. For traditional problems, which have been solved in the same way in most programming languages for years, APL suddenly offers new solutions, which appear to be light, straightforward, very general, and easy to maintain because they are easy to read.
- The readability of APL often surprises people who practise other programming languages; they probably forget that the languages they use are totally obscure for most non specialists. APL is learned and used efficiently by people who are not data processing professionals, but are instead specialists in their professional fields, such as accountancy, chemistry, insurance, logistics, finance, and biology. They have less difficulty with APL than with the problems they have to solve, and most often, they solve them with APL. They could not achieve this alone with any other programming languages, but would require the help of programming specialists … who of course know nothing of the problem domain in question.

Where is APL Typically Used?

APL is typically used in situations where there is a lot to be gained if people who understand a problem can be closely involved in developing solutions. Sometimes application code is written in the afternoon by the same people who read the latest research reports or legislation in the morning – or by members of a very small team who have overlapping skills.

In a more traditional approach, in which the specialist teams would need the help of professional programmers, such teams may find that valuable information was lost in the "process", so that several iterations would be required in order to reach a satisfactory solution. Especially when a problem has a mathematical or technical foundation, APL can turbo-charge the development cycle.

Even if there is no immediate urgency, APL allows the path between "users and coders" to be much shorter than is the case when "traditional" technologies, in which *requirement gathering*, *specification*, *architecture* and *coding* are often handled by separate teams. If you have a novel idea that you would like to investigate (or "get to market") quickly, you may reach your goal very much more easily by learning APL or employing a small team of APL developers (who will be able to "speak your language"), rather than becoming or using "programmers" to develop solutions for you.

APL is most widely used in the financial industry, which has a mathematical foundation, and rapidly changing requirements: In this environment, the use of APL can provide a significant competitive advantage.

Unfortunately some problems cannot wait!

Great flexibility and speed is the true commercial foundation for APL. With APL one can develop in direct contact with the users and involve them from the outset in the continual modification of the object of the development. Afterwards, as an application continues to evolve, it is still the speed of development which makes APL a tool especially well adapted to changing environments.

We hope you enjoyed this little trip in the magic world of APL.

If you still think that APL might be the very tool you need, you are ready to read the full text of the following tutorial. You will revisit some of the examples you have seen above, plus many, many others.

Chapter A: Getting Started

1 - Installing the Software

Before you begin to read this tutorial it is recommended that you:

- Have the manuals ready. Download them from www.dyalog.com (for free), or order a printed copy at www.lulu.com/dyalog.
- Install Dyalog APL.
- Have the demonstration files ready. Download them from http://www.dyalog.com/intro

This tutorial was written for Dyalog APL Unicode Edition, Version 12.0. However, if you have an earlier version, most of the examples will work.

In this chapter you will find practical information that may help you during your study.

1.1 Installation

The APL language uses special symbols like ⍴, ⍳, and ⍉. Because such symbols are not available on a standard keyboard, a special input mechanism is required to interpret particular keystrokes or combinations of keystrokes as APL symbols, and an output mechanism is then used to display them properly.

There are two different editions of Dyalog APL: The *Unicode* Edition, and the *Classic* Edition.

The Unicode Edition is the more modern of the two; it is better integrated with the operating environment than the Classic Edition.

However, Version 12 of Dyalog APL is the first version to offer full Unicode support. If you have to maintain applications written in earlier versions of Dyalog you will need to install the Classic Edition of Version 12. Otherwise you should install the Unicode Edition.

Details on the Classic Edition may be found in the User Guide.

The *Unicode Edition* uses standard Windows keyboard drivers which can be enabled and selected using the Windows "Language Bar", just like other "alternative" keyboards that you might use.

You have nothing special to do. The APL keyboards are added to your system as part of the installation of Dyalog APL Unicode Edition and, as a consequence, APL characters can be typed not only in the APL environment, but also in a text editor like Notepad, or in word processing software like Microsoft Word.

Two flavours of the APL keyboard are installed. The names of these keyboards are prefixed by your country code (e.g. "UK - " for United Kingdom) followed by "Dyalog AltGr" and "Dyalog Ctrl" respectively. If you use the Dyalog AltGr keyboard, you obtain APL symbols by pressing the *AltGr* key in combination with other keys on the keyboard. If you use the Dyalog Ctrl keyboard, you use *Ctrl* instead.

When you start an APL Session, you must switch to one of the APL keyboards using the Language Bar or a special "hot key" of your choice. Under Windows XP, you assign "hot keys" to input languages using the Advanced Key Settings dialog box which you reach from Control Panel using the following path:

Settings ⇨ Control Panel ⇨ Regional and Language Options
⇨ Languages ⇨ Details ⇨ Key Settings

Apart from the additional capability to enter APL symbols (using AltGr or Ctrl), the APL keyboards are otherwise completely standard. This means that in principle, you may select one of the APL keyboards as your *default input language* from the drop-down menu at the top of the Text Services and Input Languages dialog box (Settings Tab). Be warned, however, that there may be conflicts with other software that use Ctrl and/or AltGr for special purposes.

Note:

Throughout this book, it is assumed that you are using the UK - *Dyalog Ctrl* keyboard, and you will be advised to enter APL symbols using *Ctrl* + *some other key*.

If you choose instead to use the *AltGr* keyboard, you should press *AltGr* instead of *Ctrl* when so instructed. If you are using a different language (non-UK) keyboard, then *some other key* may be different.

Figure A-1

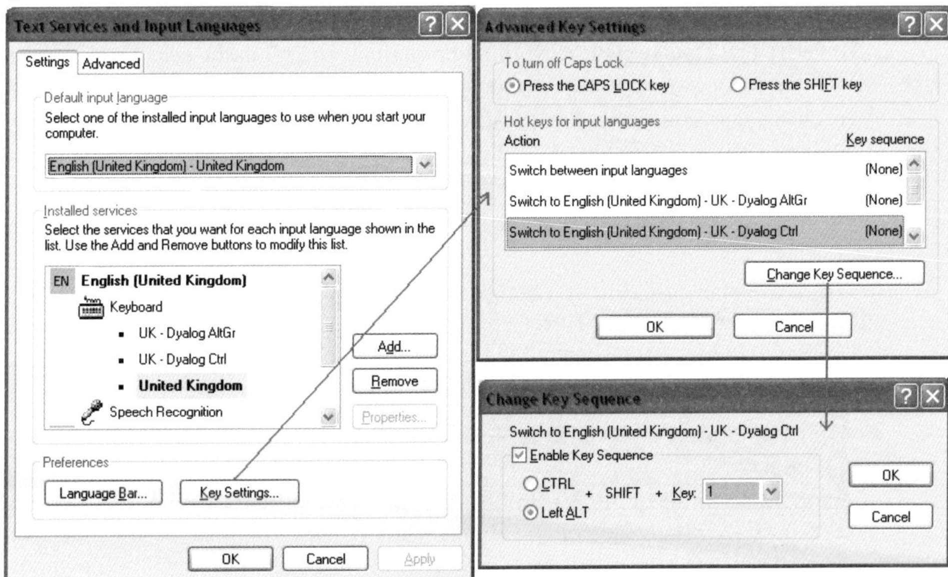

If you have any problem with the keyboard settings, refer to Dyalog's *User Guide*.

1.2 First Contact

1.2.1 - The Dyalog Working Environment

When Dyalog is started, a window appears that contains, from top to bottom (see figure A-2):

- A **MenuBar**
  This MenuBar is described in detail in the Dyalog APL User Guide, Chapter 2 "The APL Environment"; paragraph "The Session Menu Bar".
- A **Toolbar**
- A **Language bar** — We shall describe it later in 2.2.3
- An empty **working area** — at the top of which is displayed:

Version used	`Dyalog APL/W Version 12.0.2`
Edition (Classic or Unicode)	`Unicode Edition`
Current date and time	`Mon Jun 30 16:15:30 2008`
Message	`clear ws`

- Two **Statusbars** containing various indicators and status information.

1.2.2 - Check Your Installation

To verify that Dyalog APL is working properly, type 2+2 in the central (empty) area, and then press the Enter key. The answer should be 4. Be proud; this is your first APL statement!

To check that your APL keyboard and font are properly installed, try to type the special symbol "Iota" (⍳) followed by the number 7. *Iota* is obtained by pressing *Ctrl* + I. You should obtain the list of integers from 1 to 7 as shown below.

All this will be explained later, but if it worked, you can now begin the discovery of this tutorial.

Figure A-2: Dyalog's working environment

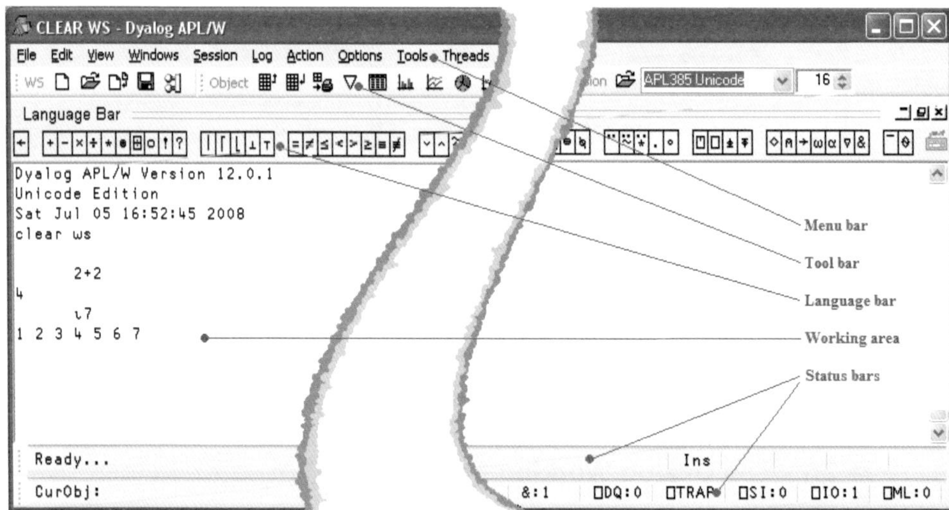

1.2.3 - The APL Language Bar

By default, Dyalog displays a language bar, docked along the top of the Session window, to facilitate your first contact with the special symbols used by the APL language. When the mouse pointer is positioned over one of the symbols in the language bar, a help message pops up that explains its name, its usage and syntax, together with the keystroke required to enter the symbol. If you click on the symbol, it is copied into the Session window at the position of your input cursor as if you had typed it using the keyboard.

Advice: After the first few hours of using APL, we recommend that you avoid using this facility and practice using the keyboard instead. If you want to become really fluent in APL, you must make the effort to learn the keystrokes that produce APL characters.

In our experience, it takes about a week to become really comfortable with the most common symbols.

1.2.4 - Key Combinations

If you do not use the language bar, you will need to use key combinations to input APL symbols. For example, *Ctrl+R* produces the symbol ⍴ (*Rho*), *Ctrl+I* produces the symbol ⍳ (*Iota*), and so on. Some symbols are obtained by *Ctrl* + *Shift* + another key.

In the keyboard layouts shown on the next page, we use the following conventions:

Figure A-3

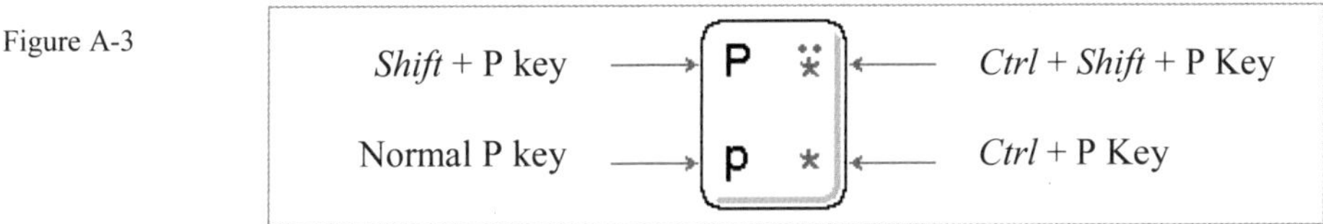

Two common UK and US English language APL keyboard layouts are illustrated below:

Figure A-4: Dyalog **UK**-Keyboard

Figure A-5: Dyalog **US** Keyboard

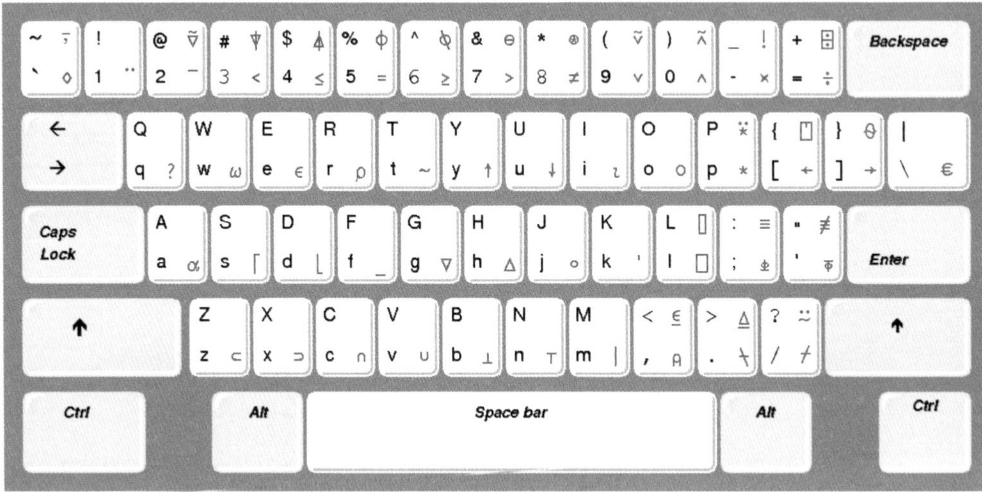

1.3 Demonstration Files

1.3.1 - The Workspace Concept

In APL, a user is given an area of memory, the ***Workspace***, in which he can create variables and programs. When the workspace is saved, all the programs and variables are saved together in a single file, in the same way as for example, a spreadsheet.

In the following pages, you will be invited to create variables, write programs, and test by yourself how the symbols work.

To relieve you of the task of entering data for your trials, most of the variables and programs used in this book are provided in a file (a *workspace*) named DyalogTutor_EN.dws.

We recommend that you download this workspace from http://www.dyalog.com/intro.
You can change its name, but we recommend that you keep the default extension "`.dws`".

Let us imagine that you have stored it under the name: `d:\mypath\myspace.dws`. Then each time you want to start a new APL practice session, you should load or reload this workspace by typing: `)Load d:\mypath\myspace` (the default extension is then optional)

Be careful: The first character of this statement is a **closing** parenthesis. This particular syntax is meaningful for what we later shall call "*System Commands*".

1.3.2 - Associated Files

In this tutorial we shall also use the following associated files.
Download them too from http://www.dyalog.com/intro:

For Chapter N about File processing:	`cellar.dcf`
	`report.txt`
	`mlk.txt`
	`nums.fun`

For Chapter Q about OLE interface with Excel	`xldemo.xls` `worldsales.xls`

For Chapter R about SALT script files	`demoscript.dyalog`
	`telefon.dyalog`
	`test.dyalog`
	`teton.dyalog`
	`experiment.7.dyalog`

Utility workspace	`Utils.dws`

1.3.3 - Print What You Have Done

During your experiments, you will probably want to print a variable or a program. Just place the cursor on the name of the variable or program, and click the button.

If ever you intend to print many objects (variables and programs), it is better to display the contents of your workspace by clicking the Workspace Explorer button . This will bring up a dialog box similar to the one illustrated below:

Figure A-8: Dyalog 's Explorer

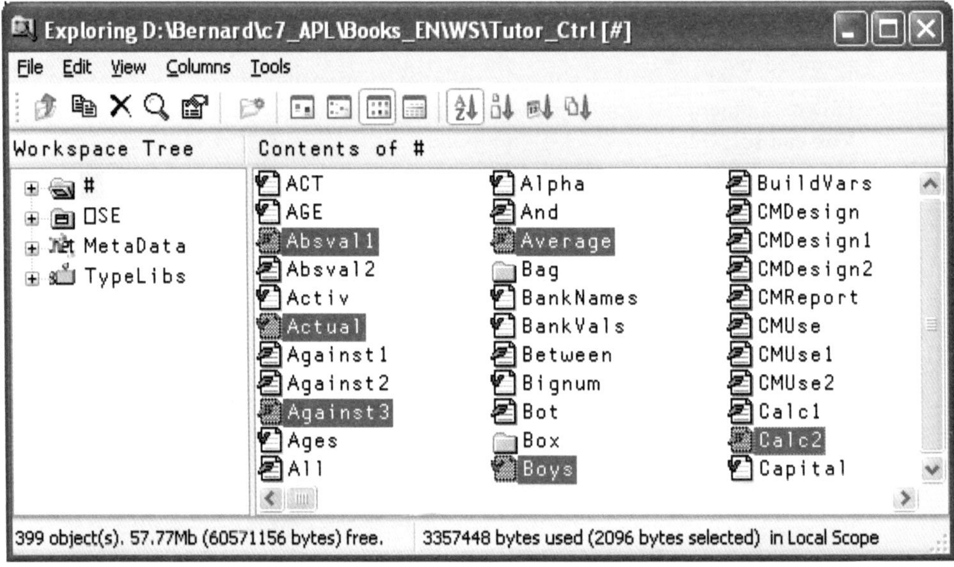

Select the objects you want to print (highlighted above), then press the right mouse button and select "Print ..." from the pop-up context menu.

You can configure various print settings, such as font, page-headers and footers using the "Print Setup" dialog box.

1.3.4 - The Session Log

While you are working, Dyalog APL stores your input (each line you enter), and the resulting output you get from the system, in a ***Session Log***. You can scroll back in that log and re-execute a line by just pressing the *Enter* key.

In fact, you can execute several lines from the Session Log in one go. To mark a line for execution, you just have to change it in some way. You can make a real alteration, or a cosmetic change that has no material effect on the expression to be executed. As soon as you make any sort of modification to the line, the colour of the text (defined using the Colours dialog box) will change. You can undo a change and restore a line to its original state, by pressing *Shift+Escape*.

To execute the marked lines press the *Enter* key. They will be executed from top to bottom, not in the order you selected them. Note however that if an expression generates an error, the remaining lines will not be executed.

The Session Log is not limited just to the current session, and you can scroll back to retrieve expressions and results from previous sessions, limited only by the size of the log. This is specified using the Log tab of the Configuration dialog box, displayed by the Options ⇨ Configuration menu.

You can scroll back in the log and permanently delete part of it (for example a large block of unwanted output). Select the part to remove, and press *Ctrl+Delete*. By default, you will be prompted for confirmation (this is a configurable option).

Using the menu Log ⇨ Print, you can print the entire log (be careful; it may be very large) or just this session's log. It may be extremely useful during the first few days to keep a printed trace of all the experiments that you have made.

1.3.5 - The Input Buffer

In addition to the Session Log (which contains a scrollable record of both input *and* output), Dyalog APL retains just the expressions that you have entered, in a separate ***Input Buffer***.

You can recall any one of the lines that you have previously executed as follows:

- To scroll back, press *Ctrl + Shift + Backspace*
- To scroll forward, press *Ctrl + Shift + Enter*

Once you have retrieved the statement you want to re-use, you can modify it (or not) and press *Enter* to re-execute it.

1.3.6 - Auto-Complete

To alleviate the chore of typing long names (of variables, functions, files), Dyalog can pop up a list of existing names beginning with the same initial character(s) as you type. This feature is called ***Auto Complete*** and is enabled, disabled and configured using the *Auto Complete* tab of the *Configuration* dialog box (Options ⇨ Configuration ⇨ Auto Complete).

To choose a name from the pop-up list, use the *Up* and *Down* cursor keys. To confirm the name that is currently selected press the *Right* cursor key (right arrow). To cancel the suggestion list, just press *Escape*.

You can configure the number of characters you must type before Dyalog makes suggestions, and change the keys used to confirm the selection or cancel the list.

2 - Working with This Tutorial

This tutorial is divided into 19 chapters named Chapter A to Chapter S. There is an additional Chapter X that contains the solutions to the exercises. In each chapter, pages are numbered starting from 1.

At the end of most chapters you will find a "*Specialist's Section*" containing advanced discussions about the symbols or methods presented in the chapter. Because these topics are for more experienced readers, they may use symbols that are not explained until later in the book.

If you are a beginner, **ignore those sections**, and skip to the next chapter.

While reading the book, reproduce the given examples on your computer, and experiment by yourself using different data; you will probably learn more from your own experimentation than from our examples.

Most chapters also include exercises; some are very simple, and some are more complex. We recommend that you do try to solve as many exercises as possible. Compare your solutions to the ones we suggest in Chapter X. APL is so rich that there may be several solutions to the same problem, the comparison is always interesting.

After Chapter D, you will be able to write small programs of your own, and you may want to print some results, input data using the Graphical User Interface (GUI), or read data from files. These topics are presented in self-contained dedicated chapters, so do not hesitate to go back and forth in the book to find the features you need.

Also have a look at the workspaces delivered with Dyalog. They are described in the User Guide, and contain some utility functions that may be useful to you.

This document is only a tutorial; everything cannot be said in these pages, and you can find additional information in the Dyalog APL manuals:

- User Guide — Installation and configuration of APL
The working environment described in detail
Utility workspaces and tutorials delivered with Dyalog APL
APL files
... and some advanced topics

- Language Reference: Describes all the symbols used in the language; Describes the structure of a program; Describes all the System Commands; Gives basic information about Object Oriented Programming
- Interface Guide: Introduction to the Graphic User Interface (GUI), with examples; APL and the Internet; OLE Automation client & server; ODBC interface with SQL Data Bases
- Object Reference: Overall description of all objects, properties, methods, and events used by the GUI interface
- .Net Interface Guide: Using the Microsoft .Net Framework

A certain number of specialised booklets will also be published to complement this tutorial; among them are:

- Object Oriented Programming
- SQAPL (Interface to Relational Databases using ODBC)
- NewLeaf (Document formatting and publishing)
- RainPro (Business and Scientific Graphics)

The manuals are available for download from *www.dyalog.com*.

We wish you pleasant reading

Chapter B: Data and Variables

When you use APL, you type an expression or a command into the session window, and the result of the expression, or a message resulting from the execution of the command, is displayed starting on the next line. So an APL "session" is a sequence of user input lines (expressions and/or commands) interleaved with the results of the expressions.

To help you see what you have done, APL initially positions the input cursor 6 spaces in from the left margin. Unless you deliberately move the cursor before you start typing, the expressions you enter into the system will therefore be indented, whereas the results of the expressions will not. For further clarity in this document, user input appears in red.

It is recommended that you go through this tutorial in front of your computer, and experiment by typing the expressions given below into the Dyalog session window. Try changing the expressions, and observe the new results.

1 - Simple Numeric Values

1.1 Our First Operations

Let's try some simple expressions (press *Enter* to have each expression evaluated):

```
      27 + 53
80
      1271 - 708
563
      644 - 832
¯188
```

Notice that APL uses a different symbol known as *high minus* (¯) to distinguish between a negative value and the function *subtract* (-). If you wish to enter a negative value, you can enter this special symbol by pressing Ctrl+ 2 (or by clicking the symbol in the "Language Bar").

Let's continue with some more expressions:

```
      86 ÷ 4                    ⇦ The Divide sign is obtained by pressing Ctrl+ =.
21.5
      59 × 8                    ⇦ The Multiply sign is obtained by pressing Ctrl+ -.
472
```

If you are familiar with other programming languages, you may be accustomed to using a slash (/) for division, and a star (*) for multiplication. Let's see what might happen if you mistakenly use * in APL:

```
      7 * 3                     ⇦ In APL the star means "Power",
343                               so that 7*3 is equivalent to 7×7×7.
```

The slash also has a different meaning in APL, we'll get to that later.

1.2 Variables

As in any other programming language, it is possible to create variables. Just choose a name and use the assignment arrow (←) to assign it a value. The value can be a single item or several items separated by spaces. The assignment arrow can be entered by pressing Ctrl+ [.

```
      Discount ← 0.15           ⇦ Read it as: Discount gets 0.15
      Years ← 1952 1943 1956 2007
      Purchased ← 4000
```

To obtain the value of a variable, just type its name (and press *Enter*), like this:

```
      Discount
0.15
      Years
1952 1943 1986 2007
```

Variable names are *case sensitive*. This means that APL considers a lower-case letter and an upper-case letter to be two different characters. So three variables named respectively VAT, Vat, and vat, would be distinct, and could contain different values. If you misspell the name of a variable, an error message will be displayed if that name is unknown:

```
      discount                  ⇦ We typed a lower-case "d", instead of "D"
VALUE ERROR                       The message "VALUE ERROR " means that the
      discount                    name discount is currently undefined.
     ^
```

Variable names must follow certain rules:

- They must contain only letters, in lower or upper-case, including some accented letters (cf. below), and the digits (0 to 9).
- The APL alphabet also includes the Greek letter Delta (∆), entered using Ctrl+H, the Underscore sign (_), and also the Underscored Delta (⍙), entered using Ctrl+.(dot).
- They cannot start with a digit.

The following variable names are valid:

`∆x`	with Delta
`Fly⍙Airlines`	with underscored Delta
`My_car_is_green`	with Underscores
`Hote273`	with digits
`Bétise_à_Cambrai`	with accented letters

But `5à7` is not valid, because it begins with a digit.

In this document, most variable names begin with an upper-case letter, with the remainder in lower-case. This is purely for consistency and ease of use.

The letters that are allowed as part of variable names are:

```
0123456789
ABCDEFGHIJKLMNOPQRSTUVWXYZ_
abcdefghijklmnopqrstuvwxyz
ÀÁÂÃÄÅÆÇÈÉÊËÌÍÎÏÐÑÒÓÔÕÖØÙÚÛÜÝß
àáâãäåæçèéêëìíîïðñòóôõöøùúûüþ
∆⍙
ABCDEFGHIKLMNOPQRSTUVWXYZ
```

Beware! Although it is permitted, the use of accented characters is not recommended because some people may be unable to enter them using their normal keyboard.

∆ and ⍙ may also cause problems if you ever want to inter-operate with other software, and are best avoided.

Finally, it is strongly recommended that you do not use the underscored letters which are only included to support old applications. Today, underscored letters are regarded as an anachronism, and are deprecated in modern versions of APL. They are not part of the Unicode character set, and are only displayed in the above list because we are cheating and using a non-standard font. When a standard Unicode font is used, the APL underscored letters correspond to the Unicode circled alphabet, which is displayed like this:

ⒶⒷⒸⒹⒺⒻⒼⒽⒾⓀⓁⓂⓃⓄⓅⓆⓇⓈⓉⓊⓋⓌⓍⓎⓏ

1.3 Operations on Variables

Variables can be used in any expression or calculation. For example, if we want to calculate the amount of the discount applied to the things we purchased, we can write:

```
      Amount ← Purchased×Discount
      Amount
600
```

When the result of an expression is assigned to a name, it is not displayed. This is why we have entered a second expression to have the value displayed. If the result of an operation is not assigned to a name, it is immediately displayed, but then the value of the result cannot be reused in another expression:

```
      Purchased × Discount
600
```

It is of course possible to change the contents of a variable. The previous value is then lost.

```
      Discount ← 0.185
```

It is possible to assign values to several variables in a single expression:

```
      (G H J) ← 30 51 49
```
⇦ G gets 30, H gets 51, and J gets 49.

This ***Multiple assignment*** is an elegant way of allocating a set of values to some distinct variables:

```
      (Colette Bernard Line Now) ← Years
      Colette
1952
      Line
1956
```

Note that it is possible to write multiple assignments without parentheses on the left:

```
      G H J ← 30 51 49
      Colette Bernard Line Now ← Years
```

Some other APL systems require the parentheses, so if compatibility across APL implementations is an issue for you, we recommend that you use parentheses in Dyalog APL as well.

2 - Arrays of Items

In APL, an *array* is a set of zero or more items. The variable `Years` that we used in the previous section is an array of 4 items.

2.1 Create a List or a Matrix

To enter a short list of items, just type them one by one separated by spaces, and assign the list to a name. For example, here is the number of TV sets sold during the last 10 days by a shopkeeper:

```
Sales ← 6 1 8 12 3 3 5 4 7 9
```

If you need to enter a very long list of items, which will not easily fit on a single line, please refer to Chapter H, Section 1, where a simple method is explained.

Imagine now that somebody has noted his income and expenses during the first six month of this year:

Month	Income	Expenses
January	4210	3121
February	4807	4284
March	3609	7543
April	5712	2601
May	2305	3364
June	4568	2784

We shall see later how we can store the names of the months; for now, let us just try to store the numeric values from the above table in a variable.

To do this, we have to give two pieces of information to the computer:

- the ***shape*** of the array: in this case, 6 rows and 2 columns
- the ***contents*** (or *items*) of the array, in row order.

The function that organises a set of items into an array of a specified shape is known as ***Reshape*** and is symbolised by the Greek letter Rho (⍴). It is easy to remember that ***R***ho can be entered using Ctrl-***R***.

The ***Reshape*** function is used as follows: `R← Shape ⍴ Contents`

For example, to obtain a 6 by 2 array of items:

```
      Money ← 6 2 ⍴ 4210 3121 4807 4284 3609 7543 5712 2601 etc...
      Money                                  ⇦ Let's verify the result.
4210 3121
4807 4284
3609 7543
5712 2601
2305 3364
4568 2784
```

2.2 Special Cases with Reshape

If there are too many items, the extra items are ignored:

```
      Contents ← 12 56 78 74 85 96 30 22 44 66 82 27
      3 3 ⍴ Contents
12 56 78
74 85 96
30 22 44                                     ⇦ The last 3 items (66 82 27) have been ignored.
```

However, if there are fewer items than implied by the shape, the list of items is reused as many times as necessary to fill the array:

```
      3 9 ⍴ Contents
12 56 78 74 85 96 30 22 44                   ⇦ We have used black and grey colours
66 82 27 12 56 78 74 85 96                     to show where the items were reused.
30 22 44 66 82 27 12 56 78
```

This property is often used to create special patterns:

```
      3 4 ⍴ 0                                ⇦ Fill an array with a single value.
0 0 0 0
0 0 0 0
0 0 0 0
      30 ⍴ 1 5 0 0                           ⇦ Repeat a pattern.
1 5 0 0 1 5 0 0 1 5 0 0 1 5 0 0 1 5 0 0 1 5 0 0 1 5 0 0 1 5
      3 4 ⍴ 2 4 6 8                          ⇦ Repeat a pattern.
2 4 6 8
2 4 6 8
2 4 6 8
```

```
      5 5 ρ 1 0 0 0 0 0                ⇦ Shift values.
1 0 0 0 0
0 1 0 0 0
0 0 1 0 0
0 0 0 1 0
0 0 0 0 1
```

2.3 Multi-dimensional Arrays

APL is not limited to arrays with two dimensions, it can handle arrays with 3, 4, indeed up to 15 dimensions.

Imagine that a company has stored the production of its assembly lines in a variable named `Prod`.

The variable contains 5 years of production, on 2 assembly lines, and for 12 months per year. To represent the 3 dimensions on the screen, the array is displayed split into sub-arrays each representing a single year, as follows:

```
      Prod
26 16 22 17 21 44 25 22 23 44 41 33
43 36 47 49 30 22 57 20 45 60 43 22
                                       ⇦ A blank line separates the sub-arrays.
44 21 58 57 17 43 47 17 43 26 53 23
29 19 23 38 53 47 38 22 40 57 35 26
                                       ⇦ Ditto.
37 27 53 26 29 46 25 26 30 20 32 16
56 55 25 47 38 27 39 59 20 28 42 25

21 57 55 44 16 54 26 16 55 56 45 45
16 55 26 20 27 55 36 39 43 38 50 16

27 23 56 41 53 60 39 47 44 47 17 28
24 35 61 26 22 35 24 20 31 35 47 37
```

This array is organised in dimensions that represent 5 years, 2 lines, 12 months: it is a three dimensional array. We can also say that its ***shape*** is `5 2 12`.

3 - Shape, Rank, and Vocabulary

3.1 Shape and Rank

The symbol ⍴, which we introduced above, can be used to obtain the lengths of the dimensions or the ***Shape*** of an array:

```
      ⍴ Years                    ⇦ Read this as "Shape of Years".
4                                ⇦ Years     has 4 items.
      ⍴ Money
6 2                              ⇦ Money     has 6 rows and 2 columns.
      Shape ← ⍴Prod
      Shape
5 2 12                           ⇦ Prod      has 5 sheets (or planes), each having
                                             2 rows and 12 columns.
```

Now, what is the shape of `Shape` ?

```
      ⍴ Shape
3                                ⇦ Prod has 3 dimensions.
```

The same result could have been obtained directly using the expression `⍴⍴ Prod`.

`Prod` has 3 dimensions; we say that its ***Rank*** is 3,
or that it is organised along 3 criteria which are: Years / Lines / Months.

```
      ⍴⍴ Money
2
```

`Money` has 2 dimensions; we say that its ***Rank*** is 2,
or that it is organised along 2 criteria which are: Months / Accounts.

Definition:

> The ***Rank*** of an array is the number of its dimensions.
> It can be obtained using the expression: ⍴⍴*Array*

3.2 Scaling Down the Ranks

Using that formula, we can see that:

`Prod`	has a shape equal to	`5 2 12`	and its rank is equal to .... `3`
`Money`	has a shape equal to	`6 2`	and its rank is equal to .... `2`
`Years`	has a shape equal to	`4`	and its rank is equal to .... `1`

It seems consistent that some array must exist which has a rank equal to ...... `0`

Such arrays are single items, like 1573 or 36.29 or the variable `Discount` used above.

```
      ⍴⍴ Discount
0
      ⍴⍴ 36.29
0
```

⇦ A single number has **no dimensions**.

We needed 3 numbers to express the shape of `Prod`, 2 numbers to express the shape of `Money`, and only 1 number to express the shape of `Years` … hence to express the shape of `1573` or `Discount`, we need **no** numbers:

```
      ⍴ 1573

```

⇦ The answer displays as a blank line: the shape of a single number is an empty array (0 items).

```
      ⍴ Discount

```

⇦ Ditto

3.3 Vocabulary

In this book, we shall use the following terms:

Array	is a generic word for any set of items (possibly containing a single item, or no items at all)		
Scalar	is a single item like	`Discount`	its rank is 0
Vector	is a list of items like	`Years`	its rank is 1
Matrix	is an array of rank 2 like	`Money`	its rank is 2
Table	is a common name for a matrix		
Cube	is a common name for 3-D arrays like	`Prod`	its rank is 3

3.4 Beware!

3.4.1 - The Shape is Always a Vector

The shape of a value is **always** a vector, even if it contains only one item or even no items at all.

```
      Shape ← ⍴Years
      Shape
4                                   ⇦ It looks like a scalar.
      ⍴⍴ Shape
1                                   ⇦ But it is of rank 1, so it is a vector.
      ⍴ Shape
1                                   ⇦ It is a vector with only one item.
```

3.4.2 - Do Not Rely on the Visual Aspect of a Variable

Although scalars, vectors, and matrices may sometimes look the same when they are displayed, they should not be confused. Consider, for example, the following vector V and matrix M:

```
      V ← 87 65 21 40
      M ← 1 4 ⍴ 87 65 21 40
```

If we display their values, they look exactly the same:

```
      V
87 65 21 40
      M
87 65 21 40
```

But they cannot easily be added or multiplied together:

```
      V+M
RANK ERROR
      V+M
     ^
```

Similarly, a scalar should not be confused with a 1-item vector or a 1-item matrix. The scalar has a rank of 0 whereas the vector is rank 1.

```
      S ←    456                    ⇦ Create a scalar.
      V ← 1⍴456                     ⇦ Create a one-item vector.
```

```
      S
456
      V
456
      ⍴⍴S
0
      ⍴⍴V
1
```

⇦ If displayed, they look the same.

⇦ But their ranks are different; the two variables should not be confused.

3.4.3 - Displaying Long Vectors

If a vector is too long to be displayed in a single line on your screen, it will be wrapped onto several lines. But to prevent possible confusion with the display of a matrix, the second line and the following lines will not be aligned at the left margin, but will be indented 6 characters to the right. For example:

```
      Bignum
446.19 231.12 253.59 115.56 262.15 271.78 1.07 180.83 166.92
      318.86 240.75 44.94 240.75 90.95 317.79 285.69 4.28 368.08
      295.32 379.85 324.21 77.04 77.04 415.16 447.26 33.17 415.16
      285.69 202.23 126.26 180.83 81.32 134.82 261.08 343.47
      157.29 335.98
```

4 - Simple Character Values

4.1 Character Vectors and Scalars

Up to now, we have used only numeric values, but we can also create textual data known as a *character array*. To identify a string of characters as text, we start and end it with a single ***Quote***:

```
      Text ← 'Today is August 14th, 2007'
      Text
Today is August 14th, 2007
      ⍴Text
26
      Trailer ← 'I type 7 trailing blanks       '
      Trailer
I type 7 trailing blanks
      ⍴Trailer
31
```

As these examples show:

- The quotes are **not** part of the text, they're just there to delimit it.
- Text can include any character: letters, digits, punctuation.
- So, `Text` and `Trailer` are vectors. They are sometimes called *Strings*.
- APL does not recognize words; a character array is simply a set of characters.
- Blank characters (spaces) are characters like any other characters; they do not have any special meaning. However, when a character array is displayed any trailing blanks are most often invisible.

A problem may occur when the text itself includes an apostrophe, for example in a sentence like "*It's raining, isn't it?*".

When you enter apostrophes as part of the text, you must double them, as shown below, to distinguish them from the delimiters:

```
      Damned ← 'It''s raining, isn''t it?'
```

This is only a typing convention, but the doubled quotes are transformed into a single apostrophe, as you can see here:

```
      Damned
It's raining, isn't it?             ⇦ The vector's size is equal to 23.
```

As mentioned above a character array can contain digits, but they are not considered to be numbers, and it is impossible to use them in a mathematical operation:

```
      Hundred ← '100'
      Hundred
100                                 ⇦ It looks like a number.
      ⍴Hundred
3                                   ⇦ But it isn't.
      Hundred + 5
DOMAIN ERROR
      Hundred+5
     ∧
```

Of course, a single character is a scalar:

```
      Singleton ← 'P'
      ⍴Singleton
                                    ⇦ Do you remember? Scalars have no dimensions.
      ⍴⍴Singleton
0                                   ⇦ Yes, it is definitely a scalar.
```

4.2 Character Arrays

We saw, some pages ago, a list of months:

```
January
February
March
April
May
June
```

We can think of this as a list of 6 words, or as a matrix of 6 rows and 8 columns (the width of "February"). Both representations are valid, and both can be used in APL; let us study them one after the other.

To enter the months as a 6 by 8 matrix, one must use the *Reshape* (`⍴`) function:

- To the left of the function we must specify the shape of the matrix we want to build: `6 8`
- To the right of the function we must specify all of the characters (including any trailing blanks) that are necessary to fill each row to the proper length:

```
      MonMat ← 6 8 ⍴ 'January FebruaryMarch   April   May     June'
```

No space was typed between `February` and `March`; do you see why?

```
      MonMat                              ⇦ Now, let us see the result.
January
February
March
April
May
JuneJanu                                  ⇦ Oops!
```

We forgot that when the right argument is too short, `⍴` reuses it from the beginning. That's the reason why the last row is wrong. We must add 4 trailing blanks.

Facility

You do not have to re-type the entire expression, just move your cursor up to the line where you defined `MonMat`, add the missing blanks, and press the *Enter* key.

APL will then copy the modified line down to the end of your session and automatically restore the original line to its original state. As a consequence, the session window always displays the sequence of expressions and results in the order in which you typed them.

```
      MonMat ← 6 8⍴'January FebruaryMarch   April   May     June    '
```

```
      MonMat
January
February
March
April
May
June                                    ⇦ That's right now!
      ⍴MonMat
6 8                                     ⇦ As expected, it is a matrix.
```

Now, to enter the months as 6 words, one must type each word between quotes, and check that each closing quote is separated from the next opening quote by at least one blank (otherwise it would be interpreted as an apostrophe – remember, the juxtaposition of two quotes in a character string is used to enter a single quote):

```
      MonVec ← 'January' 'February' 'March' 'April' 'May' 'June'
      MonVec
January  February  March April  May  June
      ⍴MonVec
6                                       ⇦ It is a vector.
```

`MonVec` is a vector of a kind that we have not seen before, the items of which are 6 sub-arrays. This kind of an array is called a ***Nested Array***.

Be patient! We shall study nested arrays very soon in this very chapter.

5 - Indexing

5.1 Traditional Vector Indexing

Our variable `Contents` contains the following items:

```
      12 56 78 74 85 96 30 22 44 66 82 27
```

To extract one of these items, you just have to specify its position, or ***Index***, between ***Square brackets***:

```
      Contents[3]
78
```

In most "traditional" languages, programmers generally use parentheses instead of brackets, but parentheses have many other different uses. In APL, parentheses have one and only one use, namely to specify the order of evaluation of a complex expression. In this respect, the use of square brackets for indexing makes APL more rigorous.

Of course, an index must follow some obvious rules: it must be an integer numeric value; it may not be negative or greater than the size of the vector. Otherwise, an "INDEX ERROR" will be reported.

It is possible to extract several items in a single operation, and in any order:

```
      Contents[3 7 1 3 3 12]          ⇦ You can see that an item can be selected
78 30 12 78 78 27                       more than once.
```

The same notation allows you to modify one or more items of the vector. The only condition is that you must provide as many replacement values as the number of items you select, or give a single replacement value to use for all the selected items:

```
      Contents[2 4 6] ← 7 11 80       ⇦ Three values replace three items.
      Contents
12 7 78 11 85 80 30 22 44 66 82 27
      Contents[8 11 12] ← 33          ⇦ One single value replaces three items.
      Contents
12 7 78 11 85 80 30 33 44 66 33 33
```

This works exactly the same on character vectors:

```
      'COMPUTER'[8 7 4 2 8 6]
REPORT
      Test ← 'BREAD'
      Test[2 4] ← 'LN'
      Test
BLEND
```

5.2 The Shape of the Result

The index may be a numeric array of any shape: scalar, vector, matrix, or an array of higher rank. To understand what happens, there is a simple rule:

> When a vector is indexed by an array, the result has exactly the ***same shape*** as the index array, as if each item of the index had been replaced by the item it designates.

This rule is easy to verify. Let us restore the initial values of `Contents`:

```
      Contents ← 12 56 78 74 85 96 30 22 44 66 82 27
```

And let us create a matrix of indices:

```
      MyIndex ← 3 5 ρ 5 5 4 4 8 6 12 6 11 12 10 6 1 4 9
      MyIndex
 5  5  4  4  8
 6 12  6 11 12
10  6  1  4  9
      Contents[MyIndex]
85 85 74 74 22
96 27 96 82 27
66 96 12 74 44
```

⇦ For example you can see that the index in row 2 column 5 was 12. So, it has been replaced by the 12th item of `Contents`, i.e. 27.

The rule remains true if the indexed vector is a character vector. For example, imagine that we have a matrix named `Planning`, in which some tasks are planned (1) or not (0) over the next 12 months:

```
      Planning
0 0 0 1 1 1 1 1 1 0 0 0
1 1 1 1 1 1 1 1 0 0 0 0
0 1 1 1 0 0 0 0 0 1 1 1
0 0 0 0 0 0 0 1 1 1 1 1
0 0 1 1 1 1 1 0 0 0 0 0
```

⇦ This is not very easy to interpret!

Let us replace the inactive periods by "-", and the busy periods by "⎕". This beautiful character, named ***Quad***, can be entered by pressing *Ctrl*+L.

```
      '-⎕'[Planning+1]
---⎕⎕⎕⎕⎕⎕---
⎕⎕⎕⎕⎕⎕⎕⎕----
-⎕⎕⎕-----⎕⎕⎕
-------⎕⎕⎕⎕⎕
--⎕⎕⎕⎕⎕-----
```

⇦ Do you understand why we added 1?

⇦ Isn't it magic?

Of course, the vector to be indexed was composed of only two characters, so the set of indices had to be composed only from the values 1 and 2. This is the reason why we added 1 to `Planning`.

All the 0's in `Planning` have been replaced by the 1st item (-), and all the 1's have been replaced by the 2nd item (⎕).

5.3 Array Indexing

Just to make some experiments, let us create a new variable, named `Tests`:

```
41 26 38
14 87 52
30 28 19
65 40 55
19 31 64
45 82 74
```

Indexing an array is very similar to the method we saw for vectors, but we now need one index for the row and one for the column; they must be separated by a ***Semi-colon***. For example, to get (or replace) the value 55 in row 4, column 3, one types:

```
      Tests[4;3]
55
```

It is of course possible to select more than one row and more than one column. If so, one obtains all the values situated at the intersections of the specified rows and columns.

```
      Tests[1 5 6;1 3]
41 38
19 64
45 74
```

The result of indexing may sometimes be surprising. Let us extract 4 values from the first column:

```
      Tests[1 2 5 6;1]
41 14 19 45
```

You probably expected the result to be displayed like a column? Really sorry!

The result of this expression is a vector, and a vector is always displayed as a row on the screen.

We shall see later that it is possible, using a little trick, to cause the result to be displayed vertically.

When you use indexing, you must specify as many indices or sets of indices as the array's rank. For a 3-D array, you must specify 3 sets of indices, separated by two semi-colons.

For example, suppose that we would like to extract the production of the 2nd assembly line, for the first 6 months of the last two years, from the array `Prod`,. Let's express that in the order of the 3 dimensions: Years/Lines/Months:

The last two years are in positions	`4 5`
The second assembly line	`2`
The first 6 months	`1 2 3 4 5 6`

```
      Prod[4 5;2;1 2 3 4 5 6]
16 55 26 20 27 55                   ⇦ The result is a matrix: 2 years/6 months.
24 35 61 26 22 35
```

Remark 1

Because we can select rows and columns, the semi-colon is necessary to tell them apart:

	`Tests[1 2;3]`	gives rows 1 and 2, column 3
whereas	`Tests[1;2 3]`	gives row 1, columns 2 and 3

Remark 2

It is also possible to select several items which are not at the intersections of the same rows or columns. To do so requires a special notation where the individual Row/Column indices of each item are embedded in parentheses. The reason for this syntax will become clear in Section 6.3.

For example, let us select `Tests[2;3]` together with `Tests[5;1]` and `Tests[1;2]`.

```
      Tests[(2 3)(5 1)(1 2)]
 52 19 26
```

5.4 Convention

To specify *all* the items of a dimension, you just omit the index for that dimension, but you must not omit the semi-colon attached to it.

In the previous example, to obtain both assembly lines we could have typed:

```
      Prod[4 5;1 2;1 2 3 4 5 6]
```

But it is shorter to type:

```
      Prod[4 5;;1 2 3 4 5 6]
```

⇦ The omitted index means "All the assembly lines".

In the same way:

```
      Prod[4 5;2;]
```

⇦ The omitted last index means "All the months".

And finally:

```
      Prod[;;1 2 3]
```

⇦ The omitted indices means "All years and lines".

This convention also applies to *replacing* specific items. For example, to change all the items in the last row of `Tests`, we could type:

```
      Tests[6;] ← 60 70 80
```

5.5 Warnings

We would like to draw your attention to some delicate details. Here is the first:

5.5.1 - Shape Compatibility

To replace several items in an array, the replacement array must have exactly the **same shape** as the array of indices they replace.

For example, suppose that we would like to replace the four "corners" of `Tests` with the values `11 22 33 44` respectively.

We **cannot** successfully execute: `Tests[1 6;1 3] ← 11 22 33 44` ; a `"LENGTH ERROR"` would be issued (note that this is a "**Shape** error").

If we had extracted these four values, the result would have been a 2 by 2 matrix:

```
      Tests[1 6;1 3]
41 38
60 80                          ⇦ Remember: row 6 was modified above!
```

So, to replace them, we cannot use a vector, as we have just tried to do. Instead we must organise the replacement array into a 2 by 2 matrix, like this:

```
      Tests[1 6;1 3] ← 2 2 ρ 11 22 33 44
      Tests
11 26 22                       ⇦ The replaced values are shown in black.
14 87 52
30 28 19
65 40 55
19 31 64
33 70 44
```

5.5.2 - Replace or Obtain All the Values

To replace **all** of the values in an array with a single value, it is necessary to use brackets in which the indices of all the dimensions have been removed.

For example, imagine that we would like to reset all the values of `Tests` to zero.

`Tests ← 0` would be **wrong**, because that would replace the matrix by a scalar.

The correct solution is `Tests[;] ← 0` ⇦ All the rows and columns are replaced by zero.

For a vector we would write: `Vector[] ← 123` ⇦ All the items are replaced by 123.

5.5.3 - "Pass-Through" Value

Imagine that we have a vector : `Vec ← 32 51 28 19 72 31`

We replace some items and assign the result to another variable: `Res ← Vec[2 4 6] ← 50`

What do we get in `Res`? Is it `Res ← Vec[2 4 6]` , or is it `Res ← 50`?

In fact, we get `50`. We say that `50` is a ***Pass-Through*** value.

5.6 The Index Function

In APL, nearly all of the built-in functions (known as *Primitive Functions*) are represented by a single symbol: `+ × ρ ÷` etc. Bracket indexing, as we introduced above, is an exception: it is represented by two non-contiguous symbols: [and]. This is one of the reasons why modern versions of APL also include an ***Index*** function.

It is represented by the symbol ⌷

Beware: This is **not** the symbol *Quad* used in our planning example a few pages ago!

In fact, it looks like a *Quad* which has been *squished*, hence its name: Squish-Quad, or ***Squad*** for short. The *Squad* is obtained with Ctrl+Shift+L.

When applied to a vector, *Index* takes a single number on its left.

```
      3 ⌷ Contents
78                                    ⇦ This is equivalent to Contents[3]
```

For now, we shall not try to extract more than one item from a vector; we need additional knowledge to do that.

For a matrix, *Index* takes a pair of values (row/column) on its left.

```
      4 2 ⌷ Tests
78                                    ⇦ This is equivalent to Tests[4;2]
```

It is possible to select several rows and several columns, using a special notation that will be explained in subsequent sections. The left argument of *Index* is now made of a list of rows followed by a list of columns, both parenthesised:

```
      (1 3 6)(1 3)⌷Tests
11 22                                 ⇦ This is equivalent to Tests[1 3 6;1 3]
30 19
33 44
```

6 - Mixed and Nested Arrays

Up to now we have dealt with only homogenous arrays: Scalars, vectors, or higher rank arrays containing only numbers or only characters. An array was a collection of what we call *simple* scalars. In the early 1980's enhanced versions of APL started to appear. They accepted a mixture of numbers and characters within the same array (so-called ***Mixed Arrays***), and arrays could contain sub-arrays as items (so-called ***Nested Arrays***).

In this chapter, we shall explore only some basic properties of *Mixed* and *Nested arrays*, just to help you understand what might otherwise appear to be unusual behaviour or unexpected error messages. We shall not go any further for now; Chapter I will be entirely dedicated to an extensive study of nested arrays.

Note that with the current widespread use of *Nested arrays*, it is now very common to refer to an "old-fashioned" array that is neither *Mixed* nor *Nested* as a *Simple array*.

6.1 Mixed Arrays

An array is described as a ***Mixed Array*** if it contains a mixture of scalar numbers and scalar characters.

It is easy to create such an array:

```
      MixVec ← 44 87 'K' 12 29 'B' 'a' 'g' 46.3
      ⍴MixVec
9                                    ⇦ This is a vector.
      MixVec
44 87 K 12 29 Bag 46.3
      MixMat ← 2 5 ⍴ MixVec
      ⍴MixMat
2 5                                  ⇦ That is a matrix.
      MixMat
44 87 K 12   29
 B  a g 46.3 44
```

6.2 Four Important Remarks

6.2.1 - In a vector like `MixVec`, each letter must be entered as a scalar: embedded within quotes, and separated from the next one by at least one blank space.

If the space is omitted, for example, if we type `'B''a''g'`, APL interprets the doubled quotes as apostrophes, which yields `B'a'g`. This is not a sequence of 3 scalars, but a 5-item vector.

6.2.2 - When `MixVec` is displayed (see above), the three letters `Bag` are joined together, like the letters in any vector of characters.

This presentation might be confused with an array of 7 items, whose 6th item is the vector `'Bag'`. That would be a *Nested Array*. We will soon learn how to investigate the structure of an array.

6.2.3 - This confusion disappears in `MixMat`. Because the items of the matrix must be aligned in columns, "B" is placed under 44, "a" under 87, and "g" under "K". Here you can easily see that the three letters `Bag` are really three independent scalars.

6.2.4 - A ***Mixed*** array is made up only of simple scalars (numbers or characters); **it is not** a *Nested Array*.

6.3 Nested Arrays

An array is said to be ***Generalised*** or ***Nested*** when one or more of its items are not *simple* scalars, but are scalars which contain other arrays. The latter may be simple arrays of any shape or rank (vectors, matrices, arrays), or they may themselves be *Nested arrays*.

A nested array can be created in a number of ways; we shall begin with the simplest one, known as ***Vector notation***, or ***Strand notation***. Here is how it works:

The items of an array are just juxtaposed side by side, and each can be identified as an item because it is:

- either separated from its neighbours by .... **blanks**
- or embedded within .... **quotes**
- or an expression embedded within................. **parentheses**
- or a .... **variable name**

Just to demonstrate how it works, let us create a nested vector and a nested matrix.

```
One ← 2 2⍴8 6 2 4          ⇦ Create two simple arrays,
Two ← 'Hello'                which will be used below.
```

```
      NesVec ← 87 24 'John' 51 (78 45 23) 85 One 69
      ⍴NesVec
8                                              ⇦ We have juxtaposed 8 items.
      NesVec
87 24  John  51  78 45 23  85  8 6  69
                               2 4
```

When displayed, this vector is a bit difficult to read. To help you understand how it is organised, we have drawn boxes around its items:

87	24	John	51	78 45 23	85	8 6 2 4	69

And now, a matrix!

```
      NesMat ← 2 3 ⍴ 'Dyalog' 44 Two 27 One (2 3⍴1 2 0 0 0 5)
      ⍴NesMat
2 3
      NesMat
 Dyalog   44  Hello
     27  8 6  1 2 0                      ⇦ It is a bit more complex to interpret.
         2 4  0 0 5
```

Here again, we have drawn boxes around the items:

Dyalog	44	Hello
27	8 6 2 4	1 2 0 0 0 5

To obtain this kind of presentation, execute the following command (remember: a command begins by a closing parenthesis):

```
      )Copy Util DISP
```

Then execute:

```
      DISP NesMat
```

The interpretation of the display is sometimes difficult for a beginner, but after some weeks (maybe months?) of experience, you will begin to understand immediately what it means.

You probably remember the mixed vector `MixVec`, which contained 3 adjacent scalars, "B", "a", and "g". Let us compare the display of `MixVec` with a 7 item nested vector, whose 6th item contains the word "Bag":

Let us enter the **nested** array ⇨ `44 87 'K' 12 29 'Bag' 46.3`
It is displayed like this ⇨ `44 87 K 12 29  Bag  46.3`

Then let's look at `MixVec` ⇨ `MixVec`
It is displayed like this ⇨ `44 87 K 12 29 Bag 46.3`

You will have observed that in the nested array the sub-vector `Bag` is separated from its neighbours not by a single space, but by two spaces: this should alert an experienced APLer that it is a nested array.

However, this difference is so small that the APL community, all over the world, uses a utility program, named `DISPLAY`, to draw boxes around arrays (nested or not), to make things clear. Let us examine it.

6.4 DISPLAY

`DISPLAY` is provided with Dyalog APL in a library workspace which itself is named DISPLAY. Because this library is by default on the *Workspace Search Path* of APL, you can easily add the DISPLAY function to your active workspace by typing the command:

```
      )copy display
```

⇦ This copies the entire workspace, but it contains only one single function: `DISPLAY`.

As you can see, applied to a simple scalar, `DISPLAY` does not produce any visible difference:

```
      DISPLAY 37
37
      DISPLAY 'K'
K
```

However, applied to a vector, `DISPLAY` draws a box around the values:

```
      DISPLAY 54 73 19
┌→────────┐
│54 73 19│
└~────────┘
```

⇦ The default presentation uses line-drawing characters to draw the box.

```
      0 DISPLAY 54 73 19
.→-------.
|54 73 19|
'~-------'
```

⇦ With the optional left argument set to 0, the function uses standard characters.

The second, rougher, form of presentation is provided for use in circumstances where the line-drawing symbols in the APL font are not displayed or printed as intended. This will depend upon your version of Windows and on the display and printer drivers you are using.

6.4.1 - Conventions

The upper-left corner of the box provides information about the **shape** of the displayed value:

- a single horizontal arrow for a vector
- two (or more) arrows for a matrix or higher rank arrays
- no arrow at all for scalars containing nested values, a concept we haven't seen up to now

The bottom-left corner of the box provides information about the **contents** of the array:

~ means that the array contains only numeric values

_ means that the array contains only characters

\+ is used for mixed arrays

∊ means that the array contains other arrays: it is a nested array

6.4.2 - Examples

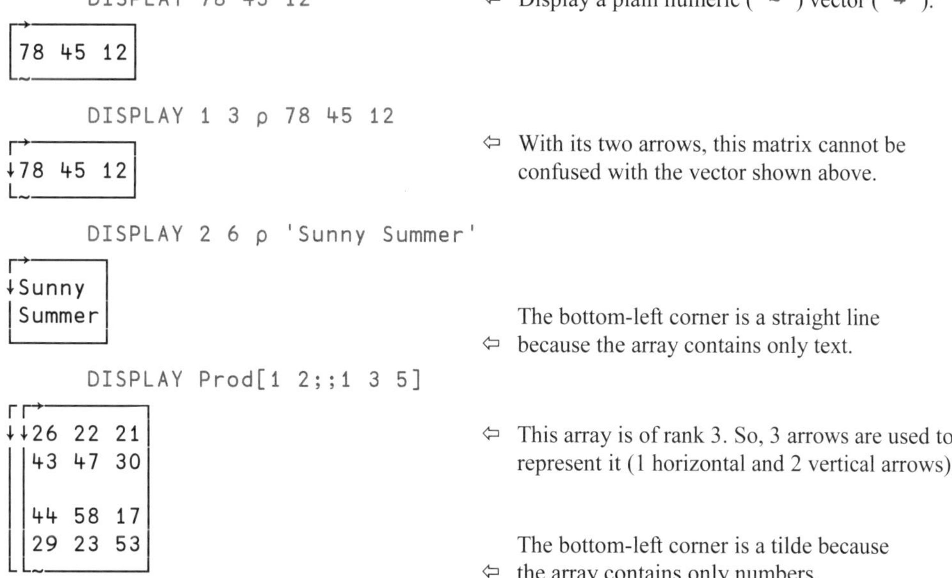

```
      DISPLAY 78 45 12
┌→───────┐
│78 45 12│
└~───────┘
```

⇦ Display a plain numeric (~) vector (→).

```
      DISPLAY 1 3 ρ 78 45 12
┌→───────┐
↓78 45 12│
└~───────┘
```

⇦ With its two arrows, this matrix cannot be confused with the vector shown above.

```
      DISPLAY 2 6 ρ 'Sunny Summer'
┌→─────┐
↓Sunny │
│Summer│
└──────┘
```

⇦ The bottom-left corner is a straight line because the array contains only text.

```
      DISPLAY Prod[1 2;;1 3 5]
┌┌→───────┐
↓↓26 22 21│
││43 47 30│
││        │
││44 58 17│
││29 23 53│
└└~───────┘
```

⇦ This array is of rank 3. So, 3 arrows are used to represent it (1 horizontal and 2 vertical arrows).

⇦ The bottom-left corner is a tilde because the array contains only numbers.

Mixed arrays are sometimes more complex to understand.

```
      DISPLAY 54 'G' 61 'U' 7 19
┌→──────────────┐
│54 G 61 U 7 19│
└+──────────────┘
```

⇦ The array is a mixed (+) vector (→), and all its items can be easily identified.

But the following array is more complex:

```
      DISPLAY 54 3 'G' 'U' 7 '3' 19
┌→───────────────┐
│54 3 GU 7 3 19│
└+───────────────┘
```

- Note that in the example above it is impossible to distinguish between the numeric value `3` and the character value `'3'`. The DISPLAY function actually tries to help us by underlining all character values, but unfortunately this coincides with the bottom border of the box. When the array being displayed becomes more complex, you will see this underlining, as the next example shows.
- The two adjacent scalars `'G'` and `'U'` are displayed side by side; a vector `'GU'` would have given a nested array, with a different representation, as you can see below:

```
      DISPLAY 54 3 'GU' 7 '3' 19
```

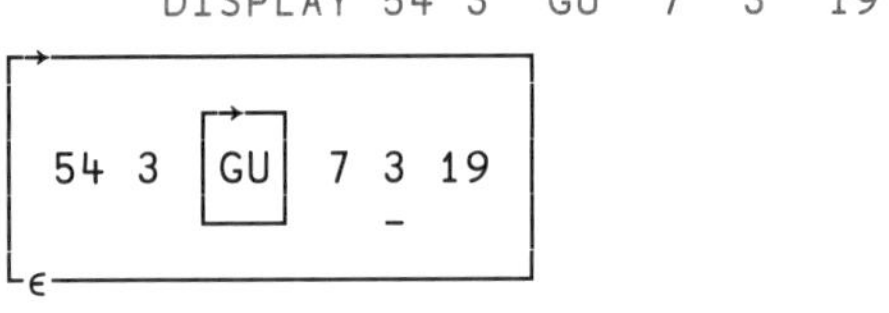

⇦ Because one of the items of this array contains a vector, the array is "nested", hence the ∊ sign at the bottom-left corner. Now the underlining of `'3'` is visible, so it is easy to see that it is a character. Since `7` is not underlined it is a number.

We shall discover more about `DISPLAY` when we study Nested arrays in detail (refer to **I-1.3**), but we can already use it to show the structure of the arrays that we have been working with. For example, our nested matrix `NesMat`:

```
      DISPLAY NesMat
```

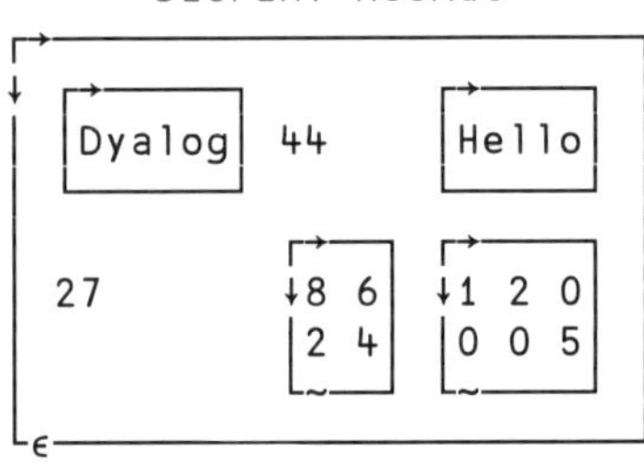

⇦ You can see that all the sub-arrays contained in `NesMat` are individually represented with the same conventions, making the interpretation easy.

6.5 Be Simple!

Up to now, the nested arrays we have met contained only "simple" items (scalars, vectors, matrices). Here is a completely weird matrix, which itself contains a small nested array made of the first two columns of `NesMat`:

```
      Weird ← 2 2⍴ 456 (NesMat[;1 2]) (17 51) 'Twisted'
      Weird
 456    Dyalog   44
            27  8 6
                2 4
17 51  Twisted
      DISPLAY Weird
```

⇦ The default presentation is difficult to interpret!

⇦ Let us use DISPLAY to make things clear!

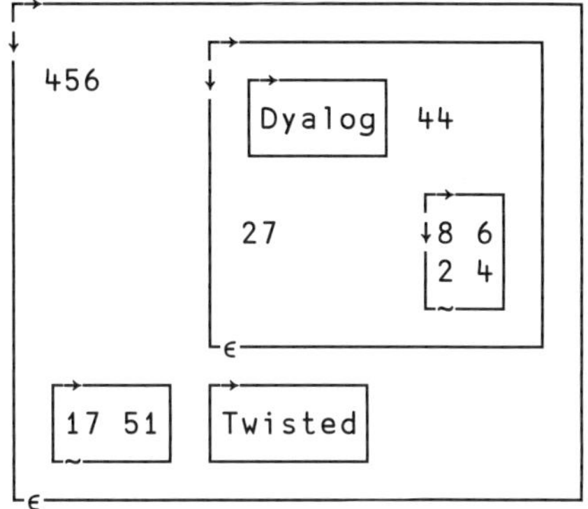

Remark

Of course, even if APL **can** handle arrays as unusual as the one above, it is **not advisable** to build such arrays! Most nested arrays have a clear and straightforward structure.

Remember: in Section 4.2 we had a list of month names to store, and we had the choice between a matrix and a vector of vectors, that is to say a nested vector.

```
      MonVec
January  February  March April  May  June
```

Because its contents are homogeneous (made up only of vectors), this array has a simple structure that is clear and easy to interpret. DISPLAY shows it like this:

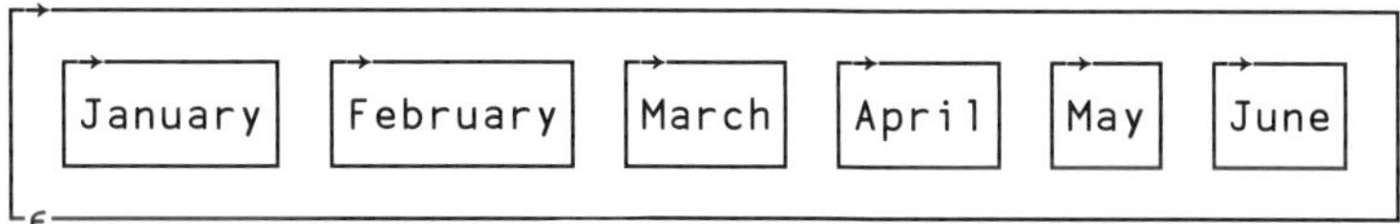

Imagine now that we want to store the ages of the children of 5 families; we could enter them like this:

```
      Children ← (6 2) (35 33 26 21) (7 7) 3 (19 14)
      Children
6 2  35 33 26 21  7 7  3  19 14
```

```
      DISPLAY Children
```

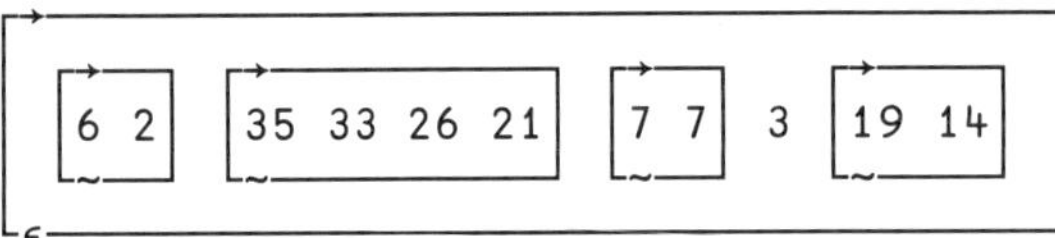

This array is not homogeneous; it is made of vectors mixed with a scalar. However, its structure is simple, and consistent. Together with the previous example, it is a pertinent usage of nested arrays.

6.6 That's *Not* All, Folks!

In this section we have only described some basic things about nested arrays. APL provides a number of functions designed specifically to manipulate nested arrays, but it would be premature to introduce these now until we have fully explored all of the basic capabilities.

Nevertheless, if you want to learn a bit more on the subject, just skip to Chapter I.

7 - Empty Arrays

An array is an ***empty array*** if the length of one or more of its dimensions is zero. Hence, it is possible to meet many different kinds of empty arrays: vectors, matrices, arrays of any rank or type.

`0⍴0`	is an empty numeric vector.
`''`	is an empty character vector, because nothing was typed between the quotes.
`' '`	is ***not*** an empty vector; we typed a blank character between the quotes. Though it is invisible, it is a character just like "B" or "Z".
`0 3⍴''`	is an empty character matrix with 0 rows, but nevertheless 3 columns.
`5 0⍴0`	is an empty numeric matrix with no columns, but nevertheless 5 rows.
`3 0 7⍴0`	is an empty numeric array of rank 3.

There are many ways to create empty arrays, as we shall discover in the following chapters.

We shall see later that empty arrays, which you may find surprising, are extremely useful in solving a large number of business problems. If fact, they are often used as the starting point (initial value) for variables that will grow by the iterative addition of new items.

The empty numeric vector is probably the most frequently used of all empty arrays. For that reason, a special symbol has been designed to represent it: ⍬ (entered by pressing Ctrl+]).

Because this symbol is made of a *Zero* with a *Tilde* on top of it, it is called ***Zilde***.

Lets us conclude this topic with a rather comforting statement:

```
      Emptiness ← ⍬                  ⇦ Let us start by an empty vector.
      Presence ← 'Friendly'          ⇦ Now, we create a text vector.
      Emptiness ⍴ Presence           ⇦ Give Presence the shape Emptiness
F                                    ⇦ ... and it works!
```

This proves that a Friendly Presence can fill up Emptiness! That's good! But can we explain it? Let's try...

In the last expression, the *Reshape* function (⍴) returns an array with the shape specified in its left argument `Emptiness`.

Since `Emptiness` is an empty vector (⍬) *Reshape* will return an array having an empty shape. Such an array is a scalar, so we know that the result of the expression will be a scalar.

Reshape will also fill the scalar with a value, taken from the right argument `Presence`. `Presence` contains the character vector `'Friendly'`, but since we only need one item to fill a scalar, we can only use the `'F'`. The rest of the character vector `'Friendly'` is not used.

In fact, the expression ⍬⍴*Array* is widely used to return the first item of an array as a scalar, and in particular to convert a 1-item vector into a scalar.

Remark Though they both are invisible when displayed, a numeric empty vector (⍬) is different from a character empty vector (' ').

8 - Workspaces and Commands

You have nearly finished this chapter and, naturally, you would like to save the variables you have created:

- In the "File" menu, select "Save" or "Save as", and use the normal procedure for saving a file.
- You can also click, in the toolbar, on the icon of a diskette (who still knows what a diskette is?), which is equivalent, in APL to "Save as".
- There is also a built-in method in APL, which may be activated through a special SAVE command or function, as will be described later.

An explanation of how APL manages your data is given below.

8.1 The Active Workspace

When you start a working session with APL, you are allotted an empty portion of memory, which is called a ***Workspace***, or ***WS*** for short. This WS is called the ***Active WS***, because it is the area of memory in which you work. You gradually fill it with variables and functions[2] as you create them.

You can ask the system to give you the list of your variables and functions. To do that, you use a ***system command***: a special word which is recognised by the APL system because its first character is a ***closing parenthesis***: `)`. Some Swedish APLers call that a "banana".

The names of system commands are not case sensitive; they can be typed in mixture of upper and lower-case characters.

Let's obtain a list of our variable names, using the command `)vars`:

```
      )vars
experiment      what    Charlebois      Contents        Damned1
Discount        Emptiness       Goof    Hundred M       MixMat
MixVec  Money   MonMat  MonVec  MyIndex NesMat  NesVec  One
Planning        Presence        Prod    Purchased       Sales
Tests   Text    Trailer Two     V       Weird   Years
```

The variables are listed in alphabetic order, but beware, the lower-case alphabet is ordered before the upper-case one (Dyalog *Classic Edition*) or after (Dyalog *Unicode Edition*). This is the reason why both the variables `experiment` and `what` are listed before `Charlebois`.

If some of these variables are no longer useful, we can delete them with the following command, in which the variable (and function) names can be listed in any order:

```
      )erase experiment What Charlebois M V Goof
not found What
      )erase what
```

We had misspelled the name of one of our variables; the system erased the other ones, and gave us a warning. Then we re-issued a command to erase the variable `what`. This example underlines the fact that although the command *name* ("erase") itself is not case sensitive, the names that it is instructed to work on are of course still case sensitive.

---

[2] In APL we try to design a computer *program*, not as a single monolithic procedure, but rather as a set of inter-connecting units known as *functions* (or *user-defined functions* to distingusish them from *primitive* or built-in functions). Each function is ideally small, self-contained, and performs a single specific task.

If you had developed functions (programs), you could list them using the command `)fns` (pronounced "funs"):

```
      )fns
Average Growth  Plus    Times
```

Remark 1

One can erase everything from the active workspace (all variables and all functions etc.) and revert to the original "clear" active workspace, by issuing the command

```
      )clear
```

This is a bit brutal: all of the contents of the WS are deleted, and no warning message is issued to notify the user of the consequence before the execution of the command. You should avoid using this command, and instead use the "Clear" button on the toolbar, which asks for confirmation. It is safer.

Remark 2

In most languages, programs must be stored (saved) independently, one after the other, and variables do not exist on their own: they live only during the execution of a program which creates, uses, and destroys them.

In APL, things are different:

- Variables have an independent existence, outside of any program execution; you have seen that it is possible to create variables and manipulate them, at will, without writing any programs.
- There may be a permanent interaction between programs and variables. Saving any part of them would be nonsense: one must save the whole context; in other words, the whole *active workspace*.

This is what we shall discover now.

8.2 The Libraries

Like in most other software environments:

- When you save a WS for the first time, you must give it a name
- Once it has been saved you need not re-specify its name when you re-save it.

  Furthermore, we advise you to not re-specify the name when you want to re-save your work, because, if you misspell it, your WS will be saved with the wrong name without you being aware of it.

To save a WS, just issue the command `)save` followed, if this is the first time, by a file name. For example:

```
      )save MyPreciousWS
C:\Action\Seminars\MyPreciousWS saved Sun Aug 12 15:36:32 2007
```

A confirmation message appears, specifying where it has been saved, and the date and time of the operation.

Of course, you can specify any path in your command, to save your WS wherever you like, but if you want to specify a full path, it is often more convenient to use the "Save" button in the toolbar, and browse through your folders.

You can have dozens of workspaces saved in various folders, according to your needs; they represent your private library.

You can also use public workspaces provided by Dyalog Ltd. as part of the APL system, workspaces downloaded from web sites, or workspaces provided by third-party developers.

You can list your workspaces using the command `)lib`.

Used alone, the command explores only the folders specified in your configuration parameters, which can be modified using the menu:

Options ⇨ Configuration ⇨ Workspace ⇨ *Workspace search path*

You can also specify explicitly in which folder the command should search:

```
      )lib c:\Action\developments\projects
Budget  Transport   Survey_3  Survey_7
```

Four workspaces were found in this folder.

8.3 Load a WS

Once a WS has been saved, it may be used again in various ways:

- You can double-click on the WS name in the *Windows Explorer*
- You can use the menu File ⇨ Open
- You can click on the "Open" icon in the toolbar
- And you can issue the system command `)load`

In all these cases, you will see the familiar file search box, in which you can browse to and select the workspace file you would like to open (or load).

You can also use the `)load` command followed by a WS name:

```
      )load myws
```

In this case APL will search for your workspace in the folders specified in your "*Workspace Search Path*" as explained above, unless you specify a full path name. If the path name includes blank characters, you **must** place the whole expression between double quotes, as in the first example below:

```
)load "d:\my documents\sixteen tons\coal"     ⇦ Double quotes are mandatory.
)load e:\freezer\mummies\ramses2              ⇦ Double quotes are not needed.
```

Remark 1

When a WS is loaded, **it replaces the active WS in memory** and becomes the new active WS. If you have not saved the variables and functions you were working on, they are definitely lost! There is no warning message.

You must be aware of this because in this respect, APL differs from most software environments, in which each new file you open is opened in a separate window.

Remark 2

When a WS is loaded, a confirmation message appears, like the following:

```
C:\Action\Seminars\MyPreciousWS saved Sun Aug 12 15:36:32 2007
```

Note that the date and time reported is the date and time when the WS was last saved.

8.4 File Extensions

The default extension of an APL WS depends on the APL system you use. For Dyalog APL, the extension is `dws`, an acronym of Dyalog WorkSpace.

This is only a default extension. When you save a WS, you can give it a different extension, like `old`, `std`, or `dev`.

If you do so, you must be aware that when you load a WS using the `)load` command, and omit the extension, the command will only search only for files with a `dws` extension.

Imagine that you have saved a WS under the name	`weekly.old`
This WS will not be found if you just issue the command	`)load weekly`
You must specify the extension:	`)load weekly.old`

All these considerations are not mandatory knowledge, since you can navigate through the file search dialog box, or through Windows Explorer to find whichever file you need.

8.5 Merge Workspaces

Suppose that you would like to use some functions or variables stored in another WS that has previously been saved. You can import them into your active WS using the command `)copy`, followed by the name of the WS and then the names of the functions and variables you want to import.

For example, imagine that you need `Screwdriver`, `Hammer`, and `Saw`, all stored in a WS named `Toolbox`. You can issue:

```
      )copy Toolbox Screwdriver Hammer Saw
```

- The WS name must be the first, and under Microsoft Windows it is not case sensitive.
- The names of the functions and variables must follow, but beware, these are always case sensitive.

If you specify only the workspace name, all its contents are imported. Be sure that all that stuff is really useful to you.

When the copy is complete, a confirmation message is issued. Like the message issued by a `)load` command, it tells you when that WS was last saved.

Of course, you can specify a path in the command; otherwise the WS is searched for in the *workspace search path* defined in your configuration. Once again, use double quotes if necessary:

```
      )copy "d:\my documents\recipes\ratatouille"
```

8.5.1 - Protected Copy

When you import the entire contents of another WS, there is a risk that it contains an object (variable or function) which has the same name, but not the same value, as an existing object in your active WS. If so, the imported object **replaces** the current one. Danger!

You can avoid this by using the `)pcopy` command, with P standing for "Protected". If there is a name conflict, the object in the active WS is not over-written, and a message tells you which objects haven't been copied. For example:

```
      )pcopy Bazaar
C:\Action\dear_customers\bazaar saved Mon Jun 27 18:44:16 2005
not copied Grub
not copied Watsit
not copied Marmite
```

8.5.2 - Intentionally Destructive Copy

We saw that an imported object may over-write an object in the active WS. This is sometimes useful!

Imagine that you loaded a certain WS:

```
      )load Goodies
```

Then you spend some hours adding new functions and variables, changing things here and there, and suddenly, you discover that you made inappropriate changes to a function named `Goof`.

You can retrieve the original function, still present in the saved version of `Goodies` with:

```
      )copy Goodies Goof
```

When imported, the original version of `Goof` will override the version you altered. Your active workspace will be correct again, and you will be able to go on with your work (but don't forget to save it!).

8.5.3 - Evolution of Your Code

Imagine that you have imported into your active WS a function named `Compute`, copied from a WS named `Utilities`. When you save your active WS, for example under the name `Budget`, the function `Compute` will be saved with it.

But now, imagine that the original version of function `Compute` contained in `Utilities` is modified, or enhanced; what happens? The copy saved with `Budget` is still the old version, and `Budget` may therefore be outdated.

This is a reason why APL allows a dynamic copy of what you need from a known reference WS. This technique will be explained in Chapter L.

8.5.4 - Active WS Identification

You can obtain the name of your current WS by issuing the command:

```
      )wsid
is d:\private\recipes\ratatouille
```

Do not be misled by the name that is reported: it just means that the contents of your active WS had initially been loaded from that WS, or have recently been saved under that name. But since it was loaded or saved, your current WS has perhaps been modified, and is no longer identical to the original copy stored in the library.

In the same way, if you see instead the message: "`is CLEAR WS`", it does not mean that your WS is clear (empty; contains nothing), but that it has not been saved yet, and hence has no name.

8.6 Exiting APL

You can close an APL session using three traditional Windows methods, and two APL system commands:

- You can click on the "Close" cross at the top-right corner of your APL window
- You can press *Alt*+F4
- You can activate the menu File ⇨ Exit
- You can issue the system command `)off`
- You can issue the system command `)continue`

The first two methods will ask if you want to save your current session configuration, a so-called *Continue WS* (this will be seen in chapter L), and the log of everything that you did during the session. The next two methods will close APL without any question or warning, and will not save your configuration. The last one will save a *Continue WS* before exiting.

In any case, always **remember to save your work** (if necessary) before you quit.

8.7 Contents of a WS

Generally speaking, a workspace contains functions (programs) and variables which interact to constitute some useful application.

The large memories of modern computers support very big workspaces, and a single WS is generally enough to store even a very complex application, or several applications. However, it is good practice to store different applications in different workspaces: accounting, budget, customer care, etc… It is not recommended that you mix several applications in a single WS.

However, if appropriate, it is possible for a function to dynamically load another workspace (without any intervention by the user), and activate a different or complementary application.

For now, a unique WS should be sufficient to contain all your experiments.

If several workspaces need to share a common set of utility programs, this can be accomplished by dynamically importing the utilities from a common source. This will be seen in Chapter L.

8.8 Our First System Commands

Just to recapitulate, here is a little summary of the system commands we've just discovered. Many other commands will be studied in Chapter L. The following conventions are used in the table:

- The command names are written using normal characters; the parameters are in *italics*
- Parameters within {braces} are optional
- *names* represents a list of variable or function names
- *wsname* is the name of a WS
- *ext* is the extension of the file. Only necessary if it is different from "`dws`"
- *path* is an optional path. If not specified, APL searches in all the directories referenced in:
  Options ⇨ Configuration ⇨ Workspace ⇨ "*Workspace Search path*"

Our First System Commands	
Command	Usage
`)vars`	Lists the variables in the active workspace.
`)fns`	Lists the user defined functions in the active workspace.
`)erase` *names*	Deletes the named objects from the active workspace.
`)clear`	Deletes everything, and leaves the active workspace empty.
`)save`	Saves the active workspace under its current name, or: Opens the File Save dialog box if the WS has no name.
`)save` {*path*}*wsname*{*ext*}	Saves the active WS under the given path/name/extension.
`)lib` `)lib` *path*	Gives the list of all workspaces in the *workspace search path.* Gives the list of all workspaces in the specified path.
`)drop` {*path*}*wsname*{*ext*}	Deletes a saved WS from disk
`)load`	Opens the File Open dialog box, from which a workspace can be selected. It will replace the active WS.
`)load` {*path*}*wsname*{*ext*}	Replaces the contents of the active WS with the referenced WS.
`)copy` {*path*}*wsname names*	Imports the named items from the specified WS into the active WS, where they may overwrite objects identically named.
`)copy` {*path*}*wsname*	Imports all the contents of the specified WS.
`)pcopy` {*path*}*wsname* {*names*}	Similar to `)copy`, but does not overwrite existing objects.
`)wsid`	Displays the name of the current (active) WS.
`)off`	Closes the APL session.
`)continue`	Saves a *Continue WS* and closes the APL session.

Exercises

Warning! *The following exercises are designed to train **you**, not the computer.*

For this reason, we suggest that you try to answer them on a sheet of paper, not on your computer. When you are sure of your answer, you can test it on the computer.

B-1 Given a scalar `S`, can you transform it into a vector containing one single item?

Or the opposite: Can you transform a one-item vector `V` into a scalar?

B-2 Given the result of the 2 expressions using the variable `X`:

```
      X
2 15 8 3
      ρX
8
```

What is `X`?

B-3 Find the result of this expression: `'LE CHAT'[7 5 2 3 4 6 7]`

This amusing example was first given in "*Informatique par telephone*" of Philip S. Abrams and Gérard Lacourly, Editions Herman, Paris 1972.

B-4 The variable `Tab` is created like this:

```
      Tab ← 2 5 ρ 9 1 4 3 6 7 4 3 8 2
```

How could you replace the values `9 6 7 2` in this variable by `21 45 78 11` respectively?

B-5

```
      X ← 1 2 9 11 3 7 8
      X[3 5] ← X[4 1]
```

What do you think is the new value of `X`?

And what happens if you now execute: `X[4 6] ← X[6 4]`

B-6 A vector of 6 items named `Mystery` is indexed like this:

```
      Mystery[3 1 6 5 2 4]
8 11 3 9 2 15
```

What is the value of `Mystery`?

B-7 One creates a vector, and selects some items from it, as shown:

```
      Vec ← 33 19 27 11 74 47 10 50 66 14
      Vec[FindMe]
47 27 19 14 50 74
```

Could you guess the value of `FindMe`?

B-8 One creates a vector, and a set of indices:

```
      Source ← 10 4 13 3 9 0 7 6 2 13 8 1 5
      Set ← 3 3 ⍴ Source[2 4 8 5 12 13 7 4]
```

Then one uses it to index the original vector:

```
      Result ← Source[Set]
```

What is the shape of `Result`?
Can you find its value?

B-9 Is there a difference between the following two vectors?

First `V1 ← 'p' 'o' 't'`

and then `V2 ← 'pot'`

B-10 Is there a difference between the following two vectors?

First `V3 ← 15 48 'Y' 'e' 's' 52`

and then `V4 ← 15 48 'Yes' 52`

B-11 Here is a very simple variable: `Two ← 2`

We use it in the following expression:

```
Foolish ← Two Two ⍴ 2 Two 'ρ' 'Two'
```

What is the shape of `Foolish`?
Can you show its value?

Solutions

The solutions are given at the end of the book, in Chapter X.

The Specialist's Section

Each chapter is followed by a "Specialist's Section" like this one.
This section is dedicated to skilled APLers, who wish to improve their knowledge.
You will find here rare or complex usages of the concepts presented in the chapter, or discover extended explanations which need the knowledge of some symbols that will be seen much further in the book

If you are exploring APL for the first time,
skip this section and go to the next chapter

Spe-1 Variable Names

Variable names must obey the rules shown in Section B-1.2.

We have seen that you may use some special characters: Delta (∆) Underscore (_), and also the underscored delta (⍙). We do not recommend these symbols; they often make programs difficult to read.

Spe-2 Representation of Numbers

Up to now, we have entered decimal numbers using the most common conventions, like `3714.12` or `0.41`

It is also possible to employ other conventions to facilitate typing.

When the magnitude of a decimal value is less than 1 it is not necessary to enter a zero before the decimal point:

`0.413`	can also been entered as	`.413`
`¯0.5119`	can also been entered as	`¯.5119`

Very large and very small numbers can be entered using ***scientific*** (or ***exponential***) ***representation***.

Using this convention, any "extreme" number can be represented by a "normal" number, the *mantissa*, multiplied by a power of 10, the *exponent*.

For example, 42781900 could be represented as 4.27819×10^{7} or 427.819×10^{5} or 42781.9×10^{4}

and 0.0000038421 could be represented as 384.21×10^{-8} or 3.8421×10^{-6}

In APL, the mantissa and the exponent are separated by the letter E.

Using this notation, one can enter very large or very small numbers.

If the magnitude of the number is not too large or too small, all its digits will be displayed:

```
      4.27819E7                       ⇦ Let us begin with rather large values.
42781900
      4278.19E4
42781900
      384.21E¯8                       ⇦ And now, some rather small values.
0.0000038421
      3.8421E¯6
0.0000038421
```

But if the numbers are very large (or very small), and would require more digits to be shown than the maximum (defined by ⎕PP, *Print Precision*) APL displays them with a "normalised" mantissa with only one integer digit, followed by the appropriate exponent:

```
      431765805838751234
4.317658058E17
      5678.1234E20
5.6781234E23
      1234.9876E¯15
1.2349876E¯12
      ¯2468.1357E¯13
¯2.4681357E¯10
```

Spe-3 The Shape of the Result of Indexing

Spe-3.1 - Rule

Suppose you are given an array of any rank `Array`

The expression `Array[A; B; C; etc...]`

always gives a result with a shape equal to `(⍴A),(⍴B),(⍴C), etc ...`

This rule makes it possible to always predict the shape of the result of an indexing operation.

For example

`Prod[2 5 3;2 1;1 2 5 6]`	would give a result of shape	`3 2 4`
`Prod[;2;⍳6]`	would give a result of shape	`5 6`

In the last example, the omitted index refers to the first dimension of `Prod` which is of length `5`.

The second index (`2`) is a scalar, and has no dimension.

That's why the shape of the result is `5 6` and not `5 1 6`

Spe-3.2 - Using Ravel to Preserve a Dimension

In a program, a matrix is indexed like this: `Mini ← Mat[Rows;Cols]`
For example `Mini ← Mat[2 9 26;50 51 80 91]`

Generally, `Rows` may contain several row numbers, and `Cols` may contain several column numbers. Applying the preceding rule, it is easy to see that we'll obtain a sub-matrix in `Mini`.

But it may be that `Rows` or `Cols` are scalars. The result of `Mat[Rows;Cols]` would then not be a sub-matrix, but a scalar or a vector. This could lead to other expressions in your function generating an error or an incorrect result, because they were written expecting matrices.

To avoid this problem, you can force an index expression to be a vector (perhaps a vector containing only one item) by using ***Ravel*** (symbol " , ") like this:

```
      Mat[,Rows ; ,Cols]   ⇦      Will always return a matrix.
```

Ravel shall be discussed in C-14.

In Section 5.3, we indexed the variable `Test` like this:

```
      Tests[1 2 5 6;1]
41 14 19 45
```

And we were surprised to see the values of a column were displayed horizontally. We can now understand why: the shape of the result is equal to `(⍴1 2 5 6),(⍴1)`. As the shape of a scalar is empty, this expression is equivalent to `(⍴1 2 5 6)` i.e. 4. The indexing operation therefore produces a vector, which is displayed on a single line of the screen.

To obtain a matrix, we must transform the column index (scalar 1) into a vector: we shall again use ***Ravel***, like this:

```
      Tests[1 2 5 6; ,1]
41
14
19
45
```

Spe-4 Multiple Usage of an Index

When an array is indexed, the same item (the second item in the example below) may be selected more than once; for example:

```
      A ← 71 72 73 74 75 76
      A[2 3 2 4 2]
72 73 72 74 72
```

If a repeated index is used to update the variable, only the last replacement value is retained:

```
      A[2 3 2 4 2]←45 19 67 33 50
      A
71 50 19 33 75 76                    ⇦ The second item was first set to 45, then to 67,
                                       and finally to 50.
```

Spe-5 A Problem With Using Reshape (ρ)

We want to create a numeric matrix with 3 rows, and as many columns as another matrix `Trix`, entirely filled with zeroes.

One solution is to first obtain the number of columns of `Trix`, using the *Drop* (↓) function:

```
      1↓ρTrix                        ⇦ Drop is discussed in G-1
8                                    ⇦ Trix has 8 columns
```

Then manually build the correct matrix using the number of columns (8) we obtained previously

```
      3 8ρ0
0 0 0 0 0 0 0 0
0 0 0 0 0 0 0 0
0 0 0 0 0 0 0 0                      ⇦ That's correct.
```

Now, let us try to build a generalized solution:

```
      nc←1↓ρTrix                     ⇦ Calculate the number of columns.
      New←3 ncρ0                     ⇦ That should be the same, no?
DOMAIN ERROR                         ⇦ What's happening then? It no longer works.
      New←3 ncρ0
     ∧
```

The reasons for the problem are as follows:

- When, in the first example, we entered the expression `3 8`, we juxtaposed two scalars, and the result was a two-item vector.

- The expression `ρTrix` in the second example returns a two-item vector (for example `5 8`). The *Drop* function leaves only one value, but the result `8` is still a one-item **vector**.
- When we then entered the expression `3 nc`, we juxtaposed a scalar to a vector. This does not return a simple vector, but a nested array.
- Unfortunately, a nested array is not a valid left argument for *Reshape*!

Solution: *Catenate* `3` and `nc` to form a simple vector, which you then use as the left argument to `ρ`.

```
      New ← (3,nc)ρ0                ⇦ Catenate is discussed in C-10.
```

A direct solution would be:

```
      New ← (3,1↓ρTrix)ρ0
```

Spe-6 Monadic Index (⌷)

In Section 5.6, we used the *Index* function with a left argument for indexing.

Used monadically (without a left argument), *Index* returns all the items of its right argument, whatever its shape:

```
      Vec ← 17 41 23 64
      ⌷ Vec                         ⇦ Equivalent to      Vec[]
17 41 23 64
      Mat ← 2 3 ρ ι6
      ⌷ Mat                         ⇦ Equivalent to      Mat[;]
1 2 3
4 5 6
```

The *Index* function may also be used with Objects (See Chapter Q, Object Oriented Programming). Applied to a an *Enumerable Property of an Object*, or an *Instance of an Object* which has such a Property as its *default* Property, the same syntax returns all the items in this collection.

For example, to obtain the names of all the sheets in an Excel workbook, one can type:

```
      XL.ActiveWorkbook.(⌷Sheets).Name
```

In this expression, `⌷Sheets` represents the collection of all those sheets.

Chapter C: Some Primitive Functions

1 - Definitions

In APL data is processed using what we call *Functions*. It is important to distinguish between:

- ***Primitive Functions*** — They are part of the APL language.
They are represented by symbols: `ρ ⍉ ⌈` ...
They cannot be modified.

- ***User Defined Functions*** — As their name implies, they are written by the user.
They are represented by names: `Average`, `Budget` ...
They can be modified.

APL has a very rich set of primitive functions. In this chapter, we will explore just a few of them; many others will follow in subsequent chapters.

In the introduction to this book, we mentioned that in traditional mathematics, some symbols can be used with a single argument or two arguments. For example:

In the expression $a = x - y$ the minus sign indicates subtraction.
Whereas in $a = -y$ the minus sign indicates the negation of y, that's different.

The first form is called the ***Dyadic*** use of the symbol.
The second form is called the ***Monadic*** use of the symbol.

It is the same in APL, where most of the symbols (functions) have a *monadic* and a *dyadic* meaning. For example:

```
Res ← ρ Var                  ⇦ Here ρ obtains the shape of a variable
Res ← Shape ρ Contents       ⇦ Here ρ creates an array with a given shape
```

There is, however, a major difference. In traditional mathematics, the symbol representing a monadic function is sometimes placed before its argument (as in: $a = -y$), sometimes after it (as in: $a = y!$), sometimes on both sides (as in: $a = |y|$), and some other conventions may be found.
In APL, the symbol representing a monadic function is **always** placed before its argument, as in `⍴Var`.

2 - Some Scalar Dyadic Functions

2.1 Definition and Examples

Scalar dyadic functions are primitive functions which have the following properties:

- They are *Dyadic* (require an argument on both sides).
- They work item by item (scalar by scalar).
- They can work on two arrays of the same shape, in which case the result also has the same shape.
- They can work on one array of any shape, and a single value (a ***scalar*** or any one-item array), in which case the result has the same shape as the non-singleton array.

The four basic arithmetic functions ***Addition***, ***Subtraction***, ***Multiplication*** and ***Division*** are scalar dyadic functions. They apply themselves between each item of the left argument and the corresponding item of the right argument, like this:

```
      5 3 2 9 + 2 6 8 4
7 9 10 13
```

⇦ The function is applied between each item of two 4-item vectors. The result is also a 4-item vector.

As an example of a function that is ***not*** a scalar function, let us look at the ***Reshape*** function. There is nothing in common between the shapes of its arguments:

```
      2 3 ⍴ 6 8 2 1 9 3
6 8 2
1 9 3
```

⇦ The left argument has 2 items, the right one has 6
⇦ and the result in this case is a matrix.

Let us explore the behaviour of the basic arithmetic functions on vectors:

```
      5 3 2 9 - 2 6 8 4
3 ¯3 ¯6 5
      5 3 2 9 ÷ 2 6 4 7
2.5 0.5 0.5 1.285714286
```

```
      Price ← 5.2 11.5 3.6 4 8.45
      Qty   ← 2 1 3 6 2
      Costs ← Price × Qty
      Costs
10.4 11.5 10.8 24 16.9
```

Scalar dyadic functions apply to arrays of any rank and shape.

As we saw in the introduction, a Sales Director makes forecasts for sales of 4 products over the coming 6 months, and assigns them to the variable `Forecast`. At the end of the 6 months, he records the actual values in the variable `Actual`. Here they are:

```
         Forecast                              Actual
            ⇩                                    ⇩
150 200 100  80  80  80              141 188 111  87  82  74
300 330 360 400 500 520              321 306 352 403 497 507
100 250 350 380 400 450              118 283 397 424 411 409
 50 120 220 300 320 350               43  91 187 306 318 363
```

For your convenience, these variables are included in the Workspace "DyalogTutor_EN.dws".

The first thing any self-respecting Sales Director will want to know is the difference between the expected and the actual results. This can be done easily by typing:

```
      Actual - Forecast
¯9 ¯12  11  7  2  ¯6
21 ¯24  ¯8  3 ¯3 ¯13
18  33  47 44 11 ¯41
¯7 ¯29 ¯33  6 ¯2  13
```

⇦ Matrix-Matrix gives a matrix of the same shape.

⇦ Remember: negative values are indicated by a high minus sign.

But remember, a scalar dyadic function may also be applied between a single value and an array of any shape.

For example, if we want to multiply `Forecast` by 2, we can type:

```
      Forecast × 2
300 400 200 160  160  160
600 660 720 800 1000 1040
200 500 700 760  800  900
100 240 440 600  640  700
```

⇦ `2 × Forecast` would do just as well.

A complete list of ***Scalar Dyadic Functions*** is given in Appendix 1.

2.2 Division By Zero

An expression such as `17÷0` leads to an error message (`DOMAIN ERROR`), because zero does not belong to the domain of valid denominators.

However, `0÷0` returns (by default) the result 1, because any number divided by itself should give 1. Nevertheless, because this is sometimes inappropriate, it is possible to change the default behaviour (see the *Specialist's Section*).

2.3 Power

In APL, the mathematical notation A^n is written `A*n`.

The function *Power* (`*`) accepts any value(s) for `n`: integer or decimal, positive, negative, or zero, according to traditional usage.

To calculate the values of : 4^2 $4^{1.4}$ 4^0 $\sqrt{4}$ $1/4$ $4^{-2.1}$ 4^5 we just need to type:

```
      4 * 2 1.4 0 0.5 ¯1 ¯2.1 5
16 6.9644 1 2 0.25 0.0544 1024
```

`0*0` gives `1`.

There is no special symbol in APL to represent a square root; it is obtained by raising a value to the power ½.

Although a few implementations of APL do support complex arithmetic, Dyalog APL does not, and it is impossible to calculate an even root of a negative number. Instead, a `DOMAIN ERROR` is issued.

2.4 Maximum & Minimum

Maximum (`⌈`) and ***Minimum*** (`⌊`) return respectively the larger of two values and the smaller of two values, whatever their signs. Because they are scalar dyadic functions, they can be applied item by item between any two compatible arrays.

```
      75 ⌈ 83
83
      19 ⌈ 11 22 ¯20 60
19 22 19 60
      52 14 ¯37 18.44 ⌊ ¯60 15 ¯40 11.23
¯60 14 ¯40 11.23
```

Minimum can be used to apply a limit to the values in an array. For example, to set a ceiling of 450 in the matrix `Forecast`, it is sufficient to type:

```
      Forecast ⌊ 450
150 200 100  80  80  80
300 330 360 400 450 450          ⇦ 500 and 520 have been limited to 450.
100 250 350 380 400 450
 50 120 220 300 320 350
```

2.5 Relationship

As in traditional mathematics, APL provides the 6 relationship functions:

`A < B`	A less than B	`A ≥ B`	A greater than or equal to B
`A ≤ B`	A less than or equal to B	`A > B`	A greater than B
`A = B`	A equal to B	`A ≠ B`	A not equal to B

These symbols are obtained by pressing the *Ctrl* key simultaneously with the keys 3 to 8, respectively.

All these 6 functions return `1` if the relation is true, or `0` if it is false.

`11 < 7`	returns	`0`
`24 ≤ 24 11 33`	returns	`1 0 1`
`5 = 9`	returns	`0`
`3 8 7 ≥ 5 8 0`	returns	`0 1 1`
`6 > 2 3⍴7 2 9 3 6 4`	returns	`2 3 ⍴ 0 1 0 1 0 1`

The results are called binary, or Boolean, values (Boolean refers to the name of the mathematician George Boole). They can be processed in many different ways and are extremely useful, as we shall soon see.

Note that none of the four symbols `< ≤ ≥ >` can be applied to character arrays.
Only `=` and `≠` can be used with character arrays, as illustrated below:

`'m' = 'm'`	returns	`1`
`'m' = 'M'`	returns	`0`
`'k' ≠ 'a'`	returns	`1`
`'sorry' ≠ 'r'`	returns	`1 1 0 0 1`

Because these functions are scalar dyadic functions, they are applied between individual letters, not words:

`'gold' = 'gulf'` returns `1 0 1 0`

For the same reason, the two words (considered as vectors) must be of equal size:

`'male' ≠ 'female'` causes a `LENGTH ERROR`

2.6 Residue

The *Residue* function, represented by `|`, returns the remainder of a division.

In the expression `R ← X|Y`, `R` is the remainder of `Y` divided by `X` (**be careful**; the arguments of *Residue* are given in the reverse order of that used by *Division* `Y÷X`).

```
      7 | 54
5
      2 | 216 47 29 28
0 1 1 0                        ⇦ This indicates which are odd and which are even values.
      7 4 11 4.3 | 54 84 119 19.6
5 0 9 2.4
```

The function can be used with negative values. The result `R` is always equal to `Y-(N×X)`, where `N` is some integer such that `R` lies between `0` and `X`, but is not equal to `X`.

```
      3 ¯5 6 ¯3 | 29 43 ¯14 ¯14
2 ¯2 4 ¯2
```

If `X` is zero, `R` is equal to `Y`.

3 - Order of Evaluation

Like other programming languages, APL allows the programmer to use parentheses to specify the order of evaluation of a complex expression. Thus the expression `5×(6+7)` means "add 6 to 7, then multiply by 5". In the absence of parentheses, most other programming languages employ rules of precedence to decide how a complex expression such as `5×6+7` would be evaluated. Typically, the result will be 37 because multiplication is given precedence over addition and is performed first.

When APL was designed, it was decided that the sheer number of primitive functions meant that a set of precedence rules would be impossibly complex to remember and apply. Instead, APL follows traditional algebraic conventions.

The solution adopted in APL is simple, and consistent with the rules we apply to calculate complex expressions in traditional algebra. Suppose, for example, that we need to calculate:

$$\log \sin \sqrt{x \div 3}$$

To do this, we would first divide x by 3, then take the square root of the result, next calculate its sine, and finally calculate the logarithm: Each function applies to the result of the entire expression to its right. This is how it is done in mathematics, and so it is in APL. The only difference is that in APL there are no exceptions!

```
      5 × 6 + 7
65
      (5×6) + 7
37
      7+5×6
37
```

⇦ First calculate `6+7`, giving `13`, then multiply by `5`, giving `65`.

⇦ Here we instruct APL to do the multiplication first.

⇦ An experienced APL programmer would probably have written the previous expression this way.

Rule

In an APL expression, each function takes as its right argument the result of the entire expression to its right. No functions have higher precedence than any others.

If the function is dyadic (takes both a left and a right argument), it takes as its left argument the array immediately to its left, delimited by the next function.

This is sometimes called "***Right to left evaluation***" (although this is not strictly correct).

If necessary, one can use ***Parentheses*** to force a different order of evaluation.

You must not be confused: each function is itself evaluated in its natural order, so `8÷4` gives 2, not 0.5! The term "*Right to Left*" only means that the first operation executed is the rightmost one.

If the order of evaluation seems strange to you at first sight, just refer to a plain English sentence: "*Take the top half of the bottom quarter*" does not mean "*Take the top half first, and then take the bottom quarter*"; it means "***First*** *split into quarters and take the bottom one,* ***then*** *split that quarter into two halves and take the top half of it*": This is exactly the way that APL works! Even in everyday English language, which we write from left to right, we implicitly use the "right to left evaluation" rule.

Let us apply this rule to some examples:

`3×5+1`	First	`5+1`	gives	`6`
	then	`3×6`	gives	`18`
`3 6⌊4+2 9>7`	First	`2 9>7`	gives	`0 1`
	then	`4+0 1`	gives	`4 5`
	and	`3 6⌊4 5`	gives	`3 5`

Warning!

In the beginning you may encounter some surprises. For example, if `V` is a vector, `1+⍴V` is different from `⍴V+1`. Let us see why, with the following vector: `V ← 5 2 7`

`1+⍴V`	First	`⍴V`	gives	`3`
	then	`1+3`	gives	`4`
`⍴V+1`	First	`V+1`	gives	`6 3 8`
	then	`⍴6 3 8`	gives	`3`

This may be completely new to people who have experience with other programming languages, and is one of the reasons why we **recommend** that you to do all of the exercises at the end of this chapter. With a little practice, you will soon find this simple rule very natural, and that you will consider it a relief that you do not have to remember complex rules for function precedence.

4 - Monadic Scalar Functions

Most of the symbols we have encountered so far also have a monadic definition; let's look at them now.

4.1 The Four Basic Symbols

We will begin with the four basic symbols: `+ - × ÷`

4.1.1 - Identity

The Plus sign used monadically is the ***Identity*** function. It returns its argument as its result:

```
      + 54 76 29
54 76 29
```

One might suppose that such a function is of no practical value, but it is sometimes used to display the value of a variable, as for example in:

```
      + Magoo ← 2 3⍴Prod
26 16 22
17 21 44
```

⇦ Without the plus sign, the value of `Magoo` would not have been displayed.

```
      + M ← 2 3⍴'abcdef'
abc
def
```

⇦ It works identically on character data, which dyadic + does not.

This feature will be used occasionally in the following pages, until we discover a different syntax.

4.1.2 - Negative

The Minus sign is the ***Negative*** function. It returns the negation of its argument:

```
      - 19 11 ¯33 0 ¯17
¯19 ¯11 33 0 17
```

4.1.3 - Signum

The Multiply symbol used monadically is the ***Signum*** function. It tells us the sign of its argument, using the following convention:

1	The value is positive
0	The value is zero
¯1	The value is negative

```
      × 19 11 ¯33 0 ¯17
1 1 ¯1 0 ¯1
```

4.1.4 - Reciprocal

No surprise: The Divide symbol gives the ***Reciprocal*** or ***Inverse*** value of its argument:

```
      ÷ 2 ¯4 .3 .25 ¯7
0.5 ¯0.25 3.333333333 4 ¯0.1428571429
```

4.2 Other Scalar Monadic Functions

4.2.1 – Exponential

The expression `*N` gives the Nth power of e, the base number of the natural logarithm.

```
      * 1 0 3 ¯1
2.718281828 1 20.08553692 0.3678794412
```

4.2.2 - Floor and Ceiling

Floor (⌊) rounds its argument down, while ***Ceiling*** (⌈) rounds its argument up, to the nearest smaller or larger integer value, respectively:

```
      ⌊ 51.384 48.962 0 ¯73.27 ¯9.99
51 48 0 ¯74 ¯10
      ⌈ 51.384 48.962 0 ¯73.27 ¯9.99
52 49 0 ¯73 ¯9
```

To round a value to the nearest integer a commonly used method is to add 0.5 and then take the *Floor*, or alternatively, to subtract 0.5 and take the *Ceiling*, as shown here:

```
       ⌊ 51.384 48.962 12.5 ¯73.27 ¯9.99 + 0.5
51 49 13 ¯73 ¯10
      ⌈ 51.384 48.962 12.5 ¯73.27 ¯9.99 - 0.5
51 49 12 ¯73 ¯10
```

The results are the same in most cases, but differ for boundary values: for example, 12.5 is rounded to 13 or 12 depending on which method is used.

4.2.3 - Magnitude (Absolute Value)

The monadic stile represents the absolute (unsigned) value of its argument, as shown:

```
      | 29.2 49.3 ¯14.8 0 ¯37.2
29.2 49.3 14.8 0 37.2
```

4.2.4 - Comparison Symbols

None of the symbols `<   ≤   =   ≥   >   ≠` have a monadic usage.

5 - Processing Binary Data

Remark

Binary values are most often produced by the comparison functions that we have already seen. However, the result of *any* function (such as addition or subtraction) which is composed only of 1s and 0s can be used as a binary (or Boolean) value, and may be used as an argument to any of the special primitive functions that apply to Boolean values.

Among the various ways of producing binary results, *Membership* appears to be one of the most interesting tools.

5.1 Membership

- ***Membership*** tells whether the items of its left argument are present (`1`) or not (`0`) in the right argument, regardless of their position in it.
- It accepts arguments of any shape or type.
- The result produced always has the same shape as the **left** argument.

Some examples will help you understand the function:

```
      23 14 41 19 ∊ 17 88 19 50 51 52 23 40
1 0 0 1
```

This means that 23 and 19 appear somewhere in the rightmost vector, whereas 14 and 41 do not. The left argument has 4 items, and so has the result.

The *Membership* function can operate on arguments of completely different shape. For example, it is possible to detect the presence of each item of a vector in a matrix, or vice versa.

In Chapter B we used a matrix containing the 6 first months of the year:

```
      MonMat
January
February
March
April
May
June
```

We can ask if certain letters are present in this matrix:

```
      'December' ∊ MonMat
0 1 1 1 0 1 1 1
```

The result shows that all the letters of `December` appear in `MonMat`, except "`D`" and lowercase "`m`" (which should not be confused with the uppercase "`M`" of March and May).

In this case we used a vector left argument and a matrix right argument. Let's try it the other way around. The following expression tells us which letters in the matrix `MonMat` appear in the vector `Century`:

```
      MonMat ∊ 'Century'
0 0 1 1 0 1 1 0
0 1 0 1 1 0 1 1
0 0 1 0 0 0 0 0
0 0 1 0 0 0 0 0
0 0 1 0 0 0 0 0
0 1 1 1 0 0 0 0
```

As you might imagine, any comparison between numbers and letters gives zero:

```
      1952 ∊ '1952'
0
      '1952' ∊ 1952
0 0 0 0
```

⇦ Remember that `'1952'` is a vector of 4 letters, none of which can be found in the number 1952.

We **recommend** that you do exercise C-22 to discover all the possibilities of *Membership*.

5.2 Binary Algebra

Binary values can be processed using half a dozen specialised primitive functions, the main ones being ***And***, ***Or***, ***Xor***, and ***Not***. Additional functions will be described in the *Specialist's Section*.

The function ***And*** is represented by the symbol `∧` (*Ctrl*+`0`), as it is in mathematics. It returns the result `1` if the left ***and*** the right arguments are both equal to 1:

```
      0 ∧ 0
0
      1 ∧ 0
0
      0 ∧ 1
0
      1 ∧ 1
1
```

⇦ This is the only case where both values are 1.

We can condense those four expressions into a single one:

```
      0 1 0 1 ∧ 0 0 1 1
0 0 0 1
```

The function ***Or*** is represented by the symbol ∨ (*Ctrl*+9), as it is in mathematics. It returns the result 1 if the left ***or*** the right argument is equal to 1.

The four possible cases are shown in the following expression:

```
      0 1 0 1 ∨ 0 0 1 1
0 1 1 1
```

Xor is an acronym for ***eXclusive Or***. It returns the result 1 if one of the arguments is equal to 1, but not if both are equal to 1.

In automation, the same function is generally represented by a circled Plus sign.

APL does not need a different symbol for the function, because ***Xor*** is the same as the comparison function that we have already met: ≠

```
      0 1 0 1 ≠ 0 0 1 1
0 1 1 0
```

The last function is the monadic function ***Not***. Represented by the *Tilde* ~ (*Ctrl*+T), it converts 0 into 1 and 1 into 0:

```
      ~ 0 1 0 0 0 1 1
1 0 1 1 1 0 0
```

Remark

- ***And***, ***Or***, and ***Xor*** are scalar dyadic functions.
- ***Not*** is a scalar monadic function.
- ***Membership*** is a dyadic function, but it is not a scalar function.

All these functions can be applied to binary data of any shape. For example, lets us see if any of those items of `Forecast`, which are greater than 350 thousand Euros, have been exceeded by `Actual` sales:

```
      + bin ← (Forecast>350) ∧ (Actual>Forecast)
0 0 0 0 0 0
0 0 0 1 0 0
0 0 0 1 1 0
0 0 0 0 0 0
```

A side note: The parentheses around the rightmost expression `(Actual>Forecast)` are not strictly needed. However, they do no harm either, so we have added them here to help you read the expression, since you may not yet be fully familiar with APL's order of evaluation.

5.3 Without

Given a vector `A` and any array `B`, the expression `A~B` returns a vector equal to `A`, but in which all items of `B` have been removed. The size and shape of `B` is immaterial, only the individual items of `B` are used.

This function is called ***Without***.

```
      'This Winter is warm' ~ MonMat
TsWtswm
```

⇦ Here, the right argument is a matrix we created earlier.

```
      'Congratulations' ~ 'ceremony'
Cgatulatis
```

⇦ The uppercase "C" is preserved because it is different from the lowercase "c".

```
      Magoo
26 16 22
17 21 44
      21 22 23 24 25 26 27 ~ Magoo
23 24 25 27
```

⇦ Of course, it also works on numbers.

6 - Processing Nested Arrays

When working with nested arrays, it is important to recognise whether or not you are using a scalar function.

6.1 Scalar *vs.* Non-scalar Functions

In Chapter B, we set up a nested vector `Children`, which is composed only of numeric items:

```
      DISPLAY Children
```

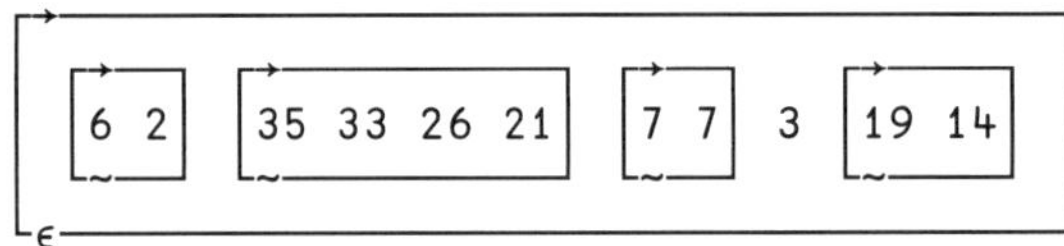

The application of scalar functions is straightforward.
For example, when we add 50 to `Children`, the value 50 is added to each of the items of `Children`. As these items are themselves scalars or vectors, adding 50 means adding 50 to each of *their* individual items. This process continues through all levels of nesting, ensuring that 50 gets added to all the individual items of `Children`. The result is therefore a structure identical to `Children`:

```
      DISPLAY Children + 50
```

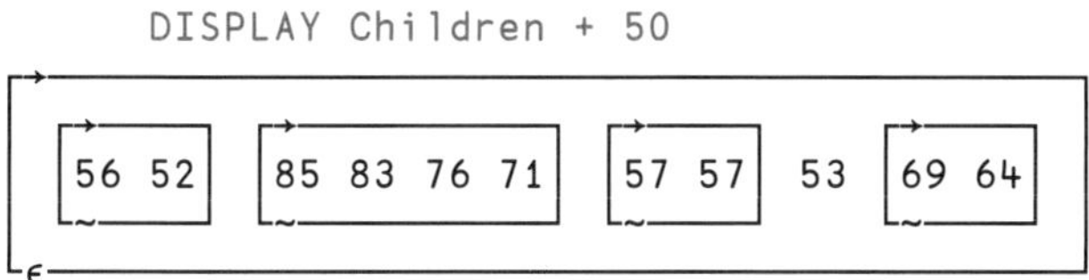

One way of expressing this behaviour is to say that the scalar functions (both the dyadic and the monadic ones) permeate down through the structure of nested arrays, until they reach the lowest-level items, and then apply themselves at this level. They are said to be ***pervasive*** functions.

Non-scalar functions, like *Membership*, are not pervasive.

```
      What ← 19 (6 2) 3 (33 26)
      What ∊ Children
0 1 1 0
```

The item (6 2) of `What` is also an item of `Children`, hence *Membership* gives the answer 1, and the same is true for the value 3.

In contrast 19 is only an item of the 5th item of `Children`; it is not an *entire* item of `Children`. Because a non-pervasive function processes each item as a whole, 19 is not the same as (19 14), so the answer is 0. The same goes for (33 26), which is only part of the second item of `Children`.

6.2 Be Careful With Shape/Type Compatibility

It is easy to add a vector of 5 scalar items to `Children`, because each of the 5 scalars can be added to the corresponding item of `Children`:

```
     Children + 10 20 30 40 50
 16 12   55 53 46 41   37 37   43   69 64
```

But if we try to add a vector of 5 sub-vectors to `Children`, we must ensure that the shape of each sub-vector is compatible with the shape of the corresponding item of `Children`:

```
     Children + (4 8) (5 7 4 9) (1 ¯1) (100 200 500) (14 51)
 10 10   40 40 30 30   8 6   103 203 503   33 65
```

If there is any incompatibility, a `LENGTH ERROR` is issued:

```
      Children+(1 2)(2 3)(3 4)(4 5)(5 6)
LENGTH ERROR
      Children+(1 2)(2 3)(3 4)(4 5)(5 6)
     ^
```

All of the items of our vector could have been added to the corresponding items of `Children` except the second one. APL has detected and signalled this error.

You must also be careful if a nested or mixed array contains character data; it will not be possible to apply any arithmetic function to the array as a whole.

7 - Reduction

7.1 Presentation

A few pages ago we calculated the costs of some purchased goods:

```
      Costs ← Price × Qty
      Costs
10.4 11.5 10.8 24 16.9
```

How much did we spend?

Mathematicians are creative people who long ago devised the symbol ∑, always with a pretty collection of indices above and below, which makes it complex to understand and difficult to type on a keyboard.

In APL, the operation is written like this:

```
      +/ Costs
73.6
```

Simple, isn't it? This expression gives the total of all the items in the vector. You can read this as "***Plus Reduction*** " of the variable `Costs`.

To gain a better understanding of the process:

When we write an expression such as	`+/ 21 45 18 27 11`
- It works as if we had written	`21 + 45 + 18 + 27 + 11`
- and we obtain the sum	`122`

In fact, it works as if we had "inserted" the symbol `+` between the values.

So, when we write `×/ 21 45 18 27 11`
- It is as if we had written `21 × 45 × 18 × 27 × 11`
- So we get the product `5051970`

Similarly, when we write `⌈/ 21 45 18 27 11`
- It is as if we had written `21 ⌈ 45 ⌈ 18 ⌈ 27 ⌈ 11`
- So we obtain the largest item `45`

And so on …

Exercise

Try to evaluate the following expression: `23⌈ ⌈ ⌈/ 17.81 21.41 9.34 16.53`

Don't panic! Remember to evaluate it symbol by symbol, from right to left.

7.2 Definition

Reduction, represented by the symbol `/`, belongs to a special category of symbols called ***Operators***.

In most programming languages the word *operator* is used to describe operations like addition, subtraction, multiplication, and so on. In APL such operations are called ***Functions***; typical examples are `+`, `-`, `×`, and `⍴`. The word *operator* has a separate meaning in APL.

In APL a ***function*** works on an **array** or between two arrays to produce a result:

```
Cost ← Price × Qty
```

Whereas an ***operator*** applies to one or two **functions** (its ***operands***) to produce what we call a *derived function*.

In the expression: `Stock ← +/ Qty`

the symbol `/` is the operator. It takes the function `+` as its single argument (operand) and produces the derived function `+/`. This derived function is then applied to `Qty`, giving a result which is assigned to `Stock`.

Please note that the argument to a monadic function is always to the right of the function, whereas the function applied to a monadic operator (its operand) is always to the left of the operator.

Many, although not all, of the APL primitive functions may be used as the operand to *Reduction*; you can even apply a user-defined function. This generality makes Reduction, and other operators, extremely powerful.

Dyalog APL provides a total of 10 such powerful *operators*, listed in appendix 4. It is also possible to write your own operators, just as it is possible to write your own functions.

7.3 Reduction of Binary Data

Among the typical usages of *Reduction* are ∧ and ∨ applied to binary data.

∧/ Bin gives the result 1 if ***All*** the items of Bin are equal to 1

∨/ Bin gives the result 1 if ***At least one*** of the items of Bin is equal to 1

+/ Bin tells us ***How many*** items of Bin are equal to 1

You can verify it on some small examples:

```
      ∧/ 1 1 1 0 1 0 1
0
      ∧/ 1 1 1 1 1 1 1
1
      ∨/ 1 1 1 0 1 0 1
1
      +/ 1 1 1 0 1 0 1
5
```

For example, in Chapter B, we created a vector named Contents:

```
      Contents
12 56 78 74 85 96 30 22 44 66 82 27
```

Are all the values greater than 20?	∧/ Contents > 20
The answer is no:	0
Is there at least one value smaller than 30?	∨/ Contents < 30
The answer is yes:	1
How many values are smaller than 30?	+/ Contents < 30
The answer is:	3

Warning! Reducing an array by a non commutative function like - or ÷ yields results which may be counter-intuitive, but which may nevertheless be useful in a number of applications.

Remember: -/ 45 9 11 2 5
is equivalent to 45 - 9 - 11 - 2 - 5

Applying APL's order of evaluation we can see that this expression is equivalent to:

```
45 - (9 - (11 - (2 - 5)))
```

The result, 50, is perhaps not what you expected.

In other languages, the result would be 18, because the expression is evaluated as:

```
(((45 - 9) - 11) - 2) - 5
```

This kind of "alternating series" can be useful for some mathematical calculations, although only rarely for business applications.

7.4 Reduction of Nested Arrays

When you apply reduction to a nested array you must check that the items of the nested array are compatible (in shape and type) with the function that you intend to apply:

```
      +/ (4 8) (1 4) 10 (9 5)         ⇦ All the items can be added together.
 24 27
      +/ (4 8) (1 4) (1 2 3) (9 5)⇦ (1 2 3) cannot be added to the other items,
LENGTH ERROR                            so APL reports an error.
      +/(4 8)(1 4)(1 2 3)(9 5)
     ^
```

7.5 *Application 1*

The employees of a company are divided into three hierarchical categories, denoted simply 1, 2, and 3. Two variables contain the salaries and the categories of these employees; i.e.:

```
Salaries     4225 1619 3706 2240 2076 1389 3916 3918 4939 2735 ...
Categories      3    1    3    2    2    1    3    3    3    2 ...
```

The employees ask for an increase in their salaries. Each category of employee requests a different percentage increase, as shown in the following table:

Category	Upgrade
1 2 3	8% 5% 2%

How much is that going to cost the company?

Let us just create a variable containing the three rates shown above:

```
      Rates ← 8 5 2 ÷ 100
      Rates
0.08 0.05 0.02
```

The first employee is in category 3, so the rate that applies to this person is:

```
      Rates[3]
0.02
```

More generally, the rates applied to all of our employees can easily be obtained like this:

```
      Rates[Categories]
0.02 0.08 0.02 0.05 0.05 0.08 0.02 0.02 0.02 0.05 0.05 0.02 etc.
```

Having the rates, we only have to multiply them by the salaries to obtain the individual increases:

```
      Salaries × Rates[Categories]
84.5 129.52 74.12 112 103.8 111.12 78.32 78.36 98.78 136.75 etc.
```

Finally, by adding them all together, we discover how much it will cost the company:

```
      +/ Salaries × Rates[Categories]
2177.41
```

Note that:

- The expression remains valid regardless of the number of employees or categories.
- The result has been obtained without writing a program (no loops, no tests).
- This expression can be phrased in the simplest possible English, namely:

  Sum the Salaries multiplied by Rates according to Categories

This illustrates how the implementation of a solution in APL can be very close to the way that the solution would be expressed in everyday language. It also shows the advantage of not having to deal with trivial and "irrelevant" matters such as looping, memory allocation, declarations, etc. before a working solution can be developed.

7.6 Application 2

Imagine now that we want to calculate the average of a set of values, for example the values contained in the variable `Contents`.

To do that, we must:

- Add all the values `+/ Contents`
- Count how many values we have `⍴Contents`
- Divide one by the other `(+/Contents) ÷ (⍴Contents)`

The result would be 56.

Again, because of APL's simple rule for the order of evaluation, the rightmost set of parentheses could be omitted.

8 - Axis Specification

8.1 Totals in an Array

8.1.1 - Processing Arrays

We have seen the result of applying reduction to vectors, but what about matrices and higher rank arrays?

As an example let us recall the array `Prod`. Its three dimensions represent respectively:

1	5 years
2	2 assembly lines
3	12 months.

We can calculate totals along any one of these 3 dimensions: Years, Lines, and Months.

We specify the dimension (or ***Axis***) between brackets after the *Reduction* symbol:

`+/[`*Axis*`] Prod`

For example, suppose that we want to calculate the total production for the five years. Years are represented by the 1st dimension of `Prod`, so we write:

```
      +/[1] Prod
155 144 244 185 136 247 162 128 195 193 188 145
168 200 182 180 170 186 194 160 179 218 217 126
```

We obtain a 2 by 12 matrix, giving the production of the 2 assembly lines, month by month.

Now, let us add up the production numbers of the two assembly lines. Lines are represented by the 2nd dimension of `Prod`, so we write:

```
      +/[2] Prod
69  52  69 66 51  66 82 42 68 104 84 55
73  40  81 95 70  90 85 39 83  83 88 49
93  82  78 73 67  73 64 85 50  48 74 41
37 112  81 64 43 109 62 55 98  94 95 61
51  58 117 67 75  95 63 67 75  82 64 65
```

We obtain a 5 by 12 matrix, with the total production of both assembly lines, month by month, in each of the 5 years.

And finally, let us calculate the annual production of each assembly line. Months are represented by the 3rd dimension of `Prod`, so we write:

```
      +/[3]Prod
334 474
449 427
367 461
490 421
482 397
```

The result is a 5 by 2 matrix, in which the columns contain the annual production of the two assembly lines in each of the five years.

8.1.2 - Axis Is Like an Operator

The dimension specified within brackets is the axis along which the function is applied.

This produces a derived function, and for this reason, the pair of *Axis* brackets is often called the ***Axis Operator***.

The syntax for *Axis* does not quite follow the general syntax for operators, but it shares all other properties with genuine operators. *Axis* takes a function as its left operand (the derived function `+/` in the last example above), the dimension specification as its "right operand" (3 in the example), and produces a derived function, which is applied to `Prod` to calculate the annual sums.

Viewed as an operator *Axis* is therefore dyadic. It is, however, important to emphasise that its "right" argument is not `Prod`, it is the expression within the brackets. This shows that a dyadic operator does not need to have two functions as operands; one of them may be an array.

8.1.3 - Processing Arrays

We shall learn more about *Axis* in Chapter J; let us first explore another simple use of this operator.

Suppose that we would like to multiply each of the rows (or columns) of a matrix by different values; we can use *Axis* to specify whether we multiply row-wise or column-wise, like this:

Here is the matrix	Let us multiply row-wise	and now column-wise
`Tam`	`Tam×[1]5 2 10`	`Tam×[2]2 5 0 2 1`
⇩	⇩	⇩

`2 3 5 8 8`
`4 6 2 5 9`
`1 4 9 7 8`
	`10 15 25 40 40`
	` 8 12  4 10 18`
	` 7 28 63 49 56`
		`4 15 0 16 8`
		`8 30 0 10 9`
		`2 20 0 14 8`

8.2 The Shape of the Result

The dimensions of `Prod` are:		5 2 12
`+/[1]Prod`	sums the 1st dimension and gives a result of shape	2 12
`+/[2]Prod`	sums the 2nd dimension and gives a result of shape	5 12
`+/[3]Prod`	sums the 3rd dimension and gives a result of shape	5 2

You can see that *Reduction* of a 3-D array gives a 2-D array, in which the summed dimension has "disappeared". This is the origin of the term "*Reduction*"; it *reduces* the *rank* of the array.

This rule will help you predict the dimensions of the result of a reduction.

Rule

When ***Reduction*** is applied along the Nth dimension of an array, the shape of the result is the same as the shape of the array, but without its Nth item.

The ***Rank*** of the result is 1 less than the rank of the original array.

Whenever you want to calculate the sum along a particular dimension of an array, think of the dimensions in terms of concrete things: Years, lines, months, etc. This should help you.

8.3 Special Notations

By default, if no axis is specified, reduction is applied along the **last** dimension of the array.

So	`+/ Prod`	is equivalent to	`+/[3] Prod`
and	`+/ Forecast`	is equivalent to	`+/[2] Forecast`

But it is also common to work along the first dimension of an array. For this reason, APL includes a special symbol for reduction along the first dimension: `⌿`

So	`+⌿ Prod`	is equivalent to	`+/[1] Prod`
and	`+⌿ Forecast`	is equivalent to	`+/[1] Forecast`

Note: if one specifies an axis after the symbol `/` or `⌿`, the function is applied along the specified *Axis*, whichever symbol is actually used. For example:

`+⌿[3] Prod`	is equivalent to	`+/[3] Prod`
`+/[1] Forecast`	is equivalent to	`+⌿[1] Forecast`

9 - Our First Program

The expression we wrote in section 7.6 to calculate the average of a set of values, is one that we may want to use time and time again. So let us store it as a program, or, to use the proper APL terminology, as a ***User Defined Function***.

There are many different ways to define functions, and these will be covered in detail in Chapter D. For now we shall use the simplest, which is perfectly suitable for straightforward calculation functions like this one. Let's type:

```
      Average ← {(+/⍵)÷(⍴⍵)}
```

`Average` is the name of the function.
It is followed by the definition, delimited by a pair of curly braces { and }.

`⍵` is a generic symbol that represents the array that will be passed as the right argument of the function.

`⍺` is a generic symbol that represents the array that will be passed as the left argument of the function, if any.

The symbols `⍵` and `⍺` are obtained using *Ctrl*+W and *Ctrl*+A, respectively.

For more complex multi-line functions it is obviously more appropriate to use a text editor. However, this is beyond the scope of this chapter.

Once defined, this function may be invoked directly, just as if it were a built-in (*primitive*) function:

```
      Average Val
31.1428571428
      Average 12 74 56 23
41.25
```

The word `Average` can now be used in any APL expression. We have enriched the vocabulary which can be used to process data in this workspace (provided that we save it).

Be patient: We shall see many other possibilities in Chapter D.

10 - Concatenation

Concatenation is a dyadic function which joins two arrays together. It is represented by comma (,). The function name is normally abbreviated to ***Catenate***, and we will use both terms.

10.1 Concatenating Vectors

Catenate is easy to understand:

```
      A ← 24 15 67 89
      B ← 11 33 75
      A,B
24 15 67 89 11 33 75
```

It is like joining two sentences together, so it is easy to remember which symbol to use.
You can see that ⍴(A,B) is equal to (⍴A) + (⍴B).

Character strings are processed in the same way:

```
      A ← 'Tell me'
      B ← 'More'
      A,B
Tell meMore
       ⇧
```

Note that there is no space inserted between the contents of the two vectors. When we join a vector of 7 characters to a vector of 4 characters, the result must have 11 characters.

When you concatenate an empty vector to another vector, the result is the same as the original:

```
      N ← 24 15 67 89
      V ← 0⍴0                  ⇦ We could use ⍬ instead.
      N,V
24 15 67 89                    ⇦ The numeric vector remains unchanged.
      A,'',B
Tell meMore                    ⇦ The text is unchanged.
```

10.2 Concatenating Other Arrays

It is possible to concatenate two arrays if their shapes are compatible. The axis along which the concatenation is to be performed must be specified, if it is different from the default.

Let us use three matrices A, B, and C:

- The shape of `A` is `3 4`   `A ← 3 4 ⍴ 'A'`
- The shape of `B` is `2 4`   `B ← 2 4 ⍴ 'B'`
- The shape of `C` is `3 3`   `C ← 3 3 ⍴ 'C'`

The possible concatenations are:

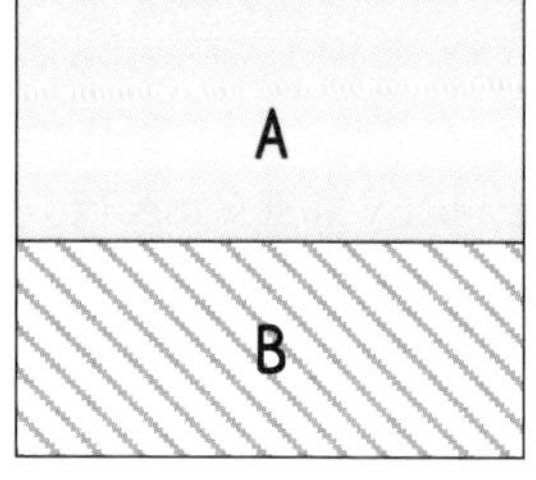

⇦ This is obtained by :
`A,[1] B`
The shape of the result is `5 4`

`B,[1] A` would have put `B` on top of `A`

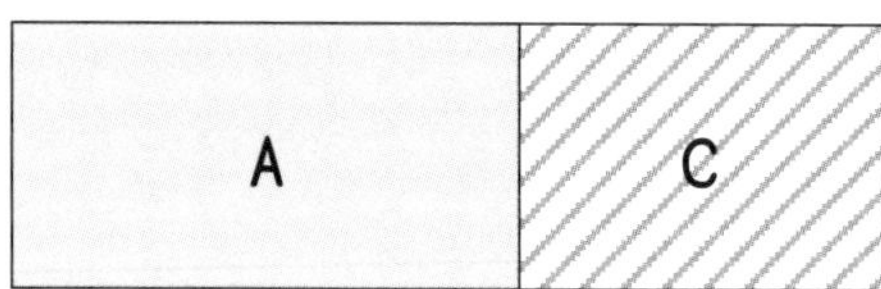

⇦ This is obtained by `A,[2] C`
The shape of the result is `3 7`

`C,[2] A` would have put `C` to the left of `A`

It is not possible to concatenate `B` and `C`, because none of their dimensions are compatible.

In the same way as for *Reduction*, the *Axis* operator indicates which dimension will change during the operation, as we can see:

In the first case:	Shape of `A`	`3 4`	
	Shape of `B`	`2 4`	
	Shape of `A,[1]B`	**`5`** `4`	⇦ The 1st dimension changes
In the second one:	Shape of `A`	`3 4`	
	Shape of `C`	`3 3`	
	Shape of `A,[2]C`	`3` **`7`**	⇦ The 2nd dimension changes

The following table shows the four possible different catenations side by side:

```
A,[1]B          B,[1]A          A,[2]C          C,[2]A
  ⇩               ⇩               ⇩               ⇩
 AAAA            BBBB            AAAACCC         CCCAAAA
 AAAA            BBBB            AAAACCC         CCCAAAA
 AAAA            AAAA            AAAACCC         CCCAAAA
 BBBB            AAAA
 BBBB            AAAA
```

Rule

> It is possible to ***Concatenate*** two arrays `A` and `B` along their ***I***th dimension provided that they have the same rank, and provided that all other dimensions have the same lengths.
>
> The operation is written like this: `A,[I] B`
>
> It is also possible to ***Concatenate*** an array `A` of rank ***N*** to another array `B` of rank ***N-1***. The concatenation **must** then be done along a dimension of `A` such that its other dimensions are strictly identical to those of `B`.

For example, it is possible to concatenate a vector to a matrix, provided that the vector has the same length as the corresponding dimension of the matrix:

```
A,[1]'JUMP'                 A,[2]'TOP'
    ⇩                            ⇩
  AAAA                        AAAAT
  AAAA                        AAAAO
  AAAA                        AAAAP
  JUMP
```

In the first example:	The shape of `A`	3 4	
	The shape of `B`	4	⇦ We **must** catenate along `[1]`
	We add one row	1	
	The shape of `A,[1]B`	4 4	⇦ The 1st dimension changes
In the second example:	The shape of `A`	3 4	
	The shape of `B`	3	⇦ We **must** catenate along `[2]`
	We add one column	1	
	The shape of `A,[2]B`	3 **5**	⇦ The 2nd dimension changes

Example 1

We can add a row of totals to the bottom of a matrix with an expression like this:

```
      Forecast,[1] (+/[1] Forecast)
150 200  100   80   80   80
300 330  360  400  500  520
100 250  350  380  400  450
 50 120  220  300  320  350
600 900 1030 1160 1300 1400
```

⇦ The parentheses are for ease of interpretation; they are not necessary.

Example 2

In a similar way, it is possible to concatenate a matrix to a 3-D array.

Suppose you have a 3-D array `A` whose dimensions are `3 4 6`, and a matrix `B` whose dimensions are `3 6`. These two arrays may be catenated together:

In this case:			
	The shape of `A`	`3 4 6`	
	The shape of `B`	`3   6`	⇦ You **must** catenate along `[2]`
	We add one layer	`  1`	
	The shape of `A,[2]B`	`3 5 6`	⇦ The 2nd dimension changes

For example we would like to append to `Prod` the production of a subcontractor, organised as an array of 5 years and 12 months.

```
      Subcon
 0  0  0  0  0  0  5  6  6  6  6  7
 7  7  7  8 10 10 10 10  8  7  8 10
10 10 12 11 12 10 11  9  6  6  6  8
 8  9 14 15 18 19 20 19 20 17 15 14
14 15 18 18 13 12 10 10 11 11 11 11
```

The shape of	`Prod`	is	`5 2 12`
The shape of	`Subcon`	is	`5   12`

They **must** be concatenated along the 2nd dimension of `Prod`
And the result will have the shape `5 3 12`

You see, it is as if `Subcon` had the length 1 along the concatenation (missing) dimension.

```
      Prod,[2] Subcon
26 16 22 17 21 44 25 22 23 44 41 33
43 36 47 49 30 22 57 20 45 60 43 22
 0  0  0  0  0  0  5  6  6  6  6  7

44 21 58 57 17 43 47 17 43 26 53 23
29 19 23 38 53 47 38 22 40 57 35 26
 7  7  7  8 10 10 10 10  8  7  8 10
```

… and so on.

10.3 Concatenating Scalars

When a scalar is concatenated to an array it is repeated as many times as necessary to match the length of the appropriate dimension of the array.

Here are two examples, using the matrix A, described above:

```
A,[1] '-'                A,[2] '*'
  ⇩                        ⇩
AAAA                     AAAA*
AAAA                     AAAA*
AAAA                     AAAA*
----
```

This property is very useful, because its saves us working out how many items are needed to match the corresponding dimension of the array.

We can also concatenate two scalars. The result is of course a two-item vector:

```
      7,9
7 9
```

10.4 Special Notations

By default, if no axis is specified catenation works along the last dimension of the array(s).

So `A,C` is equivalent to `A,[2] C`

APL also includes a special symbol that means "Concatenate along the **First** dimension"; this symbol is a comma topped by a minus sign: ⍪.
It can be obtained by *Ctrl+Shift*+@ (UK) or *Ctrl+Shift*+~ (US).

So `A⍪B` is equivalent to `A,[1] B`

If an axis is specified, the operation is processed according to the axis specification, whichever symbol (, or ⍪) is used.

So `A,[2] C` and `A⍪[2] C` are both equivalent to `A,C`
and `A,[1] B` and `A⍪[1] B` are both equivalent to `A⍪B`

11 - Replication

11.1 Basic Approach: Compression

To extract scattered values from a vector, we can use indexing:

```
      Contents[5 6 11]
85 96 82
```

We can also use a new function named ***Compression*** (or *Compress*). It takes a Boolean vector as its left argument, and any array of appropriate shape as its right argument. The items of the right argument which match the 1s in the left argument are preserved, whereas those which match the 0s are removed. It acts like a mask or a filter:

```
      0 1 1 0 / 42 15 79 66
15 79
      1 0 1 0 0 0 0 1 1/'Drumstick'
Duck
```

This is extremely useful, because we can use *Compression* to select items which match a given condition.

For example, let us extract from `Contents` the values which are greater than 80.

The Boolean vector for the left argument is obtained by `Contents>80`, and the selection is made by:

```
      (Contents>80) / Contents
85 96 82
```

Of course, the same operation can be applied to any array, provided that one specifies which axis is concerned. For example, if we have a matrix of chemical formulas:

```
      Chemistry
H2SO4
CaCO3
Fe2O3
```

```
      1 0 1 /[1] Chemistry
H2SO4
Fe2O3
```

⇦ Two rows are selected, corresponding to the two 1s in the vector on the left.

```
      1 1 0 1 0 /[2] Chemistry
H2O
CaO
FeO
```

⇦ Only 3 columns are selected; columns 3 and 5 have been removed.

Compression is an excellent tool which allows you to:

- extract some useful items from a variable,
- or remove some unwanted items from a variable, which is the same thing.

Advice

Every time you obtain a Boolean vector, you should immediately think of two major things you can do with it: ***Count*** or ***select***.

For example, using `Contents`, we can produce a Boolean vector that shows which items are smaller than 50: `bin ← Contents<50`. Then, we can:

• count the items:	`+/ bin`	gives	`5`
• select (or extract) the items:	`bin / Contents`	gives	`12 30 22 44 27`

Hint

Programmers who are new to APL and who are familiar with indexing as the natural selection mechanism may be tempted to use the Boolean selection vector to create some indexes, and then use the indices to select the desired items. This works very well, for example:

```
      ix ← bin / ⍳⍴Contents
      Contents[ix]
12 30 22 44 27
```

However this is an unnecessary complication that wastes memory and processing time, compared to the straightforward selection shown above.

11.2 Replication

In fact, *Compression* is just a special case of a more comprehensive function named ***Replication*** or ***Replicate***. Its left argument can be any vector of integer values, each of which produces the following result:

If the left item is positive	each item in the right argument is replicated the number of times specified by the corresponding item of the left argument.
If the left item is zero	the corresponding item in the right argument is suppressed.
If the left item is negative	the corresponding item in the right argument is replaced by as many "***Fill items***" as is indicated by the corresponding item in the left argument.

The concept of a "*Fill item*" is new and will be discussed in full in Chapter I on "Nested Arrays". For now, you need only to know that the fill item for a simple numeric array is 0, and the fill item for a simple character array is a space (blank).

Here are some examples, using the same left argument applied to numeric and character vectors:

```
      0 1 3 0 / 42 15 79 66           ⇦ 42 and 66 have been removed, 15 has been kept,
15 79 79 79                              and 79 has been replicated 3 times.
      0 1 3 0 / 'boat'
oaaa
      2 ¯3 1 0 / 42 15 79 66          ⇦ 15 has been replaced by 3 zeroes,
42 42 0 0 0 79                           because it is numeric.
      2 ¯3 1 0 / 'boat'               ⇦ 'o' has been replaced by 3 spaces,
bb   a                                   because it is character.
```

11.3 Scalar Left Argument

If the left argument of *Compression* or *Replication* is a scalar, it applies to all the items of the right argument.

```
      v ← 'Phew'
      1/v
Phew                                  ⇦ All the items are retained
      3/v
PPPhhheeewww                          ⇦ All the items are repeated 3 times.
      0/v
                                         All the items are removed; nothing is left.
                                      ⇦ The result is an empty vector.
```

11.4 Special Notations

Like *Reduction* and *Catenation*, *Replication* works by default along the last dimension of an array. However, it is possible for it to work on the first dimension using the symbol ⌿, which we have already seen.

For example

```
      0 1 0 ⌿ Chemistry          ⇦ Equivalent to: 0 1 0/[1] Chemistry
CaCO3
```

Beware: The result obtained this way is **not** a vector, but a matrix having only one row.

You must not confuse *Reduction* and *Replication*: Even if the symbol used is the same, they are completely different operations:

Reduction takes a function as its (left) argument (operand); it is an *operator* `+/ Contents`

Replication takes a vector as its left argument; it is a simple *function* `vec/ Contents`

12 - Position (*Index Of*)

12.1 Discovery

It is very often necessary to locate the positions of particular values in a list of items. To solve this, APL has a special function named ***Position*** (also called "***Index Of***"), represented by the Greek letter Iota (⍳). This symbol can be obtained by *Ctrl*+I (the initial letter of Iota). Let us see how it works:

```
      Vec ← 15 42 53 19 46 53 82 17 14 53 24
      Vec ⍳ 19 14 53 49 15          ⇦ We ask for the positions of 5 values in Vec
4 9 3 12 1                          ⇦ and naturally we obtain 5 answers.
```

- The result tells us that 19, 14, and 15 appear in positions 4, 9, and 1 respectively.
- The result also tells us that 53 appears in position 3. This is of course true, but it also appears in positions 6 and 10, which are not included in the result. This is a necessary restriction: If we had searched for 5 values and obtained 7 results, it would not have been possible to say where each value appears. This is the reason why ***Index Of*** returns ***only the first*** occurrence of each value.

We shall see later that this is an advantage: If instead we need to find all the positions in which a value occurs, there is another function that we can use (see section 13.2).

- Surprisingly the result tells us that 49 appears in position 12, though `Vec` has only 11 items! This is the way that *Index Of* indicates a missing value. We shall see that it is a great advantage, too.

The following rule explains how dyadic Iota works:

> In the expression: `R ← Vec ⍳ Data`
>
> - `Vec` Must be a vector.
>   It can be of any type: Numeric, character, mixed, nested.
> - `Data` Can be any array (any type, any shape, any rank).
> - `R` Has the same rank and shape as `Data`
> - The items of `R` contain the positions of the first occurrence of the corresponding items of `Data` in `Vec`
> - Items which do not appear in `Vec` give the result `1+⍴Vec`

```
      'ABC' ⍳ 57                         ⇦ A number cannot appear in a character vector.
4
      4 8 ⍳ '4 8'                        ⇦ The result contains 3 items, because the blank
3 3 3                                      space between 4 and 8 is part of the vector.
      Alpha ← 'ABCDEFGHIJKLMNOPQRSTUVWXYZ 0123456789'
      Alpha ⍳ Chemistry
8 30 19 15 32
3 38  3 15 31                            ⇦ Lower case letters give the answer 38
6 38 30 15 31                              because Alpha has 37 items.
```

And on a nested array:

```
      'Tee' (3 7) 'Golf' ⍳ 3 7 (3 7) 'Tee' 'Green'
4 4 2 1 4
```

The function *Index Of* is one of the most important primitive functions in APL. It is very flexible, and it can be used in many situations, as shown in the following examples.

Warning: In the expression `A⍳B` we search for `B` in `A`
whereas in `A∊B` we search for `A` in `B`. Do not be confused!

12.2 *Application 3*

A car manufacturer decides that he will offer his customers a discount on the catalogue price. The country has been split into 100 geographic areas, and the discount rate will depend on the geographic area according to the following table:

Area	Discount
17	9 %
50	8 %
59	6 %
84	5 %
89	4 %
Others	2 %

The first task is to calculate the discount rate to be claimed for a potential customer who lives in area `D`; for example `D ← 84`.

Let us begin by creating two variables with the values in the table above:

```
      Area     ← 17 50 59 84 89
      Discount ←  9  8  6  5  4 2
```

Let us see if 84 is in the list of favoured areas:

```
      Area ι D
4
```
⇦ Yes; 84 is the 4th item in the list.

Let us find the current rate of discount for this index position:

```
      Discount[4]
5
```
⇦ This customer can claim a 5% discount.

We could simply write: `Discount[AreaιD]`

Now, what if a customer lives in any other area such as 75, 45, or 93?

The expression `AreaιD` will for all these area codes return the result `6`, because these values are absent from `Area`.

Then `Discount[6]` will always find the rate 2%, as specified. Here we can see that it is an advantage that *Index Of* returns 1 + the number of items in the vector to be searched.

A Vector Solution

The importance of this approach to finding the discount rates is that it is vector-based. Suppose that publicity attracts crowds and that therefore D is no longer a scalar but a vector, the solution is still valid:

```
      D ← 24 75 89 60 92 50 51 50 84 66 17 89
      Discount[Area⍳D]
2 2 4 2 2 8 2 8 5 2 9 4
```

We have achieved all this without a program, neither a "loop" nor a "test". And it works for any number of areas. Readers who know other programming languages will probably appreciate the simplicity of this approach.

Generalisation

In reality, the expression that we have just written is an example of an algorithm for "*changing the frame of reference*". Don't panic, this term may seem esoteric, but the concept is simple: a list of area numbers (the initial set) is translated into a list of discount rates (the final set). The algorithm comprises only the function *Index Of* and indexing:

R← *FinalSet*[*InitialSet* ⍳ *Values*]

Let us imagine the initial set to be an alphabet composed of both lowercase and uppercase letters, and the final set to be composed of only uppercase letters, with a blank space in the middle:

```
     AlphLower
abcdefghijklmnopqrstuvwxyz ABCDEFGHIJKLMNOPQRSTUVWXYZ
     AlphUpper
ABCDEFGHIJKLMNOPQRSTUVWXYZ ABCDEFGHIJKLMNOPQRSTUVWXYZ*
```

Now, let us write a sentence; we will write it in French in order only to show what happens with missing characters.

```
      Tale ← 'Le Petit Chaperon-Rouge a bouffé le Loup'
```

If we apply the algorithm seen above, the expression will convert the text from lower to upper case:

```
      AlphUpper[AlphLower⍳Tale]
LE PETIT CHAPERON*ROUGE A BOUFF* LE LOUP
```

As one might expect, the characters - and é, which are absent from the initial alphabetic set, have been replaced by the *, the "extra" character at the end of the final set. This works because once again the final set is one item longer than the initial set.

Once more, the logical steps needed to solve the problem are easily translated into a programming solution, and the programmer can thereby direct all his attention to solving the problem.

13 - Index Generator

13.1 Basic Usage

When used as a monadic function, the symbol *Iota* generates a vector of the first N integers. It is called ***Index Generator***.

```
      ⍳ 9
1 2 3 4 5 6 7 8 9
```

If we have to extract the first 12 items of a vector Vec, we can write:

```
      Vec[1 2 3 4 5 6 7 8 9 10 11 12]
```

It is, of course, much easier to write `Vec[⍳12]`

The result can be combined with simple arithmetic operations. For example, suppose we need to produce the following list of 6 values: 115 122 129 136 143 150 (note the increments of 7). We can do this as follows:

```
          ⍳6      is   1 2 3 4 5 6
      (⍳6)-1      is   0 1 2 3 4 5
    7×(⍳6)-1      is   0 7 14 21 28 35
115+7×(⍳6)-1      is   115 122 129 136 143 150
```

More generally, any arithmetic series of integers can be produced by the following formula:

```
R ← Origin + Step × (⍳Length) - 1
```

Special Case

If `⍳N` gives a vector of length `N`, then `⍳0` should give a vector of length `0`, right? A vector having length 0 is an empty vector. Let us check:

```
      ⍳0
```

⇦ Nothing appears: It's an empty vector.

Traditionally, `⍳0` was a convenient expression to generate an empty numeric vector. Now, with modern versions of APL, it is easier to use the symbol *Zilde* (`⍬`).

Generalisation

The definition of `⍳N` given above reflects only a limited part of what this function can do; you will find more information in the *Specialist's Section* at the end of this chapter.

13.2 *Application 4*

You probably remember that the function *Index Of* returns only the *first* occurrence of a value in a vector (cf. section 12.1). Using monadic *Iota* we can build an algorithm to find *all* the occurrences.

Here is a vector, in which we would like to find the positions of the number 19:

```
      Vec ← 41 17 19 53 42 27 19 88 14 56 19 33

Vec=19     ⇨     0  0  1  0  0  0  1  0  0  0  1  0
⍳⍴Vec      ⇨     1  2  3  4  5  6  7  8  9 10 11 12
```

If we compress the second vector by the first one, the only items that will remain will be the positions of the target value:

```
      (Vec=19)/⍳⍴Vec
3 7 11
```

The same technique will work on characters. Lets us search for the letter "a" in a character vector:

```
      Phrase ← 'Panama is a canal between Atlantic and Pacific'
      (Phrase='a')/⍳⍴Phrase
2 4 6 11 14 16 30 36 41          ⇦ You can check it!
```

A Touch of Modern Maths

Having found all the "a"s, we may wish to find all the vowels.

Alas, although the expression `Phrase='a'` works because a vector can be compared with a single value, the obvious solution `Phrase='aeiouy'`[3] does not. It is not possible to make an item by item comparison of a phrase of 46 letters with "aeiouy", which has only 6 letters.

In other words: one may compare 46 letters with 46 other letters, or compare them with one letter, but not with 6 letters.

---

[3] The letter "y" is considered a vowel in many European languages.

Fortunately, the function *Membership* does exactly what we want:

```
      (Phrase ∊ 'aeiouy') / ⍳⍴Phrase
2 4 6 8 11 14 16 20 23 24 30 33 36 41 43 45
```

More generally, this algorithm can be used to search for some `Data` in a `Vector`:

```
R ← (Vector ∊ Data) / ⍳⍴Vector
```

13.3 Comparison of *Membership* and *Index Of*

We have discovered two different techniques, using the primitive functions, *Index Of*, *Membership*, and *Index Generator*, that allow us to look up one set of values in another and to determine the positions of the items of one set in the other. Depending on the problem that we have to solve, we can choose which of the two methods will be most appropriate for the job in hand. Consider the following example:

13.3.1 - Example

A company named **Blue Hammer Inc**. has subsidiaries in a number of countries; each country being identified by a numeric code. The country names are stored in a matrix named `Countries`, and the country codes are stored in a vector named `Codes`. To make things easier to read, let us show those two variables side by side:

```
 Countries            Codes
     ⇩                  ⇩

France                 50
Great Britain          43
Italy                  12
United States          83
Belgium                64
Swiss                  34
Sweden                 66
Canada                 81
Egypt                  37
etc...                etc...
```

So, Sweden is identified by 66, and Belgium is identified by 64.

All the sales made during the last month have been recorded in two vectors:

`BHCodes`	indicates in which country each sale has been made, and
`BHAmounts`	indicates the amount of each sale.

Here are the two vectors. Many countries have not sold anything, whereas some countries (like 12 and 83) have made several sales:

```
BHCodes      83  12  12  83  43  66  50  81  12  83  14  66 etc...
BHAmounts   609 727 458 469 463 219 431 602 519 317 663 631 etc...
```

13.3.2 - First Question

We would like to focus on some selected countries (14, 43, 50, 37, and 66) and calculate the total amount of their sales. Let's first identify which items of `BHCodes` are relevant:

```
      Selected ← 14 43 50 37 66
      BHCodes  ∊ Selected
0 0 0 0 1 1 1 0 0 0 1 1 0 1 0
```

⇦ Identifies sales in the selected countries only.

Then we can apply this filter to the amounts, and add them up:

```
      (BHCodes ∊ Selected) / BHAmounts
463 219 431 663 631 421
      +/ (BHCodes ∊ Selected) / BHAmounts
2828
```

An alternative solution is to find the **positions** of the selected countries, then using this set of indexes to get the amounts, and add them. The result is of course the same:

```
      Positions ← (BHCodes ∊ Selected) / ⍳⍴BHCodes
      +/ BHAmounts[Positions]
2828
```

As mentioned in Section 11 it is a kind of detour to solve this task using indexing, but here it serves to illustrate the different lookup methods.

Let us take a look at the selected countries and their positions in `BHCodes`:

```
Selected     is    14 43 50 37 66
Positions    is     5  6  7 11 12 14
```

Using *Membership*, we have obtained `Positions` which contains 6 items for the 5 countries in `Selected`. What does it tell us?

- `Positions` contains the indices of *all* of the occurrences of the selected countries in the list of sales.
- However, the items in `Positions` do not correspond to the items in `Selected` on a one-to-one basis; we cannot say that country #14 is in position 5, or country #43 in position 6, and so on.
- It does not tell us that nothing was sold in country #37. Perhaps it would have been a good idea to identify this fact?

13.3.3 - Second Question

Now, let us suppose that we want to display the names of the selected countries. To do this, we must determine the positions of the selected country codes in the entire list of country codes, and get the corresponding names.

If we use the *Membership* approach , here is what we get:

```
      Selected                          ⇦ Just to remind you of the values.
14 43 50 37 66
      Positions ← (Codes ∊ Selected) / ⍳⍴Codes
      Countries[Positions;] ,[2] Selected
France           14
Great Britain    43                     ⇦ We concatenated a numeric vector to a character
Sweden           50                       matrix; the result is a Mixed matrix.
Egypt            17
Brazil           66
```

At first sight, this **seems** to be good: all the selected countries are displayed. However, they are not in the correct order: 14 is not France but Brazil, 43 is Great Britain, but 50 is not Sweden, it is France, and so on.

The problem with this method is the lack of a one-to-one correspondence between the selected countries and their positions in the list of sales. The positions will always be in the order that the countries appear in `Countries` - because of the expression `⍳⍴Codes`. However, the order of the selection vector, the result of the expression `(Codes ∊ Selected)`, is completely independent of the order of the items in `Selected`: The expression returns the same result no matter how `Selected` is ordered.

The correct method to use in order to solve this task is to use the *Index Of* function (dyadic Iota):

```
      Positions ← Codes ⍳ Selected      ⇦ It is even a simpler expression.
      Countries[Positions;] ,[2] Selected
Brazil           14
Great Britain    43
France           50                     ⇦ That's correct now!
Egypt            17
Sweden           66
```

It is the one-to-one relationship between the items of the right argument to *Index Of* (`Selected`) and the items of its result (`Positions`) that guarantees a correct result.

13.3.4 - Comparison

The following table summarizes the most important properties of the two methods:

`Pos←(List∊Data)/⍳⍴List`	• The items in `Pos` do not have a 1-to-1correspondence with the items in `Data`. • Instead the items in `Pos` correspond to the items in `List`. • `Pos` gives all of the positions of multiple occurrences of `List` in `Data`. • `Pos` does not explicitly identify missing values.
`Pos←List ⍳ Data`	• The items in `Pos` **do** have a 1-to-1correspondence with the items in `Data`. • `Pos` ignores multiple occurrences; just gives the first. • `Pos` identifies missing values by the value `1+⍴List`.

The choice of method depends on the kind of problem you want to solve.

13.4 Idioms

The expression `(Vec∊Data)/⍳⍴Vec` is what we call an ***Idiom***; that is to say an expression which can be understood as an entity at first sight (with some practice!).

For someone who knows nothing of APL the expression above may be completely obscure (even if he has an extensive knowledge of other programming languages), and he cannot readily appreciate that an APL programmer can understand it immediately, without having to read each of the symbols one by one.

This is not a paradox. For young children, reading the word "***Daddy***" is complex: It requires the comprehension of a sequence of letters one-by-one. I presume that you no longer do that, do you? **You do not read** the letters; you understand **the word** as a whole. This is exactly the same for the above idiom.

Incidentally, it is not just the APL programmer who is capable of processing an idiomatic expression in its entirety. Dyalog APL itself includes a special *Idiom Recognition* feature that speeds up the processing of APL code for many popular idioms.

13.5 Application 5

Sometimes, a programmer needs to remove duplicate items from a vector and there is well-known idiomatic way to do this. The idiom applies equally to numeric, character and nested vectors. Let us begin with a numeric vector:

```
      Vec ← 12 89 57 46 12 50 36 37 83 46 27 12
```

The algorithm is based on the comparison of two vectors:

`⍳⍴Vec` gives the position of each item of `Vec`:

```
1 2 3 4 5 6 7 8 9 10 11 12
```

`Vec⍳Vec` may be a bit more complex to understand: We use `⍳` to identify the positions of the items of `Vec` in `Vec` itself. But because *Index Of* only returns the first occurrences, we get, for each item, the position where this value appears for the first time:

```
1 2 3 4 1 6 7 8 9 4 11 1
```

Let us write those two vectors one under the other:

`⍳⍴Vec`	`1 2 3 4 5 6 7 8 9 10 11 12`	Actual positions
`Vec⍳Vec`	`1 2 3 4 1 6 7 8 9  4 11  1`	First occurrences
`(⍳⍴Vec)=(Vec⍳Vec)`	`1 1 1 1 0 1 1 1 1  0  1  0`	Comparison

If the position of an item matches the position of its first occurrence it must be retained, otherwise it is a second (or third…) occurrence, and it must be removed. So the final algorithm is as follows:

```
((⍳⍴Vector) = Vector ⍳ Vector) / Vector
```

```
      ((⍳⍴Vec)=Vec⍳Vec)/Vec
12 89 57 46 50 36 37 83 27
```
⇦ Duplicate values have been removed.

It also works on character arrays and on nested arrays:

```
      Text ← 'All men are created equal'
      ((⍳⍴Text)=Text⍳Text)/Text
Al menarctdqu
```

Unique

Although still useful as an example, the idiom described above is now obsolescent, because a primitive function has been added to APL to perform the same task.

This function, called ***Unique***, is represented by the symbol ∪ (*Ctrl*+V) used as a monadic function:

```
      ∪ Vec
12 89 57 46 50 36 37 83 27              ⇦ It's so simple!
      ∪ Text
Al menarctdqu
      ∪ 'one' 'nine' 'five' 'nine' 'two' 'two' 'one'
 one  nine  five  two
```

13.6 *Application 6*

Some applications of *Index Generator* are extremely basic, but so useful! Suppose that you invest a certain sum of money, €6,000 for example, and you expect an interest rate of 4% p.a. How is the investment expected to grow in the next 5 years?

You will have to calculate 1.04 to the power 0, 1, 2 , 3… The *Index Generator* will help us:

```
      6000×1.04*(⍳6)-1
6000 6240 6489.6 6749.18 7019.15 7299.91
```

14 - Ravel

The function ***Ravel*** is represented by the monadic use of comma (,). Applied to any array, it returns all its items as a vector.

Naturally, if the array is already a vector, *Ravel* does not change anything.

Let us see how it works on some matrices:

```
      Tests
11 26 22
14 87 52
30 28 19
65 40 55
19 31 64
33 70 44
```

```
      ,Tests
11 26 22 14 87 52 30 28 19 65 40 55 19 31 64 33 70 44
```

The items of the matrix have been strung out and returned as a vector.

```
      Chemistry
H2SO4
CaCO3
Fe2O3
      ,Chemistry
H2SO4CaCO3Fe2O3
```

A common use of ***Ravel*** is to transform a scalar into a one-item vector. The difference between a scalar and a one-item vector is not readily obvious, until you use it as an index into a matrix.

Suppose that you need to select a particular set of columns `Cols` from the matrix `Forecast`. As long as `Cols` contains more than one value, the result will be a matrix:

```
      Cols ← 1 4 6
      Forecast[;Cols]
150  80  80
300 400 520
100 380 450
 50 300 350
```

But if `Cols` happens to have only a single value, which is a scalar, the result returned is a vector (we already mentioned this in B-5.3):

```
      Cols ← 4
      Forecast[;Cols]
80 400 380 300
```

The rank of the result may be critical if some other expression in your program expects a matrix.

To make certain that your indexing expression always returns a matrix, you must ensure that your index will always be a vector by using *Ravel*:

```
      Forecast[;,Cols]              ⇦ Whatever the rank of Cols, the result
 80                                   will always be a matrix.
400
380
300
```

Ravel can be associated with an *Axis* specifier; this will be discussed in the *Specialist's Section*.

15 - Empty Vectors and Black Holes

When we apply a scalar dyadic function to a vector and a scalar, the rule is that the result has the same size as the vector:

```
      42 75 86 31 + 10              ⇦ A scalar added to a 4-item vector
52 85 96 41                           gives a 4-item vector, too.
      'MAMMOTH' = 'M'
1 0 1 1 0 0 0
```

But what happens if the vector is empty? The rule says that the result must have the same size as the vector: Therefore it should be empty, too, regardless of the (scalar) function that we used!

```
      Hole ← ⍬                      ⇦ Any other method (like ⍳0) would be OK.
      Hole + 3
                                    ⇦ Nothing is displayed: The result is empty.
      Hole × 100
                                    ⇦ The same.
      Hole = 0

      Hole = Hole
                                    ⇦ Help! What can we do?
      ⍴Hole
0                                   ⇦ Phew! This result explains everything.
```

Empty vectors look very much like black holes: They absorb everything (but only when used with scalar functions). This may lead to some unexpected results.

Unexpected Consequences

You may remember that we wrote a function to calculate the average of a vector (see section C-9). Let us use it on a series of vectors, reducing the length of the vector each time:

```
      Average 48 73 21
47.33333333                         ⇦ OK.
      Average 48 73
60.5                                ⇦ OK.
      Average 48
                                    ⇦ No answer: The result is empty, but WHY?
```

Let us take a look at the definition of that function (double-click on its name):

```
      Average ← {(+/⍵)÷(⍴⍵)}
```

When the function processes a scalar like 48, the expression `(⍴⍵)` gives an empty result. Then, when we use this empty vector to divide into the sum, we get another empty result!

To compensate for this, we can first transform the argument of the function into a vector using *Ravel*. So, the new improved definition of the function is as follows:

```
      Average ← {(+/⍵)÷(⍴,⍵)}          ⇦ Note the comma between ⍴ and ⍵.
      Average 48
48
```

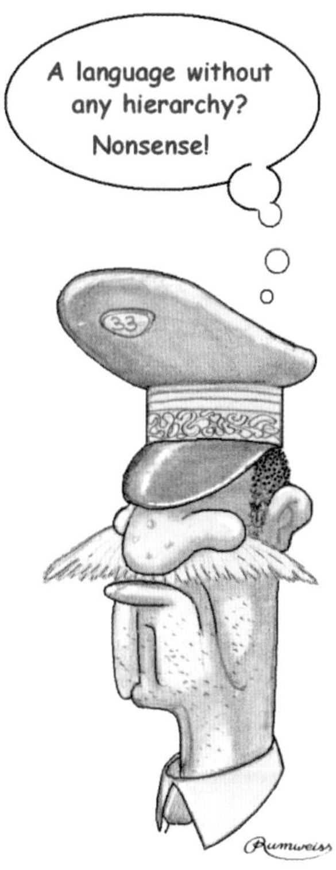

Exercises

Warning! *The following exercises are designed to train* ***you****, not the computer. For that reason, we suggest that you try to answer them on a sheet of paper, not on your computer. When you are sure of your answer, you can test it on the computer.*

C-1 Can you evaluate the following expressions?

```
3 × 2 + 6 ≠ 3 × 2
12 6 27 ⌊ 11 + ⍳3
4 5 6 ⌈ 4 + 2 5 9 > 1 6 8
7 ⌊ 25 6 17 - (2 × 3) + 9 3 5
((8 + 6) × 2 + 1) × 3 - 6 ÷3
(⍴4⌈5) + 4⌈5
```

C-2 Try to evaluate the following expressions.
Be careful: They are not as simple as might first appear!

```
2 2+2 2
2+2 2+2
2+2,2+2
2,2+2,2
```

C-3 Given the following vector: `A ← 8 2 7 5`

Compare the results obtained from the following sets of expressions:

`1+⍴A`	and	`⍴A+1`		
`1+⍳⍴A`	and	`⍳¯1+⍴A`	and	`⍳⍴A-1`

C-4 Using your knowledge of the order of evaluation in APL, re-write the following expressions without using parentheses.

```
((⍳4)-1)⌈3
7⌊(⍳9)⌈3
1+((⍳5)=1 4 3 2 5)×5
```

C-5 Given a variable `A`, find an expression which returns the answer `1` if `A` is a scalar, and `0` if it is not.

C-6 Given two scalars `A` and `B`, write an expression which gives `7` if `A` is greater than or equal to `B`, and `3` if `A` is smaller than `B`.

C-7 Given two scalars `A` and `B`, find an expression which returns:

- an empty vector — if `A` is zero, whatever the value of `B`
- 0 — if `B` is zero, but `A` is not
- 3 — if neither `A` nor `B` are zero

C-8 **Broken keyboard!**

Unfortunately, your keyboard has been damaged, and your `∧` and `∨` keys no longer work. Which other symbols could you use to replace them?

You can test your solutions on these vectors: `0 0 1 1` and `0 1 0 1`

C-9 Given these three vectors:

```
G ← 1 1 1 0 0 1
M ← 0 0 1 1 0 1
D ← 1 0 1 0 1 0
```

Evaluate the following expressions:

a) `G∨D`

b) `~G∧D`

c) `~G∨~D`

d) `D∧~G`

e) `G∧M∨D`

f) `(~D)∧(~G)`

g) `(M⌈G)=(M⌊D)`

h) `(M⌊G)≠(M⌈D)`

C-10 Evaluate the following expressions:

a) `0 < 0 ≤ 0 = 0 ≥ 0 > 0`

b) `'sugar' ∊ 'salt'`

c) `11 ≠ '11'`

d) `'14' ⍳ '41'`

C-11 How many times does the letter `"e"` appear in the following character vector?

```
Tex ← 'The silence of the sea'
```

C-12 We have conducted some experiments on a variable `Z`:

```
2 ⍴ Z        returns    1 7
+⌿ Z         returns    20
Z = 9        returns    0
                        0
                        1
                        0
```

What is the value of `Z`?

C-13 We have conducted some experiments on a variable `Z`:

```
Z = 0        returns    0 1 0 0
                        1 0 0 1
+/[2] Z      returns    20 6
+/[1] Z      returns    8 7 6 5
```

What is the value of `Z`?

C-14 What are all the **positions** of the letter "o" in the character vector specified in exercise C-11?

C-15 Given a vector `Vec` of any size and type (numeric or character), try to extract the items of `Vec` which are in the odd positions (the 1st, the 3rd, the 5th...).

C-16 How many numbers are there in the variable `Prod` used in this chapter?

C-17 How is it possible to remove all the values which do not fall between 20 (inclusive) and 30 (exclusive) from a given vector?

C-18 In a vector, we would like to replace all the values that are smaller than 20 by 20, and replace all the values that are greater than 30 by 30. How can we do that?

C-19 The following 5 expressions cannot be executed, but instead generate error messages; can you say why?

a) `3+(5-(6+2)×4`

b) `121÷(⍳4)-3`

c) `(¯X+5)*2`

d) `⍴4 5 6+2 3-1`

e) `⍳4 0 ¯4+2 0 1`

C-20 Write an APL expression which produces a vector of 17 numbers, the first being 23, with each subsequent number being equal to the preceding one plus 11.

C-21 In a shop, each product is identified by a code. You are given the list of the codes, and the corresponding prices:

```
PCodes ← 56 66 19 37 44 20 18 23 68 70 82
Prices ←  9 27 10 15 12  5  8  9 98  7 22
```

A customer gives you a list of items he intends to buy as vector of code/quantity pairs: Code-Quantity, Code-Quantity, and so on.

```
Wanabuy ← 37 1 70 20 19 2 82 5 23 10
```

Can you evaluate his bill? Note that this cannot be done easily in a single (and readable) APL expression, and you will therefore need to write several expressions.

You can check your solution: The correct answer is 375.

C-22 We have organised a lottery, and we have created four vectors:

`Tickets`	Numbers of all the tickets
`Sold`	Numbers of the tickets which have been sold
`Winners`	Numbers of the winning tickets
`Ours`	Numbers of the tickets we bought ourselves

We also have a vector named `Prizes`. It has the same length as `Winners`, and it tells us the value of the prize associated with each winning ticket.

For your convenience, these variables are provided in the workspace DyalogTutor_EN.

And now, try to answer the following 4 questions:

a) What are the numbers of the unsold tickets?

b) Are there some winning tickets which have not been sold?

c) How many winning tickets do **WE** have?

d) How much did we win?

C-23 Can you calculate all the divisors of an integer number `N`?

Solutions The solutions are given at the end of the book in Chapter X.

The Specialist's Section

Each chapter is followed by a "Specialist's Section" like this one.
This section is dedicated to skilled APLers, who wish to improve their knowledge.

You will find here rare or complex usages of the concepts presented in the chapter, or discover extended explanations which need the knowledge of some symbols that will be seen much further in the book.

If you are exploring APL for the first time,
skip this section and go to the next chapter.

Spe - 1 Division Control - ⎕DIV

We saw in Section C-2.2 that `0÷0` returns 1 because any number divided by itself should give 1.

This may sometimes be inappropriate. Suppose that we want to calculate the sales growth for 5 products, but the production of the 3rd product has not started yet, so its sales are currently zero:

```
      Before←20 31 0 120 63
      After← 22 27 0 149 59
```

The growth (in percent rounded) can be calculated like this:

```
      ⌊0.5+100× (After-Before)÷Before
10 ¯13 100 24 ¯6
```

It is rather surprising to see that we've got a 100% growth on a product that does not exist!

To avoid this dichotomy, a so-called *System variable* named `⎕DIV` is included in Dyalog APL to change the behaviour of division.

By default, `⎕DIV` is zero, but can be set to 1: `⎕DIV ← 1`.

With `⎕DIV` set to `0`	`0÷0` gives `1` Any other number divided by zero gives a DOMAIN ERROR.
With `⎕DIV` set to `1`	`0÷0` gives `0` Any other number divided by zero also gives `0`

Because `⎕DIV` is a variable, it can be localised in the header of a function. Then the particular behaviour of division remains specific to that function and its sub functions.

Spe - 2 Derived Functions

Let us sum the items of a vector: `+/Contents`

In this expression, the operator *Reduction* takes *Plus* as its argument (operand).

This pair of symbols creates a new function, a so called "***Derived function***". The derived function is in this case monadic, and it takes the variable `Contents` as its argument.

`Contents` is not the right argument of `/`; it is the argument of the derived function `+/`.

This is so true that `+/` could be parenthesised: `(+/)Contents`

It can also be given a name:

```
      AddUp ← +/
      AddUp 10 20 30
60
```

All operators create *derived functions*, i.e. functions that are derived from the function(s) they accept as operand(s).

Spe - 3 Nor & Nand

APL Boolean algebra also includes two useful functions:

Nor	(stands for Not-Or),	represented in APL by `⍱`	(made of `~` over a `∨`)
Nand	(stands for Not-And)	represented in APL by `⍲`	(made of `~` over a `∧`)

These functions give the negation of ***Or*** and ***And*** respectively.

It means that: `A⍱B` is equal to `~A∨B`
`A⍲B` is equal to `~A∧B` as shown below.

Assuming that `A ← 0 1 0 1` and `B ← 0 0 1 1`, then we can compare:

Or	`A ∨ B`	gives	`0 1 1 1`
Nor	`A ⍱ B`	gives	`1 0 0 0`
And	`A ∧ B`	gives	`0 0 0 1`
Nand	`A ⍲ B`	gives	`1 1 1 0`

Warning!

Both ∨ and ∧ are associative. It means that:

`(A∨B)∨C`	is equivalent to	`A∨(B∨C)`	and can be written `A∨B∨C`
`(A∧B)∧C`	is equivalent to	`A∧(B∧C)`	and can be written `A∧B∧C`

This is not the case for *Nor* and *Nand*:

`(A⍱B)⍱C`	is **not** equivalent to	`A⍱(B⍱C)`
`(A⍲B)⍲C`	is **not** equivalent to	`A⍲(B⍲C)`

The consequence is that if `Bin` has more than 2 items:

`⍱/Bin`	is **not** equivalent to	`~∨/Bin`
`⍲/Bin`	is **not** equivalent to	`~∧/Bin`

This is probably the reason why those two symbols are rarely used in common business applications, but they are extremely useful in electronic automation, because they represent basic logical circuits.

Spe - 4 Index Generator of Arrays

We have given a limited definition of the *Index Generator*; here is a more general presentation:

In the expression `R ← ⍳Dim`

`Dim` represents the shape of an array (the array itself need not actually exist)

`R` is the set of indexes pointing to all items of that array

The shape of `R` is given by `Dim`, and each item of `R` is the index (or set of indices) of its own items.

Some examples should help:

- If the shape of a vector is .... `5` the coordinates of its items are `1 2 3 4 5`
  They are given by .... `⍳5` ⇨ `1 2 3 4 5`
- If the shape of a matrix is........ `2 3` the coordinates of its items are pairs going from `(1 1)`, `(1 2)`, ... up to `(2 3)`
  They are given by .... `⍳2 3` ⇨
```
 1 1   1 2   1 3
 2 1   2 2   2 3
```
- If the shape of an array is... `3 2 5` the coordinates of its items are triplets, from `(1 1 1)` up to `(3 2 5)`

They are given by............. ⍳3 2 5 ⇨

```
1 1 1   1 1 2   1 1 3   1 1 4   1 1 5
1 2 1   1 2 2   1 2 3   1 2 4   1 2 5

2 1 1   2 1 2   2 1 3   2 1 4   2 1 5
2 2 1   2 2 2   2 2 3   2 2 4   2 2 5

3 1 1   3 1 2   3 1 3   3 1 4   3 1 5
3 2 1   3 2 2   3 2 3   3 2 4   3 2 5
```

More generally, any array is identical to itself indexed by *Iota* of its shape:

`Data` is identical to `Data[⍳⍴Data]`

Spe - 5 Ravel With Axis

Ravel can be used with an *Axis specifier*, using the notation: `R←,[Axis] Data`

In this expression, `Axis` can be:

- An empty vector — `R← ,[⍬] Chemistry`
- A decimal scalar, adjacent to an axis of `Data` — `R← ,[0.5] Contents`
- A subset of the axes of `Data` — `R← ,[2 3] Prod`

Spe-5.1 - Empty Axis

If `Axis` is empty, the result is obtained by appending a new dimension of size 1 to the list of `Data`'s dimensions.

It means that: if `⍴Data` is `8` then `⍴,[⍬] Data` will be `8 1`
if `⍴Data` is `3 7` then `⍴,[⍬] Data` will be `3 7 1`

Example:

```
      ,[⍬] 'PUB'
P
U
B
```

⇦ The original data is a 3 item vector.

⇦ The result is a 3 by 1 matrix
A second dimension of length 1 has been added

Spe-5.2 - Fractional Axis

If `Axis` is a fractional value, it is mandatory that it is "*adjacent*" to an existing dimension of `Data`.

This means that for an array of rank 3, the axis must be a value between 0 and 4 (exclusive).

The result is derived from `Data` by inserting a new dimension of size 1 in the list of `Data`'s dimensions. The new dimension is inserted according to the value of `Axis`.

It means that: if `⍴Data` is `8 5` then `⍴,[0.5] Data` will be `1 8 5`
`⍴,[1.5] Data` will be `8 1 5`
`⍴,[2.5] Data` will be `8 5 1`

if `⍴Data` is `7` then `⍴,[0.5] Data` will be `1 7`
`⍴,[1.5] Data` will be `7 1`

Examples:

```
      ,[1.5] 'PUB'          ⇦ The original data is a 3-item vector.
P
U                           ⇦ The result is a 3 by 1 matrix.
B
      ,[0.5] 'PUB'          ⇦ The original data is a 3-item vector.
PUB                         ⇦ The result is a not a vector, but a 1 by 3 matrix.
```

Those conventions are totally consistent with those defined for some other functions like *Laminate* or *Mix*.

The actual value of the axis specification is not used for anything other than to determine where to insert the new dimension. This means that, for example, all expressions of the form `,[1.xxx]` will have the same effect as the `,[1.5]` that we used above:

```
      ,[1.0123] 'PUB'
P
U                           ⇦ The result is the same as above.
B
```

Spe-5.3 - A List of Dimensions

If `Axis` is a subset of the axes of `Data`, it is mandatory that they are contiguous and in ascending order. It means that for an array of rank 3, the list of axes can be `[1 2]` or `[2 3]`, but neither `[1 3]` nor `[3 2]`.

The result is obtained by unravelling `Data` so that the dimensions mentioned in `Axis` are merged into a single dimension.

For example, imagine that `Data` is an array of shape `5 2 4 7`:

`,[1 2] Data`	gives a result of shape	`10 4 7`	
`,[2 3] Data`	gives a result of shape	`5 8 7`	
`,[3 4] Data`	gives a result of shape	`5 2 28`	
`,[1 2 3] Data`	gives a result of shape	`40 7`	and so on…

For example, you can try the two following operations:

`,[1 2] Prod`	gives a matrix of shape	`10 12`
`,[2 3] Prod`	gives a matrix of shape	`5 24`

Spe-5.4 - Border Cases

- If `Axis` is reduced to a single value, the operation returns `Data` unchanged.
  So: `,[1]Prod` or `,[3]Prod` both return `Prod` unchanged.
- If `Axis` contains the whole set of the axes of `Data`, the operation is equivalent to a simple *Ravel*, and gives a vector of the items of `Data`.
  So: `,[1 2 3]Prod` is strictly equivalent to `,Prod`.

For these reasons, *Ravel with axes* can only "collapse" dimensions of arrays of rank 2 or more.

Spe - 6 Residue

The formal definition of *Residue* `R ← X|Y` is the following: `R ← Y-X×⌊Y÷X+X=0`

This formula confirms what we said in Section 2.6:

- if `X` is zero, `X|Y` is equal to `Y`
- `R` and `X` will always have the same sign.

Chapter D: User Defined Functions

1 - Landmarks

1.1 Some Definitions

In previous chapters we made a distinction between the functions and operators which are part of APL, like `+ × ⌈ ⍴` (we refer to them as *primitives*), and those functions and operators that are created by the user which are represented not by a symbol but by a name, like `Average` or `Doitforme` (we say they are *user-defined*).

We also made an important distinction between *functions*, which apply to data and which return data, and *operators*, which apply to functions to produce *derived* functions (see C-7.2).

This means that we can distinguish between 4 major categories of processing tools:

Categories		Examples	Refer to
Built-in tools	Primitive functions	`+ × ⌈ ⍴`	Previous chapters
	Primitive operators	`/`	Chapter J
User-defined tools	**User-defined functions**	`Average`	This chapter
	User-defined operators		Section J-10

This chapter is devoted to user-defined *functions*. The subject of user-defined *operators* will be covered later in Chapter J.

We can further categorise user-defined functions according to the way that they process data. Firstly we can distinguish between ***Direct*** and ***Procedural*** functions.

Direct functions (commonly referred to as ***D-Fns***[4]) are defined in a very formal manner.

They are usually designed for pure calculation, without any external or user interfaces. *D-Fns* do not allow loops except by recursion, and have limited options for conditional programming.

Procedural functions are less formal, and look much more like programs written in other languages.

They provide greater flexibility for building major applications which involve user interfaces, access to files or databases, and other external interfaces. Procedural functions may take no arguments and behave like scripts.

Even though you may write entire systems with *D-Fns*, you might prefer to restrict their use to short in-line statements, for example to run {a series of functions} on *each* item of an array.

The second distinction we can make concerns the number of arguments a user-defined function can have.

Dyadic functions take two arguments, which are placed on either side of the function (`X f Y`).

Monadic functions take a single argument, which is placed to the right of the function (`f X`).

Niladic functions take no argument at all.

Ambivalent functions are dyadic functions whose left argument is optional.

1.2 Configure Your Environment

Dyalog APL has a highly configurable development and debugging environment, designed to fit the requirements of very different kinds of programmers. This environment is controlled by configuration parameters; let us determine which context will suit you best.

1.2.1 - What Do You Need?

All you need (except for love) is:

- a window in which to type expressions that you want to be executed (white Session window)
- one or more windows in which to create/modify user-defined functions (grey Edit windows)
- one or more windows to debug execution errors (black Trace window)

[4] *Direct functions or D-Fns* were originally called "*Dynamic functions*", but today the term *Direct* is preferred.

In **Classic** Dyalog mode, Edit and Trace windows can be "floating" windows which can be moved freely anywhere on your screen, as shown here:

Figure D-1

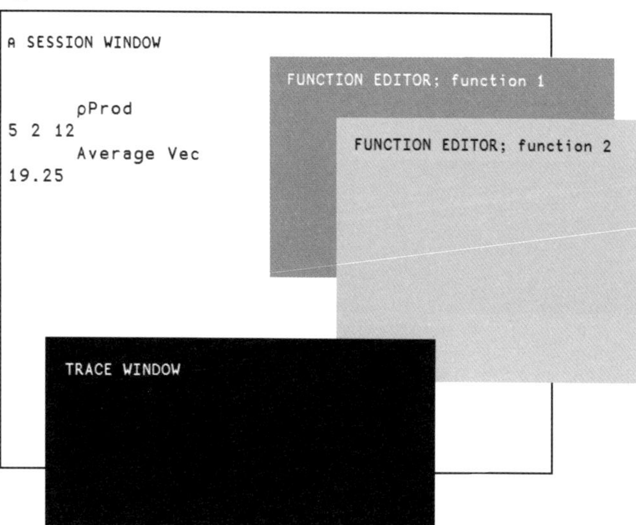

Classic mode offers two benefits:

- You can easily display more than one function at a time. This makes it convenient to Copy/Paste statements from one to another, or just to have an overall view of a collection of related functions
- You can decide to have a single trace window (as shown) or a stack of trace windows, showing which function calls which other. This will be described later.

Dyalog APL offers a second development environment scheme, more consistent with other software development tools, in which it is possible to divide the session window into three parts which can be resized, as shown here:

Figure D-2

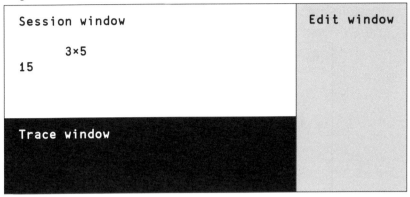

This configuration provides a single Edit window and a single Trace window, each of which is "docked" along one of the Session window borders. You can dock these windows along any of the Session window sides. For example, the figure below shows a configuration with three horizontal panes, highly suitable for entering and editing very long statements.

Figure D-3

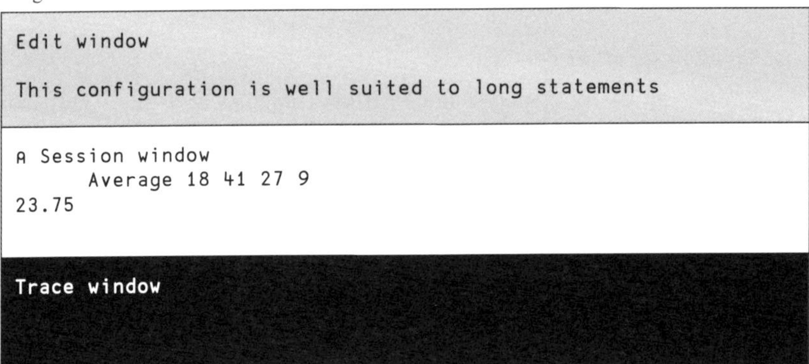

Even when this configuration is selected, it is possible to grab the border of a sub-window (Edit or Trace) and then drag and drop it the middle of the session window, as an independent floating window.

The Edit window supports the *Multiple Document Interfaces* (MDI). This means that you can work on more than one function at a time. Using the "Window" menu, you can *Tile* and *Cascade*, or you can maximize any one of the functions to concentrate solely upon it.

If you are working on a relatively small screen you may find that the "*Classic Dyalog mode*" works best for you, but it is of course up to you to decide which of the two modes you find is most convenient.

You can reconfigure your environment at any time using: Options⇨Configuration⇨Trace/Edit.

Figure D-4 - Dyalog Configuration box

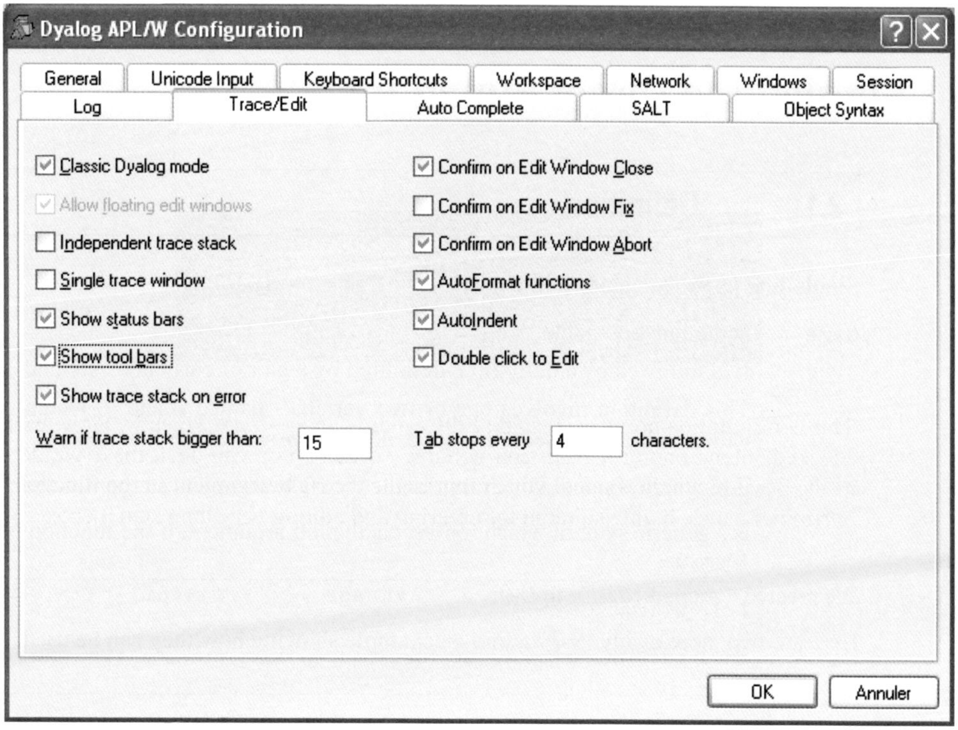

You can select "*Classic Dyalog mode*" (recommended) or not.

If selected you can decide to have multiple trace windows or select "*Single trace window*". We shall see in Section E-3.2 which option is best suited to the kind of work you are doing.

If you do not select the classic mode, the "*Single trace window*" option is hidden.

1.2.2 - A Text Editor; What For?

Some *D-Fns* can be defined by a single expression, and so do not require the use of a text editor; we used this technique in C-9 to define a function named `Average`.

A single-line *D-Fn* may be defined using assignment, which is actioned when you press the *Enter* key. This technique is clearly inappropriate for a multi-line function.

To define a multi-line function, the user must enter its statements in a separate window (the text editor), and then fix (validate, establish) the entire set of statements as a new function. To do this, the user can choose to use an external text editor, like Microsoft Notepad or Wordpad (this is explained in Chapter R), or the built-in editor delivered with Dyalog APL.

2 - Single-Line Direct Functions

2.1 Definition

Single-line *D-Fns* are created like this: `Name ← {definition}`

`Name` is the function name.
It is followed by a definition, delimited by a pair of curly braces { and }.
This definition involves one or two variables named ⍵ and ⍺, which represent the values to be processed, they are called ***arguments*** of the function.

⍵ is a generic symbol which represents the right argument of the function.

⍺ is a generic symbol which represents the left argument, if the function is dyadic.

We created a monadic *D-Fn* in C-9: `Average ← {(+/⍵)÷(⍴⍵)}`

Here are two more dyadic *D-Fns*, and an example showing how they can be used:

```
      Plus ← {⍺ + ⍵}
      Times ← {⍺ × ⍵}
      3 Times 7 Plus 9              ⇦ This is strictly equivalent to 3×7+9
48                                    the order of evaluation is the same
```

The arguments ⍵ and ⍺ are read-only (they cannot be modified) and are limited in scope to only being visible within the function itself.

The developer does not need to declare anything about the shape or internal representation of the arguments and the result. This information is automatically obtained from the arrays provided as its arguments. So, our functions can work on any arrays, as shown:

```
      12 Plus 2 3⍴⍳6                ⇦ A scalar added to a matrix returns a matrix
13 14 15                              No need to specify it
16 17 18
      7.3 Times 10 34 52 16         ⇦ A vector of integer numbers multiplied by a
scalar
73 248.2 379.6 116.8                  fractional number returns a fractional vector
```

Single-line *D-Fns* are well suited to pure calculation or straightforward array manipulation. For example, here is how we can calculate the hypotenuse of a right-angled triangle from the lengths of the two other sides:

```
      Hypo ← {(+/ω*2)*0.5}
      Hypo 4 3
5
      Hypo 12 5
13
```

2.2 Unnamed D-Fns

A *Direct function* can be defined and then discarded immediately after it has been used, in which case it does not need a name. For example, the geometric mean of a set of N values is defined as the Nth root of their product. The function can be defined (temporarily), used, and then discarded, like this:

```
      {(×/ω)*÷⍴ω} 6 8 4 11 9 14 7
7.865702202
```

This kind of function is similar to *inline* or *lambda* functions in other languages.

A special case is `{}`; this function does nothing. However, placed at the left of an expression, it can be used to prevent the result of the expression from being displayed on the screen.

2.3 Modifying The Code

Single-line *D-Fns* may be modified using the function editor, as will be explained later for procedural functions.

They can also be redefined entirely, as many times as necessary, as shown:

```
      Magic ← {α+ω}
      Magic ← {α÷+/ω}             ⇦ We create a function and then change it twice
      Magic ← {(+/α)-(+/ω)}         Only the last definition will survive.
```

Multi-line *D-Fns* will be studied later, after we have had time to practise using the function editor.

3 - Procedural Functions

Procedural functions, which are commonly referred to as *Trad-fns* (short for Traditional functions), are mainly used for complex calculations involving many variables, interactions with a user, file input/output of data, etc. They look much like functions or programs in more traditional programming languages.

3.1 A First Example

Procedural functions are composed of a *Header* and one or more *statements* (function lines), so we need to invoke a text editor to enter these as lines of text. For now, we shall use the Dyalog built-in editor.

As an example, let us see how we could define a function to calculate an average, with a technique slightly different from the one we employed in C-9.

First of all, we must choose a name for our new function. Having already used the name `Average`, let us choose `Meanval`.

Among the multiple ways of invoking the text editor let us use a very simple one: type the command `)ED` followed by a space and the name of the function to create: `)ED Meanval`

A window appears which contains only the name we chose, as shown below:

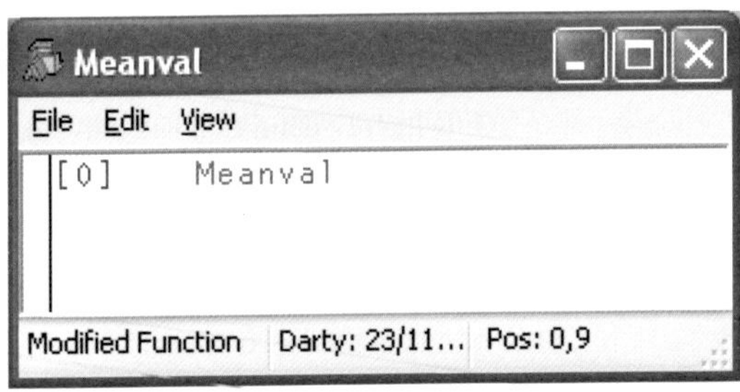

Figure D-5

First, we must specify in the header that our function will accept an array (a vector of values) on its right. We can represent the array with any valid name, for example `vec`; it is the *argument* to our function.

Normally, we would obtain the average value by the simple formula `(+/vec)÷(⍴vec)`. Here, just to produce a multi-line function, we shall split the process into a series of very simple steps, as shown below: calculate the sum, then the number of values, and divide one by the other.

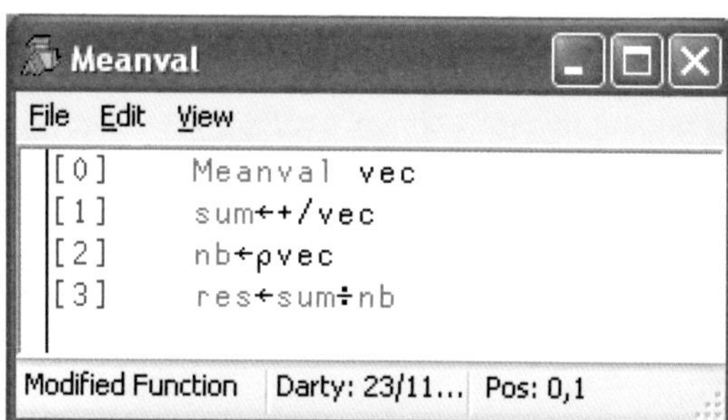

Figure D-6

Note that the presence/absence of line numbers is defined by a configuration parameter.

You can toggle line numbers on/off by pressing *Ctrl* together with the numeric keypad minus key, or by clicking [···]

Our function looks fine, and we must now make it available for execution. The term we use to describe this process in APL is to *Fix* the function. This is somewhat analogous to compilation in other programming languages. There are 2 different ways to fix the function:

- The easy way: press the *Escape* key (or activate the File⇨Exit menu).
  It may seem strange to use the *Escape* key for a positive action, but this is largely historical. *Escape* is used to fix the function and close its edit window.
- Activate the File⇨Fix menu.

  If you do so, the function is fixed, but its edit window remains open.

  This is useful only if you intend to test the function, modify it, test it again, modify again, etc, without closing the window.

Now the function exists and can be used

```
      Meanval 29 14 73 18
```

⇦ Process a vector of values
⇦ No answer; something is going wrong!

Explanation

We executed the function, and no result appeared. In fact, in our function, we have told the computer to create three variables `sum`, `nb`, and `res`, but which of them is the final result we would like to obtain? Because the flow of a function can include loops, the final result is not always the variable calculated on the last statement; the computer cannot guess!

We need a way to specify which variable is the result.

- To modify your function, just double-click on its name (or enter `)ED Meanval` again)
- Then, to the left of the header, add the text `res←` which does not mean "Put the result in `res` ", but "Return the value contained in `res`".
- Fix this modification by pressing *Escape* again.

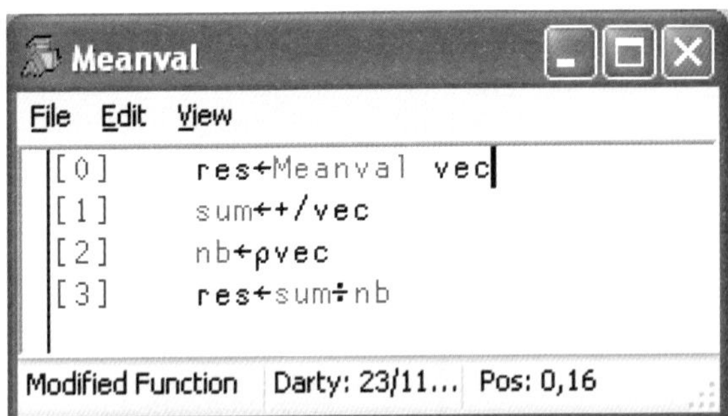

Figure D-7

Let us test it again:

```
      Meanval 29 14 73 18        ⇦ Process the same values
33.5                             ⇦ Now, a result is produced, and it is good
```

3.2 Local Names

We might think that all is now well, but this is not the case, as we shall see.

```
      vec ← 17 29 32 43          ⇦ Create a numeric vector
      Meanval vec                ⇦ Process it
30.25                              That's fine!
      nb ← 8 3 7 4 6 1 5 4       ⇦ Create a second one
      Meanval nb
4.75
      nb
8                                ⇦ Ooops, nb has been overwritten!
```

Apparently, we have a problem. Let us check the variables we used during function execution.

```
   sum    ⇨    134
   nb     ⇨    8
   res    ⇨    VALUE ERROR
   vec    ⇨    17 29 32 43
```

This needs some explanation!

Although they are no longer useful, `sum` and `nb` remain as variables in the workspace after they have been assigned values during the execution of the function:

- `sum` is correct, but is no longer useful after the function has terminated; we should find a way to prevent it from remaining in our workspace.

- The variable `nb` now contains the value (the length of the argument, in this case 8) that was calculated during the execution of the function. The value 8 has replaced the previous value of the variable that we assigned to it (`8 3 7 4 6 1 5 4`). This is really embarrassing, and should not happen!
- However, `vec` has not been overwritten, we can see that it still has its original value (`17 29 32 43`) although we applied the function to a different vector.
- And `res` no longer exists, though it has been calculated!

The reason is as follows: `vec` and `res` are temporary variable names used during function execution; they are ***Local variables***. Once execution is complete, these temporary variables are destroyed, with slightly different consequences:

- The temporary variable `res` was created during function execution. But because `res` is named as its result, when the function terminates, it returns its **value** and discards its **name**. Hence the message `VALUE ERROR` when we asked for the value of `res` after the function had finished.
- With regard to `vec`, the explanation is as follows:
  - An "external" variable `vec` already contains some values: `17 29 32 43`
  - During execution, a temporary "*local*" variable also named `vec` receives the values passed via the right argument; for example `8 3 7 4 6 1 5 4`.
  - The "external" value is hidden (we use the term *shadowed*) by the local one, so it is the local value that is visible and used during function execution.
  - At function completion, the "local" value is destroyed, revealing the "external" one which is no longer hidden by it and becomes visible again.

All the names referenced in the function header are processed as ***Local names***. Generally, these are variable names, but we shall see very soon that they can also be function names.

However, all the variables created during execution which are not referenced in the header are considered to be external references, outside the function. These names can refer to existing variables, maybe producing undesirable side effects, and they will remain after execution. They are ***Global variables***.

To avoid any unpredictable side effects, it is recommended that you declare as ***Local*** all the variables used by a function. This is done by specifying their names in the header, each prefixed by a ***semi-colon***, as shown on the following figure.

Modify your function again, as described above.

Important: Dyalog APL uses different colours for local and global names. In the previous edit windows `res` and `vec` were black, indicating that they are local names, while `sum` and `nb` were red, indicating that they are global names. You should see the colour changes while making your modifications.

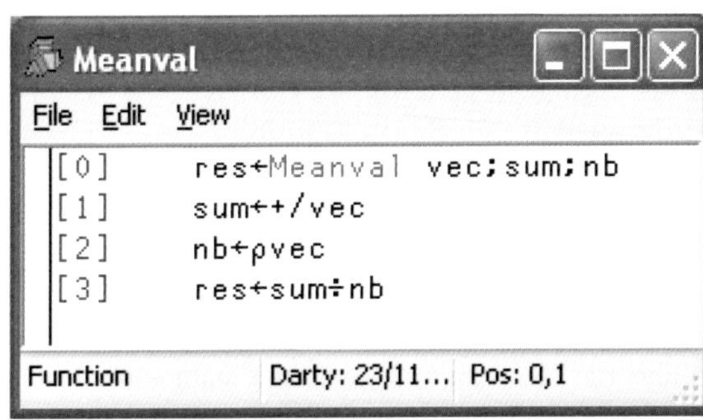

Figure D-8

The colours used here are the default ones.

You can change the colours using the Options ⇨ Colours menu

To check if this works:

- First, let us remove the inappropriate variables produced by the old version of the function:

```
      )erase sum nb vec
```

- Then let us create two vectors in the workspace:

```
      nb←'Nobody will destroy me!'
      vec←37 42 29
```

- Now we can apply our function to any set of values:

```
      Meanval 11 59 48 26 73
43.4
      nb
Nobody will destroy me!
      vec
37 42 29
```

⇦ The global value has been preserved

- Any attempt to get the values of `sum` and `res` will now cause a "`VALUE ERROR`".

Rules

- All the names referenced in the header of a function (including its result and arguments) are ***local*** to the function. They will exist only during the execution of the function.
- Operations made on local variables do not affect ***global*** variables having the same names.
- *Global* and *Local* are relative notions: when a function calls another sub function, variables local to the calling function are global for the called function.
- All the variables used in a function should preferably be declared local, unless you specifically intend otherwise.

3.3 Miscellaneous

3.3.1 - List of Functions

You can obtain a list of your variables by typing .... `)Vars`

You can obtain a list of your functions by typing .... `)Fns`

3.3.2 - Use of the Result

Once a function has been written, its result can be:

- Immediately displayed and lost:

```
      Meanval 11 59 48 26 73
43.4
```

- Included in an expression:

```
      100-3×Meanval 20 24 31 42
12.25
```

- Assigned to a variable:

```
      Janne ← Meanval 85 70 95
```

3.3.3 - Visual Representation

We saw that double-clicking on a function name invokes the editor, and allows the user to see the code. In a printed document, the conventional representation of a function is as follows:

```
     ∇ res←Meanval vec;sum;nb
[1]    sum←+/vec
[2]    nb←⍴vec
[3]    res←sum÷nb
     ∇
```

The function is delimited by a pair of ∇ symbols. This special symbol is named "***Del***" in English, or "***Carrot***" (because of its shape) in some French speaking countries. We will use this way of representing a function throughout the book.

One can obtain this representation (as a character array) using the built-in ***System function*** `⎕VR` (for "*Visual Representation*") of Dyalog APL. *System functions* are a special kind of function, provided with the development environment. The first character of their name is a **Quad** (⎕) guaranteeing that they cannot conflict with user-defined names, and they can be typed in upper or lower-case characters. They will be discussed in detail in Chapter L.

```
      ⎕vr 'Meanval'
     ∇ res←Meanval vec;sum;nb
[1]    sum←+/vec
[2]    nb←⍴vec
[3]    res←sum÷nb
     ∇
```

Note that this is quite unusual in a programming language. The result of ⎕VR is a character vector representing the source code of our function, which is now available for processing by other functions in the workspace!

3.3.4 - Invoking the Text Editor

Double-clicking a name which represents an existing item invokes the editor and displays its contents, using the colour scheme appropriate for the type of the item (function, character matrix, nested array, etc.) defined via your Options ⇨ Colours settings.

You can also invoke the editor by pressing *Shift-Enter* when the input cursor is inside or adjacent to the name. This is perhaps the most convenient way as, when working in an APL session, you tend to use the keyboard much more than the mouse.

Some items (e.g. numeric matrices, some nested arrays) may only be viewed using the editor, while others such as functions, text vectors, and text matrices can be modified. In the example below, we have invoked the editor, and changed the contents of the text matrix `Chemistry`:

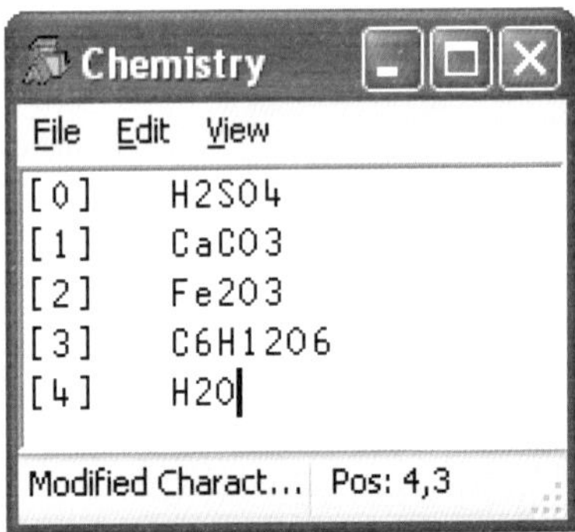

Figure D-9

The default colours are black on a white background like here.

If one saves this matrix, it will now have 5 rows and 7 columns (the length of its longest row).

If a name is currently undefined (has no value), double-clicking or pressing *Shift-Enter* on that name invokes the editor on it as if it were a new function. This is one way to create a function.

You can also invoke the editor using the command `)ED` as we did before. By default, it opens a **function** definition, but you can explicitly specify the type of a new object by prefixing its name with a special character, as shown in the table below.

Prefix	Example	Item produced
none	`)ed new`	Function
∇	`)ed ∇ borscht`	Function
-	`)ed - papyrus`	Text matrix
→	`)ed → crouton`	Simple text vector
∊	`)ed ∊ grunt`	Vector of text vectors, with one sub-vector per line

See also Appendix 2 for additional prefixes.

It is possible to open several edit windows simultaneously. For example:

`)ed Tyrex -Moose` will open one edit window to create a function named `Tyrex`, and a second edit window to create a text matrix named `Moose`.

If the object specified by the name already exists, the prefix (if specified) is ignored, and the editor is invoked according to the existing type of the object.

There are some other ways to invoke the editor:

- Use `⎕ED` instead of the command `)ED`. For example: `⎕ED 'Clown'`.
  `⎕ED` is a *System function*. This concept will be discussed in Chapter L.
- Type a name, or put the cursor on an existing name, and activate the menu: Action ⇨ Edit
- Type a name, or put the input cursor on an existing name, and click ∇

3.4 Second Example

You will remember that in Chapter C we had two variables named `Forecast` and `Actual` representing sales of 4 products over 6 months.

It would be nice to interlace the columns of those two matrices to make it easier to compare forecast and actual sales for the same month. Furthermore, because this might be useful for other pairs of matrices, let's create a general function to do the job; let's call it `Interlace`.

```
        Forecast                                 Actual
           ⇩                                        ⇩
150 200 100  80  80  80                 141 188 111  87  82  74
300 330 360 400 500 520                 321 306 352 403 497 507
100 250 350 380 400 450                 118 283 397 424 411 409
 50 120 220 300 320 350                  43  91 187 306 318 363
```

The result we would like to obtain is shown below. For illustrative purposes, `Forecast` numbers are shown in black and and `Actual` in grey:

```
150 141 200 188 100 111  80  87  80  82  80  74
300 321 330 306 360 352 400 403 500 497 520 507
100 118 250 283 350 397 380 424 400 411 450 409
 50  43 120  91 220 187 300 306 320 318 350 363
```

The first thing you must decide is how this function will be used:

- Will you pass both matrices on the right: `Interlace Forecast Actual`
- or one on the left and one on the right: `Forecast Interlace Actual`

Both solutions are valid; it is only a question of personal taste and ease of use. Our first function was monadic; let us make this one dyadic.

Having decided on the calling syntax, we can invoke the editor as described earlier, and type the function header as shown below:

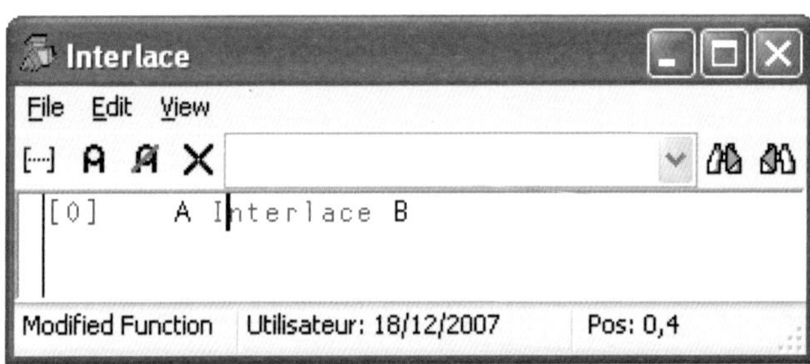

Figure D-10

Notice the toolbar that was absent in previous editor examples.
The toolbar can be switched on (the default) or off at will using the configuration dialog box:

Options ⇨ Configuration

and then:

Trace/Edit ⇨ Show toolbars

The names given to the arguments do not matter to the APL system: `A` and `B`, `Left` and `Right`, `X` and `Y` are perfectly valid names and are obviously easier to recall than `Potatoes` or `Ocarina`. However, you should pick names which help you remember what the function is doing. For example, in a general-purpose function like this, you should probably avoid using too specific names like `Forecast` and `Actual`: that would imply that this function only works on arrays containing Forecast and Actual data. Such names might also confuse the distinction between local and global names.

How shall we interlace our two matrices? We suggest the following steps:

- Calculate the size of the result `R`. It will be a matrix with as many rows as `A` and `B`, but twice as many columns .... `size ← 1 2×⍴B`
- Create `R` filled with zeroes .... `R ← size⍴0`
- Calculate the indices of its even columns .... `even ← 2×⍳(⍴B)[2]`
- Fill the even columns with `B` .... `R[;even]←B`
- Calculate the indices of the odd columns, and fill them with `A` .. `R[;even-1]←A`

The final function could be written as follows. Do not forget to localize your variables, and specify the name of the result in the function header.

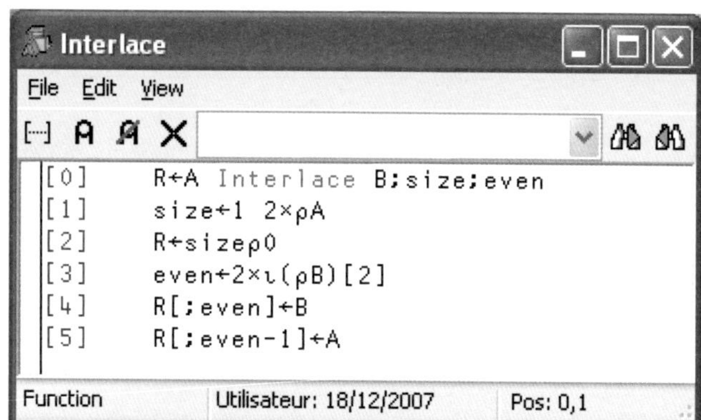

Figure D-11

We can now apply the function to any pair of variables, provided they have the same size:

```
      (2 3⍴⍳6) Interlace (2 3⍴5 7 0 2 8 9)
1 5 2 7 3 0
4 2 5 8 6 9
      Forecast Interlace Actual
150 141 200 188 100 111  80  87  80  82  80  74
300 321 330 306 360 352 400 403 500 497 520 507
100 118 250 283 350 397 380 424 400 411 450 409
 50  43 120  91 220 187 300 306 320 318 350 363
```

Another possible syntax

If you had decided instead to make the function monadic, it could have been written like this (the modified parts are in black, and the rest is in grey):

```
      ∇ R←Interlace Couple;A;B ;size;even
[1]     (A B)←Couple                        ⇦ Split the argument into 2 variables
[1]     size←1 2×⍴A
[2]     R←size⍴0
[3]     even←2×⍳(⍴B)[2]
[4]     R[;even]←B
[5]     R[;even-1]←A
      ∇
```

You are now ready to solve simple problems; we **strongly recommend** that you try to solve all the following exercises before you continue further in this chapter.

Exercises

D-1 Write a dyadic function `Extract` which returns the first N items of any given vector. The value N and the vector itself will be the left and right arguments, respectively:

```
      3 Extract 45 86 31 20 75 62 18
45 86 31
      6 Extract 'can you do it?'
can yo
```

D-2 Write a dyadic function which ignores the first N items of any given vector, and only returns the remainder, as shown:

```
      3 Ignore 45 86 31 20 75 62 18
20 75 62 18
      6 Ignore 'can you do it?'
u do it?
```

D-3 Write a monadic function which returns the items of a vector in reverse order:

```
      Reverse 'snoitalutargnoc'
congratulations
```

D-4 Write a monadic function which appends row and column totals to a numeric matrix.

For example, if `Mat` is the matrix:

```
75 14  86 20
31 16  40 51
22 64  31 28
```

Then `Totalise Mat` should give:

```
 75 14  86 20 195
 31 16  40 51 138
 22 64  31 28 145
128 94 157 99 478
```

D-5 Write a monadic function which returns the lengths of the words contained in a text vector:

```
      Lengths 'This seems to be a good solution'
4 5 2 2 1 4 8
```

D-6 Write a dyadic function which produces the series of integer values between the limits given by its two arguments:

```
      17 To 29
17 18 19 20 21 22 23 24 25 26 27 28 29
```

D-7 Develop a monadic function which puts a frame around a text matrix. For the first version, just concatenate minus signs above and under the matrix, and vertical bars down both sides. Then, update the function to replace the four corners by four Plus signs. For example:

```
      Frame Towns
+----------+
|Canberra  |
|Paris     |
|Washington|
|Moscow    |
|Martigues |
|Mexico    |
+----------+
```

Finally, you can improve the appearance of the result by changing the function to use line-drawing symbols. You enter line-drawing symbols using the *Ctrl* key in conjunction with the numeric keypad (Dyalog APL *Classic Edition*), or by using `⎕UCS` (*Unicode Edition*). The horizontal and vertical lines are `⎕UCS 9472 9474` and the four corners are `⎕UCS 9484 9488 9492 9496`:

```
      Frame2 Towns
```

D-8 It is very likely that the function you wrote for the previous exercise works on matrices but not on vectors. Can you make it work on both?

```
      Frame 'We are not out of the wood'
┌──────────────────────────┐
│We are not out of the wood│
└──────────────────────────┘
```

D-9 Write a function which replaces a given letter by another one in a text vector. The letter to replace is given first; the replacing letter is given second, like this:

```
     'tc' Switch1 'A bird in the hand is worth two in the bush'
A bird in che hand is worch cwo in che bush
```

D-10 Modify the previous function so that it commutes the two letters:

```
      'ei' Switch2 'A bird in the hand is worth two in the bush'
A berd en thi hand es worth two en thi bush
```

3.5 Calls to Sub-Functions

The statements which constitute the body of a user-defined function can themselves call functions: primitive or user-defined. This clearly means that a function can call other functions without any special procedural technique.

Let us suppose that you successfully solved exercise D-6 above, so that you now have a function `To` to produce a list of integer values between two limits:

```
      408 To 413
408 409 410 411 412 413
```

Now, let us imagine a company with a turnover which has more or less grown over 12 years. The variable `Tome` represents its TurnOver in Millions of Euros.

```
      Tome ← 56 59 67 64 60 61 68 73 78 75 81 84
```

We want to calculate the difference between each year and the next. This can be obtained by subtracting the following two vectors:

```
 v1     59 67 64 60 61 68 73 78 75 81 84
-v2     56 59 67 64 60 61 68 73 78 75 81
        --------------------------------
  =      3  8 ¯3 ¯4  1  7  5  5 ¯3  6  3
```

The first one can be obtained by `Tome[2 To 12]`, the second one by `Tome[1 To 11]`. If we want to generalise the expression, all we need do is replace 12 by `⍴Tome`.

The following function is very poorly written, but this is intentional:

```
     ∇ Z←Willitwork Y;v1;v2
[1]    v1←Y[2 To ⍴Y]                ⇦ We use sub-function To
[2]    v2←Y[1 To (⍴Y)-1]            ⇦ Once more
[3]    Z←v1-v2
     ∇
```

Obviously, it is necessary that "`To`" has been written before we can use "`Willitwork`".

```
      Willitwork Tome               ⇦ Of course it works!
3 8 ¯3 ¯4 1 7 5 5 ¯3 6 3
```

In this example "`To`" has been written as an independent defined function. However for very small calculations like this, the sub-function can be defined as a *Direct function*, inside the calling function. Let us show how this might be done:

```
      )erase To                     ⇦ We can get rid of To

     ∇ Z←Willitwork2 Y;v1;v2 ;To
[1]    To←{(⍺-1)+⍳⍵-⍺-1}            ⇦ First, we define the sub-function
[2]    v1←Y[2 To ⍴Y]                ⇦ Now we can use it
[2]    v2←Y[1 To (⍴Y)-1]
[3]    Z←v1-v2
     ∇
```

It is good practice to localise the name of the sub-function, to avoid any potential conflict with an existing name outside the frame of reference of the function. If you fail to localise `To` in the function header, and then run `Willitwork2` while there is another function named `To` *outside it*, the *outer* `To` will be overwritten. If there was a variable named `To`, our function `Willitwork2` would have generated an error on line `[1]` (because you are not allowed to overwrite a variable with a function).

Of course, a much better solution, which doesn't use a sub-function, would have been the following:

```
      ∇ Z←Willitwork3 Y;index
[1]     index←ι(ρY)-1
[2]     Z←Y[index+1]-Y[index]
      ∇
```

Recursion: If a function calls itself, it is said to be *recursive* (see Section 9).

4 - Flow Control

4.1 Overview

Apart from extremely simple calculations, most programs rely on certain statements being executed only if a given condition is satisfied (conditional execution), or on a set of statements being executed again and again, until a given limit is reached (looping). The APL language offers a special set of syntactic elements to control the flow of statements.

In the very first versions of APL, the only way to implement conditional execution and looping was to use the symbol → (*branch arrow*). This was used to jump from one statement to another, skipping over other statements (conditional execution) or jumping back to repeat a set of statements again (looping). The branch arrow is equivalent to the GOTO statement in other languages, and was once the only way to control execution flow in an APL program. Contemporary versions of APL include a special set of keywords which offer a much more flexible, easy to use, and easy to read way to control the flow of execution. They are also very similar to those used in most other languages. These are known as ***Control structures***.

We shall begin by using control structures and then introduce you later to the old way of programming, only because you may come across it in some existing programs, and because it sometimes offers shorter or more convenient ways of doing things.

Control structures are blocks of statements which begin and end with special keywords. These keywords are all **prefixed** with a ***colon***, like `:If` or `:Repeat` .

The keywords can be typed in lower or upper case, but Dyalog APL will always store and display them using a fixed spelling convention, with an upper case first letter, and the following letters in lower case. Composite keywords like "`EndIf`" or "`GoTo`", are shown with the first letter of the second word also in uppercase.

Opening keywords are used to begin the conditional execution or repeated execution of a block of statements.

Usually (but not always), the block is ended by a keyword starting with `:End`.

The sets of opening/closing keywords are shown here.

```
:If ............ :EndIf
:For ........... :EndFor
:Select ........ :EndSelect
:Repeat ........ :Until
     or......... :EndRepeat
:While ......... :EndWhile
     or......... :Until
:Trap........... :EndTrap
:With........... :EndWith
:Hold........... :EndHold
```

The primary keywords shown above can be complemented by additional keywords which qualify more precisely what is to be done.

```
:Else
:ElseIf
:AndIf
:Orif
:Case
:Caselist
:Until
```

And finally, some keywords may be used to conditionally alter the flow of execution within a control structure.

```
:GoTo
:Return
:Leave
:Continue
```

The following keywords will not be studied in this chapter:

`:Trap ... :EndTrap`	concerns event processing	See Chapter M
`:With ... :EndWith`	concerns the GUI interface	See Chapter P
	and namespaces	See Chapter O
`:Hold ... :EndHold`	concerns *multithreading*	

4.2 Conditional Execution

4.2.1 - Simple Conditions .... (:If / :EndIf)

The clauses `:If` and `:EndIf` delimit a block of statements (Block **1** in the diagram below), which will be executed only if the condition specified by the `:If` clause is satisfied, as illustrated below:

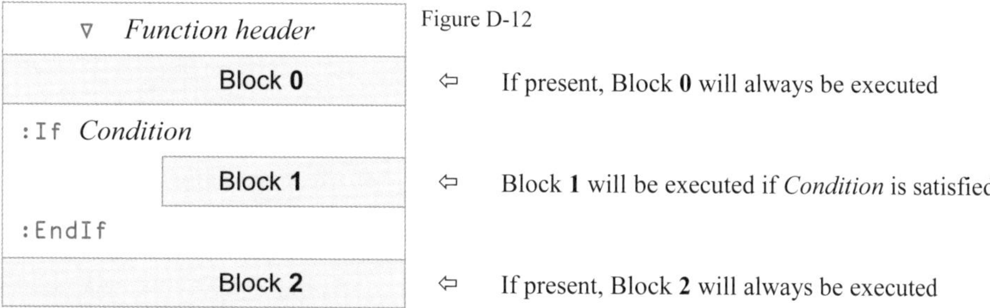
∇ Function header
Block 0
:If Condition
Block 1
:EndIf
Block 2
⇦ If present, Block 0 will always be executed
⇦ Block 1 will be executed if Condition is satisfied
⇦ If present, Block 2 will always be executed
Figure D-12

Condition is any expression whose result is a Boolean **scalar** or one item array. For example:

`Code∊List` or `Price>100` or `Values∧.=0`

Example

Our keyboard has been damaged: we can no longer use the *Absolute value* key. Perhaps a function could replace it? Here is a version using a `:If` clause:

```
     ∇ Y←Absval1 Y
        :If Y<0
            Y←-Y
        :EndIf
     ∇
```

If the argument is positive (or zero), the function does nothing, and just returns the argument it received. If the argument is negative, it returns the corresponding positive value.

4.2.2 - Alternative Processing .... (:If / :Else / :EndIf)

In the previous example if *Condition* is satisfied, Block **1** is executed; otherwise nothing is done. But sometimes we would like to execute one set of statements (Block **1**) if *Condition* is satisfied, or an alternative one (Block **2**) if it is not.

For this, we use the additional keyword `:Else` as shown below:

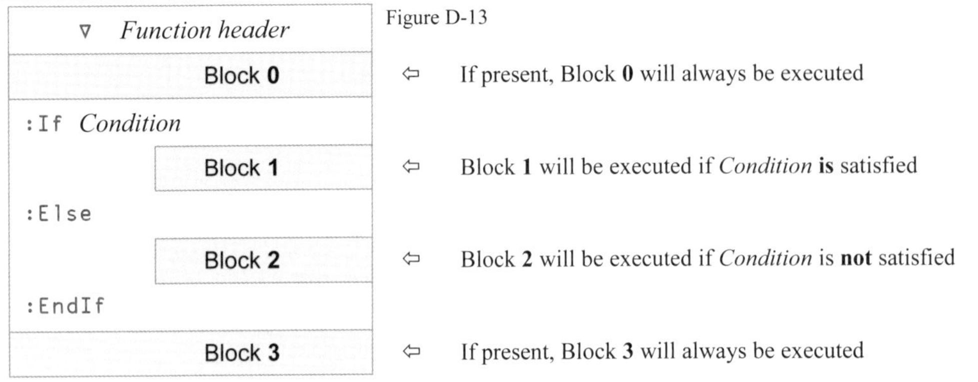
∇ Function header
Block 0
:If Condition
Block 1
:Else
Block 2
:EndIf
Block 3
⇦ If present, Block 0 will always be executed
⇦ Block 1 will be executed if Condition is satisfied
⇦ Block 2 will be executed if Condition is not satisfied
⇦ If present, Block 3 will always be executed

Figure D-13

Example

Let us try to solve the classic equation: $ax^2+bx+c=0$, given the values of a, b, and c.

```
     ∇ Z←QuadRoot abc;a;b;c;delta
       (a b c)←abc
       delta←(b*2)-4×a×c                ⇦ Calculate the discriminant
       :If delta≥0                      ⇦ If positive, calculate the roots
           Z←(-b)+1 ¯1×delta*0.5
           Z←Z÷2×a
       :Else                            ⇦ If negative, issue a message
           Z←'No roots'
       :EndIf
     ∇
      Quadroot ¯2 7 15
¯1.5 5
      Quadroot 4 2 3
No roots
```

4.2.3 - Composite Conditions.. (:OrIf / :AndIf)

Multiple conditions can be combined using the Boolean functions "OR" and "AND".

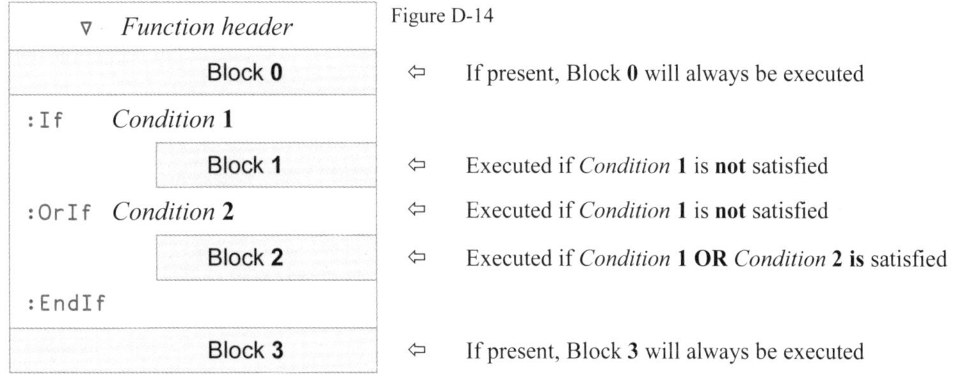
∇ Function header
Block 0
⇦ If present, Block 0 will always be executed
:If Condition 1
Block 1
⇦ Executed if Condition 1 is not satisfied
:OrIf Condition 2
⇦ Executed if Condition 1 is not satisfied
Block 2
⇦ Executed if Condition 1 OR Condition 2 is satisfied
:EndIf
Block 3
⇦ If present, Block 3 will always be executed

Figure D-14

In many cases, the same result could be obtained by a more traditional APL approach using `∨`:

`:If` (*Condition* **1**) `∨` (*Condition* **2**)

However, suppose that Block **1** and/or *Condition* **2** needs a lot of computing time.

- The traditional APL solution will always evaluate both *Condition* **1** and *Condition* **2**, combine the results, and decide what to do.
- With the "`:OrIf`" technique, if *Condition* **1** is satisfied, Block **2** will be immediately executed, and neither Block **1** nor *Condition* **2** will be evaluated. This may sometimes save a lot of processing time.

Note that the optional Block **1** may be useful to prepare the variables to be referenced in *Condition* **2**.

We have a similar structure with the `:AndIf` clause:

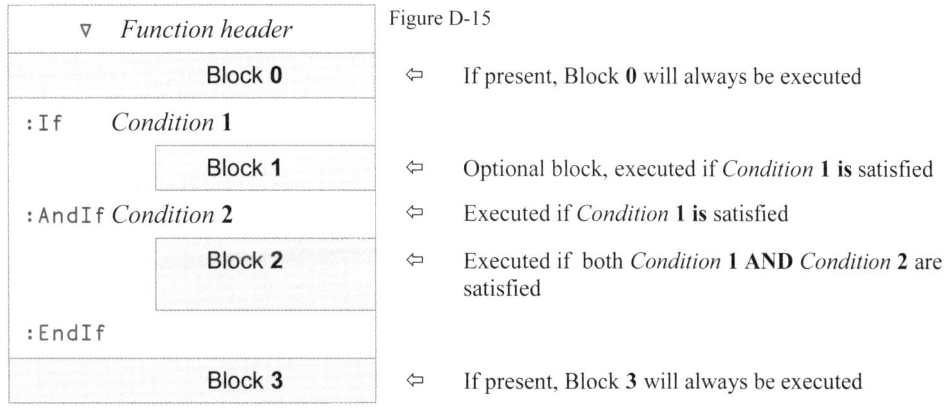
∇ Function header
Block 0
⇦ If present, Block 0 will always be executed
:If Condition 1
Block 1
⇦ Optional block, executed if Condition 1 is satisfied
:AndIf Condition 2
⇦ Executed if Condition 1 is satisfied
Block 2
⇦ Executed if both Condition 1 AND Condition 2 are satisfied
:EndIf
Block 3
⇦ If present, Block 3 will always be executed

Figure D-15

In many cases, the same result could be obtained by a more traditional APL approach using ∧:

:If (*Condition* **1**) ∧ (*Condition* **2**)

However, it may be that *Condition* **2** cannot be evaluated if *Condition* **1** is not satisfied. For example, we want to execute Block **2** if the variable "VAR" exists and is smaller than 1000. It is obvious that VAR<1000 cannot be evaluated if the variable does not exist. The two conditions must be evaluated separately:

```
:If 2=⎕NC'VAR'              ⇦ True if VAR is a variable, cf. section 7.3.3
:AndIf VAR<1000             ⇦ Will not be executed if VAR is not a variable
...
:EndIf
```

If *Condition* **1** is not satisfied neither Block **1** nor *Condition* **2** will be executed. This may also save some computing time.

Note that you may not combine :OrIf and :AndIf within the same control structure; the following code will generate a SYNTAX ERROR.

```
:If        Width<20
:AndIf     Length<100
:OrIf      Height<5
           Surface←0
:Else
           Surface←Width×Length
:EndIf
```

4.2.4 - Cascading Conditions .... (:ElseIf / :Else)

Sometimes, if the first condition is not satisfied, perhaps a second or a third one will be. In each case, a different set of statements will be executed. This type of logic may be controlled by one or more ":ElseIf" clauses. And if none of these conditions are satisfied, perhaps another block of statements is to be executed; this may be controlled by a final ":Else", as we have seen earlier.

Depending on the problem, ":Else" may be present or not. If there is no ":Else" clause and no condition has been satisfied, nothing will be executed inside the :If block.

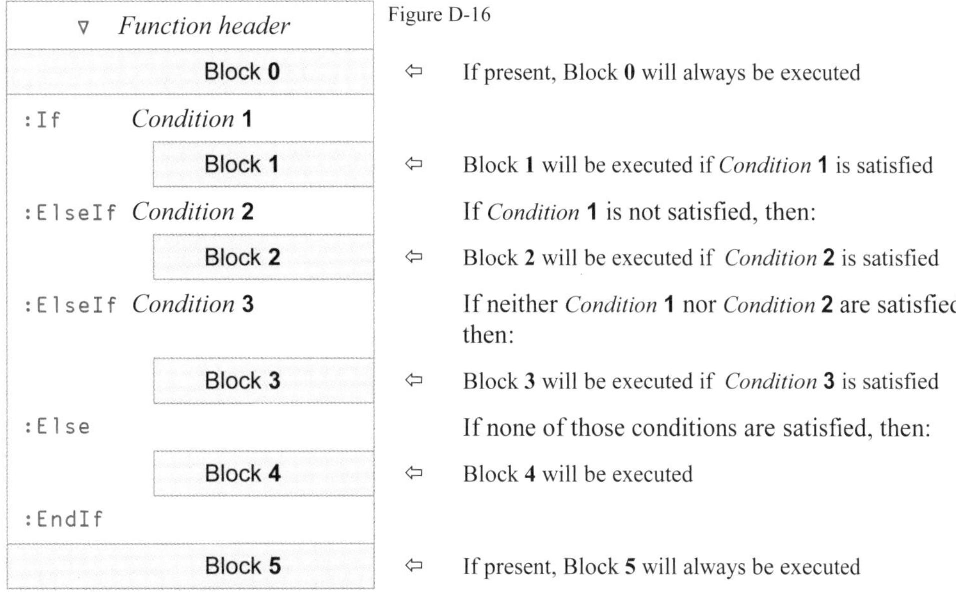
∇ Function header
Block 0
:If Condition 1
Block 1
:ElseIf Condition 2
Block 2
:ElseIf Condition 3
Block 3
:Else
Block 4
:EndIf
Block 5
⇦ If present, Block 0 will always be executed
⇦ Block 1 will be executed if Condition 1 is satisfied
If Condition 1 is not satisfied, then:
⇦ Block 2 will be executed if Condition 2 is satisfied
If neither Condition 1 nor Condition 2 are satisfied, then:
⇦ Block 3 will be executed if Condition 3 is satisfied
If none of those conditions are satisfied, then:
⇦ Block 4 will be executed
⇦ If present, Block 5 will always be executed

Figure D-16

The conditional blocks **1** to **4** above are thus mutually exclusive. As soon as a condition is satisfied, the next block of statements is executed, and execution will continue with the code below the closing keyword "`:EndIf`", **even** if any other of the subsequent conditions could also be satisfied.

For example, suppose that the first condition is: `Var<100` and the second is: `Var<200`.

If `Var` happens to be equal to 33, it is both smaller than 100 and 200, but only the block of statements attached to `Var<100` will be executed.

4.2.5 - Alternative Solutions

Now you know how to use control structures to write conditional expressions. However, this does not mean that you always *have* to use control structures. The richness of the APL language often makes it more convenient to express conditional calculations using a more mathematical approach.

For example, suppose that you need to comment on the result of a football or rugby match by displaying "*Won*", "*Draw*", or "*Lost*", depending on the scores of the two teams. Here are two solutions:

Solution 1

```
    ∇ Z←X Against1 Y
      :If X>Y
          Z←'Won'
      :ElseIf X=Y
          Z←'Draw'
      :Else
          Z←'Lost'
      :EndIf
    ∇
```

Solution 2

```
    ∇ Z←X Against2 Y ;which
      which←2+(X>Y)-(X<Y)
      Z←(3 4⍴'LostDrawWon ')[which;]
    ∇
```

Which solution you prefer is probably a matter of taste and previous experience, both yours and of whoever is to read and maintain the programs you write.

4.3 Disparate Conditions

4.3.1 - Clauses .... (`:Select` / `:Case` / `:CaseList`)

Sometimes it is necessary to execute completely different sets of statements, depending on the value of a specific *control expression*, hereafter called the *control value*.

To achieve this, we use "`:Select`", with additional "`:Case`" or "`:CaseList`" clauses.

The sequence begins with `:Select` followed by the *control expression*.

It is followed by any number of blocks, each of which will be executed if the *control value* is equal to one of the values specified in the corresponding clause:

- `:Case` for a single value
- `:CaseList` for a list of possible values

The sequence ends with `:EndSelect`.

You can have as many `:Case` or `:CaseList` clauses as you need, and in any order.

If there is no "`:Else`" clause and the control variable is not equal to any of the specified values, nothing is executed.

The blocks are mutually exclusive. The `:Case` statements are examined from the top, and once a match is found and the corresponding block of statements has been executed, execution will continue with the first line after the `:EndSelect` statement - even if the *control value* matches other `:Case` statements.

Figure D-17

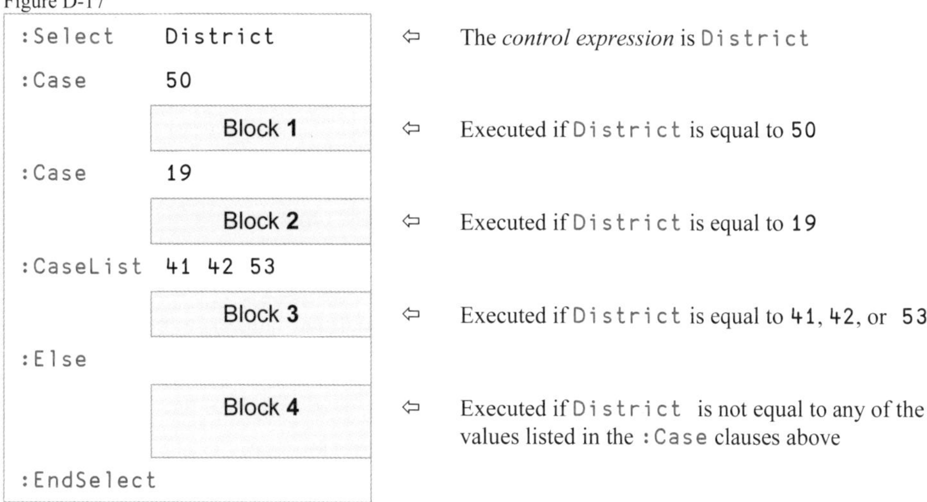
:Select District
:Case 50
Block 1
:Case 19
Block 2
:CaseList 41 42 53
Block 3
:Else
Block 4
:EndSelect
The *control expression* is District
Executed if District is equal to 50
Executed if District is equal to 19
Executed if District is equal to 41, 42, or 53
Executed if District is not equal to any of the values listed in the :Case clauses above

4.3.2 - Remark

Values specified in `:Case` or `:CaseList` clauses can be numbers, characters, or even nested arrays:

`:CaseList 'yes' 'no' 'doubt'`	3 possible values
`:CaseList (2 7)(5 1)'Null'`	3 different possible vectors
`:Case 'BERLIN'`	1 single word
`:Caselist 'PARIS'`	5 possible letters

Be careful with the last two examples where a character vector is used:

- If the keyword is `:Case`, the control value must match the entire character vector `"BERLIN"`.
- If the keyword is `:CaseList`, the control value may be any one letter out of the 5 letters in `"PARIS"`. Any subset, like `"PAR"` will not be recognised as matching.

4.3.3 - Attention

The control value must be **strictly** identical to the value(s) specified in the `:Case` clause(s).

For example, in the preceding diagram, there is a clause `:Case 50` (scalar).

If the control value is equal to `1⍴50` (a one-item vector), it is not strictly identical to the specified array (the scalar `50`), and the corresponding set of statements will **not** be executed.

4.4 Predefined Loops

4.4.1 - Basic Use .... (:For / :In / :EndFor)

In many iterative calculations a set of statements is repeated over and over again, and on each iteration a new value is given to a particular variable. We will refer to this variable as the *control variable*.

If the values of the control variable can be predefined before the beginning of the loop, we recommend that you use the :For clause, with the following syntax:

:For *Control variable* :In *List of values*

The keyword :For is followed by the control variable name.

In the same statement, the keyword :In is followed by an expression returning the list of values to be assigned to the control variable on each iteration. Here is an example:

Figure D-18

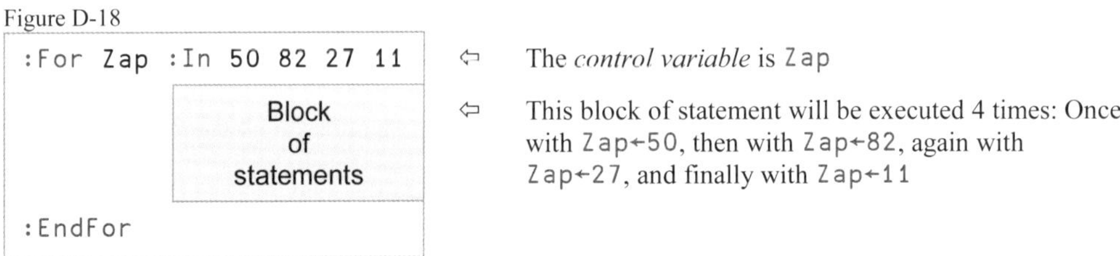

:For Zap :In 50 82 27 11
Block of statements
:EndFor
⇦ The *control variable* is Zap
⇦ This block of statement will be executed 4 times: Once with Zap←50, then with Zap←82, again with Zap←27, and finally with Zap←11

Generally, the block of statements makes some reference to the *control variable*, for example, as part of a calculation, but this is not mandatory.

This technique has one great advantage: the number of loops is predefined, and it is impossible to accidentally program an endless loop.

4.4.2 - Control of Iterations

The values assigned to the control variable can be whatever values are needed by the algorithm:

A list of numeric values .... 66+4×⍳20

A nested vector .... (5 4)(3 0 8)(4 7)(2 5 9)

A list of letters .... 'DYALOG'

A list of words .... 'Madrid' 'Paris' 'Tokyo' 'Ushuaia'

It is also possible to use a *set* of control values, rather than just a single one.

For example, with: `:For (Code Qty) :In (5 8)(2 3)(7 4)`

The loop will be executed first with `Code ← 5` and `Qty ← 8`
then with `Code ← 2` and `Qty ← 3`
and finally with `Code ← 7` and `Qty ← 4`

In most cases this kind of iterative process is executed to completion. However, it is possible to take an early exit when some condition or other is met. This can be done using the `:Leave` clause, or using an explicit branch like `→0` or `→(Total=0)/Next`. These methods will be explained later.

A special variant of `:In` named `:InEach` is explained in the Specialist's Section at the end of this chapter.

Example

Let us try to find all the possible divisors of a given integer. We can divide that value by integers starting from 1, up to the number itself. If the division gives an integer result, the integer can be appended to the vector of results, which has been initialised as an empty vector.

```
     ∇ Z←Divisors1 Y;res;div
       Z←θ                      ⇦ Start with an empty vector
       :For div :In ⍳Y          ⇦ All possible control variable values
           res←Y÷div            ⇦ Calculate the quotient
           :If res=⌊res         ⇦ Is it integer?
               Z←Z,div          ⇦ If yes, keep div as a valid divisor
           :EndIf
       :EndFor
     ∇
      Divisors1 3219
1 3 29 37 87 111 1073 3219
```

This example hopefully shows that it is straightforward to write simple, predefined loops using control structures. If you are used to other programming languages that do not offer array processing features, you may even find this way of writing programs very natural.

However, it turns out that many simple, predefined loops like this one are very tightly coupled to the structure or values of the data that they are working on: The number of items in a list, the number of rows in a matrix, or, as in the example, the number of integers less than or equal to a particular value.

In such cases it is very often possible to express the entire algorithm in a very straightforward way, without any explicit loops. Usually the result is a much shorter program that is much easier to read, and which runs considerably faster than the solution using explicit loops.

For example, in the example above it is possible to replace the loop by a vector of possible divisors produced by the *Index generator*. The algorithm is unchanged, but the program is shorter, and runs about 10 times faster:

```
     ∇ Z←Divisors2 Y;res;bin
       res←Y÷⍳Y                        ⇦ Divide by all possible integers in one go
       bin←res=⌊res                    ⇦ Test all the results
       Z←bin/⍳Y                        ⇦ Select those giving integer quotients
     ∇

      Divisors2 3219
1 3 29 37 87 111 1073 3219             ⇦ We get the same results, of course
```

Of course, sometimes the processing that is to take place inside the loop is so complex that it is infeasible to rewrite the program so that it doesn't use an explicit loop. Likewise, if there is a dependency such that the calculations taking place in the nth iteration are dependent on the results produced in the $(n-1)^{th}$ iteration, it is in general necessary to program an explicit loop.

4.5 Conditional Loops

In the previous section we used the term "Predefined loops", because the number of iterations was controlled by an expression executed before the loop starts. It is also possible to program loops which are repeated until a given condition is satisfied.

Two methods are available: `:Repeat ... :Until`
`:While ... :EndWhile`

The two methods are similar, but there are some important differences:

- `:Repeat` - When the loop is initialised, the condition is **not** yet satisfied (generally).
  - The program loops until this condition **becomes** satisfied.
  - The "Loop or Stop" test is placed at the **bottom** of the loop.
  - The instructions in the loop are executed at least once.
- `:While` - When the loop is initialised, the condition **is** (generally) satisfied.
  - The program loops as long as it **remains** satisfied.
  - The "Loop or Stop" test is placed at the **beginning** of the loop.
  - The instructions in the loop are not necessarily executed at all.

4.5.1 - Bottom-Controlled Loop.................................... (`:Repeat` / `:Until`)

The control variables involved in the test are often initialised before the loop begins, but they can be created during the execution of the loop, because the test is placed at the bottom.

Then the block of statements delimited by `:Repeat` / `:Until` is executed repeatedly up to the point where the condition specified after `:Until` becomes satisfied.

This condition may involve one or more variables. It is obvious that the statements contained in the loop must modify some of those control variables, or import them from an external source, so that the condition is satisfied after a limited number of iterations. This is the programmer's responsibility.

Figure D-19

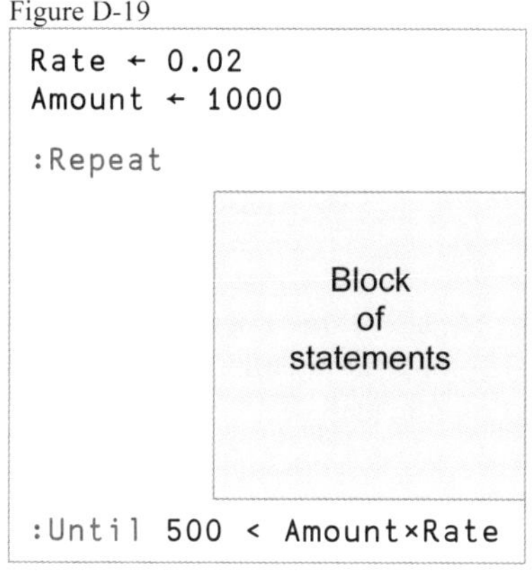

⇦ Some variables are initialised.

⇦ This block will be executed repeatedly, until the final condition is satisfied.

It **must** contain statements which modify one or more of the variables involved in the final test, or you will have created an infinite loop.
For example: `Amount ←` *Instruction*
`Rate ←` *Instruction*

⇦ When the final condition is satisfied, the loop stops

The test is made on the bottom line of the loop, immediately after `:Until`, so the loop is executed at least once.

The "Loop or Stop" control is made at the bottom of each loop, but it is also possible to add one or more intermediate conditions which cause an exit from the loop using a "`:Leave`" clause or a *branch arrow* (this will be explained in 5.3).

Example

In this example we will read a text file.

We have not yet seen how we can actually do that, but for the moment let us assume that we have available three functions: `OpenFile` opens the file and returns a "handle" (which is just a number) that identifies the open file, `ReadFile` reads a number of characters sequentially from the file, and `CloseFile` closes the file after it has been used. How these functions may be programmed is not important for this example.

The function that reads from the file will only return a limited number of characters at a time, so if the file is larger than that we must continue to collect chunks until nothing more is returned:

```
     ∇ text←ReadTextFile filename;handle;newtext
       text←''                       ⇦ Start with an empty vector
       handle←OpenFile filename      ⇦ Open the file
       :Repeat
           newtext←ReadFile handle   ⇦ Read a chunk of text
           text←text,newtext         ⇦ Add it to the result
       :Until 0=⍴newtext             ⇦ Finished if we did not get anything
       CloseFile handle              ⇦ Close the file
     ∇
```

Special case

It is possible to replace `:Until` by `:EndRepeat`. However, because there is no longer a pre-specified exit condition, the program would loop endlessly. For this reason it is necessary to employ intermediate tests to exit the loop when using this technique.

4.5.2 - Top-Controlled Loop .... (`:While` / `:EndWhile`)

Because the test is now placed at the top of the loop, control variables involved in the test must be initialised before the loop begins.

Then the block of statements limited by `:While` / `:EndWhile` will be executed repeatedly as long as the condition specified after `:While` remains satisfied.

This condition may involve one or more variables. It is obvious that the statements contained in the loop must modify some of those control variables so that the condition is satisfied after a limited number of iterations. This is the programmer's responsibility.

Figure D-20

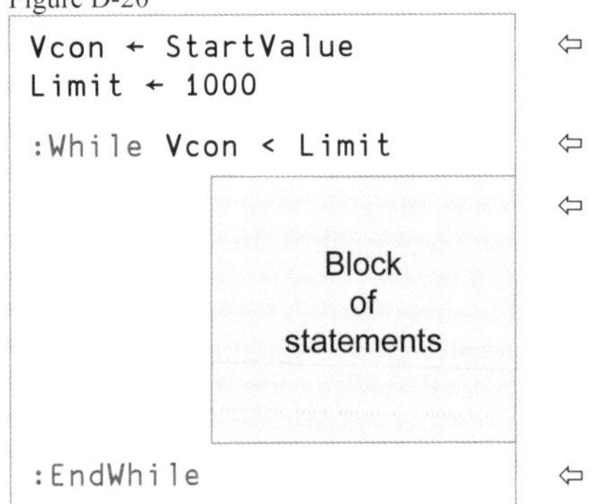

⇦ Some variables are initialised

⇦ A test decides whether the loop must go on or not

⇦ This block will be executed repeatedly, as long as `Vcon` is smaller than `Limit`.

It **must** contain statements which modify one or more of the variables involved in the test.
For example: `Vcon ← Vcon + Number`
`Limit ← Limit + 1`

⇦ Sometimes replaced by an `:Until` clause

A test is made in the top line of the loop, immediately after `:While`, so it is possible that the block of statements inside the loop will never be executed.

The "Loop or Stop" control is made at each beginning of a new loop, but it is also possible to add a second control at the bottom of the loop by replacing "`:EndWhile`" by a clause "`:Until`", as we did for the `:Repeat` loop.

4.6 Exception Control

4.6.1 - Skip to the Next Iteration .... (:Continue)

In any kind of loop (For-EndFor / Repeat-Until / While-EndWhile) this clause indicates that the program must abandon the current iteration and skip to the next one.

In a :For-loop	this means that the next value(s) of the control variable(s) are set, and the execution continues from the line immediately below the :For-statement.
In a :Repeat-loop	this means that the execution continues from the line immediately below the :Repeat-statement.
In a :While-loop	this means that execution continues from the line containing the :While-statement.

4.6.2 - Leave the Loop... (:Leave)

In any kind of loop this clause causes the program to skip the current and all remaining iterations, abort the loop immediately, and continue execution from the line immediately below the bottom end of the loop.

4.6.3 - Jump to Another Statement .... (:GoTo)

This clause is used to explicitly jump from the current statement to another one, with the following syntax:

:GoTo *Destination*

In most cases, *Destination* is the ***Label*** of another statement in the same program.

A *Label* is a word placed at the beginning of a statement, and followed by a colon. It is used as a reference to the statement. It can be followed by an APL expression, but for readability, it is recommended that you put a label on a line of its own. For example:

```
[14]    Next:                        ⇦ Next  is a Label
[15]     Val←Goal-Val÷2
```

Next is considered by the interpreter to be a variable, whose value is the number of the line on which it is placed (14 in our example). It is used as a destination point both by the traditional *Branch arrow* and by the :GoTo clause, like this:

```
               :GoTo Next            ⇦ Do not type the colon after the label here
Equivalent to  →Next                 ⇦ This will be studied in Section 5
```

The following conventions apply to the *Destination* of a jump:

Figure D-21

Destination	**Consequence of** `:GoTo` *Destination* or `→` *Destination*
Valid label	Skip to the statement referenced by that label.
0	Quit the current function, and return to the calling environment.
⍬	Do not skip at all, but continue on to the next statement.

4.6.4 - Quit This Function .... (`:Return`)

This clause causes the function to terminate immediately, and has exactly the same effect as `→0` or `:GoTo 0` (explained later). Control returns to the calling environment.

4.7 Endless Loops

Whatever your skills you may inadvertently create a function which runs endlessly. Usually this is due to an inappropriate loop definition.

However, sometimes execution may appear to take an inordinate amount of time, not because APL is unneccessarily executing the same set of statements again and again in an endless loop, but because it has to process a very large amount of data.

Fortunately you can interrupt the execution of a function using two kinds of interrupts: weak and strong. Let us see what this means.

4.7.1 - A Time Consuming Function

Let us consider the function below:

```
∇ Endless;a;b;i;r
  i←0
  :Repeat
      b←15000-a←⍳10000
      a←1000 1000⍴1.07×a
      b←1000 1000⍴1.07×b
      r←+/,(a×a∊b)⌈(b×b∊a)
      ⎕←i←i+1
  :Until i=20
∇
```

This function is not really endless, but `Endless[6]` needs a lot of computing time because it processes two rather large matrices, each made of one million floating-point values.

`Endless[7]` displays the iteration number, so that you will see the program running.

Depending on the speed of your computer each iteration may take from 1 to 5 seconds.

Don't run it yet!

4.7.2 - Weak and Strong Interrupts

If you issue a ***Weak interrupt***, the computer will complete the execution of the statement that it is currently processing. Then it will halt the function before executing the next statement. We recommend using a weak interrupt, because it allows the user to restart the function at the very point it was interrupted (see Chapter E).

If you issue a ***Strong interrupt***, the computer will complete the execution of the APL primitive that it is currently processing. Then it will interrupt the function before executing the next primitive.

For example, in the `Endless` function shown above, it could calculate `a∊b`, and stop before executing the multiplication `a×a∊b`. Of course, if the user restarts the statement, it will be executed again in its entirety (it is impossible to resume execution in the middle of a statement).

Note that it is impossible to interrupt the execution of a primitive like `a∊b` itself, and sometimes the execution of a primitive may take a long time.

4.7.3 - How Can You Generate an Interrupt?

A *Weak interrupt* can be generated by pressing *Ctrl* together with the "*Pause/Attn*" (or "*Pause/Break*") key on your keyboard.

Alternatively, you can also select the Action ⇨ Interrupt menu option in the APL menubar.

Otherwise, both *Weak* and *Strong interrupts* can be generated using the menu obtained by clicking on the APL icon in the *Notification area* of your *Taskbar (also known as the System Tray)*, at the bottom right of your screen, as shown below:

Figure D-22

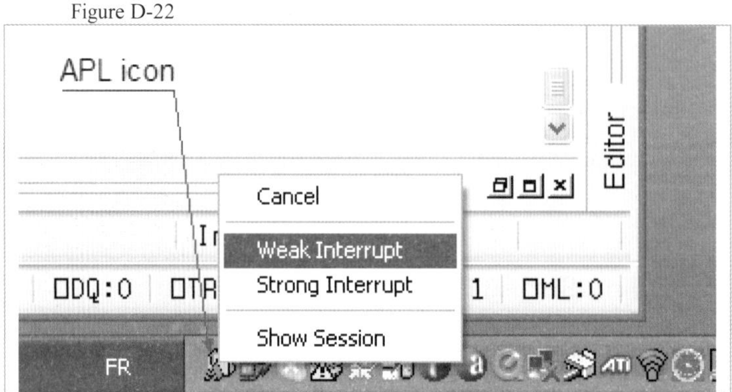

Be patient! Because the loop needs a lot of computing resources, there may be a few seconds delay from when you click the APL icon until this menu appears. Then there may be a few more seconds delay after you select Weak or Strong Interrupt before the interrupt actually occurs.

Now, let's test it.

4.7.4 - First a Weak Interrupt

Run the function, and after one or two iterations, press *Ctrl+Pause*.

```
      Endless                    ⇦ Run the function
1                                ⇦ Iteration numbers are displayed
2
3                                ⇦ Press Ctrl+Pause

Endless[7]                       ⇦ After a few seconds, the program stops
```

The message issued means that the function has been interrupted just before executing line number `[7]`, and you can be sure that line `[6]` has been finished entirely.

If you run Dyalog APL with the default configuration, a trace window is displayed with the function in yellow on black, while the next statement to be executed is white on red.

You can see that the function was interrupted just before executing line `[7]` ⇨

Figure D-23

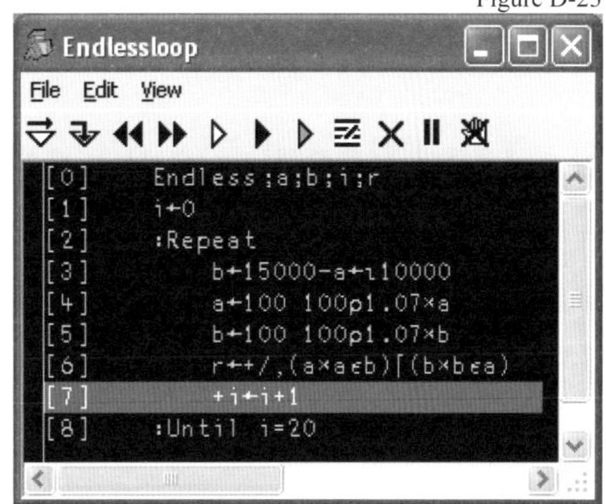

To back out from the interrupted state of execution, press the *Escape* key as many times as needed, or execute the command `)Reset`, which will be explained in the next chapter.

Then **try again** to interrupt that function using the menu associated with the APL icon in the *Notification area*.

4.7.5 - And Now a Strong Interrupt

Run the function again, and after some seconds or some iterations, activate the menu associated with the APL icon in the *Notification area*. It may take a few seconds before the options become selectable (white on blue), but then choose "Strong Interrupt".

The result is slightly different, as you can see here:

```
      Endless
1
2
3
4
INTERRUPT
Endless[6] r←+/,(a×a∊b)⌈(b×b∊a)
                          ^
```

You can see that the function was interrupted while executing statement `[6]` ⇨

Figure D-24

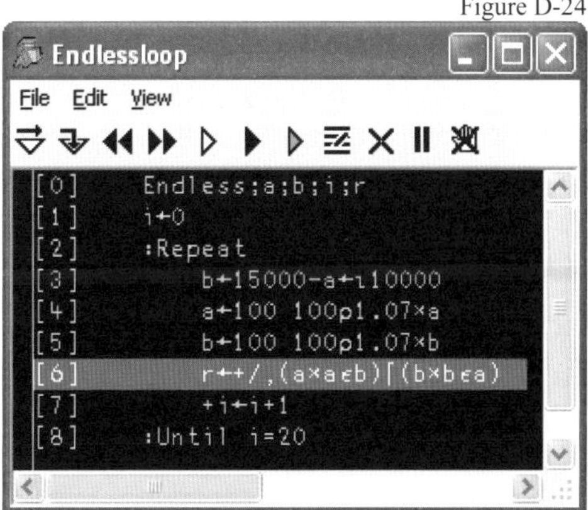

The caret under the message clearly indicates that the function has executed `b∊a`, and was then interrupted just before the multiplication.

5 - Traditional Flow Control

5.1 Conditional Execution

In early versions of APL, a unique symbol, the ***Branch arrow*** (→) provided the only means to override the order in which statements were executed. Today you should only use this mechanism when maintaining code which is already written in this style.

The *branch arrow* works in exactly the same way as the `:GoTo` clause.

→ *Destination* and `:GoTo` *Destination* are strictly equivalent.

Destination should **always** be a ***Label***. Remember: a *Label* is a word placed at the beginning of a statement, and **followed** by a ***colon***. Specifying a statement number (i.e. `→47`) would become invalid as soon as you add or remove lines before that line number.

5.1.1 - Equivalent of `:If ... :EndIf` Controls

Using small tricks it is possible to use → to program conditional execution.

Just remember that jumping to an empty *Destination* does nothing, so that statements are executed sequentially.

Consider the following program:

```
[10]     Any statement
[11]     →(~Price≥10)⍴Cheap            ⇦ This simulates an :If clause
[12]     Any statement
....     ...
[19]     Any statement
[20]    Cheap:                         ⇦ This label acts as an :EndIf clause
[21]     Any statement
```

Suppose that `Price` is equal to 7; let us see how the statement works:

`Price≥10`	is	`0`	
`~Price≥10`	is	`1`	
`Cheap`	is	`20`	A label is considered to be a variable, in this case 20
`1⍴Cheap`	is	`20`	
`→20`	make the program jump to statement `[20]`		

Now, suppose that `Price` is equal to 33

`Price≥10`	is	`1`	
`~Price≥10`	is	`0`	
`0⍴Cheap`	is	`⍬`	Empty result
`→⍬`	the program does not jump, and statement `[12]` is processed normally		

So, when `Price<10` is satisfied, the program skips statements `[12 to 19]`, otherwise it executes them.

This kind of conditional jump can be summarised like this:

→(~ *Condition*)⍴ *Destination*

Using control structures, we would have written:

```
[10]     Any statement
[11]      :If Price≥10
[12]         Any statement
....         ...
[19]         Any statement
[20]    :EndIf
[21]     Any statement
```

We have programmed something equivalent to an `:If ... :EndIf` control structure, but it is less easy to read.

5.1.2 - Equivalent of `:If` ... `:Else` ... `:EndIf` Controls

Suppose we want to create a monadic function which performs the following operations:

- It says "Hello".
- It displays "Even" or "Odd", depending on the parity of its argument.
  This can be obtained using *Residue* (see Section C-2.6).
- If even, it calculates the half of the value and displays it.
- If odd, it calculates 1 plus three times the value, and displays it.
- … and finally it says "Good bye".

We could write the function without any flow control, but we are here to compare two flow control techniques, so let us use them:

With Control structures

```
      ∇ Syra1 Y
[1]     'Hello'
[2]     :If 0=2|Y
[3]         Y'is Even'
[4]         'Calculated:'(Y÷2)
[5]     :Else
[6]         Y'is Odd'
[7]         'Calculated:'(1+3×Y)
[8]     :EndIf
[9]     'Good bye'
      ∇
```

With Branch arrow

```
      ∇ Syra2 Y
[1]     'Hello'
[2]     →(0=2|Y)/Even
[3]     Y'is Odd'
[4]     'Calculated:' (1+3×Y)
[5]     →Quit
[6]    Even:
[7]     Y'is Even'
[8]     'Calculated' (Y÷2)
[9]    Quit:
[10]    'Good bye'
      ∇
```

Of course, both functions work properly, as you can see:

With Control structures

```
      Syra1 28
Hello
28  is Even
 Calculated: 14
Good bye
```

With Branch arrow

```
      Syra2 87
Hello
87  is Odd
 Calculated: 262
Good bye
```

If we compare the code, the use of *Control structures* produces more readable code, with a clear organisation of statement blocks. The use of *Branch arrows* requires a lot of labels (for which it may be difficult to find meaningful names…), the statement blocks can be placed in any order, and the programmer must take care not to overlap segments of code. For example, if statement `[5]` had been forgotten in `Syra2`, when an odd argument is processed, the function would first display for example "`15 is Odd`" , calculate 46, and immediately after would display "`15 is Even`".

Advice: Prefer control structures.

5.1.3 - Loops

With *Control structures*, we have three techniques to control loops: `For`, `Repeat`, and `While`. When we use *Branch arrows* the only possibility is to branch back to the beginning of the loop, and include a conditional exit, using the same technique as above.

Among many possible approaches, here are two typical constructs.

- In the first approach, a test is placed at the bottom of the iterative part. As long as the condition is true, the program skips back to the label at the start of the block; when it becomes false, the program goes on and executes the statements which follow the test.

It is very similar to `:Repeat` ... `:Until`, with the difference that `Until` is followed by the "exit" condition, while here the branch arrow is followed by the "loop again" condition.

Figure D-25

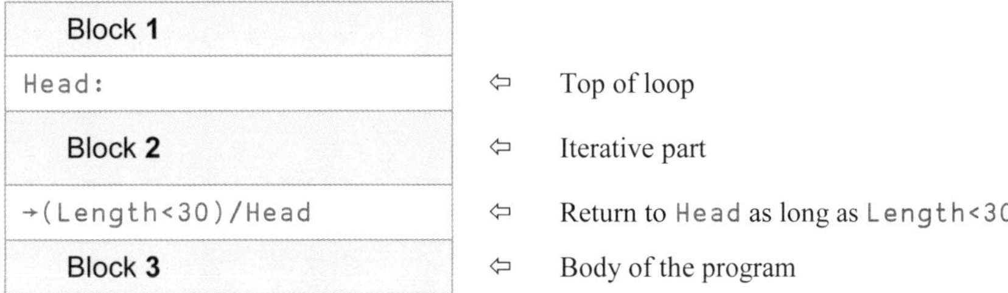

- In the second approach, a branch arrow placed at the bottom causes an unconditional jump to the start of the loop. The loop must therefore include a test that causes a jump to a label placed outside of the loop.

  It is very similar to `:Repeat` ... `:EndRepeat`. If the conditional exit is placed at the very top of the loop, it is very similar to `:While` ... `:EndWhile`.

Figure D-26

Block 1		
`Begin:`	⇦	Top of loop
Block 2		
`→(Amount=0)/Body`	⇦	Test to exit the loop
Block 3	⇦	Executed as long as `Amount≠0`
`→Begin`	⇦	Bottom of loop; jump back to the head
`Body:`	⇦	Destination label to exit the loop
Block 4		

5.1.4 - Other Conditional Expressions

Using a branch arrow, the way to program conditional jumps is to write an expression which returns the value of the destination label (jump), an empty vector (no jump), or zero (quit the function).

Since the expression following the branch arrow is an ordinary APL expression, one can imagine a large number of different expressions which will provide the branch arrow with an appropriate destination.

For example: *condition*`/Label`, *condition*`↑Label`, *condition*`⍴Label` will all return the value of `Label` if the condition is satisfied, or an empty vector if it is not.

Here are some typical examples:

Jump if true or continue if false

→(*Condition*)/*Destination*

→(*Condition*)⍴*Destination*

→*Destination*×⍳*Condition*

→(*Condition*)↑*Destination* ⇦ This symbol will be studied in the next chapter

You shall discover some other conditional executions in the Specialist's section.

Jump if false or continue if true

→(*Condition*)↓*Destination* ⇦ This symbol will be studied in the next chapter

Jump if true or quit the function if false

→*Destination*×*Condition*

5.2 Multiple Conditions

5.2.1 - Transform a Value into a Destination

Because it is possible to jump to different parts of a function depending on the result of an expression it is even possible to write a program that is similar to `:Select` ... `:Case` ... `:EndSelect`.

Consider the following expression:

→(*Dest1*,*Dest2*,*Dest3*)[*Value*]

Whether *Value* is equal to 1, 2 or 3, this statement will produce a jump to the corresponding destination. If *Value* is an empty vector, the program will not jump, so it will execute the next statement.

If we combine this observation with the use of dyadic *Iota* we can easily test for other values than 1, 2, 3. For example, suppose that we need to jump to 3 different locations depending on the value of a variable named `Value`. We could write:

```
 →( Case1,Case2,Case3,Case3,CaseElse )[100 20 30 0 ι Value]
Case1:
 ...
 →EndSelect
Case2:
 ...
 →EndSelect
Case3:
 ...
 →EndSelect
CaseElse:
 ...
 →EndSelect
EndSelect:
```

This is equivalent to this control structure block:

```
 :Select Value
 :Case 100
    ...
 :Case 20
    ...
 :CaseList 30 0
    ...
 :Else
    ...
 :EndSelect
```

5.2.2 - Multiple Conditions and Destinations

```
→((Cond1),( Cond2),( Cond3))/Dest1,Dest2,Dest3
```

Conditions and destinations are concatenated to return a Boolean vector to the left of the *Compress* function, and a vector of destinations (line numbers) to the right of it. The program jumps to the destination attached to the **first** satisfied condition, even if several conditions are satisfied.

This is because the branch arrow accepts a vector of values (destinations) as its right argument. However, it ignores everything but the first item in the vector.

Therefore this statement is similar to:

```
:If Cond1
   ...
:ElseIf Cond2
   ...
:ElseIf Cond3
   ...
:EndIf
```

5.3 Modern and Traditional Controls Cooperate

It is sometimes convenient to mix modern and traditional flow control in order to simplify the code.

Consider a loop in which we must terminate the execution of the function if the condition `X<3` becomes satisfied.

With modern control structures, the function could be written like this:

```
:Repeat
    Statements
    :If X<3
        :Return                 ⇦ Exit from the function
    :EndIf
    Statements
:EndRepeat
Body ...
```

Because each opening clause must be paired with a closing one, the exit test needs 3 lines; this is a bit heavy. It is possible to use fewer statements using an explicit branch:

```
:Repeat
    Statements
    :Goto (X<3)/0               ⇦ Simpler , but perhaps less readable (remember
    Statements                    that a jump to 0 means exit from the function)
:EndRepeat
Body ...
```

The exit statement could also have been written

```
    →(X<3)/0
```

since the branch arrow and the `:Goto` keyword are equivalent.

Something very similar could be written if we need to leave a loop when a given condition, for example `A=B`, becomes satisfied:

Using control structures

```
:Repeat
    Statements
    :If A=B
        :Leave
    :EndIf
    Statements
:EndRepeat
Body ...
```

Control structure with a traditional branch

```
 :Repeat
     Statements
     →(A=B)/Hell
     Statements
 :EndRepeat
Hell:
 Body ...
```

Remark Branching using → or `:GoTo` is not recommended as a general tool for programming flow control. It is explained here mainly in order to help you understand existing code, and to show that the technique may be useful and feasible in special situations. You should in general either use control structures or use statements which do not require conditions.

Caution! Colons are placed **before** a keyword (`:For`), but **after** a label (`Next:`)

6 - Input, Output, and Format

Up to now, our functions processed values passed as arguments, and returned results which could be used in an expression, assigned to a variable, or displayed. But a function can also get data from other sources, and/or it can produce results which are not APL variables, but, for example, printed material, or data files. In this section you will learn some useful techniques to write such functions.

This section will also help you use data that you may already have stored in Excel worksheets or in text files on disk.

6.1 Some Input and Output Methods

Here are some of the most typical methods used by a function to get data or output results.

Some Input/Output methods	Input	Output	§
A function returns a result, it is displayed at function completion		X	
A function can also display intermediate values during execution		X	6.3
A function can use or modify a global variable	X	X	6.4
It can exchange data with a spreadsheet, like Microsoft Excel	X	X	6.5
It can read or write data from/to a file (or a database)	X	X	6.6
A function can print data on a printer		X	6.7
A function can exchange data with a graphical user interface	X	X	6.8
A function can get data typed by the user on the keyboard	X		6.9
A function can use Internet facilities to input or output data	X	X	

All of these possibilities will not be explained here; we shall limit our investigations to some simple methods that you may test immediately, using some utility functions which are provided in the associated workspace.

We also provide some text files and spreadsheets that you can use for experimentation:

Excel workbooks:	`xldemo.xls` `worldsales.xls`
Text files	`mlk.txt` `report.txt`

We recommend that you place those files in a reference directory where they will be preserved, and copy them to a test directory where you will be able to make some experiments and modify them at will.

Also create a global variable in your WS with the path to that test directory, to avoid repeating it in all the tests you will do.
For example: `MyPath←'d:\mydir\apltests\'`

In the following sections we will refer to the variable `MyPath`.

6.2 Format

In the preceding pages, we found that we can display, on the screen, any kind of results: numbers, text, or a mixture of numbers and characters in nested arrays. Now we shall try to output data to external media, like graphic interfaces, disk files, or printers. Most of those media only accept text. For example, it is impossible to send numbers to a printer: we must first convert them to printable characters.

The APL language includes two such conversion tools: a function named ***Format***, represented by the symbol `⍕`, and a *System function* named `⎕FMT`.

These facilities will be studied in detail in Chapter F, but we will introduce here the basic use of *Format*.

6.2.1 - Monadic Format

Monadic *Format* converts any array (numbers, characters, and nested arrays) into its character representation. The result is exactly the same as what you see when you display the array in the APL session, because in fact, APL internally uses monadic *Format* to display arrays.

- Character values are not converted: they remain unchanged.
- Numeric and nested values are transformed into vectors or matrices of characters.

```
      ⍴⍕'album'                          ⇦ A character vector is unchanged
5
      ⍴Chemistry                         ⇦ Chemistry is a character matrix
3 5
      ⍴⍕Chemistry                        ⇦ It is not modified by ⍕
3 5
      ⍴52 69 76                          ⇦ This numeric vector has 3 items
3
      ⍕52 69 76
52 69 76                                 ⇦ Once converted, it is an 8-item character vector
      ⍴⍕52 69 76
8
```

In Chapter B we used a 2 by 3 nested matrix named `NesMat`. It can be converted into text:

```
      ⍴ NesMat                           ⇦ The nested matrix had 2 rows and 3 columns
2 3
      ⍴u ← ⍕NesMat                       ⇦ Once converted into text, it is 20 characters wide
3 20                                       and it has 3 rows, because the second row
      u                                    contained two small matrices
 Dyalog   44  Hello
     27  8 6  1 2 0
         2 4  0 0 5
```

6.2.2 - Dyadic Format

Dyadic *Format* applies **only** to numeric values. It converts them into text in a format controlled by the left argument, which is made up of two numbers:

- The first number indicates the number of characters (the width of the output) to be used to represent each numeric value.
- The second number indicates how many decimal digits will be displayed.

Let us make some experiments with the following matrix:

```
      MN
 608.1    928.24 1293.14  849.95      ⇦ This is the normal display, and this is also how
1127.84   970.27 1249    1168.29        monadic Format would present it.
 775.12 1065      670.69 1091.7
      8 2⍕MN                          ⇦ Each number will be represented by 8 characters,
  608.10  928.24 1293.14  849.95        right aligned, with 2 decimal digits.
 1127.84  970.27 1249.00 1168.29
  775.12 1065.00  670.69 1091.70
      ⍴8 2⍕MN                         ⇦ The result has of course 3 rows and 32 columns
3 32                                    (4 times 8 characters).
```

```
      6 0⍕MN
   608   928  1293   850
  1128   970  1249  1168
   775  1065   671  1092
      ⍴6 0⍕MN
3 24
```

⇦ Each number will be represented by 6 characters right aligned, with no decimal digits.

⇦ The result has 3 rows and 24 columns.

Remarks Values are not truncated, but **rounded.**

Any attempt to apply dyadic ⍕ to characters will cause a `DOMAIN ERROR`

Format will be studied in detail in Chapter F.

6.3 Displaying Intermediate Results

During normal execution, most applications do not use the session window (the development environment); all input/output is typically done with more user-friendly interfaces. However, during the development of an application, it may be useful for experimental purposes to have a function display intermediate results.

This can be accomplished in 3 different ways:

- If the result of an expression is not assigned to a variable, it is displayed:

  ```
  [3]    'The cost is: ',(9 2⍕ Val),' US Dollars'
  ```

  This text vector is not assigned to a name, so it will be displayed on the screen.

- It is possible to display the value of a variable using the identity function (monadic + sign), but this applies only to the leftmost calculated value in an statement:

  ```
  [8]    +Sel←(vector>0)/vector←Old,New
  ```

  The result of the expression is assigned to a variable (`Sel`), and displayed. Please note that it is not considered good programming practice to assign a value to a variable and then reference the variable elsewhere in the same expression. However, you may encounter existing code that looks like this.

- Any intermediate result can be displayed by assigning it to the ***Quad*** symbol (⎕), and this assignment can be placed anywhere in the middle of an statement:

  ```
  [5]    VAT←(⎕←+/Purchased)×⎕←Rates[⎕←Segment]
  ```

  Three values will be displayed one after the other, on three successive lines of the screen, in the order that the respective expressions are evaluated:

First	`Segment`
then	`Rates[Segment]`
and finally	`+/Purchased`

  We **recommend** that you use this last method, which is the most explicit, and which can be easily detected by any text search utility function.

6.4 Using Global Variables

A function can use (input) or modify (output) the contents of one or more variables which are global to it. The variables may be completely global, or they may be local to a calling function (so-called *semi-global* variables).

For example, as we suggested earlier, a global variable may contain a path used by dozens of functions in a workspace:

```
MyPath ← 'g:\common\finance\archives\2007\'
```

It will be possible for any function to use this path to prefix some file names:

```
File1 ← MyPath,'sales.xls'
File2 ← MyPath,'customers.txt'
```

Storing common parameters like a folder path in global variables can often be very convenient. For example, it makes it very easy to have the system use another set of files, without changing any functions. This technique can for example be used to switch between running on test data and on production data.

Similarly, a function can output values into global variables, which may be used by many other functions sharing the same workspace:

CountryCode ← *Any expression*

CountryPrefix ← *Any expression*

Currency[index] ← *Any expression*

Those 3 variables may again be localised at a higher level, in a calling function, or they may be global to the whole workspace.

You must be very cautious when using this technique:

- Maintenance of functions using global variables is complex because it is difficult to keep track of the different statements which use or update those variables.
- If an error occurs, and if several functions can modify these global variables, it may be very difficult to determine which of them had last modified a variable involved in the error.
- If function execution is interrupted and restarted, global values set before the interruption may conflict with new ones calculated in a different context. For example, if the function increments a global variable in line `[1]`, but crashes in line `[2]`, and you restart the function, you will have the global variable incremented twice instead of once, as you had expected. Such errors are *very* nasty, as they can lead to other errors or breakdowns much later in the execution. It can be close to impossible to find the causes of such errors.

Such a technique should be restricted to a limited number of variables, clearly identified and documented by any convenient method: a common name prefix, an automated system of references, etc.

Sometimes when starting an application it is necessary to read a lot of settings from a file and make the settings available to all the programs that constitute the application. In such a situation it would make sense to write a program to read the settings from the file and store them in global variables in the workspace.

Advice: Whenever possible, favour explicit exchange of values through arguments and results.

6.5 Exchanging Data With an Excel Worksheet

Many applications are based on an intelligent partnership between Excel and APL:

- Some users enter data in a set of worksheets with a predefined structure.
- APL reads the sheets, and processes the data with much greater power, precision and flexibility than Excel is capable of.
- Finally, APL outputs results into one or more worksheets, in which the user can modify the presentation, define additional simple calculations, and produce simple graphs.

To help you explore those techniques, we provide (in Utils_01.dws) two functions that will help you exchange data with an Excel worksheet:

- `XLGet` imports data from a worksheet into your WS
- `XLPut` exports data to a worksheet

These functions have been developed for learning purposes, and you can use them for light applications.

The workspace "loaddata.dws", distributed as part of the Dyalog APL system, contains a set of professional grade functions to read from and write to text files, Excel workbooks, SQL databases, and XML files.

"loaddata.dws" contains the functions `LoadXL` and `SaveXL`, which are similar to `XLGet` and `XLPut`, but with a slightly different syntax.

6.5.1 - Importing Data

`XLGet` Has the following syntax: *Variable* ← `XLGet` *Fileid Sheet Range*

Where:

Variable is any variable you wish to create or modify.

Fileid is the full path and name of the workbook.
For example: `'c:\mydir\subdirectory\mydata.xls'`

Sheet is the name of the worksheet inside the workbook, for example `'Sales'`
If left empty, the function will read the active worksheet.

Range is the part you want to get, specified using Excel notation, for example `'B4:H8'`
If empty, the function will read all the contents of the selected sheet.

Examples

```
Val1 ← XLGet (MyPath,'worldsales.xls') 'Madrid' ''
Val2 ← XLGet (MyPath,'xldemo.xls') '' 'A5:E10'
```

In the first example, we get all the contents of the `Madrid` sheet (no *Range* was specified).

In the second one, we get a small part (A5 to E10) of the active worksheet (no *Sheet* specified).

As one cannot predict which was the active worksheet when the workbook was last saved, this second method should be reserved to single-sheet workbooks.

6.5.2 - Exporting Data

`XLPut` Has the following syntax: *Values* `XLPut` *Fileid Sheet StartCell*

Where:

Values are the values to write to the target worksheet.

Fileid has the same meaning as in `XLGet`.

Sheet is the name of an existing worksheet in that workbook. It will be modified.
If empty, a new worksheet will be inserted, with a default name.

StartCell is the top left cell to be written; for example `'E5'`.
The function will automatically deduce the corresponding *Range* from *StartCell* and ⍴*Values*.

Example

```
Val1 ← 'Fiat' 'Venturi' 'Opel' , (3 3⍴⍳9)
Val1 XLPut (MyPath,'worldsales.xls') 'Denver' 'A16'
```

Don't modify this workbook further, as it will be used again in Chapter Q.
If you want to experiment further, you can use a copy of this workbook or a different one.

6.6 Reading or Writing a Text File

Files can have many different formats. Some contain integer or decimal numbers, some contain APL variables (vectors, arrays, nested values), as we shall see in Chapter N, but most files contain plain text.

In this chapter, we shall limit our investigations:

- to text files, which can be viewed and modified using a text editor like Microsoft Notepad,
- to rather small files that can be read or written as a whole in a single operation (depending on your workspace size, you can easily read/write several thousands of lines of text).

Such a file can be considered as a long text vector containing special line separation characters ("*carriage return*" and "*line feed*"). For that reason, when edited with Notepad, they look more or less like APL character matrices.

Except for special purposes, to exchange data between APL and a text file, one needs to:

- convert the data read from a file as a character vector into a more convenient APL character array (read),
- or convert an APL character array into a special character vector with embedded line separators (write).

Those conversions require some techniques we haven't seen yet. This is the reason why we give you some predefined functions. You will find them in a workspace named Files.dws, delivered with Dyalog APL. It contains a *Namespace* (you can read about namespaces in Chapter O) which itself contains the functions. To use them, you must:

- Copy the *Namespace* containing them (be careful with the case): `)copy files Files`
- Set an access path to the *NameSpace* contents: `⎕Path ← 'Files'`

`ReadAllText`	Reads the contents of a text file and returns a charatcer vector. The lines of the text are separated by two special characters: *Carriage Return* and *Line Feed*.
Syntax	*Result* ← `ReadAllText` *Path*,*Fileid*
Example	`Dream ← ReadAllText MyPath,'mlk.txt'`
`ReadAllLines`	Reads the contents of a text file and returns a nested vector of character vectors, one vector per line of text in the file.
Syntax	*Result* ← `ReadAllLines` *Path*,*Fileid*
Example	`Dream ← ReadAllLines MyPath,'mlk.txt'`
`PutText`	Writes a character matrix (or vector) to a file. If a file with the same name already exists, it is replaced by the new file. The function returns the number of characters written to the file.
Syntax	*Number* ← *TextMatrix* `PutText` *Path*,*Fileid*
Example	`Number ← Chemistry PutText MyPath,'newfile.txt'`

The workspace "loaddata.dws", distributed as part of the Dyalog APL system, contains a set of professional grade functions to read from and write to text files, Excel workbooks, SQL databases, and XML files.

"loaddata.dws" contains two functions `LoadText` and `SaveText` to complement the set of functions described above. `LoadText` and `SaveText` are designed to work with comma separated files (.CSV files) and fixed field width text files.

We have only used text files. Dyalog APL also includes an advanced file system designed to work very easily and efficiently with APL arrays, as well as a generalised interface to SQL databases. The APL file system is described in chapter N. The SQL interface is not described in this tutorial; please refer instead to the specialised brochures.

6.7 Printing Results on a Printer

An APL function can print data on a printer using the resources provided by the system.

However, many parameters need to be specified: orientation of the paper, position of what you want to print, font shape, size, body, colour, etc., and these details must be specified for all the things you expect to print on a page. This is a bit too soon for a beginner.

Most people prefer to use predefined utility software, like ***NewLeaf***, a built-in component of Dyalog APL, which allows you to easily print thousands of pages, produce PDF files, and produce attractive business reports.
We strongly recommend you to have a quick look at Chapter S, to discover both *Newleaf* and ***RainPro***, another powerful software to produce very convenient business graphics..

For now, we would like to give you a very basic tool which just allows you to print limited character matrices. All the parameters are defaulted:

- The printer is your default printer.
- The font, "APL385 Unicode", is a fixed pitch font, which displays data in the same tabular presentation as the APL session.
- Depending on whether you print in "Portrait" or "Landscape" orientation, the function will print 60 or 40 lines of text per page, and the width of your matrix will also be limited to 75 or 110 characters.

The function accepts the matrix to print as a right argument, and `'L'` or `'P'` (the default) as optional left argument; for example:

`Print XG10`	Where `XG10` is a given text matrix
`'L' Print 5 0⍕20 22⍴Tickets`	The numeric vector `Tickets` is converted to a text matrix and printed in Landscape

6.8 Using a Graphical User Interface

We shall see later in this tutorial (Chapter P) how easy it is to create graphic user interfaces (GUI) which allow both input and output of information.

In the example shown below, the user can select a currency, a customer typology, a geographic zone, etc. These actions interact with the application and can be transformed into values assigned to some variables. This is an example of using a GUI for **input** purposes.

When the user presses the "*Select*" button, the associated application performs some operations, and displays a list of customers with some figures. This is an example of using a GUI for pure **output** if the grid has been specified "*Read only*", or **Input/Output** if the user is also allowed to modify the values in the cells.

Figure D-27

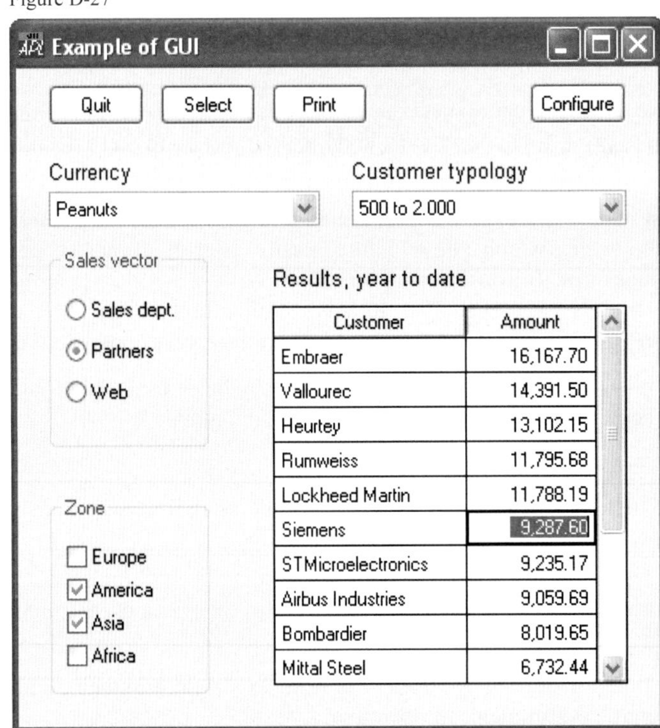

6.9 Requesting Values From the Keyboard

Here again, if the user of an application is required to enter some input data, this is often done via some user friendly GUI interface like the previous one, or from a web page. However, during the development phase or for a light application, it may be simpler to use a very basic Question/Answer mode.

Two symbols are used to request input from the user:

Quad `val ← ⎕` is used to enter one or more numbers.

Quote-Quad `val ← ⍞` is used to enter any string of characters.

6.9.1 - Quad Evaluated Input

This first method is no longer in common use, but can be useful when prototyping an application which needs to request input. Also, you can easily accidentally type ⎕ in the session and activate Quad evaluated input, so it is worth studying briefly.

Quad causes a pause in the execution of a function, and allows the user to type any kind of expression. That expression is ***evaluated*** like any APL expression entered in the session, and its ***result*** is the result of the ***Quad*** function.

- When a function executes a *Quad*, it displays ⎕: at the left margin of the screen to inform the user that he or she is expected to enter one or more values.
- If any error occurs during evaluation, the input *Quad* is redisplayed over and over again, until the user succeeds in entering a valid expression.

In the following example, a function is supposed to count how many items of its right argument there are between two limits. These limits could be passed via a left argument, but in this case we choose to ask the user to enter them during execution of the function:

```
     ∇ Prompt1 Vector;lim1;lim2;nb
[1]    'What are the limits?'
[2]    (lim1 lim2)←⎕
[3]    nb←+/(Vector>lim1)∧(Vector<lim2)
[4]    (⍕nb),' values are comprised between ',(⍕lim1),' and ',⍕lim2
     ∇

      Prompt1 Salaries
What are the limits?              ⇦ Prompting message
⎕:                                ⇦ Prompt
      2000 2500                   ⇦ The user's answer
5 values are comprised between 2000 and 2500
```

Let us make an error while executing the function again

```
      Prompt1 Salaries
What are the limits?
⎕:
      mylims                      ⇦ We tried to answer with a variable name, but that
VALUE ERROR                         variable does not exist. An error message is
issued.
      mylims                        This is not very user friendly!
     ∧                              Then the user is automatically requested again to
⎕:                                ⇦ provide a value.
      ⌊0.5+0.9 1.1×Average Salaries
4 values are comprised between 2653 and 3243
```

The expression has been evaluated (using a variable, a defined function, and some primitives) and the result (`2653 3243`) has been assigned to `lim1 lim2`.

Hint: If you accidentally start evaluated input in the session, hit *Ctrl+Break* to generate an interrupt.

6.9.2 - Quote-Quad Character Input

Quote-Quad allows the user to enter a string of characters. That string is returned as the result of the ***Quote-Quad*** function.

If the user types nothing and just presses the *Enter* key, the returned value is an empty text vector.

```
     ∇ Prompt2;tex
[1]    'Type any string of characters'
[2]    tex←⍞
[3]    '"',tex,'" is a vector of length ',⍕⍴tex
     ∇

      Prompt2
Type any string of characters
Are you serious?
"Are you serious?" is a vector of length 16
```

You can see that the *Quote-Quad* does not display any prompt sign.

Advice Avoid using *Quad* evaluated input.
Quote-Quad remains useful for quick tests, the development of light interactive functions, or scripting applications which work with redirected input and output.

7 - Syntax Considerations

7.1 Comments & Statement Separators

7.1.1 - Comments

It is possible to write comments in a function to make it easier to read, explain how it should be used, and help future maintenance or evolutions.

Comments begin with the symbol ***Lamp***: ⍝ (because it "illuminates" the code)

They can be placed alone on a dedicated line, or to the right of any statement, including the function header. All the characters placed to the right of the *Lamp* are ignored by the interpreter.

7.1.2 - Statement Separators

Several statements can be placed on the same line of a function, using the statement separator ***Diamond*** ⋄. Statements are executed **starting from the leftmost one**.

Putting several statements on a same line does not save computing time, and generally does not improve the readability of a function. It should be reserved for short, straightforward statements.

The diamond separator can also be used in ***Multithreaded programming*** to force the execution of a set of statements without any switch to another thread. But this is outside the scope of this tutorial.

Example

Let us demonstrate these concepts on the function `Interlace`, written some pages ago:

```
     ∇ R←A Interlace B;size;even    ⍝ This is just a demo
      ⍝ A & B are matrices of the same shape
       size←1 2×⍴A
       R←size⍴0                     ⍝ Build a matrix full of zeroes
       even←2×⍳(⍴B)[2]              ⍝ Calculate the even column numbers
       R[;even]←B ⋄ R[;even-1]←A    ⍝ Interlace
     ∇
```

We have placed some comments: in the header, on a dedicated line, and to the right of some statements. We have also grouped the last two statements on a single line, separated by a *Diamond*.

This separator is often used in a loop to execute a statement and quit the function or skip to another statement:

```
      New ← Old+20 ◇ →0
or:   Total ← 0 ◇ →Mummy                ⇦ Mummy is a label
```

7.2 Why Should a Function Return a Result?

During the execution of a function, any result which is not assigned to a variable name is immediately displayed on the screen; we used that in our functions `Syra1` & `Syra2`.

So, let us compare two very similar functions and their usage:

This one returns a result	This one does not

`∇ Z←X Plus Y`
`[1]    Z←X+Y`
`∇`
	`∇ X PlusNoRes Y`
	`[1]    X+Y`
	`∇`

`      6 Plus 8` `14`	`      6 PlusNoRes 8` `14`

Apparently, both functions work very well:

- The left one calculates a local variable `Z`, which has been declared to be the function result. The function returns the value of `Z` as its result, and because the result is not assigned or used, it is displayed on the screen.
- The right one calculates `X+Y`. Because this sum it is not assigned, it is immediately displayed.

But now, let us try to include these functions in more complex expressions:

`      10×6 Plus 8`
`140`
	`      10×6  PlusNoRes 8`
	`14`
	`VALUE ERROR`
	`      10×6 PlusNoRes 8`
	`    ∧`

Something went wrong!

- The leftmost function returns a result. The result is available to the calling expression, in this case as the right argument to the multiply function, so that we obtained the answer we wanted.
- But the rightmost function returns no result. The value calculated in the 1st statement is just displayed (though we did not need it); it is **not returned** as a result. So, the multiply function has an argument on its left (10), but nothing on its right, hence the error message.

Advice:

> Whenever you can, write functions which produce an explicit result.
> You can always throw the result away if you don't need it.

7.3 Different Types of Functions

7.3.1 - What Is an Explicit Result?

We have seen that some functions (like `Average`, or `Plus`) return a result; we describe the result as being ***Explicit.*** It means that once the function has been executed, the result is passed on to the next part of the expression which is being evaluated or, if there is none, it is displayed on the screen.

Some other functions (like `PlusNoRes`) do not return an explicit result. This does not mean that they do nothing; perhaps they read or write data from/to a file or an Excel worksheet, perhaps they print a graph on a printer, or perhaps they build a graphic user interface. All these consequences which arise from the execution of the function can be called ***Implicit*** or hidden results. Anything that happens during the execution of a function and that is not communicated directly in the function's result is generally called a *side effect* of the function (and perhaps its sub-functions).

7.3.2 - Six Major Types of Functions (Valence)

The number of arguments of a function is termed its ***Valence***.

You have already met functions with one or two arguments (Monadic or Dyadic), you can also write functions which take no arguments at all; they are called ***Niladic***. Though they do not receive values through arguments, they can process data introduced via the various techniques described in Section 6.

Depending on whether or not they return an explicit result, functions can be classified as follows:

Valence	With an explicit result	Without an explicit result
Niladic	`∇ Z ←    Function`	`∇     Function`
Monadic	`∇ Z ←    Function Y`	`∇     Function Y`
Dyadic	`∇ Z ← X Function Y`	`∇   X Function Y`

Niladic functions which return no result are very similar to programs written in other languages.

The functions which we have already written can be classified as follows:

Syntax	With result	Without result
Niladic		`Endless`
Monadic	`Meanval / Willitwork`	`Syra1 / Syra2`
Dyadic	`Interlace / Plus / Times`	`PlusNoRes`

7.3.3 - Ambivalent Functions

Most APL symbols are used to represent both monadic and dyadic primitive functions. For example, the symbol `⍴` represents both the *Shape* (`⍴A`) function and the *Reshape* (`A⍴B`) function, and `⌈` represents both *Ceiling* (`⌈A`) and *Maximum* (`A⌈B`). These symbols are said to be ***Ambivalent***.

To write an *ambivalent* user-defined function the name of the left argument in the header, is sspecified within braces (to show that it is optional), like this:

```
∇ Result ← {Left} Function Right
```

We are now faced with a problem; this function must work correctly whether or not a left argument is provided, so we must test for its presence. To test for the current use of a name, we can use the *System function* `⎕NC`. Traditionally NC stands for ***Name Class***, but we will here use the term ***Name Category*** in order to avoid confusion with the class concept used in Object Oriented Programming.

We shall see in Chapter L that: the *Name Category* of a variable name is 2
the *Name Category* of a function name is 3
the *Name Category* of an unused name is 0

So, we must include in the function the expression: `⎕NC 'Left'`

- If a left argument was provided, the answer will be 2.
- If no left argument was provided, the answer will be 0 (even if the workspace contains a global function or variable named `Left`, because `Left` is here a local name).

Just to check that it works, let us write a useless ambivalent function:

```
      ∇ {Left} Useless Right
[1]     ⎕NC'Left'
      ∇
       23 Useless 78
2                                        ⇦ This means that a left argument is present.
       Useless 71
0                                        ⇦ This means that no left argument was provided.
```

7.3.4 - Example

The following function rounds a numeric value to its Nth decimal digit:

```
      ∇ Res←N Round Val
[1]     Res←⌊0.5+Val×10*N
[2]     Res←Res÷10*N
      ∇
       2 Round 41.31875 82.92413 127.71625
41.32 82.92 127.72
       2 0 3 Round 41.31875 82.92413 127.71625
41.32 83 127.716
```

Now, suppose that we usually want to round values to the second decimal digit; we can decide that if we do not specify a left argument, this will be the default behaviour of our function. The necessary modifications appear in black:

```
        ∇ Res←{N}Round Val
[1]     ⍝ Rounds "Val" to its "Nth" decimal
[2]     :If 0=⎕NC'N'
[3]         N←2     ⍝ By default, if omitted, N is set to 2
[4]     :EndIf
[5]     Res←⌊0.5+Val×10*N
[6]     Res←Res÷10*N
      ∇
```

Now, the left argument is optional, and an `:If … :EndIf` clause detects its presence. If absent `N` is set to 2. The expressions shown below illustrate the two ways in which the function can be used. This function really is ambivalent.

```
       2 0 3 Round 41.31875 82.92413 127.71625
41.32 83 127.716
       Round 41.31875 82.92413 127.71625
41.32 82.92 127.72
```

7.3.5 - Shy Result

A ***Shy*** result is a result which is returned, but not displayed.

Consider a function which deletes a file from disk and returns a result equal to 1 (file deleted) or 0 (file not found). Usually, one doesn't care if the file did not exist, so the result is not needed. But sometimes it may be important to check whether the file really existed and has been removed. So, sometimes, a result is useless, and sometimes it is useful … this is the reason why shy results have been invented.

A shy result is specified by putting the name of the result in braces:

```
∇ {Result} ← X Function Y
```

Let us write a demonstration function:

```
      ∇ {Z}←A ShyFun B
[1]     Z←A×B
      ∇
        17 ShyFun 3                  ⇦ The result is returned, but not displayed.
        ⎕←17 ShyFun 3                ⇦ Here we explicitly ask for the result to be shown.
51
        10×17 ShyFun 3               ⇦ The result can be used for any calculation.
510
```

7.3.6 - An Argument Used as a Result

It is possible to use the same name for the result as one of the arguments. For example, these are two valid headers:

```
∇ X←X Fun Y     or     ∇ Y←X Fun Y
```

This may be useful when a condition causes the function to terminate without any processing. Suppose that you want to repeatedly divide the right argument by 2, until the result becomes odd. A simple loop will do it, but if the argument is already odd, the loop stops immediately, and the result is equal to the argument:

```
      ∇ Y←DivideIt Y
[1]     :While 0=2|Y                 ⇦ As long as Y is even, we divide it
[2]         Y←Y÷2
[3]     :EndWhile
      ∇
```

If Y is even the loop is executed at least once.
If Y is odd the function exits immediately and returns the unmodified value of Y as its result.

7.4 Nested Argument and Result

7.4.1 - Nested Right Argument

Both the left and right arguments of a function can be nested vectors, as shown here:

```
      Function 'London' 'UK' 7684700 40
```

A composite argument of this sort is often split (dispatched) into a number of separate local variables using multiple assignment, as illustrated in the first statement of this example:

```
     ∇ Dispatch Vector;town;country;population;prefix
[1]    (town country population prefix) ← Vector
[2]    Other statements
     ∇
```

A more elegant way to achieve the same thing is to specify the composite nature of the argument directly, as follows:

```
     ∇ Dispatch (town country population prefix)
[1]    town
[2]    country
[3]    population
[4]    prefix
     ∇
```

Using this syntax, the items of the right argument are automatically allocated into local variables, as you can see:

```
      Dispatch 'London' 'UK' 7684700 40
London
UK
7684700
40
```

Important: This special syntax applies **only to the Right argument**, not to the left one.

If a nested vector is passed on the left it can be split (dispatched) by multiple assignment, as suggested earlier.

7.4.2 - Choice of Syntax

When a function `Fun` is to receive two values `A` and `B`, you now have the choice between two syntaxes:

Dyadic:	`∇ A Fun B`	for example	`∇ R ← A Plus B`
Monadic:	`∇ Fun (A B)`	for example	`∇ R ← Add A B`

The dyadic way has the advantage that the function can be used with *Reduction*, while the monadic version cannot.
For example, we can use `Plus` in this kind of expression: `Plus/14 10 52 1 12 43`

7.4.3 - Nested Result

Similar notation can be applied to the result of the function. Suppose that you want to return a vector of 3 separate (local) variables (named `one`, `two`, and `three`) as the result of the function. One way is to declare that the function returns a single named result, and to assign the 3 local variables into the result before the function terminates. Another approach is to simply declare the structure of the result in the header as illustrated below. As these names (`one`, `two`, and `three`) appear in the header; they are local.

```
     ∇ (one two three) ← Left NestedRes Right
[1]    one←Left+Right
[2]    two←Right[Left]
[3]    three←two×one[1]                ⇦ Ever seen such a stupid function?
     ∇
```

```
      DISPLAY  3 NestedRes 12 45 78
┌→─────────────────────┐
│ ┌→────────┐          │
│ │15 48 81 │ 78 1170  │
│ └~────────┘          │
└∊─────────────────────┘
```

7.5 Choice of Names

The names that you use to specify the arguments and the result of a function may be any valid APL name:

For example: `∇ Cain ← Adam PLUS Eve`
or: `∇ Dumb ← Man WITHOUT Voice`

However, it is recommended that you use simple names, names that are easy to remember, and names that are consistent from one function to the other. This is especially important if several people have to maintain a common set of functions; any of them should be able to understand immediately which variables represent the arguments and which the result…

This recommendation is really about adopting a strict *naming convention*, and this applies to any serious programming project, whether it uses APL or not.

Here are some simple conventions that you might consider:

`∇ Z ← X Function Y`	Often used by English-speaking developers
`∇ R ← G Function D`	Often used by French-speaking developers
`∇ R ← A Function B`	and so on…

However, we advise you to adopt meaningful words to indicate the nature of the arguments; for example:

`NumVec` or `TexVec`	For numeric or character vectors
`NumMat` or `TexMat`	For numeric or character matrices

We also recommend that you avoid modifying the arguments in the body of the function: otherwise you could make maintenance much more difficult.

8 - Multi-Line Direct Functions

The Direct functions we wrote in Section 2 were limited to a single statement; we will now use the text editor to define multi-line Direct functions.

8.1 Characteristics

- Generally, the opening and closing braces are placed alone on the first and last lines. This is not mandatory, it is just a convention.
- Like procedural functions, they can be commented at will.
- One can create as many variables as needed: they are automatically deemed to be local variables. Note that this is opposite to procedural functions, in which names are considered global, unless they are localised.
- The arguments `⍵` and `⍺` retain the values passed to them as argument and may not be changed.
  Any attempt to modify them causes a `SYNTAX ERROR` to be reported, except when *defaulting the left argument* (cf. Section 8.3.1).
- As soon as an expression generates a result that is not assigned to a name or used in any other way, the function terminates, and the value of that expression is returned as the result of the function. If the function contains more lines they will not be executed.
- *Control structures*, *branch arrows*, and *labels* cannot be used in D-fns.

Let us write a function, deliberately broken up into several statements, to calculate an average value:

```
     ∇ DirFun1←{              ⍝ Even the header can be commented
[1]         vector←,⍵         ⍝ If ⍵ is a scalar
[2]         size←⍴vector
[3]         sum←+/vector
[4]         sum÷size                    ⇦ This will be our result
[5]         sum×size                    ⇦ This line will not be executed
[6]    }
     ∇

      DirFun1 3 9 4 7 6
5.8
```

You can check that any attempt to reference the values of `vector`, `size` or `sum` generates a `VALUE ERROR`, as they are local variables.

You can also see that statement `[5]` has not been executed, because the result of statement `[4]` **is** the final result, and the function terminated there. Such superfluous statements should be avoided, as they will sooner or later cause unnecessary confusion.

As a debugging tool, it is possible to modify statements to display intermediate results, like any other function,:

```
[2]         ⎕←size←⍴vector
[3]         ⎕←sum←+/vector

      DirFun1 13 29 34 27 51
5
154
30.8
```

Be careful: If you display the value calculated in line `[4]`, the value calculated in that line is no longer unused, and execution would now continue in line `[5]` - an example of the confusion mentioned above:

```
[2]         ⎕←size←⍴vector
[3]         ⎕←sum←+/vector
[4]         ⎕←sum÷size

      DirFun1 13 29 34 27 51
5
154
30.8
770                                     ⇦ The result is now the value calculated in line [5]!
```

8.2 Guards

We said that control structures or traditional branch arrows cannot be used in *D-Fns*. However, it is possible to have a *D-Fn* conditionally calculate a result, by using a ***Guard***.

A *Guard* is any expression which generates a one-item Boolean result, followed by a colon.

The expression placed to the right of a *Guard* is executed only if the *guard* is true. This syntax is similar to an `:If … :ElseIf … :ElseIf … :Else … :EndIf` control structure.

For example, this function will give a result equal to `'Positive'`, `'Zero'`, or `'Negative'` if the argument `⍵` is respectively greater than, equal to, or smaller than zero:

```
Sign←{
    ⍵>0: 'Positive'
    ⍵=0: 'Zero'
    'Negative'                    ⇦ This will not be executed if ⍵ is positive or zero!
 }
```

8.3 Syntax Considerations

8.3.1 - Default Left Argument

A dyadic *D-Fn* can always be used monadically; syntactically, its left argument `⍺` is always optional. If the left argument is not present it is possible to assign a default value to `⍺` by a normal assignment, for example: `⍺←10`. The assignment will not be carried out if `⍺` already has a value.

Consider a function which calculates the Nth root of a number, but which is normally used to calculate square roots (N=2). You can specify that the default value of the left argument (when omitted) is 2, as follows:

```
Root←{
    ⍺←2                       ⇦ When omitted ⍺ is set to 2
    ⍵*÷⍺                      ⇦ In any case calculate a root using ⍺
    }
    4 Root 625                ⇦ If specified, ⍺ is used
5                               5 is the 4th root of 625
    Root 625                  ⇦ If not specified, ⍺ takes the default value 2
25                              and the square root is calculated
```

The expression to the right of `⍺←` is evaluated only if the function has been used monadically. For this reason the expression should not have any side effects, as illustrated by this (silly) example:

```
     ∇ Silly←{
[1]          a←1              ⇦ Always executed
[2]          ⍺←a←2            ⇦ Not executed if ⍺ already has a value
[3]          a                ⇦ Let us see the value of "a"
[4]      }
     ∇
      Silly 0                 ⇦ ⍺ is not specified
2                             ⇦ As set in line [2]
      0 Silly 0               ⇦ Now ⍺ is specified
1                             ⇦ As set in line [1]; line [2] has not been
                                 executed
```

8.3.2 - Shy Result

Like procedural functions, *D-Fns* may produce a *shy result*. This happens when the last expression that is evaluated is assigned to a (local) name, as opposed to just leaving the result of the expression unassigned. Here is an example:

```
Function←{
    Any statement              ⇦ Here are the normal statements
    ...
    ⍵>10:var← Any value        ⇦ If the Guard is true, the function will terminate,
    The body of the function     and var will be returned as a shy result.
    Dum←...    }               ⇦ This is the last statement and it is assigned; the result will be shy.
```

`var` and `Dum` are dummy variables, because they cannot be used anymore: the statements in which they are assigned are the last ones executed.

8.3.3 - Local Sub-Functions

We have already defined a direct sub-function in a procedural function (see `Willitwork2` in Section 3.5), and we localised it in the function header. This can be done too in *D-Fns*, but note that in *D-Fns*, sub-functions, like variables, are localised automatically.

In the function below, we calculate the square root of the average of the squares of some numbers. Each of those three steps is done by a sub-function:

```
rms←{
    Root←{⍵*0.5}               ⇦ Define Root
    Mean←{(+/⍵)÷ρ,⍵}           ⇦ Define Mean
    Square←{⍵×⍵}               ⇦ Define Square
    Root Mean Square ⍵         ⇦ Apply these 3 functions to argument ⍵
}
      rms 15 20 34 19 15 21 14
20.71576349
```

9 - Recursion

A function is ***Recursive*** when it calls itself, generally to calculate the Nth step of an algorithm from its $(N-1)^{th}$ step.

For example, the factorial of N can be defined as N times the factorial of N-1. Of course, some condition must specify when the process is supposed to stop. In our example, the factorial of 1 is not calculated, but set to 1. A recursive function could be written as follows:

```
     ∇ Z←Fact N
[1]    Z←1
[2]    →(N<2)/0
[3]    Z←N×Fact N-1                ⇦ The function calls itself
     ∇

      Fact 8
40320
```

Be careful

Recursive solutions are generally very elegant, however:

- Because a function may call itself a great number of times before it reaches the exit condition, this technique may need a lot of memory if the function works on huge arrays.
- When the function calls itself, the variables calculated during one step must not interfere with the calling context. You must carefully localise all your variables (which is the reason for the possible large memory consumption, as the local variables in all recursions may exist at the same time).

Recursion is never mandatory. A recursive function can always be re-written using looping instead of recursion.

Recursion in D-Fns

D-Fns, like procedural functions, can be recursive. A function can refer to itself explicitly (by its own name), but one can also use the special symbol ∇ to represent this self-call.

For example, one can calculate a factorial with a recursive function; it can be defined with two equivalent notations, one using its name, and one using the implicit self-reference *Del* (or *Carrot*):

```
DFact1←{                          DFact2←{
     ⍵=1:1                              ⍵=1:1
     ⍵×DFact1 ⍵-1                       ⍵×∇ ⍵-1
}                                 }

      DFact2 7
5040
```

An implicit self-reference using ∇ needs less interpretative overhead, and therefore it may execute more quickly. Moreover, it will continue to work even if the function is renamed.

10 - Synonyms

Synonyms are defined on the spot by associating a new name with an **existing** primitive, defined, or derived function. For example:

```
      Shape ← ⍴                  ⇦ Synonym of a primitive function
      Mean ← Average             ⇦ Synonym of a defined function
      Sum ← +/                   ⇦ Synonym of a derived function
```

From now on, one can use the words `Shape`, `Mean`, and `Sum` instead of the corresponding expressions:

Normal expressions

```
      +/12 47 31 23
113
      ⍴Prod
5 2 12
      Average 12 47 31 23
28.25
```

Using synonyms

```
      Sum 12 47 31 23
113
      Shape Prod
5 2 12
      Mean 12 47 31 23
28.25
```

Remark 1

It is important to notice that this is not a way of creating a **new** function by assembling a collection of symbols or functions together. For example, we defined a synonym for `⍴`, because it is a single function, but we cannot do the same for `Rank`, because that would need the use of two primitive functions.

`Rank ← ⍴⍴` would cause a `SYNTAX ERROR`

`Sum ← +/` is not an exception because `+/` represents a single *derived function*

Remark 2

When defining a synonym, the contents of the original function are not duplicated.
For example, if you type `Copy ← Meanval` the word `Copy` just contains a link to `Meanval`, but the code of `Meanval` is not duplicated.

As evidence of this, if you try to display the code of `Copy` using `⎕VR 'Copy'`, you will see the code of `Meanval`, as shown below:

```
      Copy ← Meanval                 ⇦ Create the synonym
      ⎕vr 'Copy'
     ∇ res←Meanval vec;sum;nb        ⇦ Though this is the Visual Representation of Copy
[1]    sum←+/vec                       this is the header of Meanval
[2]    nb←⍴vec
[3]    res←sum÷nb
     ∇
```

Furthermore, if you were to modify some statement in `Meanval` (for example to multiply the result by 100), `Copy` is still pointing to the same code, and the two functions remain the same:

```
      ⎕vr 'Copy'
     ∇ res←Meanval vec;sum;nb
[1]    sum←+/vec
[2]    nb←⍴vec
[3]    res←100×sum÷nb                ⇦ The modification was made in Meanval but
     ∇                                 Copy points to this new code
```

Warning!

Some typing errors may create involuntary synonyms:

For example, you intended to type: `Val ← Average 41 11 19`

But you inadvertently pressed the *Enter* key and just typed: `Val ← Average`

You created a synonym! And now, if you try again to enter the correct expression, it doesn't work:

`Val ← Average 41 11 19` would cause a `SYNTAX ERROR` because `Val` is now a function!

In such a case, the only thing you can do is: `)erase Val`

More generally, once a *Synonym* has been defined, it cannot be modified using Dyalog's function editor. Unless a new function assignment is made one can only delete and recreate it.

11 - About the Text Editor

Most of the features of the built-in Dyalog APL editor are very similar to those of other familiar editors, but some are very specific, and we therefore provide a brief description of the specific editing facilities of Dyalog APL.

11.1 What Can You Edit?

The following table shows the different item types that can be displayed using the text editor. Some of them can be modified (Editable), some others cannot: they can only be viewed

The table contains a list of the item types, the default foreground and background colours (FCol / BCol) used to represent them, and a Yes or No depending on whether they can be modified or not.

Item type	FCol	BCol	Editable
Function	*various*	White	yes
Character matrix	Green	Black	yes
Character vector	Black	White	yes
Vector of text vectors	Blue	Black	yes
Any numeric array	White	Grey	no (*)
Mixed array	Blue	Grey	no
Object representation (⎕OR)	White	Red	no

(*) Note that numeric matrices can be edited using the numeric editor tool. Just place the cursor on the variable name and click on the ▦ button. This does not apply to vectors or higher rank variables.

11.2 What Can You Do?

11.2.1 - Cut / Copy / Paste

It is possible to Cut / Copy / Paste text inside an edit window, but also from one edit window to another one. It is also possible to copy text from the session window and paste it into any function, operator, or editable variable, or the reverse. So, if you have entered some experimental expressions in the session, you can drag and drop them into a defined function.

The standard Windows clipboard is used, so you can also copy and paste between Dyalog APL and other applications, or between multiple Dyalog APL sessions.

Some older APL keyboard layouts are in conflict with the newer Windows shortcuts for Cut, Copy and Paste (*Ctrl*+X, *Ctrl*+C and *Ctrl*+V). If these keystrokes produce APL characters, use the Edit menu, or use the three following shortcuts, which are the original Windows shortcuts:

Cut	*Shift+Delete*
Copy	*Ctrl+Insert*
Paste	*Shift+Insert*

11.2.2 - Drag/Drop Restrictions

You may *move* or *copy* text using drag/drop, but the following behaviour applies:

- If you drag/drop text within the same Edit window, the default operation is a *move*. If you press the Ctrl key at the same time, the operation is a *copy*.
- If you drag/drop text from one window to another window, the operation is always a *copy*.
- If you drag/drop text within the Session window, the operation is always a *copy*.

11.2.3 - Open a New Line or Statement

The simplest way to open a new line is as follows: place the cursor at the left or right end of a line, check that the keyboard is in *Insert* mode (the default), and press the *Enter* key.

It is also possible to activate the menu Edit ⇨ Open Line, or depress *Ctrl+Shift+Insert*.

11.2.4 - Delete a Line or Statement

The simplest way to delete a single line is to press *Ctrl+Delete*, or use Edit ⇨ Delete line.

To delete a block of lines, just select the text with the keyboard or with the mouse, and press the *Delete* key.

11.2.5 - Exit the Editor

We have already seen the three main ways of leaving the editor:

- Press the *Escape* key, or activate the menu option File ⇨ Exit. This fixes the modifications and closes the edit window.
- Press *Shift+Escape* or activate File ⇨ Abort. This leaves the editor without saving the modifications; they are lost.
- File ⇨ Fix fixes the modifications but does not close the edit window.

11.3 Undo, Redo, Replay

11.3.1 - Undo

As long as the contents of an Edit window have not been fixed, it is possible to undo all the modifications made since the last fix.

To ***undo*** modifications, you can:

- Press *Ctrl+Shift+BackSpace* as many times as needed
- Or activate the menu Edit ⇨ Undo

When all the modifications have been removed, a warning dialog box displays "No more".

This is similar to the *Ctrl-Z* keyboard shortcut available in many other Windows programs.

11.3.2 - Redo

Having used ***undo***, it is possible to restore the changes that you have undone, one by one.

To ***redo*** modifications, you can:

- Press *Ctrl+Shift+Enter* as many times as needed
- Or activate the menu Edit ⇨ Redo

When all the modifications have been restored, a warning dialog box displays "No more"

It must be emphasised that the *Undo/Redo* facility applies only to the current window. If some pieces of text have been copied to another window, the contents of the other window are not affected by the *Undo* or *Redo* operations.

This is similar to the *Ctrl-Y* keyboard shortcut available in many other Windows programs.

11.3.3 - Replay Input Lines

The same keyboard shortcuts (*Ctrl+Shift+BackSpace* and *Ctrl+Shift+Enter*) can be used to scroll up and down the statements that you have previously entered into the session window. For example, suppose you have typed:

```
(Prod×1.07)-⌈/,Forecast
```
Result
```
250 17⍴BigNum
```
Result
```
5 10 3 17⍴Boys
```
Result

Suppose now that you want to re-execute the first statement with 1.17 instead of 1.07. You *could* scroll back through the considerable amount of output (generated by the 3 expressions) to find this statement. However instead, you can search just through the *input* statements (only the lines that you have entered, excluding any output), which are stored in a dedicated Input History buffer:

- Press *Ctrl+Shift+BackSpace* to scroll back through the Input History buffer as many times as needed.
- Press *Ctrl+Shift+Enter* to scroll forward, if you went too far back.

Once you have found the line, you can change it (or not) and then execute it again by pressing the *Enter* key.

The size of this dedicated buffer is controlled by the following configuration parameter:

Options ⇨ Configuration ⇨ Log ⇨ History buffer size [Kb]

11.3.4 - Advice

When you type into any of the lines displayed on your session screen, these lines are marked as *active*, even if you havn't actually changed anything. All *active* lines will be executed again from top to bottom when you press the *Enter* key.

If you want to de-activate one of them, place the cursor on it and press *Shift+Escape*. You can do the same if you do not want to execute something you typed.

11.4 Miscellaneous

11.4.1 - Reformat

When writing a long function with many control structures, it is convenient to see the lines indented. Indentation is easily lost during editing, but you can reformat the function at any time by pressing *Ctrl+Keypad Slash* (/), or by selecting the menu item Edit ⇨ Reformat.

11.4.2 - Show/Hide Line Numbers

Whether or not you prefer to have line numbers displayed is just a question of taste. This is controlled by the configuration parameter:

Options ⇨ Configuration ⇨ General ⇨ Show line numbers

This configuration parameter determines the status when Dyalog APL is started. If you change the setting it will not have any effect until next time Dyalog APL is started.

Regardless of this parameter setting you can always toggle line numbers on/off in the current session in one of the following ways:

- Press *Ctrl+Keypad minus*
- Press the [···] button.in the session toolbar
- In your edit window, activate: View ⇨ Line numbers

The change immediately applies to all edit windows, but will not be remembered when the Dyalog APL session is closed.

11.4.3 - Localise Names

To avoid forgetting to add a name to the list of local names in the function header, you can declare it local/global when typing it.

- The easy way: when typing the name, press *Ctrl+Up*. This toggle works when the cursor is placed on the name or on its borders (just before or just after).
- The heavy way: in your edit window, activate: Edit ⇨ Toggle local name

11.4.4 - Comment / Uncomment Lines

It is often useful to (perhaps temporarily) neutralise a set of statements in the middle of a function.

Just select the corresponding statements with the mouse or with the keyboard, and use the Edit menu:

Edit ⇨ Comment selected lines	to neutralise the statements
Edit ⇨ Uncomment selected lines	to activate them again

You can also use *Ctrl-Alt-,* (*Ctrl-Alt-Comma)* to comment them all at once, and *Ctrl-Alt-. (Ctrl-Alt-Period)* to uncomment them all.

12 - SALT

Up to now, all the functions and operators we defined were created with an APL code editor, and stored in an APL workspace.

This monolithic *one-workspace* approach to application development works well for small applications developed by single programmers, but is often inappropriate for large applications developed by teams of programmers. Some groups have tackled this problem by storing code in ancillary workspaces or special files. Code is then copied dynamically into the main workspace when required, using techniques that will be explained later.

Had the same application been developed in a more traditional language, programs would be entered and modified using a text editor, stored in separate text files, and maintained independently from one another under the aegis of a *source-code management* system that allows the team of programmers to coordinate their activities and keep track of changes.

This type of application development approach is also available in Dyalog APL, using a source code management system named ***SALT***, for *Simple APL Library Toolkit*.

SALT makes it possible to store sets of APL functions, operators, and variables in text files that may be edited and managed using either the built-in APL code editor or industry standard tools. This makes it easier to share code between projects and teams of developers.

To take full advantage of this new technique of developing applications, you should first learn about *Namespaces* and related topics, notations, and commands. For this reason, *SALT* will be studied in Chapter R.

Don't worry,
we have a First-Aid kit
in Chapter E
!?
{(+/⍵)÷⍴⍵}

Exercises

D-11 Write a multi-line *direct* function which displays the greatest value in a numeric matrix, and its position (Row and Column) in the matrix, for example:

```
      MaxPlace Actual
The greatest value: 507, is in row 2, column 6
```

D-12 Conversions from Celsius to Fahrenheit degrees and back can be done using the following formulas:

```
F ← 32+9×C÷5          C ← 5×(F-32)÷9
```

Can you program a function that makes the conversion `C→F` or `F→C` according to its right argument?

```
      86 32 212 Convert 'F-C'
30 0 100
      7 15 25   Convert 'C-F'
44.6 59 7
```

D-13 Summing the items of a vector is so simple in APL (`+/vec`), that one cannot understand why this simple problem needs a loop in traditional languages! Just for fun, can you program such a loop in APL? Use control structures.

```
      +/ 31 37 44 19 27 60 42
260
      LoopSum  31 37 44 19 27 60 42
260
```

D-14 In exercise D-3, you were asked to reverse the order of a vector of items. Even if it is a strange idea, can you do the same operation using a loop, moving letter after letter?

```
      ReverLoop 'The solution without loop was much better'
retteb hcum saw pool tuohtiw noitulos ehT
```

D-15 In a given numeric matrix with `N` columns, we would like to insert subtotals after each group of `G` columns (where `G` is a divisor of `N`).

Try to write a function to do that, following these 3 steps:

- Reshape the matrix so that it fits in `G` columns only, with the necessary number of rows to contain all the values.
- Concatenate, on the right, the totals of each row.
- Then reshape again that new matrix to obtain the final result.

In the examples below, the original matrix appears in grey, and the inserted subtotals appear in black:

```
      Twelve
51 40 18 90 72 75 13  4 35 18 95 29
85 20 87  6 60  3 53 73 32 34 10 36
40 60 56 33 60  3 15 60 63 18 63  5
      3 SubSum Twelve
51 40 18 109 90 72 75 237 13  4 35  52 18 95 29 142
85 20 87 192  6 60  3  69 53 73 32 158 34 10 36  80
40 60 56 156 33 60  3  96 15 60 63 138 18 63  5  86
      6 SubSum Twelve
51 40 18 90 72 75 346 13  4 35 18 95 29 194
85 20 87  6 60  3 261 53 73 32 34 10 36 238
40 60 56 33 60  3 252 15 60 63 18 63  5 224
```

D-16 This is a very classic problem: we want to partition a text vector each time a given separator is found, and make a matrix from these pieces. We will see later a solution without a loop, but for the moment, sorry, you will need a loop.

```
      '/' Sorry 'You/will/need a/loop/to solve/this/exercise'
You
will
need a
loop
to solve
this
exercise
```

D-17 Given any positive integer N, derive from it a series of values, like this:

- The first item is the number N itself
- If the current value of N is **even**, the next value will be N÷2
- If the current value of N is **odd**, the next value will be 1+3×N

It appears that after a certain number of iterations, the final value of N will be 1.

This property, which has never been proven, is known as the *Syracuse* (or Collatz or Ullam) *conjecture*. In mathematics, a conjecture is a theory which appears to always be true, but nobody has been able to prove that it must be true.

Can you write a function to calculate the values generated from a given start value:

```
      Syracuse 37
37 112 56 28 14 7 22 11 34 17 52 26 13 40 20 10 5 16 8 4 2 1
```

You can write it using loops or recursion, and write a procedural or a direct function.

The Specialist's Section

Each chapter is followed by a "Specialist's Section" like this one.
This section is dedicated to skilled APLers, who wish to improve their knowledge.

You will find here rare or complex usages of the concepts presented in the chapter, or discover extended explanations which need the knowledge of some symbols that will be seen much further in the book

If you are exploring APL for the first time,
skip this section and go to the next chapter

Spe-1 Shadowed Names

A name can be localised in a Trad-function only if the programmer explicitly specifies its name in the function header. But a function can dynamically define new variables or new functions, using Execute (⍎) and ⎕FX.

So during function execution, names of new variables and functions may be created dynamically. They could not therefore be localised explicitly when the function was written, but they can be localised, or ***Shadowed*** dynamically at run-time.

One or more names can be shadowed using the System function ⎕SHADOW, which accepts a vector of names separated by blanks, or a matrix of names, with one name per row (but **not** a nested vector of names). For example:

`Dummy` is the textual representation of a niladic function named `Demonstration`, as a character matrix (also know as the function's *Canonical Representation*):

```
Demonstration
'This is just'
'a demo function'
```

`Ombra` is a function with no localised names:

```
      ∇ CanRep Ombra Text
[1]     ⎕SHADOW Text,' ',CanRep[1;]
[2]     ⍎Text,'←1'
[3]     ⍎⎕FX CanRep
[4]     ∘ ⍝ Intentional error
      ∇
```

Let us execute it: `Dummy Ombra 'New'`

[1] The function shadows "New" and "Demonstration"
[2] It dynamically creates a variable named "New"
[3] It fixes a new function named "Demonstration" and executes it

When the function is interrupted in [4], it is easy to see that those items have been created. But when the function completes, New and Demonstration disappear: they were only local names.

Spe-2 Loop Control

Loops programmed with traditional branch arrows are controlled by the APL statements. Loops using *Control structures* are controlled by the interpreter. For that reason, if you trace loops programmed with Repeat, or For, you will see that the first statement of the loop is executed only once, the following iterations execute only the "useful" statements. It is different for a While loop, because the test is placed in the first statement.

This has a surprising consequence. Imagine a For loop, using a control variable named Again which is supposed to take three successive values: 12 54 86.

But the programmer erroneously alters the value of Again during execution:

```
     ∇ Mess;Again
[1]    :For Again :In 12 54 86
[2]        Again
[3]        Again←'Who modified me?'
[4]        Again
[5]    :End
     ∇
```

```
      Mess
12
Who modified me?                    ⇦ At each iteration, Again is modified
54                                  ⇦ But it is automatically reset to the correct value
Who modified me?                      at each new iteration
86
Who modified me?
```

Spe-3 Labels and the Branch Arrow

Spe-3.1 - Niladic Arrow

A niladic *Branch arrow* → means: quit the current execution, i.e. quit the current function and all the calling functions, whatever the depth of the execution stack.

This is different from branching to zero `→0` which means: quit the current function and resume execution in the calling environment.

When an execution is interrupted, a niladic *Branch arrow* clears its execution stack.

When an evaluated input value is requested by a *Quad* (⎕), a niladic *Branch arrow* stops the request and forces an exit from the function and from all the calling functions.

Note, however, that a niladic Branch arrow only clears the most current execution stack. If several functions have been interrupted and new ones started without first clearing the execution stack, you may have several active stacks. Each stack is identified by an asterisk to the right of the name of the interrupted function:

```
      )si                          ⇦ Show all three execution stacks
#.foo[4]*
#.goo[1]
#.foo[4]*
#.goo[1]
#.foo[4]*
#.goo[1]
      →                            ⇦ Clear the uppermost stack, leaving two
      )si
#.foo[4]*
#.goo[1]
#.foo[4]*
#.goo[1]
      )reset                       ⇦ This will clear all execution stacks in one go
      )si
```

Spe-3.2 - Branch to a Wrong Label

We said that a *Label* is processed as a numeric ***local variable*** which takes its value from the line number on which it appears. For example, if a function contains the statement:

```
[23]    Next: NewPrice←OldPrice×(1-Discount)
```

Then `Next` is a numeric value equal to 23. It is like a "read only variable", since you cannot modify it: Any assignment to `Next` would cause a SYNTAX ERROR. However, the value of `Next` will change if some lines are deleted or inserted before line 23.

For this reason, the statements `→Next` and `:GoTo Next` are equivalent to `→23` - but only as long as the label `Next` appears in line no. 23!

We also said that a branch to zero causes an exit from the current function. This is also the case for any jump to a line number which is outside the number of lines in the function. For example `→50` would terminate any function which has less than 50 lines.

Now imagine two functions, one calling the other:

```
     ∇ MainFun
[1]     Any statements
...
[12]    SubFun
[13]    'You are back!'
...
[87]  Special: Instruction
...
     ∇
```

```
     ∇ SubFun
[1]     Any statements
...
[9]     :GoTo Special
[10]    'This will not work'
     ∇
```

- When `MainFun` is executed, "`Special`" immediately becomes a read-only variable whose value is 87.
- When `SubFun` is called, `Special` is local to `MainFun`, but global to `SubFun`, so it is visible, and is equal to 87.
- When evaluated, the jump `:GoTo Special` (or `→Special`) is equivalent to `:GoTo 87`.
- But because the function has only 10 lines this will terminate `SubFun`.
- Execution then continues at `MainFun[13]`, not at `MainFun[87]`.

Conclusion: Be very careful when using labels and un-localised names in general!

Spe-4 Other Conditional Execution

In the course of this Chapter you have learned how to program conditional execution, using control structures or traditional branching techniques.

APL provides two other methods: The *Execute* function and the *Power* operator.

Spe-4.1 - Conditional Execution Using Execute

The function *Execute* (`⍎`) will be studied in Chapter F; it executes any character vector given as a right argument, as if it were an expression that had been typed into the APL session window. But if the vector is empty, nothing will be executed. This feature can be used to conditionally execute a statement. Let us consider the following expression:

```
⍎(Diff<Limit)/'Range←¯5 5'
```

If `(Diff<Limit)`is satisfied:

`1/'Range←¯5 5'` gives `'Range←¯5 5'`
and `⍎'Range←¯5 5'` will execute the expression, so `Range` will be set to `¯5 5`.

If `(Diff<Limit)`is **not** satisfied,

`0/'Range←¯5 5'` gives an empty vector,
and `⍎''` does nothing, so `Range` will not be assigned.

More generally, one can write: ⍎(*Condition*)/*Text*

When the expression on the right contains quotes, they must be doubled, and the expression may become more complex to read. Using *Execute* will in general compromise the ability to analyse the code in order to, for example, search for references to a given function or global variable. For these reasons, and also because executed expressions may run slightly slower than ordinary statements, this technique should be avoided. It is mentioned only because it has been used for years by many programmers, before better tools became available in APL.

Advice: Prefer control structures.

Spe-4.2 - Conditional Execution Using the Power Operator

The *Power operator* (⍣) will be studied in Chapter J; it must not be confused with the *Power function* (*).

Power executes a given function *N* times. Of course, if *N* is equal to 1, the function is executed once, and if *N* is 0, the function is not executed at all. For example, in 7.3.4, we wrote a function which rounds a vector of values:

```
      A ← 37                              ⇦ Let us prepare two variables
      Vec ← 17.4269 69.8731 82.3137
      Round Vec                           ⇦ This is the normal use of Round
17.43 69.87 82.31
      (Round⍣(A>20))Vec                   ⇦ When the right argument of Power is 1
17.43 69.87 82.31                           Round is applied once
      (Round⍣(A>80))Vec                   ⇦ When the right argument of Power is 0
17.4269 69.8731 82.3137                     Round is not applied: the vector is unchanged
```

We must separate the operator's right argument from the resulting derived function's argument.

We can use a "no-op" function like + as a separator or use parentheses.

More generally, one can write: {*LeftOp*} (*Function*⍣(*Condition*)) *RightOp*

Spe-5 Name Category of Synonyms

The System function *Name Category* (⎕NC) indicates if a name currently represents a variable, a function, an operator, and so on.

When applied to a nested vector of names, it returns an extended result, which gives more precision. For example:

```
      ⎕nc 'Round' 'Average'
3.1 3.2
```

`3.1`	means that	`Round`	is a *Procedural* function
`3.2`	means that	`Average`	is a *Direct* function

Let us now create some synonyms:

```
      SynRound←Round              ⇦ Synonym of a Procedural defined function
      SynAverage←Average          ⇦ Synonym of a Direct defined function
      Rho←ρ                       ⇦ Synonym of a Primitive function
      Sum←+/                      ⇦ Synonym of a Derived function
```

```
      ⎕NC 'SynRound' 'SynAverage' 'Rho' 'Sum'
3.1  3.2  3.3  3.3
```

This makes clear that:

- Synonyms of defined functions have the same *Name Category* as the corresponding defined functions.
- Synonyms of *primitive* or *derived* functions have a *Name Category* equal to 3.3

Spe-6 Bare Output

When using *Quote* (⎕) to input data the prompt and the user's answer appear on different lines on the screen.

When using a *Quote-Quad* (⍞) to input data, it is possible to force the system to issue the user with a prompt and collect his or her input on the same line of the screen. This is done by first assigning the prompt (a character vector) to ⍞, and then referencing ⍞. When the assignment and reference is performed like this as successive operations, the system does not throw a new-line after the prompt, and the user-input is collected on the same line as the prompt. This is called "*Bare Output*".

Here is an example:

```
      ⍞←'This is my question:' ⋄ Z←⍞
This is my question:And this is my answer
```

In this example, the question appears on the screen (here in black), and the user answered on the same line (in red).

What we get in `Z` is the complete line: Question + Answer:

```
      Z
This is my question:And this is my answer
```

Using *Take* and *Drop*, it is possible to remove the question, like in this demonstration function:

```
     ∇ Z←Demo;FN;NA;CY
        ⍞←20↑'First name ............'
        FN←20↓⍞
        ⍞←20↑'Name ..................'
        NA←20↓⍞
        ⍞←20↑'Country................'
        CY←20↓⍞
        Z←FN,' ',NA,' ',CY
     ∇

      Demo
First name .........Charles
Name ...............Darwin        ⇦ The answers are well aligned
Country.............UK
Charles Darwin UK                 ⇦ We get only the user's answers
```

Spe-7 :InEach

The control phrase `:For` ... `:In` can be used to assign values to several control variables. One can also use `:InEach` which assigns one item from each of a set of nested values to the corresponding control variable. Sometimes `:In` is more convenient than,`:InEach` and sometimes the reverse is true, as we will now show:

Let us assume that data for an invoice is represented as a number of lines, each with a quantity and a price:

```
      Invoice1 ← (10 100)(20 200)(30 300)
```

Then we can process each line in a loop using this function:

```
     ∇ z←Process1 Invoice
        :For (q p) :In Invoice
            q×p          ⍝ "Process" this invoice line
        :EndFor
     ∇

      Process1 Invoice1
1000
4000
9000
```

Some day somebody decides to deliver the invoice data in a slightly different way: First all quantities, then all prices:

```
      Invoice2 ← (10 20 30)(100 200 300)
```

Then we only need to modify our processing function to use `:InEach` instead of `:In`:

```
     ∇ z←Process2 Invoice
[1]    :For (q p) :InEach Invoice
[2]        q×p          ⍝ "Process" this invoice line
[3]    :EndFor
     ∇

      Process2 Invoice2
1000
4000
9000
```

Rules:

In `:For Vars :InEach NesVec`	`⍴Vars` is equal to the shape of `NesVec`.
In `:For Vars :In NesVec`	`⍴Vars` is equal to the shape of each **item** in `NesVec`.

Chapter E: First Aid Kit

It's a pity, but it is impossible to develop applications that work perfectly. Applications always contain errors due to programming mistakes, incorrect use of function calls, or external reasons, such as a missing file or the abnormal termination of an external (non-APL) piece of code.

All these problems may interrupt the normal processing of an application, and require immediate corrective action. The aim of this chapter is to give you the basis to deal with these situations, and work through the experience.

Later, in Chapter M you will see that it is possible to trap and hide unpredictable errors or events, in order to provide a safe environment for the user.

Because APL is an interpreted language, program execution is not aborted, just suspended when an exception occurs. Then the programmer has access to all the application variables, and can diagnose the problem. If he can modify the code or correct some environmental dependency, he may be able to restart the program from the very point it had been interrupted, until a new exception occurs, and so on. This gives great flexibility when debugging applications.

In this chapter, you will learn how to:

- interpret error messages,
- interpret the information provided by various system indicators,
- trace the execution of an application step by step,
- set *break-points* in strategic places to help debugging.

A forgotten comma, an incorrect axis, a missing parenthesis, a scalar where you expected a vector, can all cause an error and it may sometimes be very difficult for a beginner to understand the reason. Try to get help from people who have a better understanding of APL: you will save time, and learn a lot from them.

1 - When an Error Occurs

1.1 Our First Error

Even when you use a function, that is in itself perfectly correct, errors may occur if you call it with arguments that are not consistent with the function's requirements. We will use this type of mistake to illustrate what happens when an error occurs.

In the previous chapter, we wrote a function to interlace two matrices of the same shape. This function works perfectly if you stick to its rules, but what happens if you call it with matrices that *don't* have the same shape?

1.1.1 - Your Environment and Indicators

Let us try to interlace `Forecast` (4 rows / 6 columns) with a 3 by 5 matrix, and see what happens:

```
      Forecast Interlace 3 5⍴⍳15
LENGTH ERROR
Interlace[4] R[;even]←B
               ^
```

⇦ First, an error message is issued

Simultaneously a trace window appears
⇩

Figure E-1

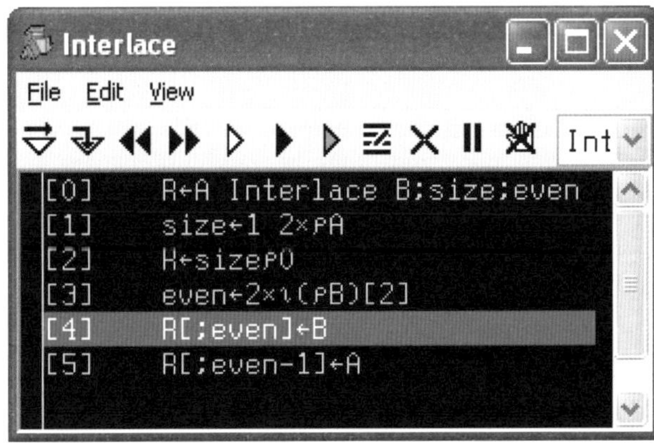

And in the lower right corner of your session screen, you can see information displayed in red

⇩

Ins | MO
¯RAP | ⎕SI:1 | ⎕IO:1

APL will preserve the entire execution context (local variables, and program status indicators); so that you can resume function execution once the error has been diagnosed and repaired.

Let us now examine the meaning of these things.

1.1.2 - The Diagnostic Message

The ***Diagnostic Message*** is displayed on three rows of the screen which show:

- The type of error (explained in Section 2.1).
- The function name [and line number] - the statement that can't be executed.
- A caret which is placed where the statement was interrupted.

A *System function* named ⎕DM returns the latest *Diagnostic Message*. It is a 3-item nested vector, with a sub-vector for each of the 3 lines, as shown below:

```
      DISPLAY ⎕DM
```

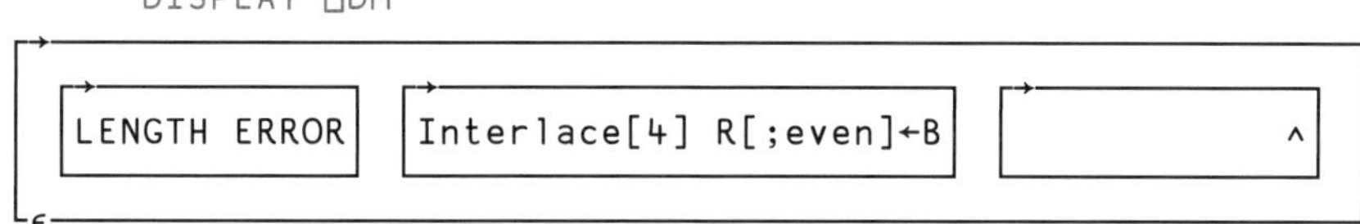

```
┌→──────────────────────────────────────────────────────────────────────┐
│ ┌→───────────┐ ┌→─────────────────────────┐ ┌→─────────────┐ │
│ │LENGTH ERROR│ │Interlace[4] R[;even]←B│ │               ^│ │
│ └────────────┘ └──────────────────────────┘ └──────────────┘ │
└∊──────────────────────────────────────────────────────────────────────┘
```

⎕DM retains this value until a new error occurs to replace it, or until we explicitly clear it.

1.1.3 - State Indicator and Line Counter

Whenever function execution is interrupted for any reason, Dyalog APL keeps track of the exact point where the interrupt occurred in the ***State Indicator*** (SI for short). This value of the State Indicator may be obtained using a system command or a system function:

System command	**System function**
`)SI` `#.Interlace[4]*`	`⎕SI` `Interlace`

The *system function* ⎕SI returns a nested vector containing only the names of interrupted functions; in this example only one name appears.

The *system command*)SI reports, for each function in the execution stack:

- A path (here #.) which will be explained later, in Chapter O. Ignore it for now.
- The function name (Interlace).
- The number of the statement on which function execution has stopped [4].
- An asterisk which means that this function has been interrupted.

What you see in red in the bottom right-hand corner of your session (⎕SI:1) is the number of functions referenced in the *State Indicator*. Normally, this number should be zero, and displayed in black; as soon as an error or an interrupt occurs, it is displayed in red as a warning.

APL also keeps, in a ***Line Counter***, the list of function lines waiting for execution. In this case there is only one. It can be obtained from the *System function* ⎕LC:

```
      ⎕LC
4                                ⇦ A function has been interrupted on line 4
```

1.1.4 - The Trace Window

If you are running Dyalog APL using the default *Tracer* behaviour, a window pops up, with the function text displayed in yellow on a black background, and the statement in error shown in white on red.

If it does not appear spontaneously, just press *Ctrl+Enter*.

Then activate: Options⇨Configuration⇨Trace/Edit, and select "*Show trace stack on error*".

We shall see later how this trace window can be used. **Do not close it** for the moment.

1.1.5 - You Can See the Local Variables

Your cursor may not be in this (Trace) window: it may remain in the session window, so that you can conveniently enter expressions to diagnose what has happened. If the trace window *does* have the focus you can just switch the focus to the session window and work there, without closing the trace window.

Because the function has been interrupted, all its local variables are visible:

- You can look at their values.
- You can even modify them (sometimes this may help).

```
      ⍴B
3 5
      size                       ⇦ The future result size is correct.
4 12
      ⍴R[;even]                  ⇦ But we cannot assign the 3 rows of B
4 5                                into the 4 rows of R.
```

1.1.6 - What Can We Do?

Obviously, in this case there is nothing we can do: the function is correct, we just misused it! We could perhaps forget about it and go on to do something else. However, if we do so, APL will retain the entire execution stack of functions and local variables in its interrupted state. If we are not going to continue debugging, we should really clean up by getting the system out of this state.

There are 3 ways to achieve this. If you want to try out all three of them, you will need to reproduce the same error after each exit operation:

- First option: close the trace window. You can use the standard Windows methods to close it, or you can click on it to give it the focus, and then press *Escape* to close it.
- Second option: type a branch arrow → in the session window (see Chapter D, Section Spe-3).
- Third option: execute the `)Reset` command in the session window.

Whichever option you chose, you can verify that:

- Both `)SI` and `⎕SI` now give an empty result.
- The red indication `⎕SI:1` is replaced by a black `⎕SI:0` in the session status bar.
- However, there is a little difference: with the first two methods, `⎕DM` retains its value (and keeps track of the latest error), while `)Reset` also clears `⎕DM`.

1.2 Cascade of Errors

We shall now see what happens when an error occurs in a sub-function.

1.2.1 - Preparation

A palindrome is a string of characters which remains the same when it is reversed, after any non-alphabetic characters (including spaces) have been removed.

For example: `Cigar: toss it in a can. It is so tragic`
or `Was it a car or a cat I saw?`

We shall try to write a function which detects whether or not a given string of characters is a palindrome. We are going to use two sub-functions:

`Upper` removes all non-alphabetic characters, and transforms the remaining letters into upper-case characters:

```
     ∇ Z←Upper text;low;up;all
[1]    low←'abcdefghijklmnopqrstuvwxyz'
[2]    up ←'ABCDEFGHIJKLMNOPQRSTUVWXYZ'
[3]    all←low,up
[4]    text←(text∊all)/text
[5]    Z←(up,up)[all⍳text]
     ∇
Upper 'Visit New York'                ⇨ VISITNEWYORK
```

`Reverse` reverses the items of a vector. This is one possible solution to exercise D-3, written by someone who was unaware that APL has a *reverse* primitive (see Chapter G):

```
     ∇ Z←Reverse vec;index
[1]    index←(1+⍴vec)-⍳⍴vec
[2]    Z←vec[index]
     ∇
```

```
Reverse 'Demonstration'              ⇨ noitartsnomeD
```

`Palindrome` compares the upper-cased original vector and its reversed version:

```
     ∇ Z←Palindrome vector;torvec
[1]    vector←Upper vector
[2]    torvec←Reverse vector
[3]    Z←∧/torvec=vector
     ∇
```

Let's try it out:

```
      Palindrome 'Was it a car or a cat I saw?'
1                                              ⇦ This a palindrome.
      Palindrome 'Am I a palindrome?'
0                                              ⇦ This is not a palindrome.
```

Now, in `Palindrome` we decide to replace `Reverse` by `ReverBug`, a deliberately faulty and obtuse version. Not only does it use an unnecessary loop, but it includes some (intentional) errors:

```
     ∇ Z←ReverBug Vec;From;To ⍝ Intentionally faulty
[1]    Z←(⍴Vec)⍴'?'
[2]    From←0
[3]    :Repeat
[4]        From←Frm+1
[5]        To←(⍴Vec)-From
[6]        Z[To]←Vec[From]
[7]    :Until From=⍴Vec
     ∇
```

All these functions are provided in the associated workspace.

1.2.2 - Let Us Create More Errors

First, let us execute the little function `Plus`, shown below, with incorrect arguments, so as to obtain a `LENGTH ERROR`:

```
     ∇ Z←X Plus Y
[1]    Z←X+Y
     ∇
```

```
      5 1 7 Plus 6 2 9 4
LENGTH ERROR
Plus[1] Z←X+Y
       ∧
```

As in the previous example:

- An error message is issued, and a trace window pops up.
- ⎕SI:1 is now displayed in red in the status bar, and)SI contains one line.
- ⎕LC contains the value 1 (the function is interrupted on line 1).

We shall intentionally ignore this error. **Do not close** the trace window.

And now, let us execute Palindrome. An error is immediately reported.

```
      Palindrome 'Was it a car or a cat I saw?'
VALUE ERROR
ReverBug[4] From←Frm+1                ⇦ The word From has been misspelled.
                ∧
```

- A second error message is issued.
- In the bottom right corner of our session, we now have the information ⎕SI:3.
- ⎕LC contains three values: 4 2 1.
- And we now have 3 trace windows instead of one:
  - One window contains Plus, unchanged.
  - A second window contains Palindrome, on a grey background.
  - And on top of that, a window contains ReverBug.

Figure E-2

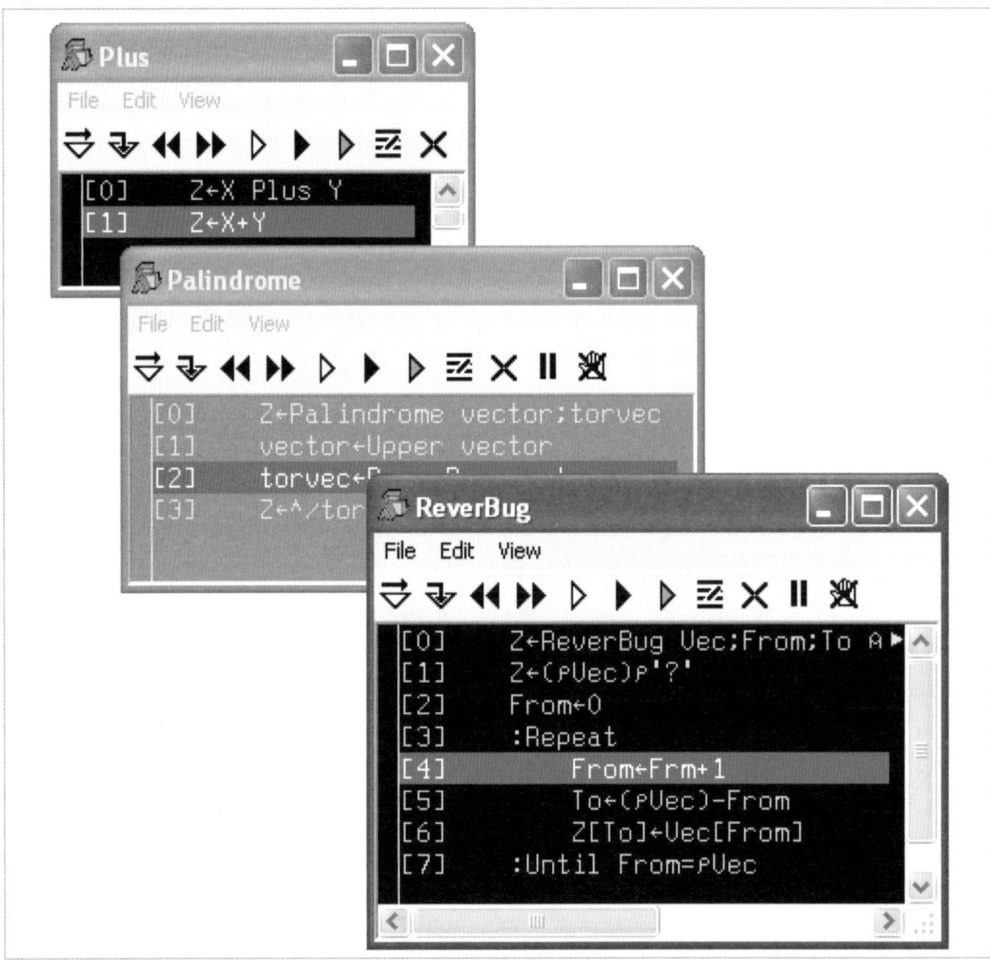

Let us consult the indicators we know. ⎕DM still shows the latest known error, and ⎕SI gives the names of the three interrupted functions, the last one being displayed first:

```
      ⎕DM
VALUE ERROR  ReverBug[4] From←Frm+1                         ^
      ⎕SI
ReverBug  Palindrome  Plus
```

```
      )SI
#.ReverBug[4]*                  ⇦ The star means that this function is interrupted.
#.Palindrome[2]                 ⇦ There is no star to the right of this one, it is
"pending".
#.Plus[1]*                      ⇦ This function has also been interrupted.
```

As you can see, `)SI` is a stack. Starting from the bottom, it indicates that `Plus` was interrupted on line `[1]`. Then `Palindrome[2]` has called `ReverBug`, and finally `ReverBug` caused an error in line `[4]`.

Both `⎕SI` and `⎕LC` report the most recently interrupted function first, followed by the others.

`Palindrome` has not itself generated an error: it is just waiting for the completion of `ReverBug`. The `Palindrome` function is said to be ***Pending***.

For that reason:

- There is no star to the right of `Palindrome` in `)SI`.
- The background of its trace window is grey instead of black.

1.2.3 - Switch to Edit Mode

In this case, the error is obvious and we can try to correct it, but the text displayed in the trace window cannot be edited directly; we must first turn the trace window into an edit window.

To do this, ensure that your cursor is over an empty space in the session window (it must not be over another name) and then:

- just double-click (on nothing),
- or press *Shift+Enter.*

Alternatively, you can switch focus to the trace window and place the cursor before the start of any function line and press *Shift+Enter.*

All three methods turn the black trace window into a white edit window.

You can now modify the incorrect statement (change `Frm` into `From`), and press *Escape* to fix the modification. The system switches back to the black trace window, showing the newly corrected statement.

1.2.4 - Continue Execution

After making the correction, you can choose to either:

- Restart the function from the interruption point.
- Or continue by tracing its execution, statement by statement, to see what happens.

Let us choose the first option. This can be achieved using one of the following methods:

- First method: in the session window, execute `→⎕LC`, which is equivalent to `→4 2 1`. The branch arrow ignores the two last numbers, so the program resumes execution from line number 4 in the function at the top of the stack (`ReverBug` in this case).
- Second method: in the trace window toolbar, press the ▶ (*Continue execution*) button.

The function restarts but, unfortunately, a second error immediately appears:

```
INDEX ERROR
ReverBug[6] Z[To]←Vec[From]
              ∧
```

The indicators are nearly the same; they now tell us that the function is no longer interrupted on line 4, but on line 6.

To diagnose the problem, we can look at the values of our local variables. We can either double-click on their names (which will open each one in a new window), or just type their names in the session; let us use the latter approach:

```
      Z                              ⇦ Something is wrong: the first letter (W) should
ASITACARORACATISAW?                    be in the last position where the "?" is.
      ⍴Vec                           ⇦ We had an argument with 19 letters.
19
      From                           ⇦ And we are trying to move the 19th letter.
19
      To                             ⇦ But the last index equal to zero causes an error.
0
```

Our statement in line `[5]` calculated the wrong index! It would be insufficient to correct the statement and continue with the current execution, because the variables are already wrong. A better solution would be to exit from `ReverBug`, and restart from where `Palindrome` called it.

If we want to return to the calling function, we cannot execute `)Reset` nor `→`, because that would cause a complete exit both from `ReverBug` and from `Palindrome`. The only way back is to ensure that the `ReverBug` trace window has the focus and then press *Escape* to get out of `ReverBug` and return to `Palindrome`.

We are now back in the calling environment:

```
      )si
#.Palindrome[2]*
#.Plus[1]*
```

Notice that `ReverBug` is no longer present in the state indicator and that the asterisk is now displayed alongside `Palindrome`, because `Palindrome` is now the interrupted function.

Let us modify the 5th statement of ReverBug like this: To←(1+⍴vec)-From

Then, resume the execution of Palindrome exactly as we restarted Reverbug:

- Execute →⎕LC in the session.
- Or press the ▶ (*Continue execution*) button in the trace window toolbar.

```
      →⎕LC                                  ⇦ Restart the execution.
1                                           ⇦ Final result: Yes, it is a palindrome!

      )SI
#.Plus[1]*                                  ⇦ We still have an old interrupted function.

      ⎕DM
 INDEX ERROR  ReverBug[6] Z[to]←vec[from]          ^
```

As you can see, ⎕DM does not report the stack of errors, just the last one that occurred.

The best thing we can do now to restore a clean environment is to execute:

```
      )Reset
```

1.3 Information and Actions

1.3.1 - Indicators

When an error occurs, a number of program status indicators are available for the developer's use. Not all of them will be described here; we shall just explore the most useful ones.

)SI	*State indicator*	List of suspended functions with line numbers and state.
⎕SI	*State indicator*	Nested vector of suspended functions names.
⎕DM	*Diagnostic message*	3-item nested vector which reports the message associated with the very latest error.
⎕LC	*Line Counter*	Numeric vector containing the line numbers of functions that are pending or suspended and waiting for execution, the last one being displayed first – the same order as ⎕SI.
⎕EN	***Event Number***	Every type of error or exception is identified by a number. The number of the very latest error is reported by ⎕EN.

Here are some very common *Event Numbers*; they will be explained in the next Section:

```
 1      WS FULL
 2      SYNTAX ERROR
 3      INDEX ERROR
 4      RANK ERROR
 5      LENGTH ERROR
 6      VALUE ERROR
11      DOMAIN ERROR
```

A full list of *Event Numbers* is given in Appendix 6.

1.3.2 - Some Possible Actions

`→⎕LC` Continue the interrupted function from the very statement on which it was interrupted.

`→0` Quit the interrupted function, and return to its calling environment, which may be the session, or a calling function. In the latter case execution will be resumed in the calling function.

`→` Quit the interrupted function and all its calling functions, and return to the session. If other functions are suspended, they remain in the *State Indicator*.

`)Reset` Quit **all** suspended functions, reset the *State Indicator*.
`⎕SI`, `⎕DM`, and `⎕LC` are reset to empty vectors, and `⎕EN` is set to zero.

1.4 Why Should You Reset Your State Indicator?

Please change the 5th statement of `ReverBug` back to reproduce the second error:

Instead of the correct statement: `To←(1+⍴vec)-From`
introduce the error again: `To←(⍴vec)-From`

In the previous chapter, exercise D-6, we asked you to write a dyadic function which returns the list of integer values in the range specified by its two arguments. For example:

```
      17 To 25
17 18 19 20 21 22 23 24 25
```
⇦ It works; you're a genius!

Now, let us run our erroneous function: `ReverBug 'This function does not work'`

An error occurs, but we decide not to reset the *State Indicator*.

Let us now execute our little function To again:

```
      17 To 29
17  0  29                          ⇦ Horror: it no longer works!
      DISPLAY 17 To 29
                                   ⇦ It returns an incorrect result.
```

In fact, our To function is no longer visible; it is hidden by the To variable, which is local to the erroneous function. At the present time, To refers to a one-item vector whose value is zero. That explains the result we obtained.

As soon as we reset the *State Indicator*, the local variables of ReverBug disappear, and the function can be invoked again:

```
      )Reset                       ⇦ Reset the execution stack.
      24 To 30
24 25 26 27 28 29 30               ⇦ Who said that it did not work?
```

So, having a "dirty" state indicator can easily lead to a lot of confusion.

You should also be aware that because APL preserves the full context in which a function stopped or crashed, all the local variables are retained too; this may require a lot of memory space!

Recommendation When a function crashes, always try to clear the stack if you can:

- Try to correct the problem, and resume execution.
- Or, if that is impossible, abort it and reset the execution context by executing)Reset.
- If you can't fix it now, Dyalog will allow you to)SAVE the workspace and try again later.

2 - Most Frequent Error Messages

2.1 Execution Errors

For each common error, we shall give you the most probable reason for the error, some rare cases which may be difficult to debug, and suggest some immediate experiments that you can carry out to help diagnose the problem.

Among the 6 most common errors, 4 are really easy to diagnose, but the last two ones are a bit more complex.

2.1.1 - VALUE ERROR .... (⎕EN=6)

You used a name which does not have a value; it does not represent a variable, a function, or an operator.

Here are some possible reasons:

- Perhaps you misspelled the variable (or function) name, entered the incorrect mixture of upper and lower case characters, or confused the letter "O" with the digit "0", etc.
- You tried to use the result of a function which actually produces no result because in its header line you forgot to specify the name that represents its result. See D-7.2.
- You tried to reference one of the local variables of a function before it was assigned a value. Remember that all the names referenced in the function header are local, including the result.
- Another common cause is an erroneous function header, as explained below.

For example, you intended to create a function named `Travel`, with two arguments named `West` and `East`. When you entered the header, you forgot the space between `Travel` and `East`, so that the function looks like this:

```
      ∇ Z←West TravelEast
[1]     Z←West-East
      ∇
```

Instead, you have defined a monadic function named `West`, with a right argument named `TravelEast`. When you try to use `Travel`, it does not exist, and you get an error.

If you suspect that this has occurred, and you can remember the syntax of the function, check to see if you have a different function whose name is the same as your intended left argument.

If you do not spot it immediately, you can use the (*Search*) tool, provided in the Dyalog APL toolbar or via the menu, Tools ⇨ Search.

In the *Advanced* tab, type the name that you want to search for (here circled in red), deselect "*Match Whole Word*", and, if you are not sure of the case, also deselect "*Match Case*", then click on "*Find now*". You should then discover what the name of the misspelled function really is.

Figure E-3

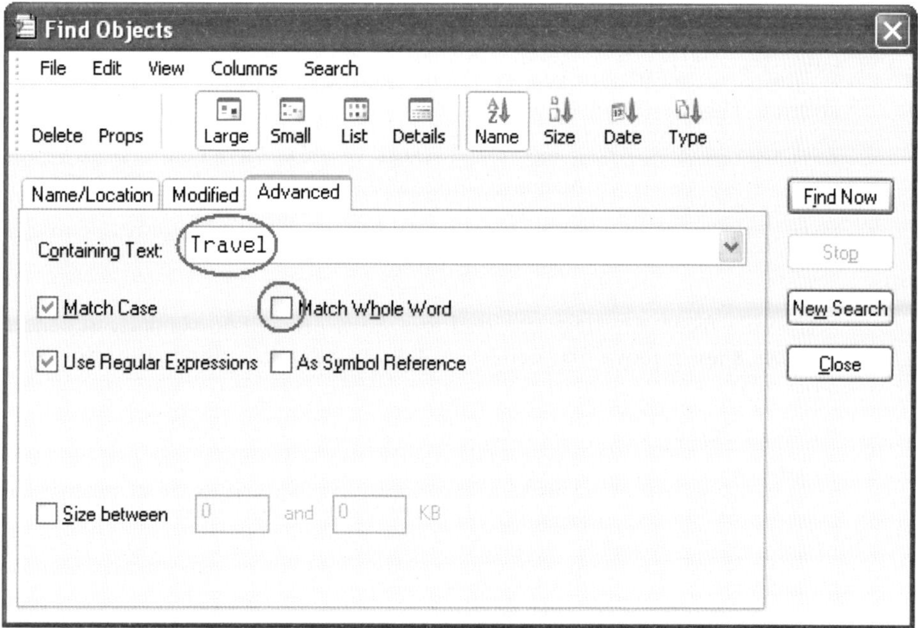

2.1.2 - LENGTH ERROR .... (⎕EN=5)

A *Length Error* usually involves two arguments, because their shapes are inconsistent for a given operation. For example:

```
4 6 8 + 3 7
```

Suggestion If an operation like `X+Y` causes a *Length Error*, look at the shapes of both arguments `X` and `Y`, and see if they are compatible with one another.

Also remember that:

- A matrix with only one row looks like (but is not) a vector: see B-3.4.2.
- A matrix or vector with only one element looks like (but is not) a scalar: see B-3.4.2.
- An incorrectly specified axis may also cause such an error. For example:

Let us create:	`MatA←3 4⍴⍳12`	and	`MatB←5 4⍴⍳16`	
Both	`MatA,MatB`	and	`MatA,[2]MatB`	would cause a *Length Error.*
But	`MatA⍪MatB`	or	`MatA,[1]MatB`	will work.

2.1.3 - RANK ERROR .... (⎕EN=4)

A *Rank Error* means that you tried to do something which is not consistent with the *Rank* of an array. This may involve one or more variables. Here are some common examples:

`Forecast[3 5]` Is incorrect, because `Forecast` is a matrix, not a vector. A semi-colon is needed somewhere: `[;3 5]` or `[3;5]`, or `[3 5;]`.

`Matrix+Vector` This cannot work, even if `Matrix` has only one row, and looks very much like a vector.

Sometimes incorrect syntax can lead to a *Rank Error*. For example, to concatenate the two matrices shown above, the correct syntax is: `MatA,[1]MatB`. But now, suppose that you write:

`MatA[1],MatB` The comma is in the wrong place, and APL tries to calculate `MatA[1]`
This leads to a *Rank error* because `MatA` is a matrix, and not a vector.

Suggestion If a statement causes a *Rank Error*, look at the shapes of all the arrays involved in the expression.

2.1.4 - INDEX ERROR.. (⎕EN=3)

You tried to index a variable, but your index was wrong. For example, you tried to get the 20th element of a vector which has only 17 elements.

This occurs when the index (or one of the items of the index) is:

- Smaller than or equal to zero.
- Greater than the length of the variable, along the specified axis.
- Not an integer.

`Forecast[5;5]` This is wrong. `Forecast` has 6 columns, but only 4 rows: the second index is good, but the first one is not.

The same diagnostic message is issued when an *Axis* is not correct, except that a non-integer axis is required for *Laminate*. For example:

`MatA,[3]MatB` This cannot work, because `MatA` does not have 3 dimensions.

`Vector,[2]100` A vector has only one dimension. Here again, an *Index Error* occurs.

Suggestions

If the error occurs in an indexing operation like `Var[`*IndexA*`;`*IndexB*`;...]`, look at the shape of `Var`, and check if *IndexA*, *IndexB*, etc. contain values which are compatible with the size of `Var`.

If the error occurs in an *Axis* specification like `+/[`*Axis*`]Var` or `VarA,[`*Axis*`]VarB`, look at the shape(s) of the variable(s) involved in the operation, and check that *Axis* is compatible.

2.1.5 - DOMAIN ERROR .... (⎕EN=11)

This error is much more complex to diagnose.

It usually means that some function cannot be applied to a particular value or type of data; the data is outside the *domain* in which the function is designed to operate. Here are some very common circumstances in which a `DOMAIN ERROR` occurs:

`Values ÷ Div` This is perfectly correct; except if `Div` contains one or more zeroes and `Values` does not contain zero in the same places.

`You + Me` Is correct; except if one of the arguments is not numeric. Beware: this may be difficult to see when a variable contains numeric characters such as `'0123456789'`. Hint: for a simple array `You` the expression `0=1↑0⍴You` returns `1` if the array is numeric, and `0` if it is character.

`Values[Index]` The same problem if `Index` contains characters or non-integer values.

`Bin1 ⍲ Bin2` The symbol `⍲` is a Boolean operation; it would cause a `DOMAIN ERROR` if either argument contains values other that 0 and 1.

`×/ ⍳Max` If `Max` is too big the result would be larger than the largest number that the computer can represent.

More generally, all these statements are in themselves perfectly correct when applied to appropriate data. However, they may fail when applied to other, inappropriate data.

Suggestion

Do not worry too much about the syntax of your statement: it is probably good. You should instead try to determine which values are appropriate to the operation, and check whether the actual values are within the operation's domain.

2.1.6 - SYNTAX ERROR .... (⎕EN=2)

This error may also be a difficult one. It means that a statement is ill-formed! Do not worry about your data: the problem arises from the statement itself.

Typically, the reason is that you have entered the wrong number of parentheses, quotes, or brackets: check that your parentheses, quotes, brackets are well balanced.

Here are some incorrect expressions: `(A+B)×C)` or `'ISN'T IT?'` or `Vec[Set[Old]`

Some other typical sources of *Syntax* errors:

- Monadic use of a dyadic primitive or user-defined function: `Interlace Actual` or: `<45 67`
- Use of the upper minus sign with a name: `¯5` is correct; `¯Var` is not. One should write `-Var`
- A missing `:End` clause in a *control structure*, or other inappropriate use of control structures.

2.1.7 - WS FULL.. (⎕EN=1)

You have probably tried to create an array that would be larger than the amount of available memory in the workspace.

- If it happens on *Reshape* (`Shape⍴Contents`), check whether the left argument is much bigger than you anticipated.
- If it happens on *Compress/Replicate* (`Numbers/Variable`), check that the left argument does not contain large numeric values:
  `101101/Variable` is not the same as: `1 0 1 1 0 1/Variable`

A `WS FULL` may also happen when a recursive function working on a large amount of data calls itself a large number of times. If this happens, consider whether a plain loop might be a safer solution.

2.2 Some Other Errors

2.2.1 - Can't Fix

This is not an execution error. It happens only when you try to define a function, and APL cannot fix it because its header is incorrect. Here are some things you should check:

- Check that all your local variables are separated by semi-colons and not by some other characters (dot, comma, blank …), and check that there is no extra semi-colon to the right:

  `FUN Rarg ;loca,locb;locc` is invalid: there is a comma instead of a semi-colon.
  `FUN Rarg ;loca;locb;locc;` is invalid: there is an extra semi-colon.

- Check that you havn't tried to specify a nested left argument. This is only allowed for the right argument:

  `Left FUN (one two three)` is correct.
  `(one two three) FUN Right` is invalid.

- Check the name of your function. If the name you have chosen is already in use as a variable, you cannot redefine the name as a function.

2.2.2 - Not Saved, This Ws Is…

You started with a clear workspace, and spent hours developing a set of functions. At the end of the day you decide to save it:

```
      )save D:\Washington\APL\WS\Bidou
Not saved, this ws is CLEAR WS
```

Don't panic! This does not mean that your workspace is empty and that you have lost all your work; it is just a friendly warning.

It so happens that in this case a saved workspace named `BIDOU` already exists, and Dyalog APL refuses to overwrite it with the active workspace.

Had your workspace been named `Tartempion`, the warning message would have been:

```
Not saved, this ws is Tartempion
```

But because you started with a `CLEAR WS` and you have not explicitly renamed the workspace, APL will not allow you to save it until you give it a name. Hence the message:

```
Not saved, this ws is CLEAR WS
```

For this reason, always prefer the "Windows" or "Windows-like" procedure when saving your workspace, using a file search dialog box.

3 - Trace Tools

3.1 Invoke and Use the Tracer

3.1.1 - Invoke the Tracer

In the default configuration for the Tracer, accessed by Option⇨Configuration⇨Trace/Edit, the option "*Show trace stack on error*" should be selected. This means that as soon as an error occurs, a trace window pops up, as we saw in the previous sections. If this option is not selected, you must invoke the tracer manually when needed.

When an error occurs, check that your cursor is on an empty line (it should be), and just press *Ctrl+Enter* or activate Action⇨Trace in the toolbar. This is called a "***Naked Trace***".

But sometimes it is better to anticipate that there will be errors, and trace the execution from the beginning. You can type any valid statement and instead of pressing *Enter* to execute it, press *Ctrl+Enter* (the easy way) or activate Action⇨Trace in the session toolbar to trace it. All the functions referenced by this statement will be traced.

Using this technique, you can trace the execution of a function from the very beginning.

3.1.2 - Trace Actions

All of the things you can do may be actioned using the keyboard or the little toolbar which appears on top of the trace window. In the table below, you will find the icons displayed on these buttons, what they do, and the equivalent keyboard shortcuts. Preferably use the keyboard: you will save time.

Figure E-4

Icon	Usage	Keyboard shortcut
	Execute this statement	*Enter*
	Execute this statement and **trace** the sub-functions	*Ctrl+Enter*
	Go back to the previous statement	*Ctrl+Shift+BackSpace*
	Skip this line (do not execute it)	*Ctrl+Shift+Enter*
	Continue the trace automatically	
	Continue execution, without tracing	→⎕LC
	Restart all threads	
	Edit the variable or function pointed to by the cursor	*Shift+Enter*
	Quit this function, and return to its environment	*Escape*
	Interrupt (when in "*Continue trace*" mode)	
	Remove *break-points* (see Section 3.3)	

3.1.3 - Trace Strategies

Usually, the tracer is employed to execute a function step by step, by repeatedly pressing the *Enter* key. At each step, you can check the values of your variables. You might perhaps monitor the values of certain significant variables, each in its own window, and see how they change when the function is executed, step after step, or in continuous mode.

When the current statement includes a call to one or more user-defined sub functions, you must decide how it should be processed:

- If you are confident in those sub functions and have no doubt about them, just press the *Enter* key, and the current line will be executed.
- If you think that a sub function requires investigation, press *Ctrl+Enter* or click on the "*Trace into expression*" button. This will open the Tracer on each of the sub functions in turn. You can continue tracing to any depth of function call.

In the example shown in figure E-5 below, we traced the execution of `Palindrome`.

```
      Palindrome 'Just to show a function call'
```

On its 1st statement, it calls `Upper`: we did not trace it, but executed it by pressing *Enter*.

On its 2nd statement, it calls `ReverBug`: we decided to trace it as shown above and to display the values of `From`, `To` and `Z`. Here is the window configuration after 16 executions of the loop:

Figure E-5

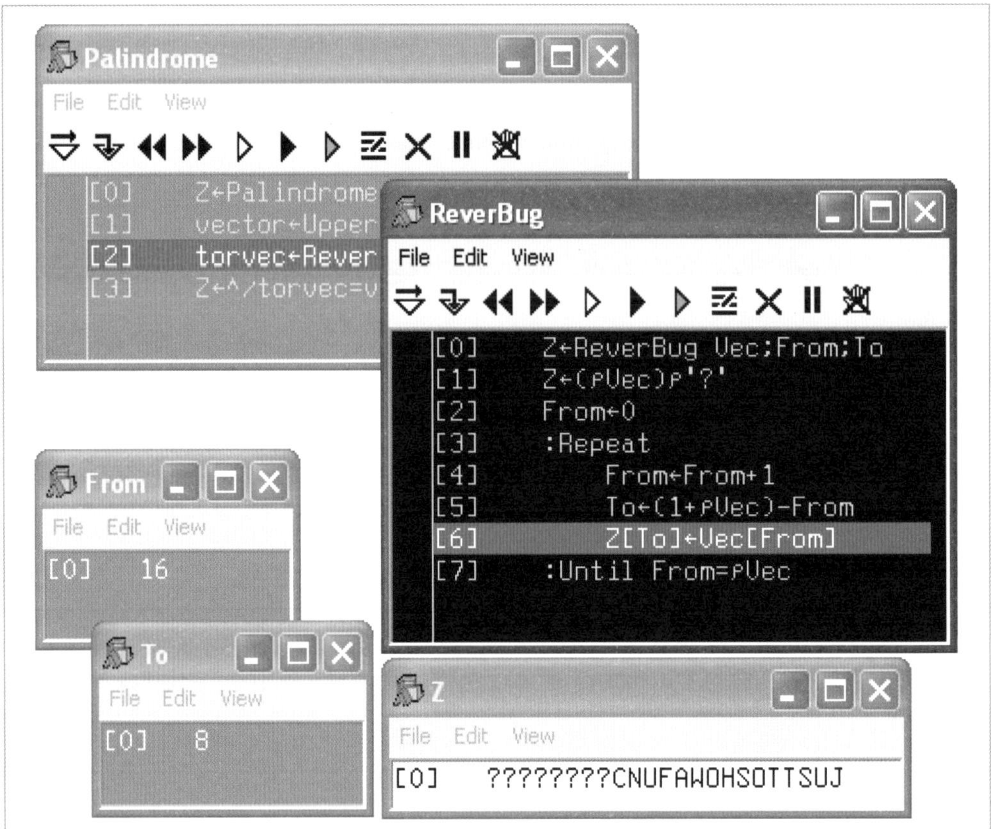

You can see that `Palindrome` is on a grey background because it is pending. It has called `ReverBug`, and once the variables were calculated for the first time we opened three edit windows to see their values changing loop after loop.

You can also move the red line to skip some statements:

- **Backward** if you want to re-execute some statements after you have changed some parameters or variables, or changed the code, etc. Press *Ctrl+Shift+BackSpace* , or use the "*Go back one line*" button.
- **Forward**, to skip some insignificant statements. Press *Ctrl+Shift+Enter*, or use the "*Skip current line*" button.

Sometimes an error appears only after an unpredictable number of iterations, and tracing the execution statement after statement would take much too long. In a situation like this, you can display some important variables as shown above, and run the function in automatic mode (press the "*Continue trace*" button). You can then stop execution with the "*Interrupt*" button when a given variable is about to take what you suspect might be a critical value.

When you have finished your investigations you can:

- Resume execution automatically by pressing the "*Continue execution*" button, or by executing `→⎕LC`.
- Abort the execution by pressing the "*Quit*" button, or by typing `→0`, or `→` , or `)Reset`, depending on your intentions.

3.2 Choose Your Configuration

If your program is interrupted in a very deep stack of functions, you will get as many trace windows as you have suspended functions. Those windows may occupy most of the screen. Sometimes this default behaviour may be unhelpful.

This is why the configuration panel offers the option "*Single trace window*". If this option is selected, there is only a single trace window. When the execution enters a sub function, or returns to its calling function, the contents of the trace windows are replaced by the new current function.

This setting may be convenient when big functions call other big functions, deeply. But it is not very convenient when tracing recursive functions.

It is up to you to decide which configuration is most convenient for you. In any case, this can be changed dynamically, without restarting APL.

3.3 Break-points and Trace-controls

3.3.1 - Set Break-points

When one wants to investigate the behaviour of a set of statements nested in a very deep sub-function, the best option is to run the main function but tell the system to interrupt the execution just before a particular statement is executed. To achieve this, one can place ***break-points*** (sometimes names ***Stops***) on one or more statements.

When you edit or trace a function, you normally have a blank column to the left of the function body, as shown below. If this is not the case, activate the menu View⇨Stop (deselect the two other options: "*Trace*" and "*Monitor*").

Figure E-6

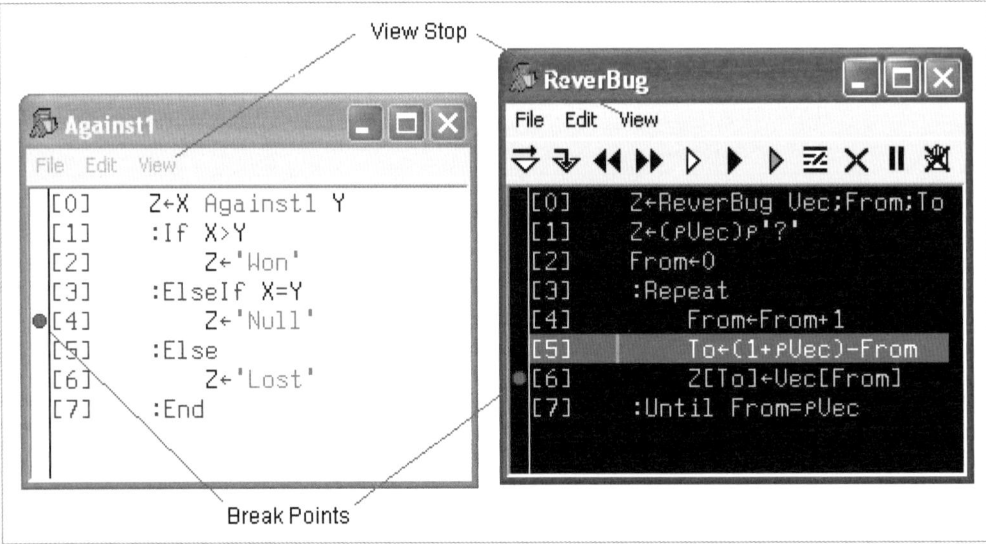

You can set or remove break-points by clicking the mouse in this column, on the line on which you wish to toggle the break-point. A red dot shows that the break-point is set. You can set and clear break-points in edit windows as well as in trace windows, and they can be changed at any time.

When one of the marked functions is executed, it stops before each break-point:

```
      ReverBug 'Just for fun'
ReverBug[6]
```
⇦ We have stopped on line [6].

```
      ⎕DM
  #.ReverBug[6] Z[To]←Vec[From]
```
⇦ The function is just stopped, so there is no error reported in ⎕DM, just the statement.

You can then make all the experiments you need to do, and restart the function at will, in continuous or trace mode.

3.3.2 - Remove Break-points

Each break-point can be removed individually with the mouse, as explained before. But after a long period of testing and debugging, it may be difficult to remember where break-points were set, and it is unacceptable to hand over a finished application to the end-user if it contains break-points.

For this reason, always remove all the break-points by clicking the button. This button removes all of the break-points from all of your functions, throughout the entire workspace.

In fact you may choose to display up to 3 blank columns to the left of the function body to show break-points, trace-controls, and monitored lines too. To do this, check or clear the Trace, Stop and Monitor items shown in the *View* menu.

When you move the mouse-pointer into this area, its shape changes to a red circle (break-point), a yellow circle (trace-control; see 3.3.3) or a clock (monitored line; this will be explained in Chapter L, paragraph Spe-9), to indicate which of these will be set or cleared when you click the mouse.

3.3.3 - Trace-controls

Earlier, we saw a very convenient way of tracing functions. There is another debugging technique in which functions are executed normally; no trace windows are employed and there is no need to execute statements step by step. To set this up, **before** execution, the developer sets trace-controls on selected statements in one or more functions. Whenever a line marked by a trace-control is executed, the last value calculated on that line will be displayed in the session, without interrupting execution. Let us explore this technique.

First, in `Palindrome`, let us replace `ReverBug` by another looping function, `ReverLoop` (see below), a possible solution to exercise D-14 and one that is more appropriate for this test.

In the View menu of any function, for example `Palindrome`, select "*Trace*" just as we selected "*Stop*" earlier. An additional column will open to the left of the function body, in which you can set trace-controls (yellow dots).

Let us set trace-controls on lines 1 and 2 of `Palindrome`, and 3 of `ReverLoop`, as shown below:

Figure E-7

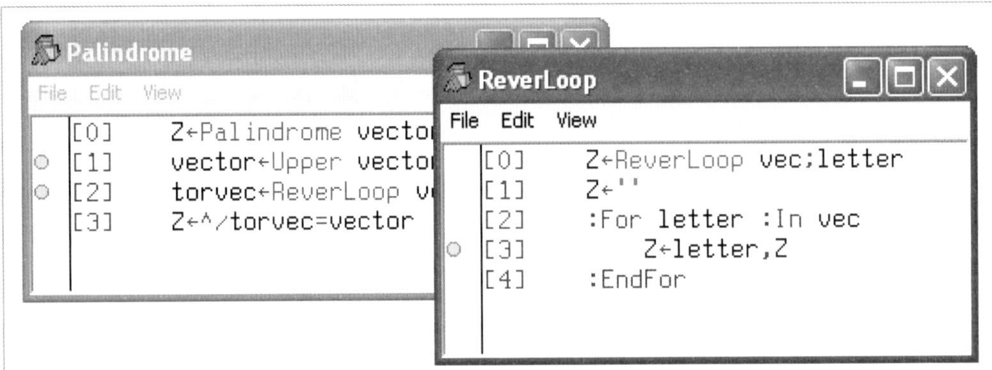

We can now close these windows and execute the function. Each time a statement, on which a trace-control is set, is executed, Dyalog APL displays the name of the function, the line number, and the last value calculated on that line:

```
      Palindrome 'Boring'
 Palindrome[1]  BORING           ⇦ The result of Upper
 ReverLoop[3]  B                 ⇦ The result of the first loop in ReverLoop
 ReverLoop[3]  OB
 ReverLoop[3]  ROB
 ReverLoop[3]  IROB
 ReverLoop[3]  NIROB
 ReverLoop[3]  GNIROB            ⇦ The result of the last loop
 Palindrome[2]  GNIROB           ⇦ The value of torvec
0                                ⇦ The final result
```

In fact, for each trace-control, depending on the context, APL displays:

- The last value calculated in that line `Value←Statement`
- The result of a branch statement `→(Condition)/Value`
- The "*pass-through*" value of an assignment `Vec[Index]←Value`

As you might imagine, if the traced functions perform many loops, this approach may produce pages and pages of output, especially if the results are large. In this case, you will probably most often prefer the previous method.

Trace-controls can be removed one-by-one as described above or, more conveniently, all at once by clicking the [button icon] button.

3.3.4 - Intentional Interruption

When an application is running in its normal production context, it is possible that some unexpected circumstances may cause it to crash at an unpredictable point. To cater for this eventuality, it is common practice to set a general error trap, using the techniques described in Chapter M, and halt execution in a controlled manner at a predefined point in the program, so that the developer is able to diagnose and correct the problem.

To deliberately make a function stop under program control, one can use `⎕Stop` (see the next section), or generate an intentional error. The latter is probably easier, even for a beginner. There are many ways to do this, but a common one is to jump to a dedicated erroneous statement containing the single character "∘", or *Jot*, obtained by pressing *Ctrl*+J:

```
[14]    ∘
```

This symbol alone does not mean anything, so it causes a `SYNTAX ERROR`. You may encounter this in existing applications.

3.4 System Functions

Break-points and *trace-controls* can also be set and removed using two system functions, which share the same syntax:

Lines `⎕Trace` '*Function*'
Lines `⎕Stop` '*Function*'

For example: `1 2 9 ⎕Trace 'Palindrome'` ⇦ 9 will be ignored for this function
or: `4 6 0 ⎕Stop 'ReverBug'`

Where:

- Numbers outside the range of available statements are ignored.
- Zero means that a *break-point* or a *trace-control* will be placed immediately prior to exiting from the function.

Both functions return a numeric vector indicating the lines in which *break-points* or *trace-controls* have been actually set, as a shy result. If a new set of values is provided, it replaces the previous one. For example:

```
      ⎕←4 6 0 ⎕Stop 'ReverBug'      ⇦ Display the shy result.
0 4 6                               ⇦ The result is in ascending order.
      ⎕←5 ⎕Stop 'ReverBug'          ⇦ We change our mind.
5                                   ⇦ The previous list has been replaced.
```

The monadic usage of these functions returns the current stop or trace settings for a function:

```
      ⎕Stop 'ReverBug'
5
      ⎕Trace 'Palindrome'
1 2
```

⇦ The value 9, out of range, has been ignored.

The break-points and trace-controls can be removed by specifying an empty vector:

For example: `⍬ ⎕Trace 'Palindrome'`

or: `⍬ ⎕Stop 'ReverBug'`

What now?

This is enough for the moment. With a little practice, you should be able to diagnose and correct programming errors. But if you intend to program very professional end-user applications, you must protect your code against unexpected circumstances. This can be done using "*Exception processing*".

Please refer to Chapter M, which usefully complements the present one.

Exercises

There are no exercises in this chapter. Enjoy the break!

What kind of APLer are you now?

Beginner

The Specialist's Section

Each chapter is followed by a "Specialist's Section" like this one.
This section is dedicated to skilled APLers, who wish to improve their knowledge.

You will find here rare or complex usages of the concepts presented in the chapter, or discover extended explanations which need the knowledge of some symbols that will be seen much further in the book

If you are exploring APL for the first time,
skip this section and go to the next chapter

Spe-1 Value Errors

Spe-1.1 - Namespaces

If a VALUE ERROR occurs when you reference a function name, for example `GetText`, perhaps this function is not "visible" because it is located in a different *Namespace*. Check to see if you have some *Namespaces* by typing the command `)OBS`, and search through them to find the function.

Imagine that `GetText` exists in a *Namespace* called `Files`. You have two ways to execute it from the *root* namespace:

- Give its full path when calling the function: `Files.GetText` *Argument*
  or: `#.Files.GetText` *Argument*
- Set a global path to this *Namespace* `⎕PATH←'Files'`
  Then call the function normally `GetText` *Argument*

Spe-1.2 - Nightmare

You expected to define a function named `Travel` and wrongly defined a function named `West` (see Section 2.1.1):

```
     ∇ Z←West TravelEast
[1]    Z←West-East
     ∇
```

If you try to execute `West`, (for example, type: `West 100`), you will get a `VALUE ERROR` on the first statement if `East` does not exist as a global variable.

But suppose that you *do* have a numeric global variable named `East`. Then the first statement will be executed successfully, and `West` will call itself recursively, endlessly applying to the same argument (`-East`), with no exit condition, until the execution stack fills up the workspace. You will then have an error message like "*The current trace stack is 395967 levels deep,* etc.". In the status field that displays the depth of the State Indicator, you will see a high value.

Trying to do anything at this point, even a naked branch, may not work simply because you have run out of workspace, and APL will issue `WS FULL` on any attempt to resolve the situation.

Just type `)Reset` to get out of this nightmare, then go and have a strong cup of coffee.

While drinking it, you can think about how you learned in section D-4.7 to interrupt a function, so that you do not have to wait for the workspace to be eaten up before you can regain control, if (read: when) this happens again.

Spe-2)SINL

When diagnosing a problem, you generally use `)SI`. However, you can obtain additional information with `)SINL`, which also gives all the **local** names used by the suspended functions, whether or not they have already been calculated. NL stands for "Name List'.

For example, when `Palindrome` crashes:

```
      )SINL
#.ReverBug[4]*  Vec     Z       From    To
#.Palindrome[2] vector  Z       torvec
```

When the crash occurred `To` and `torvec` did not exist, but their names are nevertheless reported by `)SINL`.

Spe-3 Namespaces and Indicators

Spe-3.1 - Extended State Indicator

When a function crashes, the information reported by `)SI` includes the full path to the functions on the execution stack. This is why all the lines begin with a *Hash*: the *Root* namespace identifier.

For example, suppose that we write a function named `MyFile`, which calls `GetText` which is located in the *Namespace* `Files`, and this last function crashes:

```
      )SI
#.Files.GetText[3]*              ⇦ This function runs in a Namespace.
#.MyFile[1]                      ⇦ The calling function is at the Root level.
```

Note that ⎕SI only reports the function names, not the full paths to them. You can obtain that information using the *Extended* SI, represented by the system function ⎕XSI, as shown:

```
      ⎕XSI
 #.Files.GetText  #.MyFile
```

This may help you to open a function in the editor, even if it is being executed in a different *Namespace* reached using ⎕CS.

For example, you could edit the functions in the stack using:

```
      ⎕ED ⎕XSI                  ⇦ To edit all the functions.
      ⎕ED 1⊃⎕XSI                ⇦ To edit only the first one.
```

Spe-3.2 - Namespace Indicator

A function located in a *Namespace* can be called from any other namespace. It may be important to know from where it was called. This information is given by ⎕NSI.

Let us consider the following scenario:

A workspace contains two *Namespaces*: ToolBox contains some user-defined functions. Files is a Dyalog provided set of utilities.

This workspace contains the following function:

```
     ∇ Z←Application FileName;Sink
[1]    Sink←'Any top level statements'
[2]    Z←#.ToolBox.Control FileName
     ∇
```

This main program calls Control (located in ToolBox):

```
     ∇ Z←Control FileName;Sink
[1]    Sink←'Any ToolBox statements'
[2]    ⎕CS'#'
[3]    Z←Files.GetText GloPath,FileName
     ∇
```

And on the line before Control calls GetText (located in the *Namespace* Files), it switches execution (it is running in #.ToolBox) to the *Root* namespace (⎕CS'#') in order to execute the expression Files.GetText from #.

When we try to apply the main function to a missing file, an error occurs:

```
      Application 'milk.txt'
FILE NAME ERROR
GetText[3] tn←name ⎕NTIE 0
          ^
```

⎕SI only reports the suspended functions: `GetText Control Application`

This is a bit poor, because we cannot see whether or not these three functions are in the same *Namespace*. However, ⎕XSI and ⎕NSI give us more information:

```
⎕XSI ⇨    #.Files.GetText  #.ToolBox.Control  #.Application
⎕NSI ⇨    #  #  #
```

⎕XSI Indicates *where* each function is *located*: `GetText` in `Files`, and `Control` in `ToolBox`.

⎕NSI Indicates *from where* each function has been *called*:

`Application`	was of course executed in the *Root*.
`Control`	was called by `Application` from the *Root*, using its full path.
`GetText`	was called by `Control`. But because that function had just executed `⎕CS'#'`, it was running in the *Root Namespace*. So, `GetText` was finally called from the *Root*, too.

This explains why the three functions have been called from the *Root*.

The traditional *State Indicator* has also been extended in Dyalog APL:

```
      )SI
#.Files.GetText[3]*
[#] #.ToolBox.Control[3]          ⇦ The [#] means that
#.Application[2]                    there has been a switch to that namespace.
```

Let us change `Control` a little so that this function no longer executes its last line in the *Root* namespace (the second statement is commented out). This needs some minor changes to the third statement so that it can "see" the global names:

```
     ∇ Z←Control FileName;Sink
[1]    Sink←'Any statement'
[2]    ⍝   ⎕CS'#'
[3]    Z←#.Files.GetText #.GloPath,FileName
     ∇
```

Of course, the execution fails again, but we now get slightly different information:

```
⎕XSI ⇨    #.Files.GetText  #.ToolBox.Control  #.Application
⎕NSI ⇨    #.ToolBox  #  #
```

Nothing has changed in ⎕XSI (the functions are still located in the same places), but now ⎕NSI reports that GetText was no longer called from the *Root*, but was called from ToolBox where Control was executing. This is also visible in the *State Indicator*:

```
      )SI
#.Files.GetText[3]*
#.ToolBox.Control[3]                    ⇦ The [#] has disappeared
#.Application[2]
```

Chapter F: Execute & Format Control

1 - Execute

1.1 Definition

Execute is a monadic function represented by ⍎; its dyadic use will be explained in the Specialist's Section at the end of this Chapter.

Execute takes a character vector (or scalar) as its argument.

If the character vector represents a valid APL expression, *Execute* will just … execute it, as if it had been typed on the keyboard. Otherwise, an error will be reported.

```
      Letters ← '5×6+2'               ⇦ This is a plain character vector.
      Letters
5×6+2
      ⍎ Letters                       ⇦ Let us execute it.
40
```

The argument can contain any valid expression:

- Numeric or character constants, or variables
- Left arrows (assignment) or right arrows (branch)
- Primitive or defined functions and operators
- Calls to other *Execute* functions

In the expression below, *Execute* calls a defined function and creates a new variable:

```
      ⍎ 'New ← 3 + Average 8 9'
      New                             ⇦ A new variable has been created.
11.5
```

If the expression returns a result it will be used as the result of *Execute*.

For example:

```
      Res ← ⍎ 'Average 10 11 12'
      Res
11
```

We could just as well have written: `⍎ 'Res ← Average 10 11 12'`

Beware!

Note that if the argument does not return a result, it can still be executed, but *Execute* will not return a result, and any attempt to assign it to a variable or to use it in any other way will cause a `VALUE ERROR`.

Assuming that `PlusNoRes` is a function which does not give a result:

These expressions will work	These expressions will fail...	... because they are equivalent to:
`⍎''`	`Res←⍎''`	`Res←`
`⍎'    '`	`Res←⍎'    '`	`Res←`
`⍎'→There'`	`Res←⍎'→There'`	`Res← →There`
`⍎'3 PlusNoRes 5'`	`Res←⍎'3 PlusNoRes 5'`	`Res←3 PlusNoRes 5`

1.2 Some Typical Uses

1.2.1 - Convert Text into Numbers

Execute may be used to convert characters into numbers. One common application of execute is to convert numeric data, stored as character strings in a text file (for example, a .csv file), into binary numbers. You can just read in a string such as “123, 456, 789” and execute it to obtain the corresponding 3-item vector:

```
      ⍎'123 456 789'
123 456 789
```

We saw in Chapter D that *Format* can be used to convert numbers to characters; the reverse can be done using *Execute*. This explains why those two functions are represented by "reversed" symbols, as shown here:

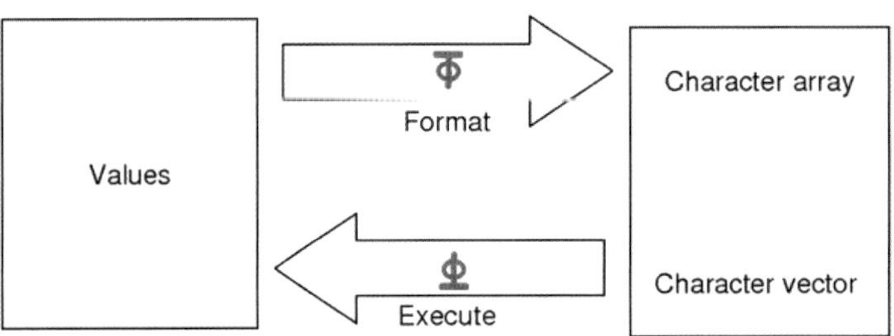

There is, however, a major difference: *Format* can be applied to matrices, whereas *Execute* can only be applied to vectors.

```
      BirthDate ← 'October 14th, 1952'
      +/ ⍎ ⍞←BirthDate[9 10,13+⍳5]
14 1952                          ⇦ These are 7 characters.
1966                             ⇦ They have been converted to numbers and added.
```

Because *Execute* can only be applied to vectors, a matrix of numeric characters can only be converted after it has been ravelled. But to avoid characters of one row being attached to those of the previous row, it is necessary to catenate a blank character before ravelling.

Given the character matrix `Mat` shown here ⇨

```
 845
1237
 933
2607
```

Ravel would give .... `8451237 9332607`

The correct conversion will be obtained by first catenating a blank, as shown below:

```
      ⍎,Mat,' '
845 1237 933 2607
```

1.2.2 - A Safer and Faster Solution

Using *Execute* to convert characters into numbers may cause errors if the characters do not represent valid numbers. So, we strongly recommend that you instead use `⎕VFI` (for *Verify and Fix Input*). This is a specialised *System function* that performs the same conversion, but securely, and is about twice as fast as *Execute*. `⎕VFI` will be studied in Chapter L.

1.2.3 - Other Uses

Execute can be used for many other purposes, including some that may be considered to be rather advanced programming techniques. Some examples are provided in the Specialist's Section at the end of this chapter:

- Conditional execution (rather obsolete)
- Case select (also obsolete)
- Dynamic variable creation

1.3 Make Things Simple

The vector submitted to *Execute* is often constructed by catenating pieces of text, or tokens.

These tokens may contain quotes (which must then be doubled), commas, parentheses, etc. But to build the final expression, you will also need quotes (to delimit the tokens), commas (to concatenate them), parentheses, and so on.

By now, the expression is becoming extremely complex. It may be difficult to see if a comma is part of a token or is being used to concatenate two successive tokens. It may be hard to see whether or not the parentheses and quotes are properly balanced. If the final expression is correct, it doesn't matter, but if it is wrong, maintenance may be difficult.

To simplify maintenance, it is good practice to assign the text to a variable before executing it. If the operation fails for any reason, you can just display the variable to see if it looks correct. For example, here is a statement involving *Execute*:

```
⍎'Tab',(⍕Size),'←(4 ',(⍕Size),'⍴'') '''
```

That's rather obscure! If any problem occurs, it will be difficult to spot the cause.

Let us insert a variable just before the *Execute* function:

```
⍎Debug←'Tab',(⍕Size),'←(4 ',(⍕Size),'⍴'') '''
```

If any problem occurs, it will be easy to see if the value of `Debug` is what we expected.

For example, if `Size` is `43`, `Debug` will contain: `Tab43←(4 43⍴') '`.

Obviously, this is not a correct statement, so it would fail if we tried to execute it.

2 - The Format Primitive

The *Format* primitive function has already been briefly described in Chapter D, Section 6.2. We shall cover it in more depth in this section.

2.1 Monadic Format

Monadic *Format* converts any array, whatever its value, into its character representation. This applies to numbers, characters, and nested arrays. The result is exactly the same as you would see if you displayed the array on your screen, because APL internally uses monadic *Format* to display arrays.

- Character arrays are not converted; they remain unchanged.
- Numeric and nested arrays are converted into vectors or matrices of characters.

```
      ⍴Chemistry                    ⇦ Chemistry is a character matrix.
3 5
      ⍴⎕←⍕Chemistry                 ⇦ It is not modified by ⍕.
H2SO4
CaCO3
Fe2O3
3 5
      ⍴52 69 76                     ⇦ This numeric vector has 3 items.
3
      ⍴⎕←⍕52 69 76
52 69 76                            ⇦ Once converted, it is an 8-character vector.
8
```

In Chapter B, we used a 2 by 3 nested matrix called NesMat. It can be converted into text:

```
      ⍴ NesMat                      ⇦ The nested matrix had 2 rows and 3 columns.
2 3
      ⍴⎕← ⍕NesMat                   ⇦ Once converted into text, it is 20 characters wide
 Dyalog   44   Hello                  and it has 3 rows, because the second row of
     27   8 6   1 2 0                 NesMat contained two small matrices.
          2 4   0 0 5
3 20
```

2.2 Dyadic Format

2.2.1 - Definition

Dyadic *Format* applies **only** to numeric values; any attempt to apply it to characters will cause a DOMAIN ERROR.

The general syntax of *Format* is: *Descriptor* ⍕ *Values*

Where *Values* can be an array of any *Rank*.

It converts numbers into text in a format controlled by the left argument, the *Descriptor*.

The *Descriptor* is made up of two numbers:

- The first number indicates the number of characters to be assigned to each numeric value; or to put it another way, the width of the field in which each numeric value is to be represented.
- The second number indicates how many decimal digits will be displayed.

```
      MN
 608.1    928.24 1293.14  849.95
1127.84  970.27 1249     1168.29
 775.12 1065      670.69 1091.7
```

⇦ This is the normal display, and this is also how monadic *Format* would present it.

```
      8 2⍕MN
  608.10  928.24 1293.14  849.95
 1127.84  970.27 1249.00 1168.29
  775.12 1065.00  670.69 1091.70
----'----|----'----|----'----|--
```

⇦ Each number will be represented by 8 characters, right aligned, with 2 decimal digits.

⇦ To help you count the characters, we have drawn a ruler (which is not part of the result).

```
      ⍴8 2⍕MN
3 32
```

⇦ The result has of course 3 rows and 32 columns (8 characters for each of the 4 columns).

```
      6 0⍕MN
   608   928  1293   850
  1128   970  1249  1168
   775  1065   671  1092
```

⇦ Here, each number will be represented by 6 characters, right aligned, with no decimal digits.

```
      ⍴6 0⍕MN
3 24
```

⇦ The result has 3 rows and 24 columns.

Remark You can see that the numbers to be formatted are **rounded** rather than truncated when the specified format does not allow the full precision of the numbers to be shown.

2.2.2 - Overflow

If a column is not wide enough to represent some of the numbers, these numbers will be replaced by asterisks:

`Small` is the following matrix:

```
 207.11    ¯33.24 1293.14   732.55
3302.12 32406.74   833.6   8231.52
 306.91  4231.8    ¯18.23    78.02
```

This format gives a nice presentation:

```
      9 2⍕Small
 207.11    ¯33.24  1293.14
732.55
3302.12 32406.74    833.60
8231.52
 306.91  4231.80    ¯18.23
78.02
```

If we reduce the width of the columns, the value in row 2, column 2 is adjacent to the value on its left. This is difficult to read:

```
      8 2⍕Small
 207.11   ¯33.24 1293.14   732.55
3302.1232406.74  833.60 8231.52
 306.91 4231.80  ¯18.23    78.02
```

If we further reduce the width of the columns, the largest value cannot be represented and is replaced by asterisks. Some other numbers are now adjacent to their neighbours

```
      7 2⍕Small
 207.11 ¯33.241293.14 732.55
3302.12******* 833.608231.52
 306.914231.80 ¯18.23  78.02
```

Remark To calculate the width required to represent a number you must allow for the minus sign, the integer digits, the decimal point, and as many decimal digits as specified in the *Descriptor*.

2.2.3 - Multiple Specifications

One can define a different format for each column of numbers. Each format definition is made of 2 numbers, so if the matrix has N columns, the left argument must have 2×N items:

```
      4 0 12 2 9 3 7 0⍕ MN
 608       928.24 1293.140    850
1128       970.27 1249.000   1168
 775      1065.00  670.690   1092
----'-----|----'-----|----'-----|--
```

⇦ In this case, each column has its own format: 4 0, then 12 2, then 9 3, and 7 0. Some columns are narrow, some are wide; some have decimal digits, and some have not.

⇦ This ruler is not part of the result.

If the format descriptor (the left argument) does not contain enough pairs of values, it will be repeated as many times as needed, provided that the width of the matrix is a multiple of the number of pairs.

In other words, in Desc ⍕ Values, the residue (⍴Desc)|2×¯1↑⍴Values must be equal to 0 (otherwise a LENGTH ERROR is reported).

```
      8 0 5 0⍕MN
     608  928     1293  850
    1128  970     1249 1168
     775 1065      671 1092
```

⇦ Columns 3 and 4 re-use the format used for columns 1 and 2. This is equivalent to: 8 0 5 0 8 0 5 0⍕MN

2.2.4 - Scalar Descriptor

When the *Descriptor* is reduced to a simple scalar, it specifies the number of decimal digits. The columns are formatted in the smallest width compatible with the values they contain, plus one separating space. For example:

```
      2⍕3302.1275 306  813.6  81231.752
 3302.13 306.00 813.60 81231.75
      3⍕Small
  207.110    ¯33.240 1293.140   732.550
 3302.120 32406.740  833.600 8231.520
  306.910  4231.800  ¯18.230    78.020
```

⇦ Numbers are displayed with 3 decimal digits.

Each column is separated from the preceding one (and from the left margin) by a single space.

This technique is convenient for experimental purposes, to have the most compact possible presentation, but you cannot control the total width of the final result.

3 - The ⎕FMT System Function

The *Format* primitive function is inadequate for producing professional looking output, such as one may require for common business purposes, because:

- Negative values are represented by a high minus sign, which is rather unusual outside the APL world.
- A large value, like 5244172.68, is displayed in a single unpleasant block, where it should be segmented like this: 5,244,172.68.
- National conventions differ from one country to another. It would be convenient if the value shown above could be written 5,244,172.68 or 5 244 172,68 or again 5.244.172,68.
- It would be nice if negative values could have different styles of presentation, depending on the usage and the context: -427 or (427).

For all these reasons, the ⍕ primitive is sometimes inappropriate, and it is better to use a *System function* named ⎕FMT (where FMT also stands for *Format*).

3.1 Monadic Use

Monadic ⎕FMT, like its primitive counterpart, converts numbers into text, without any specific control over the formatting.

The result of ⎕FMT is **always** a matrix, even if it is applied to a numeric scalar or vector. This is different from ⍕:

```
      ⍴⍕ 523 12 742
10
      ⍴⎕FMT 523 12 742
1 10
```

The general presentation is the same, except for some very special cases.

3.2 Dyadic Use

3.2.1 - Overview

Like ⍕, dyadic ⎕FMT accepts a *Descriptor* for its left argument: *Descriptor* ⎕FMT *Values*

The right argument (*Values*) can be:

- a scalar, a vector, a matrix, but, unlike ⍕, **not** a higher rank array
- a nested scalar or a nested vector, whose items are simple arrays (not nested) of rank not greater than 2

If *Values* is a nested vector, each of its items must be homogeneous (either character or numeric). In other words, an item of *Values* may not itself be of mixed type.

The *Descriptor* is a character vector, made of a succession of elementary descriptors separated by commas; for example:

```
'I6,4A1,F8.2' ⎕FMT Codes Boys Price
```

Each elementary descriptor is made up of:

- A letter, the *Specification*, specifying the data representation (integer, decimal, character).
- Numeric values which specify the width and the shape of the result.
- *Qualifiers* and *Affixtures*, used to specify further details of the formatting.
- Sometimes a *Repetition factor*, to apply the same description to several columns.

These elementary descriptors are used one after the other, from left to right, and applied to successive values (or columns of values).

Usually each array specified on the right has its own specific descriptor on the left.

For example, in the statement above:

'I6'	applies to..................................	Codes
'4A1'	applies to the 4 columns of.......	Boys
'F8.2'	applies to..................................	Price

However, an elementary descriptor can apply to several arrays if they are to share the same formatting, or a single array can require several descriptors when each of its columns is to be formatted differently.

Matrices are formatted normally, whereas vectors are transposed **vertically**, into columns.

3.2.2 - Specifications I and F

These specifications are used to display numeric values: I for Integers
F for Fractional

with the following syntax:

*r*I*w* *w* = the width (the number of characters) dedicated to each column of numbers
r = the number of columns to which this format specification is to be applied (this is the repetition factor mentioned earlier)

*r*F*w.d* *w* = the width (the number of characters) dedicated to each column of numbers
d = the number of decimal digits to display
r = the repetition factor

Let us work on this numeric matrix MN:

```
 608.1    928.24 1293.14  849.95
1127.84   970.27 1249    1168.29
 775.12  1065     670.69 1091.7
```

And the vector Price that we used in Chapter C: 5.2 11.5 3.6 4 8.45

```
      'I4,2F9.1,I8,F6.1' ⎕Fmt MN Price
 608    928.2   1293.1     850   5.2
1128    970.3   1249.0    1168  11.5
 775   1065.0    670.7    1092   3.6
                                 4.0
                                 8.4
```

Comments

I4 The first column of MN is displayed 4-characters wide, as integers (the values are rounded)

2F9.1 Two columns are displayed 9-characters wide, with only one decimal digit

I8 The last column of MN is displayed 8-characters wide, as integers

F6.1 The vector is displayed vertically 6-characters wide, with 1 decimal digit

- Vectors are displayed vertically
- Numbers are rounded to the nearest value
- ⎕FMT tolerates the fact that Price has more items than the number of rows in MN

In the Specialist's Section you will see that you can also display numeric values using scientific (or Exponential) format, using the E specification, which is very similar to F.

3.2.3 - Specification A

This specification is used to format characters (mnemonic: A = Alphabet) with the following syntax:

rAw   *w* = the width (the number of characters) dedicated to each column of characters
r = the number of columns to which this format applies (the repetition factor)

Let us again use these two variables: MonMat ⇩ Chemistry ⇩

```
January     H2SO4
February    CaCO3
March       Fe2O3
April
May
June
```

```
      '8A1,A4,9A1' ⎕fmt MonMat  Chemistry
January    H2SO4
February   CaCO3
March      Fe2O3
April
May
June
----ı----|----ı--
```

⇦ To help you count the characters, we have drawn a ruler.

8A1 The 8 columns of MonMat are displayed in 8 columns, each of which is 1-character wide.

A4 The first column of Chemistry, displayed in a 4-character wide column, produces a separation of 3 blanks.

9A1 The subsequent columns of Chemistry are displayed in (up to) 9 columns, each of which is 1-character wide.

Remarks

- Specifications (I F A ...) must be specified in upper case (i f a would cause errors).
- We specified 9A1 though we had only 4 remaining columns to format, with no problems; ⎕FMT ignores excess repetition factors.

But, what would happen if the first descriptor was larger than necessary?

```
      '10A1,A4,4A1' ⎕fmt MonMat  Chemistry
January H2   SO4
FebruaryCa   CO3
March   Fe   2O3
April
May
June
```

- 10 columns (8 from `MonMat` and 2 from `Chemistry`) are displayed in columns which are each 1-character wide.
- The next column of `Chemistry` is displayed in a column which is 4-characters wide.
- The last two columns of `Chemistry` are displayed in columns which are each 1-character wide (again we have specified more columns than are needed).

In the following expression, a single descriptor applies to all the columns of the right argument:

```
      'A3' ⎕FMT Chemistry
  H  2  S  O  4
  C  a  C  O  3
  F  e  2  O  3
```

⇦ Each character is formatted in a 3-character wide column, and right-justified.

3.2.4 - Specification X

Suppose that we want to number the rows by displaying the characters `'123'` to the left of `Chemistry`. The following method would produce a poor presentation:

```
      'A1,5A1' ⎕FMT '123' Chemistry
1H2SO4
2CaCO3
3Fe2O3
```

⇦ `'6A1'` would produce the same result.

To separate the digits on the left from `Chemistry`, we could specify a different format for the first column of `Chemistry`. It is however simpler to include a specific descriptor for the separation; this is the role of the `X` specification.

*r*X*w*   *w* = the width (the number of characters) of the blank column to insert
          r = the repetition factor

For example, to insert a blank column that is 3-characters wide we can specify:

```
      'A1,X3,5A1' ⎕FMT '123' Chemistry
1   H2SO4
2   CaCO3
3   Fe2O3
```

`'X3'` and `'3X1'` are synonymous, but the first description is simpler.

3.2.5 - Text Inclusion Specification

It is sometimes convenient to separate two columns of the formatted result by a string of characters.

This string of characters must be inserted in the format description, embedded between a pair of delimiters. You can choose from the following delimiters:

< *characters* >
⊂ *characters* ⊃
¨ *characters* ¨
⎕ *characters* ⎕
⍞ *characters* ⍞

Of course, if the delimiters are ⊂ ⊃, the character string cannot contain ⊂ or ⊃. Similarly for the other pairs of delimiters.

For the remainder of this Chapter, we shall only use ⊂ ⊃ or < >.

Let us use the `Rates` variable that we specified earlier (`0.08 0.05 0.02`) to calculate a result and display it. In the example below, the inserted characters are shown in black:

```
      Res ← MN[;4]×Rates
      For ← '⊂| ⊃,5A1,⊂ | ⊃,4F8.2,⊂ ×⊃,I2,⊂% =⊃,F7.2,⊂€⊃'
      For ⎕FMT Chemistry MN (Rates×100) Res
| H2SO4 |   608.10  928.24 1293.14  849.95 × 8% =   68.00€
| CaCO3 |  1127.84  970.27 1249.00 1168.29 × 5% =   58.41€
| Fe2O3 |   775.12 1065.00  670.69 1091.70 × 2% =   21.83€
```

This format specification contains 9 descriptors. To avoid a single long statement, it is possible to prepare the description, save it in a variable, and use it later, as shown above.

3.2.6 - Specification G – The Picture Code

The specifications we saw earlier (`I F X A`) are very similar to those used in the "FORMAT" statement in a very popular scientific language, FORTRAN. Another traditional language, COBOL, uses a different approach in its "PICTURE" statement.

The `G` specification in APL is very similar to the COBOL "PICTURE" statement.

In this specification, the letter `G` is followed by any string of characters, in which the characters `Z` and `9` represent the positions in which numeric digits are to be placed in the output.

The string is delimited by the same delimiters that we use for the text inclusion specification:

< > or ⊂ ⊃ or ¨ ¨ or ⎕ ⎕ or ⍞ ⍞

It works as follows:

- All the values are rounded to the nearest integer (no decimal digit will be displayed).
- Each digit replaces one of the characters Z or 9 included in the G format string.
- Unused 9's are replaced by zeroes, while unused Z's are replaced by blanks.
- All characters to the left of the first Z or 9, or to the right of the last Z or 9 are reproduced verbatim.
- Characters inserted between some Z's or 9's are reproduced only if there are digits on both sides.

Some examples may help:

Let us describe the formatting of this matrix Mat:

```
75 14 86 20
31 16 40 51
22 64 31 28
```

```
      '4G⊂(9999) + ⊃' ⎕FMT Mat
(0075) + (0014) + (0086) + (0020) +
(0031) + (0016) + (0040) + (0051) +
(0022) + (0064) + (0031) + (0028) +
```

Each descriptor "9" has been replaced by a digit of Mat, or by a zero, and all the other characters have been reproduced from the model.

```
      MN
 608.1    928.24 1293.14  849.95
1127.84   970.27 1249    1168.29
 775.12 1065     670.69 1091.7
      '4G⊂ 9999⊃'⎕FMT MN
 0608 0928 1293 0850
 1128 0970 1249 1168
 0775 1065 0671 1092
```

⇦ Each value is padded by leading zeroes, and the decimal digits are lost.

```
      '4G⊂ ZZZ9⊃'⎕FMT MN
  608  928 1293  850
 1128  970 1249 1168
  775 1065  671 1092
```

⇦ Small values are not padded by zeroes, but blanks.

Decimal digits can be displayed only if we convert the values into integers, and insert "artificial" decimal points between the Z's or 9's.

```
      'G⊂ ZZZZ9.99⊃' ⎕FMT 100×MN
   608.10    928.24  1293.14   849.95
  1127.84    970.27  1249.00  1168.29
   775.12   1065.00   670.69  1091.70
      'G⊂Value ZZ-ZZ/Z9⊃' ⎕FMT 621184 654 8 19346
Value 62-11/84
Value     6/54
Value        8
Value  1-93/46
```

⇦ As we said earlier, the symbols placed between descriptors Z and 9 are displayed only if they are surrounded by digits.

This characteristic is useful when displaying numbers according to national conventions:

```
      'G⊂ZZZ,ZZZ,ZZ9.99⊃' ⎕FMT 32145698710 8452 95732 64952465
321,456,987.10
          84.52                ⇦ Anglo-American presentation
         957.32
     649,524.65
      'G⊂ZZZ ZZZ ZZ9,99⊃' ⎕FMT 32145698710 8452 95732 64952465
321 456 987,10
          84,52                ⇦ French presentation
         957,32
     649 524,65
```

Here is a surprising example:

```
      'G⊂Simon ZZ Garfunkel ZZ⊃' ⎕FMT 4562.31 8699.84
Simon 45 Garfunkel 62
Simon 87
```

- The two numbers have been rounded like this: `4562 8700`.
- Because vectors are shown in columns we get one printed line per item in the vector.
- On the first line `4562` has been split into `45` and `62`.
- On the second line `8700` has been split into `87` and `00`.
- But because we used a descriptor `Z`, these zeroes have been replaced by blanks.
- Then `Garfunkel` is no longer between non-blank digits and therefore not reproduced.

3.2.7- Specification T

Specification `X` was used to specify an offset between a field and its left neighbour.

Specification `T` (where `T` stands for Tabular) specifies a position from the left margin. This makes it easy to position data in a sheet.

```
      'I2,T15,5A1,T30,4I6' ⎕FMT (75 91 34) Chemistry MN
75            H2SO4             608   928  1293   850
91            CaCO3            1128   970  1249  1168
34            Fe2O3             775  1065   671  1092
----'----|----'----|----'----|----'----|----'----|---
         10        20        30        40        50
```

As you can see, `Chemistry` starts at the 15th position, and the first column of `MN` starts at the 30th position, but occupying 6 characters per column it is right-aligned at the 35th character.

3.2.8- Specification K

Specification Kn is used to multiply a value by 10^n before it is displayed.

`'F12.2'⎕fmt 123.45`	would give	`123.45`
`'K3F12.2'⎕fmt 123.45`	would give	`123450.00`
`'K¯1F12.2'⎕fmt 123.45`	would give	`12.35`

In the first statement no K was used and the value remained as is. In the second statement, the value has been multiplied by 1000, and in the last one, it has been divided by 10 (and rounded afterwards).

Because specification G only displays integer values, it is often convenient to use specification K to multiply decimal values by a power of 10 to obtain the correct display, as shown here:

```
      'G<ZZZ ZZZ ZZ9.99>'⎕FMT 75435.39 66054.17 7.2 1673.08
        754.35
        660.54                          ⇦ This representation gives the wrong idea about
the
          0.07                            values.
         16.73
      'K2G<ZZZ ZZZ ZZ9.99>'⎕FMT 75435.39 66054.17 7.2 1673.08
     75 435.39
     66 054.17                          ⇦ The values have bee multiplied by 100, hence
          7.20                            producing the correct representation.
      1 673.08
```

3.3 Qualifiers and Affixtures

Specifications I, F, and G can be associated with *Qualifiers* and *Affixtures*:

Qualifiers modify the presentation of numeric values.

Affixtures print additional characters when some conditions are satisfied.

Qualifiers and *Affixtures* must be specified to the **left** of the specification they modify.

3.3.1 - Qualifiers

B	Replaces zero values by Blanks.
C	Separates triads of characters by Commas in the integer part of a number.
L	Aligns the value to the Left of its field.

Z — Fills up the left part of the zone reserved for a field with Zeroes.

Ov⊂*text*⊃ — Replaces Only the specific value *v* with the given *text*. If omitted, *v* is assumed to be zero. So replacing zeroes with a special text string is easy.

S⊂*cs*⊃ — Replaces characters with Substitution characters.
cs is a list of couples of characters, where: *c* is the original character; *s* is the substitute character

This applies only to the replacement of the following characters:

- `.` The decimal separator.
- `,` The thousands separator produced by qualifier C.
- `*` The overflow character used when a value is greater than the space allowed for it.
- `0` The fill character produced by qualifier Z.
- `_` The character indicating lack of precision (see the Specialist's Section).

3.3.2 - Examples of Qualifiers

```
      'ZI2,2(⊂/⊃,ZI2)' ⎕FMT 1 3⍴ 9 7 98
09/07/98
```

⇦ Values have been padded with zeroes on their left.

Note that a repetition factor may be applied to a list of specifications enclosed by parentheses.

```
      'CF13.2' ⎕FMT 74815926.03
74,815,926.03
```

⇦ Groups of 3 digits are separated by commas (Anglo-American presentation).

```
      'S<, .,>CF13.2' ⎕FMT 74815926.03
74 815 926,03
```

In this last example, commas have been replaced by blanks, and the decimal point has been changed into a comma, using the S qualifier, to obtain a French presentation.

Let us use the following numeric matrix Yop:

```
178.23       0    ¯87.64
     0 ¯681.19   42
```

```
      'BF9.2' ⎕FMT Yop
  178.23              ¯87.64
          ¯681.19     42.00
```

⇦ Zero values have been replaced by blanks.

```
      'O<none>F9.2' ⎕FMT Yop
  178.23       none   ¯87.64
    none  ¯681.19     42.00
```

Here, the qualifier O (the letter O) was used to replace zeroes (assumed by default) by "*none*". To replace any other specific value with a text string, the value should follow the qualifier, as shown in this example:

```
      'O42<Error>F9.2' ⎕FMT Yop
  178.23       0.00   ¯87.64
    0.00  ¯681.19     Error
```

⇦ 42 has been replaced.

3.3.3 - Affixtures

`M⊂`*text*`⊃`	Replaces the `M`inus sign to the **left** of negative values with the given *text.*
`N⊂`*text*`⊃`	The given *text* will be added to the **right** of negative values.
`P⊂`*text*`⊃`	The given *text* will be added to the **left** of `P`ositive or zero values.
`Q⊂`*text*`⊃`	The given *text* will be added to the **right** of positive or zero values.
`R⊂`*text*`⊃`	The given *text* will be repeated as many times as necessary to entirely fill the printing zone, then the digits are overlaid on top. Positions which are not occupied by the digits allow the text to appear. In other words, the *text* will act as a background for the formatted value.

It is important to note that the width of the text added by an *affixture* must be counted in the total width reserved for the column.

3.3.4 - Examples of Affixtures

```
      'M⊂(⊃N⊂)⊃F10.2' ⎕FMT Yop
 178.23       0.00    (87.64)
   0.00   (681.19)      42.00
```

⇦ `M⊂(⊃` will replace the minus sign with `(` and `N⊂)⊃` adds `)` on the right side.

With affixtures `M` and `N`, negative values have been placed between parentheses, in accordance with common accounting practice, but now they are no longer aligned with the positive values. To achieve this, we should place a blank to the right of positive values, using affixture `Q`:

```
      'M⊂(⊃N⊂)⊃Q⊂ ⊃F9.2' ⎕FMT Yop
 178.23     0.00   (87.64)
   0.00  (681.19)   42.00
      'R⊂\⊃I6' ⎕FMT Yop
\\\178\\\\\0\\\¯88
\\\\\0\\¯681\\\\42
```

⇦ Vacant positions are filled by a replacement character.

Remarks

- Qualifiers and Affixtures can be cumulated, and can be placed in any order.
  For example: `'S<, .,>CΓ13.2' ⎕FMT` *Values*
  and `'CS<, .,>F13.2' ⎕FMT` *Values*
  are strictly equivalent.

- Blanks can be inserted between specifications, qualifiers, and affixtures.
  For example `'BS<, .,>CF13.2' ⎕FMT` *Values*
  and `'B S <, .,> C F 13.2' ⎕FMT` *Values*
  give exactly the same result

- A repetition factor can apply to a group of descriptors placed between parentheses:

```
'10A1,I4,3(A1,F8.2,I3),CF13.2'  ⎕FMT Values
'4(I2,F6.2),X3,8A1,5(I6,A1,X3)' ⎕FMT Values
```

- Various errors may occur, all signalled by the message `FORMAT ERROR`. Here are some frequent errors:
    - A numeric value is matched with an `A` specification.
    - Character data is matched with a specification other than `A`.
    - The format specification is ill-shaped. Check that delimiters and parentheses are well balanced.
    - In decimal specifications (`F` and `E`), the specified width is too small, so the decimal digits cannot be represented.

Dyalog APL programming is pure Art

The Specialist's Section

Each chapter is followed by a "Specialist's Section" like this one.
This section is dedicated to skilled APLers, who wish to improve their knowledge.

If you are exploring APL for the first time
please skip this section and go to the next chapter

Spe-1 Execute

Spe 1.1 - Name Conflict

Suppose that we would like to switch two letters inside a word. Let us write a function which accepts the index of the letters to switch as its left argument, and the **name** of an existing variable as its right argument.

It is important to note that the function works on the **name** of the variable, not on its **value**:

```
      Word ← 'MORAL'                 ⇦ This is our variable.
      3 5 Exchange 'Word'            ⇦ We pass its name to the function
      Word
MOLAR                                ⇦ and its contents have been changed.
```

Here is the function we wrote to obtain this result:

```
     ∇ Index Exchange VarName;V;text
[1]    V←⌽Index
[2]    text←VarName,'[Index]←',VarName,'[V]'
[3]    ⍎text
     ∇
```

In our example `VarName` was equal to `'Word'`, so that statement `[2]` assigned the following to `text`:

```
      'Word[Index]←Word[V]'          ⇦ When executed, this statement exchanged
                                       two letters in the variable named Word.
```

All is well up to now. But now, let us try again on another variable:

```
      V←'RATS'
      1 2 Exchange 'V'
      V
RATS                                 ⇦ This is wrong, we should have obtained ARTS
```

The reason is that our statement `[2]` now returns: `'V[Index]←V[V]'`

But V is the name of a local variable in the function. When the last statement is executed, it exchanges items inside that **local** variable, not in the global one, which remains unchanged!

In other words, be careful when *Execute* is expected to work on global names, as there may be a risk of conflict with local names. In order to reduce this risk programmers sometimes use complex and weird names for the local names in such functions.

Spe 1.2 - Conditional Execution

For many years *Execute* has been used to conditionally execute certain expressions in a function.

- The general form .... ⍎(*Condition*)/'*Statement*'
- Example.............................. ⍎(Quantity>80)/'Discount←7'

If the condition is satisfied, *Compress* returns the character string unchanged, and the statement is then executed. On the other hand, if the condition is not satisfied, *Compress* returns an empty vector, and *Execute* does nothing.

This form is now considered obsolete and should be replaced by an :If .... :Endif control structure.

```
:If Quantity>80
    Discount←7
:Endif
```

Spe 1.3 - Case Selection

Execute is sometimes used to select one case from a set of cases.

Consider the following scenario: a program allows the user to extrapolate a series of numeric values. He has the choice between three extrapolation methods: Least Squares, Moving average, and a home made method. Each can be applied using one of three functions: LeastSqr, MovAverage, HomeXtra. We want to write a function that takes the method number (1 to 3) as its left argument, and the values to extrapolate as its right argument. You can compare two programming techniques:

```
     ∇ R←Method Calc1 Values
[1]    :Select Method
[2]    :Case 1
[3]        R←LeastSqr Values
[4]    :Case 2
[5]        R←MovAverage Values
[6]    :Case 3
[7]        R←HomeXtra Values
[8]    :EndSelect
     ∇
```

```
     ∇ R←Method Calc2 Values;Fun
[1]    Fun←(3 11⍴'LeastSqr   MovAverage HomeXtra   ')[Method;]
[2]    R←⍎Fun,' Values'
     ∇
```

Let us analyse how `Calc2` works: Suppose that the user has chosen the 3rd method. Statement `[1]` places the 3rd word `HomeXtra` plus 3 trailing blanks in `Fun`.

Once this character vector is catenated to `' Values'`, we obtain: `'HomeXtra    Values'`

Then, *Execute* calls the appropriate function and returns the desired result.

This form too is considered obsolete and should be avoided, if only for clarity.

Spe 1.4 - Dynamic Variable Creation

Some very specific applications may require that a program creates variables whose names depend on the context. This may seem a bit artificial, but imagine that we have three variables:

- `Prefix` is the following text matrix:

```
Prod
Price
Discount
Orders
```

- `Suffix` is a vector:

```
'USA'
```

- `Numbers` is a numeric matrix:

```
623 486 739 648
108 103 112  98
  7   6   7   5
890 942 637 806
```

And we now want to create variables named `ProdUSA`, `PriceUSA`, and so on, and fill them with the corresponding values. A simple loop should do that:

```
     ∇ BuildVars(Mat Vec Val);row;name
[1]     :For row :In ⍳1↑⍴Mat
[2]         name←Mat[row;],Vec
[3]         name←(name≠' ')/name
[4]         ⍎ ⎕← name,'←Val[row;]'
[5]     :End
     ∇
```

Let us see the debugging output that we have added to line `[4]`:

```
      BuildVars (Prefix Suffix Numbers)
ProdUSA←Val[row;]
PriceUSA←Val[row;]
DiscountUSA←Val[row;]
OrdersUSA←Val[row;]
```

Spe 1.5 - Dyadic Execute

In the dyadic use of *Execute* the left argument must be the name of a *Namespace*. The statement provided as the right argument will then be executed in the *Namespace* specified as the left argument. For example:

```
      'ToolBox' ⍎ text1        ⇦ Execute the statement in the ToolBox namespace.
      '⎕SE'     ⍎ text2        ⇦ Execute the statement in the session namespace.
      '#'       ⍎ text3        ⇦ Execute the statement in the root namespace.
```

Spe-2 Formatting data

Spe 2.1 - Lack of Precision

If the number of specified significant digits exceeds the computer's internal precision, low order digits are replaced with an underscore (_). This character can be replaced by another one, using specification S. For example: S<_?>.

```
      'F20.1' ⎕FMT 1E18÷3                ⇦ Normal
333333333333333__._
      'S<_?>F20.1' ⎕FMT 1E18÷3           ⇦ Substituted
333333333333333??.?
```

Spe 2.2 - Scientific Representation

If the second item of a pair of *Format* descriptors is negative (e.g. 9 ¯3⍕Var), numbers are formatted in *Scientific* notation (also described as *Exponential* notation; see Section B-Spe-2), with as many significant digits in the mantissa as specified by the descriptor:

```
      11 ¯3⍕ Small
   2.07E2     ¯3.32E1      1.29E3      7.33E2
   3.30E3      3.24E4      8.34E2      8.23E3
   3.07E2      4.23E3     ¯1.82E1      7.80E1
      11 ¯5⍕ Small
 2.0711E2  ¯3.3240E1   1.2931E3   7.3255E2
 3.3021E3   3.2407E4   8.3360E2   8.2315E3
 3.0691E2   4.2318E3  ¯1.8230E1   7.8020E1
```

Spe 2.3 - Specification E

This specification in the left argument to ⎕FMT is used to display numeric values, but in scientific (or E*xponential*) form.

Its syntax is very similar to the syntax of the F specification:

*r*E*w.s*   *w* = the width (in number of characters) dedicated to each column of numbers
s = the number of significant digits displayed in the mantissa
r = the repetition factor

```
      'E12.4' ⎕FMT 12553 0.0487 ¯62.133
   1.255E4
   4.870E¯2
  ¯6.213E1
----'----|--                               ⇦ Added ruler
```

You can see that each number is represented by 12 characters, with exactly 4 significant digits. However, in order to make room for larger exponents the last column is left blank.

The result is *normalized*; i.e. there is always one digit before the decimal point, the other ones are after it.

```
      'E16.7' ⎕FMT 2 2⍴ 98675342 0.004257 ¯15 649
    9.867534E7      4.257000E¯3
   ¯1.500000E1      6.490000E2
----'----|----'----|----'----|--
```

Spe 2.4 - Formatting Using the Microsoft.Net Framework

Dyalog APL has an interface to *Microsoft.Net*, which is introduced in Chapter Q. The *.Net Framework* includes a vast collection of utility programs, including functions to interpret and format data according to rules defined for a given *locale*, or *culture* or *language* (which you can customise using Control Panel ⇨ Regional and Language Options). For example:

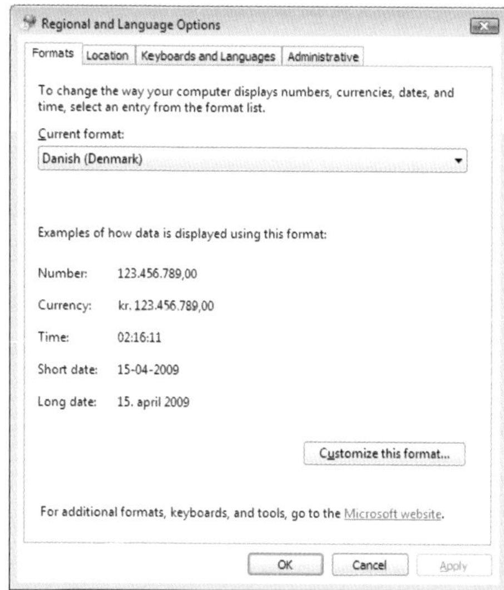

The following examples briefly illustrate some of the capabilities of the `String.Format` method.

```
      ⎕USING←''                          ⇦ Declares our intention to use .Net.
      ⎕← cc← System.Globalization.CultureInfo.CurrentCulture
da-DK                                    ⇦ In fact, cc is an object.
      cc.EnglishName                     ⇦ Extract the value of a property of cc.
Danish (Denmark)
```

The `String.Format` function takes three arguments: An instance of the `NumberFormatInfo` class, a format string, and a vector of data. An appropriate `NumberFormatInfo` instance (i.e. the one that is the default for the current culture), can be obtained from the `NumberFormat` property of our instance of the `CurrentCulture` object `cc`.

`String.Format` returns a string, which appears in APL as a character vector:

```
      pi←○1
      System.String.Format cc.NumberFormat '{0:F}' (,pi)
3,14
```

The `0` in `{0:F}` is an index (selecting the first item in the data array), and `F` specifies fixed-point formatting. The default number of digits and the decimal separator to use are specified in the `NumberFormatInfo` object, which has a number of properties that we can inspect, if we need to know more about how numbers are formatted in the selected culture:

```
      cc.NumberFormat.(NumberDecimalSeparator NumberDecimalDigits)
 ,  2
```

Of course, we don't have to use the default format; we can also specify the number of decimal digits that we want. In the following string we format the first number as a fixed-point number with 5 decimal digits and the 2nd as a currency amount with 2 digits (C2):

```
      format←'Pi is {0:F5} and I have {1:C2}'
      System.String.Format cc.NumberFormat format (pi×1 2)
Pi is 3,14159 and I have kr. 6,28
```

We also don't have to use the current culture, we can select any of the cultures known to Windows:

```
      us←⎕NEW System.Globalization.CultureInfo (⊂'en-US')
      System.String.Format us.NumberFormat format (pi×1 2)
Pi is 3.14159 and I have $6.28
```

We can format dates:

```
      ⎕← mar1← ⎕NEW System.DateTime (2009 3 1 11 55 0)
01-03-2009 11:55:00
      System.String.Format cc.NumberFormat '{0:D}' (,mar1)
1. marts 2009
```

There is also a wide variety of options and parameters for formatting dates, for example:

```
      format←'Short date: {0:d}, Custom date: {0:dd MMMM yy hh:mm}'
      System.String.Format cc.NumberFormat format (,mar1)
Short date: 01-03-2009, Custom date: 01 marts 09 11:55
```

In the case of dates (and many other classes), the `System.DateTime` class itself has a `ToString` method which hooks up to the same underlying functionality:

```
      mar1.ToString '{yyyy, dd MMMM}' us
{2009, 01 March}
      mar1.ToString '{dd MMMM yy}'
{01 marts 09}
```

The .Net base classes generally also contain a function called `Parse`, which performs the inverse operation:

```
      System.Double.Parse '3,14'
3.14
      System.Double.Parse '3.14' us
3.14
      System.DateTime.Parse '1 march 2009 11:55'
01-03-2009 11:55:00
```

The examples above have only scratched the surface of the wide variety of formatting options which are available. More documentation of the available formatting options is available on line at http://msdn.microsoft.com (search for "formatting types").

Chapter G: Working on Data Shape

In most programming languages the programmer has to declare the dimensions of an array statically, and it is often only possible to operate on the individual items using programmer-written loops.

In contrast to this, because APL processes arrays in their entirety, it is important to be able to manage the dimensions of an array dynamically. This is why this chapter presents a certain number of new tools that will help you perform these tasks.

We have already studied functions which create arrays with specific shapes:

Reshape	`A⍴B`	of course!
Concatenate	`A,B`	creates a new array by gluing two arrays together
Ravel	`,B`	creates a vector from any array
Compress	`A/B`	selects parts of an array
Replicate	`A/B`	generally replicates the items of an array
Indexing	`A[B]`	creates a new array, often with modified dimensions
Index function	`A⌷B`	creates a new array, often with modified dimensions

1 - Take and Drop

1.1 Take and Drop Applied to Vectors

1.1.1 - Starter

Two functions, ***Take*** (`↑`) and ***Drop*** (`↓`), can be used to extract or remove the number of items specified in the left argument, starting from the beginning of a vector if the left argument is positive, or from the end of the vector if it is negative.

Take Extracts the vector's head or tail, depending on the sign of the argument.
Drop Removes the vector's head or tail, and hence selects the remaining part.

Let us test these functions on some vectors of numbers or characters:

```
      Nums
56 66 19 37 44 20 18 23 68 70 82
      4↑Nums                           ⇦ With a positive left argument n the function
56 66 19 37                              extracts the first n items.
      5↑'My name is Bond'                It works on any kind of data (numbers, text)
My na                                    including nested arrays.
      2↑Children
 6 2   35 33 26 21                     ⇦ This is nested (2 & 4 items, respectively).
      ¯3↑Nums                          ⇦ With a negative left argument n, it extracts the
68 70 82                                 last n items of the vector, in their normal
      ¯6↑'Mississippi'                   order (not reversed).
ssippi
      4↓Nums                           ⇦ With a positive left argument n this function
44 20 18 23 68 70 82                     removes the first n items, and returns the tail.
      5↓'My name is Bond'
me is Bond
      ¯7↓Nums                          ⇦ With a negative left argument n, it removes the
56 66 19 37                              last n items and returns the head.
      ¯6↓'Mississippi'
Missi
```

1.1.2 - Remark

You will have noticed that `4↑Nums` and `¯7↓Nums` both gave the same result: `56 66 19 37`.

At first sight it would appear that there is no need for both of these functions, and that one or other of *Take* and *Drop* is redundant. There are, however, some differences that make it necessary to have both functions, as we will soon see.

1.1.3 - Be Careful

Do not confuse these two expressions:

`¯3↑Nums`	Takes the **last** three items of the vector, and gives:	`68 70 82`
`-3↑Nums`	Takes the **first** three items, and then changes their sign:	`¯56 ¯66 ¯19`

The result of *Take* or *Drop* applied to a vector remains a vector, even if it has only one item:

```
      ⍴1↑Nums                          ⇦ Although the results of these expressions
1                                        would contain only one item, they are
      ⍴10↓Nums                           not scalars, but 1-item vectors.
1
```

1.1.4 - Produce Empty Vectors

Of course, if you take no items, or if you drop all the items, the result is an empty vector, of the same type (numeric or character) as the original array:

```
      0↑Cash
                          ⇦ Empty result
      22↓Cash
                          ⇦ Ditto
      14↓'Empty'
```

1.1.5 - Take More Cash Than You Have

The *Take* function has a very special property: it allows you to take more items than there really are. If so, it pads the result with ***Fill items***; zeroes for a numeric vector, and blanks for a text vector:

```
      Cash ← 45 23 18 92
      7↑Cash                    ⇦ We took too many items; three zeroes have been
45 23 18 92 0 0 0                 appended to the vector.
      ¯9↑Cash                   ⇦ Starting from the tail, the zeroes are placed
0 0 0 0 0 45 23 18 92             before the existing items.
      12↑'Invisible'            ⇦ Three blank spaces have been appended, on the
Invisible                         right, but they cannot be seen.
      ¯12↑'Visible'             ⇦ Starting from the right, 5 blanks are appended
     Visible                      to the left, and they are visible.
```

In fact, the concept of *Fill item* is a bit more complex than this; it will be studied in detail in Section I-7.

The concept of "taking more than you have" is sometimes referred to as ***Overtaking***. This is an application of *Take* that cannot be performed using *Drop* alone.

This property applies equally to empty vectors; they are filled with as many zeroes or blanks as specified. This means that the result will be different for empty numeric and empty character vectors:

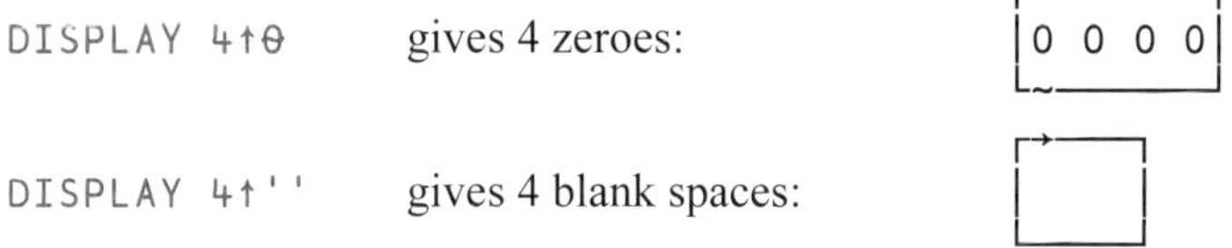

DISPLAY 4↑⍬ gives 4 zeroes:

DISPLAY 4↑'' gives 4 blank spaces:

1.2 Three Basic Applications

1.2.1 - Determine the Type of a Variable

The property we have just seen can be used to determine whether an array is numeric or character, provided that it is simple and homogeneous (neither *mixed* nor *nested*). The method is simple: create an empty vector "filled" with the array (`0⍴⍵`), then take one item of it (`1↑`), and compare with 0. This will return 1 (true) for a numeric array, and 0 (false) for a character array. A little dynamic function will do that for us:

```
      Typeof ← {0=1↑0⍴⍵}                ⇦ Define the function.
      Typeof Nums
1                                       ⇦ This vector is numeric.
      Typeof MonMat
0                                       ⇦ This matrix is made of characters.
```

This function wouldn't work on a mixed or nested variable. We shall see in Chapter I that APL has a *Type* primitive function that does the job much better.

1.2.2 - Change a Vector into a Matrix

Sometimes you want a variable `Var` to be a matrix, although you are not sure of its current rank.

If it is already a matrix, you want to leave it unchanged, and if it is a vector, you want to change it into a one-row matrix. The following function should help:

```
      HorMat ← {(¯2↑1,⍴⍵)⍴⍵}
      ⍴HorMat 3 5⍴⍳5 VerMat             ⇦ A matrix remains unchanged.
3 5
      ⍴HorMat 'This is a vector'        ⇦ A vector is transformed.
1 16
```

Explanation: We first append 1 to the shape of the argument, this gives 1 3 5 for the matrix, and 1 16 for the vector. Next, we keep only the last two items, this gives 3 5 for the matrix, and 1 16 for the vector. The final *Reshape* returns an unchanged matrix, or transforms a vector into a matrix.

We can change vectors into 1-column matrices with a very similar function, which also leaves matrices unchanged:

```
      VerMat ← {(2↑(⍴⍵),1)⍴⍵}
      ⍴VerMat 'Will it be vertical?'    ⇦ This time, a vector is changed into a
20 1                                      vertical 1-column matrix.
```

1.2.3 - Calculate Growth Rates

Let us imagine a business with a turnover which has grown over 12 years.
The variable Tome is TurnOver in Millions of Euros.

```
      Tome ← 56 59 67 64 60 61 68 73 78 75 81 84
```

We want to calculate the difference between each year and the next; how do we achieve this?

```
1↓Tome          gives 59 67 64 60 61 68 73 78 75 81 84
¯1↓Tome         gives 56 59 67 64 60 61 68 73 78 75 81
```

All that remains is to subtract the results of these expressions one from the other, item by item:

```
      (1↓Tome)-(¯1↓Tome)
3 8 ¯3 ¯4 1 7 5 5 ¯3 6 3
```

Without any program or loop; all very simple!

If instead of subtraction we used division, we would calculate (with some obvious adjustments) the rates of growth instead of the differences. Let us put that in a small defined function, and apply it:

```
      Growth ← {100×((1↓⍵)÷(¯1↓⍵))-1}
      2⍕Growth Tome
5.36 13.56 ¯4.48 ¯6.25 1.67 11.48 7.35 6.85 ¯3.85 8 3.70
```

1.3 Take and Drop Applied to Arrays

1.3.1 - Use Without Axis

The functions *Take* and *Drop* can be applied to any array so long as the left argument contains as many items as the number of dimensions of the array. That is to say:

In the expressions N↑Array and N↓Array, (⍴N) must be equal to ⍴⍴Array.

We shall work on the following matrix Mat:

```
13 52 33 81
42 62 70 47
51 73 28 19
```

We take 2 rows starting from the top, and 3 columns starting from the left.

```
      2 3↑Mat
        ⇩
     13 52 33
     42 62 70
```

We drop 1 row starting from the top, and 2 columns starting from the right.

```
      1 ¯2↓Mat
         ⇩
       42 62
       51 73
```

We take 5 rows starting from the bottom, and 3 columns starting from the left.

```
¯5 3↑Mat
    ⇩
 0  0  0
 0  0  0
13 52 33
42 62 70
51 73 28
```

We drop 1 row starting from the bottom, and 3 columns starting from the left.

```
¯1 3↓Mat
    ⇩
   81
   47
```

As expected, with `¯5 3↑Mat`, two extra rows have been added on the top of `Mat`, because we asked for 5 rows starting from the bottom.

With the expression `¯1 3↓Mat`, we have dropped 3 columns, so only one is left, but it is still a 1-column matrix; it has not been changed into a vector.

As for vectors, it is often possible to use *Take* or *Drop* interchangeably to obtain the same result:

```
2 ¯3↑Mat
    ⇩
52 33 81
62 70 47
```

```
¯1 1↓Mat
    ⇩
52 33 81
62 70 47
```

1.3.2 - Take and Drop With Axis

If one or more of the array dimensions is to remain unchanged, one need only specify the parameters for the other dimensions (the ones to be changed), together with the dimensions (the axes) themselves.

For example, suppose that we want to extract the first two rows of a matrix.

If we know its shape, that's rather easy: `2 4↑Mat`

But if we don't know its shape in advance, the expression is more complex: `(2,¯1↑⍴Mat)↑Mat`

Alternatively, using an axis specification, it becomes easy again: `2↑[1]Mat`

Here are some more examples:

```
      7↑[2]Mat
13 52 33 81 0 0 0
42 62 70 47 0 0 0
51 73 28 19 0 0 0
```

⇦ Take 7 columns, whatever the number of rows.

```
      ¯1↓[1]Mat
13 52 33 81
42 62 70 47
```

⇦ Drop the last row, whatever the number of columns.

```
      3 6↑[1 3]Prod
26 16 22 17 21 44
43 36 47 49 30 22

44 21 58 57 17 43
29 19 23 38 53 47

37 27 53 26 29 46
56 55 25 47 38 27
```

⇦ Take 3 years and 6 months (axes 1 and 3) in Prod, whatever the number of assembly lines (axis 2).

2 - Laminate

We have previously used *Catenate* to glue one array to another; let us now look at a new method.

We shall work with the following two character matrices:

```
      Boys                Girls
       ⇩                    ⇩
      Mark                 Suzy
      Paul                 Anna
      Bill                 Jane
```

Because it does not change the *Rank* of an array, the *Catenation* of those two matrices will give another matrix, as we saw in Chapter C:

```
   Boys,Girls             Boys⍪Girls
       ⇩                    ⇩
    MarkSuzy               Mark
    PaulAnna               Paul
    BillJane               Bill
                           Suzy
                           Anna
                           Jane
```

If both matrices have exactly the same shape, it is possible to join them together along a new dimension to make a three-dimensional array. Because this operation produces a result of higher rank than its arguments, it is called ***Laminate*** rather than *Catenate*.

The symbol representing *Catenate* and *Laminate* is the same (,), but when the comma is used as *Laminate* it is always used with a fractional *Axis*.

The two arrays we intend to *Laminate* have the same shape: `3 4`. Because we are going to laminate 2 arrays, the new dimension will have a length of `2`, and the shape of the result will be some combination of `3 4` and `2`. Let us examine all the possibilities:

Result shape Explanation

Result shape ⇩	Explanation
3 4	The original dimensions of the two components.
2 3 4	The new dimension is inserted before the 1st dimension.
3 **2** 4	The new dimension is inserted between the 1st and the 2nd dimension.
3 4 **2**	The new dimension is inserted after the 2nd dimension.

To obtain these 3 different results, we shall use *Laminate* with a fractional axis to specify where the new dimension is to be inserted:

`Boys,[0.5]Girls`	will produce a result of shape	**2** 3 4
`Boys,[1.5]Girls`	will produce a result of shape	3 **2** 4
`Boys,[2.5]Girls`	will produce a result of shape	3 4 **2**

Here are the 3 cases:

```
Boys,[0.5]Girls
      ⇩
    Mark
    Paul
    Bill

    Suzy
    Anna
    Jane
```

```
Boys,[1.5]Girls
      ⇩
    Mark
    Suzy

    Paul
    Anna

    Bill
    Jane
```

```
Boys,[2.5]Girls
      ⇩
     MS
     au
     rz
     ky

     PA
     an
     un
     la

     BJ
     ia
     ln
     le
```

In fact, the value of the axis specifier just identifies the *position* of the new dimension relative to the values 1 and 2, so it could be any other fractional value between 0 and 1, or 1 and 2, or 2 and 3, respectively.

Hence, the 3 results above could have equally been obtained by:

```
Boys,[0.295]Girls
Boys,[1.643]Girls
Boys,[2.107]Girls
```

Of course, it would be somewhat obtuse to use such axis specifications, and programmers conventionally use "`n.5`" values, like the ones in our examples.

2.1 Application to Vectors and Scalars

Now that we understand the reason for the fractional axis, which is perhaps initially somewhat surprising, we can apply *Laminate* to all kind of arrays.

2.1.1 - Laminate Applied to Vectors

Let us use both character and numeric vectors:

```
t1←'tomatoes' ◇ t2←'potatoes' ◇ n1←14 62 32 88 47 ◇ n2←10×⍳5
```

If we catenate them, we still obtain vectors

```
      t1,t2                                n1,n2
        ⇩                                    ⇩
 tomatoespotatoes                 14 62 32 88 47 10 20 30 40 50
```

But if we instead laminate them, we obtain matrices with either 2 rows or 2 columns:

```
      t1,[0.5]t2                    n1,[0.5]n2
          ⇩                             ⇩
       tomatoes                   14 62 32 88 47
       potatoes                   10 20 30 40 50

      t1,[1.5]t2                    n1,[1.5]n2
          ⇩                             ⇩
          tp                           14 10
          oo                           62 20
          mt                           32 30
          aa                           88 40
          tt                           47 50
          oo
          ee
          ss
```

Of course, since we are working with 1-dimensional arrays we cannot specify an axis equal to or greater than 2.

2.1.2 - Laminate Scalars with Vectors

Scalars can be laminated with any array: they are repeated as many times as necessary to match the length of the new dimension.

```
      n1,[0.5]0
14 62 32 88 47
 0  0  0  0  0
```

```
      1,[1.5]n1
1 14
1 62
1 32
1 88
1 47
```

This can be used, for example, to underline a title:

```
      Title←'Laminate is good for you'
```

Without *Laminate*, we must create a matrix with 2 rows, and as many columns as the length of `Title`, filled with `Title` itself, followed by as many dashes as the length of `Title`: boring!

```
      (2,⍴Title)⍴Title,(⍴Title)⍴'-'
Laminate is good for you
------------------------
```

Now, with *Laminate*, we just have to laminate a single dash; it will be repeated as many times as necessary.

```
      Title,[0.5]'-'
Laminate is good for you
------------------------
```

2.2 Applications

2.2.1 - Interlace Matrices

Do you remember that, in Chapter D, we wrote a function to interlace two matrices? It is no longer relevant; we can solve the problem more simply using *Laminate*.

Take a look to the result of `Boys,[2.5]Girls` above. You will see that the boys' names are on the left, the girls' names are on the right. If we reshape that result with appropriate dimensions, we shall obtain `Boys` and `Girls` interlaced ☺ :

```
      (1 2×⍴Boys)⍴Boys,[2.5]Girls
MSaurzky
PAanunla                              ⇦ It is not easy to read, but it works!
BJialnle
```

We can apply the same technique to matrices of forecasts and actuals:

```
      (1 2×⍴Forecast)⍴Forecast,[2.5]Actual
150 141 200 188 100 111  80  87  80  82  80  74
300 321 330 306 360 352 400 403 500 497 520 507
100 118 250 283 350 397 380 424 400 411 450 409
 50  43 120  91 220 187 300 306 320 318 350 363
```

2.2.2 - Show Vectors

Suppose that we have four vectors containing information about certain people: their age, their salary, their marital status, and their number of children:

```
TheirAge       ⇨ 52 30 47 63 29 35 28
TheirSalary    ⇨ 2437 1382 1780 1989 2819 4312 2106
TheirStatus    ⇨ MSMMDMSS
TheirChildren  ⇨ 3 0 2 4 2 1 1
```

The output shown above is not ideal, because each individual vector is displayed using its own natural format, and it is extremely difficult to connect the four related items to a specific person. We can have these values displayed much better if we create a matrix.

To produce a matrix we will need to laminate two of the vectors, and catenate the others (in rows or in columns). The results are much easier to read:

```
      TheirAge⍪TheirSalary⍪TheirStatus⍪[0.5]TheirChildren
  52   30   47   63   29   35   28
2437 1382 1780 1989 2819 4312 2106
   M    S    M    M    D    M    S
   3    0    2    4    2    1    1
      TheirAge,TheirSalary,TheirStatus,[1.5]TheirChildren
52 2437 M 3
30 1382 S 0
47 1780 M 2
63 1989 M 4
29 2819 D 2
35 4312 M 1
28 2106 S 1
```

In these examples, there is only one *Laminate*, followed by as many *Catenates* as needed.

3 - Expand

3.1 Basic Use

You remember that simple *Compress* uses a Boolean vector of 1's and 0's as a mask to include or exclude specific items of an array.

Simple ***Expand*** (specified by the \ symbol) also uses a Boolean vector of 1's and 0's, but the 0's *insert* new items into the array. It is used as follows:

R ← *Pattern\Argument*

In this form, the Boolean vector left argument contains a 1 for each item of the right argument, and a 0 for each item to insert. For example:

```
      1 1 0 1 0 0 1 1 1 \11 28 32 40 57 69
11 28 0 32 0 0 40 57 69
      1 1 0 1 0 0 1 1 1 \'Africa'
Af r  ica
```

If the right argument is numeric, *Expand* inserts zeroes, and if it is a character vector, *Expand* inserts blanks as *Fill items*. For mixed or nested arrays, the concept of *Fill items* is more complex, and will be explained in Chapter I, Section 7.

3.2 Extended Definition

If the left argument *Pattern* is not a simple Boolean vector, but contains integers other than just 0's and 1's the properties of *Expand* are as follows:

- For each **positive** item in *Pattern*, the corresponding item in the argument is replicated as many times as is specified by that value.
- Each **negative** item in *Pattern* inserts an equivalent number of *Fill items* (zeroes or blanks) in the same position.
- **Zero** items in *Pattern* mean the same as ¯1, and they each insert one fill item.

This new definition is fully compatible with the Boolean case we described before. Here is an example:

```
      1 1 0 3 ¯2 1 1 1  \11 28 32 40 57 69
11 28 0 32 32 32 0 0 40 57 69
```

The first two items remain unchanged. Then a zero inserts a zero in the result. The next value is repeated 3 times, and the value `¯2` inserts 2 zeroes. The last 3 items are unchanged.

The same thing can be done using a character vector:

```
      1 1 0 3 ¯2 1 1 1 \'expand'        ⇦ Because the patterns 0 and ¯1 produce the same
ex ppp  and                                effect, we can obtain the same result
      1 1 ¯1 3 0 0 1 1 1\'expand'          with a different pattern.
ex ppp  and
```

Naturally, the function can work on any shape of array, provided one specifies along which axis it is to be applied.

```
      1 1 0 1 1 1\[2]Chemistry          ⇦ We insert one column.
H2 SO4
Ca CO3
Fe 2O3
      1 0 1 0 1\[1]Chemistry            ⇦ We insert some rows.
H2SO4                                      This is a common use of Expand.

CaCO3

Fe2O3
      1 ¯3 1 1 1 0 3\[2]Chemistry       ⇦ Three columns are inserted, and the last
H   2SO 444                                column is repeated 3 times.
C   aCO 333
F   e2O 333
```

Expand can also be used on scalars; they are repeated as many times as necessary to fit the number of positive values in the pattern:

```
      0 0 1 1 0 0 1 1 \'A'              ⇦ Equivalent to 0 0 1 1 0 0 1 1\'AAAA'
  AA  AA
      0 1 3 ¯2 1 1 \71
0 71 71 71 71 0 0 71 71
```

3.3 Expand Along First Axis

By default, *Expand* works on the last dimension of an array. To work on the first dimension, one can use the function ⍀

```
      1 1 ¯2 1⍀Chemistry
H2SO4
CaCO3


Fe2O3
```

If one places an axis indication after the symbol `\` or `⍀`, the operation is processed according to the *Axis* operator, whichever of the two symbols is used. For example:

`Vec⍀[3]Prod`	and	`Vec\[3]Prod`	are equivalent to	`Vec\Prod`
`Vec\[1]Forecast`	and	`Vec⍀[1]Forecast`	are equivalent to	`Vec⍀Forecast`

4 - Reverse and Transpose

APL is also well endowed with functions which pivot data about an axis, and the axis is suggested by the shape of the symbol used. The functions apply to both numeric and character data. In the examples we are going to use a character matrix called `Towns`.

The symbols `⌽` and `⊖` are used for two variants of the same function which is called ***Reverse***, or sometimes ***Mirror***, because it reverses data like a mirror.

The `⍉` function is called ***Transpose***.

Initial Variable	Left-right reversal (*Mirror*)	Top-bottom reversal (*Mirror*)	Switch Rows & Columns (*Transpose*)
`Towns`	`⌽Towns`	`⊖Towns`	`⍉Towns`

`Canberra`
`Paris`
`Washington`
`Moscow`
`Martigues`
`Mexico`
	`  arrebnaC`
	`     siraP`
	`notgnihsaW`
	`    wocsoM`
	` seugitraM`
	`    ocixeM`
		`Mexico`
		`Martigues`
		`Moscow`
		`Washington`
		`Paris`
		`Canberra`
			`CPWMMM`
			`aaaoae`
			`nrssrx`
			`bihcti`
			`esioic`
			`r nwgo`
			`r g u`
			`a t e`
			`  o s`
			`  n`

The symbols used (`⌽ ⊖ ⍉`) are self-describing, no effort is required to remember any of them because the position of the bar clearly indicates which kind of transformation they stand for.

The symbols are obtained as follow:

`⌽`	⇨	*Ctrl*+*Shift*+5
`⊖`	⇨	*Ctrl*+*Shift*+7
`⍉`	⇨	*Ctrl*+*Shift*+6

If you insert an axis specification after the symbols ⌽ or ⊖, the operation is processed according to the *Axis* operator, whichever of the two symbols is used. So:

⌽[1]*matrix*	and	⊖[1]*matrix*	are both equivalent to	⊖*matrix*
⌽[2]*matrix*	and	⊖[2]*matrix*	are both equivalent to	⌽*matrix*

Remarks

Transpose has no effect on a vector, because it has only one axis:

```
      ⍉'I shall not move'
I shall not move
```

Transpose cannot be modified by an axis specifier, because it always operates on all of the dimensions of its argument.

Transpose can be applied to arrays of any rank; let us try it with a 3-D character array:

```
      You ← Boys,[0.5]Girls
      ⍉You
MS
PA
BJ

au
an
ia

rz
un
ln

ky
la
le
      ⍴You
2 3 4
      ⍴⍉You                    ⇦ You can see that ⍴⍉You is equal to ⌽⍴You
4 3 2
```

5 - Rotate

The symbols ⌽ and ⊖ also have a dyadic use, which shifts the items of the right argument in a circular manner.

The dyadic functions are called ***Rotate***.

5.1 Rotate Vectors

When applied to vectors, ⌽ and ⊖ work in exactly the same way; we shall use ⌽ in our examples:

R ← *N* ⌽ *Vector*

When *N* is positive, the first *N* items of *Vector* are moved to the end. In other words, the vector is rotated to the left.

When *N* is negative, the last *N* items of *Vector* are moved to the beginning. In other words, the vector is rotated to the right.

```
      6⌽'What did they do to my song?'
id they do to my song?What d            ⇦ The first 6 items have been moved;
                                          they are shown in grey.
      ¯10⌽'What did they do to my song?'
o my song?What did they do t            ⇦ The 10 last items have been moved
                                          to the front of the vector.
```

Rotate can of course be applied to numeric vectors as well.

```
      Nums
56 66 19 37 44 20 18 23 68 70 82
      3⌽Nums
37 44 20 18 23 68 70 82 56 66 19
```

Do not confuse the following two expressions. The first one moves the last 3 items to the beginning, whilst the second expression moves the first 3 items to the end, and then changes the sign of the result (we saw something very similar with *Take* in Section G-1.1.3). It is all about being careful with the normal and the high minus symbols!

```
      ¯3⌽Nums
68 70 82 56 66 19 37 44 20 18 23
      -3⌽Nums
¯37 ¯44 ¯20 ¯18 ¯23 ¯68 ¯70 ¯82 ¯56 ¯66 ¯19
```

5.2 Rotate Higher-Rank Arrays

When applied to a matrix or higher-order array ⌽ works on the last dimension, while ⊖ works on the first dimension. This default behaviour can be overridden by an *Axis* specification. To obtain a rotation along any other dimension, the *Axis* specification is mandatory.

Rotate can be applied to any array, but we shall only demonstrate its application to matrices.

5.2.1 - Uniform Rotation

In its simplest form, *Rotate* applies the same rotation to all the rows or columns of a matrix; let us see the result produced on a character matrix. The shifted rows or columns are shown in grey:

```
      MonMat                           2⊖MonMat
January                          March
February                         April
March                            May
April                            June
May                              January
June                             February

      2⌽MonMat                        ¯2⊖MonMat
nuary Ja                         May
bruaryFe                         June
rch   Ma                         January
ril   Ap                         February
y     Ma                         March
ne    Ju                         April
```

5.2.2 - Multiple Rotations

It is possible to apply a different rotation to each of the rows or to each of the columns.

In this case, the rotation is no longer indicated by a single value, but by a vector which specifies the amount by which each row or column will be moved.

```
Chemistry                  ¯1 0 2 ⌽ Chemistry
  ⇩                          ⇩
H2SO4                      4H2SO     ⇦ The last character is moved to the head.
CaCO3                      CaCO3     ⇦ This row remains unchanged.
Fe2O3                      2O3Fe     ⇦ The first two characters are sent to the
```
end.

```
MonMat                     1 0 2 ¯2 0 0 2 2 ⊖MonMat
  ⇩                          ⇩
January                    Far ar
February                   Mereua
March                      Aayuh
April                      Mpnrl
May                        Janc  y
June                       Jubi  ry
```

5.2.3 - Application

Rotate can provide very simple solutions to many tasks. For example, let us count how many blanks appear at the end of each row of `MonMat`:

```
      +/' '=MonMat
1 0 3 3 5 4
```

We can then use these values to move the blanks to the beginning of each row, thereby right-justifying the matrix:

```
      (-+/' '=MonMat)⌽MonMat
 January
February
   March
   April
     May
    June
```

6 - Dyadic Transpose

Dyadic Transpose is interesting only for arrays of rank higher than 2. It rotates an array as if to show it from different angles.

Remember our variable called `Prod`. It is an array with 3 dimensions, which are respectively 5 years, 2 assembly lines, and 12 months.

Suppose we now want to reorganise it into an array of 2 assembly lines, 5 years, and 12 months: a dyadic transposition can do that for us.

The left argument of *Dyadic Transpose* specifies the position that you want each dimension to appear in the result.

The shape of `Prod` was `OldShape ← 5 2 12`

The required shape is `NewShape ← 2 5 12`

So the transposition vector will be `2 1 3`

Years becomes 2nd,
Lines becomes 1st,
Months remains as the 3rd dimension

```
      2 1 3⍉Prod
26 16 22 17 21 44 25 22 23 44 41 33
44 21 58 57 17 43 47 17 43 26 53 23
37 27 53 26 29 46 25 26 30 20 32 16
21 57 55 44 16 54 26 16 55 56 45 45
27 23 56 41 53 60 39 47 44 47 17 28

43 36 47 49 30 22 57 20 45 60 43 22
29 19 23 38 53 47 38 22 40 57 35 26
56 55 25 47 38 27 39 59 20 28 42 25
16 55 26 20 27 55 36 39 43 38 50 16
24 35 61 26 22 35 24 20 31 35 47 37
```

Alternatively, if we want to reorganise it into an array of 2 assembly lines, 12 months, and 5 years, the method will be the same:

The required new shape is `2 12 5`

Because these dimensions are all different from the originals, the transposition vector can be generated using dyadic *Iota* (this does not work when two or more dimensions are equal):

```
      TV←2 12 5 ⍳ ⍴Prod
      TV
3 1 2
      TV⍉Prod
26 44 37 21 27
16 21 27 57 23
22 58 53 55 56
17 57 26 44 41
21 17 29 16 53
44 43 46 54 60
25 47 25 26 39
22 17 26 16 47
23 43 30 55 44
44 26 20 56 47
41 53 32 45 17
33 23 16 45 28

43 29 56 16 24
36 19 55 55 35
47 23 25 26 61
49 38 47 .. ..        and so on…
```

What kind of APLer are you now?

Exercises

G-1 You are given a matrix named `XG1`:

```
1 9 5 3 6
5 4 8 2 3
7 7 6 2 6
```

Try to produce each of the three following matrices, using first only *Take*, and then only *Drop*:

```
5 3 6        5 4 8 2        9 5 3
8 2 3        7 7 6 2        4 8 2
                            7 6 2
```

G-2 With `XG1` again, how could you produce this:

```
1 9 5 3 6 0
5 4 8 2 3 0
7 7 6 2 6 0
0 0 0 0 0 0
```

G-3 Write a function which "highlights" all the vowels of a given character vector by placing an arrow under them:

```
      ShowVowels 'This function works properly'
This function works properly
  ↑    ↑   ↑↑    ↑       ↑  ↑   ↑
```

G-4 Some matrices are mainly filled with zeroes, like the matrix `XG4` shown here. These are called *sparse matrices*.

```
0 0 8 0 0 3 0
0 7 0 0 0 0 0
6 0 2 0 0 0 1
0 0 0 0 4 0 0
```

A large sparse matrix may occupy a lot of memory. To reduce the memory consumption, we can ravel the matrix, retaining only the positive values together with their position in this vector:

Ravel the matrix ⇨ 0 0 8 0 0 3 0 0 7 0 0 0 0 0 6 0 2 0 5 etc…

Keep the positive values ⇨ 8 3 7 6 2 1 etc…

and their positions ⇨ 3 6 9 15 17 21 etc…

If now we add the shape of the matrix on the left, we have all the necessary information to restore the original matrix when required:

```
4 8 3 7  6  2  1  4
7 3 6 9 15 17 21 26
```

⇧ Shape of the original matrix

Can you write:

- A function which creates this compact form. Let us call the function `Contraction`.
- A function `Restore` which retrieves the original matrix from its compact form?

G-5 In a given character vector, we would like to replace all the occurrences of a given letter with blanks:

```
      Phrase
Panama is a canal between Atlantic and Pacific
      'a' Whiten Phrase
P n m  is   c n l between Atl ntic  nd P cific
```

Find a solution using *Expand*.

G-6 Write a dyadic function to centre a title above a character matrix, like this:

```
      '2007' Ontop MonMat
  2007
--------
January
February
March
etc...
```

G-7 You are given a matrix called `XG7`:

```
oeornlhtu
 n siduot
hf uogYti
```

What is the result of the expression: `¯3 ¯1 3⌽(-2 1 0 1 0 2 1 2 0)⊖XG7`

G-8 You are given a Boolean vector like `XG8`:

```
1 0 0 1 1 1 0 1 0 0 0 1 1 0 0 0 0 1 1 0 0 0 0 1 0 0
```

We would like to find a list of *N* contiguous zeroes in this vector. Write a function which gives the position of the first zero of the first such list found. If there is no list of *N* zeroes, the function is supposed to return 0. Loops are (of course) strictly forbidden!

`3 Free XG8` should give `9`

`6 Free XG8` should give `0`

`4 Free XG8` should give `14`

G-9 XG9 is a long matrix of names:

```
Emily
Luciano
Paul
Oxana
Thor
Carmen
Veronica
William
Vladimir
Monica
Colette
```

Write a function to split this matrix into slices, and position these slices one next to the other, like this:

```
      3 Split XG9
Emily   Thor     Vladimir
Luciano Carmen   Monica
Paul    Veronica Colette
Oxana   William
```

The number of slices is passed as the left argument, and a blank is inserted between the slices.

G-10 You are given a numeric vector XG10:

```
      XG10 ← 22 22 74 74 74 74 30 65 65 65 19
```

It has the same number of items as there are names in the variable XG9 which you used in the previous exercise. It is composed of groups of identical codes.

Can you write a function which displays side by side this vector of codes and the associated matrix of names, with an empty line inserted each time the code changes, like this:

```
      XG10 Expand XG9
22  Emily
22  Luciano

74  Paul
74  Oxana
74  Thor
74  Carmen

30  Veronica

65  William
65  Vladimir
65  Monica

19  Colette
```

The Specialist's Section

Each chapter is followed by a "Specialist's Section" like this one.
This section is dedicated to skilled APLers, who wish to improve their knowledge.

If you are exploring APL for the first time,
skip this section and go to the next chapter

Spe - 1 More About Laminate

Here is a more formal definition of the conditions required to laminate two variables `A` and `B`.

In the expression: `R ← A,[axis]B`

- It is mandatory that `(⍴A)≡(⍴B)`, unless one of them is a scalar
- `axis` must be a value between `⎕IO-1` and `⎕IO+⍴⍴A`
- The shape of `R` is given by the expression: `((⌊axis)↑⍴A),2,((⌊axis)↓⍴A)`

Examine the second rule: it is obvious that `axis` can be negative if the *Index origin* is set to 0. The axis can also be negative for *Mix* and *Ravel with axis*.

Let us use the following two vectors:

```
A ← 41 27 88 11
B ← 39 63 12 69
```

Now let us try to produce this matrix:

```
41 27 88 11
39 63 12 69
```

With a "normal" `⎕IO` set to 1 we would write `A,[0.5]B`

With `⎕IO` set to 0, the expression becomes `A,[¯0.5]B`

Spe - 2 Dyadic Transpose

Spe-2.1 - Conditions

We said that *Dyadic Transpose* can be thought of as a way to observe an array from different positions. For this usage there is a certain rule to follow.

To transpose an array `R ← A⍉B`

this condition must be met: `A[⍋A]≡⍳⍴⍴B`

In other words: `A` must be composed of all the values of `⍳⍴⍴B` taken in any order.

Spe-2.2 - Diagonal Sections of an Array

Dyadic Transpose can also be used to select the items from an array which have two or more identical coordinates. Such selections are called "*Diagonal sections*" of the array.

For example, let us use the following array:

```
      ⎕← A ← 3 3 4⍴⍳36
 1  2  3  4
 5  6  7  8
 9 10 11 12

13 14 15 16
17 18 19 20
21 22 23 24

25 26 27 28
29 30 31 32
33 34 35 36
```

The expression `1 1 2⍉A` gives

```
 1  2  3  4
17 18 19 20
33 34 35 36
```

⇦ These values are shown in black in the display of `A` here above.

We have specified that both the first and second dimension are to become the first dimension of the result. This conflict is resolved by extracting the items on the diagonal between the dimensions which are merged.

The items on this diagonal have identical first and second coordinates, very much like the identical nature of the first and second values in the left argument `1 1 2⍉A`. The result is a diagonal section of the "cube".

The expression `2 2 1⍉A` would give the same result, but transposed:

```
      2 2 1⍉A
1 17 33
2 18 34
3 19 35
4 20 36
```

Rules

This special use of `A⍉B` must also follow some rules:

`(⍴A)≡(⍴⍴B)`	as always
`∧/A∊⍳⍴⍴B`	as always
`∧/(⍳⌈/A)∊A`	means that the items of `A` must be consecutive integers, starting from 1

So, for the array A shown above, the only possible sections are:

```
1 1 1     1 1 2     1 2 1     1 2 2
2 1 1     2 1 2     2 2 1
```

If the required conditions are satisfied, the selection is processed in two steps:

- **First step**: the left argument A is examined to see which of the coordinates are identical.

  For example, a left argument equal to 1 2 1 or 2 1 2 will select items which have their first and third coordinates identical. A left argument equal to 1 1 2 or 2 2 1 will select items which have their first two coordinates identical.

  `1 2 2⍉A` and `2 1 1⍉A` would select the items which have their last two coordinates equal, that is:

  ```
   1  6 11
  13 18 23
  25 30 35
  ```

  So, now we know which items from B we must work with in the next step.

- **Second step**: the selected values are repositioned using a normal dyadic transposition, the left argument of which is composed of the unique values of A obtained by `∪A`.

  For example, we said that both `1 2 2⍉A` and `2 1 1⍉A` would select the same set of values, shown here above. This little matrix will then be transposed using a left argument equal to `1 2` (the matrix remains unchanged) or `2 1` (the matrix is transposed):

  ```
   1 2 2⍉A                  2 1 1⍉A
     ⇩                         ⇩
   1  6 11                 1 13 25
  13 18 23                 6 18 30
  25 30 35                11 23 35
  ```

We recommend that you check out all the possibilities!

Spe-2.3 - Diagonal Section of a Matrix

In the case of a matrix, the only possible diagonal section is specified by 1 1. It selects what is called the main diagonal of the matrix.

For example, `1 1⍉ Forecast` would select the values printed in black below:

```
      Forecast
150 200 100  80  80  80
300 330 360 400 500 520
100 250 350 380 400 450
 50 120 220 300 320 350
      1 1⍉ Forecast
150 330 350 300
```

Chapter H: Special Syntax

1 - Modified Assignment

Changes to a variable frequently involve modifying its current value, and such expressions naturally contain two references to its name:

```
A ← A+1
Positions ← Positions,New
```

If the variable has a long name, its repetition causes the expression to be rather lengthy too:

```
Currency_Ctrl_Flags ← Currency_Ctrl_Flags ∨ Bin
```

If you want to change just part of the variable using indexing, there is even more repetition:

```
Mytable[Rows;Columns] ← Mytable[Rows;Columns]×2
```

Dyalog APL has a unique feature that allows you to avoid this type of repetition; it is called ***Modified Assignment.***

In an expression that uses *Modified Assignment*, the name of the variable to be modified appears just once, at the beginning of the expression. This is followed by the function to be used to change its value, then the assignment arrow, and then the array that specifies the amount by which the original value of the variable is to be changed. This array would otherwise appear as the right argument of the function.

`A←A+1`	can be written as	`A +← 1`
`Positions ← Positions,New`	can be written as	`Positions ,← new`

Using *Modified Assignment*, the other two expressions can be re-written as follows:

```
Currency_Ctrl_Flags ∨← Bin
Mytable[Rows;Columns] ×← 2
```

Modified Assignment is concise and can reduce errors (such as misspelling the variable name in the second part of the expression).

However, there is a disadvantage to *Modified Assignment*: When reading a statement it is very easy to miss the function to the left of the assignment arrow and assume that the statement contains a plain assignment.

Application

Modified Assignment can be used to enter a very long list of values, which would otherwise exceed the screen width, as illustrated in the following example:

```
      vec  ← 52 17 39 77 40 17 29 0 0 14
      vec ,← 80 12 31 46 100 51 49 43 21
      vec ,← 17 18 19 63 61 70 44 0 20 11   etc...
      vec
52 17 39 77 40 17 29 0 0 14 80 12 31 46 100 51 49 43 21 17 18 19
      63 61 70 44 0 20 11
```

2 - Multiple Assignment

It is possible to assign several values to several variables at the same time. This is as true for nested arrays as it is for simple arrays.

```
      (A B C) ← 23 41 56
      (D E F) ← (20 61) (2 2⍴1 2 3 4) 'Africa'
```

These two instructions are equivalent to the following assignments:

```
A ⇨   23                 D ⇨   20 61
B ⇨   41                 E ⇨   1 2
C ⇨   56                       3 4
                         F ⇨   Africa
```

The variables D and F are vectors, and E is a matrix: they are not nested. This technique, called ***Multiple Assignment***, is a simple way to split the contents of a simple or nested vector into several variables.

Of course, the number of variable names must be equal to the length of the vector to the right of the assignment arrow.

As we have already mentioned in Chapter B, for clarity and also for compatibility with other APL systems, we recommend that you parenthesize the names of the variables to the left of the arrow. However, this is not mandatory in Dyalog APL, and you may come across the following syntax, especially in environments in which compatibility with other APL systems is not an issue:

```
      A B C ← 23 41 56
```

This technique can be combined with the *Modified Assignment* seen above. For example, we can update A, B, and C (which we have just set to 23, 41, and 56, respectively) as follows:

```
      (A B C) + ← 57 (19 ¯16) (2 3⍴⍳6)
      A B C
80  60 25   57 58 59
            60 61 62
```

3 - Selective Assignment

3.1 Quick Overview

Let us consider the following matrix Mat:

```
13 52 33 81
42 62 70 47
51 73 28 19
```

It is easy to select (extract) the first row and half of the second row:

```
      6⍴Mat
13 52 33 81 42 62
```

But, until now, it would have been much more complex to modify these items. Previously, we would have had to use two steps:

```
      Mat[1;]←37 38 11 12
      Mat[2;1 2]←20 88
      Mat
37 38 11 12
20 88 70 47
51 73 28 19
```

⇦ Modified values appear in black
Unchanged values are in grey

Now, we will introduce ***Selective Assignment***. The purpose of *Selective Assignment* is to provide a concise way to specify that a selected part (and only that selected part) of an array is to be assigned a new value. In *Selective Assignment*, the expression that specifies (selects) the part of the array to be changed, appears in parentheses to the left of the assignment arrow. The replacement array appears on the right.

Let us restore Mat to its original state, and try out this new technique:

```
      Mat ← 3 4ρ13 52 33 81 42 62 70 47 51 73 28 19
      (6ρMat) ← 37 38 11 12 20 88
      Mat
37 38 11 12
20 88 70 47
51 73 28 19
```

It is important to realise that the replacement array does not necessarily have the same shape as the indices of the replaced portion of `Mat`, which in any case are not necessarily rectangular. Instead, the replacement array must have the same shape as the result of the selection expression. In this case, `6ρMat` would have produced a 6-item vector, so the replacement array must be a 6-item vector, too.

This is also true if we select/replace a sub-matrix of `Mat`, using *Take*:

```
      ¯2 3↑Mat
20 88 70                          ⇦ The selected portion is a matrix
51 73 28
      (¯2 3↑Mat) ← 2 3ρ10×ι6      ⇦ So we must replace it with a matrix of the same shape
      Mat
37 38 11 12
10 20 30 47
40 50 60 19
```

We can even try using a nested replacement array, here using *Drop*:

```
      (1 1↓Mat) ← 2 3ρ'To' 'be' 'or' 'not' 'to' 'be'
      Mat
37   38  11  12
10   To  be  or
40  not  to  be
```

3.2 Available Primitives

This technique cannot be used with every primitive function; only the following selection functions are allowed. When appropriate, these functions can however be used with an *Axis* specification.

ρ	Reshape
/ and ⌿	Compress / Replicate
↑	Take
↓	Drop
,	Ravel

⌽	and	⊖	Reverse, Rotate
		⍉	Transpose (Monadic and Dyadic)
		⊃	Disclose, Pick
\	and	⍀	Expand
		⌷	Index

Examples

One of the most interesting selection tools is *Compress*. Let us restore `Mat` again.

```
      Mat ← 3 4⍴13 52 33 81 42 62 70 47 51 73 28 19
```

How can we negate all the values which are smaller than 40?

```
      ((,Mat<40)/,Mat) ×← ¯1
      Mat
¯13 52 ¯33  81
 42 62  70  47
 51 73 ¯28 ¯19
```

⇦ In this example, we simultaneously use *Selective* and *Modified* assignments

We can also use *Compress* to replace vowels scattered throughout a matrix:

```
      ((,MonMat∊'aeiouy')/,MonMat)←'_'
      MonMat
J_n__r_
F_br__r_
M_rch
Apr_l
M__
J_n_
```

⇦ These modifications would require several instructions if we could not use a selective assignment

Using *Dyadic Transpose*, it is possible to select and modify a diagonal in a matrix.

```
      (1 1⍉Mat) ← 0
      Mat
 0 52 ¯33  81
42  0  70  47
51 73   0 ¯19
```

To replace all the items in a matrix with the values contained in a vector, we now have two methods:

The obvious	`Mat ← (⍴Mat)⍴Vector`
Selective assignment, using *Ravel*	`(,Mat) ← Vector`

Chapter I: Nested Arrays (Continued)

1 - First Contact

1.1 Definitions

We have already met *Nested* arrays in Chapter B; let us just remind ourselves of some definitions:

An array is said to be ***Generalised*** or ***Nested*** when one or more of its items are not simple scalars, but scalars containing "enclosed" arrays (this term will be explained soon).

Such an array can be created in many ways, although until now we have only covered the simplest one, called ***Vector notation***, or ***Strand notation***. Using this notation the items of an array are just juxtaposed, and **each** item can be identified as a separate item because:

- it is separated from its neighbours by **blanks,** or
- it is embedded within **quotes,** or
- it is an expression embedded within **parentheses,** or
- it is a **variable name**, or the name of a niladic function which returns a result.

Just to demonstrate how it works, we will create a nested vector and a nested matrix:

```
      One ← 2 2⍴8 6 2 4
      Two ← 'Hello'
      NesVec ← 87 24 'John' 51 (78 45 23) 85 One 69
      NesMat ← 2 3⍴'Dyalog' 44 Two 27 One (2 3⍴1 2 0 0 0 5)
      DISPLAY NesVec
┌→─────────────────────────────────────────┐
│         ┌→───┐    ┌→───────┐    ┌→──┐    │
│ 87 24   │John│ 51 │78 45 23│ 85 ↓8 6│ 69 │
│         └────┘    └~───────┘    │2 4│    │
│                                 └~──┘    │
└∊─────────────────────────────────────────┘
```

```
      DISPLAY NesMat
```

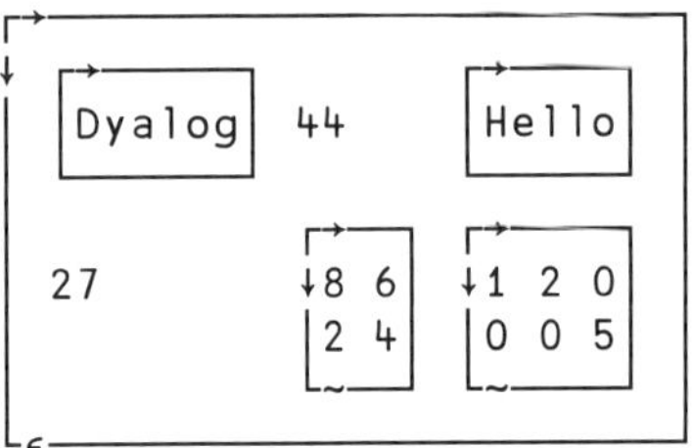

Later, we will provide a more formal description of this notation.

1.2 Enclose & Disclose

It seems so easy to create and work with nested arrays; couldn't we turn a simple array into a nested array by for example replacing one item of a simple matrix with a vector, like this?

```
      Mat ← 2 3⍴87 63 52 74 11 62  ⇦ Create a simple matrix
      Mat[1;2] ← 10 20 30          ⇦ Try to change it into a nested array
LENGTH ERROR
      Mat[1;2]←10 20 30
     ∧
```

It doesn't work!

We cannot replace **one** item with an array of **three** items.

`Mat[1;2]` is a scalar. We can only replace it with a scalar.

1.2.1 - Enclose

Let us now use a little trick to make the assignment above work. We just have to zip up the 3 values into a single "bag", using a function called ***Enclose***, represented by the symbol `⊂`.

Then we will be able to replace one item by one bag!

```
      Mat[1;2] ← ⊂10 20 30
      Mat
87  10 20 30  52               ⇦ Now it works!
74         11  62
```

We can of course do the same with character data, but we now know that an expression like `Mat[2;3] ← 2 4⍴'JohnPete'` is incorrect; we must enclose the array like this:

```
      Mat[2;3] ← ⊂2 4⍴'JohnPete'
      DISPLAY Mat
```

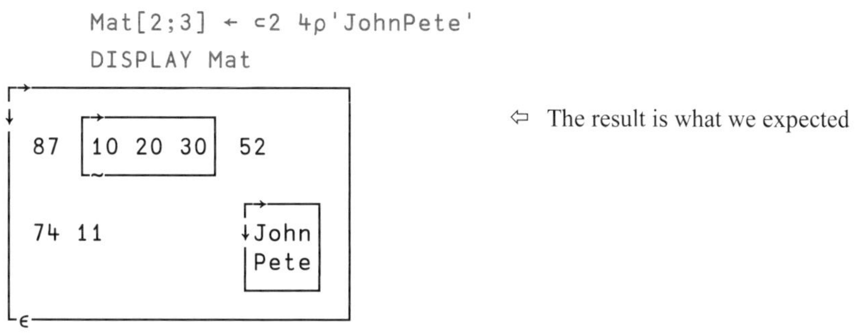

⇦ The result is what we expected

The result of *Enclose* is always a scalar - cf. Section 1.2.4 below.

1.2.2 - Disclose

If we look at the contents of `Mat[2;3]`, we see a little 2 by 4 matrix, but if we look at its shape, we see that it surprisingly has no shape. Its rank is zero, so it must be a scalar!

```
      Mat[2;3]
John
Pete
      ⍴Mat[2;3]
                                        ⇦ Nothing! Its shape is empty
      ⍴⍴Mat[2;3]
0                                       ⇦ And its rank is zero
```

The explanation is obvious: we have put this little matrix into a bag (a scalar), so we now see the bag, and not its contents. If we want to see its contents, we must extract them from the bag, using a function called ***Disclose***, which is represented by the symbol `⊃`.

```
      ⍴⊃Mat[2;3]
2 4                                     ⇦ Right, we now have access to the matrix
      ⍴⍴⊃Mat[2;3]
2                                       ⇦ And its rank is two, as expected
```

We experience the same behaviour if we try to extract one item from a nested vector.

Let us recall the nested vector `NesVec`, which we built in Chapter B:

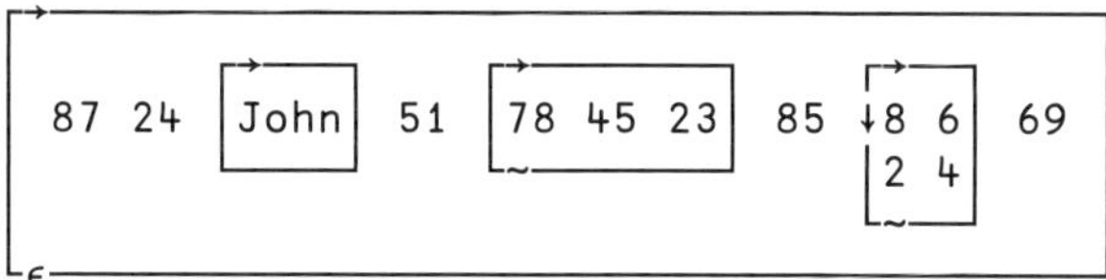

We can use similar expressions to the ones we used on `Mat`:

```
      ⍴NesVec[5]
                                  ⇦ It looks like a scalar;
                                    it is a scalar, containing an enclosed vector.
      ⍴⊃NesVec[5]
3                                 ⇦ Once disclosed, we gain access to its contents
```

In fact, this should not have come as a complete surprise to us. Earlier we learned that the shape of the result of an indexing operation is identical to the shape of the indices. In this case (as well as in the matrix case above), the index specifies a scalar. Hence it would be incorrect to expect anything other than a scalar as the result of the indexing operation!

1.2.3 - Mnemonics

It is easy to remember how to generate the two symbols for *Enclose* and *Disclose* on a US or UK keyboard:

Disclose	⊃	is generated by	Ctrl+X	like	eXtract
Enclose	⊂	is generated by	Ctrl+Z	like	Zip-up

These symbols are often called *Left Shoe* and *Right Shoe* (⊂⊃), but you should preferably use the terms *Disclose* and *Enclose* when you read code.

1.2.4 - Simple and Other Scalars

We know that the result of enclose is **always** a scalar, but there is a difference between enclosing a scalar number or character, and enclosing any other array.

When appropriate, we shall now use four different terms:

Simple scalar A single number or letter (rank zero).

Enclosed array A scalar: the result of enclosing anything other than a simple scalar.

Item A scalar: an item of an array, whether it is a simple scalar or an enclosed array.

Nested array An array in which at least one of the items is an enclosed array.

Always remember these important points:

- *Enclose* does nothing to a simple scalar - it returns the scalar unchanged. The same for *Disclose*.
- All items of an array are effectively scalars, whether they are simple scalars or enclosed arrays: their rank is 0, and their shape is empty.

- A single item can be replaced only by another single item: a simple scalar, or an array of values zipped up using *Enclose* (to form an enclosed array).
- *Vector notation* (*Strand notation*) avoids the use of *Enclose*, because of the conventions used to separate individual items one from one another.

Let us create four vectors:

```
A ← 'Coffee'
B ← 'Tea'
C ← 'Chocolate'
V ← A B C
```

The last statement is just a simpler way to write: `V ← (⊂A),(⊂B),(⊂C)`

So we can see that each of the items of `V` is an enclosed character vector.
Thus, `⍴V[1]` is `⍬`, not `6`.

Here is another example:

```
NesVec[1 5 6] ← 'Yes' 987 'Hello'
DISPLAY NesVec
```

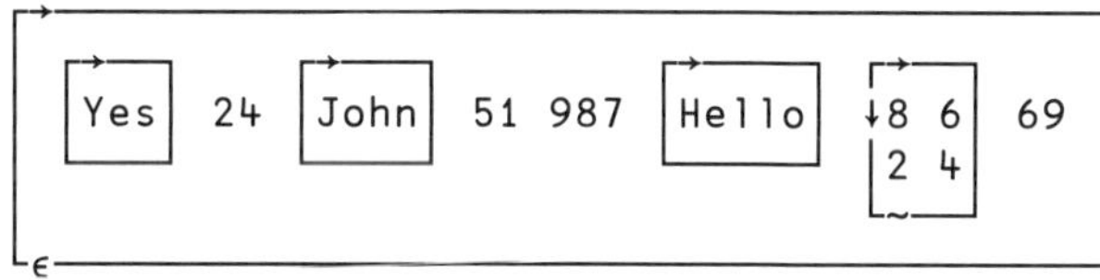

If we type an additional *Enclose*, the result is very different: it effectively adds an extra "bag" around "Hello", as shown below.

```
NesVec[1 5 6]←'Yes' 987 (⊂'Hello')
DISPLAY NesVec
```

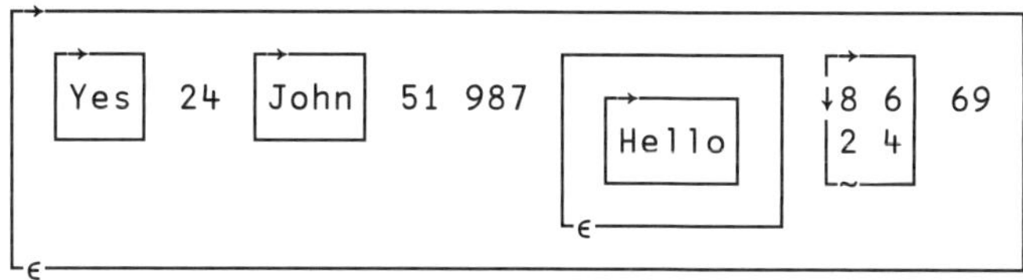

Please undo this last modification to `NesVec`, as we will use its previous value below.

1.3 More About DISPLAY

We have already seen the function `DISPLAY` and its main characteristics in Section B-6.4. We now need to explore some additional characteristics of it.

1.3.1 - Conventions

The following conventions are used in the character matrix that `DISPLAY` returns:

A simple scalar has no box around it.

All other arrays are shown with a surrounding box. The upper-left hand corner of the box describes the *shape* of the array. It can be:

- a simple line for a scalar that is an enclosed array .... −
- a single arrow, for a vector .... →
- one or more vertical arrows for matrices and higher rank arrays...... ↓ or ↓↓
- a horizontal circled minus for an array with empty last axis .... ⊖
- a vertical circled bar for an array with another empty axis .... ⌽

The bottom-left hand corner of the box describes the *nature* of the array:

- a simple line for character contents.. −
- a tilde for numeric contents... ~
- a *Plus* symbol for mixed contents.. +
- a *Membership* symbol for nested arrays .... ∊
- a ***Del*** symbol (or *Carrot*) for `⎕OR` arrays... ∇
- a hash for *Namespace* references.. #

We have not yet studied the last two concepts (`⎕OR` and namespaces); you can ignore them for now.

1.3.2 - Change the Default Presentation

By default, the boxes are drawn with special line-drawing characters, but you can provide a zero left argument to force the function to use alternative (standard APL) characters:

Default or the left argument set to 1	**With the left argument set to 0**
`DISPLAY 'New'`	`0 DISPLAY 'New'`
⇩	⇩

```
┌→──┐        .→--.
│New│        |New|
└───┘        '---'
```

As mentioned previously, the default presentation looks a lot better on the screen, but line-drawing symbols can be problematical under Windows, for example when trying to print them. Nevertheless, we will use this form of output from now on.

1.3.3 - Distinguish Between Items

Now that we have discovered the existence of scalars which are enclosed arrays, we can use `DISPLAY` to distinguish between the two kinds of scalars:

```
      DISPLAY 34
34
```

⇦ `DISPLAY` draws no box around a simple scalar.

```
      DISPLAY NesVec[6]
┌─────────┐
│ ┌→────┐ │
│ │Hello│ │
│ └─────┘ │
└∊────────┘
```

⇦ The 6th item of `NesVec` is an enclosed vector, so its corners are marked with a simple line and an ∊. It contains a second box whose corners tell us that `Hello` is a character vector.

`NesVec[6]` is a scalar containing a vector.

```
      DISPLAY ⊃NesVec[6]
┌→────┐
│Hello│
└─────┘
```

⇦ If we *Disclose* the item, we obtain a simple vector

1.3.4 - Empty Arrays

Here is how `DISPLAY` identifies some empty arrays:

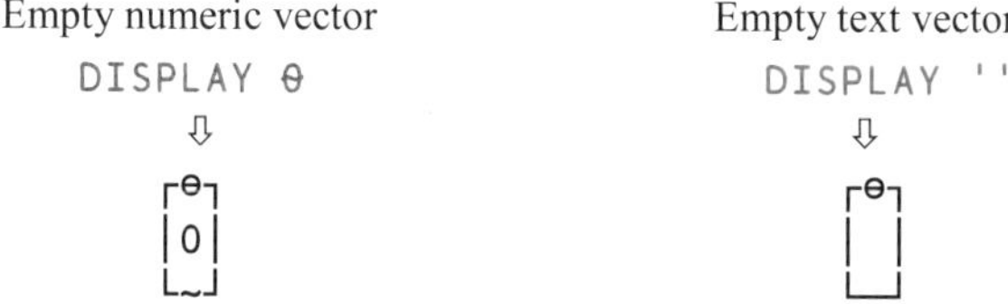

Empty numeric vector — `DISPLAY ⍬`

Empty text vector — `DISPLAY ''`

These are vectors, because there is no vertical arrow, and the ⊖ sign indicates that they are empty. At the bottom of the boxes the symbols ~ and – show that an empty numeric vector and an empty character vector are different. One contains a zero, the other contains a blank. This indicates the type of the array, which is a property of an array even when the array is empty (see section I-7 for more about *fill* items).

We can see the same kind of output for empty matrices:

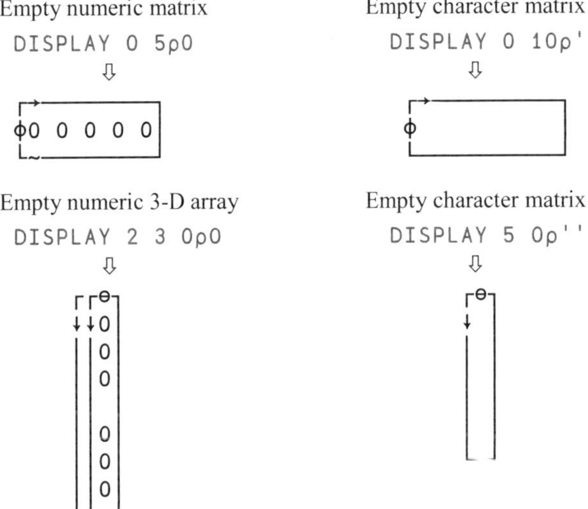

Empty numeric matrix
DISPLAY 0 5⍴0
Empty character matrix
DISPLAY 0 10⍴''
Empty numeric 3-D array
DISPLAY 2 3 0⍴0
Empty character matrix
DISPLAY 5 0⍴''

The output for the empty numeric 3-D array contains 2 sets of 3 zeroes, to show that its shape is 2 3 0.

2 - Depth & Match

2.1 Enclosing Scalars

Applied to a simple scalar, *Enclose* does nothing: the enclose of a simple scalar is the same simple scalar:

```
DISPLAY 35            DISPLAY ⊂35
    ⇩                      ⇩
    35                     35
```

However, when applied to any other array, *Enclose* puts a "bag" around it:

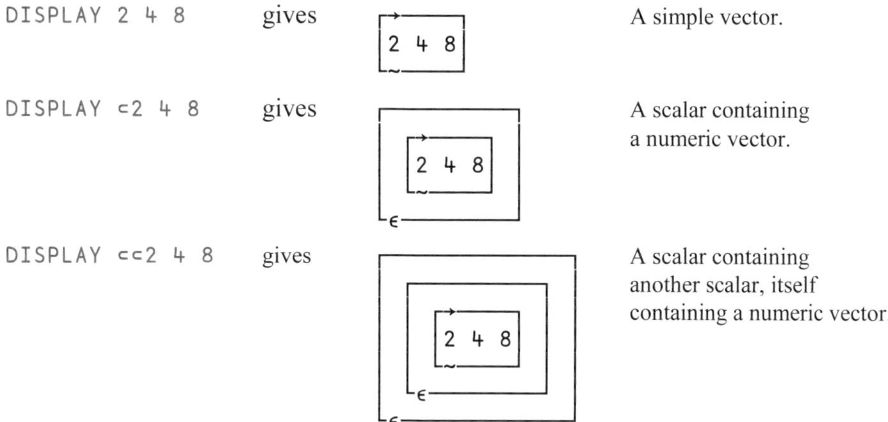

DISPLAY 2 4 8 gives
2 4 8
A simple vector.
DISPLAY ⊂2 4 8 gives
2 4 8
A scalar containing a numeric vector.
DISPLAY ⊂⊂2 4 8 gives
2 4 8
A scalar containing another scalar, itself containing a numeric vector.

2.2 Depth

Suppose that we write a function `Process`, which takes as its argument a vector consisting of: the name of a town, the number of inhabitants, a country code, and the turnover of our company in that town.

For example: `Process 'Lyon' 466400 'FR' 894600`

For the purpose of this example, the function will just display the items it receives in its argument. We choose to write it with the following syntax:

```
     ∇ Process vec;town;pop;coun;tov
[1]    (town pop coun tov)←vec
[2]    (15↑'Town =')town
[3]    (15↑'Population =')pop
[4]    (15↑'Country=')coun
[5]    (15↑'Turnover=')tov
     ∇
```

Perhaps this is not the smartest thing we could do, but we did it!

Now, let us execute the function and verify that it works properly:

```
      Process 'York' 186800 'GB' 540678
 Town =           York
 Population =     186800
 Country=         GB
 Turnover=        540678
```

This looks promising, but what will happen if the user forgets one of the items that the function expects? Let's test it:

```
      Process 'York' 186800 'GB'
LENGTH ERROR
Process[1] (town pop coun tov)←vec
                ^
```

⇦ As we might expect, an error message is issued: we cannot put 3 values into 4 variables!

Let us add a little test to our function to check whether or not the right argument has 4 items.

Here is the new version; the parts which have not been modified are shown in grey:

```
    ∇ Process vec;town;pop;coun;tov
[1]   :If 4=⍴vec
[2]       (town pop coun tov)←vec
...
[6]       (15↑'Turnover=')tov
[7]   :Else
[8]       'Hey, dude, weren''t you supposed to provide 4 values?'
[9]   :End
    ∇
```

It seems to work well now:

```
      Process 'York' 186800 'GB'
Hey, dude, weren't you supposed to provide 4 values?
```

But one day the user forgets all but one of the items, and just types the name of the town:

```
      Process 'York'
 Town =          Y
 Population =    o
 Country=        r
 Turnover=       k
```

⇦ Our test *did* work, but not as expected, because the shape of `'York'` itself is 4...

This trivial example shows that when nested arrays are involved, it is not sufficient to rely on the shape of an array; we need additional information: specifically, is it a simple or a nested array? To help distinguish between simple and nested arrays, APL provides a function named ***Depth***. It is represented by the monadic use of the symbol `≡`.

Depth

> The *Depth* of a simple scalar is 0.
>
> The *Depth* of any other array of any shape is 1, if all of its items are simple scalars. We call such an array a *simple array*, so we can instead say:
>
> The *Depth* of a non-scalar, simple array is 1.
>
> The *Depth* of any other array is equal to the depth of its deepest item plus 1.
>
> The *Depth* is positive if the array is uniform (all of its items have the same depth), and negative if it is not.

Another intuitive definition of ***Depth*** is this: `DISPLAY` the array and count the number of boxes you must pass to reach its deepest item.

Here are some examples:

```
      ≡ 540678
0                                   ⇦ A scalar has a depth of 0.
      ≡ 15 84 37 11                 ⇦ This vector contains only simple scalars
1                                     Its depth is 1.
      ≡ Towns
1                                   ⇦ The same for matrices and higher rank arrays.
      ≡ Prod                          When they contain only simple scalars
1                                     their depth is 1.
```

Now, let us consider this nested vector:

```
      ≡ Vec1 ← (4 3) 'Yes' (8 7 5 6) (2 4)
2
```

It is composed of 4 enclosed vectors, each of depth 1 - so `Vec1` has depth 2. Now let us change the expression slightly:

```
      ≡ Vec2 ← (4 3) 'Yes' (8 7 5) 6 (2 4)
¯2
```

This vector is no longer uniform: it contains four enclosed vectors and one simple scalar, so its depth is negative. The *magnitude* of the depth has not changed, since it reports the highest level of nesting.

In this context the word "uniform" only means that the array contains items of the same **depth**.

`Vec2` is not uniform:	because it contains vectors (depth=1) mixed with a scalar (depth=0).
`Vec1` is uniform:	because all its items are vectors (depth=1), even though they do not have the same shape, the same type, and certainly not the same content.

2.3 Match & Natch

As you might imagine, it would be rather complex to write a program to determine if two arrays are strictly identical, especially when they are nested. For this reason, APL provides the function ***Match***, which is represented by the dyadic use of the traditional mathematical symbol ≡. It returns 1 if its arguments are strictly identical, and 0 if they are not:

```
      14 25 36 ≡ 1 3⍴14 25 36       ⇦ A simple = would have caused a RANK ERROR
0
      (1 2) 'Yes' ≡ (1 2) 'Yes'
1
```

The "opposite" function of *Match* is ***Not-Match***, or simply ***Natch***, which is represented by the symbol ≢. It returns 1 if its arguments are not strictly identical - otherwise 0.

```
      (1 2) 'Yes' ≢ '1 2' 'Yes'
1
      ⍬ ≢ ⍳0
0
      ⍬ ≢ ''
1
```

⇦ Though expressed differently, these two arrays are identical.

⇦ However, numeric and character empty arrays are different.

3 - Each

3.1 Definition and Examples

To avoid the necessity of processing the items of an array one after the other in an explicitly programmed loop, one can use a monadic operator called ***Each***, which is represented by a dieresis (¨) symbol.

As its name implies, *Each* applies the function on its left (its *operand*) to each of the items of the array on its right (if the function is monadic), or to each pair of corresponding items of the arrays on its left and right (if the function is dyadic).

Let us try it with some small nested vectors and a monadic function:

```
      Vec3 ← (5 2) (7 10 23) (52 41) (38 5 17 22)
      Vec4 ← (15 12) 71023 (2 2⍴⍳4) (74 85 96)
      Vec5 ← (7 5 1) (19 14 13) (33 44 55)
      ⍴Vec3
4
      ⍴¨Vec3
 2  3  2  4
```

⇦ The shape of Vec3

⇦ The shape of *each* of the items in Vec3

We can do the same with the second vector:

```
      ⍴¨Vec4
 2     2 2  3
      DISPLAY ⍴¨Vec4
```

⇦ Beware! One item of Vec4 is a scalar, so its shape is empty, as shown here:

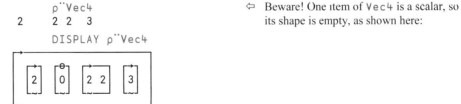

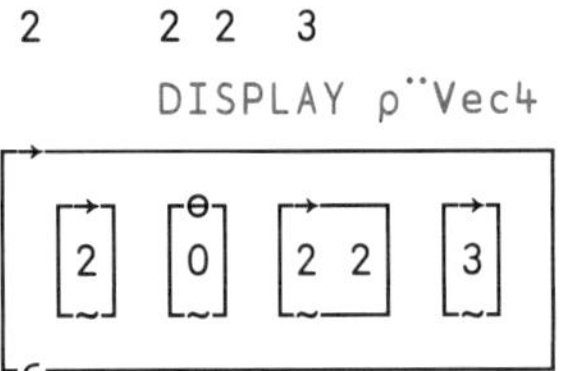

```
┌→──────────────────────┐
│ ┌→┐ ┌⊖┐ ┌→──┐ ┌→┐     │
│ │2│ │0│ │2 2│ │3│     │
│ └~┘ └~┘ └~──┘ └~┘     │
└∊──────────────────────┘
```

If the function specified as the operand to *Each* is dyadic the derived function is also dyadic. As usual, if one of the arguments is a scalar, the scalar is automatically repeated to match the shape of the other argument. For example, to take the first three letters of a character vector called `Text`, we would write `3↑Text`. So we can use *Each* to take the first three letters of each vector in a set of character vectors:

```
      3↑¨MonVec
 Jan  Feb  Mar  Apr  May  Jun
```

Naturally, the operand to *Each* can also be a *User Defined Function*, provided that it can be applied to all of the items of the argument array(s):

```
      Average¨Vec3
 3.5  13.33333333  46.5  20.5
```

Remark In fact, *Each* is a bit more than a "hidden" loop.

Please remember that all items of an array are scalars - either simple scalars or enclosed arrays. So, in an expression like `⍴¨Vec5`, shouldn't we expect the result to be just a list of 3 empty vectors, since the shape of a scalar is an empty vector?

No, the *Each* operator is smarter than that. For each item of the argument array, the item is first *Disclosed* (the "bag" is opened), the function is applied to the disclosed item, and the result is *Enclosed* to again form a scalar (i.e. put into a new bag). Finally, all the new bags (scalars) are arranged in exactly the same structure (rank and shape) as the original argument array to form the final result. So:

```
      ⍴¨Vec5
 3  3  3
```

Is in fact equivalent to:

```
      (⊂⍴⊃Vec5[1]), (⊂⍴⊃Vec5[2]), (⊂⍴⊃Vec5[3])
 3  3  3
      (⍴¨Vec5) ≡ (⊂⍴⊃Vec5[1]),(⊂⍴⊃Vec5[2]),(⊂⍴⊃Vec5[3])
1
```

If the operand to *Each* is a dyadic function, the corresponding items of the left and right arguments are both disclosed before applying the function.

We have seen that the operand to *Each* may be a primitive function or a user-defined function. It may also be a *Derived function* returned by another operator. For example, in the following expressions the operand to *Each* is not `/`, but the derived function (`+/`):

```
      +/¨Vec3                    ⇦ Sums the numbers inside each item of the vector.
7 40 93 82
      +/¨Vec4                    ⇦ It still works, even though one item is a matrix.
27 71023  3 7  255
```

Beware: In some cases the same derived function can be applied with or without the help of *Each*, but the result will not be the same at all:

```
      DISPLAY Vec5
```

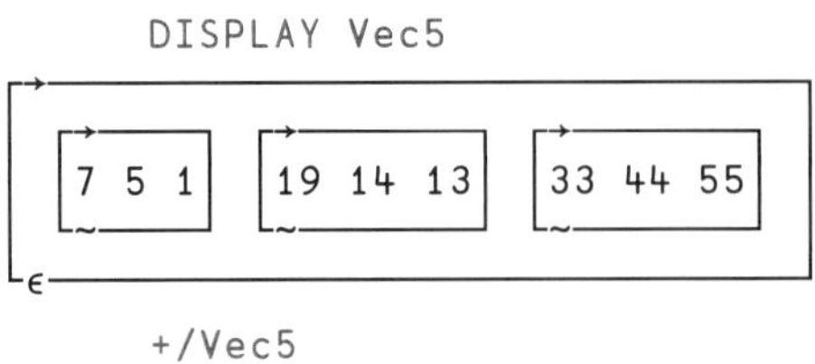

```
      +/Vec5
 59 63 69                        ⇦ The result is the sum of the 3 sub-vectors.
      +/¨Vec5                    ⇦ The result is the sum of each of the 3 sub-vectors.
13 46 132
```

The Use of *Each*

Each is a "loop cruncher". Instead of programming loops, you can in APL apply any function to each of the items of an array, each of which may contain a complex set of data.

This operator is also useful combined with *Match* when a simple equal sign would have caused an error. For example, to compare two lists of names:

```
      'John' 'Julius' 'Jim' 'Jean' ≡¨ 'John' 'Oops' 'Jim' 'Jeff'
1 0 1 0
```

When used inappropriately the *Each* operator can sometimes use a large amount of memory for its intermediate results, so you may need to use it with some care.

Suppose that we have a huge list `ToverCust` of turnover amounts, one item per customer (we have more than 5,000 of them!). Each item contains a matrix having a varying number of rows (products) and 52 columns (weeks). Our task is to calculate the total average turnover per week per customer. No problem:

```
      ToverPerWeek←(+/¨+⌿¨ToverCust)÷52
```

However, if `ToverCust` is very large and we do not have much workspace left, the above expression may easily cause a `WS FULL` error.

The reason is that the intermediate expression `+⌿¨ToverCust` produces a list of 52 amounts per customer, and that may require more workspace than we have room for.

Instead we can put the entire expression into a function. As is often the case in APL, the hard part of writing a function is finding a good name for it. Fortunately we can get by without a name here:

```
      ToverPerWeek←{(+/+⌿⍵)÷52}¨ToverCust
```

Because we have "isolated" the entire logical process in the function and used *Each* to loop through the items one by one, we will at most have only one customer's data "active" at any time, and each intermediate result (a 52 item vector) will be thrown away before recalculating that for the next customer. The result of each function call is just one number, so it is much less likely that we will run into `WS FULL` problems.

3.2 Three Compressions!

In the following we will show three expressions which look similar, but their results are very different. Let us first recall that `Vec5` consists of 3 vectors, each containing 3 items:

```
      Vec5
 7 5 1   19 14 13   33 44 55
```

What is the result of a *Compression*?

```
      1 0 1/Vec5
 7 5 1   33 44 55
      DISPLAY 1 0 1/Vec5
```

⇦ The vector `1 0 1` applies to the three items of `Vec5`, eliminating the second one.

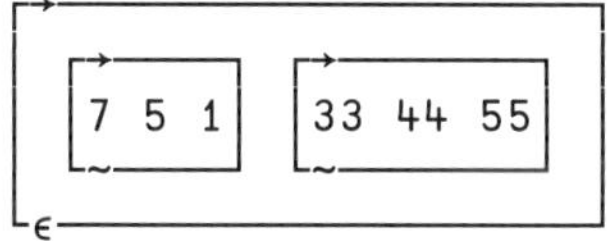

⇦ As said above, the compression applies to the items of `Vec5`, as it would to any vector. So, the second item has been removed.

```
      1 0 1/¨Vec5
 7 5 1     33 44 55
      DISPLAY 1 0 1/¨Vec5
```

⇦ You think the result is the same? Are you sure? It is not displayed the same way.

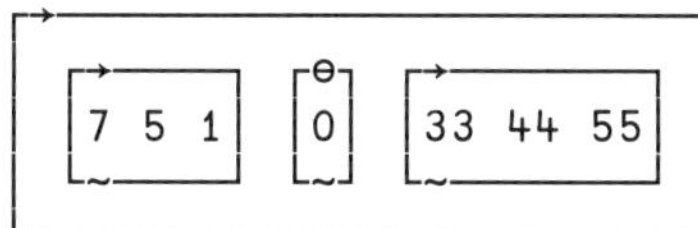

⇦ Things are different here: each item of `1 0 1` is applied to each sub-vector, like this:
`1` applied to 7 5 1 gives 7 5 1,
`0` applied to 19 14 13 gives an empty vector,
`1` applied to 33 44 55 gives 33 44 55,
Thanks to `DISPLAY`!

There is a third way of using *Compress*:

```
      DISPLAY (⊂1 0 1)/¨Vec5
```

⇦ Now the entire mask `1 0 1` is applied to each sub-vector.
The 2nd item of each sub-vector has been removed.

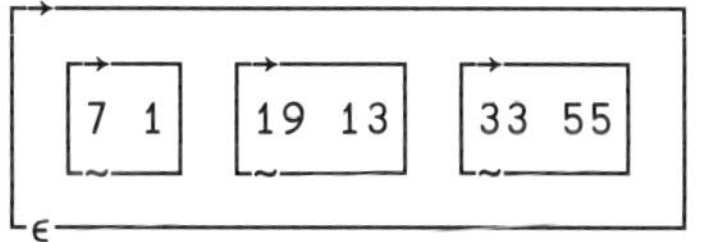

4 - Processing Nested Arrays

We have already seen a number of operations involving nested arrays; we shall explore some more in this section. Because nested arrays generally tend to have a rather simple, or at least uniform, structure, we can illustrate the operations using our little vectors.

4.1 Scalar Dyadic Functions

You can refer to Section C-6.1 concerning the application of scalar dyadic functions to nested arrays.

However, let us here explore again how *Each* applies to scalar dyadic functions:

```
      Vec5
7 5 1  19 14 13  33 44 55
      Vec5 + 100 20 1
107 105 101  39 34 33  34 45 56
      Vec5 +¨ 100 20 1
107 105 101  39 34 33  34 45 56
      Vec5 +¨ ⊂100 20 1
107 25 2  119 34 14  133 64 56
      Vec5 + ⊂100 20 1
107 25 2  119 34 14  133 64 56
```

⇦ 100, 20, and 1 are added to the three sub-vectors, respectively.

⇦ 100 is added to the first, 20 to the second, and 1 to the last: the result is the same.

⇦ The entire vector 100 20 1 is added to each of the three sub-vectors.

⇦ Same result: The scalar on the right is extended to match the shape of the left.

In fact, *Each* is superfluous when using it with scalar dyadic functions, because they are ***Pervasive***, cf. section C-6.1.

4.2 Juxtaposition vs. Catenation

When you *catenate* a number of arrays, for example `V ← A,B,C`, you create a new array with the **contents** of `A`, `B`, and `C` catenated together to make a single new array, as we have seen many times before.

Let us use a small vector and see how it works:

```
      Small ← 3 4 5
```

```
1 2,Small,6 7        gives    ┌→────────────┐
                              │1 2 3 4 5 6 7│
                              └~────────────┘
```

⇦ A simple vector

What happens here is of course that first the 3-item vector `Small` and the 2-item vector `6 7` are combined into one 5-item vector. Then this 5-item vector is combined with the 2-item vector `1 2` to form the resulting 7-item vector. Both the final and the interim results are simple.

We can now explain what happens when you *juxtapose* two or more arrays (*Strand notation*), for example `V ← A B C D E`: each array is enclosed, and the resulting scalars are catenated together.

Such an expression produces a vector made of as many items as we have arrays on the right.

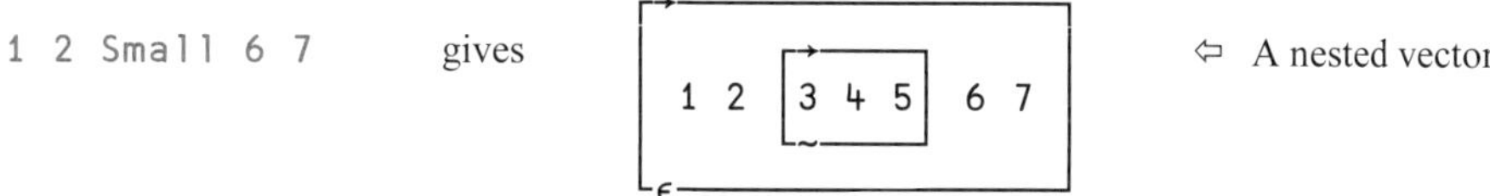

This is what we call *Vector notation* or *Strand notation*. In this case, we juxtaposed 5 arrays, so we created a nested array of length 5.

What happens here is that each of the 5 arrays is first enclosed, and then the resulting 5 scalars are catenated together to produce the 5-item vector. Please remember that enclosing a simple scalar does not change it, so you can only see the difference for the array `Small`.

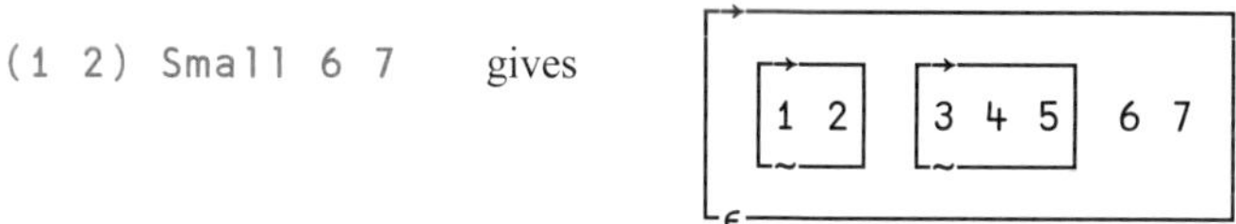

Here, we juxtaposed 4 arrays, two of which are vectors. It is again an example of *Strand notation*.

In other words, juxtaposition works on arrays seen as building blocks, while catenation works on the contents of the arrays.

It may help you to know that there is a strict relationship between catenation and *Strand notation*:

`A B C`	is strictly identical to	`(⊂A),(⊂B),(⊂C)`
`(1 2) Small,6 7`	gives exactly the same result as `(1 2) Small 6 7`, but for a very different reason:	

In fact, `Small` is **not** catenated to the vector `6 7` as in the first example above. To read this expression correctly, we must refer to the comma as an APL function:

- Its right argument is the vector `6 7`, of course.
- Its left argument is whatever is on its left, up to the next function symbol. As there is no such function (parentheses are not functions), the left argument is the result of the entire expression to the left of the comma, i.e. the 2-item vector `(1 2) Small`.

So, the result is that the 2-item vector `(1 2) Small` is combined with the 2-item vector `6 7` to form the resulting 4-item vector.

Remember this: When interpreting an expression you must never "break" a sequence of juxtaposed arrays (a *Strand*), even if it is a nested vector.

So, the left argument to *Catenate* is in this example:

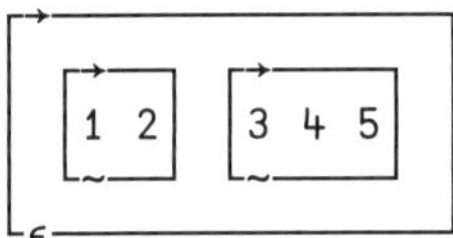

When *Catenate* is executed, the two items of this argument are catenated to the two items `6` and `7` of the right argument, making the same 4-item nested vector as in the previous example.

What is the result of the expression: `(1 2),Small (6 7)` ?

4.3 Characters and Numbers

We have a character matrix `MT` and a numeric matrix `MN`:

```
  MT                                MN
  ⇩                                 ⇩
Francis          608.1    928.24 1293.14   849.95
Carmen          1127.84   970.27 1249     1168.29
Luciano          775.12 1065      670.69 1091.7
```

We would like to have them displayed side by side.

4.3.1 - Solution 1

The first idea is to just type `MT MN`

```
      MT MN
 Francis     608.1    928.24 1293.14   849.95
 Carmen     1127.84   970.27 1249     1168.29
 Luciano     775.12 1065      670.69 1091.7
```

The format of the result is not ideal; some values have 2 decimal digits, and some have only one or none. But there is a much more important problem. Imagine that we would like to draw a line on the top of the report. We can catenate a single dash along the first dimension:

```
      '-'⍪MT MN                     ⇦ We could have written: '-',[1]MT MN

- Francis    608.1    928.24 1293.14   849.95
  Carmen    1127.84   970.27 1249     1168.29
  Luciano    775.12 1065      670.69 1091.7
```

⇧ Look here!

This is not what we expected: the dash has been placed on the left, not on the top! The reason is that the expression `MT MN` does not produce a matrix, but a 2-item nested vector. And when one catenates a scalar to a vector, it is inserted before its first item or after the last one to produce a longer vector. This cannot produce a matrix, unless *Laminate* is used, but we shall not try that now.

4.3.2 - Solution 2

Well, if juxtaposition doesn't achieve what we want, why shouldn't we catenate our two matrices?

```
      MT,MN
Francis   608.1    928.24 1293.14   849.95     ⇦ It is almost the same presentation,
Carmen   1127.84   970.27 1249     1168.29       but not exactly: this is a matrix!
Luciano   775.12 1065      670.69 1091.7
```

Now, let us try to draw the line.

```
      '-'⍪MT,MN
-------        -       -       -       -
Francis   608.1    928.24 1293.14   849.95     ⇦ Horrible!
Carmen   1127.84   970.27 1249     1168.29       What happened?
Luciano   775.12 1065      670.69 1091.7
```

When we catenated `MT` (shape 3 7) with `MN` (shape 3 4), we produced a 3 by 11 matrix.
So, when we further catenated a dash on top of it, the dash was repeated 11 times to fit the last dimension of the matrix. This is why we obtained 7 dashes on top of the 7 text columns, and 4 dashes, each on top of each of the 4 numeric columns. This is still not what we want!

4.3.3 - Solution 3

The final solution will be the following: convert the numbers into text, using the *Format* function, and then catenate one character matrix to another character matrix:

```
      '-'⍪MT,9 2⍕MN
-------------------------------------------  ⇦ The line is where we want it
Francis    608.10    928.24   1293.14    849.95
Carmen    1127.84    970.27   1249.00   1168.29
Luciano    775.12   1065.00    670.69   1091.70  ⇦ The numbers are nicely formatted
```

Exercise

Try to deduce the results of the following 3 expressions (depth, rank, shape), and then verify your solutions on the computer:

```
(⊂MT) (⊂MN)
(⊂MT),(⊂MN)
MT,⊂MN
```

4.4 Some More Operations

Let us use `Vec5` once more: `Vec5 ← (7 5 1)(19 14 13)(33 44 55)`

4.4.1 - Reduction

```
      +/Vec5
 59 63 69
```

⇧ Notice the space here!

The three enclosed arrays (scalars) have been added together, and the result is therefore an enclosed array (a scalar). You can tell this from the output, because the first value (59) is not displayed at the left margin, but indented 1 character.

```
      DISPLAY +/Vec5
┌──────────────┐
│ ┌→────────┐  │
│ │59 63 69 │  │
│ └~────────┘  │
└∊─────────────┘
```

⇦ The result we obtained is an enclosed vector (a scalar)

We know that the reduction of a vector (rank 1) produces a scalar (rank 0), and this rule still applies here.

To obtain the *contents* of the (enclosed) vector, we must disclose the result:

```
      DISPLAY ⊃+/Vec5
┌→───────┐
│59 63 69│
└~───────┘
```

The same thing can be observed if we try to collect all the values contained in `Vec5` into a single vector, by catenating them together:

```
      DISPLAY ,/Vec5
```

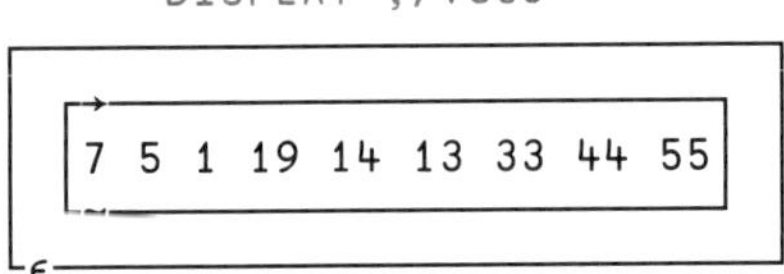

⇦ It worked, but here again we might want to disclose the result: `⊃,/Vec5`

4.4.2 - Index Of and Membership

The *Index Of* function (dyadic ⍳) may be used to search for (find the position of) items in a nested vector:

```
      Vec5 ⍳ (19 14 13)(1 5 7)
2 4
```

⇦ This is correct: the first vector appears in Vec5 as Vec5[2], and the second vector is not present.

But beware, there is a booby trap:

```
      Vec5 ⍳ (19 14 13)
4 4 4
```

⇦ (19 14 13) is not a nested array. Vec5 is searched for each of these 3 numbers individually, and they are not found.

```
      Vec5 ⍳ ⊂19 14 13
2
```

⇦ This gives the expected answer

It is also important to be aware of this when using *Membership*:

```
      (3 4 5)(7 5 1) ∊ Vec5
0 1
      (7 5 1) ∊ Vec5
0 0 0
      (⊂7 5 1) ∊ Vec5
1
```

4.4.3 - Indexing

The rules we saw about indexing remain true: when one indexes a vector by an array, the result has the same shape as the array. If the vector is nested, the result is generally nested too:

```
      DISPLAY Vec4
┌→──────────────────────────────────────────┐
│ ┌→────┐         ┌→──┐  ┌→────────┐        │
│ │15 12│  71023  ↓1 2│  │74 85 96 │        │
│ └~────┘         │3 4│  └~────────┘        │
│                 └~──┘                     │
└∊──────────────────────────────────────────┘
      DISPLAY Vec4[2 2⍴ 4 2 1 3]
┌→───────────────────────┐
↓ ┌→───────┐             │
│ │74 85 96│  71023      │
│ └~───────┘             │
│ ┌→────┐       ┌→──┐    │
│ │15 12│       ↓1 2│    │
│ └~────┘       │3 4│    │
│               └~──┘    │
└∊───────────────────────┘
```

We have also seen, in Section B-5.3, that a nested array can be used as an index. For example, to index items scattered throughout a matrix, the array that specifies the indices is composed of 2-item vectors (row & column indices):

```
      Tests
11 26 22
14 87 52
30 28 19
65 40 55
19 31 64
33 70 44
      Tests[(2 3)(5 1)(1 2)]
52 19 26
      Tests[2 2⍴(2 3)(5 1)(1 2)]
52 19
26 52
```

Let us try to obtain the same result with the *Index* function, or *Squad*:

`(2 3)(5 1)(1 2) ⌷ Tests`	This cannot work. *Squad* expects a 2-item vector: a list of rows and a list of columns.
`(2 3)(5 1)(1 2) ⌷¨ Tests`	This won't work: each item of the left argument cannot be associated with a corresponding item of `Tests`, because they do not have the same shape.

```
      (2 3)(5 1)(1 2)⌷¨⊂Tests
52 19 26
```

This last expression worked correctly. **Each** couple of indices is applied to `Tests` as a whole because it has been enclosed, and therefore the scalar on the right is extended to match the 3-item vector on the left.

4.4.4 - Always Keep In Mind the Following Rules

- The items of a nested array are scalars and are therefore always processed as scalars.

  In the expression `(5 6)(4 2)×10 5`

  `(5 6)` is multiplied by `10`, and `(4 2)` is multiplied by `5`

- A single list of values placed between parentheses is not a nested array:

  `(45 77 80)` is not a nested array. The parentheses do nothing here.

- An expression is always evaluated from right to left, one function at a time. Note that strands can be easy to miss when determining what the left argument of a function is:

  In the expression `2×A 3+B`

  The left argument of the *Plus* function is not `3` alone, but the vector `A 3`

Before we go any further with nested arrays, we recommend that you try to solve some exercises.

Exercises

I-1 You are given 3 numeric vectors:

```
A ← 1 2 3
B ← 4 5 6
C ← 7 8 9
```

Try to predict the results given by the following expressions in terms of depth, rank, and shape. Then check your results using `DISPLAY`.

a) `A B C × 1 2 3`

b) `(10 20),A`

c) `(10 20),A B`

d) `A B 2 × C[2]`

e) `10×A 20×B`

I-2 Same question for the following expressions:

a) `+/A B C`

b) `+/¨A B C`

c) `1 0 1/¨A B C`

d) `(A B C)⍳(4 5 6)`

e) `1 10 3 ∊ A`

f) `(⊂1 0 1)/¨A B C`

g) `1 10 3 ∊ A B C`

I-3 Create the following nested array: `NA ← 1 2 (2 2⍴3 4 5 6)7 8`

What are the results of:

```
+/NA
,/NA
```

5 - Split and Mix

We saw that in some cases we can choose to represent data either as a matrix or as a nested vector; remember `MonMat` and `MonVec`.

Two primitive monadic functions are provided to switch from one form to the other:

Mix (↑) Returns an array of higher *Rank* and lower *Depth* than that of its argument.

Split (↓) Returns an array of lower *Rank* and higher *Depth* than that of its argument.

5.1 Basic Use

Let us apply ***Mix*** to two small vectors:

```
      VTex ← 'One' 'Two' 'Three'
      VNum ← (6 2) 14 (7 5 3)
      DISPLAY RTex← ↑ VT
```

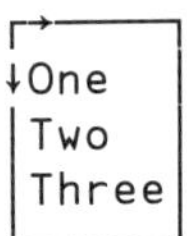

⇦ We converted a nested vector: *Depth* = 2 / *Rank* = 1
into a simple matrix: *Depth* = 1 / *Rank* = 2

```
      DISPLAY RNum← ↑ VNum
```

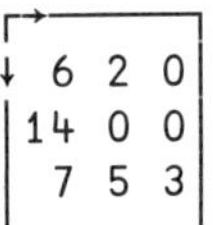

⇦ We converted a nested vector: *Depth* = ¯2 / *Rank* = 1
into a simple matrix: *Depth* = 1 / *Rank* = 2

Of course the operation is possible only because the shorter items are padded with blanks (for text) or zeroes (for numbers), or more generally by the appropriate *Fill Item* (this notion will be explained soon).

The last example above shows that when we say that the depth is reduced, we actually mean that the *magnitude* of the depth is reduced.

And now, let us apply ***Split*** to the matrices we have just produced:

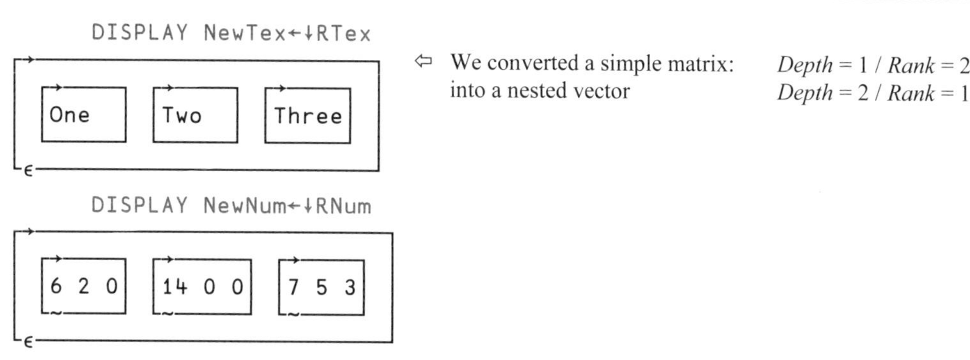

DISPLAY NewTex←↓RTex

DISPLAY NewNum←↓RNum

Note that the two new vectors (`NewTex` and `NewNum`) are not identical to the original ones (`VTex` and `VNum`) because when they were converted into the matrices `RTex` and `RNum`, the shorter items were padded. When one splits a matrix, the items of the result all have the same size.

Mix applied to heterogeneous data

The examples shown above represent very common uses of *Mix* and *Split*. However, it is of course also possible to apply the functions to heterogeneous data:

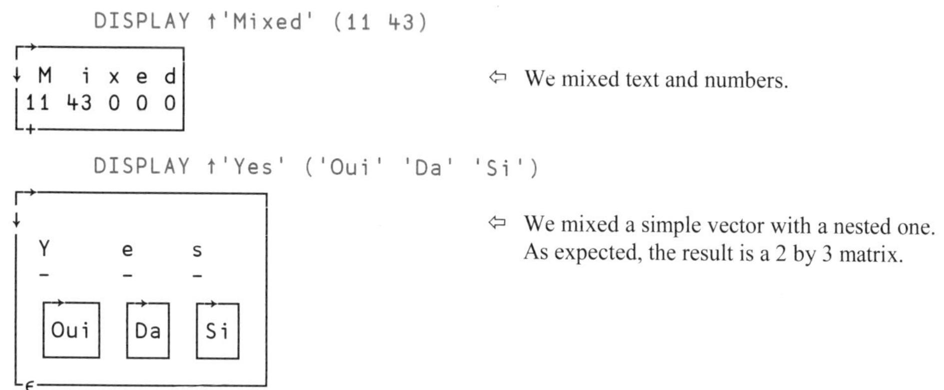

DISPLAY ↑'Mixed' (11 43)
M i x e d
11 43 0 0 0
⇦ We mixed text and numbers.
DISPLAY ↑'Yes' ('Oui' 'Da' 'Si')
Y e s
Oui
Da
Si
⇦ We mixed a simple vector with a nested one.
As expected, the result is a 2 by 3 matrix.

5.2 Axis Specification

5.2.1 - Split

When we apply the function *Split* to an array its rank will decrease, so we must specify which of its dimensions is to be suppressed. As usual, if we don't specify it explicitly, the default is to suppress the last dimension.

Let us work on `Chemistry`, a matrix we used earlier:

```
H2SO4
CaCO3
Fe2O3
```

In this case there are two possible uses of *Split*; we can apply it either to the 1st dimension or to the 2nd dimension.

```
      ↓[1]Chemistry
 HCF  2ae  SC2  OOO  433          ⇦ The matrix is split column-wise.
      ↓[2]Chemistry               ⇦ The matrix is split row-wise.
 H2SO4  CaCO3  Fe2O3
      ↓Chemistry
 H2SO4  CaCO3  Fe2O3              ⇦ As always, the default is along the last axis.
```

5.2.2 - Mix

The use of *Mix* is a bit more complex, because it adds a new dimension to an existing array. So does the function *Laminate*, and the two functions use the same convention to specify where to insert the new dimension.

If we apply the function *Mix* to a 3-item nested vector of vectors, in which the largest item is an enclosed 5 item vector, the result must be either a 5 by 3 matrix, or a 3 by 5 matrix (the default).

In the same way as for *Laminate*, a new dimension is created, which can be inserted before or after the existing dimension. The programmer decides this by specifying an axis:

`[0.5]` inserts the new dimension **before** the existing one, and results in a 5 by 3 matrix,
`[1.5]` inserts the new dimension **after** the existing one, and results in a 3 by 5 matrix.

```
      ↑[0.5]'One' 'Two' 'Three'
OTT
nwh
eor
  e
  e
      ↑[1.5]'One' 'Two' 'Three'     ⇦ This is the default
One
Two                                 ⇦ Equivalent to ↑'One' 'Two' 'Three'
Three
```

Let us now work with a nested matrix,

```
      ⎕ ← Friends ← 2 3⍴'John' 'Mike' 'Anna' 'Noah' 'Suzy'  'Paul'
 John  Mike  Anna
 Noah  Suzy  Paul
```

The shape of this matrix is 2 3, and its items are all of length 4. So, *Mix* can produce three different results, according to axis specifications as follows:

With this axis ⇩	the new dimension is inserted ⇩	and it returns an array of shape ⇩	
[2.5]	**after** 2 3	2 3 4	⇦ The default
[1.5]	**between** 2 **and** 3	2 4 3	
[0.5]	**before** 2 3	4 2 3	

Each of these 3 cases is illustrated below. To help you understand them, we have written the same name (Suzy) in bold letters each time:

```
↑[2.5]Friends        ↑[1.5]Friends        ↑[0.5]Friends
     ⇩                    ⇩                    ⇩
   John                 JMA                  JMA
   Mike                 oin                  NSP
   Anna                 hkn
                        nea                  oin
   Noah                                      oua
   Suzy                 NSP
   Paul                 oua                  hkn
                        azu                  azu
(This is the default)   hyl
                                             nea
                                             hyl
```

In the first example, the names are placed "horizontally" as rows in 2 sub-matrices.

In the second case, they are placed "vertically" in columns.

The third case is more difficult to read; the names are positioned perpendicularly to the matrices, with one letter in each. You might like to imagine that the letters are arranged in a cube, and that you are viewing it from 3 different positions.

6 - First & Type

We have not mentioned this before (because up to now we have only used it on 1-item arrays), but *Disclose* actually discloses just the *first* item of an array. All other items are ignored. For this reason, the function is also called ***First***.

```
      ⊃26 (10 20 30) 100
26
```

```
      ⊃'January' 'February' 'March' ...
January
      ⊃2 2⍴'Dyalog' (2 2⍴⍳4) 'APL' 100
Dyalog
```

We shall also soon need to know whether an array is made of numbers, of characters, or both. This information may be found using the function ***Type***, which is the monadic use of the symbol `∊`.

The *Type* function returns an array having exactly the same structure as its argument: shape, rank, depth, for all levels of nesting. The resulting array contains a zero for each numeric scalar, and a blank for each character scalar in the argument array.

When applied to a nested array, the result may be rather difficult to interpret, because the blanks are, by definition, invisible when displayed:

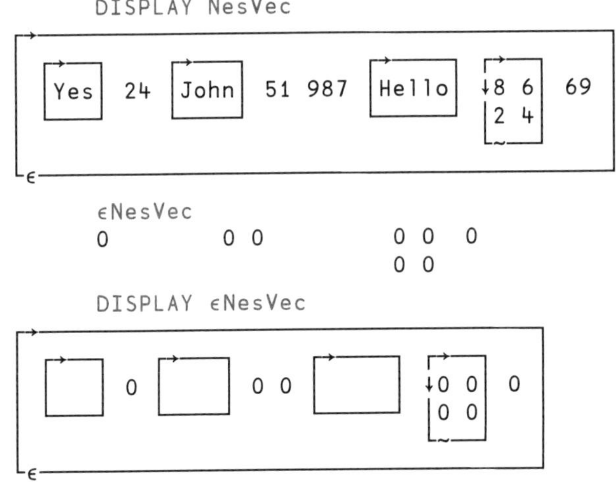

7 - Prototype, Fill Item

Some operations like *Expand* or *Take* may insert new additional items into an array. Up to now, things were simple; numeric arrays were expanded with zeroes, and character arrays were expanded with blanks. But what will happen if the array contains both numbers and characters (a mixed array), or if it is a nested array?

We need a variable to experiment a little:

```
      Hogwash ← 19 (2 2⍴⍳4) (3 1⍴'APL') (2 2⍴5 8 'Nuts' 9)
```

What would be the result of expressions like `6↑Hogwash` or `1 1 0 1 0 1\Hogwash`?

In general, when expanding an array, APL inserts *Fill Items*, and it does so using the *Prototype* of the array.

Definitions

> The ***Prototype*** of an array is defined as the *Type* of its *First* item: `∊⊃Array`
>
> In other words, the prototype of an array is its first item, in which all the numbers are replaced by zeroes and all characters are replaced by blanks, through all levels of depth.
>
> The *Prototype* of an array is used as a ***Fill Item*** whenever an operation needs to create additional items.

The first item of `Hoqwash` is a number, so its *Prototype* is a single zero. If we lengthen the vector using *overtake*, it will be padded with zeroes (fill items):

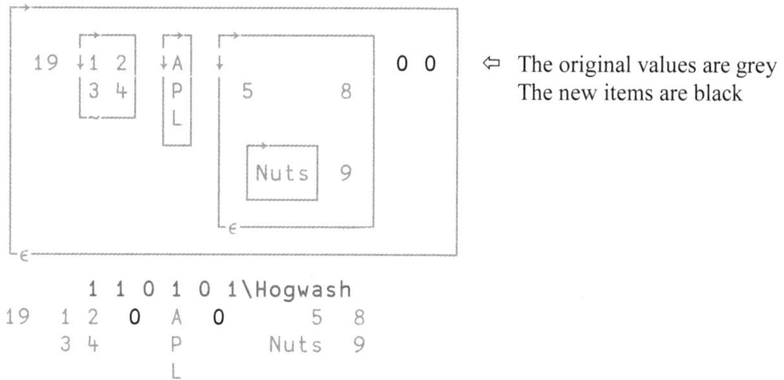

⇦ The original values are grey
The new items are black

```
      1 1 0 1 0 1\Hogwash
19  1 2  0  A  0      5  8
    3 4     P       Nuts  9
            L
```

Let us rotate the vector by one position: `Hogwash ← 1⌽Hogwash`

Now, the first item is a numeric matrix, and the prototype of `Hogwash` is:

```
      ∊⊃Hogwash
0 0
0 0
```

If we take 6 items from `Hogwash` two such matrices will be added:

```
      DISPLAY 6↑Hogwash
```

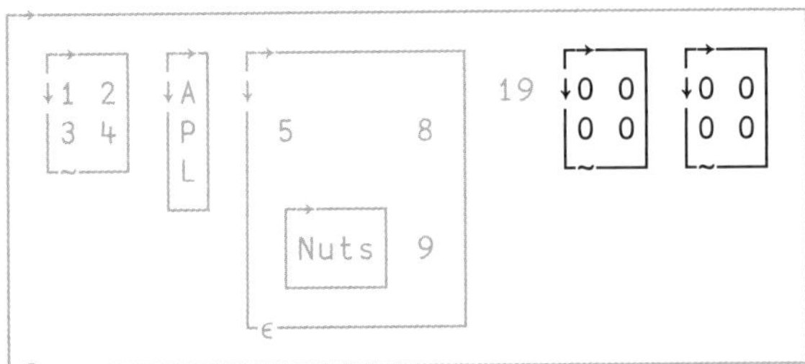

Let us rotate the variable once more: `Hogwash ← 1⌽Hogwash`

Now the first item is a little 3 by 1 character matrix containing the letters "APL". So the *Prototype* will be a 3 by 1 character matrix containing three blanks. This is the array that will be used by *Expand* as the fill item. Let us verify it:

```
      DISPLAY 1 1 0 1 0 1\Hogwash
```

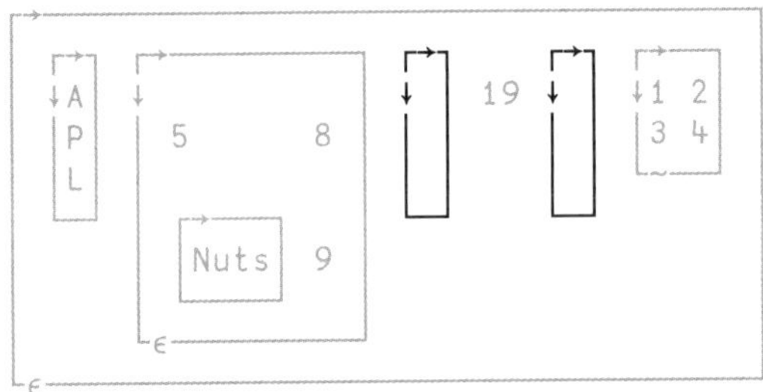

If we repeat the rotation, the first item will be a nested matrix. So, the prototype (and hence also the fill item) will be a 2 by 2 nested matrix. Let us again try *Take*:

```
      Hogwash←1⌽Hogwash
      DISPLAY 6↑Hogwash
```

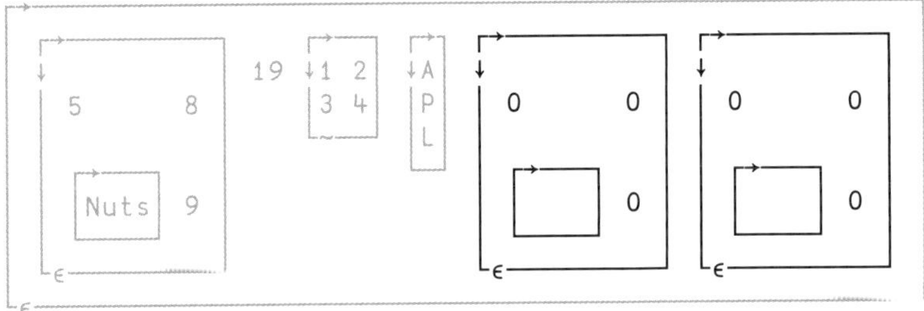

Obviously, fill items are generally only useful for arrays whose items have a uniform structure.

8 - Pick

8.1 - Definition

Whenever you need to select one (and only one) item from an array you can use the dyadic function ***Pick***, represented by the symbol (⊃). What makes *Pick* different from an ordinary indexing is that it is possible to "dig into" a nested array and pick an item at any level of nesting, and that it discloses the result. The latter is probably the reason why *Pick* and the monadic function *Disclose* use the same symbol. The syntax of *Pick* is as follows:

R← *Path* ⊃ *Data*

The left argument is a scalar or a vector which specifies the *Path* that leads to the desired item. Each item of *Path* is the index or set of indices needed to reach the item at the corresponding level of depth of the array.

The operation starts at the outermost level and goes deeper and deeper into the levels of nesting. At each level, the selected item is disclosed before applying the next level of selection.

We shall work with the nested matrix `Weird`, which we created in Section B-6.5:

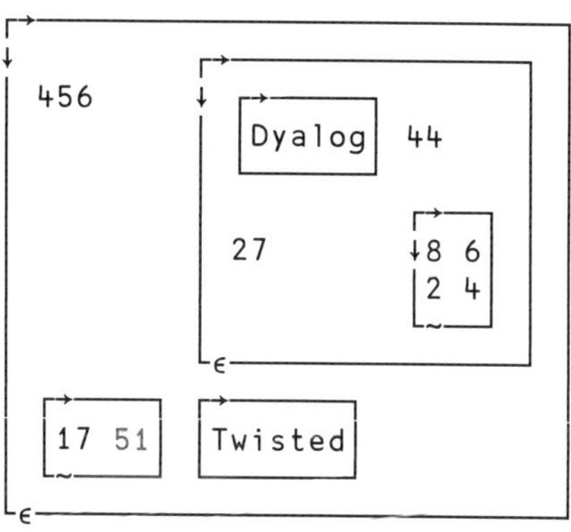

⇦ Let us try to select the value 51

To select the `51` we must first select the vector located in row 2, column 1 of the matrix, and then select the second item of that vector. This is how we express this selection using *Pick*:

```
      (2 1) 2 ⊃ Weird
51
```

The left argument `(2 1) 2` is a 2-item vector because we need to select at two levels of nesting.

Using simple indexing and explicit disclosing we need a much more complicated expression to obtain the same selection:

```
      ⊃(⊃Weird[2;1])[2]          ⇦ In this special case, the leftmost ⊃ is not required.
51
```

We can also select the letter "g" within the text "Dyalog". To do so we must first select the matrix located in row 1, column 2. Within this matrix we must select the character vector located in row 1, column 1, and finally we must select the sixth item of that character vector:

```
      (1 2) (1 1) 6 ⊃ Weird
g
```

This time the left argument is a 3-item vector because we need to select at three levels of nesting:

- `(1 2)` is the set of indices for the selection at the outermost level of depth,
- `(1 1)` is the set of indices for the selection at the 2nd level of depth, and
- `6` is the index for the selection at the 3rd level of depth.

Using simple indexing this selection is almost obscure:

```
      ⊃(⊃(⊃Weird[1;2])[1;1])[6]
g
```

8.2 - Beware!

The left argument to *Pick* is a vector with as many items as the depth at which we want to select an item. Each item of the left argument has a number of items corresponding to the rank of the sub-item at the corresponding depth at which it operates.

If we remove the last item of *Path* in the example above the selection will stop one level above the level at which it stopped before. This means that we would select the entire character vector "Dyalog" instead of just the letter "g":

```
      (1 2) (1 1) ⊃ Weird
Dyalog
```

Yes, we selected the entire character vector. Please note again that the result has been disclosed, so that a simple array is returned in this case, instead of scalar which is an enclosed vector.

If we instead remove the last two items of *Path* we might expect to select the entire 2 by 2 nested matrix containing the character vector "Dyalog":

```
      (1 2) ⊃ Weird
RANK ERROR                              ⇦ It does not work!
      (1 2)⊃Weird
     ^
```

The reason for this is a problem that we have seen before:

In the expression `(1 2) (1 1) ⊃ Weird` the item `(1 2)` is a scalar (an enclosed vector) because we use *Strand notation*. The left argument to *Pick* has two items, because we want to select an item at the 2nd level.

In the expression `(1 2) ⊃ Weird` we do not have a *Strand*, so the argument `(1 2)` is not enclosed. It is a (simple) 2-item vector and therefore only suitable for selection at the 2nd level. The `RANK ERROR` is reported because we try to use a scalar `1` as an index at the outermost level. However, at this level the array is a matrix, so 2 items are needed to form a proper index at this level.

We want to select at the outermost level, so the left argument to *Pick* must have exactly one item. Therefore we must explicitly enclose the vector, leading to the correct expression:

```
      (⊂1 2) ⊃ Weird
 Dyalog    44
     27   8 6
          2 4
```

We still need two indexes inside the enclosure because at the outermost level the array is a matrix.

The expression we used before (without the explicit *Enclose*) is inappropriate for the array `Weird`, but it would work fine with a different array; for example, to take the first item of a nested vector, and then select the second item of it, as shown here:

```
      (1 2)⊃'Madrid' 'New York' 'London'
a                                       ⇦ We selected the "a" of "Madrid".
                                          The parentheses are superfluous here.
```

In this expression an *Enclose* would be wrong, as we need to select at two levels. However, at each level we only need one index, as we select from vectors at both levels.

8.3 - Important

As mentioned previously, *Pick* returns the **contents** of the specified item, not the scalar which contains it.

Let us refer to the original value of `Hogwash` (i.e. before we rotated it above). It looks as if `2⊃Hogwash` and `Hogwash[2]` display the same value:

```
 1 2
 3 4
```

This is deceptive: the first expression (`2⊃Hogwash`) returns the 2 by 2 matrix contained in `Hogwash[2]`, while the other merely returns the 2nd item of `Hogwash`, which is an enclosed matrix:

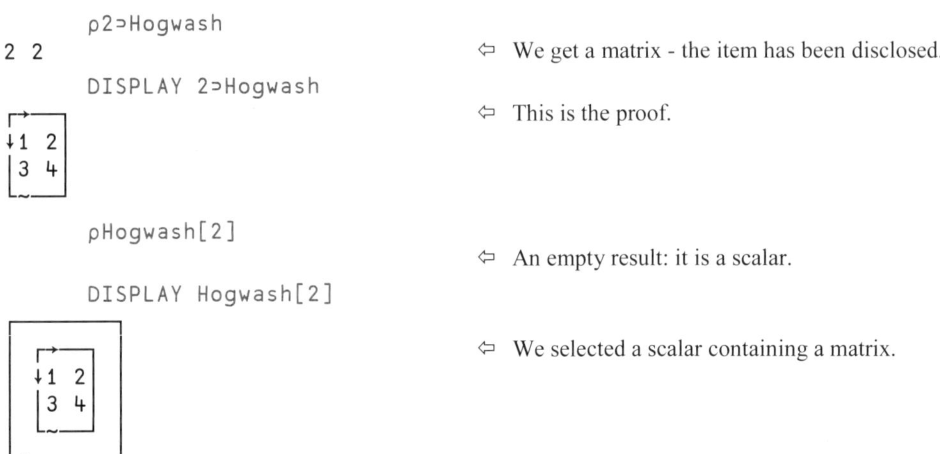

```
      ⍴2⊃Hogwash
2 2                                ⇦ We get a matrix - the item has been disclosed.
      DISPLAY 2⊃Hogwash
┌→──┐                              ⇦ This is the proof.
↓1 2│
│3 4│
└~──┘

      ⍴Hogwash[2]
                                   ⇦ An empty result: it is a scalar.
      DISPLAY Hogwash[2]
┌─────────┐
│ ┌→──┐   │                        ⇦ We selected a scalar containing a matrix.
│ ↓1 2│   │
│ │3 4│   │
│ └~──┘   │
└∊────────┘
```

8.4 - Selective Assignment

When one wants to modify an item deep inside an array it is important to remember that *Pick* returns a disclosed result.

For example, let us try to replace the number 5 with the character vector "Five" in the 4th item of `Hogwash`.

If we wanted to extract the value 5, we would just write: `4 (1 1)⊃Hogwash`

To replace it, we use the same expression in a normal selective assignment:

```
      (4 (1 1)⊃Hogwash) ← 'Five'
      Hogwash
19  1 2  A   Five  8              ⇦ And it works, though we haven't enclosed
    3 4  P   Nuts  9                the replacement value!
         L
```

8.5 - An Idiom

Suppose you have a nested vector: `nv ← (3 7 5)(9 7 2 8)(1 6)(2 0 8)`
You can select one of its items with: `2⊃nv ⇒ 9 7 2 8`

But how can you select two (or more) items, for example the 2nd and the 4th item?

`2 4⊃nv` does not work; it selects only one item: the 4th item of the 2nd item, the number `8` in this case.

`2 4⊃¨nv` would work if `nv` had exactly two items: each value of the left argument could then be applied to each item of `nv`. However, this is not what we want here, and since `nv` has more than 2 items we would see a `LENGTH ERROR`.

`2 4⊃¨⊂nv` will work because each item of the left argument will be applied to `nv` as a whole, so we will select the 2nd and the 4th items:

```
      DISPLAY 2 4⊃¨⊂nv
```

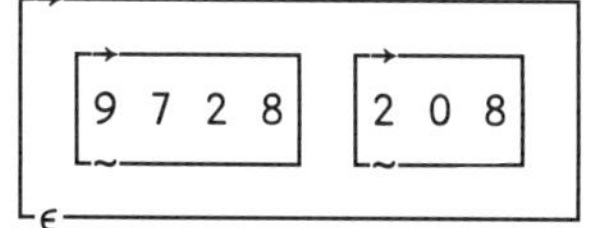

This expression is known as the "*Chipmunk idiom*", probably because of the eyes and moustaches of the combined symbol: `⊃¨⊂`

9 – Partition & Partitioned Enclose

The primitive function ***Partitioned Enclose*** is the dyadic use of the *Left Shoe* (`⊂`). It is used to group the items of an array into a vector of nested items, or enclosures, according to a specified pattern. It is used as follows:

R← *Pattern* ⊂ *Array*

or R← *Pattern* ⊂[*Axis*] *Array*

Like a few other operations related to nested arrays, *Partitioned Enclose* does not have the same definition and the same usage in the different APL systems supplied by Dyalog Ltd and IBM Corp.

For the reasons and consequences of those differences, please refer to the *Specialist's Section* of this chapter. Both definitions have some advantages.

In Dyalog APL the programmer can switch from one definition to the other by setting a *System variable* called ⎕ML (where ML stands for "*Migration Level*") to an appropriate value.

9.1 The Dyalog Definition

The default value of ⎕ML is zero, meaning that *Partitioned Enclose* follows Dyalog's definition.

According to this definition the *Pattern* must be a Boolean vector with the same length as the specified axis of the array to be partitioned. It breaks the array up into nested items as follows:

- Each enclosure starts with the item that corresponds to a 1 in the pattern, and finishes with the item before the item corresponding to the next 1, or with the last item in the array.
- As a consequence of this, because the first enclosure begins with the item corresponding to the first 1, any leading items of the array that correspond to leading 0's in the pattern will not appear in the result.

```
      OUT ← 'Once Upon a Time'
      ⎕ ← bin ← OUT=' '
0 0 0 0 1 0 0 0 0 1 0 1 0 0 0 0
      DISPLAY bin ⊂ OUT
```

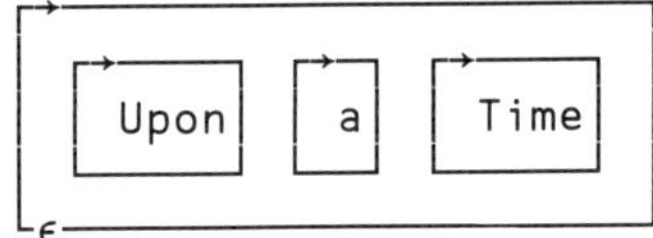

⇦ Not only is the first word ignored, but each word also starts with a preceding blank. This may not be exactly what you want.

With a matrix, things are very similar, except that one needs to specify along which axis the enclosures will be applied:

```
      DISPLAY 1 0 1 0 0 ⊂[2] Chemistry
```

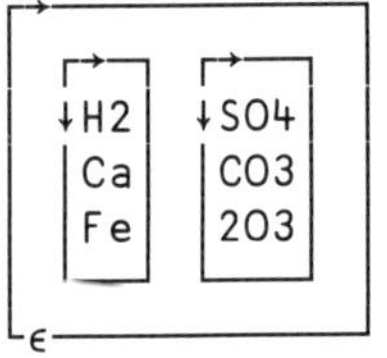

⇦ As usual, the last dimension is the default, Therefore this is equivalent to:
`1 0 1 0 0 ⊂ Chemistry`

```
      DISPLAY 1 0 1 ⊂[1]  Chemistry
```

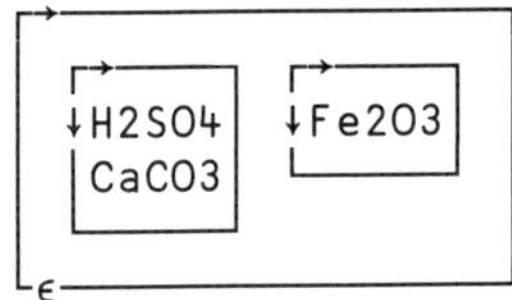

⇦ The result is a vector of the enclosed items.

9.2 The IBM Definition

This version of the function, called "*Partition*" in IBM's definition, can be used in Dyalog APL provided that ⎕ML is set to 3.

In this version, *Pattern* must be a vector of positive or zero integers, with the same length as the specified axis of the array to be partitioned. It operates as follows:

- The first enclosure starts with the first item of the array.
- Each enclosure ends when the next value of *Pattern* is greater than the current one.
- The items which correspond to 0's in *Pattern* are removed.

9.2.1 - Working on Vectors

We shall work with characters, but of course we could have worked with numbers just as well.

```
      ⎕ML←3                              ⇦ Switch to a more IBM-compatible environment
      Pattern ← 3 3 3 7 7 1 1 0 3 3 3 9 2 1 1 0
      DISPLAY Pattern ⊂ 'Once upon a time'
┌→──────────────────────────────────┐
│ ┌→──┐ ┌→───┐ ┌→──┐ ┌→───┐ │
│ │Onc│ │e up│ │n a│ │ tim│ │
│ └───┘ └────┘ └───┘ └────┘ │
└∊──────────────────────────────────┘
```

The 4 enclosures correspond to the 3 increments: 3⇨7, 0⇨3, 3⇨9, and the tail of the vector. You will also notice that two characters have disappeared, because they corresponded to zeroes in the pattern.

This definition can be used to group the items of a vector according to a given vector of keys, provided that the keys are ordered in ascending order. For example:

```
      Area ← 22 22 41 41 41 41 57 63 63 63 85 85
      Cash ← 17 10 21 45 75 41 30 81 20 11 42 53
      DISPLAY Area ⊂ Cash
┌→─────────────────────────────────────────────────────────┐
│ ┌→────┐ ┌→──────────┐ ┌→─┐ ┌→───────┐ ┌→────┐ │
│ │17 10│ │21 45 75 41│ │30│ │81 20 11│ │42 53│ │
│ └~────┘ └~──────────┘ └~─┘ └~───────┘ └~────┘ │
└∊─────────────────────────────────────────────────────────┘
```

This definition is also extremely convenient to divide a character string into a vector of strings on the basis of a separator. For example, let us partition a vector at each of its blank characters:

```
      Phrase
Panama is a canal between Atlantic and Pacific
      Phrase≠' '
1 1 1 1 1 1 0 1 1 0 1 0 1 1 1 1 1 0 1 1 1 1 1 1 1 0 etc...
      DISPLAY (Phrase≠' ') ⊂ Phrase
┌→─────────────────────────────────────────────────────────────────────┐
│ ┌→─────┐ ┌→─┐ ┌→┐ ┌→────┐ ┌→──────┐ ┌→───────┐ ┌→──┐ ┌→──────┐ │
│ │Panama│ │is│ │a│ │canal│ │between│ │Atlantic│ │and│ │Pacific│ │
│ └──────┘ └──┘ └─┘ └─────┘ └───────┘ └────────┘ └───┘ └───────┘ │
└∊─────────────────────────────────────────────────────────────────────┘
```

The blanks have been removed, because they matched the zeroes, and a new enclosure starts at the beginning of each word, corresponding to the increment 0⇨1. As you might imagine, this is extremely useful in many circumstances. One can write a function to do it, with the separator passed as a left argument:

```
      Cut←{⎕ML←3 ⋄ (~⍵∊⍺)⊂⍵ }
      ⎕ML←0                           ⇦ As ⎕ML is local to Cut, the function can be
      ↑' 'Cut Phrase                     executed in a standard environment.
Panama
is
a
canal
between
Atlantic
and
Pacific
```

In fact, we wrote the function to accept not just a single separator, but a list of separators, by replacing the perhaps more obvious `(⍵≠⍺)` by `(~⍵∊⍺)`. Now we can use it like this:

```
      ↑'mw'Cut Phrase
Pana
a is a canal bet
een Atlantic and Pacific
```

9.2.2 - Working on Higher-Rank Arrays

Although the IBM version of *Partition* is very simple, and clearly useful when it is applied to vectors, the situation is more complex when it is applied to matrices or higher-rank arrays. This is in contrast to Dyalog's definition, which works on any rank arrays in a very straightforward and obvious way. We shall not study the more complex application of IBM's definition here; if you are interested, please refer to the *Specialist's Section* at the end of this chapter.

10 - Union & Intersection

In mathematics, one uses the two functions *Union* and *Intersection* to compare two sets of values. Dyalog APL provides the same functions, with the same symbols as the ones used in mathematics:

Union (A∪B) Returns a vector containing all the items of A, followed by the items of B which do not appear in A. Both A and B must be scalars or vectors. Equivalent to A,B~A.

Intersection (A∩B) Returns a vector containing the items of A that also appear in B. Both A and B must be scalars or vectors. Equivalent to (A∊B)/A.

```
      15 76 43 80 ∪ 11 43 15 20 76 93
15 76 43 80 11 20 93
      'we' 'are' 'so' 'happy' ∩ 'are' 'you' 'so' 'tired?'
 are  so
```

Note that these functions do not remove duplicates (because in mathematics, all the items of a set are supposedly distinct):

```
      1 1 2 2 ∪ 1 1 3 3 5 5
1 1 2 2 3 3 5 5
      'if' 'we' 'had' 'had' 'a' 'car' ∩ 'have' 'you' 'had' 'lunch' '?'
 had  had
```

11 - Enlist

Enlist is a monadic function that exists as a primitive only in the IBM and IBM-compatible implementations of APL. It is represented by the Epsilon symbol (∊). In a standard Dyalog APL environment (⎕ML←0), monadic ∊ returns the *Type* of an array (see Section 6 above), but it is possible, by setting ⎕ML to 1 (or higher), to simulate a more IBM-compatible environment. Then monadic ∊ will then act as the *Enlist* function, and the *Type* function will no longer be available.

Enlist returns a vector of all the simple scalars contained in an array. This could at first sight look very much like *Ravel*, but it is *not* the same for nested arrays. *Ravel* just rearranges the top-level items of an array, while *Enlist* removes all levels of nesting and returns a simple vector. Let us compare the two functions:.

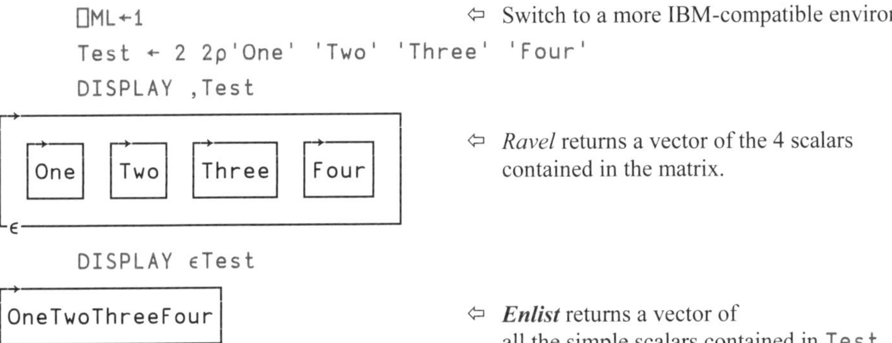

```
      ⎕ML←1                                    ⇦ Switch to a more IBM-compatible environment.
      Test ← 2 2⍴'One' 'Two' 'Three' 'Four'
      DISPLAY ,Test
┌→──────────────────────────────────┐
│ ┌→──┐ ┌→──┐ ┌→────┐ ┌→───┐        │         ⇦ Ravel returns a vector of the 4 scalars
│ │One│ │Two│ │Three│ │Four│        │           contained in the matrix.
│ └───┘ └───┘ └─────┘ └────┘        │
└∊──────────────────────────────────┘
      DISPLAY ∊Test
┌→──────────────────┐
│OneTwoThreeFour    │                           ⇦ Enlist returns a vector of
└───────────────────┘                             all the simple scalars contained in Test.
```

Enlist is very useful. To avoid the task of changing the value of ⎕ML again and again (and remembering to change it back), one can package up the primitive as a small *Dynamic function* with an appropriate (local) value of ⎕ML:

```
      ⎕ML←0
      Enlist←{⎕ML←1 ⋄ ∊⍵}
      DISPLAY Enlist Weird
┌→─────────────────────────────────────────────┐
│456 Dyalog 44 27 8 6 2 4 17 51 Twisted       │
└+─────────────────────────────────────────────┘
```

What kind of APLer are you now?

Exercises

I-4 You are given two vectors. The first contains the reference codes for some items in a warehouse. Identical codes are grouped, but not necessarily in ascending order. The second vector contains the quantities of each item sold during the day or the week. For example:

```
I4Ref ← 47 47 83 83 83 83 83 29 36 36 36 50 50
I4Qty ←  5  8  3 18 11  1  6 10 61 52 39  8 11
```

Can you calculate how many items of each reference code have been sold?
Preferably, use *Partition*.
In this particular example, the result should be: `13 39 10 152 19`

I-5 You are given two character matrices with the same number of columns. Let us call them `I5Big` and `I5Small`.

You are asked to find where the rows of `I5Small` appear in `I5Big`, i.e. for each row in `I5Small` find the index of the same row in `I5Big`. For those rows of `I5Small` which do not appear in `I5Big`, you can return the value 0, or `1+1↑⍴I5Big`.

I-6 You are given a long character vector, called `I6Text`. We would like to extract a part of it as a *simple* character vector. The extract is defined as a number of sub-vectors, each being 5 characters long, and starting at the positions given by the vector `I6Start`.

For example:

```
I6Text←'This boring text has been typed just for a little experiment'
I6Start←6 27 52
```

You should find: `borintypedxperi`

I-7 This exercise is the same as I-6, but instead of extracting 5 characters each time you are asked to extract a variable number of characters, specified by the variable `I6Long`. Using the same example as in I-6 and this additional variable:

```
I6Long ← 3 8 4
```

You should find: `bortyped juxper`

The Specialist's Section

Each chapter is followed by a "Specialist's Section" like this one.
This section is dedicated to skilled APLers, who wish to improve their knowledge.

If you are exploring APL for the first time,
skip this section and go to the next chapter

Spe-1 Compatibility and Migration Level

Spe-1.1 - Migration Level

In the early 1980s, a number of "second-generation" APL systems evolved to support nested arrays. Dyalog APL entered the market just as these systems were starting to appear, and decided to adopt the APL2 specification that IBM had been presenting to the world. In the event, unfortunately, the APL2 specification changed very late in this process, after Dyalog had more or less released Dyalog APL (or so the story goes). As a result, there are some minor differences between the dialects.

Just to give you an idea of the sometimes subtle differences, let us take a look at the expression `A B C[2]`, where `A`, `B`, and `C` are three vectors, for example:

```
A ← 1 2 3
B ← 4 5 6
C ← 7 8 9
```

The expression `A B C[2]` is ambiguous; it may be interpreted in two different ways:

- Does it mean: create a 3-item vector made of `A`, `B`, and the second item of `C`?
- Or does it mean: create a 3-item vector made of `A`, `B`, and `C`, and then take the second item of it (that is to say `B` enclosed)?

IBM chose the first interpretation, and in an IBM-compatible implementation of APL the result would be `(1 2 3) (4 5 6) 8`.

In Dyalog APL, indexing is a function like any other function, and it takes as its argument the entire vector on its left. The result is therefore `⊂4 5 6` (`⊂` because strand notation nested the items).

As a minor player at the time, Dyalog wished to move the product in the direction of APL2, and in order to help the people who needed to use both IBM's APL2 and Dyalog APL, and to make it easier to migrate an application from APL2 to Dyalog, a compatibility feature was introduced into Dyalog APL via a special ***System Variable*** named ⎕ML, where the letters ML stand for "***Migration Level***".

The default value for ⎕ML is zero, meaning "the Dyalog way".

To use code written according to IBM's conventions, it is possible to set ⎕ML to higher values (1, 2, or 3), and obtain an increasing (but not total) level of compatibility with IBM's APL2. Today, Dyalog has become a major player in the APL market. Pressure on Dyalog users to move in the direction of APL2 has faded and many users prefer the Dyalog definitions. The unfortunate result of the story is that, depending on the roots of an application, code may be written to use any one of the possible migration levels.

In this book we only use the standard conventions of Dyalog APL (the most widely used if APL2 compatibility is not an important issue), but we shall mention how some operations could be written with IBM's notation.

It should be emphasized that when you select a non-zero value for ⎕ML the "Dyalog way" of operation will no longer be available for the primitive functions that are sensitive to the selected value of ⎕ML.

Remember this: ⎕ML is a normal system variable. It can be localised in a function header or in a dynamic function, so that its influence is restricted to that function.

Spe-1.2 - A List of Differences

This list is not a complete list of language differences between IBM APL2 and Dyalog. It only lists the features of Dyalog APL that can be made to function like those of APL2 by setting ⎕ML appropriately.

Operation	Dyalog's implementation	IBM's implementation	Comments
Mix	R←↑[n]Var with n decimal	R←⊃[n]Var with n integer or decimal	Same behaviour, different symbols. IBM's definition requires ⎕ML≥2.
Split	R←↓[n]Var	R←⊂[n]Var	Same behaviour, different symbols. IBM's definition requires ⎕ML≥1
Partition	R←Pat⊂[n]Var with Pat Boolean	R←Pat⊂[n]Var with Pat integer	Same syntax, but different behaviour, cf. Section 9. IBM's definition requires ⎕ML≥3.
First	R←⊃Var	R←↑B	Same behaviour, different symbols. IBM's definition requires ⎕ML≥2.
Type	R←∊Var	R←↑0⍴⊂Var	No special symbol in IBM's definition. The IBM expression requires ⎕ML≥2.
Enlist		R←∊Var	No Dyalog equivalent. Requires ⎕ML>0
Depth	R←≡Var	R←≡Var	If the items of Var have non-uniform depths the IBM definition returns the absolute value of the depth rather than a negative value. IBM's definition requires ⎕ML≥2.
⎕TC	Backspace, Linefeed, Newline	Backspace, Newline, Linefeed	IBM's definition requires ⎕ML≥3.

Spe-2 The IBM Partition on Matrices

We studied IBM's *Partition* function applied to vectors in Section 9.2.1; it appeared to be extremely useful.

Its use is much more complex when applied to other arrays. Let us just try it on a matrix:

```
      1 1 2 2 2 ⊂[2]Chemistry
 H2  SO4
 Ca  CO3
 Fe  2O3
```

Don't be mislead by this result, which looks very much like the result that we obtained using Dyalog's definition. It is much more complex. IBM's *Partition* operates along the specified axis, but it also separates all the items along the other axis, as if the matrix were seen through a grid.

```
      DISPLAY 1 1 2 2 2 ⊂[2]Chemistry
```

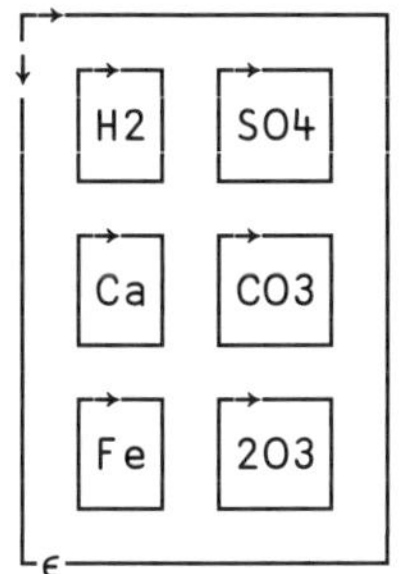

⇦ Not only do we observe a partition of the columns, but the rows are also separated.

```
      DISPLAY 1 2 2 ⊂[1]Chemistry
```

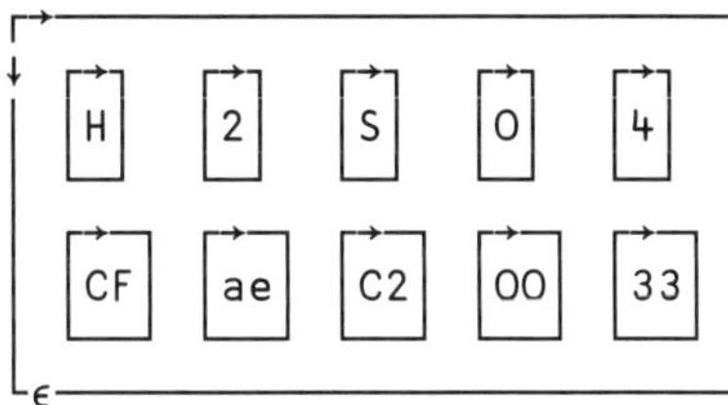

⇦ The first row is separated from the next two, but the columns have also been grouped.

Spe-3 Ambiguous Representation

DISPLAY is an essential tool to understand the structure of a variable. But sometimes even DISPLAY is insufficient:

```
      DISPLAY V ← 5 8 '7' 9
┌→──────┐
│5 8 7 9│
└+──────┘
```

In this form, the dash which should tell us that 7 is a character is indistinguishable from the dashes used to draw the box. We just know that one (or more) of the four items is character, because the *Plus* symbol tells us that this array is mixed.

A convenient way to distinguish between numbers and letters is to look at the *Type* of the items and compare it with 0 (numbers) or ' ' (letters):

```
      ' '= ∊ V
0 0 1 0
```

Spe-4 Pick Inside a Scalar

Suppose that one item of a nested variable is a vector which has been enclosed twice, and we would like to select one value out of its contents. For example, how can we select the letter "P" in the following vector:

```
      DISPLAY nv←(3 5 2)(⊂'CARPACCIO')(6 8 1)
```

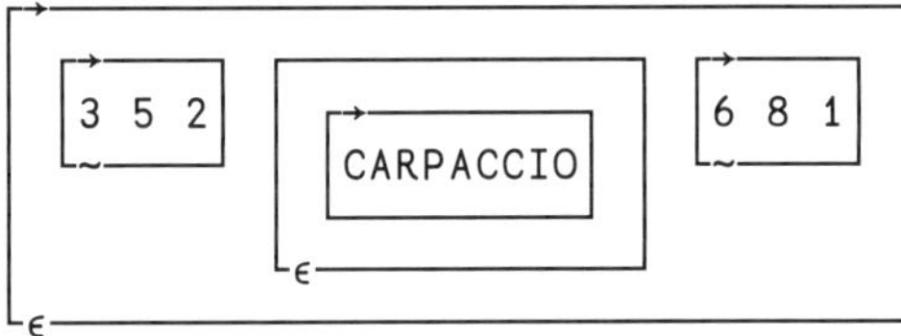

`2 1 4 ⊃nv` is incorrect because the second item of nv is an enclosed scalar. The index 1 would have been appropriate for a one-item vector, but not for a scalar.

The correct answer is:

```
      2 ⍬ 4 ⊃ nv
P
```

Chapter J: Operators

1 - Definitions

1.1 Operators & Derived Functions

We have already seen some operators: *Reduce* (described in section C-7), *Axis* (C-8), and *Each* (I-3). Let us define precisely what they are:

- There are built-in (*primitive*) operators and user defined operators.
- An ***Operator*** is similar to a function, but rather than working on arrays to produce a result which is also an array, an operator works on functions (and sometimes an array) to produce a new function.
- The new function generated by the operator and its argument(s) is called a ***Derived Function***. The *Derived Function* can be applied to arrays, in the same way as any other function.
- The arguments passed to the operator are sometimes referred to as *operands*, to distinguish them from the arguments to the derived function. However, in this tutorial we will use the term *argument* for both, as there is little chance of confusing them.
- Monadic operators take a single argument on their **left**.
  This is in contrast to monadic *functions*, which take their argument to the *right*.
- Dyadic operators have two arguments (operands), one on each side.
  The arguments to an operator are usually functions, but it is not uncommon for *user defined* operators to take one function and one array argument.
- The *Derived Function*, in turn, can be monadic, dyadic, or ambivalent.
- Neither of the functions supplied as arguments to an operator nor the resultant *Derived Function* can be niladic.

For example, in the expression `+/3 5 6` the *Reduce* operator (`/`) *operates on* the function *Plus* to produce the derived function *Plus Reduce*.
This derived function is then applied to `3 5 6` to produce a result.

Beware!

You must not be confused by the fact that some symbols are used to represent both a function and an operator. This is the case for / and \.

Let us compare these two expressions: (a) `1 1 0 1 0 / 6 2 9 4 5`
(b) `+ / 6 2 9 4 5`

In (a), the Slash (/) represents the dyadic *function Compress* because both arguments to the / are arrays.

In (b), the same symbol represents *Reduce*, *which* is an *operator*, because the left argument to the / is a function.

The association of + with / creates a *Derived Function* which could be parenthesised as `(+/)` even though it is not necessary to do so.

For clarification, we can define a synonym for the derived function: `Sum ← +/`

- Until now, we have only considered it as a *monadic* derived function: `+/ 6 2 9 4 5`
  This can be made more evident by using the synonym: `Sum 6 2 9 4 5`
- But, we shall soon see that it may also be used as a *dyadic* function `2 +/ 6 2 9 4 5`
  Or, using the synonym: `2 Sum 6 2 9 4 5`

So, we can say that this *derived function* is *ambivalent*.

1.2 Sequences of Operators

Derived functions behave exactly like plain primitive functions. So, they can be the argument of a second (and a third…) operator:

```
      +/¨ (3 4 6)(4 9 7 1)(3 1)
13 21 4
```

The left argument of *Each* is the derived function `(+/)`, so we could have written:

```
      Sum¨ (3 4 6)(4 9 7 1)(3 1)
```

Now, suppose that we no longer want to add up vectors, but three small matrices instead:

```
          A                    B                   C
          ⇩                    ⇩                   ⇩

        1 2 3                 1 0              8 3 4 2 0
        4 5 6                 0 1              0 3 5 1 7
                              0 1              3 6 2 1 7
                              1 0
```

Because they are matrices, we must specify the axis along which we add them up. Of course we could use the two symbols / and ⌿, but if the arrays had been of a higher rank an explicit axis specification might have been necessary. It could also be that we just prefer an explicit axis specification. If so, a third level of operator[5] can be added:

```
      +/[2]¨A B C                  ⇦ Or      (((+/)[2])¨)A B C
 6 15  1 1 1 1  17 16 19
      +/[1]¨A B C                  ⇦ Or      (((+/)[1])¨)A B C
 5 7 9  2 2  11 12 11 4 14
```

Operator 1 is /
"Operator" 2 is []
Operator 3 is ¨

1.3 List of Built-in Operators

Dyalog APL has a rich set of built-in operators. You will find a full list with detailed syntax and examples in Appendix 4.

2 - More About Some Operators You Already Know

2.1 Reduce

Up to now, we have used *Reduce* with rather basic functions (+ × ⌈ ∧), but it can also be used, less obviously, with functions, like *Reshape*, *Compress*, and *Replicate*. In these cases, the derived function typically takes a 2-item nested vector as its argument, and the effect is to insert the function (the argument to the operator) between the two items of this vector.

Just remember this:

Since	`+/ (2 4 3)(7 1 5)`	is equivalent to	`⊂(2 4 3) + (7 1 5)`
then	`⍴/ (2 4 3)(7 1 5)`	is equivalent to	`⊂(2 4 3) ⍴ (7 1 5)`

Here is an example of *Reduction* by *Reshape*:

```
      ⍴/ (2 5)(3 1 9 4 1 0 7)
 3 1 9 4 1
 0 7 3 1 9
```

---

[5] Although the *Axis specification* shares some properties with operators, it is a special syntactical element and not really an operator, cf. Section 2.3. below.

This *looks* very much like `(2 5) ⍴ (3 1 9 4 1 0 7)`, but the result is not a matrix. It is a scalar containing a *nested* matrix, for the reason already seen in I-4.4.1: The reduction of a vector always gives a scalar.

Now, here is a *Reduction* by *Compression*, another by *Replication*, and one by *Index Of*:

```
      // (1 1 0 1 0 1 1) 'Strange'
 Stage
```

Here again this looks like `(1 1 0 1 0 1 1) / 'Strange'` but the result is a scalar.

```
      // (1 1 0 4 0 1 2) 'Strange'
 Staaaagee
      ⍳/ (2 6 1 7) (2 4⍴3 7 8 4 2 5 6 0)
 5 4 5 5
 1 5 2 5
```

2.2 *n*-Wise Reduce

2.2.1 - Elementary Definition

The derived functions of *Reduce* can be used with two arguments.
This form is called ***n-Wise Reduce***.

When applied to vectors *n-Wise Reduce* has the following syntax:

R ← *Scope* ■/ *Vector*

where ■ denotes a dyadic function.

This special kind of *Reduce* splits the vector into slices of length equal to *Scope*, and reduces each slice using the specified function, so, for example:

`2 ×/ 8 10 7 2 6 11`	means	`(×/8 10) (×/10 7) (×/7 2) (×/2 6) (×/6 11)`
	i.e.	`(8×10) (10×7) (7×2) (2×6) (6×11)`
	and gives	`80 70 14 12 66`

`3 +/ 8 10 7 2 6 11`	means	`(+/8 10 7) (+/10 7 2) (+/7 2 6) (+/2 6 11)`
	i.e.	`(8+10+7) (10+7+2) (7+2+6) (2+6+11)`
	and gives	`25 19 15 19`

The size of the result is, of course, `(1+⍴Vector)-Scope`.

We can try this with other functions that give nested results:

`2 ,/ 8 10 7 2 6 11`	means	`(,/8 10) (,/10 7) (,/7 2) (,/2 6) (,/6 11)`
	i.e.	`(8,10) (10,7) (7,2) (2,6) (6,11)`
	and gives	`8 10  10 7  7 2  2 6  6 11`

```
2 ρ/ 2 4 1 3 7        means      (ρ/2 4) (ρ/4 1) (ρ/1 3) (ρ/3 7)
                      i.e.       (2ρ4)   (4ρ1)   (1ρ3)   (3ρ7)
                      and gives  4 4   1 1 1 1   3   7 7 7
```

The same result would have been obtained using *Replicate*: `2 // 2 4 1 3 7`

2.2.2 - Full Definition

The general syntax is `R ← ` *Scope* `■/[`*Axis*`]` *Array*

where ■ stands for any dyadic function.

- The *Array* is split into slices along the specified *Axis*.
- The left argument *Scope* can be positive (as in the examples above), zero, or negative.
- If *Scope* is positive, *Reduce* is applied to slices of length equal to *Scope*.
- If *Scope* is zero, the result is an array with the same shape as *Array*, except that its length along the axis selected by *Axis* is incremented by 1, and it is filled with the *Identity Item* for the function ■. This is explained in section Spe-1.4 (*Specialist's Section*).
- If *Scope* is negative, each slice is reversed before *Reduce* is applied.

Here are some examples which use this matrix `Tam` ⇨

```
2 3 5 8 8
4 6 2 5 9
1 4 9 7 8
```

```
      2 ⌈/ Tam                    ⇦ Obtains the largest items of 2 adjacent columns
3 5 8 8
6 6 5 9
4 9 9 8

      2 +⌿ Tam                    ⇦ Adds up pairs of adjacent rows
6  9  7 13 17
5 10 11 12 17

      0 +/ Tam
0 0 0 0 0 0                       ⇦ Returns a matrix with one more column,
0 0 0 0 0 0                         filled with zeroes (identity item of addition)
0 0 0 0 0 0

      0 ×/[1] Tam
1 1 1 1 1                         ⇦ Returns a matrix with one more row, filled
1 1 1 1 1                           with ones (identity item of multiplication)
1 1 1 1 1
1 1 1 1 1

      ¯2 -/ 11 14 15 21 23 30 28 34  ⇦ Obtains the differences between adjacent values
3 1 6 2 7 ¯2 6                         (14-11)(15-14)(21-15)(23-21) etc...
```

2.3 Axis

Strictly speaking, axis is not an operator. It has different syntax (consisting of two brackets enclosing a numeric value to the right of a function) and applies in different ways depending on the function that it modifies. However, applying a function "with axis" does apply a transformation and produces a derived function, and it is common to think of axis as an operator.

It is possible to use *Axis* with any of the *Scalar Dyadic Functions*. This can be useful for example to add the items of a vector to each of the rows of a matrix, or multiply the columns of a matrix by different values:

```
     Tam              Tam +[1] 8 6 9          Tam ×[2] 2 5 0 2 1
      ⇩                      ⇩                        ⇩

2 3 5 8 8             10 11 13 16 16            4 15 0 16 8
4 6 2 5 9             10 12  8 11 15            8 30 0 10 9
1 4 9 7 8             10 13 18 16 17            2 20 0 14 8
```

The list of all *Scalar Dyadic Functions* is given in Appendix 1.

The following functions can use the *Axis* operator:

Monadic Functions	Description
↑ and ↓	Mix and Split
⌽ or ⊖	Reverse
,	Ravel with axis
⊂	Enclose with axis, Partitioned Enclose
⊂ and ⊃	APL2-like Split and Mix (⎕ML>1, cf. Chapter I, Section Spe-1)

Dyadic Functions	Description
+ × ⌈ ∧ ≤ etc…	All *scalar dyadic functions*
↑ and ↓	Take and Drop
/ or ⌿	Compress & Replicate
\ or ⍀	Expand and Scan (*see next section*)
⌽ or ⊖	Rotate
, or ⍪	Catenate
, or ⍪	Laminate
⊂	Partitioned Enclose

3 - Scan

3.1 Definition

Scan is represented by the symbol \ or ⍀. Its most general syntax is: R ← ■\[*Axis*]*Array* where ■ stands for any appropriate dyadic function.

To understand how it works, let us apply it to a vector.

The Nth item of +*Vector* is equal to the *Reduction* of the first N items of *Vector*.

More generally, the Nth item of ■*Vector* is equal to ■/N↑*Vector*.

```
      +\ 3 6 1 8 5
3 9 10 18 23
```

As you can see:

the 1st item is equal to	+/3	giving	3
the 2nd item is equal to	+/3 6	giving	9
the 3rd item is equal to	+/3 6 1	giving	10
the 4th item is equal to	+/3 6 1 8	giving	18
the 5th item is equal to	+/3 6 1 8 5	giving	23

The method is of course the same for a multiplication:

```
      ×\ 3 6 1 8 5
3 18 18 144 720
```

Warning! It would be a mistake to always try to deduce the value of each item in the result from its immediate left neighbour. While it is possible to do this for commutative functions like addition and multiplication, it is not appropriate for non-commutative functions like subtraction:

```
      -\ 3 6 1 8 5
3 ¯3 ¯2 ¯10 ¯5
```
⇦ The result is **not** `3 ¯3 ¯4 ¯12 ¯17` as one might first imagine

the 1st item is equal to	`-/3`	giving	`3`	
the 2nd item is equal to	`-/3 6`	giving	`¯3`	
the 3rd item is equal to	`-/3 6 1`	giving	`¯2`	`(3-(6-1))`
the 4th item is equal to	`-/3 6 1 8`	giving	`¯10`	
the 5th item is equal to	`-/3 6 1 8 5`	giving	`¯5`	

So, be careful when using *Scan* with non-commutative functions.

When applied to matrices or higher rank arrays, *Scan* works along the specified axis. If the axis specification is omitted, \ works along the *last* axis and ⍀ works along the *first* axis.

```
      +\[2] Tam
2  5 10 18 26
4 10 12 17 26
1  5 14 21 29
```
⇦ This can also be written as `+\Tam`

```
      +\[1] Tam
2  3  5  8  8
6  9  7 13 17
7 13 16 20 25
```
⇦ This can also be written as `+⍀Tam`

3.2 Scan with Binary Values

Scan is very useful when applied to binary values.

```
      ∨\ 0 0 0 0 1 1 0 1 0 0 1 1
0 0 0 0 1 1 1 1 1 1 1 1
```

Because the function *Or* gives the result 1 as soon as one of its arguments is 1, *Or-Scan* repeats the first 1 up to the end of the vector.

```
      ∧\ 1 1 1 1 0 1 1 0 0 1 1 0
1 1 1 1 0 0 0 0 0 0 0 0
```
⇦ The vector reverts to zero on the first zero

```
      <\ 0 0 0 0 1 1 0 1 0 0 1 1
0 0 0 0 1 0 0 0 0 0 0 0
```
⇦ Marks the position of the first 1

```
      ≤\ 1 1 1 1 0 1 1 0 0 1 1 0
1 1 1 1 0 1 1 1 1 1 1 1
```
⇦ Marks the position of the first zero

3.3 Applications

Scan can be used to solve common problems in a very simple way:

3.3.1 - Inflate Values

Someone forecasts investments in a foreign country for the next 5 years:

```
      Inv ← 2000 5000 6000 4000 2000
```

But the country in question suffers from inflation, and the inflation rates are forecasted as follows:

```
      Inf ← 2.6 2.9 3.4 3.1 2.7
```

The cumulative consequence of these inflation rates can be calculated by multiplying them all with a "*Multiply-Scan*":

```
      7 3⍕ ×\ 1+Inf÷100
  1.026  1.056  1.092  1.125  1.156
```

Now, the investments expressed in "future values" would be:

```
      9 2⍕ Inv × ×\1+Inf÷100
  2052.00  5278.77  6549.90  4501.96  2311.76
```

Finally, the year after year cumulated investment may be obtained by an "*Add-Scan*":

```
      9 2⍕ +\ Inv × ×\1+Inf÷100
  2052.00  7330.77 13880.67 18382.63 20694.39
```

As you can see, we employed two *Scans* in the same expression.

3.3.2 - Remove Leading/Trailing Blanks

One often has to remove leading (or trailing) blanks from a character vector. We can use the "*Or-Scan*" to do it. The details of the method are shown here:

```
      LB ← '    Remove my 4 leading blanks'
      LB≠' '
0 0 0 0 1 1 1 1 1 1 0 1 1 0 1 0 1 1 1 1 1 1 1 0 1 1 1 1 1 1
      ∨\ LB≠' '
0 0 0 0 1 1 1 1 1 1 1 1 1 1 1 1 1 1 1 1 1 1 1 1 1 1 1 1 1 1
      (∨\LB≠' ')/LB
Remove my 4 leading blanks
```

This can be coded in a small utility function: `CutBlanks ← {(∨\' '≠⍵)/⍵}`
This expression is recognised by Dyalog APL as an *Idiom*, and processed very quickly.

To remove trailing blanks, it would suffice to reverse the vector, remove leading blanks as above, and then reverse it back again.

4 - Outer Product

4.1 Definition

Imagine that you have calculated the multiplication table for the integers 1 to 9; you could present it like this:

×	1	2	3	4	5	6	7	8	9
1	1	2	3	4	5	6	7	8	9
2	2	4	6	8	10	12	14	16	18
3	3	6	9	12	15	18	21	24	27
4	4	8	12	16	20	24	28	32	36
etc...	etc...								
9	9	18	27	36	45	54	63	72	81

The task of calculating this table consists of taking pairs of items of two vectors, (the column and row headings) and combining them with the function at the top left. For example 3 times 7 gives 21 (shown here in red above). Once the operation has been repeated for all the possible pairs, one obtains what is called, in APL, the ***Outer Product***.

We can change the values and replace the multiplications by additions:

+	8	5	15	9	11	40
5	13	10	20	14	16	45
4	12	9	19	13	15	44
10	18	15	25	19	22	50
3	11	8	18	12	14	43

Outer Product is a dyadic operator represented by a dot (.)
Its arguments are:

- On its right: The dyadic function involved (multiplication or addition in the examples above)
- On its left: A small circle named ***Jot*** (∘). This character is obtained using Ctrl+J
  In this specific case, it is a "non-operation" which just takes the place of the left argument.

So, the two operations above can be written like this:

```
      (⍳9) ∘.× (⍳9)
1  2  3  4  5  6  7  8  9
2  4  6  8 10 12 14 16 18
3  6  9 12 15 18 21 24 27
etc ...
8 16 24 32 40 48 56 64 72
9 18 27 36 45 54 63 72 81
```

```
      5 4 10 3 ∘.+ 8 5 15 9 11 40
13 10 20 14 16 45
12  9 19 13 15 44
18 15 25 19 21 50
11  8 18 12 14 43
```

4.2 Extensions

4.2.1 - Other Functions

The function used in an outer product can be any primitive or user-defined dyadic function, so *Outer Product* is an operator of amazing power.

Imagine you have written a little function to calculate the length of the hypotenuse of a right-angled triangle from the lengths of the other 2 sides given as the left and right argument:

```
      Hypo ← {((⍺*2)+(⍵*2))*0.5}
      3 Hypo 4
5
```

You can test it on a number of combinations of lengths in one expression like this:

```
      8 3⍕ 3 6 12 ∘.Hypo 4 1 8 7 5
   5.000   3.162   8.544   7.616   5.831
   7.211   6.083  10.000   9.220   7.810
  12.649  12.042  14.422  13.892  13.000
```

Now let's have some fun with relational functions:

(⍳5) ∘.= (⍳5)	(⍳5) ∘.< (⍳5)	(⍳5) ∘.≥ (⍳5)
1 0 0 0 0 0 1 0 0 0 0 0 1 0 0 0 0 0 1 0 0 0 0 0 1	0 1 1 1 1 0 0 1 1 1 0 0 0 1 1 0 0 0 0 1 0 0 0 0 0	1 0 0 0 0 1 1 0 0 0 1 1 1 0 0 1 1 1 1 0 1 1 1 1 1

We shall study some applications of *Outer Product* like `∘.<` or `∘.⌊` in section 3.3.

Some other *Outer Products* like `∘.⍴`, `∘.,` or `∘./` produce nested arrays; we have shown them in grey frames in order to make it easier to see the structures:

```
      3 4 2 ∘.⍴ 6 3 7
```

6 6 6	3 3 3	7 7 7
6 6 6 6	3 3 3 3	7 7 7 7
6 6	3 3	7 7

```
      3 0 2 ∘./ 5 1 7
```

5 5 5	1 1 1	7 7 7
5 5	1 1	7 7

```
      3 1 2 ∘., 6 3 0 7
```

3 6	3 3	3 0	3 7
1 6	1 3	1 0	1 7
2 6	2 3	2 0	2 7

```
      3 2 4 ∘.↑ 5 8 4
```

5 0 0	8 0 0	4 0 0
5 0	8 0	4 0
5 0 0 0	8 0 0 0	4 0 0 0

4.2.2 - Other shapes and types of data

We have so far applied *Outer Product* to numeric vectors; it can of course also be used with character data, and higher rank arrays. When applied to higher rank arrays, the result becomes quickly very big, because each item of the left array has to be combined with each item of the right one.

In an operation like `R ← A ∘.■ B`, the shape of `R` is equal to `(⍴A),(⍴B)`

```
      ⎕← Left ← ↑'DIMITRI' 'GUNTHER'
DIMITRI
GUNTHER
      Right ← 'VERONICA'
      Left ∘.= Right
  V E R O N I C A
D 0 0 0 0 0 0 0 0
I 0 0 0 0 0 1 0 0
M 0 0 0 0 0 0 0 0
I 0 0 0 0 0 1 0 0
T 0 0 0 0 0 0 0 0
R 0 0 1 0 0 0 0 0
I 0 0 0 0 0 1 0 0

G 0 0 0 0 0 0 0 0
U 0 0 0 0 0 0 0 0
N 0 0 0 0 1 0 0 0
T 0 0 0 0 0 0 0 0
H 0 0 0 0 0 0 0 0
E 0 1 0 0 0 0 0 0
R 0 0 1 0 0 0 0 0
```

⇦ To help you understand how this result has been calculated, the arguments are shown too, in grey.

⇦ We have combined an array of shape....... 2 7
with an array of shape 8
So the shape of the result is.................. 2 7 8

As an exercise, try to produce the same display, with the arguments actually included in the result as shown here...

4.3 *Applications*

4.3.1 - Dispatching Items into Categories

Suppose the vector `Ages` contains the ages of 400 respondents to an opinion poll. We want to find out how many people there are in each of the following age groups:

0 - 25 - 30 - 35 - 45 - 50 - 55 - 65 or above.

Here is an extract of the data:

```
Ages    ⇨  32 19 50 33 23 65 46 26 31 58 51 23 51 36 28 42 ... etc
Limits  ⇨  0 25 30 35 45 50 55 65
```

We will use the *Outer Product* `Limits °.< Ages`, and here are the first items calculated, using the data shown above:

<	32	19	50	33	23	65	46	26	31	58	51	23	51	36	28	42	34	... etc
0	1	1	1	1	1	1	1	1	1	1	1	1	1	1	1	1	1	
25	1	0	1	1	0	1	1	0	1	1	1	0	1	1	1	1	1	
30	1	0	1	1	0	1	1	0	1	1	1	0	1	1	0	1	1	
35	0	0	1	0	0	1	1	0	0	1	1	0	1	1	0	1	0	
45	0	0	1	0	0	1	1	0	0	1	1	0	1	0	0	0	0	
50	0	0	0	0	0	1	0	0	0	1	1	0	1	0	0	0	0	etc.
etc																		

If we add up this binary matrix from left to right, we obtain for each row the number of people who are older than 0 years, older than 25 years, 30 years, etc. This is the expression:

```
Cum ← +/ Limits ∘.< Ages
```

With the cut-down example above, the value of `Cum` would be: `17 14 12 8 6 4`

In other words there are 12 people older than 30. But among them, 8 are older than 35. In order to know how many people are between 30 and 35, it is necessary to calculate 12-8, to obtain 4.

To calculate this for all categories, it is necessary to make a series of subtractions as shown here:

```
  17 14 12 8 6 4        This is Cum
- 14 12  8 6 4 0        This is Cum without its first item, and followed by zero
----------------        Let us subtract
=  3  2  4 2 2 4        The result is obtained by the expression Cum - 1↓ Cum,0
```

The two expressions that do it all are therefore:

```
      Cum ← +/ Limits ∘.< Ages
      Cum - 1↓ Cum,0
56 32 56 104 63 38 37 14
```

Without any programming, it works whatever the number of people or categories.

Isn't it like magic?

The second statement above (`Cum - 1↓ Cum,0`) calculates the differences between all pairs of adjacent values. This is exactly what *n-Wise Reduce* does. So, we could instead write the following even simpler expression:

```
      2 -/ Cum
56 32 56 104 63 38 37 14
```

It would even be tempting to put everything into one single expression:

```
      2 -/ +/ Limits ∘.< Ages
56 32 56 104 63 38 37 14
```

Once again, APL allows us to find original atypical solutions to some traditional problems.

4.3.2 - Draw a Bar Chart

Imagine that you have to represent a list of values with a bar chart. Perhaps you will use dedicated graphical software, and you'd be right, but just have a look at this elegant solution, which again uses an *Outer Product*.

Here is the list of values that we want to chart: `Nums ← 1 3 0 7 9 8 5 4 2 3 1`

Let us first calculate the vertical scale.
It is made of the integers from 9 to 1 in reverse order and can be obtained by:

```
      ⌽ ⍳ ⌈/ Nums
9 8 7 6 5 4 3 2 1
```

Then, let us compare this scale to the values; an *Outer Product* will build columns of 1's up to the correct height:

```
      (⌽⍳⌈/Nums) ∘.≤ Nums
0 0 0 0 1 0 0 0 0 0 0
0 0 0 0 1 1 0 0 0 0 0
0 0 0 1 1 1 0 0 0 0 0
0 0 0 1 1 1 0 0 0 0 0
0 0 0 1 1 1 1 0 0 0 0
0 0 0 1 1 1 1 1 0 0 0
0 1 0 1 1 1 1 1 0 1 0
0 1 0 1 1 1 1 1 1 1 0
1 1 0 1 1 1 1 1 1 1 1
```

And to draw the graph, we can index a two-character vector, exactly as we did in section B-5.2:

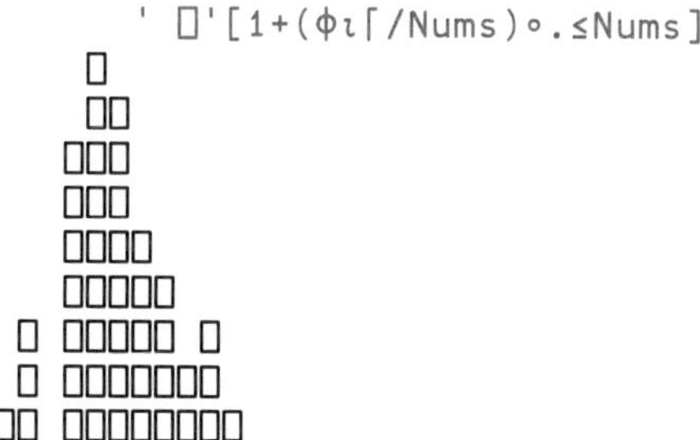

4.3.3 - Decreasing Refunding

Some students have spent money to buy expensive books for their studies.

```
      Exp ← 740 310 1240 620 800 460 1060
```

Their university agrees to refund them, but places the following limits on the refunding rates:

For expenses from 0 to 500 the rate is 80%
For expenses from 500 to 900 the rate is 50%
For higher expenses, nothing is paid.

We could say exactly the same thing in a somewhat different way:

For expenses from 0 to 900 we get 50%
Starting again from **0** to 500 we get an **additional** .. 30%

Even if this rule may seem strange, both methods give the same result. For example, a student who spent 740€ would get:

With the "traditional" rule (80% of 500) + (50% of 240)..... 400 + 120 = **520**
With our "foolish" rule (50% of 740) + (30% of 500)..... 370 + 150 = **520**

Now, let us limit the expenses to the given maxima:

```
      Exp ∘.⌊ 900 500
740 500
310 310
900 500
620 500
800 500
460 460
900 500
```

⇦ The first column contains the expenses limited to 900, and the second contains the expenses limited to 500

According to our modified rules, we must pay 50% of the first column plus 30% of the second, we can multiply the columns by `0.5 0.3` (using an *axis* operator) and add them:

```
      +/ (Exp∘.⌊900 500) ×[2] 0.5 0.3
520 248 600 460 550 368 600
```

And the total refund is of course:

```
      +/ +/ (Exp∘.⌊900 500) ×[2] 0.5 0.3
3346
```

If we laminate the original vector, we can see the expenses and the refunding:

```
      Exp,[0.5] +/(Exp∘.⌊900 500)×[2]0.5 0.3
740 310 1240 620 800 460 1060
520 248  600 460 550 368  600
```
⇦ Check, it works!

Outer Product

Exercise

J-1 Let us try to generalise the method used here above.

In our example, we had chosen a very simple case, because we had only two slices, and all the students used the same scale. Let us now imagine a slightly more complex case:

- the students are classified in 3 categories, which have different refunding rates
- we now have 4 different expense ranges

The new conditions are expressed with the traditional notation, in a table:

Limits ⇨	0 to **600**	600 to **1.100**	1.100 to **1.500**	1.500 to **2.000**
Students classified **1**	100%	100%	80%	50%
Students classified **2**	100%	70%	30%	10%
Students classified **3**	80%	60%	20%	5%

Try to write a function `Refund` to solve this problem.
Using loops is strictly prohibited, and could be punished with high severity!

You can test your solution with these variables, available in "DyalogTutor_EN.dws":

`StudExp` Vector of students expenses
`StudCat` Vector of the categories of each student
`StudRates` The table of rates, topped by the expense limits, as shown below:

```
      StudRates
600 1100 1500 2000        ⇦ The first row contains the limits
100  100   80   50        ⇦ The next 3 rows contain rates per category
100   70   30   10
 80   60   20    5
```

The syntax could be: `StudRefund (StudRates StudCat StudExp)`

If you want to check your solution, here are the first 10 answers you should obtain:

```
Expenses    ⇨  2300 1030 460 380 1700 1900 440 1050 2380 1600
Categories  ⇨     3    2   3   3    1    1   1    1    1    2
Refunding   ⇨   885  901 368 304 1520 1620 440 1050 1670 1080
```

5 - Inner Product

Inner Product is a generalisation of what mathematicians call *Matrix product*, a tool considered by most students as extremely abstract, full of bizarre notations, like $\Sigma a_{ij}.b_{jk}$, and obviously far removed from everyday problems. You will discover that:

- the concept is really simple, nearly obvious
- it can be applied to many real life problems

A simple example will help us.

5.1 A Concrete Situation

A company intends to open a series of hotels and resorts in four countries. This requires serious investments over a period of five years. The following table shows these investments (in millions of dollars, of course!)

⇩ Countries\Years ⇨	Year 1	Year 2	Year 3	Year 4	Year 5
Greece	120	100	40	20	0
Brazil	200	150	100	120	200
Egypt	50	120	220	350	600
Argentina	0	80	100	110	120

These figures are contained in a matrix named `Invest`

These investments will be supported by the company itself plus 2 banks, each taking a certain percentage of the total, depending on the evaluation of each project. The following table shows how the risks are shared:

Percentages ⇘	Greece	Brazil	Egypt	Argentina
Bank 1	50	10	20	30
Bank 2	20	60	40	30
Company	30	30	40	40

Those percentages are contained in a matrix named `Percent`

We would like to calculate, year by year, how much each of the 3 partners is engaged in this project. For example, let us try to evaluate the contribution of Bank 2 during Year 3.

For Greece,	the bank will bring	20%	of	40 =	8
For Brazil,	the bank will bring	60%	of	100 =	60
For Egypt,	the bank will bring	40%	of	220 =	88
For Argentina,	the bank will bring	30%	of	100 =	30
	Total invested =				186

This result could have been obtained by the sum of four products:

```
      +/ Percent[2;] × Invest[;3]÷100
186
```

We should repeat that algorithm for all the rows of `Percent`, and all the columns of `Invest`: this is precisely what an *Inner Product* does.

And because it ***adds*** series of ***products***, it will be expressed by a dot (the operator) between a plus and a multiply sign, like this:

```
      Percent +.× Invest÷100
 90 113 104 125 176
164 182 186 249 396
116 155 170 226 348
```

In the presentation below, we have detailed the elementary products which lead to the calculation for bank 2 in year 3:

						Y 1	Y 2	Y 3	Y 4	Y 5
Greece	8				←	120	100	40	20	0
Brazil		60			←	200	150	100	120	200
Egypt			88		←	50	120	220	350	600
Argentina				30	←	0	80	100	110	120
	↑	↑	↑	↑	↘					
Bank 1	50	10	20	30		90	113	104	125	176
Bank2	20	60	40	30		164	182	186	249	396
Company	30	30	40	40		116	155	170	226	348

This presentation has a great advantage: It clearly shows the relations that exist between the 3 matrices:

- The left argument has as many columns as the right one has rows.
- The result has as many rows as the left argument, and as many columns as the right one.

As you can see row *x*, column *y* of the result is calculated from row *x* of the left argument and column *y* of the right argument.

These rules will be generalised in the next section.

5.2 Definitions

The syntax of *Inner Product* is `R ← X ■.● Y`

The *Inner Product* is represented by a dot (.)
■ and ● represent two appropriate dyadic functions (either primitive or user-defined).

The arguments may be arrays of any rank: Scalars, vectors, matrices, or higher rank arrays. The shape of the arguments and the shape of the result follow very simple rules.

- The length of the last dimension of the left argument must be equal to the length of the first dimension of the right argument.
  In other words: `(¯1↑⍴X)` must be equal to `(1↑⍴Y)`
- The shape of the result is the catenation of the arguments' shapes, in which the common dimension has disappeared.
  In other words: `(⍴R)` is equal to `(¯1↓⍴X),(1↓⍴Y)`

Of course, as usual, scalars are repeated to fit the appropriate size.

Let us represent scalars by `S`, vectors by `V`, matrices by `M`, and higher rank arrays by `A`.
The table below shows the shape of the result of some *Inner Products*:

`R←X ■.● Y`	Shape of X	Shape of Y	Shape of R
`A←A ■.● A`	2 3 8	8 5 4	2 3 5 4
`M←M ■.● M`	3 5	5 8	3 8
`V←M ■.● V`	4 7	7	4
`V←V ■.● M`	4	4 7	7
`S←V ■.● V`	10	10	⍬

5.3 Typical Uses of Inner Products

5.3.1 - Two Simple Problems

Many students imagine that matrix products are complex things, reserved for mathematicians, and far removed from everyday life. This opinion should be reconsidered: Very simple problems can be solved using *Inner Product*.

`HMS` is a variable which contains duration in Hours, Minutes, and Seconds: `HMS ← 3 44 29`

We would like to convert it into seconds. We shall see 3 methods just now, and a 4th method will be given in another chapter.

A horrible solution	`(3600×HMS[1]) + (60×HMS[2]) + HMS[3]`
A good APL solution	`+/ 3600 60 1 × HMS`
An excellent solution with *Inner Product*	`3600 60 1 +.× HMS`

The second and third solutions are equivalent in terms of number of characters typed and performance. But **we recommend** that you use the third one: It will help you become familiar with *Inner Product* so that after a certain period, it will become part of your toolkit as an APL programmer.

Here is a very similar example. Two vectors represent the prices of a certain number of goods, and the quantities we bought:

```
Price   ⇨     6  4.2  1.5  8.9  31  18
Qty     ⇨     2  6    3    5    1    0.5
```

To calculate how much we paid, we can use the beginner's solution, or a solution with a simple *Inner Product*; they give the same result, of course.

The beginner's solution	`+/ Price × Qty`
A solution with *Inner Product*	`Price +.× Qty`

Just to show how it works, let us again use the presentation used for our Banks/Investments example:

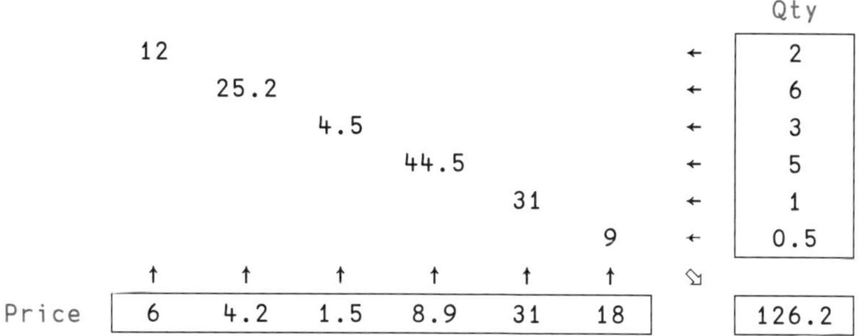

5.3.2 - A Useful Family

Used with comparison functions, *Inner Product* offers 18 extremely useful derived functions.

`Ages` is a vector containing the ages of 400 persons. In the same way as we did in section C-7.3 we can answer some elementary questions:

Question	**Solution**	**Answer**
Are all these people younger than 65?	`∧/ Ages < 65`	`0` (No)
Is there at least one person younger than 20?	`∨/ Ages < 20`	`1` (Yes)
How many people are younger than 20?	`+/ Ages < 20`	`24`

We can now replace *Reduce* in these examples by *Inner Product*, like this:

Question	**Solution**	
Are all these people younger than 65?	`Ages ∧.< 65`	
Is there at least one person younger than 20?	`Ages ∨.< 20`	
How many people are younger than 20?	`Ages +.< 20`	Clever, isn't it ?

These expressions can be read as:

Are the ages *all smaller* than 65?	`∧.<`	means "all smaller"
Is there *at least* one age *smaller* than 20?	`∨.<`	means "at least one is smaller"
How many ages are *smaller* than 20?	`+.<`	means "how many are smaller"

In those three expressions we have combined `∧`, `∨`, and `+` with `<`. We could just as well combine them with all the comparison symbols, giving 18 different *Inner Products*, as shown in this table:

■.●		Right argument ●					
		`<`	`≤`	`=`	`≥`	`>`	`≠`
Left argument	`∧`	`∧.<`	`∧.≤`	`∧.=`	`∧.≥`	`∧.>`	`∧.≠`
	`∨`	`∨.<`	`∨.≤`	`∨.=`	`∨.≥`	`∨.>`	`∨.≠`
	`+`	`+.<`	`+.≤`	`+.=`	`+.≥`	`+.>`	`+.≠`

5.3.3 - A Special Case

In this family of *Inner Products*, `∧.=` is particularly interesting, because it answers the question "*Are all those values equal?*". For example, applied to vectors of same length:

```
      'customer' ∧.= 'customer'
1                                        ⇦ Of course!
      'customer' ∧.= 'cucumber'
0                                        ⇦ Hope you had no doubt about it?
```

Let us use this property to search for a word in a matrix of words:

```
      Words
CONTACT
COLUMNS
FORTUNE
PRODUCT
COLONEL
PROVIDE
MACHINE
TYPICAL
```

If we combine this 8 by 7 matrix with a 7-item vector, compatibility rules are obeyed, and the result will be a 8-item vector:

```
      Words ∧.= 'PRODUCT'
0 0 0 1 0 0 0 0
```
⇦ We found the word in the 4th position

The shape of `Words` is 8 7
The shape of `'PRODUCT'` is................................. 7
The common dimension disappears,..................... ⇧
and the result is of length.....................................8

Now, let us search for 3 words:

```
      Three
MACHINE
COMFORT
PRODUCT
      Words ∧.= ⍉Three
0 0 0
0 0 0
0 0 0
0 0 1
0 0 0
0 0 0
1 0 0
0 0 0
```
⇦ We must transpose the matrix to be compliant with the compatibility rules

⇦ We found 2 words, and one is missing

That's not too bad, but it would perhaps be more useful to obtain the positions of these words.

If we multiply the first column by `⍳8`, we obtain `0 0 0 0 0 0 7 0`
And if we sum the result, we get 7, the position of the word we are looking for!

We can repeat this for the three columns, once again using *Inner Product*:

```
      (⍳1↑⍴Words) +.× Words ∧.= ⍉Three
7 0 4
```

Please note, however, that this method will not work very well if the left argument contains duplicates. For example:

```
      Words2
CONTACT
COLUMNS
MACHINE                         ⇦ Also found in row 7
PRODUCT
COLONEL
PROVIDE
MACHINE                         ⇦ Also found in row 3
TYPICAL
      Words2 ∧.= ⍉Three
0 0 0
0 0 0
1 0 0
0 0 1
0 0 0
0 0 0
1 0 0
0 0 0
      (⍳1↑⍴Words2) +.× Words2 ∧.= ⍉Three
10 0 4
```

The first item in the result is the *sum* of the positions in which the first word in `Three` was found. Applying another very frequently used method we can obtain a result very similar to that produced by *Index Of*. By this we mean that it returns the index to the *first* found occurrence in `Words2` of the words in `Three`, and that it returns 1 + the number of rows in `Words2` for words not found.

This method uses another operator *Scan* that we have seen earlier. Using *Or Scan* along the first axis makes it possible to identify the first row in which a match is found:

```
      ∨⍀ Words2 ∧.= ⍉Three
0 0 0
0 0 0
1 0 0
1 0 1
1 0 1
1 0 1
1 0 1
1 0 1
```

When we subtract the number of 1's in each column from the number of rows we get one less than the row number containing the first 1. So, the final expression becomes:

```
      (1+1↑⍴Words2) - +⌿ ∨⍀ Words2 ∧.= ⍉Three
3 9 4
```

The first and last words are found in row 3 and 4, respectively. The second word is not found, so the result is 1 + the number of rows we searched.

The converse to the expression `∧.=` is `∨.≠`. It looks for *different* values instead of for *equal* values. Let us look at one simple example:

```
      Words2 ∨.≠ ⍉Three
1 1 1
1 1 1
0 1 1
1 1 0
1 1 1
1 1 1
0 1 1
1 1 1
```

A 1 means that this word in Three does not match the word in this line of Words2. So, if a row contains all 1's the word in that row does not match any of the words in Three. Using *And Reduce* along the second axis pinpoints the rows of Words2 for which this is true:

```
      ∧/ Words2 ∨.≠ ⍉Three
1 1 0 0 1 1 0 1
      (∧/ Words2 ∨.≠ ⍉Three) ⌿ Words2
CONTACT
COLUMNS
COLONEL                         ⇦ These words are not found in Three
PROVIDE
TYPICAL
```

5.3.4 - Similar Applications

Very often it is desirable to find out whether any rows (or columns) of a matrix contain all blanks or all zeroes; or alternatively whether any rows or columns contain at least one non-zero number or non-blank character.

To solve the first task we can use the same *Inner Product* as we used in most of the previous section (∧.=), and to solve the second one we can use the converse, which we introduced at the end of the previous section (∨.≠).

Suppose we have a matrix of characters MC, and a matrix of numbers MN.

MC ∧.= ' '	says which	rows	contain	all blanks
MN ∧.= 0	says which	rows	contain	all zeroes
' ' ∧.= MC	says which	columns	contain	all blanks
MC ∨.≠ ' '	says which	rows	contain	at least one non-blank character
0 ∨.≠ MN	says which	columns	contain	at least one non-zero number

and so on…

5.3.5 - Shortest Routes in a Graph

Finding the shortest routes in a graph is a very classical problem to which *Inner Product* offers an elegant solution. Imagine 6 points in a town. They can be joined via a certain number of paths, according to the figure below.

Because of one-way streets, the length of the path from one point to another may be different from the length of the return path, or one of the paths may be missing.

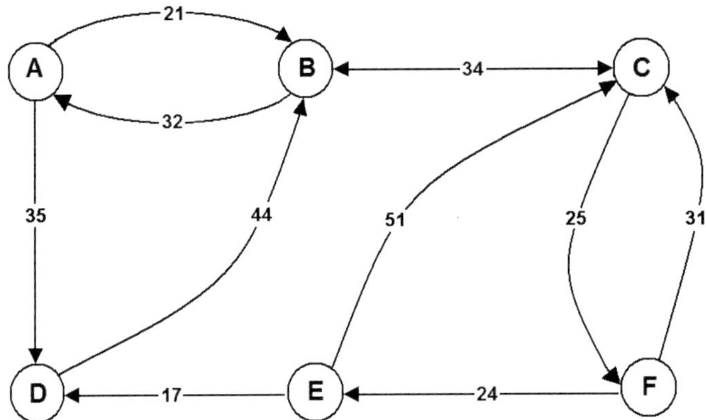

We can create a matrix with the distances between the points. The missing paths will be represented by a very high value (`1000` in this case) to dissuade anyone from using them:

Origin	Destination					
	A	B	C	D	E	F
A	0	21	1000	35	1000	1000
B	32	0	34	1000	1000	1000
C	1000	34	0	1000	1000	25
D	1000	44	1000	0	1000	1000
E	1000	1000	51	17	0	1000
F	1000	1000	31	1000	24	0

Values in this matrix represent paths of length 1 (in one step), so let us call it `L1`:

```
      L1
   0   21 1000   35 1000 1000
  32    0   34 1000 1000 1000
1000   34    0 1000 1000   25
1000   44 1000    0 1000 1000
1000 1000   51   17    0 1000
1000 1000   31 1000   24    0
```

Now, can we get from some point to another in two steps? For example, there is no direct route in one single step from E to B; can we get there in two steps?

Let us consider all the possible pairs of routes from E to B:

Routes				**Total**
First step		Second step	Distances	**distance**
E ⇨ A	+	A ⇨ B	1000 + 21	1021
E ⇨ B	+	B ⇨ B	1000 + 0	1000
E ⇨ C	+	C ⇨ B	51 + 34	85
E ⇨ D	+	D ⇨ B	17 + 44	61
E ⇨ E	+	E ⇨ B	0 + 1000	1000
E ⇨ F	+	F ⇨ B	1000 + 1000	2000

Finally, one can see that we have added the lengths of paths starting from E to the lengths of paths arriving at B. But, as we have accepted "null" paths (E to E, or B to B), this matrix takes into account both 1-step and 2-step routes. As you can see, this can be obtained by adding the 5th row of `L1` (from E to any point) to its 2nd column (from any point to B), like this:

```
      L1[5;] + L1[;2]
1021 1000 85 61 1000 2000
```

Only two routes really exist, because they are smaller than 1000, they are of length 85 and 61. Of course, we shall choose the shortest one: `⌊/ L1[5;]+L1[;2]`

To obtain all the minimum routes in one or two steps, we have just to repeat this calculation for all the rows and columns: An *Inner Product* by the *Minimum* of *Sums* will do that.

```
      ⎕ ← L2 ← L1 ⌊.+ L1
   0 21 55   35 1000 1000
  32  0 34   67 1000   59
  66 34  0 1000   49   25
  76 44 78    0 1000 1000
1000 61 51   17    0   76
1000 65 31   41   24    0
```

The result shows new routes, for example from A to C, or B to F, or D to A, etc…
We can now repeat the operation, and find the shortest routes in 1, 2, or 3 steps:

```
      ⎕ ← L3 ← L2 ⌊.+ L1
 0 21 55 35 1000  80
32  0 34 67   83  59
66 34  0 66   49  25
76 44 78  0 1000 103
93 61 51 17    0  76
97 65 31 41   24   0
      L4 ← L3 ⌊.+ L1
```

⇦ `L2 ⌊.+ L2` would give the same result

⇦ It is still impossible to go from A to E and from D to E.
A fourth step is necessary.

```
      ' ABCDEF' , 'ABCDEF' ⍪ L4
   A  B  C  D   E   F
A  0 21 55 35 104  80
B 32  0 34 67  83  59
C 66 34  0 66  49  25
D 76 44 78  0 127 103
E 93 61 51 17   0  76
F 97 65 31 41  24   0
```

⇦ Now we can go from any point to any other
An additional inner product would show that it is not possible to find shorter routes.

The solution is elegant, but has a shortcoming: We found, for example, that the shortest path from D to E is of length 127, and that it requires 4 steps, but we do not know which ones those four steps are.

5.3.6 - Is a Graph Contiguous?

In some development projects involving large graphs, it is sometimes necessary to check whether all the points belong to a single graph; the danger being that, due to an error in data, the graph can be divided into two or more sub-graphs that are not connected to each other.

To check for "continuity", the graph can be represented by a binary matrix in which the ones represent the existing links and the zeroes the missing ones. The graph is contiguous if any point can be linked to any other, through a finite number of steps.

The matrix G1 represents the graph shown above.

The diagonal is now set to 1, because any point is of course connected to itself ⇨

```
1 1 0 1 0 0
1 1 1 0 0 0
0 1 1 0 0 1
0 1 0 1 0 0
0 0 1 1 1 0
0 0 1 0 1 1
```

Let us see if a point can be linked to another in two steps, for example C to E.

This route exists if we can find a link from C to A ***and*** then from A to E, ***or*** from C to B ***and*** then B to E, ***or*** ... and so on.

Repeated for all points, the connectivity matrix in two steps can be obtained using an *Inner Product* by ***Or*** and ***And***:

```
      ⎕ ← G2 ← G1 ∨.∧ G1
1 1 1 1 0 0
1 1 1 1 0 1
1 1 1 0 1 1
1 1 1 1 0 0
0 1 1 1 1 1
0 1 1 1 1 1
```

⇦ In fact, G2 is equal to L2<1000

⇦ Some points still cannot be linked to some other ones.
We must repeat the operation again.

```
      ⎕ ← G3 ← G2 ∨.∧ G1
1 1 1 1 0 1
1 1 1 1 1 1
1 1 1 1 1 1
1 1 1 1 0 1
1 1 1 1 1 1
1 1 1 1 1 1
```

⇦ This is much better, however, A cannot be linked to E in 3 steps, nor D to E. An additional step is necessary.

A fourth step `G4 ← G3 ∨.∧ G1` would lead to a matrix full of ones, meaning that the graph cannot be split into separate sub-graphs.

5.4 Other Uses of Inner Product

We saw above some common uses of *Inner Product*, but there are many other useful *Inner Products*, using primitives or even user defined functions.

`Vec <.> 1⌽Vec` Tests whether a numeric vector is in ascending order.

`Num <.< Lims` Tests whether the number `Num` is between two limits given in `Lims`

As for *Outer Product*, some applications of *Inner Product* produce nested arrays, as you can see with these two small matrices:

```
    a                    b
    ⇩                    ⇩
  2 4 1              3 0 2 5
  1 3 5              1 7 7 2
                     6 0 4 2
```

`a ,.+ b` gives:

5 5 7	2 11 1	4 11 5	7 6 3
4 4 11	1 10 5	3 10 9	6 5 7

`a +., b` gives:

7 10	7 7	7 13	7 9
9 10	9 7	9 13	9 9

5.5 *Application*

We have a certain number of points, the coordinates (*x y*) of which are given by a nested vector:

```
      Coords ← (0 2) (¯1 2) (¯2 1) (¯1 0) (¯1 ¯1) (1 ¯3) (2 ¯2) (2 0)
      (X Y) ← ↓[1] ↑Coords              ⇦ Let us split these coordinates into vectors of
      X,[0.5]Y                            X and Y coordinates, respectively
0 ¯1 ¯2 ¯1 ¯1  1  2 2
2  2  1  0 ¯1 ¯3 ¯2 0
```

This figure shows where these points are placed in a coordinate system, and the polygon we get when we connect the points:

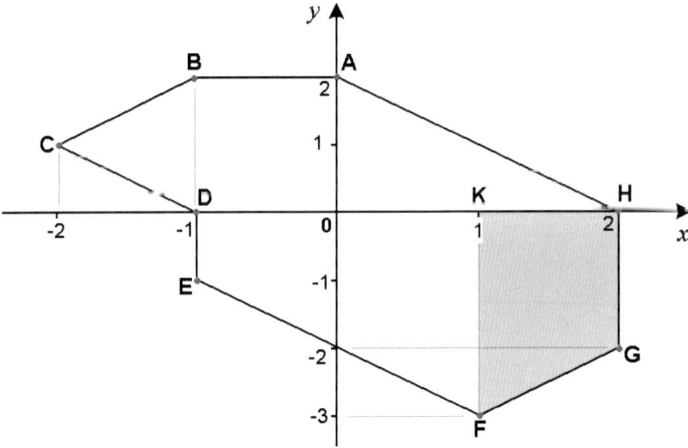

The ***area*** of the polygon can be calculated by adding the areas of the trapeziums delimited by the polygon and the horizontal axis, like the grey trapezium FGHK.

- Their base lengths are calculated by subtracting adjacent values in `X` . . . . `X - 1⌽X`
- They must be multiplied by half of the sums of adjacent values in `Y` .... `(Y + 1⌽Y) ÷2`

In other words, we must ***add*** the ***products*** of bases by heights: It is obviously an inner product.

```
      (X-1⌽X) +.× (Y+1⌽Y)÷2
11.5
```

What about the ***perimeter*** now? We must add all the individual segments.
Each segment like BC or FG can be calculated using Pythagoras' theorem: $a^2+b^2 = c^2$

We shall calculate the length of horizontal and vertical sides by subtracting adjacent values in `X` and `Y`, as we did for `X` in the previous example. Let us put these lengths in `Segs`:

```
Segs ← (X-1⌽X),[1.5](Y-1⌽Y)   gives     1  0
                                         1  1
                                        ¯1  1
                                         0  1
                                        ¯2  2
                                        ¯1 ¯1
                                         0 ¯2
                                         2 ¯2
```

Now, in each small right-angled triangle, we must add the squares of both sides, to obtain the squares of hypotenuse: *Add* the *squares* will be our first *Inner Product*: `Segs +.* 2`
Then we have to add the square roots of these hypotenuses. *Add* the *square roots* will be our second *Inner Product*.

```
      (Segs +.* 2) +.* 0.5        ⇦ This solution uses the same product twice
13.89949494
```

Inner Product

Exercises

J-2 You are given the matrix M:

```
8 2 5 1 4
3 7 1 5 0
4 3 6 0 6
```

Calculate the following expressions, and check on the computer:

a) `⌈/ M`

b) `⌊/ +/ M`

c) `×/ ⌊/[1] M`

d) `×/ ⍴M`

J-3 Calculate:

a) `-\ 1 1 1 1 1 1`

b) `-\ 5 4 3 2 1`

c) `×/ +\ 6⍴1`

J-4 Calculate:

a) `∧/ 1 1 1 0 1 1`

b) `∧\ 1 1 1 0 1 1`

c) `=/ 0 1 1 1 0 1 1`

d) `=\ 0 1 1 1 0 1 1`

J-5 When we execute `×\vec` we obtain `7 14 70 210 840`
What is the value of `vec`?

J-6 Broken keyboard! The Iota (`⍳`) key of your keyboard does not work. How could you create the list of the first `N` integers?

J-7 Let us call *a*, *b*, and *c* the three sides of a triangle, and *p* its half-perimeter, equal of course to 0.5×(*a*+*b*+*c*). Believe it or not, the area of that triangle is equal to the square root of:

$$p \times (p-a) \times (p-b) \times (p-c)$$

Can you write a function to calculate the area of a triangle, given the lengths of its sides?

J-8 We would like to know whether all the items of a vector are different. Among the many possible solutions, could you find one using *Outer Product*, and another one using *Inner Product*? The result must of course be a Boolean 0 or 1.

J-9 What would be the result of: `2 =/ 'MASSACHUSSETTS'`

J-10 Try to find a word in a vector of characters. Your function should give the positions of the first letter of the word in the vector. For example:

```
      'CAN' In 'CAN YOU CANCEL MY FLIGHT ON AIR CANADA?'
1 9 33
```

The word "`CAN`" starts in positions 1 9 and 33.
There are several solutions which do not need a loop; try to find one.

J-11 For a certain number of people, you are given two vectors:

- `Status` is their marital status (S=Single, M=Married, D=Divorced, W=Widow, U=Unknown)
- `Gender` is their gender (M=Male, F=Female)

Write a function to count how many people there are in each category, like in this example:

```
      Gender CrossCount Status
20 26 17 7 5
17 34 23 2 7
```

```
   D  M  S U W
F 20 26 17 7 5
M 17 34 23 2 7
```

⇦ In a second step, you can add legends

```
         D  M  S U  W  Total
F       20 26 17 7  5     75
M       17 34 23 2  7     83
Total   37 60 40 9 12    158
```

⇦ Then, you can also add totals

6 - Compose

Compose is a dyadic operator which combines its arguments (operands) to form one single, composite operation. One can regard it as an easy way of specifying an inline "mini-function". As such, it does not really add functionality to the language that could not be obtained by other means; it is just a very convenient notation.

Compose is represented by a *Jot* (∘); the keystroke to obtain it is *Ctrl-J*.

This operator has 4 different forms:

Form 1	■∘● Y	Both arguments are monadic functions. The derived function is monadic. Equivalent to ■ ● Y
Form 2	*n*∘● Y	The left argument is a value, the right one is a dyadic function. The derived function is monadic. Equivalent to *n* ● Y
Form 3	■∘*n* Y	The left argument is a dyadic function, the right one is a value. The derived function is monadic. Equivalent to Y ● *n*,
Form 4	X ■∘● Y	The left argument is a dyadic function, the right one is a monadic function. The derived function is dyadic. Equivalent to X ■ ● Y

Because APL's syntax makes it very easy to "chain" function calls together, as the equivalent expressions above demonstrate, the *Compose* operator is rarely used alone. Most often it is used together with the *Each* operator, as this may give important advantages for execution time and memory consumption. Using *Compose* also makes it easy and convenient to create a derived function to be used together with the *Reduction* operator. We will explain these uses in the examples below.

6.1 Form 1

Form 1 ■∘● Y — Both arguments ■ and ● must be *monadic* functions. The function ● must return a result; the function ■ needs not do so. The derived function is monadic

Quite often you would like to apply two monadic functions to each item of an array. This is very easy to do, with the help of the powerful *Each* operator.

Let us look at the simple example in which we just want to find the rank of each item of the variable `Weird`:

```
      ⍴¨ ⍴¨ Weird
 0  2
 1  1
```

In the expression above the first `⍴¨` creates a (potentially) big array containing the shape of each item of `Weird`. Then the second `⍴¨` gets the shape of each of the items of the intermediate result. Remember; the rank of an array is the *shape of the shape* of the array.

This is inefficient for two reasons: Firstly, APL must allocate memory to hold the intermediate array, which will be discarded as soon as the entire expression has been evaluated. Secondly APL must internally loop through a potentially large number of items twice.

With the help of *Compose* we can eliminate both problems: APL only needs to traverse the array once, applying both functions to each item in succession. During the processing of each item only a very small intermediate array will be created holding the shape of each item, and it will be discarded before processing the next item:

```
      ⍴∘⍴ ¨ Weird
 0  2
 1  1
      +/∘⍳ ¨ 2 4 7
3 10 28
```

⇦ This expression applies the composite function `⍴⍴` to all the items of the variable, and returns their ranks

⇦ Here, we add up the items of `⍳2`, those of `⍳4` and finally those of `⍳7`

In the last example above, the left argument of *Compose* is itself a derived function of *Reduce*.

In the example below, both arguments are user defined functions:

```
      sqrt ← {⍵*0.5}
      sqrt∘Average ¨ (11 7)(8 11)(21 51)(16 9)
 3  3.082207001  6  3.535533906
```

6.2 Form 2

Form 2 *n*∘● Y

The left argument is a value, while ● must be a *dyadic* function
The function ● does not need to return a result
The derived function is monadic

This use of *Compose* allows the programmer to "*bind*" the function ● to a fixed left argument, *n* , while its right argument will be provided by Y.

```
      3∘↑ ¨ (⍳5) 'Houston' (21 53 78 55) (11 22)
 1 2 3  Hou  21 53 78  11 22 0
```

This expression applies 3↑ to each of the items of the right argument. So far this is not a very good example, as the expression would work and give the same result even without using *Compose*:

```
      3↑¨ (⍳5) 'Houston' (21 53 78 55) (11 22)
 1 2 3  Hou  21 53 78  11 22 0
```

However, binding the value 3 to *Take* makes it possible to combine the function with yet another function, so that we can again obtain the advantage of one loop and reduced memory usage:

```
      ⌽∘(3∘↑) ¨ (⍳5) 'Houston' (21 53 78 55) (11 22)
 3 2 1  uoH  78 53 21  0 22 11
```

6.3 Form 3

Form 3 ■∘*n* Y

The left argument ■ is a *dyadic* function; the right one is a value
The function ■ does not need to return a result
The derived function is monadic

This use of *Compose* is very similar to the previous one. It "*binds*" the function ■ to a fixed right argument, *n* , while the ***left*** argument of ■ is provided by Y.

In other words (■∘*n)* Y is equivalent to Y■*n*. Though Y was passed on the right, it is processed as if it were the (missing) left argument of the function ■.

For example

```
      (*∘0.5) 16 81 169
4 9 13
```

⇦ Once bound to 0.5, the *Power* function behaves like a square root function which applies to its right argument.

In this form, the derived function must be parenthesised so that the argument `0.5` is separated from the right argument `16 81 169`.

`16 81 169*0.5` and `{⍵*0.5} 16 81 169` would give the same result.

6.4 Form 4

Form 4 `X ■∘● Y` The left argument ■ must be a *dyadic* function
The right argument ● must be a *monadic* function
The function ● must return a result; the function ■ needs not do so
The derived function is dyadic

This use of *Compose* is very similar to Form 1.

Here is an example of composition of *Multiplication* and monadic *Iota*:

```
      DISPLAY 2 5 4 ×∘⍳ ¨ 2 4 3
┌→──────────────────────────────────────┐
│ ┌→──┐ ┌→──────────┐ ┌→─────┐ │
│ │2 4│ │5 10 15 20│ │4 8 12│ │
│ └~──┘ └~──────────┘ └~─────┘ │
└∊──────────────────────────────────────┘
```

Another example: The "*Golden mean*" can be calculated by this infinite series:

`1 +÷ 1 +÷ 1 +÷ 1 +÷ 1 +÷ 1 +÷ 1 +÷ 1 +÷ 1` etc...

As you can see, we have inserted `+÷` between the items of a series of ones. This operation is a *Reduction* by `+÷`, but the *Reduce* operator only accepts a single function on its left. To overcome this we can "glue" the two functions together using *Compose*, thereby creating a single, derived function that may be used together with *Reduce*:

```
      +∘÷ / 1 1 1 1 1 1
1.625                              ⇦ Poor approximation, but it works!
      +∘÷ / 50⍴1
1.618033989                        ⇦ A nearly perfect result
```

7 - Commute

As its name implies, ***Commute*** (⍨) is a monadic operator which commutes the arguments of its *derived function*.

For example....... `4 ÷ 2` gives `2`,
but..................... `4 ÷⍨ 2` is equivalent to `2÷4` and gives `0.5`

- `X ■⍨ Y` is equivalent to `Y ■ X`
- When used monadically, `■⍨Y` is equivalent to `Y ■ Y`

For example `⍴⍨ 3` is equivalent to `3⍴3` and gives `3 3 3`

Based only on these simple examples one might think that *Commute* is useless (typing `⍴⍨3` is no easier than typing `3⍴3`). However, *Commute* may be used to reduce the number of parentheses needed in an expression.

For example, we want to create a vector like `3⍴3` or `5⍴5`, using the last item of `StudRates`.

A direct approach would be:
```
((⍴StudRates)⌷StudRates)⍴(⍴StudRates)⌷StudRates
```

Commute allows a simpler expression:
```
⍴⍨(⍴StudRates)⌷StudRates
```

It is not only for "cosmetic" reasons that it is desirable to avoid repeating an expression. It also means that the interpreter only has to evaluate the expression once, possibly saving some execution time. Furthermore, avoiding a verbatim repetition of a piece of code improves maintainability considerably. If the expression needs to be modified it is simply too easy to forget to modify all instances of it, or to make mistakes in some of the modifications.

Some APL programmers still prefer to use an intermediate variable or an inline direct function to obtain the same benefits in terms of efficiency and maintainability:

```
A ← (⍴StudRates)⌷StudRates
A⍴A
{⍵⍴⍵} (⍴StudRates)⌷StudRates
```

It is mostly a matter of taste which of the possible solutions different programmers prefer. The case illustrates that the APL language typically allows the same task to be solved in many different ways.

8 - Power Operator

Power is a *dyadic* operator represented by ⍣ (Ctrl-Shift P), which produces a *derived function* that is either monadic, dyadic, or ambivalent, depending on the function used as the left argument. Again depending on the left argument, the derived function may return a result or not.

The general syntax is: `{R} ← {X} (■⍣n) Y` **(Form 1)**

or: `{R} ← {X} (■⍣●) Y` **(Form 2)**

Power operates as follows:

8.1 - Elementary Use (Form 1)

If the right argument *n* is a numeric integer scalar, the left argument function ■ is applied *n* times to argument `Y` (monadic use) or to `X` and `Y` (dyadic use).

n **must** be separated from the right argument. For example, the derived function could be surrounded by parentheses.

Imagine we have a little matrix `mat`:

```
1 2 3
8 0 4
7 6 5
```

And we write a function to spin it a quarter of a turn: `Spin ← {⊖⍉ ⍵}`

```
      Spin mat
3 4 5
2 0 6
1 8 7
      Spin Spin mat
5 6 7
4 0 8
3 2 1
```

Of course, after 4 executions, the matrix would return to its original position.

We can spin the matrix any number of times using the *Power* operator:

```
      (Spin⍣14) mat                ⇦ 14 spins are equivalent to a double-spin
5 6 7
4 0 8
3 2 1
```

Power can give us a way of calculating a Fibonacci series:

```
      fibo ← {⍵,+/¯2↑⍵}
      (fibo⍣10) 1
1 1 2 3 5 8 13 21 34 55 89
```

8.2 - Conditional Execution (Form 1)

As a special case, when *n* is Boolean, the function is applied (1) or not applied (0). It causes a conditional execution of the function.

```
      (⌊⍣1) 23.73 42.25
23 42                          ⇦ The truncation was executed
      (⌊⍣0) 23.73 42.25
23.73 42.25                    ⇦ Nothing was done
```

For example, a function has been written in such a way that it works only on nested vectors, but sometimes its right argument `Rop` is a simple vector (not nested) or even a scalar. So one must: *Ravel* `Rop` (if it is a scalar), *Enclose* it, then *Ravel* it again to produce a vector, or do nothing if `Rop` is already a nested vector. The following expression will perform the necessary transformations:

```
(,∘⊂∘, ⍣ (1=≡,Rop) ) Rop       ⇦ Here (1=≡,Rop) gives a binary result so that
                                 (,⊂,) will be executed only if that result is 1
```

Note that in the example above we make good use of the newly introduced *Compose* operator. The left argument to the *Power* operator is a derived function that combines three functions into one, making it suitable as the left argument to the *Power* operator.

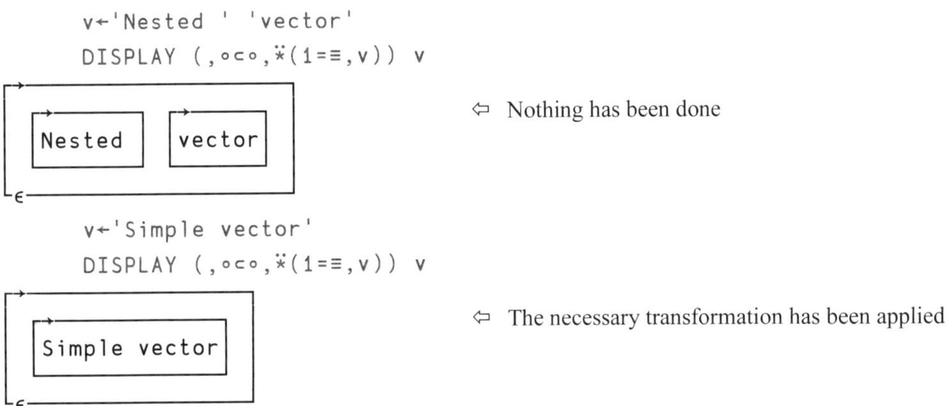

v←'Nested ' 'vector'
DISPLAY (,∘⊂∘,⍣(1=≡,v)) v
Nested
vector
⇦ Nothing has been done
v←'Simple vector'
DISPLAY (,∘⊂∘,⍣(1=≡,v)) v
Simple vector
⇦ The necessary transformation has been applied

Whether one prefers to use *Power* to write such a compact conditional expression, or to use a traditional control structure (`:If` ... `:EndIf`) is mostly a matter of taste. Some may find the former easier to write and read than the other, while others may prefer the latter.

8.3 - Left Argument (All Forms)

If a left argument `X` is provided (dyadic usage) it is bound as the left argument to ■ (the function to the left).

In other words: `X(■ ⍣ ●)Y` is equivalent to `(X∘■ ⍣ ●)Y`

Be careful: This may lead to some errors of interpretation:

```
      3(× ⍣ 4)2
162
      3×3×3×3×2
162
```

⇦ and not `3×2×2×2×2` as one might imagine!

8.4 - Inverse Function

If the right argument *n* is **negative** the function executed by the *Power* operator is not ■, but its **inverse** function - if such an inverse function exists and APL knows about it. If the inverse function to ■ is not known to APL, a DOMAIN ERROR will be reported. In particular, APL is not able to find the inverse function to user defined functions, and some primitive functions have no inverse function.

The inverse function is applied (| *n*) times.

The function ■ may be an appropriate primitive function or an expression consisting of such primitive functions combined with primitive operators among:

Compose	∘	*Axis*	[*n*]
Each	¨	*Scan*	\
Outer Product	∘.	*Power*	⍣
Commute	⍨		

```
      (+\ ⍣ ¯1) 3 4 9 15 19
3 1 5 6 4
      +\ 3 1 5 6 4
3 4 9 15 19
```

⇦ We obtain the inverse of "*Plus-Scan*"

⇦ Just to confirm

If `Rop` is the following matrix

```
10  4 14  8
25 10 35 20
15  6 21 12
```

```
      2 5 3 (∘.× ⍣ ¯1)Rop
5 2 7 4
```

⇦ This is the vector which, combined with `2 5 3` by an *Outer Product*, would give back `Rop`

8.5 - Fixpoint, and Use with Defined Operators

Here are two additional features of the *Power* operator:

- In its Form 2, *Power* has two argument functions: `{X}(■⍣●)Y`
- *Power* can also be associated with defined operators

These two types of use require an advanced knowledge of APL and of *User-defined Operators*. They will not be presented now, but in the *Specialist's Section*. Have a look at it when you feel ready.

9 - Spawn

9.1 Main Features

The monadic operator ***Spawn*** is represented by an Ampersand (`&`). It executes a function asynchronously from the main flow of execution in a separate sequence of instructions known as a *Thread*.

If the main flow of execution and the function executing in the separate thread are both using the CPU heavily, nothing is gained by starting a separate thread. On the contrary, the two threads will be competing for the same resource - the CPU, which requires some overhead. But if one of the threads involves waiting time in which it cannot make use of the CPU, the other thread may use the CPU, which otherwise would have been idle. In such cases a considerable improvement of the application's perceived performance may be observed.

There are many situations in which a thread may be waiting and not able to make good use of the CPU: It may be waiting for user input, a file operation, a response from a web client or server, or a response from a database manager, to give just a few examples.

Spawn is itself monadic, but its derived function is monadic, dyadic, or ambivalent, according to the definition of the left function argument. This function (and hence the derived function) may not be niladic.

Spawn returns as a *Shy result* the number of the thread in which the task is executed.

The main execution flow is executing in thread number 0, so the first time one launches a new thread, it is executed in thread number 1. Let us execute `⍳5` in a separate thread:

```
      ⎕← ⍳& 5                    ⇦ The Quad forces the shy result to be displayed
1                                ⇦ As expected it was executed in thread 1
1 2 3 4 5                        ⇦ Then the function result is displayed
```

Once a thread number has been used it will not be used again in this session: The thread number will be incremented every time *Spawn* is used:

```
      ⎕← ÷& 2 5 10               ⇦ Parallel execution of ÷2 5 10
2                                ⇦ The thread number was incremented
0.5 0.2 0.1
```

In these examples, the derived function was monadic; let us now use a dyadic function argument, and try to execute `2 3 7 × 4 6 5` in a separate thread:

```
      R ← 2 3 7 ×& 4 6 5
8 18 35
```

Warning!

Looking at the previous example you could think that `R` contains the result of the function call, but it does not:

```
      R                          ⇦ The result is the thread number!
3
```

If you think about it, it should not come as a surprise that the result of starting a new thread is not the result of the function call. If that had been the case the main execution thread would have had to stop and wait until the execution of the function had completed - and we would not have had any parallel execution at all!

So, if we cannot get hold of the result of the function call when starting it using the *Spawn* operator, how can we get hold of it later, when we assume that the function has completed execution?

The answer is the monadic *System function* `⎕TSYNC` (*Thread Synchronization*). It takes an array of thread numbers as its argument. It then causes the thread in which it is executing to stop and wait until all the threads listed in the argument have completed execution. Then it returns an array of the same shape as the right argument, each item containing the result of the function call executed in the corresponding thread.

Let us build a simple example using the system function `⎕DL` (*Delay*), which simply stops execution for approximately a specified number of seconds. `⎕DL` returns a result - the exact length of the delay.

```
      ⎕ ← Thread ← ⎕DL& 10       ⇦ A new thread #4 will just waste 10 seconds
4                                ⇦ This is displayed immediately
      ⎕ ← ⎕TSYNC Thread          ⇦ Will wait until the 10 seconds have passed
10.045                           ⇦ The result returned by ⎕DL
```

It will never really make sense to use primitive functions with *Spawn*, as this will only slow the system down. In practice, *Spawn* is always used to start user-defined functions in situations where you don't mind that your main thread slows down a little while a job is done in the background. For example, you might start a function which prepares a print job and let it run in the background. Your application will possibly run more slowly until the print job is completed, but you can avoid having to make your user wait until the print job is finished. If the user is typing in data for the next job, the slowdown may not even be noticeable.

Programming using multiple threads is complex and requires great care. In particular, you have to be careful about what happens to global or semi-global variables that can be seen by more than one thread. Dyalog contains several mechanisms for controlling and synchronizing the execution in threads. The *Spawn* operator and `⎕TSYNC` are just the two most basic ones. We will not go into further detail about the others here; please refer to the Dyalog help file if you are interested in learning more about using multiple threads in Dyalog.

9.2 Special Syntax

Suppose we have three functions: `DyaFun` is dyadic
`MonaFun` is monadic
`NilFun` is niladic

`47 DyaFun& 60` will execute `Dyafun` in a separate thread.
The derived function is dyadic: `47 (DyaFun&) 60`

`MonaFun& 33` will execute `Monafun` in a separate thread.
The derived function is monadic: `(MonaFun&) 33`

`NilaFun&` **will not work**; it will cause a `VALUE ERROR`! Why?

The reason is that the APL syntax does not allow operators to be used with niladic functions. If you think about the other operators we have seen so far, you will see that using them with niladic functions does not make sense. Although there is really no specific reason why it should not be possible to run a niladic function in a separate thread, you cannot do so, because to specify a niladic function as the argument to the *Spawn* operator would violate the consistency of the APL syntax.

Don't worry, we have solutions!

Two possible ways to execute a niladic function in a separate thread are:

`⍎& 'NilaFunc'` The argument of *Spawn* is the *Execute* function (`⍎`) and the argument of the *derived function* is the name of the function we would like to execute: `'NilaFunc'`.
Finally, this will launch `⍎'NilaFunc'` in a new thread, and it works as expected!

`{NilaFunc}& 0` Here `NilaFunc` is embedded in a direct function, which is always ambivalent. A dummy right argument is provided, but ignored (any value will do).

Spawn can be used in conjunction with *Each* (¨) to launch several parallel threads in one expression.

10 - User-Defined Operators

As we have seen APL offers a set of primitive *functions*, and you can write your own *user defined* functions. Likewise for *operators*: Dyalog APL has a set of primitive operators, and you can write your own *user defined* operators.

10.1 Definition Modes

As we saw for functions, operators can be defined directly (*Direct Operators*) or by using the function editor.

10.1.1 - Direct Operators

A direct operator is defined like a direct function, with a few extra conventions:

`⍺⍺` represents the left argument (the left operand) of the operator
`⍵⍵` represents the right argument (the right operand) of the operator

`⍺` is the left argument of the *derived function*
`⍵` is the right argument of the *derived function*

Using these conventions, suppose that we want to simulate *Inner Product*; we could write:

```
INPRO ← {⍺ ⍺⍺.⍵⍵ ⍵}
```

To see if it works, we can just check that we obtain the same results as with the primitive Inner Product:

```
      Percent +INPRO× Invest
 9000 11300 10400 12500 17600
16400 18200 18600 24900 39600
11600 15500 17000 22600 34800
      Words ∧INPRO= 'COLONEL'
0 0 0 0 1 0 0 0
```

⇦ αα is set to +, and ⍵⍵ is set to ×
and as usual: α is set to `Percent`
⍵ is set to `Invest`

10.1.2 - Using the Function Editor

If the operator is to be defined with a function editor, the names of the arguments for the operator (its operands), which may be functions or arrays, must be attached to the name of the operator by a pair of parentheses. The name(s) of the argument(s) to the derived function are specified on either side of the parentheses. Here are the possible header structures for a defined operator:

Dyadic operator	Dyadic derived function	`X (f OPER g) Y`
	Monadic derived function	`(f OPER g) Y`
	Ambivalent derived function	`{X} (f OPER g) Y`
Monadic operator	Dyadic derived function	`X (f OPER) Y`
	Monadic derived function	`(f OPER) Y`
	Ambivalent derived function	`{X} (f OPER) Y`

Neither a defined operator nor its derived function can be niladic.

10.2 Some Basic Examples

Just to experiment a little, let us define a dyadic operator with a dyadic derived function.

```
      ∇ R ← X (f OPER g) Y
[1]   R ← (X f X)g(Y f Y)
      ∇
      5 ×OPER+ 8
89
      5 +OPER× 8
160
```

⇦ Equivalent to `(5×5) + (8×8)`

⇦ Equivalent to `(5+5) × (8+8)`

You probably remember that we used a *Multiply-Scan* to calculate a vector of inflation rates, which we then used to calculate the future values of investments given as current values (see section 3.3.1). We could just as well have used the rates to calculate the current values if we knew the future values. So why not create an operator that can be used to transform future values into current values, or the inverse; let us name it `INDEF` (for INflate/DEFlate).

The derived function arguments will be the inflation rates (left) and the investment values (right).

```
      ∇ R ← Rates (action INDEF) Values
[1]     R ← Values action ×\1+Rates÷100  ∇
```

Example values: `Inv` .... `2000 5000 6000 4000 2000`

`Inf` .... `2.6 2.9 3.4 3.1 2.7`

We can use it to calculate the future values using multiplication:

```
      2⍕ Inf ×INDEF Inv
 2052.00 5278.77 6549.90 4501.96 2311.76
```

Using divide we can do the inverse:

```
      2⍕ Inf ÷INDEF 3200 4300 3800 2500 2500
 3118.91 4072.92 3480.97 2221.25 2162.86
      Inf ÷INDEF Inf ×INDEF Inv
2000 5000 6000 4000 2000
```

⇦ Forward & back...

Section Spe-3.2 describes an interesting user-defined operator.

The Specialist's Section

Each chapter is followed by a "Specialist's Section" like this one.
This section is dedicated to skilled APLers, who wish to improve their knowledge.

If you are exploring APL for the first time, skip this section and go to the next chapter

Spe-1 Reduction Applied to Empty Vectors

Spe-1.1 - Identities

Suppose we have two numeric vectors a and b.

For example:

```
a ← 2 4 1
b ← 7 3 6
```

You can see that `+/ a,b` is equal to `(+/a) + (+/b)`

```
      +/ 2 4 1
7
      +/ 7 3 6
16
      +/ 2 4 1, 7 3 6
23                          ⇦ Yes, 7+16 = 23
```

Similarly `×/ a,b` is equal to `(×/a) × (×/b)`

```
      ×/ 2 4 1
8
      ×/ 7 3 6
126
      ×/ 2 4 1, 7 3 6
1008                        ⇦ Yes, 8×126 = 1008
```

When b is empty, `a,b` is equal to a, and the last equivalence leads to:

`×/a` is equal to `×/ a,⍬` which is equal to `(×/a) × (×/⍬)`

From the last expression we can deduce that the multiplication by `(×/⍬)` does not change anything. In other words, `×/⍬` must be the *identity item* of multiplication (1).

Using the same chain of reasoning it follows that `(+/⍬)` must return 0, the identity item of addition.

More generally, if ■ represents any dyadic, commutative function, we can say that:

	`■/ a,b`	is equal to	`(■/a) ■ (■/b)`
So:	`■/ a,⍬`	is equal to	`(■/a) ■ (■/⍬)` and also equal to `■/a`
It follows that	`■/⍬`	must return the *identity item* of the function ■.	

Spe-1.2 - Rule

> The reduction of an empty vector by any dyadic and commutative **primitive** function ■ returns the *identity item* of that function (0 for *Addition*, 1 for *Multiplication*, etc…).
>
> If ■ has no identity item, a `DOMAIN ERROR` is issued.

Spe-1.3 - Examples

Some *identity items* are obvious:

`+/⍬` is `0`

`×/⍬` is `1`

Some others may need a little explanation:

`⌊/⍬` is the largest possible value, because any other number compared to it is smaller. On a 32-bit Intel-based PC this value is `1.797693135E308`.

`⌈/⍬` is the smallest possible value, because any other number compared to it is larger. On a 32-bit Intel-based PC this value is `¯1.797693135E308`.

Spe-1.4 - Non-commutative Functions

For non-commutative functions things are not that simple. Because you will in general get different results if you swap the arguments to a non-commutative function, a value that works as an identity item if used as left argument cannot be expected to be an identity item when used as right argument.

So, a non-commutative function may have

1) an identity item that works only as left argument (a *left* identity item)
2) an identity item that works only as right argument (a *right* identity item)
3) no identity item at all

Examples:

`*/⍬` has the *right* identity item `1`, as any number raised to the power of 1 gives the number itself, but it has no *left* identity item

`⌽/⍬` has the *left* identity item `0`, as a zero-rotation leaves any array unchanged, but it has no *right* identity item

`//⍬` has the *left* identity item `1`, as any array compressed by `1` is preserved, but it has no *right* identity item

The full list of identity items is given in Appendix 5.

Spe-1.5 - Application to n-Wise Reduction

The properties described above explain the results returned by *n-Wise Reduction* when its left argument is 0.

Let us just explore how it processes vectors:

We saw earlier that the result size is: `(1+⍴Vector) - Scope.`

If `Scope` is 0, the result size is: `(1+⍴Vector)`

And if `Scope` is 0, the *slices* are all empty. Hence the result is composed of *identity items* of the function in question (if it exists, of course).

With `vec ← 3 2 6 1 8`

`0 +/ vec` returns `0 0 0 0 0 0`

`0 ×/ vec` returns `1 1 1 1 1 1`

Spe-2 Index Origin and Axis operator

Changing *Index Origin* has an impact on the use of *Axis*. For example:

With the default value `⎕IO←1` one writes: `+/[1]M` `⌽[3]A` `A,[1]B` `+\[2]M`

With `⎕IO←0` one must write: `+/[0]M` `⌽[2]A` `A,[0]B` `+\[1]M`

For this reason, when an operation applies to the first or the last dimension of an array, we recommend using the special symbols rather than specifying an axis, as they work independently of `⎕IO`:

To apply the function along the last dimension (the default), use: `/` `,` `⌽` `\`

To apply the function along the first dimension, use: `⌿` `⍪` `⊖` `⍀`

We already mentioned (section G-Spe-1) that a fractional *Axis* used with *Laminate, Ravel with axis,* and *Mix* sometimes has to be negative when ⎕IO is set to zero. For example:

	With ⎕IO←1	With ⎕IO←0
Laminate two vectors to produce a matrix:	`A,[0.5]B`	`A,[¯0.5]B`
Ravel with axis a matrix to produce a 3-D array	`,[0.5]M`	`,[¯0.5]M`
Mix a nested vector to create a matrix:	`↑[0.5]A B`	`↑[¯0.5]A B`

Spe-3 The Power Operator

Spe-3.1 - Form 2 of *Power*, and Fixpoint

In its form 2, *Power* has two functions as arguments: `{X} (■⍣●) Y`

The right argument ● must be a dyadic function that returns a Boolean scalar. The left argument ■ is applied repeatedly like this;

Y_{n+1} ← {X} ■ Y_n

until the condition Y_{n+1} ● Y_n returns *True* (1).

If the condition never returns *True*, the derived function will continue to execute *ad-infinitum*. The only way that it can be stopped is by a *Strong Interrupt*.

When ● is = or ≡, the result is called the *Fixpoint* of the function ■.

It is important to understand that, during the process, the result produced by one execution becomes the Y argument for the next iteration, so the value of Y changes, while the value of X (if any) doesn't.

To demonstrate this, let us use this extremely stupid function: `Stupid ← {? (⎕←⍵) + ⎕←⍺}`

The function returns a random integer between 1 and the sum of its two arguments. This random number may be smaller than the right argument, or not. Let us use this limit condition as a *Fixpoint*:

```
10 (Stupid ⍣ <) 20
```

Execution might proceed as follows:

	X	Y_n	Result (Y_{n+1})	
Step 1	10	20	28	
Step 2	10	28 ←	33	⇦ The new value of Y is the previous result
Step 3	10	33 ←	34	
Step 4	10	34 ←	14	⇨ Y_{n+1} is smaller than Y_n; the process stops here

If we had used = instead of < as the right argument, many more iterations might have been necessary, because the probability of a match is much smaller.

For all the many mathematic iterative calculations that "converge" towards a final limit, this use of the *Power* operator is certainly something you should consider.

Here is the example of the "*Golden mean*" (already seen in section 6.4). The process is supposed to converge until Y_{n+1} is exactly equal to Y_n. This is of course impossible in theory, but remember that the comparison precision is limited by the *Comparison Tolerance* ⎕CT, so in practice we will reach a point at which Y_{n+1} is indistinguishable from Y_n:

```
      1 +∘÷ ⍣ = 1
1.618033989
```

Spe-3.2 - Using User-Defined Operators

Power can be used with user-defined operators, to produce interesting processing tools.

In mathematics and physics, there are many cases in which one must apply a first operation, then a second one, and then the inverse of the first one.

For example, in electricity, the effective resistance of N resistors connected in parallel is the inverse of the sum of the inverses of the individual resistors' resistances. By chance, the operation ÷ is its own inverse.

If the resistances of 5 resistors connected in parallel are `2 50 7 4 10` Ohms, respectively, the effective resistance can be calculated easily as:

```
      ÷ +/ ÷r
0.9873060649
```

Instead of this simple solution, we will create a defined operator to link the three operations:

```
              DUAL ← {⍵⍵⍣¯1 ⍺⍺ ⍵⍵ ⍵}
```

As you can see, the operator first applies the right function `⍵⍵` to `⍵`, then the left one `⍺⍺`, and finally the inverse of the right function (`⍵⍵⍣¯1`).

Now, this `DUAL` operator can be applied to many problems, for example:

- Calculate the effective resistance of a set of resistors connected in parallel, of course. We just have to use ÷ for the right argument and `+/` for the left one:

  ```
        +/ DUAL ÷ 2 50 7 4 10
  0.9873060649
  ```

- Calculate the geometric mean of a list of values:

  ```
        Average DUAL ⍟ 13 29 17 33 18 24 11
  19.3208312
  ```

- Calculate the standard deviation of a series of values, for example `Ages`:

  ```
        (Average DUAL (×⍨))(Ages-Average Ages)
  12.83040822
  ```

Spe-4 Defined Operators

The arguments of a defined operator are typically functions, but they may also be arrays. If so, it is important to use parentheses to distinguish the arguments of the operator from those of the derived function:

```
      5 (3 OPER +) 7                 ⇦ Equivalent to (5 3 5) + (7 3 7)
12 6 12
      5 (× OPER 2) 7                 ⇦ Equivalent to (5×5) 2 (7×7)
25 2 49
      DISPLAY 5 (1 OPER 2) 7         ⇦ Equivalent to (5 1 5) 2 (7 1 7)
┌→──────────────────┐
│ ┌→────┐   ┌→────┐ │
│ │5 1 5│ 2 │7 1 7│ │
│ └~────┘   └~────┘ │
└∊──────────────────┘
```

None of the primitive operators take arrays as both arguments; at least one must be a function.

Spe-5 The Result of an Inverse Function

As shown in Section 8.4 above, the derived function returned by the *Power* operator is the *inverse* of its left operand when the right operand is negative.

Therefore, the following identity is usually true for a function ■ for which an inverse function exists:

```
Y ≡ {X}(■ ⍣ ¯1) {X} ■ Y
```

For example:

```
      2 ≡ (÷⍣ ¯1) ÷2
1
```

However, where several possible inverses exist, the "simplest" is chosen. For example:

```
      2⊥1 1
3
      2⊥0 1 1                        ⇦ The 0 does not change the result.
3
      2 (⊥⍣¯1) 3                     ⇦ The inverse function does not return the 0.
1 1
      1 1 ≡ 2 (⊥⍣¯1) 2⊥1 1           ⇦ Here the identity holds true.
1
```

```
      0 1 1 ≡ 2 (⊥⍣¯1) 2⊥0 1 1        ⇦ Not here; the result has been "simplified".
0
      2⊤3
1                                     ⇦ Notice that this is different from 2(⊥⍣¯1)3
```

The last example shows that the use of inverse decode rather than encode allows you to let the system decide how many digits are needed.

Chapter K: Mathematical Functions

1 - Sorting and Searching Data

1.1 Sorting Numeric Data

1.1.1 - Sorting Numeric Vectors

Two primitive functions are provided to sort data:

Grade Up ⍋ returns the set of indexes required to sort the array in ascending order

Grade Down ⍒ returns the set of indexes required to sort the array in descending order

Here is an example:

```
      Vec ← 4 6 2 11 7 6 5 9 6 8
      ⍋Vec
3 1 7 2 6 9 5 10 8 4
```

Notice that ⍋ does not actually return a sorted (i.e. re-ordered) array. Instead, we obtain a set of indexes which tells us that:

the smallest item is .... the 3rd item
then comes .... the 1st item
then .... the 7th item
then .... the 2nd, 6th, and 9th, which are all equal
etc…
and the largest item is .... the 4th item

To obtain `Vec` sorted in ascending order, we must index it by these values, as shown here:

```
      Vec[⍋Vec]
2 4 5 6 6 6 7 8 9 11
```

As you might imagine, *Grade Down* sorts the vector in descending order:

```
      Vec[⍒Vec]
11 9 8 7 6 6 6 5 4 2
```

When several items of the argument are equal, they are ordered from left to right.

For this reason, `⍒Vec` is equal to `⌽⍋Vec` only if the values in `Vec` are all different. This is not the case for our vector:

```
      ⍋Vec
3 1 7 2 6 9 5 10 8 4
      ⌽⍋Vec
4 8 10 5 9 6 2 7 1 3
      ⍒Vec
4 8 10 5 2 6 9 7 1 3
```

⇦ In black: The indexes of the three 6's

Special Use

You may rightfully wonder why *Grade Up* and *Grade Down* return indexes instead of sorted data. There are of course good reasons for it, as we will show here.

Firstly, the availability of the intermediate result of the sorting process opens up possibilities for interesting and useful manipulations. Here is one example:

Given a vector of discrete values (no duplicates), the expression `⍋⍋V` (or `⍋⍒V`) indicates which position the items of `V` would occupy if they were sorted in increasing (or decreasing) order.

```
      Class ← 153 432 317 609 411 227 186 350
      ⍋⍒ Class
8 2 5 1 3 6 7 4
```

This means that 153 is the last value in the hierarchy (the smallest), 432 is the 2nd (nearly the greatest value), … 609 is the first (the highest), … and so on.

Secondly, it makes it much easier to sort complementary arrays (e.g. arrays that represent columns in a database table) in the same order. Suppose, for example, that we would like to sort our familiar lists of prices and quantities in ascending order of quantity:

```
      Price ← 5.2 11.5 3.6 4 8.45
      Qty   ← 2 1 3 6 2
      Ix ← ⍋ Qty
      Price ← Price[Ix]
      Qty   ← Qty[Ix]
```

1.1.2 - Sorting Numeric Matrices

Grade Up and *Grade Down* can be used to sort the **rows** of a matrix.

In this case, they sort the rows by giving the highest "weight" to the leftmost columns, and the lightest "weight" to the rightmost one. Both functions return a vector of row indexes, which can be used to sort the matrix (do not forget the semicolon when indexing).

Original matrix	Sorted matrix	
Bof	Bof[⍋Bof;]	**Comments**
2 40 8	2 33 9	You can see that the first column is sorted in ascending order.
8 31 7	2 40 8	
5 55 2	2 40 9	
2 33 9	5 52 9	Then, if the first value is the same, the items of the second column are in ascending order.
7 20 2	5 55 1	
8 12 6	5 55 2	
7 20 1	7 18 8	
5 55 1	7 20 1	Finally, when the first two columns contain the same values, rows are sorted according to the last column.
5 52 9	7 20 2	
2 40 9	7 21 1	
7 18 8	8 12 6	
7 21 1	8 31 7	

1.2 Sorting Characters

1.2.1 - Using the Default Alphabet

When applied to characters, the monadic forms of *Grade Up* and *Grade Down* refer to an "implicit" alphabetic order. This collating sequence of characters depends on the version of Dyalog that you use:

- In *Classic Editions* of Dyalog it is given by a specific *System variable* known as the "***Atomic Vector***", or ⎕AV (described in chapter L).
- In *Unicode Editions* (Version 12 and later) it is the numerical order of the corresponding Unicode code points.

```
      Text ← 'Grade Up also works on Characters'
      Text[⍋Text]
aaaacdeehklnoooprrrrssstwCGU        ⇦ The result obtained in the Classic Edition
CGUaaaacdeehklnoooprrrrssstw        ⇦ The result obtained in the Unicode Edition
```

In the *Classic* Edition, the Dyalog ⎕AV has the lower case characters (a-z) located in positions 18-43 (⎕IO=1) and the upper case ones (A-Z) at positions 66-91; so all the lower case letters sort before all the upper case letters. In the *Unicode* Edition, the code points are respectively A-Z (65-90) and a-z (97-122), so all the upper case letters sort before all the lower case ones. This is why we obtained 2 different results.

For this reason, sorting characters using the default alphabet should be reserved for text that contains only lower case or only upper case letters, or matrices where upper and lower case letters appear in the same columns, as in the following example:

```
Towns           Towns[⍋Towns;]

Canberra        Canberra
Paris           Martigues        ⇦ The names are sorted correctly because all letters
Washington      Mexico             in each column are of the same case (all are upper
Moscow          Moscow             case, or all are lower case)
Martigues       Paris
Mexico          Washington
```

The default sorting doesn't work on the following matrix of Trade Marks (real or invented). This example has been produced using the *Unicode* edition; the *Classic* edition would have given a different result:

```
TM              TM[⍋TM;]

IVECO           IVECO            ⇦ This name comes first, because the upper case "V"
Toyota          Imperio            comes before the lower case "m".
absolitude      TRUELIFE         ⇦ Toyota should appear before TRUELIFE, but "R"
TRUELIFE        Toyota             comes before "o" in the default alphabet.
Imperio         absolitude       ⇦ This word should be the first, but lower-case
                                   letters come after upper-case ones.
```

1.2.2 - Using an Explicit Alphabet

To avoid this kind of problem, it is advisable to use the dyadic versions of the sorting primitives, which take an explicit alphabet as their left argument. Let us try this:

```
      Xal ← 'aAbBcCdDeEfFgGhHiIjJkKlLmMnNoOpPqQrRsStTuUvVwWxXyYzZ '
      TM[Xal⍋TM;]
absolitude
Imperio
IVECO                            ⇦ That's great: The names are now correctly sorted
Toyota
TRUELIFE
```

Alas, our satisfaction will be short lived! Imagine that "IVECO" becomes "iveco".
In our alphabet, a lower-case "i" comes before the upper-case "I", and we would obtain:

```
absolitude
iveco                            ⇦ That's wrong again!
Imperio
truelife                         ⇦ Oops - this is also wrong!
Toyota
```

As you can see we have the same problem with "TRUELIFE", now that it has been changed into "truelife". It should still be placed after "Toyota", but the lower case "t" causes it to be placed before the upper case "T" in "Toyota".

There is fortunately a solution to this annoying problem. Instead of a vector, let us organise our alphabet into a matrix, as shown here:

```
      Mal
abcdefghijklmnopqrstuvwxyz          ⇦ Although you cannot see it, note that the last
ABCDEFGHIJKLMNOPQRSTUVWXYZ            column contains a blank in both rows.
```

Now, "i" and "I" have the same "weight" because they are placed in the same columns of the alphabet. The same is true for "t" and 'T". When sorting a matrix, the lower case letters and the upper case letters will now be sorted identically.

```
      TM[Mal⍋TM;]
absolitude
Imperio                             ⇦ Phew, now it works!
iveco
Toyota
truelife
```

Note that if we had both "Imperio" and "imperio" in the matrix, "imperio" would come first, because "i" is in the first row of the alphabet matrix, while "I" is in the second row of our alphabet.

1.3 Finding Values

Find (also named ***Search***) is a primitive function represented by an underscored Epsilon: `⍷`.

It allows you to search for an array `X` in an array `Y`: `R ← X ⍷ Y`

The result `R` is a Boolean array with the same shape as `Y`, with a 1 at the starting point of each occurrence of `X` in `Y`. For example:

```
      ⎕← where← 'at' ⍷ 'Congratulations'       ⇦ Search for a text in a vector.
0 0 0 0 0 1 0 0 0 1 0 0 0 0 0
      'Congratulations',[0.5]where             ⇦ Show the correspondences.
C o n g r a t u l a t i o n s
0 0 0 0 0 1 0 0 0 1 0 0 0 0 0
```

Find can of course also be applied to numeric arrays. Here, we search for a vector of 3 numbers in a longer vector:

```
      2 5 1 ⍷ 4 8 2 5 1 6 4 2 5 3 5 1 2 2 5 1 7
0 0 1 0 0 0 0 0 0 0 0 0 0 1 0 0 0
```

The rank of `Y` can be higher than the rank of `X`. For example, we can search for a vector in a matrix:

```
      Car                      'tan' ⍷ Car
It is important          0 0 0 0 0 0 0 0 0 0 0 1 0 0 0
for John to get          0 0 0 0 0 0 0 0 0 0 0 0 0 0 0
an Italian car,          0 0 0 0 0 0 0 0 0 0 0 0 0 0 0
with a big fuel          0 0 0 0 0 0 0 0 0 0 0 0 0 0 0
tank, leathered          1 0 0 0 0 0 0 0 0 0 0 0 0 0 0
seats, HiFi set          0 0 0 0 0 0 0 0 0 0 0 0 0 0 0
for his journey          0 0 0 0 0 0 0 0 0 0 0 0 0 0 0
in Brittany.             0 0 0 0 0 0 0 1 0 0 0 0 0 0 0
```

The opposite is also permitted (i.e. the left argument having a higher rank than the right argument), but would not be very useful. The result would be only zeroes.

2 - Encode and Decode

APL offers two primitives, ***Encode*** (⊤) and ***Decode*** (⊥), to convert numeric values from their decimal (normal) form to a representation in any other number system, and back again.

Because we may not be very familiar with this kind of calculation, it may seem that only mad mathematicians should invest their time studying such conversions. In fact, these functions are used rather frequently to solve common problems.

But before studying them, we need to present some basic notions.

2.1 Some Words of Theory

2.1.1 - Familiar, But Not Decimal

`8839` is a simple number, represented in our good old decimal system. But if `8839` represents a number of seconds, it could just as well be expressed as: `2` hours, `27` minutes, and `19` seconds.

`2 27 19` is the representation of `8839` in a non uniform number system based on 24 hour days, each divided into 60 minutes, each divided into 60 seconds.

The second representation is more familiar to us, but is **not** a decimal representation: The value has been expressed in a complex *base* or *radix*; we shall say that it is **coded** (even though it is familiar).

Converting `8839` into `2 27 19` is called ***Encode*** because the result is not decimal.
Converting `2 27 19` into `8839` is called ***Decode*** because the result is decimal.
We shall say that `24 60 60` is the *Base* of the number system of `2 27 19`.

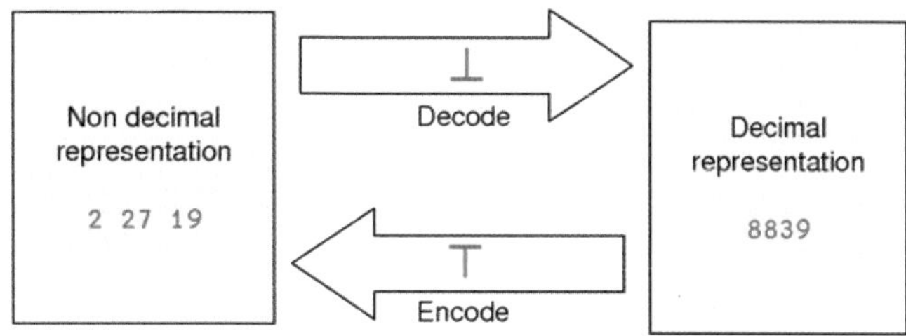

2.1.2 - Three Important Remarks

- In this case encoding a scalar (`8839`) produces a vector (`2 27 19`). In general, the representation of a decimal scalar in a non-decimal base cannot be expected to be a single number. It will always be an array of the same shape as the left argument to the *Encode* function, and in all but very special cases this left argument will be a vector or a higher rank array.

  For example, a binary value cannot be written 101011 (this is a decimal number); it must be written as a vector of binary digits: 1 0 1 0 1 1.

- The items of an encoded value can be greater than 9. In our examples, we had items equal to 27 and 19. But they are always smaller than the corresponding item of the *Base*. Would you say that that you spent 2 hours and 87 minutes to do something? Certainly not, because 87 is greater than 60; you would say 3 hours and 27 minutes.

- No matter whether days were made of only 18 hours, or they were made of 36 hours, 8839 seconds would still be represented as 2 hours, 27 minutes, 19 seconds.

  This leads to the following rule: The first item of the base vector is never taken into account **when decoding**, but it is always used for **encoding**.

2.1.3 - Base and Weights

Given the *Base* vector 24 60 60 and a value 2 27 19, one can *Decode* it (obtain its decimal representation) by any of the following three formulas:

```
(3600×2) + (60×27) + 19
+/ 3600 60 1 × 2 27 19
3600 60 1 +.× 2 27 19
```

The last formula clearly shows that decoding a set of values is nothing else than an *Inner Product*. This is important, because it means that the same shape compatibility rules will apply.

The values `3600 60 1` are the *Weights* representing how many seconds are in an hour, in a minute, and in a second. They can be obtained from the *Base* vector as follows:

```
Weights ← ⌽ 1,×\ ⌽ 1↓Base
```

This formula confirms the remark we made earlier: The first item of the *Base* vector is not used when decoding a value. However, it is needed in order to do the reverse operation (encoding) using the same *Base* vector.

Once the weights are calculated, we can define the relationship between *Decode* and *Inner product*:

Base ⊥ *Values* is equivalent to *Weights* +.× *Values*

2.2 Using Decode & Encode

2.2.1 - Decode

Decode is represented by ⊥. It accepts the *Base* vector directly as its left argument so that you do not have to calculate the weights:

```
      Base ← 24 60 60
      Base ⊥ 2 27 19
8839
```

Because the first item of the base vector is not used when decoding we could have obtained the same result in this way:

```
      Base0 ← 0 60 60
      Base0 ⊥ 2 27 19
8839
```

Example

Eggs are packaged in boxes, each containing 6 packs of 6 eggs.

If we have 2 full boxes, plus 5 packs, plus 3 eggs, we can calculate the total number of eggs using any of the following expressions, each giving the same result (105):

```
      (36×2) + (6×5) + 3
      +/ 36 6 1 × 2 5 3
      36 6 1 +.× 2 5 3
      6 6 6 ⊥ 2 5 3
```

In this very special case, our *Base* is uniform (6 6 6), and we can write the last expression in a simpler way. As usual, the scalar value is reused as appropriate:

```
      6 ⊥ 2 5 3                ⇦ We decode 2 5 3
105                            ⇦ 2 5 3 is the base 6 representation of 105
```

2.2.2 - Shape Compatibility

We said that *Decode* is nothing but a plain *Inner Product*, so the same shape compatibility rules must be satisfied.

Imagine that we have to convert two durations given in hours, minutes, and seconds, into just seconds. The first duration is 2 hours, 27 minutes, and 19 seconds, and the second one is 5 hours, 3 minutes, and 48 seconds. When we put those durations into a single variable, it is natural to express the data as a matrix, as shown here:

```
      ⎕← HMS ← 2 3 ⍴ 2 27 19 5 3 48
2 27 19
5  3 48
```

But we cannot combine a 3 item vector (Base ← 24 60 60) with a 2-row matrix (HMS).

Base ⊥ HMS would cause a LENGTH ERROR. We must transpose HMS in order to make the lengths of the arguments compatible:

```
      Base ⊥ ⍉HMS          ⇦ The length of Base is equal to the length of the first
8839 18228                   dimension of ⍉HMS. The same rule applies to Inner product.
```

2.2.3 - Encode

As an example of encoding a decimal number, we can encode 105 into base 6:

```
      6 6 6 ⊤ 105
2 5 3
```

Please note that specifying a scalar 6 as the left argument in the expression above does not give the same result:

```
      6 ⊤ 105
3
```

The reason is that it is not really possible for APL to "reuse the scalar as appropriate" here, because what does appropriate mean in this case? The left argument to *Encode* defines the number of digits in the new number system, so if we want or need three digits we must specify three 6's.[6]

We can as well convert a number of seconds into hours, minutes, and seconds, like this:

```
      24 60 60 ⊤ 23456
6 30 56
```

However, when converting 3 values the results must be read carefully:

```
      Base ⊤ 8839 18228 7205
 2  5 2
27  3 0
19 48 5
```

Do not read these results horizontally: 8839 seconds are **not** equal to 2 hours, 5 minutes, and 2 seconds! You must read the result **vertically**, and you will recognise the results we got earlier: `2 27 19`, `5 3 48`, and `2 0 5`.

2.2.4 - Limited Encoding

The shape of the result of `Bases ⊤ Values` is equal to `(⍴Bases),(⍴Values)`.

No specific rule is imposed on the arguments' shapes, but if the last dimension of the base is too small, APL proceeds to a limited encoding, as shown below:

```
24 60 60 ⊤ 8839    is    2 27 19    ⇦ Full conversion
   60 60 ⊤ 8839    is      27 19    ⇦ Truncated result
      60 ⊤ 8839    is         19    ⇦ Ditto
```

The last two results are truncated to the length of the specified base vector, but nothing indicates that they have been truncated. To avoid potential misinterpretation, it is common to use a leading zero as the first item of the base:

```
0 24 60 60 ⊤ 123456    is    1  10  17  36
   0 60 60 ⊤ 123456    is       34  17  36
      0 60 ⊤ 123456    is         2057  36
         0 ⊤ 123456    is           123456
```

The first conversion states that 123456 seconds represent 1 day, 10 hours, 17 minutes, and 36 seconds; this conversion is normal.

In the second conversion (limited to hours), 1 day + 10 hours gave 34 hours.

The third conversion was limited to minutes, and the given duration is equal to 2057 minutes and 36 seconds. It should be obvious that this conversion was limited.

---

[6] In Chapter J, Section Spe-5, you will find an example showing a clever way to have APL itself figure out the number of digits needed to properly encode a number.

2.2.5 - Using Several Simultaneous Bases

If one needs to encode or decode several values in several different bases, *Base* will no longer be a vector, but a matrix. However, this is a bit more complex and will be studied in the *Specialist's Section*.

2.3 Applications

2.3.1 - Condense or Expand Values

It is sometimes convenient to condense several values into a single one. In general this does not save much memory space, but it may be more convenient to manipulate a single value rather than several. This can be achieved by decoding the values into a decimal number.

Say, for example, that you have a list of 5 rarely used settings that you need to save in a relational database. Instead of creating 5 columns in the database table to hold the settings you could decode the 5 values into a decimal integer and save it in a single database column.

Often it is convenient to select a base made of powers of 10, corresponding to the maximum number of digits of the given values, for example:

```
      100 1000 10 100 ⊥ 35 681 7 24
35681724
```

That single value `35681724` contains the same information as the original vector, and because all base values used are powers of 10 it is fairly easy to recognize the original numbers.

The conversion base was built like this:

100	for	35	which has 2 digits
1000	for	681	which has 3 digits
10	for	7	which has only one digit
100	for	24	which has 2 digits

The base vector must of course be built according to the largest values that can appear in each of the items - not just from an arbitrary number as in our small example.

The reverse transformation may be done by coding the value using the same base:

```
      100 1000 10 100 ⊤ 35681724
35 681 7 24
```

A similar technique may be used to separate the integer and decimal parts of positive numbers:

```
      0 1 ⊤ 127.83  619.26  423.44 19.962
127      619      423      19            ⇦ Integer part
  0.83     0.26     0.44    0.962        ⇦ Decimal part
```

2.3.2 - Calculating Polynomials

Let us recall the example about packing eggs:

`6 ⊥ 2 5 3` We can say that we used *Decode* to calculate `(2×6*2)+(5×6)+3`

In other words, using traditional math notation, we calculated $2x^2+5x+3$ for $x=6$

This example shows that *Decode* can be used to calculate a polynomial represented by the coefficients of the unknown variable, sorted according to the decreasing powers of the variable.

For example, to calculate $3x^4+2x^2-7x+2$ for $x=1.2$ we can write:

```
      1.2 ⊥ 3 0 2 ¯7 2
2.7008
```

Don't forget zero coefficients for the missing powers of x (here, we have no term in x^3).

This is equivalent to: `(1.2 * 4 3 2 1 0) +.× 3 0 2 ¯7 2`

To calculate the value of a polynomial for several values of x, the values must be placed in a vertical 1-column matrix, to be compliant with the shape compatibility rules. For example, to calculate the same polynomial for x varying from 0 to 2 by steps of 0.2, we could write:

```
      X ← 0.2 ×  1+ ⍳11
      X
0 0.2 0.4 0.6 0.8 1 1.2 1.4 1.6 1.8 2
      2⍕ (11 1⍴X) ⊥ 3 0 2 ¯7 2
 2.00 0.68 ¯0.40 ¯1.09 ¯1.09 0.00 2.70 7.64 15.58 27.37 44.00
```

The results have been displayed with only 2 decimal digits, using an appropriate *Format*.

What a Surprising Base!

Let us calculate $4x^4+2x^3+3x^2-x-6$ for $x=¯1.5$

```
      ¯1.5 ⊥ 4 2 3 ¯1 ¯6
15.75
```

⇦ We used a negative decimal base. That may seem strange, but it is mathematically correct.

2.3.3 - Calculating Positions in a Matrix

Suppose that we want to locate the items of a vector (for example: `18 63 57 80 51`) in a matrix:

```
      Mat
86 63 73 72 99 88 24
31 35 51 59 84 41 27
42 54 47 29 18 16 57
80  4 53 50 95 75 55
```

```
      Vals ← 18 63 57 80 51            ⇦ The values to search for.
      ⎕ ← Pos ← (,Mat)⍳Vals            ⇦ We use dyadic Iota, but note that Mat has been
19 2 21 22 10                            converted to a vector first.
```

To transform this result into 5 row-column indices, we can employ *Decode*, using the shape of our matrix as the decoding base. But we must first subtract 1 because a number system starts from zero, while the dyadic *Iota* starts from 1, and then add the 1 again afterwards[7].

```
      1 + (⍴Mat) ⊤ Pos-1
3  1  3  4  2                          ⇦ Rows
5  2  7  1  3                          ⇦ Columns
```

However, we have a problem when searching for a value that does not appear in `Mat`, like 77.

First `(,Mat) ⍳ 77` would give `29`

then `(⍴Mat) ⊤ 29-1` would give `0 0`

and `1+(⍴Mat)⊤29-1` would give `1 1` ⇦ This is wrong, of course.

This can be easily corrected by a minor adaptation:

```
      Vals ← 86 63 77 80 51
      Pos ← (,Mat) ⍳ Vals
      (Pos≤⍴,Mat) ×[2] (⍴Mat) ⊤ Pos-1
 1  1  0  4  2                         ⇦ Missing values are now reported as being in
 1  2  0  1  3                           row zero and column zero.
```

2.3.4 - Right-aligning Text

We mentioned that *Decode* could be replaced by an *Inner product*, using the following equivalence:

Base `⊥` *Values* is equivalent to *Weights* `+.×` *Values*

with: *Weights* `← ⌽1,×\⌽1↓` *Base*

What happens if the base vector contains one zero (or more)?

```
      ⌽1,×\⌽1↓ 10 8 5 3 10 2
2400 300 60 20 2 1                     ⇦ This is the calculation with a non-zero base.
      ⌽1,×\⌽1↓ 10 8 0 3 10 2
0 0 60 20 2 1                          ⇦ This is what happens if we insert a zero.
```

We can see that the weights to the left of a zero are all forced to become zero.

In other words: `10 8 0 3 10 2 ⊥` *Values*

is strictly identical to: ` 0 0 0 3 10 2 ⊥` *Values*

[7] If the system variable *Index Origin* (`⎕IO`) is set to zero, dyadic *Iota* will also count from zero, cf. chapter L. However, the default value of *Index Origin* is 1, hence dyadic *Iota* counts from 1 in the default configuration.

Let us use this discovery to right-align some text containing blanks.

```
      Text                                  Text=' '
This little                          0 0 0 0 1 0 0 0 0 0 0 1 1 1 1 1 1 1
text contains both                   0 0 0 0 1 0 0 0 0 0 0 0 0 1 0 0 0 0
embedded and                         0 0 0 0 0 0 0 0 1 0 0 0 1 1 1 1 1 1
trailing blanks                      0 0 0 0 0 0 0 0 1 0 0 0 0 0 0 1 1 1
```

If we use the rows of this Boolean matrix as decoding bases, the result above states that the ones placed to the left of a zero will not have any effect, and our bases will therefore be equivalent to:

```
                                     0 0 0 0 0 0 0 0 0 0 0 1 1 1 1 1 1 1
                                     0 0 0 0 0 0 0 0 0 0 0 0 0 0 0 0 0 0
                                     0 0 0 0 0 0 0 0 0 0 0 0 1 1 1 1 1 1
                                     0 0 0 0 0 0 0 0 0 0 0 0 0 0 0 1 1 1
```

With that matrix of bases the expression `(Text=' ')⊥1` gives the result `8 1 7 4`, which is one more than the necessary rotation. Furthermore, we must rotate right, i.e. a negative number of positions. So, the final solution is:

```
      (1-(Text=' ')⊥1)⌽Text
       This little
text contains both
      embedded and
   trailing blanks
```

⇦ The result is perfect.
This is a really original usage of *Decode*.

Another example uses the same property of *Decode*: Given a Boolean vector `bin`, one can find how many 1s there are to the right of the last zero using this expression: `bin⊥bin`.

3 - Randomised Values

Random numbers are often used for demonstration purposes, or to test an algorithm. Strictly speaking, "Random" would mean that a set of values is completely unpredictable. This is of course not the case for numbers generated by a computer: They are by definition perfectly deterministic!

However, the values produced by an algorithm may appear to a human being as if they were random values when, given a subset of those numbers, the human is unable to predict the next values in the sequence.

If this first condition is satisfied, and if all of the unique values in a long series appear approximately the same number of times, these values can be qualified as *pseudo-random* values or *Randomised* values.

In APL, the question mark (`?`) is used to produce pseudo-random numbers.

3.1 Deal: Dyadic Usage

The dyadic usage of the question mark is named ***Deal***.

The expression

```
Number ? Limit
```

produces as many pseudo-random **integer** values as specified by `Number`, all among `⍳Limit`, and **all different**.

For this reason, `Number` cannot be greater than `Limit`.

The name of the function *Deal* relates to dealing cards. When you are dealt a hand of cards, the cards that you get are (hopefully!) arbitrary, but you cannot be given the same card twice.

Here are some examples:

```
      7 ? 52                          ⇦ Dealing a hand of 7 cards.
30 16 10 11 9 14 26
      7 ? 52                          ⇦ Executing the same expression again gives a
29 31 26 4 28 1 36                      different set of values.
      12 ? 12                         ⇦ It is possible to find 12 different values all
3 10 4 11 1 5 2 7 12 9 8 6              smaller than or equal to 12.
      13 ? 12                         ⇦ But 13 different integers smaller than or
DOMAIN ERROR                            equal to 12 is impossible, and causes an error.
```

3.2 Roll: Monadic Use

The monadic use of the question mark is named ***Roll***. The name relates to rolling a dice.

In the expression

```
? Array
```

where `Array` represents any array of positive integer values, each item `A` of `Array` produces a pseudo-random value within the list `⍳A`, so that the result is an array of the same shape as `Array`. Each item of the result is calculated independently of the other items.

```
   Mat                  ?Mat
75 14 86 20          49 14 75 12
31 16 40 51          11  1 19 13
22 64 31 28          12 47 23 27
```

For example, 75 has produced a value between 1 and 75 (49), 14 has produced a value between 1 and 14 (14 itself). Because each of the resulting values has been calculated separately, some of them may be repeated several times (this is the case for 12 here).

If the argument is made of a repeated single value `V`, the result is an array made of values all taken from `⍳V`. This makes it possible to produce any number of values within the same limits.

For example:

```
      ? 10⍴6
4 5 1 1 4 5 1 3 1 3
```

⇦ Simulates rolling a dice 10 times.

```
      ? 4 8⍴20
18 20 18 13 15 18  4 15
 2 16 17 19  9  9 13  2
 2  2 16 16  9  2  5  8
18 14 19 12  3  2 13 19
```

⇦ In this example, a 4 by 8 matrix is filled with 20s.

Then for each 20 a pseudo-random value is found.

You can see that many values are repeated.

3.3 Derived Uses

3.3.1 - Decimal Random Values

We have seen that the values produced by *Deal* and *Roll* are always integer values extracted from `⍳V`, where `V` is a given limit.

However, it is possible to obtain a set of integer or decimal values between any limits, just by adding a constant, and dividing by some appropriate value.

Imagine that we would like to obtain 50 decimal values, with 2 decimal digits, all between 743 and 761, inclusive. We could follow these steps:

- Let us first calculate integer values starting from 1: `set ← ? 50⍴ 1+100×761-743`
- Those values are between 1 and 1801
- If we add `(100×743)-1` (74299) we obtain values between 74300 and 76100.
- Once divided by 100, they give decimal values between 743 and 761 inclusive.

```
      Lims ← 743 761
      set ← ? 50⍴ 1+100× --/Lims
      set +← (100×⌊/Lims)-1
      set ÷← 100
      set
749.68 755.12 751.05 747.54 758.35 757.17 ... etc .... 758.6 753.22 760.92
      (⌊/set) , ⌈/set
743.27  760.98
```

⇦ The limits are well respected

3.3.2 - Sets of Random Characters

Random characters can be obtained by indexing a set of characters by a random set of integer values smaller than or equal to the size of the character string, as shown here:

```
      alpha←'abcdefghijklmnopqrstuvwxyz'
      alpha[?3 15⍴26]
uweqyxbroyzmnuq
jupsibbfkkbitog
pdguzfpnvouigyz
```

4 - Some More Maths

4.1 Logarithms

The base `B` logarithm of a number `N` is calculated like this: `L ← B⍟N`.

The value of `L` is such that `B*L` gives back the original number `N`. Here are some examples:

```
      10⍟1000                 ⇦ The base 10 logarithm, also called the decimal logarithm.
3
      10*3                    ⇦ The inverse operation.
1000
      3⍟81                    ⇦ The base 3 logarithm of 81.
4
      3*4                     ⇦ The inverse operation.
81
      10⍟2
0.3010299957
```

The monadic form of the logarithm function (`⍟`) gives the *Natural* (or *Napierian*) logarithm of a number:

```
      ⍟10
2.302585093
      *1
2.718281828                   ⇦ The base of the natural logarithm.
      ⍟*1
1
      (*1)⍟10                 ⇦ This left argument is superfluous.
2.302585093
```

The relationship between the natural and the base B logarithms of a number is described by the following formulas:

Given:
```
            N ← ⍟A
            L ← B⍟A
            e ← *1            ⇦ The base of the natural logarithm =
2.71828182845....
```
Then:
```
            N = L × ⍟B
```
and:
```
            L = N × B⍟e
```

4.2 Factorial & Binomial

The product of the first N integers, or the ***Factorial*** of N, is written as N! in traditional mathematics. APL uses the same symbol for the function, but in APL a monadic function is always placed to the left of its argument.

So *Factorial* looks like this in APL: !N.

As in mathematics, !0 is equal to 1.

```
      !0 1 2 3 4 5 6 7
1 1 2 6 24 120 720 5040
```

If N is a decimal number, !N gives the *Gamma* function of N+1. This is explained in the *Specialist's Section*.

The monadic function !N represents the number of possibilities when sorting N objects. But if one picks only P objects among N objects, the number of possible ***Combinations*** is given by:

```
      (!N) ÷ (!P) × (!N-P)
```

This can be obtained directly using the dyadic form of !: P!N

For example, taking 13 playing cards out of 52 can be done in 13!52 ways, that is to say 635,013,559,600 (that's a lot!).

If P is greater that N, P!N gives a 0 result.

The formula (0,⍳N)!N gives the coefficients of $(x+1)^n$, this is the reason why P!N is called ***Binomial***. One can obtain a set of coefficients with the following expression:

```
      X ← ⍳5
      ⍉(0,X)∘.!X
1 1  0  0 0 0
1 2  1  0 0 0
1 3  3  1 0 0        ⇦ For example: (x+1)³ ⇨ 1x³+3x²+3x+1
1 4  6  4 1 0
1 5 10 10 5 1
```

4.3 Trigonometry

4.3.1 - Multiples of π

The common constant Pi (or π) is very useful in many mathematical and technical calculations. It can be obtained via the primitive function ***Circle*** (the symbol ○), which gives multiples of Pi.
The symbol ○ is sometimes called ***Orange*** because it is all round, and placed on the O key of the keyboard (*Ctrl-O*). Do not confuse it with the little circle ∘ (*Jot*) used in *Outer product*.

π×N can be obtained by: ○N

```
      ○ 1 2 0.5
3.141592654 6.283185307 1.570796327
      ○ ÷3
1.047197551
```

This last expression gives, in traditional mathematical notation: π /3

Beware! Do not be mislead. This does not mean that the symbol ○ alone represents π and that we divided it by 3. This just means that the function ○ is applied to ÷3, that is, the reciprocal of 3.

4.3.2 - Circular and Hyperbolic Trigonometry

Using the dyadic form of *Circle*, one can obtain all the possible direct and inverse functions of circular and hyperbolic trigonometry.

The trigonometric function is designated by the left argument to ○ according to the table below. You can see that positive left arguments refer to direct trigonometric functions, while negative arguments refer to their inverse functions. Values from 1 to 3 calculate circular functions, and values from 5 to 7 calculate hyperbolic functions.

Direct Trigonometric Functions	
Fun	Fun ○ X
0	(1-X*2)*0.5
1	*sin* X
2	*cos* X
3	*tg* X
4	(1+X*2)*0.5
5	*sh* X
6	*ch* X
7	*th* X

Inverse Trigonometric Functions	
Fun	Fun ○ X
¯1	*arcsin* X
¯2	*arccos* X
¯3	*arctg* X
¯4	(¯1+X*2)*0.5
¯5	*argsh* X
¯6	*argch* X
¯7	*arth* X

For example:

`2○X`	means	*cos* `X`
`5○X`	means	*sh* `X`
`¯2○X`	means	*arccos* `X`
`0○Val`	calculates |*cos* `X`| if `Val` = *sin* `X`, or |*sin* `X`| if `Val` = *cos* `X`
`4○Val`	calculates |*ch* `X`| if `Val` = *sh* `X`
`¯4○Val`	calculates |*sh* `X`| if `Val` = *ch* `X`

For direct circular trigonometry (`Fun` = `1`, `2`, or `3`), the value of `X` must be in *Radians*, and for inverse circular trigonometry (`Fun` = `¯1`, `¯2`, or `¯3`) the returned result is in *Radians*.

4.3.3 - Some Examples

```
      2○ 0,○÷6 3
1 0.8660254038 0.5
```
⇦ cosine of: 0, π /6, and π /3, respectively.

```
      1 2 3 ○ ○÷3
0.8660254038    0.5    1.732050808
      ⇧              ⇧          ⇧
```
sin π /3 *cos* π /3 *tg* π /3

⇦ Here, we calculate 3 different functions for π /3.

```
      (¯3○1) = ○÷4
1
```
⇦ This confirms that *arctg* 1 is equal to π /4.

```
      1 2 ○ ○÷2
1 6.123031769E¯17
```
⇦ This calculates *sin* π /2 and *cos* π /2.

The very last result shows that the algorithms used to calculate the circular or hyperbolic values sometimes lead to very minor rounding approximations. The second value is in fact very close to zero.

4.4 GCD and LCM

4.4.1 - Greatest Common Divisor (GCD)

When applied to binary values the symbol `∨` represents the *Or* Boolean function.

The same symbol can be applied to numbers other than 0 and 1. Then it calculates their ***Greatest Common Divisor*** (or *GCD*). It is a *Dyadic Scalar Function*: Applied to arrays of the same shape it gives a result of the same shape; applied between a scalar and any array it gives a result of the same shape as the array, and the scalar value is reused as needed.

```
      15180 ∨ 285285 ¯285285 47
165 165 1
```
⇦ The result is always positive. There is no common divisor for 15180 and 47 other than 1.

```
      5180 0 28 ∨ 6142 41 19
74 41 1
```

⇦ As always, if one of the items of the argument to ∨ is 0, the corresponding item from the other argument is returned (41 in this case).

```
      5178 417 28 ∨ 7.4 0.9 1.4
0.2 0.3 1.4
```

4.4.2 - Lowest Common Multiple (LCM)

When applied to binary values the symbol ∧ represents the *And* Boolean function.

The same symbol can be applied to numbers other than 0 and 1. Then it calculates their ***Lowest Common Multiple*** (or *LCM*). It is also a *Dyadic Scalar Function.*

```
      152 1 6183 ¯519 0 ∧ 316 8 411 24 16
12008 8 847071 ¯4152 0
```

4.5 Set Union and Intersection

Mathematical Set Theory describes the following two functions:

Intersection A∩B gives the items common to two sets of values A and B.
Union A∪B gives the items that are *either* in set A *or* in set B.

The same functions are found in Dyalog, using the same symbols. They only work on scalar and vector arguments:

```
      'Hey' 'give' 'me' 53 'Dollars' ∩ 53 'Euros' 'not' 'Dollars'
53  Dollars
      'Hey' 'give' 'me' 53 'Dollars' ∪ 53 'Euros' 'not' 'Dollars'
 Hey  give  me  53  Dollars  Euros  not
```

In contrast to mathematical sets APL vectors are ordered and may contain duplicates, which makes a couple of conventions necessary:

For *Intersection* the result is in the order that the items appear in the left argument, including duplicates. In fact, the result is equal to the left argument, but with all items that are not found in the right argument removed:

```
      1 1 2 2 3 3 ∩ 2 3
2 2 3 3
```

For *Union* the result is always the left argument, followed by all items of the right argument that are not already found in the left argument - including duplicates:

```
      1 1 2 2 3 3 ∪ 2 2 2 4 4 4 6 6 6
1 1 2 2 3 3 4 4 4 6 6 6
```

5 - Domino

5.1 Some Definitions

5.1.1 - Identity Matrix

Any number multiplied by 1 is the same number. Similarly, a matrix multiplied by a Boolean matrix of the same shape, containing only 1s along its main diagonal, remains unchanged.

If `M` is	and if `I` is	then `M+.×I` is	

`12 50  7`
`44  3 25`
`30 71 80`
	`1 0 0`
	`0 1 0`
	`0 0 1`
		`12 50  7`
		`44  3 25`
		`30 71 80`
			⇦ This result is equal to `M`

We say that `I` is the *Identity item* for the multiplication of 3 by 3 matrices. One can define a similar *Identity item* for a square matrix of any size.

5.1.2 - Inverse Matrices

If we multiply 4 by 0.25 or 0.25 by 4, we obtain 1, which is the *Identity item* for multiplication. Alternatively, we can say that 0.25 is the reciprocal, or inverse, of 4, and vice versa.

Given that `I` is the *Identity item* for matrix multiplication, if we can find two matrices `MAT` and `TAM` whose product is `I`, we can say that these two matrices are each the inverse of the other:

If `MAT` is	and if `TAM` is	then `MAT+.×TAM` is

`1   0 2`
`0   2 1`
`0.5 3 1.5`
	` 0     ¯3     2`
	`¯0.25 ¯0.25  0.5`
	` 0.5   1.5  ¯1`
		`1 0 0`
		`0 1 0`
		`0 0 1`

Both `MAT+.×TAM` and `TAM+.×MAT` would give the same result; `MAT` and `TAM` are really each the inverse of the other.

Here is a second example with 2 by 2 matrices:

`M1`	`M2`	`M1+.×M2`
`2 1` `4 1`	`¯0.5  0.5` ` 2   ¯1`	`1 0` `0 1`

For the moment, we defined inverses only for square matrices. We shall see later (Specialist's Section, § 4) that it is also possible to define inverses for non-square matrices.

5.2 Matrix Inverse

5.2.1 - Monadic Domino

APL provides a ***Matrix Inverse*** primitive function, represented by the symbol ⌹. Because of its appearance, this symbol is named ***Domino***.

Monadic *Domino* returns the inverse of a matrix:

```
      ⌹ MAT
¯8.558701407E¯16 ¯3     2
¯2.500000000E¯1  ¯0.25  0.5
 5.000000000E¯1   1.5  ¯1
```

Calculating the inverse of a matrix is a complex operation, and the precision may decrease as the number of operations grows, resulting in some degree of approximation. This is the case above. The top left value should have been zero, but is only very close to it. Being so close to 0, it is displayed using scientific notation, which is then applied to all other values in that column.

To make results like the one above easier to read, we will hereafter present the results in a rounded form, as shown below:

```
      ⌹ MAT
 0     ¯3     2                      ⇦ As expected, this is the value of TAM
¯0.25 ¯0.25  0.5
 0.5    1.5  ¯1
```

Remember, you can always use *Format* to display rounded values, for example:

```
      2⍕ ⌹MAT
  0.00 ¯3.00  2.00
 ¯0.25 ¯0.25  0.50
  0.50  1.50 ¯1.00
```

5.2.2 - Singular Matrices

In normal arithmetic, zero has no inverse, and ÷0 in APL causes a `DOMAIN ERROR`.

In the same way, some matrices cannot be inverted; they are said to be *Singular*.

```
      ⌹ ⎕ ← 3 3⍴1 3 5 3 4 15 2 7 10
1 3  5
3 4 15
2 7 10
DOMAIN ERROR                              ⇦ This error message means that our matrix cannot
      ⌹ ⎕←3 3⍴1 3 5 3 4 15 2 7 10           be inverted: It is singular.
      ∧
```

5.2.3 - Solving a Set of Equations

Here is a set of three linear equations with three unknowns x y, and z, written using traditional mathematical notation:

$$\begin{aligned} ^{-}8 &= 3x + 2y - z \\ 19 &= x - y + 3z \\ 0 &= 5x + 2y \end{aligned}$$

This set of equations can be represented using a vector for the constants and a matrix for the coefficients of the three unknowns, as shown below:

```
      Cons ← ¯8 19 0
      ⎕← Coefs ← 3 3⍴3 2 ¯1 1 ¯1 3 5 2 0
3  2 ¯1
1 ¯1  3
5  2  0
```

To solve the above set of equations, we must find a vector of three values `XYZ` such that:

`Cons` is equal to `Coefs +.× XYZ`

We can find such a solution provided that the matrix `Coefs` has an inverse, i.e. that it is non-singular.

Let us multiply both sides of the equation by the inverse of `Coefs`:

If	`Coefs +.× XYZ`	is equal to	`Cons`
then	`(⌹Coefs) +.× Coefs +.× XYZ`	is equal to	`(⌹Coefs) +.× Cons`

Knowing that `(⌹Coefs)+.×Coefs` gives the identity matrix (let's call it `I`), the expression can be reduced further:

Since	`(⌹Coefs) +.× Coefs +.× XYZ`	is equal to	`(⌹Coefs) +.× Cons`
then	`I +.× XYZ`	is equal to	`(⌹Coefs) +.× Cons`
and consequently	`XYZ`	is equal to	`(⌹Coefs) +.× Cons`

Eureka! We found a way of calculating the values we had to find:

```
      ⎕← XYZ ← (⌹Coefs) +.× Cons
2 ¯5 4                                    ⇦ You can check. This is correct!
```

More generally: *Solutions* ← (⌹ *Coefficients*) +.× *Constants*

Note that in the formula above we multiply *Constants* by the inverse (or reciprocal) of a matrix. Multiplying by the reciprocal of something is usually known as division, so perhaps this is true here as well? Yes it is, and we'll show that in the next section.

5.3 Matrix Division

The dyadic form of *Domino* implements matrix division, so it can do exactly what we have just done: It can easily solve sets of linear equations like the one shown above:

```
      Cons⌹Coefs                    ⇦ Equivalent to (⌹Coefs) +.× Cons
2 ¯5 4                              ⇦ We found the same solution as before.
```

Naturally, this method works only if the coefficient matrix has an inverse. In other words, the set of equations must have a single solution. If there is no solution, a `DOMAIN ERROR` will be reported.

We can summarise this as follows:

Given a system of `N` linear equations with `N` unknowns, let the matrix of the coefficients of the unknowns be named *Coefficients*, and the vector of constants be named *Constants*, the system can be solved using matrix division like this:

Solutions ← *Constants* ⌹ *Coefficients*

5.4 Two or Three Steps in Geometry

5.4.1 - A Complex Solution to a Simple Problem

To begin with, we invite you to study a complicated method to solve a simple problem. Our intention is then to generalise this method to develop a solution for an everyday problem in statistical studies.

The goal is to find the coefficients of a straight line passing through two points `P` and `Q`, of which the coordinates are given below:

```
X ← 2 4    vector of P and Q X-coordinates    ⇦ See figure K-1 below
Y ← 2 3    vector of P and Q Y-coordinates
```

Figure K-1

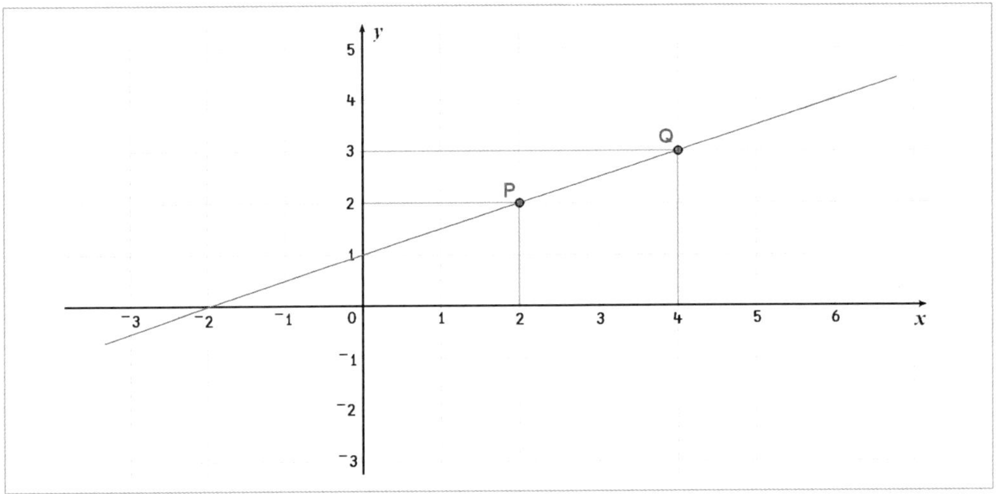

The general equation describing a straight line is $y = ax + b$. With our two points given, the following is obtained:

$2 = 2a + b$
$3 = 4a + b$

⇦ This is a set of two linear equations in which the unknowns are a and b

Let us solve this set of equations by the method demonstrated in the previous section.

The vector of constants (formerly named `Cons`) is now given by `Y`.................. `2 3`

The matrix `M` of the coefficients of the unknowns (formerly `Coefs`) is:...........

```
2 1
4 1
```

This matrix `M` can be obtained from the vector `X` like this................................. `M← X,[1.5]1`

Now a and b can be calculated using the method we saw above...................... `C← Y⌹M`

If we replace `M` by the expression used to calculate it from `X`, we can write ..... `C← Y⌹X,[1.5]1`

```
      X ← 2 4
      Y ← 2 3
      ⎕← C← Y⌹X,[1.5]1
0.5 1
```

You can easily check on the figure that these are the values we looked for. The equation for this line is (in traditional notation): y = `0.5`x `+ 1`

Do you find this method tedious? You are right, but now let us discover its scope.

5.4.2 - Calculating Additional Y-coordinates

Having found the coefficients of the line shown in the previous section, let us try to calculate the Y-coordinates of several points for which the X-coordinates are known:

The coefficients of our line were obtained by this calculation: .... `C← Y⌹M`
We saw earlier that it is strictly equivalent to .... `C← (⌹M) +.× Y`

Let us left-multiply both terms of this expression by `M`:

If	`C`	is equal to	`(⌹M)+.×Y`	
then	`M+.×C`	is equal to	`M +.× (⌹M)+.×Y`	where again `M+.×(⌹M)` is equal to `I`
so	`M+.×C`	is equal to	`I+.×Y`	
or	`M+.×C`	is equal to	`Y`	

This exposition shows that the Y-coordinates `Y` of some points placed on a line defined by coefficients `C` can be calculated from their X-coordinates `X` by the formula `M+.×C` or, in a more explicit form:

```
Y ← (X,[1.5]1) +.× C
```

Y-coordinates ← (*X-coordinates*,[1.5]1) +.× *Coefficients*

Let us apply this technique to a set of points:

```
      (0 ¯2 3 6,[1.5]1) +.× C
1 0 2.5 4
```

⇦ You can check it in the diagram.

5.5 Least Squares Fitting

5.5.1 - Linear Regression

Our line was defined by two points. What happens if we no longer have 2 points, but many? Of course there is a high probability that these points are not aligned.

As an example, suppose that we have twelve employees; we know their ages and salaries:

```
      AGE,[0.5]SAL
  20   21   28   31   33   34   36   37   40   44   45   51
3071 2997 2442 3589 3774 3071 3108 5291 5180 7548 5772 5883
```

(Salaries are given in Peanuts, a currency used more and more in many companies).

We shall place the ages on the X axis, and salaries on the Y axis (see figure K-2)

This time, matrix `AGE,[1.5]1` will have more rows (12) than columns (2), and the set of equations has no solution, which confirms that no single straight line can join all those points.

In this type of situation, it may be desirable to define a straight line which best represents the spread of points. Generally a straight line is sought such that the sum of the squares of the deviations of Y-coordinates between the given points and the line is minimised. This particular line is called the *Least Squares line* or a *Linear regression*.

To find this line, we shall use *Domino* once more. The expression used to calculate the coefficients of a line passing through two points can be applied to a rectangular matrix, and *Domino* gives the coefficients of the *Least Squares line* passing through the set of points. Isn't it magic?

For the given points, here is the calculation:

```
      ⎕← C← SAL ⌹ AGE,[1.5]1
134.9457203 ¯412.600208                    ⇦ Equation: y = 134.9x - 412.6
```

Let us calculate the rounded salaries located on the line, at the same X-coordinates as the given points:

```
      0⍕ (AGE,[1.5]1) +.× C
2286 2421 3366 3771 4041 4176 4445 4580 4985 5525 5660 6470
```

Figure K-2

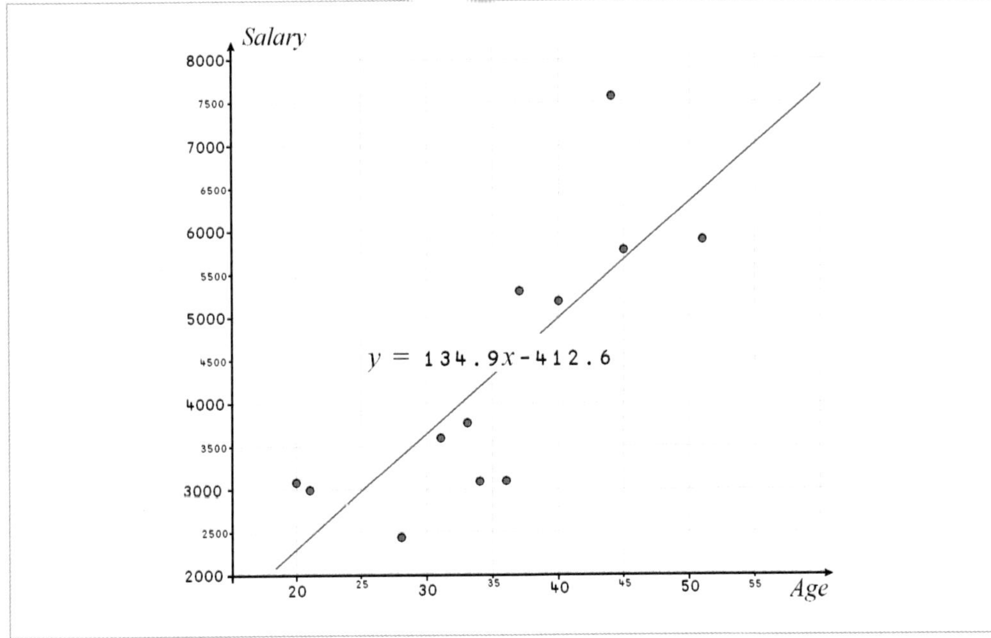

5.5.2 - Extension

In the previous example, we measured the effect of a single factor (age) on a single observation (salary) using a linear model.

What if we want to use the same model to explore the relationship between several factors and a single observation?. The following example is inspired by a controller in IBM France who tried to see if the heads of his commercial agencies had "reasonable" expense claim forms.

- The amounts were stored in.. `Amounts`

He tried to measure the effect of 4 factors on these expenses amounts:

- The number of salesmen in each agency .... `NbMen`
- The size of the area covered by each agency... `Radius`
- The number of customers in each agency .... `NbCus`
- The annual income produced by each agency .... `Income`

In other words, he tried to find the vector `TC` of 5 theoretical coefficients C1 to C5, which most closely satisfies the following equation:

```
Amounts = (C1×NbMen) + (C2×Radius) + (C3×NbCus) + (C4×Income) + C5
```

Here is the data:

Amounts	NbMen	Radius	NbCus	Income
40420	25	90	430	2400
23000	20	50	87	9000
28110	24	12	72	9500
32460	28	12	210	4100
25800	14	30	144	6500
33610	8	30	91	3300
61520	31	120	207	9800
44970	17	75	161	4900

Let us apply exactly what we did on ages and salaries, and calculate the following variables:

- Matrix of factors............................ `Fact ← NbMen,Radius,NbCus,Income,[1.5]1`
- Coefficients of the least squares line .... `2⍕TC ← Amounts⌹Fact`

```
1154.23 362.14 ¯99.39 ¯3.33 31193.65
     C1     C2     C3    C4       C5
```

- Y-coordinates of points on that least squares line .... `YLS ← Fact+.×TC`
- Differences .... `Diff ← Amounts-YLS`
- The same in percentages.. `Pcent ← 100×Diff÷YLS`

And finally, display all the data, with a "-" sign for those who are much higher that the least squares line (supposed to be bad managers), and a "+" sign for those who are significantly below that line (supposed to be excellent managers):

```
      Flag ← '+ -'[1++/Pcent∘.>¯10 10]
      Title ← 29↑'   Real Normal   Diff      %'
      Title⍪(7 0⍕Amounts,YLS,Diff,[1.5]Pcent),Flag
   Real Normal   Diff      %
  40420  41914  ¯1494     ¯4
  23000  33773 ¯10773    ¯32+      ⇦ This one is really thrifty!
  28110  24455   3655     15-
  32460  33335   ¯875     ¯3
  25800  22264   3536     16-      ⇦ This one wastes money!
  33610  31260   2350      8
  61520  57229   4291      7
  44970  45660   ¯690     ¯2
```

5.5.3 - Non-linear Adjustment

In this last example we used independent factors and tried to combine them with a linear expression. We could as well have used vectors linked one to the other by any mathematical expression, like `Results←(C1×Var)+(C2×Var*2)+(C3×⍟Var)+C4` (if this makes sense):

A typical case is trying to fit a set of points with a polynomial curve. Here are 8 points:

```
      X← ¯1 ¯1 0.5  1.5  2 2 3 4
      Y← ¯3 ¯1 0   ¯1   ¯1 1 3 5
```

A linear regression would give a line with the following coefficients:

```
      2⍕ Y ⌹ X,[1.5]1
1.22 ¯1.31
```

The right argument was obtained by laminating 1 to `X`; we could just as well have obtained it with the following *Outer Product*: `X∘.*1 0` because `X*0` gives 1, and `X*1` gives `X`:

Now, instead of taking only powers 1 and 0 of `X`, we could extend the scope of the powers up to the third degree (for example): `X∘.*3 2 1 0`

We would then obtain not the coefficients of a straight line but those of a third degree polynomial curve (shown in figure K-3 below):

```
      2⍕ C←Y⌹X∘.*3 2 1 0
0.10 ¯0.16 0.58 ¯1.07
```

In other words, this set of points can be approximated by: $0.1x^3 - 0.16x^2 + 0.58x - 1.07$

Figure K-3

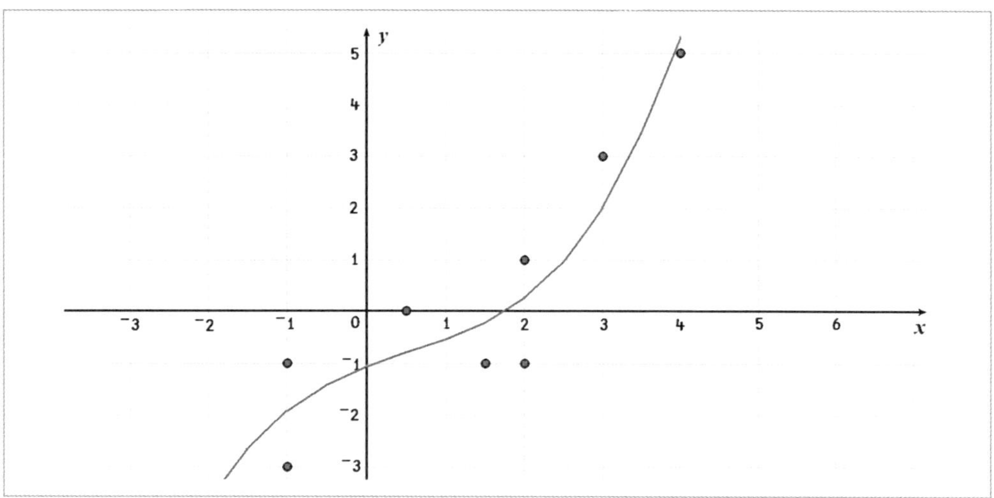

Exercises

K-1 Can you predict (and explain) the results of these two expressions:

a) `0 ⊥ 12 34 60 77 19`

b) `1 ⊥ 12 34 60 77 19`

K-2 In a binary number system, a group of 4 bits represents values from 0 to 15. Those 4 bits represent the 16 states of a base 16 number system, known as the hexadecimal number system. This system is very often used in computer science, with the numbers 0-9 represented by the characters "0" – "9", and the numbers 10-15, represented by the characters "A" to "F".

Write a function to convert hexadecimal values into decimal, and the reverse. Let us decide that hexadecimal values are represented as 4 character vectors:

```
      H2D '1A5C' 'C20F' 'EB79'
6748 49679 60281
      D2H 6748 49679 60281
 1A5C  C20F  EB79
```

K-3 Create three variables, filled with random integers, according to the following specifications:

a) A vector of 12 values between 8 and 30, without duplicates.

b) A 4 by 6 matrix filled with values between 37 and 47, with possible duplicates.

c) A 5 by 2 matrix filled with values between ¯5 and 5, without duplicates.

K-4 Create a vector of 15 random numbers between 0.01 and 0.09 inclusive, with 3 significant digits each, with possible duplicates.

K-5 What will we obtain by executing this expression: `10+?(10+?10)⍴10`

K-6 We would like to obtain a vector of 5 items, chosen randomly without duplicates among the following values:

```
List ← 12 29 5 44 31 60 8 86
```

K-7 Create a vector with a length randomly chosen between 6 and 16, and filled with random integers between 3 and 40 inclusive, with possible duplicates.

K-8 The value of *cos x* can be calculated by the following formula, written with traditional mathematical notations:

$$\cos x = x^0/0! - x^2/2! + x^4/4! - x^6/6! + x^8/8! - x^{10}/10! \text{ etc...}$$

Can you write an APL expression which executes this calculation, up to the power `2×N` ?

K-9 Try to evaluate the following expressions, and then check your result on the computer:

a) `(1○ ○÷4)*2`

b) `2×0.5+¯2 ○ 1 ○ 0.5`

K-10 Find the solution to this set of equations:

$$\begin{aligned} x - y &= 5 \\ y - 2z &= ^{-}7 \\ z - x &= 2 \end{aligned}$$

K-11 Three variables a, b, and c meet the following conditions:

```
a-b+3c   = 13
4b-2a    = ¯6
a-2b+2c  = 10
```

Can you calculate the value of 3a + 5b - c

The Specialist's Section

Each chapter is followed by a "Specialist's Section" like this one.
This section is dedicated to skilled APLers, who wish to improve their knowledge.

If you are exploring APL for the first time,
skip this section and go to the next chapter

Spe - 1 Encode and Decode

Spe 1.1 - Special decoding

If you replace *Decode* by the equivalent *Inner product*, you can easily check these surprising properties:

```
0⊥v      is equivalent to     ⊖ρ¯1↑v
1⊥v      is equivalent to     +/v
```

When dealing with integers the values are normally smaller than the corresponding items of the *Base*. For example, it would be unusual to say that a time is equal to 7 hours 83 minutes and 127 seconds. However, *Decode* works perfectly on such values:

```
      24 60 60 ⊥ 7 83 127
30307
```

And, though we did not mention it, *Encode* (like *Decode*) accepts decimal and/or negative bases:

```
      (3ρ5.2) ⊤ 160.23
5 4 4.23
```

Spe 1.2 - Processing Negative Values

Imagine that we want to encode some numbers in any base, with 6 digits. We will choose base 10, so that the result is readily understandable:

```
(6ρ10) ⊤ 17        gives        0 0 0 0 1 7
```

Now let us try to predict the result of `(6⍴10)⊤¯17`. Knowing that `17+¯17` is `0`, it would be reasonable to expect that `((6⍴10)⊤17) + ((6⍴10)⊤¯17)` also returns a result that is "zero" in some way - for example `6⍴0`?

In other words, we are looking for a 6-item vector that, when added to `0 0 0 0 1 7`, gives `6⍴0`. The real challenge is that the items of the vector must only contain the digits `0-9`!

Let's see what happens:

```
(6⍴10) ⊤ ¯17        gives       9 9 9 9 8 3
```

These results may seem a bit surprising. In base 10, when the sum of two digits exceeds 9, a carry is produced, which is used when adding the next digits to the left, and so on. When adding the encoded values of `17` and `¯17`, here is how the values are processed:

```
 1 1 1 1 1 1                 ⇦ The numbers carried to the left
   0 0 0 0 1 7
+  9 9 9 9 8 3
 -------------
= 1 0 0 0 0 0 0
```

If only 6 digits are kept, as agreed, you can see that the result is composed only of zeroes.

That would be the same for 431:

```
   (6⍴10) ⊤  431     gives       0 0 0 4 3 1
   (6⍴10) ⊤ ¯431     gives       9 9 9 5 6 9
and the sum is                 1 0 0 0 0 0 0
```

We can observe the same behaviour in any other base. For example, in base 5:

```
   (6⍴5) ⊤  68       gives       0 0 0 2 3 3
   (6⍴5) ⊤ ¯68       gives       4 4 4 2 1 2        Remember that, in base 5,
and the sum is                 1 0 0 0 0 0 0     ⇦  3+2 gives 0, with 1 carried!
```

The rule remains true for decimal values:

```
   (5⍴10) ⊤  15.8    gives       0 0 0 1 5.8
   (5⍴10) ⊤ ¯15.8    gives       9 9 9 8 4.2
and the sum is                 1 0 0 0 0 0
```

This may lead to a few frustrations during decoding if precautions are not taken:

```
   10⊥(6⍴10)⊤ 143    gives              143     ⇦ This is what we expected
   10⊥(6⍴10)⊤¯143    gives           999857     ⇦ This may seem wrong
and the sum is                      1000000
```

The result obtained is such that the sum of 143 and 999857 gives 10^6.

If one needs to encode and later decode values among which some may be negative, it is advisable to provide one more digit than is necessary, and to test its value. In many computers the internal representation of positive numbers begins with a 0-bit, and negative values start with a 1-bit. The same principle applies to the decoded values. In base 10, positive values begin with the digit 0, and negative ones with a 9. We can deduce from this a general function to decode values encoded in a uniform base:

```
     ∇ Z←Base Decode Values;P
[1]    Z←Base⊥Values
[2]    P←1↑⍴Values
[3]    Z←Z-(Base*P)×(Z>¯1+Base*P-1)
     ∇
      test ← (6⍴10) ⊤ ¯417.42 26 32 ¯1654 0 3.7 ¯55
      10⊥test
999582.58 26 32 998346 0 3.7 999945       ⇦ Negative values are wrongly decoded.
      10 Decode test
¯417.42 26 32 ¯1654 0 3.7 ¯55             ⇦ Negative values are correctly decoded.
```

Spe 1.3 - Multiple Encoding/Decoding

It is possible to decode a value using several bases simultaneously:

```
      ⎕← BB← ⍉4 3⍴5 10 6
 5  5  5  5                    ⇦ The different bases are placed one under the
10 10 10 10                      other in a matrix.
 6  6  6  6
      BB ⊥ 4 1 3 2
542 4132 920                   ⇦ Interpreting 4 1 3 2 in 3 different bases
```

In this very specific case, the 3 bases were all uniform; a simple vertical matrix with one digit per row would have given the same conversion:

```
      (3 1⍴5 10 6)⊥4 1 3 2
542 4132 920
```

Similarly, it is possible to see how a single number could be represented in several bases:

```
      (5 3⍴5 10 2) ⊤ 27
0 0 1
0 0 1                          ⇦ These three columns represent 27 in bases 5, 10,
1 0 0                            and 2, respectively.
0 2 1
2 7 1
```

Rules: The arguments of *Encode* and *Decode* must obey the following rules:

In `R ← Bases ⊥ Mat` ⇨ `(⍴R)` is equal to `(¯1↓⍴,Bases),1↓⍴Mat`

In `R ← Bases ⊤ Mat` ⇨ `(⍴R)` is equal to `(⍴Bases),⍴Mat`

Let us convert (encode) the following matrix `Seconds` into hours, minutes and seconds:

```
      Seconds
1341 5000 345
3600  781  90
      24 60 60 ⊤ Seconds
 0  1  0                    ⇦ Hours
 1  0  0

22 23  5                    ⇦ Minutes
 0 13  1

21 20 45                    ⇦ Seconds
 0  1 30
```

Spe - 2 Random Link

Spe 2.1 - Making Random Numbers Predictable or Unpredictable

The algorithm used to create randomised numbers is described in detail in the next section. It uses an initial seed value, contained in the system variable `⎕RL` (where `RL` stands for *Random Link*). Each time a new value is generated this seed value is changed so that the next value will be different. When you `)SAVE` a workspace, the random link is also saved. However, each time Dyalog APL is started, or each time the active workspace is cleared by `)CLEAR`, the *Random Link* is reset to a predefined value, equal (by default) to `7*5` (`16807`).

For this reason, if an expression using pseudo-random values is executed immediately after APL has been started, the expression will give the same result on each such occasion. This can be useful if for example we want to reproduce the same experimental conditions, but it can also be a disadvantage if we really would like random values.

To reproduce a given set of random values, one can dynamically set `⎕RL` to any desired value (perhaps `⎕RL←7*5`, or any other value in the range 1 to 2147483646):

```
      OLDRL ← ⎕RL               ⇦ Store the current value of ⎕RL
      ? 5⍴40                    ⇦ Get five random values.
37 9 18 26 3
      ? 5⍴40                    ⇦ The same expression produces a different set
27 6 7 27 17                      of values each time it is executed.
      ⎕RL ← OLDRL               ⇦ But if we restore the original value, we obtain the
      ? 10⍴40                     same set of 10 randomised values.
37 9 18 26 3 27 6 7 27 17
```

Since the randomised values are so predictable, how do we ensure that we get different values each time the same APL job is started?

A common approach is to set the *Random Link* to a value derived from the current timestamp, ⎕TS, for example:

```
      ⎕RL ← 24 60 60 1000 ⊥ ¯4↑⎕TS
```

Another simple algorithm is not to touch the *Random Link* directly, but instead ask for as many random values as the "seconds" item of the current timestamp (⎕TS[6]) reports. These numbers will not be used, but ⎕RL will be changed an unpredictable number of times and will therefore be set to an unpredictable value (at least unpredictable among the 60 possible values):

```
      ⎕RL
16807                                ⇦ The standard initial value.
      Sink ← ⎕TS[6]?100              ⇦ Generate an arbitrary number of random values.
      ⎕RL
282475249                            ⇦ ⎕RL has been changed to an "arbitrary" value.
```

Spe 2.2 - Algorithm

Here is the algorithm used by APL to create a randomised scalar (an array would need loops). We have written the algorithm for *Roll*; the algorithm for *Deal* is just an extension.

```
      ∇ Z←Roll N
[1]     ⎕RL←(¯1+2*31)|⎕RL×7*5
[2]     Z←⎕IO+⌊N×⎕RL÷2*31
      ∇
```

The first instruction prepares the seed used for the next number. *Residue* is used to ensure that the result will always be smaller than (¯1+2*31). Consequently, ⎕RL÷2*31 always returns a value in the range 0-1. Multiplied by the argument, it produces a result strictly smaller than N, and by adding ⎕IO we get the desired result.

You can compare our function to the primitive function; they work identically:

⎕RL←7*5 ?10 2 ⎕RL 282475249 ?10 8	⎕RL←7*5 Roll 10 2 ⎕RL 282475249 Roll 10 8

Spe - 3 Gamma and Beta Functions

In mathematics, the *Gamma* function of a variable x is defined by the following formula:

$$\Gamma(x) = \int_0^\infty t^{x-1} e^{-t} dt$$

This function satisfies the recurrence relationship: $\Gamma(x) = x \times \Gamma(x\text{-}1)$

If x is integer, $\Gamma(x)$ is equivalent to $(x\text{-}1)!$

In APL, monadic `!N` gives the *Gamma* function of `N+1`.

```
      ! 2.4 3 3.2 3.4
2.981206427 6 7.756689536 10.13610185
```

The dyadic form of `!` gives the *Binomial* function, which satisfies the following identity with the mathematical *Beta* function:

β`(A,B)` is identical to: `÷B×(A-1)!A+B-1`

Spe - 4 Domino and Rectangular Matrices

In section 5.1.2 we used square matrices to define what a matrix inverse is. But in section 5.5.1 we used *Domino* on a rectangular matrix; this requires some explanation. In the following sections we shall define what we mean by a "left inverse" and a "right inverse" to a given matrix.

Note: *Domino* uses Housholder transformations, a technique based on Lawson & Hanson algorithm, an extension of Golub & Businger algorithm.

Spe 4.1 - Left Inverse of a Matrix

Let us recall the context: We intended to investigate a vector of values.

`Y` was a vector of values to investigate (for example a vector of expenses amounts).

`M` was a rectangular matrix containing a set of columns containing observations.
(For example: Number of salesmen, size of the area, number of customers, and so on…).

`C` was the coefficients of a "*Least Squares line*". They should be such as the sum of the squares of differences between points on this line and the given points `Y` is minimal.

In mathematics three major properties can be demonstrated:

- The coefficients `C` can be obtained from `Y` by means of a linear regression or, in other words, an *Inner product* involving a matrix `Inv`: .... `C←Inv+.×Y`
- This matrix `Inv` is unique
- It can be obtained by the following formula: .... `Inv←(⌹ (⍉M)+.×M)+.×(⍉M)`

In this formula, the product `(⍉M)+.×M` gives a square matrix, even if `M` is rectangular. This is why we can calculate its inverse matrix using *Domino*.
If we refer to the definition of dyadic *Domino*, ... `(⌹A)+.×B` can be written: `B⌹A`

So, the formula giving `Inv` can also be written: .... `Inv←(⍉M)⌹ (⍉M)+.×M`

Let us see what happens if we multiply that formula by `M` on its right:

Given that	`Inv`	is equal to	`(⌹ (⍉M)+.×M)+.×(⍉M)`
then	`Inv+.×M`	is equal to	`(⌹ (⍉M)+.×M)+.×(⍉M) +.×M`
Let us replace	`(⍉M)+.×M`	by	`U`
then	`Inv+.×M`	is equal to	`(⌹U)+.×U` which is the identity matrix `I`

Since `Inv+.×M` gives an identity matrix, we know that `Inv` is a true ***left inverse*** for `M`.

Rule: The *left inverse* `Inv` of a matrix `M` can be obtained by:

```
Inv ← (⌹ (⍉M)+.×M) +.× ⍉M
```

This can be easily verified with the data we used in section 5.5.2, where our matrix of explanatory factors (`M` here above) was calculated as follows:

```
      ⍴Fact ← NbMen,Radius,NbCus,Income,[1.5]1      ⇦ Our matrix of factors.
8 5
      ⍴Inv ← (⌹ (⍉Fact)+.×Fact) +.× ⍉Fact           ⇦ Its left inverse.
5 8
```

The shape compatibility is satisfied, and we can multiply these matrices:

```
      ⌊0.5+ Inv +.× Fact
1 0 0 0 0                  ⇦ Once rounded, one can see it is an identity
0 1 0 0 0                    matrix: Inv is really a left inverse for Fact
0 0 1 0 0
0 0 0 1 0
0 0 0 0 1
```

Spe 4.2 - Pseudo Right Inverse

We just saw that `Inv` is a left inverse for `M`; is it also a right inverse?

We calculated the coefficients `C` of the least squares line using this formula: .... `C←Inv+.×Y`

Then we calculated the coordinates of points located on that line by: .... `YLS←M+.×C`

Let us replace `C` by its definition from the first formula:............................... `YLS←M+.×Inv+.×Y`

If `Inv` was a true right-inverse of `M` the product `M+.×Inv` would give an identity matrix `I`, and `YLS` would be equal to `Y`. This is not the case: The difference is not zero, but is such that the sum `+/(Y-YSL)*2` is minimised.

In the expression `Y-YLS`, let us replace: `YLS` by `M+.×Inv+.×Y`

Then replace `Y` by `I+.×Y` (this does not change anything)

We reach the conclusion that `Y-YSL` is equal to `(I+.×Y)-(M+.×Inv+.×Y)`

Using `Y` as a common factor, this can be written like this: `(I-M+.×Inv)+.×Y`

If `+/(Y-YSL)*2` is minimised, `+/((I-M+.×Inv)+.×Y)*2` should be minimised too.

This property must remain true whatever the value of `Y`, including the case where `Y` equals 1. This means that the value of `Inv` (calculated independently of `Y`) is such that it minimises the expression:

```
+/(I-M+.×Inv)*2
```

We can say that `Inv` is a ***pseudo right-inverse*** matrix for `M` minimising `+/(I-M+.×Inv)*2`.

In APL, *Domino* has been extended to calculate such an inverse: `Inv ← ⌹M`

Spe 4.3 - Summary

In APL, a matrix `M` having more rows than columns has an inverse, which can be obtained by `⌹M`. This value is strictly equal, within rounding errors, to any of the following formulas:

```
      Inv ← (⌹ (⍉M)+.×M) +.× ⍉M
and   Inv ← (⍉M) ⌹ (⍉M)+.×M
```

This matrix is a ***true left inverse*** of `M`, which means that the product `(⌹M) +.× M` gives an identity matrix.

This matrix is also a ***pseudo right inverse*** of `M`. That is to say that the product does not give an identity matrix, but a matrix `J` such that the sum `+/(I-J)*2` is minimised.

The result of this is to minimise any expression of the form: `+/((I-M+.×Inv)+.×Y)*2` whatever the value of `Y`.

This last property explains why *Domino* may be used to calculate linear, multi-linear, or polynomial regressions.

Spe 4.4 - Scalars and Vectors

A scalar S is treated in such a way that ⌹S is equal to ÷S with the exception that 0÷0 equals 1, while 0⌹0 signals a DOMAIN ERROR.

Vectors are treated like single column matrices:

```
      ⎕← CEV← ⌹ VEC←2 ¯1 0.5
0.380952381 ¯0.1904761905 0.09523809524
      CEV +.× VEC
1
      VEC +.× CEV
1
```

Mathematics applied to Finance

Chapter L: System Interfaces

1 - Overview

1.1 Commands, System Variables, and System Functions

Functions and operators, both primitive and defined, give us ways of processing data. We also need tools to control the environment in which these functions execute, or to get information about this environment. For example, we may need to know the list of existing variables or functions, delete some of them, or get today's date just to print it on a report.

- Some of the actions can be performed using ***System Commands***, like `)VARS` or `)SAVE`.
- Some can be performed using ***System Variables*** or ***System Functions***, like `⎕IO` or `⎕FMT`.
- Some can be performed in both ways, sometimes with small differences.
- Some can be performed using Windows facilities, like clicking a button on the toolbar. This topic was discussed in section B-8, and we shall not mention it again.

System Commands, *System Variables*, and *System Functions* will together be called ***System Interfaces***.

There are more than 100 of such system interfaces, and we shall study some of them here:

- Some *System Interfaces* have been or will be studied in chapters dedicated to particular topics. For example `⎕F`*xxx* and `⎕N`*xxx* functions will be studied in the chapter dedicated to file processing; `⎕W`*xxx* functions will be studied with the GUI interface.
- Some *System Interfaces* are described in specialised brochures concerning, for example, Object Oriented Programming, and will not be described in this tutorial.
- Some rarely used *System Interfaces* will not be presented at all. If necessary, you can refer to the User Guide or to the on-line help.

Terminology In this chapter we will use the general term *object* to refer to a variable, function, or operator. This should not be confused with the more formal definition of an *Object* which is used in object oriented programming.

1.2 Common Properties

System Interfaces share some unusual properties:

- Like primitive functions and operators they are built into the system and therefore available in any workspace.
- Their names begin with a special character, followed by a name or an acronym. For *System Commands* the special character is a right (closing) parenthesis, for *System Functions* and *System Variables* the special character is *Quad* (⎕). Examples:

`)LOAD`	*System Command* for LOADing a workspace
`⎕LOAD`	*System Function* for LOADing a workspace
`⎕TS`	for Time Stamp
`⎕IO`	for Index Origin
`⎕AV`	for Atomic Vector

  At first this may look a little strange, but it is also very practical. It is one of the fundamental design principles of APL that there should not be any reserved names, so it is important that these *system* names do not conflict with any user-defined names.
- Their names are not case sensitive (but their arguments may very well be, if they, for example, refer to function or variable names).

System Commands are very special in two ways:

- They can only be executed by typing an expression into the Session, not from within a function or operator - not even using the *Execute* function. This is why there is some overlap between *System Commands* and *System Functions*; the latter may be executed in functions and operators. Note however that in some cases a system command and its corresponding system function may work slightly differently, as described later in this Chapter.
- When they require a folder path and/or a workspace name as an argument, and the path or the workspace name contain blanks, the entire file specification must be enclosed between a pair of double quotes ("like this"). Otherwise the commands would not be analysed properly by the system (blanks separate arguments to system commands) and would therefore fail. For example:

`)LOAD "d:\my data\results\year 2008"`	is correct
`)LOAD  d:\my data\results\year 2008`	would fail

System Variables also have some special properties:

- They are always present and cannot be erased.
- They have a default value which can be modified by the user.
- Like ordinary variables they can be localised in a function header and within the function may take a local value that is different from the global value.

- However, an ordinary variable that is localised in the function header has no default value, and an attempt to use it before it has been assigned a value will result in a `VALUE ERROR`. In contrast to this a localised system variable inherits its global value as its default value. This means that it is safe to reference a localised system variable even if it has not been assigned a value in the function. However in general it is best practice to assign it explicitly in the function in which it is localised, before you use it.

1.3 Organisation

In Appendix 7 & 8 you can find an overall list of all *System Interfaces.*

Because of the large number of system interfaces we have decided to combine the descriptions of *System Commands* with those of *System Variables* and *Functions* when they refer to similar operations, and we have grouped them in the following overall sections:

- 2 - Workspace Management
- 3 - Object Management
- 4 - Environment Control & Information
- 5 - Function Definition and Processing
- 6 - Debugging and Exception Trapping
- 7 - Calculation Control
- 8 - Character Processing, Input/Output
- 9 - Miscellaneous

2 - Workspace Management

- 2.1 Workspace Identification `)WSID` `⎕WSID`
- 2.2 Startup Expression `⎕LX`
- 2.3 Load a Workspace `)LOAD` `⎕LOAD` `)XLOAD`
- 2.4 Import Objects `)COPY` `⎕CY` `)PCOPY`
- 2.5 Explore a Workspace Library `)LIB`
- 2.6 Clear the Active Workspace `)CLEAR` `⎕CLEAR`
- 2.7 Save a Workspace `)SAVE` `⎕SAVE`
- 2.8 Memory Space Available `⎕WA`

2.1)WSID & ⎕WSID — Workspace Identification

2.1.1 - Conventions

The full identification of a workspace, which is used when the workspace is saved or loaded, is composed of a folder path, the workspace name, and a file extension. This can be represented like this:

wsid = {path} + wsname + {extension}

Under Windows, it is not necessary to specify the extension because if you omit it the default extension `DWS` (**D**yalog**W**ork**S**pace) is added automatically. Any other extension is allowed. If you want to name the workspace without an extension, you must include the dot (and nothing else) after the name. Under UNIX and LINUX, there is no default extension, and nothing is added to the name you specify.

In many cases the folder path is optional, too; this will be discussed in the following pages.

2.1.2 - Get Identification

The identity of the active workspace can be obtained using either a system variable or a system command:

```
      ⎕WSID                              ⇦ Query the current name
D:\Rumweiss\c7_APL\WS\Book_12
      ⍴⎕WSID
35                                       ⇦ The result is a vector
```

We could have obtained the same information by executing: `)WSID`

What we get identifies the file from which the active workspace was loaded, or in which it has been saved most recently.

If the active workspace has not yet been given a name, its identity is reported as `CLEAR WS`. This does not necessarily mean that the workspace is empty. It may well contain variables, functions, etc., but it has not yet been saved or given a name.

2.1.3 - Change Identity

The identity of a workspace is often referred to verbally as its *wsid* – pronounced "wussid". One can change the *wsid*, including a new folder path, and a new extension, if needed. This new *wsid* will be used the next time this workspace is saved.

```
      ⎕WSID ← 'G:\Secure\WS\Budget.old'    ⇦ Change path, name, and extension
```

The same could have been obtained by: `)WSID G:\Secure\WS\Budget.old`

With the system command `)WSID` do not forget to enclose the new *wsid* between a pair of double quotes if it contains any blanks.

2.2 ⎕LX Startup Expression

Each workspace has a system variable named `⎕LX`, containing a character vector which by default is empty. You can assign it a character vector containing an APL expression. This expression is automatically executed when the workspace is loaded, and before the control is given to the user.

This is the reason why the variable is called ***Latent Expression***.

A common approach is to set `⎕LX` to the name of a function, which then will be started automatically as soon as the workspace is loaded from a file. This may be used, for example to start an application without any action from the user, or to prepare some variables, or to display a welcome message.

To see how it works, let us write a function which displays a message and initialises a variable.

```
      ∇ Starter
[1]     ''
[2]     'Welcome aboard this WS'
[3]     Date←100⊥3↑⎕TS
      ∇
```

Then, let us assign the name of this function to `⎕LX`, and save the workspace:

```
      ⎕LX ← 'Starter'
      )save
d:\bernard\action\temp\Joke saved Sun Mar 16 11:01:50 2008
```

For the moment, nothing happens.
Now, some days later we load that workspace, and here is what will happen then:

```
      )load Joke
d:\bernard\action\temp\Joke saved Sun Mar 16 11:01:50 2008

Welcome aboard this WS
      Date
20080320
```

⇦ The message is immediately displayed

⇦ And if we ask for the variable `Date`, it has been updated

It may happen that a developer changes a few details in a workspace and saves it under another name, again and again … so that after some weeks or months, he has a lot of similar workspaces. In these circumstances `⎕LX` may be helpful: It can be used to display a message and remind the reader about the actual contents of this WS:

```
      ⎕LX ← '''Temporary version with new depreciation rules'''
      )SAVE
```

But why three levels of quotes? The outermost level of quotes delimits the string to be executed. Inside, a second set of quotes is used to delimit the message, but because those quotes are themselves embedded within the outer quotes, they must be doubled.

In other words:	`⎕LX ← 'Text'`	would execute a **function** (or variable) named `Text`
whereas:	`⎕LX ← ''Text''`	would cause a `VALUE ERROR` or a `DOMAIN ERROR`
but:	`⎕LX ← '''Text'''`	will display the string `'Text'`

The execution of a *Latent Expression* may sometimes be undesirable. For example, if the programmer needs to maintain an application workspace it may not be appropriate to run the initialisation program when the workspace is loaded for maintenance. The programmer might also wish to trace through the initialisation function itself in order to locate a problem with it.

To avoid the execution of `⎕LX` at load time, use `)XLOAD` rather than `)LOAD`, as shown in the next section. If you are investigating an unknown workspace for the first time, it is wise to use `)XLOAD` and inspect the *Latent Expression* rather than "risking it".

2.3)LOAD,)XLOAD & ⎕LOAD — Load a Workspace

2.3.1 - Normal Loading

This command replaces the contents of the active workspace by the specified workspace, which had previously been saved to a file.

Beware: Everything in the active workspace will effectively be destroyed, and no warning message will be issued.

The syntax is: `)LOAD` {*wsid*}
`⎕LOAD` '*wsid* '

- If the extension is missing, "dws" is assumed under Windows.
- If the folder path is missing, Dyalog APL will search through the directories specified by the "*Workspace Search Path*" which is set in the configuration dialog box:
  Options ⇨ Configure ⇨ Workspace ⇨ *Workspace search path*
- If the system command is issued without any *wsid*, the file search dialog box will be activated, so that the user can browse for the appropriate file.

Once the workspace is loaded into memory, its *Latent expression* is executed.

Please refer to section Spe-2 to see how `⎕LOAD` may work together with `⎕SAVE`.

2.3.2 - Loading Without the Execution of ⎕LX

To avoid the execution of the *Latent Expression*, one can use `)XLOAD` instead of `)LOAD`. There is no equivalent system function. This is sometimes called "*Quiet Load*".

2.4)COPY,)PCOPY & ⎕CY Import Objects

2.4.1 - Normal Copy

The syntax is: `)COPY` {*wsid* {*objects*}}
{*objects*} `⎕CY` '*wsid*'

This command allows you to import (copy) all or selected objects from a stored workspace into the active workspace. If no objects are specified in the command, all objects from the stored workspace will be copied, otherwise only the specified objects (variables, functions, operators, or namespaces) will be copied.

The list of objects to copy is specified:

- As a list of names, separated by blanks, for the system command
- As a matrix of names, or a list of names separated by blanks, for the system function. A single name can be specified as a vector.

```
)COPY "H:\Common Data\JP Morgan" Rates Depreciate Compare
```

The objects `Rates`, `Depreciate`, `Compare` will be copied from the workspace `JP Morgan.dws`. Because the *wsid* includes blanks, it has been enclosed within double quotes.

```
Companies ← ↑'Areva' 'Exxon' 'Mittal' 'Boeing' 'SAAB'
Companies ⎕CY 'G:\Secure\WS\Budget'
```

The objects mentioned in the left argument will be copied from `Budget.dws`.

2.4.2 - Exceptions

System variables are **not copied**, unless they are explicitly specified; for example:

```
)COPY G:\Secure\WS\Budget Boeing Nokia ⎕LX Compute ⎕CT
```

Objects contained in a *Namespace* can be copied, provided one gives the correct path:

```
)COPY Test Utilities.Prt.Print Utilities.Smooth
```

If one or more of the specified objects do not exist in the saved workspace:

- The system command reports their names in a warning message beginning by `"Not found"`
- The system function reports a `DOMAIN ERROR`

If the system command `)COPY` is issued with no *wsid*, the file search dialog box will be opened. However in this case, there is no provision to select specific objects to be copied; the contents of the entire workspace will be copied.

Beware: Any existing, global objects in the active workspace with the same names as copied objects will be replaced, with no warning.
To avoid this, one can use `)PCOPY`.

2.4.3 - Protected Copy

The command `)PCOPY` behaves much like `)COPY`, but if there is a name conflict, the objects of the active workspace will not be destroyed, and an information message will tell you which objects haven't been copied. There is no equivalent system function.

2.5)LIB Explore a Workspace Library

The syntax is `)LIB` *{path}*

This command lists the names of Dyalog APL workspaces contained in the given folder.

If no folder is specified, the workspaces in the user's workspace search path are listed. In this case, the listing is divided into sections identifying the individual folders. The current folder is identified by a simple dot (".").

Note: It is impossible to rely on the extension of a file to decide whether it is a workspace or not: Some workspaces may have an extension different from "dws", and not all files having a "dws" extension can be trusted to be APL workspace files.

For that reason, when the command `)LIB` is issued, Dyalog APL opens all the files located in the specified folder(s) and examines their internal structure. If the folder(s) contain hundreds of files this may take a significant amount of time.

2.6)CLEAR & ⎕CLEAR Clear the Active Workspace

The syntax is:

```
)CLEAR
⎕CLEAR
```

This system command and this system function destroy the active workspace, and replace it by a "clear" (i.e. empty) workspace containing no defined objects (variables, functions, operators, namespaces, etc.). However, the empty workspace will contain all the built-in system variables, whose values will be reset to their defaults.

Beware: If you have changed some variables or functions in the active workspace, they will be discarded by the command (whether `⎕CLEAR` or `)CLEAR`) without any warning message. For this reason, we recommend that you use the "Clear" button in the session toolbar, which requires confirmation.

2.7)SAVE & ⎕SAVE Save a Workspace

The syntax is: `)SAVE {wsid}`
`⎕SAVE 'wsid'`

The active workspace can be saved as a file by the system command `)SAVE` as well as by the system function `⎕SAVE`.

If the active workspace already has a name (because it has already been saved to a file, or loaded from a file, or assigned a name by `)WSID` or `⎕WSID`) you can use the command `)SAVE` without specifying the name. This will save the current state of the workspace to the same file (overwriting the previous content of the file). If this is your intention, it is wiser not to specify the (same) path and name, to avoid the possibility of misspelling it:

```
      )save
d:\bernard\action\temp\example saved Wed Mar 19 11:53:56 2008
```

The system function `⎕SAVE` does not offer this possibility; it requires the *wsid.*

If the workspace has never been saved (a "clear" workspace), or if it should be saved under a different *wsid*, the new identity must be specified. By "different *wsid*" we mean that either the path, or the name, or the extension is different.

```
      )save g:\shared\april\Poker.old
g:\shared\april\Poker.old saved Wed Mar 19 13:27:06 2008
```

The system function can do the same. It returns a shy result:

```
      ⎕save 'g:\shared\april\Poker.old'
```

The shy result returned from `⎕SAVE` is a Boolean scalar 1 in the workspace in which the save operation takes place. Please refer to section Spe-2 for more information about `⎕SAVE` and what happens when the saved workspace is subsequently loaded.

If the file identified by the new *wsid* already exists, the system command `)SAVE` will refuse to overwrite the file (to avoid the accidental destruction of an existing workspace that you had forgotten about) with one of the following warning messages:

`Not saved, this WS is CLEAR WS`	When the active WS has never been saved
`Not saved, this WS is BUDGET`	When the active WS already has another name

If you get one of the above error messages, either `)SAVE` the workspace using a different name or use the system command `)WSID` to give the active workspace the correct name before using `)SAVE`. The system function `⎕SAVE` is different; it will overwrite the file without complaining.

2.8 ⎕WA Memory Space Available

⎕WA is a niladic system function that returns the total free space in the working area, in bytes. For example: 65149212

When Dyalog is started a certain amount of memory is allocated. As workspaces are loaded and objects are created and destroyed, the amount of memory consumed grows (and occasionally shrinks) subject to a pre-defined maximum value. This is a parameter that can be viewed and changed in:

Options ⇨ Configure ⇨ Workspace ⇨ *Maximum workspace size (kB)*

So, what ⎕WA reports is this maximum value, less the space occupied by functions, variables, operators, etc. in the active workspace.

As a side effect, each time ⎕WA is invoked Dyalog APL carries out an internal reorganisation of the workspace in order to maximise and determine the free space, as follows:

- Any un-referenced memory is discarded. This process is known as *garbage collection*.
- Numeric arrays are converted to their most compact form. For example, a numeric array containing only the values 0 and 1 will be converted to Boolean representation, in which each value only occupies one bit.
- All remaining used memory blocks are copied to the low address end of the working area, leaving a single free block at the high address end. This process is known as *compaction*.

3 - Object Management

- 3.1 Object Lists)VARS)FNS)OPS)OBS ⎕NL
- 3.2 Name Category ⎕NC
- 3.3 Delete Objects)ERASE ⎕EX
- 3.4 Object Size ⎕SIZE

3.1)VARS,)FNS,)OPS,)OBS & ⎕NL Object Lists

3.1.1 - System Commands

The programmer can define different types of objects. For each type, a specific system command gives the list of those objects in the active workspace:

- Variables)VARS
- Defined functions)FNS
- Defined operators)OPS
- Namespaces)OBS may also be spelled)OBJECTS

The concept of *Namespaces* will be studied later (Chapter O).

By default, these commands list all objects of their respective type:

```
      )VARS
Charlebois      Contents        Damned1 Discount        Emptiness
Goof    Hundred M       MixMat  MixVec  MonMat  MonVec  Money
MyIndex NesMat  NesVec  One     Planning        Presence        Prod
Purchased       Sales   Tests   Text    Trailer Two     V
Weird   Years   experiment      what
```

The object names are listed in alphabetic order, but this order is different in the *Unicode* and the *Classic* editions of Dyalog. In the *Unicode Edition*, all uppercase letters are ordered before any lowercase ones. This is the reason why all the variables from Goof to Years are listed before experiment in the example above. In the *Classic* edition all lowercase letters are ordered before any uppercase ones, so experiment would have been ordered before Charlebois, for example.

It is also possible to specify a letter after the command, to list only the names starting with that letter or a later one. For example:

```
      )FNS S
Search  Show    ShyFun  Sorry   Spin    Split   StudRepay       SubSum
Switch  Syra    Syracuse        Time    Top     Totalise        Tox
Typeof  Underline       Upper   VerMat  Whiten  Willitwork
```

3.1.2 - Name List

The system function ⎕NL (for *Name List*) returns the names of specific categories of objects in the active workspace.

It accepts, as a right argument, one or more numbers. Each number refers to a particular category of objects:

1	Labels	(see Remark 1 below)
2	Variables	
3	Functions	
4	Operators	
8	Events	(see Remark 2 below)
9	Namespaces	(see Remark 2 below)

Categories 8 and 9 refer to concepts that we have not seen yet.

The category numbers are the same as the ones reported by the system function ⎕NC.

So ⎕NL 2 returns the list of all our variables in the active workspace
⎕NL 3 returns the list of all our functions
⎕NL 2 3 4 returns the list of variables, functions, and operators

The result is a matrix of names, with one name per row, sorted in the order of ⎕AV.
If the argument (or one of its items) is negative, ⎕NL returns a nested vector instead:

```
      ⎕NL 4
DUAL
INDEF                                   ⇦ A matrix of operator names
INPRO
OPER
      ⎕NL ¯4
 DUAL  INDEF  INPRO  OPER               ⇦ The same names, in nested form
```

By specifying a list of letters as a left argument, one can obtain only the names beginning with one of those letters, sorted in the order of ⎕AV:

```
      'BU' ⎕NL 2 ¯3
BankNames  BankVals  Between  Bignum  Bot  Boys
      BuildVars  USA  Underline  Upper  UpperCase
```

Note that this is quite different behaviour from that of the related system commands, shown in the previous section, when a starting letter is given.

Remark 1 ⎕NL 1 returns a list of *Labels*. Labels are not defined until the functions containing them are executing, so in a session with no suspended functions ⎕NL 1 will return an empty result. But if some functions are suspended, their labels are defined (they are like read-only variables), and ⎕NL 1 will return the list of all labels present in all suspended functions.

Remark 2 We shall see later that variables, functions, and operators, are not the only possible categories of objects. Dyalog APL can also process *Namespaces*, COM, GUI or .Net objects, and also *Events*, *Methods*, *Properties* associated with them (see the section on ⎕NC).

To support these many kinds of objects, each category has been subdivided into sub-categories. For example, Category 2 (variables) is divided into:

2.1 Normal variable
2.2 Field
2.3 Property
2.6 External or Shared variable

⎕NL has been extended to obtain all or part of a category:

⎕NL 2 returns objects of all the sub-categories (2.1 to 2.6)
⎕NL 2.3 returns only objects of the specified sub-category (*Properties*)

Warning! ⎕NL 2 and)VARS are not absolutely equivalent.
See section Spe-1 in the Specialist's Section for more information.

3.2 ⎕NC Name Category

Names are classified in a number of main categories, some of which are divided into sub-categories. Traditionally these categories have been called *Name Classes* (this is what NC stands for in ⎕NC), but here we will use the term *categories*, in order to avoid confusion with the term *class* as used in object oriented programming.

The possible categories are shown in the table below:

Category	Category Name	Sub-category	Description
¯1		*none*	Invalid name
0		*none*	Unused (free) name
1	Labels	*none*	
2	Variables	2.1	Variable
		2.2	Field
		2.3	Property
		2.6	External or Shared variable
3	Functions	3.1	Procedural function
		3.2	Direct function
		3.3	Derived or Primitive function
		3.6	External function
4	Operators	4.1	Procedural operator
		4.2	Direct operator
8	Events	8.6	External event
9	Namespaces	9.1	Created using ⎕NS or)NS
		9.2	Instance
		9.4	Class
		9.5	Interface
		9.6	External Class
		9.7	External Interface

The *System function* ⎕NC accepts a matrix of names with one name per row (or a single name as a vector) and returns the category number for each name. For example:

```
      ⎕NC ↑ 'Salaries' 'Palindrome'
2 3                                      ⇦ Salaries is a variable,
                                           while Palindrome is a function
```

We can now understand why in section D-7.3.3 we used ⎕NC to see whether the left argument of an *ambivalent* function had been provided (answer 2) or not (answer 0).

When used with a simple (not nested) right argument, like the matrix produced by *Mix* for the example below, ⎕NC gives only the main categories of those names, as shown here:

```
      ⎕nc ↑ 'Palindrome' 'Average' 'Forecast' 'OPER' 'DUAL'
3 3 2 4 4
```

This means that we have two functions, one variable, and two operators.

When used with a nested right argument, ⎕NC gives the sub-categories of the names, as shown here:

```
      ⎕nc 'Palindrome' 'Average' 'Forecast' 'OPER' 'DUAL'
3.1 3.2 2.1 4.1 4.2
```

This answer gives much more detailed information:

Palindrome	is a procedural function
Average	is a direct function
Forecast	is a variable
OPER	is a procedural operator
DUAL	is a direct operator

This also works for a single name, provided that it is enclosed:

```
      ⎕nc ⊂'Palindrome'
3.1
```

Note In addition, negative values in the result returned by ⎕NC identify names of methods, properties and events that are inherited through the class hierarchy of the current class or instance. These concepts belong to the object oriented extensions to the APL language that have been implemented in Dyalog, but which are not covered in this tutorial.

3.3)ERASE & ⎕EX Delete Objects

To remove objects (variables, functions, operators, namespaces, etc.) from the active workspace, one can use:

The command	)ERASE	followed by a list of names, in any order
The function	⎕EX	followed by a matrix of names with one name per row (or a simple vector or scalar for a single name)

The command elicits no positive confirmation message, but will report if a name is missing (perhaps misspelled):

```
      )Erase Plus Data Globish
not found Data
```

⎕EX produces a *shy* Boolean result:

1 For a well-formed name that is now available (if there was previously an object with this name, it has been erased).
0 For a name that is not available (because the name is ill-formed, or an existing object with this name could not be erased).

```
      ⎕ ← ⎕EX¨ 'SubSum' 'Spin' '⎕IO' 'Absent' '6teen'
 1  1  0  1  0
```

The first, second and fourth names are valid. The third and fifth are not; "⎕IO" is the name of a system variable, and system variables and system functions cannot be erased, and "6teen" is an invalid name.

Note that even if a name does not represent an existing object, like "Absent", the answer is still 1 because the name is now (as before) available.

Note 1 If a function is executing while being erased, it continues to run until its execution has been completed. However, the name becomes immediately available for re-use.

Note 2 ⎕EX and)ERASE are not absolutely equivalent.
See Section Spe-1 in the Specialist's Section for more information.

3.4 ⎕SIZE Object Size

⎕SIZE returns the amount of memory space that one or more objects (e.g. variables or functions) occupies. The answer is given in bytes; zero indicates that no object of this name exists in this workspace:

```
      ⎕SIZE 'ReverBug'                    ⇦ Applied to a function name
644
      ⎕SIZE ↑'Prod' 'Grumpf' 'Girls'
144 0 32                                  ⇦ 'Grumpf' does not represent an existing object
```

4 - Environment Control & Information

- 4.1 Current Date & Time ⎕TS
- 4.2 Print Precision ⎕PP
- 4.3 Index Origin ⎕IO
- 4.4 Account Information ⎕AI
- 4.5 Programmable Function Keys ⎕PFKEY

4.1 ⎕TS Current Date & Time

⎕TS (acronym for ***Time Stamp***) is a niladic system function that returns a seven item numeric vector containing the current date and time, according to the computer's clock, in the following order:

Year - Month - Day - Hours - Minutes - Seconds - Milliseconds

```
      ⎕TS
2008 3 15 14 20 7 296
```

⇦ If the host system does not allow such a high precision, milliseconds are reported as zero.

4.2 ⎕PP Print Precision

⎕PP is a system variable holding the maximum number of significant digits used to display numeric values when no particular format is specified.

⎕PP may be assigned any integer in the range 1 to 17. Its default value in a clear workspace is 10

```
      ⎕PP
10
      1952÷117 ¯19
16.68376068 ¯102.7368421
      ⎕PP ← 17
      1952÷117 ¯19
16.683760683760685 ¯102.73684210526316
      ⎕PP ← 6
      1952÷117 ¯19
16.6838 ¯102.737
```

⇦ Default value (for the `10` line)

⇦ 10 digits are shown, plus the decimal point and the negative sign.

⎕PP is used as an implicit argument by monadic *Format* (⍕) and monadic ⎕FMT.

When numbers are formatted using the dyadic versions of ⍕ and ⎕FMT, ⎕PP is ignored:

```
      ⎕PP ← 6
      14 11⍕31÷253 37
 0.12252964427 0.83783783784          ⇦ ⎕PP has been ignored.
```

⎕PP is also ignored when displaying integers:

```
      ⎕PP ← 6
      3184×1175 25319
3741200 80615696                      ⇦ We obtained more than 6 digits.
```

4.3 ⎕IO Index Origin

By default the origin of any set of indexes is 1, but this can be changed by means of the system variable ⎕IO. For example:

```
      ⎕IO
1                                     ⇦ Default value of ⎕IO
      vector ← 32 15 77 98 40
      vector[1 5]                     ⇦ This works as usual.
32 40
      ⍳7
1 2 3 4 5 6 7
      ⎕IO ← 0                         ⇦ If we set ⎕IO to zero, everything changes;
      vector ⍳ 32 40                  ⇦ 32 is no longer in position 1, but in position 0.
0 4
      vector[0 4]
32 40
      ⍳7
0 1 2 3 4 5 6                         ⇦ And now ⍳7 starts from 0, and stops at 6.
```

Beware!

Using ⎕IO←0 may sometimes be convenient, but it may also cause surprises because all the functions that work on indexes or that use an *Axis* specification are affected:

⍋vector	would give	2 1 5 3 4	with ⎕IO set to 1 (the default)
	but would give	1 0 4 2 3	with ⎕IO set to 0

Now, when you concatenate two matrices, the expression Boys,[1]Girls would not place them one under the other, but side by side, giving:

```
MarkSuzy
PaulAnna
BillJane
```

To obtain them one under the other, one should write: `Boys,[0]Girls`

The same for *Reduction*: `+/[1]2 3⍴⍳6` gives `3 12`
`+/[0]2 3⍴⍳6` gives `3 5 7`

Coding may be affected. For example, when searching for a value `N` in a vector `V` using *Index Of* (dyadic *Iota*), we would like to check that the value was found.

In origin 1, the check is `(V⍳N)≤⍴V`
In origin 0, we must change this to: `(V⍳N)<⍴V` We must modify our code

Laminate is also affected.

Normally, to laminate two vectors one under the other, we should write: `A,[0.5]B`
With `⎕IO` set to zero, that would place the vectors side by side in a matrix of 2 columns.

To obtain the desired result we must subtract 1 from the axis: .... `A,[¯0.5]B`

```
      'Hello',[¯0.5]'World'
Hello
World
```

The same consideration also applies to *Mix* (`↑`).
These are the only cases where an *Axis* can be negative.

Recommendation: In most cases it is possible to write expressions that work no matter what is the value of `⎕IO`. However, this will unavoidably clutter up the code and make it less readable and maintainable. We therefore recommend that you decide on either 1 or 0 as your global index origin, and then stick to it throughout your application. If you need to deviate from the global setting in a part of the application, do not forget to localise `⎕IO` in the appropriate functions.

4.4 ⎕AI Account Information

`⎕AI` is a niladic system function that returns a vector of 4 integer items:

`⎕AI[1]` is the user identification (usually 0 under Windows)
`⎕AI[2]` is the total computing time spent during the session, in milliseconds
`⎕AI[3]` is the total elapsed time for the session
`⎕AI[4]` is the keying time, the time during which the keyboard was available for input

```
      ⎕AI
0 359 215984 215796
```

The first item may be useful when sharing files, to identify who is accessing a given file. It is also known as the *Network ID*. It is a parameter that may be viewed and set in:

Options ⇨ Configure ⇨ Network ⇨ *Network ID*

The second and third items may be useful to compare the performance of two similar programs.

4.5 ⎕PFKEY Programmable Function Keys

⎕PFKEY associates a sequence of keystrokes with a function key. When the user subsequently presses that key, it is as if he had typed the associated keystrokes one by one.

This function has a monadic and a dyadic use:

R ← ⎕PFKEY *KeyNumber*	Returns the current setting of the specified key
R ← '*Characters*' ⎕PFKEY *KeyNumber*	Defines a new setting for the specified key

In the second use (dyadic) the result R is identical to the left argument. Because this is generally useless, the result is often assigned to a dummy variable.

The key number is an integer scalar in the range 0-255. On a Windows-based computer 1 to 12 correspond to the top row F1-F12 keys, 13-24 to *Shift*-F1-F12, 25-36 to *Ctrl*-F1-F12, and 37-48 to *Shift-Ctrl*-F1-F12.

If the key has not been defined previously, the monadic use (query) returns an empty character vector.

In the dyadic use, the left argument is a simple or nested character vector defining the new setting of the key. This new value is returned in the result R.

The items of that argument are either character scalars or enclosed 2-item character vectors which specify special input codes.

In the Unicode Edition, these codes can be found in the dialog box Options ⇨ Configure ⇨ *Keyboard Shortcuts*.

In the Classic Edition, the codes can be found in the *Input Translate Table*. The *Input Translate Table* is a text file with the file extension ".DIN" that resides in the *aplkeys* sub-folder within the Dyalog installation folder. You can examine the files *uk.din* or *us.din* to find codes for special keys, and you can read more about *Input Translate Tables* elsewhere.

Example 1

Imagine we enter the following statement:

```
Garbage ← '2+2'⎕PFKEY 3
```

The key F3 is now defined, and if we press it, we will see the characters "2+2" appear on the screen as if we had typed them, with the cursor positioned immediately to the right of the last 2:

```
2+2|
   ⇧ Cursor
```

To have this statement executed, we need to press the *Enter* key.

To have the *Enter* actioned automatically we can program F3 to virtually "type" not only 2+2 but also the *Enter* key. To achieve this, we use the appropriate *Input code*. In the section "Special functions" of the *Input Translate Table*, we can see that the action "Enter" is represented by the code "ER". To make this 2-item code represent a single keystroke, we must enclose it. So:

'2+2',⊂'ER' represents 4 keystrokes: "2+2" followed by the *Enter* key

We can redefine our function key like this:

```
Garbage ← ('2+2',⊂'ER')⎕PFKEY 3
```

And now, if we press F3 again, it automatically displays **and** executes our statement:

```
      2+2
4
```

Example 2

In order to restart an interrupted function at the very point where it was interrupted, one possibility is to type →⎕LC and press the *Enter* key.

If we want to program key F9 to do this for us we just have to enter:

```
Garbage ← ('→⎕LC',⊂'ER') ⎕PFKEY 9
```

With this technique, one can easily program some function keys to execute frequently-used system commands like:)VARS,)FNS,)OPS,)OBS,)RESET, etc.

Programmable function keys are recognised in any of the three types of windows (Session, Edit and Trace windows) provided by the Dyalog APL development environment.

Example 3

In this section we have repeatedly assigned a result that we are not at all interested in to a dummy variable named Garbage. There is another technique to avoid seeing unwanted results without creating an unwanted name. It makes use of the simplest possible direct function: It does not do anything; it just absorbs the value as its right argument, but it does not return a result. Using this technique we can write the expression shown in Example 2 above like this:

```
{} ('→⎕LC',⊂'ER') ⎕PFKEY 9
```

5 - Function Definition and Processing

- 5.1 Edit Objects)ED ⎕ED
- 5.2 Function Representations ⎕CR ⎕NR ⎕VR ⎕OR
- 5.3 Function Creation ⎕FX
- 5.4 Name Shadowing ⎕SHADOW
- 5.5 Locking a Function ⎕LOCK
- 5.6 Internal References ⎕REFS
- 5.7 Function attributes ⎕AT

In this section we will describe how these system commands and system functions may be used to work with user defined functions. However, everything we say also applies to user defined operators, even if we do not say so explicitly in the following paragraphs.

5.1)ED & ⎕ED Edit Objects

To create a new function or variable, we earlier used the system command)ED. One can also use the system function ⎕ED.

There is a difference, however. When using)ED to create a new object, one can specify the type of object to create by prefixing the name with a special symbol (cf. section D-3.3.4). This is also possible with ⎕ED, but the symbol is specified in the left argument.

5.2 ⎕CR, ⎕NR, ⎕VR & ⎕OR Function Representations

A function (or operator) can be displayed in 4 ways. Three of them are character representations, while the last one is a special internal representation. Each serves a different purpose.

The way that a function is entered in the editor and the way that APL displays it may be different. When you open a function for editing, Dyalog will have "cleaned it up", so that the body of the function is presented in a standard form:

- Unnecessary blanks are removed, except for leading indentation of control structures and the blanks in comments.
- Control structure keywords like ":ElseIf" are "normalised", with each word beginning with an uppercase letter, as in: ":For", ":Select", ":While", ":EndFor", etc,

- System variables and system functions are in upper case letters: ⎕TS, ⎕CR, ⎕PFKEY, etc
- If the function contains *Labels*, they are aligned at the left margin, and the statements not containing labels are indented one character (or more if they are embedded in control structures).

Hint: During an edit session you may have made so many and such complicated changes that the text has become severely muddled, and you wish you could have the nice and clean formatting that APL will provide when the function is saved and re-opened. Your wish can easily be fulfilled - just select the menu item Edit ⇨ Reformat or press the / key on your numeric pad.

5.2.1 - Canonical Representation

The ***Canonical Representation*** of a function or an operator (⎕CR) is a text matrix containing the source code text of the function/operator (i.e. a "normalised" presentation of the characters you typed to define it):

```
      Mat ← ⎕CR 'DemoCR'
      ⍴Mat
12 53
      DISPLAY Mat
┌→─────────────────────────────────────────────────────┐
↓ Y←DemoCR Y;Last;Next                                 │
│ ⍝ Just to demonstrate what ⎕CR means                 │
│ →(Y=0)/Process                                       │
│ 'Zero is not a valid argument' ⋄ →0                  │
│Process:Y←,Y           ⍝ Label at the left margin     │
│ :While 1<Last←Y[⍴Y]   ⍝ Indented statement           │
│     :If 0=2|Last      ⍝ Preserved indentation blanks│
│         Y←Y,Last÷2                                   │
│     :Else             ⍝ Normalised Keywords          │
│         Y←Y,1+3×Last                                 │
│     :End                                             │
│ :End                                                 │
└──────────────────────────────────────────────────────┘
```

If the argument to ⎕CR is the name of a variable, or a *Locked* function or operator, or an external function, or is undefined, the result is an empty matrix whose shape is 0 0.

This matrix representation is useful when one function needs to process the text of one or more other functions, for example in order to search for a given word, or to dynamically modify some statements, and then transform it back into a function using ⎕FX (cf. section 5.3).

5.2.2 - Nested Representation

The ***Nested Representation*** of a function (⎕NR) is a nested text vector containing the same characters as ⎕CR, with the same normalisation, except that the trailing blanks are removed:

```
      u ← ⎕NR 'Palindrome'
      ⍴u
4
      DISPLAY u
┌→─────────────────────────────────────────────────────────────────── ... etc ...
│ ┌→───────────────────────────┐ ┌→────────────────────┐ ┌→──── ...
│ │ Z←Palindrome vector;torvec │ │ vector←Upper vector │ │ tor  ...
│ └────────────────────────────┘ └─────────────────────┘ └───── ...
└∊────────────────────────────────────────────────────────────── ...
```

5.2.3 - Vector Representation

The ***Vector Representation*** of a function (⎕VR) gives the same visual representation as the ones used in this book, with beginning and ending *Del* characters (∇, "carrots") and statement numbers to the left. ⎕VR is a simple text vector containing "*NewLine*" characters (⎕UCS 13) at the end of each statement, so that the display continues at the left margin.

```
      ⍴Visu ← ⎕VR 'Palindrome'
122                              ⇦ It is a simple vector.
      +/Visu = ⎕UCS 13
4                                ⇦ It contains 5 lines of text separated by 4
```
NewLines.

```
      Visu
     ∇ Z←Palindrome vector;torvec
[1]    vector←Upper vector
[2]    torvec←ReverBug vector
[3]    Z←∧/torvec=vector
     ∇
```

This representation is very convenient to display a function and copy it into documentation or into a book.

5.2.4 - Object Representation

The ***Object Representation*** of a function (⎕OR) is used to convert a function, operator or namespace to a special form that may be assigned to a variable and/or stored on a file.

```
      Orep ← ⎕OR'Palindrome'
```

- Orep is a scalar of depth 1.
- The type of that object (∊Orep) is itself.

```
      ⍴⍴ Orep ← ⎕OR'Palindrome'    ⇦ It is a scalar
0
      ≡ Orep                        ⇦ Its depth is 1
1
```

These unique characteristics distinguish the result of ⎕OR from any other object.

If displayed, the *Object Representation* of a function has the same visual appearance as its ⎕VR.

```
      Orep
     ∇ Z←Palindrome vector;torvec
[1]    vector←Upper vector
[2]    torvec←ReverBug vector
[3]    Z←∧/torvec=vector
     ∇
```

Applied to a variable, the result of ⎕OR '*variable*' is its value unchanged.

```
      ⎕OR 'Boys'
Mark
Paul
Bill
```

⎕OR can be used to store functions and operators in *Component files* in order to quickly load them into the workspace when required, cf. chapter N. It is significantly faster than using ⎕CR, ⎕NR, or ⎕VR.

5.3 ⎕FX Function Creation

Given any of the possible representations of a function or operator (⎕CR, ⎕NR, ⎕VR, or ⎕OR), ⎕FX can be used it to *Fix* (create) the corresponding function, whatever the technique used to produce that representation.

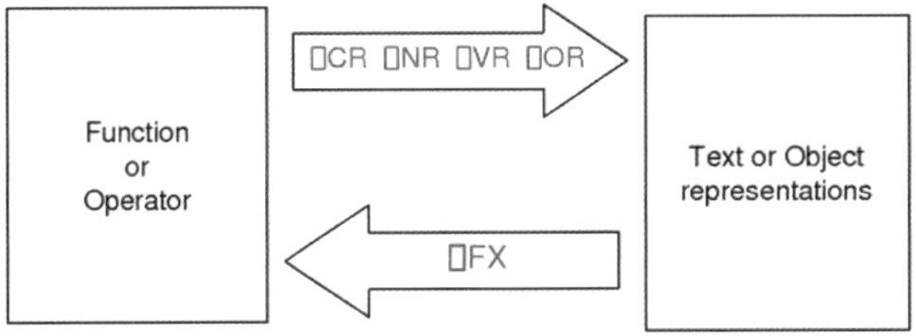

⎕FX returns a *shy* result which is the name of the function just created.

If the function cannot be created because there is an error in the representation, the result is the row number in the canonical representation in which the first error was detected.

```
      ⎕NC 'Divide'                ⇦ There is no function with this name
0
      ρ matrix←↑'z←a Divide b' 'z←a÷b'
2 12
```

```
      matrix                    ⇦ We just created a text matrix very similar to
z←a Divide b                      a canonical representation.
z←a÷b
      ⎕ ← ⎕FX matrix            ⇦ Let us "Fix" it, and explicitly ask for the result.
Divide                          ⇦ The result is the name of the function just created.
      ⎕NC 'Divide'
3                               ⇦ This is the proof that we created a function.
      36 Divide 12              ⇦ Now we can use it.
3
```

If a function already exists with the chosen name, it is replaced by the newly fixed function without any warning.

⎕FX can be used to restore and use functions stored on a *Component file* (generally using their *Object Representations*), or for example to generate sets of functions whose code can be dynamically built from a character array by a master function.

5.4 ⎕SHADOW Name Shadowing

A name can be localised in a function header by the programmer. But a function can also dynamically define new variables or new functions, by the means of Execute (⍎) and ⎕FX.

In some cases such variables or function names cannot be localised statically, because their names are not known to the programmer. Instead they can be localised dynamically; we use the term ***Shadowed***.

For an example, see Chapter D, section Spe-1.

5.5 ⎕LOCK Locking a Function

It is possible to hide the source code of one of more functions or operators from another APL developer. This may be used to prevent piracy, or just to prevent the code from being (accidentally) changed by unauthorized people.

The monadic syntax is: ⎕LOCK '*name*' where "*name*" is the name of a function.

Once locked, the function can be used, but it cannot be edited. Stop or trace vectors, formerly set by the ⎕STOP and ⎕TRACE functions, or set manually, are cancelled.

Warning! A locked function **cannot** be unlocked: Remember to store an unlocked copy somewhere before you lock it!

⎕LOCK also has a dyadic use: *protection* ⎕LOCK '*name*'
where "*protection*" specifies to what extent the function code is hidden.

This left argument may be 1, 2, or 3 (the default) with the following meaning:

1 The object may not be displayed and you may not obtain its character form using any of the functions ⎕CR, ⎕VR or ⎕NR. The object, and any objects it calls, may be suspended as usual, but the content of the function or operator lines will not be displayed in the trace windows.

2 Execution cannot be suspended with the locked function or operator in the state indicator. On suspension of execution the state indicator is cut back to the statement containing the call to the locked function or operator. It is still possible to obtain the function or operator's character representation.

3 You can neither display the locked object nor suspend execution within it.

Locks are additive, so that

```
1 ⎕LOCK'FOO'
2 ⎕LOCK'FOO'
```

is the same as:

```
3 ⎕LOCK'FOO'
```

5.6 ⎕REFS Internal References

This system function gives a list of all the names referenced inside a function, including the function name itself, its arguments, result, labels, variables, and called functions and operators, but excluding distinguished names of system variables and functions (even if they are localised).

The syntax is: `R← ⎕REFS Y`

`Y` must be a simple character scalar or vector, identifying the name of a function or operator, or the object representation form of a function or operator.

`R` is a simple character matrix, with one name per row, sorted in alphabetic order.

For example, applied to the function `DemoCR` used in this chapter, we would obtain:

```
      ⎕REFS 'DemoCR'
DemoCR                    ⇦ Function name
Last                      ⇦ Local variable
Next                      ⇦ Local variable (unused)
Process                   ⇦ Label
Y                         ⇦ Argument & result
```

5.7 ⎕AT Function Attributes

The attributes of a function or operator refer to its syntax and other useful information.

The syntax is: `R ← {X} ⎕AT Y`

`Y` is a simple character scalar, vector or matrix, or a vector of character vectors representing the names one or more defined functions or operators.

- Used dyadically with `X` equal to 1, 2, 3, or 4, this function closely emulates IBM's APL2 implementation. This will not be studied here; please refer to Dyalog's on-line help.
- Used monadically, `⎕AT` returns information that is more appropriate for Dyalog APL.

The result is a 4 column matrix with the same number of rows as names in `Y`, containing the following attribute information:

In the first column `R[;1]`, each item is a 3-item integer vector representing the function header syntax, with the following conventions:

1	Function result	0 1 ¯1	The object has no result The object has an explicit result The object has a shy result
2	Function valence	0 1 2 ¯2	The function has no arguments (*Niladic*) **Or** this is not a function The function is *Monadic* The function is *Dyadic* The function is *Ambivalent* or is a *D-Fun*
3	Operator valence	0 1 2	This is not an operator The operator is *Monadic* The operator is *Dyadic* or is a *D-Op*

For example:

`∇ FOO`	would be described by:	`0 0 0`
`∇ Z←FOO`	would be described by:	`1 0 0`
`∇ {Z}←A FOO B`	would be described by:	`¯1 2 0`
`∇ {A} FOO B`	would be described by:	`0 ¯2 0`
`∇ {Z}←(F OP G)B`	would be described by:	`¯1 1 2`

Note that for operators the first two items (function result and valence) describe the operator's *derived function*.

In the second column `R[;2]`, each item is the timestamp (in `⎕TS` form) of the time the function was most recently fixed. For *Direct* functions and operators defined by an assignment (without using the editor), this information is set to `7⍴0`, as shown in the third row of the example below. If they later are modified using the editor, the timestamp will be updated.

In the third column `R[;3]`, each item is the current `⎕LOCK` state of the function:

0 Not locked
1 Cannot display function
2 Cannot suspend function
3 Cannot display or suspend

In the last column `R[;4]`, each item is a character vector giving the network ID of the user who last fixed (edited) the function. For *Direct* functions and operators defined by an assignment (without using the editor), this information is empty.

In the example below, to facilitate the interpretation, we have presented the results in columns, though this is not how they will appear on your screen:

```
      ⎕AT 'Interlace' 'ReverLoop'  'Average' 'DUAL'

 1  2 0    2007 12 18 15  8 39 0    0   InterFluences
 1  1 0    2008  1 15 18  4 25 0    0   User
 1 ¯2 0       0  0  0  0  0  0 0    0
 1 ¯2 2    2007 11 23 17 24 27 0    0   InterFluences
```

6 - Debugging and Event Trapping

Most *System Interfaces* related to debugging facilities have already been studied in the preceding chapters, or will be studied soon in a dedicated chapter:

	Interface	Symbol	Refer to
•	Diagnostic Message	`⎕DM`	`E-1.1.2`
•	Line Counter	`⎕LC`	`E-1.1.3`
•	State indicator	`⎕SI` & `)SI`	`E-1.1.3`
•	State indicator with Name List	`)SINL`	`E-Spe-2`
•	Clear stack	`)RESET`	`E-1.3.1`
•	Event Number	`⎕EN`	`E-1.3.1`
•	Set/Query Breakpoints	`⎕STOP`	`E-3.4`
•	Set/Query Trace points	`⎕TRACE`	`E-3.4`
•	Extended State Indicator	`⎕XSI`	`E-Spe-3.1`
•	NameSpace State Indicator	`⎕NSI`	`E-Spe-3.2`
•	Exception trapping	`⎕TRAP`	`M-2.3`
•	Exception signal	`⎕SIGNAL`	`M-3`
•	Exception Message	`⎕EM`	`M-2.1`

7 - Calculation Control

7.1 Already Studied

We have already studied some *System Interfaces* relating to calculation control in the preceding chapters:

Interface	Symbol	Refer to
• Division control	⎕DIV	C-Spe-1
• Migration level	⎕ML	I-9
• Random link	⎕RL	K-Spe-2

7.2 ⎕CT Comparison Tolerance

Imagine you have a desktop calculator with a calculation precision limited to 5 digits.

If so	1÷3	would give	0.33333
and then	3×1÷3	would give	0.99999

It appears that 3×1÷3 is not equal to 1, and the expression 1=3×1÷3 would return 0! Something mathematically true may no longer be true if limited by the computer's precision.

Of course the precision of modern computers is much higher than this, but please be aware of the following:

- The internal representation of many values would require an infinite number of bits, very much like 1÷3 would require an infinite sequence of decimal digits in our decimal system. When limited by their internal representations, such values are rounded, and give rise to very small inaccuracies. For example, a not very exotic value like 0.1 cannot be represented exactly in the binary representation used by most computers' processors.
- Some mathematical calculations may require a large number of operations; then the unavoidable inaccuracies may add up, or even be multiplied by large numbers, and hence become visible. For examples of this, please recall the calculations of a matrix inversion (section K-5.2.1) and a trigonometric function (section K-4.3.3).

In order to compensate for inaccuracies due to the limited precision of numbers APL considers two numbers to be equal if the difference between them is within a (small) range (or tolerance level).

This tolerance level is defined by the system variable `⎕CT` (for *Comparison Tolerance*). It is possible to adjust the size of the tolerance level by assigning a value to `⎕CT`.

Two numbers `A` and `B` will be considered equal if: `(|A-B)≤⎕CT×(|A)⌈(|B)`. In other words, they are declared equal if the *relative* difference between them is smaller than or equal to `⎕CT`.

- `⎕CT` may be assigned any value in the range from `0` to `16*¯8`.
- A value of `0` ensures exact comparison.
- The value in a clear workspace is `1E¯14`.

```
      ⎕CT                              ⇦ Default configuration
1E¯14
      1 = 1.00000000000001  1.0000000000001
1 0
      ⎕CT←1E¯15 ⋄ 1 = 1.00000000000001  1.0000000000001
0 0
      ⎕CT←1E¯13 ⋄ 1 = 1.00000000000001  1.0000000000001
1 1
```

The choice of `1E¯14` for the default value is a compromise: With too low a value two numbers which differ only because of the limited precision of the computer would be considered different, and with a too large value too many numbers that are "really different" would be considered equal.
The computer's precision is approximately `2E¯16`, so the default value `1E¯14` is sufficiently larger than that to compensate for many inaccuracies, while still small enough to allow numbers with up to approximately 14 significant digits to be considered different.

An area in which the limited precision of the computer may really become a problem is in applications dealing with large monetary amounts in low valued currencies. For example, the two values hereafter are considered equal, even though their last three digits differ:

```
      5678901234567893 = 5678901234567949
1
```

Comparison Tolerance does not apply to comparisons between integers, but the two numbers above are too large to be stored as 32-bit integers, and are thus represented as floating-point values in Dyalog APL.

The following functions use *Comparison Tolerance* as an implicit parameter:

All the comparison functions	`< ≤ = ≥ > ≠`
Match and Natch	`≡ ≢`
Floor and Ceiling	`⌊ ⌈`
Index Of and Membership	`⍳ ∊`
Unique	`∪`
Without	`~`
Union and Intersection	`∪ ∩`

7.3 ⎕DL Delay

⎕DL is used to make a function pause for a certain number of seconds before continuing. The function takes the desired number of seconds as its right argument, and returns as a shy result the exact length of the pause, in seconds (which may deviate slightly from the requested time, but will always be greater than or equal to the requested delay).

```
      ⎕DL 2
```

If necessary, the pause can be interrupted by a strong interrupt.

⎕DL can for example be used to slow down a loop to have it wait for external conditions without using computer resources. Another use is in a test environment to simulate that two programs (on the same or on different computers) run at different speeds.

8 - Character Processing, Input/Output

- 8.1 Atomic Vectors ⎕AV ⎕AVU
- 8.2 Unicode Conversions ⎕UCS
- 8.3 Terminal Control ⎕TC
- 8.4 Alphabet & Digits ⎕A ⎕D
- 8.5 Null Item ⎕NULL

8.1 ⎕AV & ⎕AVU Atomic Vectors

In earlier versions of Dyalog APL (prior to Version 12) and in Version 12 *Classic Edition*, characters were always stored in one byte each, as an index into the vector of all 256 possible characters, called the *Atomic Vector*, or ⎕AV.

⎕AV was useful to get some special characters which cannot be entered via the keyboard. For example, line-drawing characters are normally typed by pressing the *Ctrl* key in conjunction with one of the numeric pad keys. But if the keyboard has no numeric pad, they can be obtained from ⎕AV[220+⍳11]. The horizontal and vertical bars are in ⎕AV[226 231], and the 9 other ones are in the following order:

```
3 3⍴⎕AV[220+3 10 2 7 5 8 4 9 1]   ⇨   ┌┬┐
                                      ├┼┤
                                      └┴┘
```

In the *Unicode Edition* (Version 12 and after), ⎕AV is now **obsolete**, and it is recommended that you do not use it any more. In *Unicode*, characters are internally represented by numbers or ***code points***, which allow representing about 100.000 characters, including characters used in all of the world's languages, and some special character sets like the APL one. Each code point occupies 1, 2, or 4 bytes.

⎕AV still exists, but only to allow old code which references it to continue to run. The *Unicode Atomic Vector* ⎕AVU defines ⎕AV as a list of 256 *code points*. If you are migrating from Classic to Unicode, you can redefine ⎕AVU so that it corresponds to the font that you were using in Classic, so that data that you read from files or workspaces created by Classic are correctly translated to Unicode.

8.2 ⎕UCS Unicode Conversions

The function ⎕UCS (*Universal Character Set*) converts characters into code points and vice versa:

```
      ⎕UCS 'Dyalog APL'
68 121 97 108 111 103 32 65 80 76
      ⎕UCS ⎕UCS 'Dyalog APL'
Dyalog APL
      ⎕UCS 123 40 43 47 9077 41 247 9076 9077 125
{(+/⍵)÷⍴⍵}
      ⎕UCS 3 3⍴⎕AV[220+3 10 2 7 5 8 4 9 1]
9484 9516 9488
9500 9532 9508
9492 9524 9496
```

⇦ The code points for the line-drawing characters shown above.

We can observe that ⎕AV is identical to ⎕UCS ⎕AVU.

⎕UCS has also a dyadic use, to translate Unicode characters into one of three standard variable-length Unicode encoding schemes, UTF-8, UTF-16 and UTF-32. For example:

```
      'UTF-8' ⎕UCS '⍺'
226 141 186
```

This means that the alpha character (⍺), which has code point number 9082, is represented as the above three bytes when encoded using UTF-8. Please refer to the on-line help for more information on these conversions.

8.3 ⎕TC Terminal Control

Some characters cannot be entered between quotes from the keyboard; this is the case for control characters like *Enter*, *Backspace*, *Escape*, etc.

Three of these special characters are returned by a niladic system function named ⎕TC:

In the default configuration, ⎕TC returns .... Backspace, Linefeed, Newline.
In an IBM-like configuration (with ⎕ML←3), the order is:..... Backspace, Newline, Linefeed.

With the introduction of Unicode support and ⎕UCS, ⎕TC has become obsolete. We strongly recommend using ⎕UCS, with the following equivalences:

Backspace	⎕UCS 8	
Linefeed	⎕UCS 10	These equivalences are independent of ⎕ML
Newline	⎕UCS 13	

8.4 ⎕A & ⎕D Alphabet & Digits

It is sometimes necessary to use the vector of upper case letters; it is given by ⎕A.

Similarly, the vector of numeric digits 0 to 9 is given by ⎕D.

Because the names of system functions are not case-sensitive, both ⎕A and ⎕a return the uppercase alphabet; there is no system function that returns the lower case alphabet. You can obtain it using ⎕UCS:

```
      ⎕A,'/',⎕D,'/',⎕UCS 96+⍳26
ABCDEFGHIJKLMNOPQRSTUVWXYZ/0123456789/abcdefghijklmnopqrstuvwxyz
```

8.5 ⎕NULL Null Item

⎕NULL is a reference to a null item, which may be returned across the COM interface.

For example, ⎕NULL is what you get when you import (read) all or part of an Excel worksheet when some cells are empty. The following statements will be studied later in this book, but you can test them. Just replace "MyBook" by the path and name of one of your Excel workbooks:

```
      xl←⎕NEW'OleClient'(⊂'ClassName' 'Excel.Application')
      xl.Workbooks.Open⊂'MyBook.xls'
      Contents←xl.ActiveWorkbook.ActiveSheet.UsedRange.Value2
```

The result in Contents is a nested matrix in which each item corresponds to one cell in the worksheet. All items corresponding to empty cells contain the scalar ⎕NULL. ⎕NULL is displayed as [Null]; in the example below the empty cells have been printed in black to make them more visible. Similarly, you must use ⎕NULL when you want to update a worksheet cell to become empty.

```
      Contents
     2011  [Null]    [Null]      Sales  [Null]  [Null]  [Null]
 Updated   [Null]  November         10    2007  [Null]  [Null]
    Year   Coffee       Tea  Chocolate    Soda   Sugar  Totals
  Germany    8607       562       3200    3210     816   16395
    Italy    9200    [Null]       2800    3300     850   16150
   Canada    9500       600     [Null]    3600     860   14560
   France   10000       600     [Null]    4000     870   15470
   Others     340       120       1050     830     410    2750
   Totals   37647      1882       7050   14940    3806   65325
```

To produce a "map" of filled and empty cells, you can use: `~Contents∊⎕NULL`

For the example above the result would be:

```
1 0 0 1 0 0 0
1 0 1 1 1 0 0
1 1 1 1 1 1 1
1 1 1 1 1 1 1
1 1 0 1 1 1 1
1 1 1 0 1 1 1
1 1 1 0 1 1 1
1 1 1 1 1 1 1
1 1 1 1 1 1 1
```

`⎕NULL` is a *Namespace Reference* (or *Ref* in short); this concept will be explained in chapter O, section 2.1. It is seen like a scalar containing a reference to a *Namespace*:

```
      ⍴⎕null                    ⇦ Its shape is empty

      ≡⎕null                    ⇦ Its depth is zero
0
      DISPLAY ⎕null
[Null]
```

`⎕NULL` may be used in any context that accepts a *Namespace Reference*, in particular:

- As the argument to a defined function.
- As an item of an array.
- As the argument to all primitive functions that do not require numeric arguments like, for example: `≡`, `≢`, `=`, `≠`, `⍴`, `⊂`, `⊃`, etc...
- However: It is not recommended that you use `⎕NULL` as a general null value marker in arrays other than those used to communicate with COM components. Introducing a `⎕NULL` into a numeric array will turn it into an array of references, and make it very inefficient to handle.

9 - Miscellaneous

9.1 ⎕OFF &)OFF Quit APL

This system function or command terminates an APL session. Note that you are not prompted by a dialog box to save your work or be given the opportunity to re-consider.

⎕OFF is used to have a function close the application and return to the calling environment (Windows or Unix).

9.2 ⎕SH, ⎕CMD,)SH &)CMD Host System Commands

⎕SH and ⎕CMD are synonyms and stand for "Shell" and "Command", respectively. Those two commands are used to ask the host system (DOS or UNIX) to execute a command and return the result to the APL session.

If the command produces output, the output is returned as a nested vector, with one vector per line of text. When displaying the result, you can make it more readable if you first transform it into a matrix, as shown:

```
      u←⎕SH 'set'
      ↑u
ALLUSERSPROFILE=C:\Documents and Settings\All Users
APPDATA=C:\Documents and Settings\Utilisateur\Application Data
CLASSPATH=.;C:\Program Files\Java\jre1.5.0_10\lib\ext\QTJava.zip
CLIENTNAME=Console
CommonProgramFiles=C:\Program Files\Fichiers communs
COMPUTERNAME=INTERFLUENCES
ComSpec=C:\WINDOWS\system32\cmd.exe
```

... and so on.

This technique is not recommended under Windows, at least in a production environment, because it needs to first initialise a DOS command environment: It is slow, and it may be somehow fragile, as it is sensitive to the exact configuration of the environment. Please refer to the on-line help description of ⎕CMD for the Windows environment or ⎕SH for the Unix environment. If you need to use Windows functionality it is better to use ⎕NA to access it directly from one of the many DLLs that are provided with Windows.

One can also use the equivalent system commands:)SH and)CMD.

9.3 ⎕PW Page Width

This command is used to define the number of characters which can be displayed on the screen on a single line of text before it is folded onto a new line. For example:

```
      ⎕pw
35
      50⍴'123456789 '
123456789 123456789 123456789 12345
      6789 123456789
```

By default, when APL is started it is set the same as your last session configuration but it can be modified:

```
      ⎕PW←120
```

Then it can be saved in the *Session Namespace* ⎕SE using the menu Session ⇨ Save.

If you close your Dyalog session using the Windows shortcut key *Alt-F4*, or by clicking on the close button in the upper right hand corner of the window, you will see a pop-up window in which you are asked whether you wish to save the session configuration.

Figure L-1

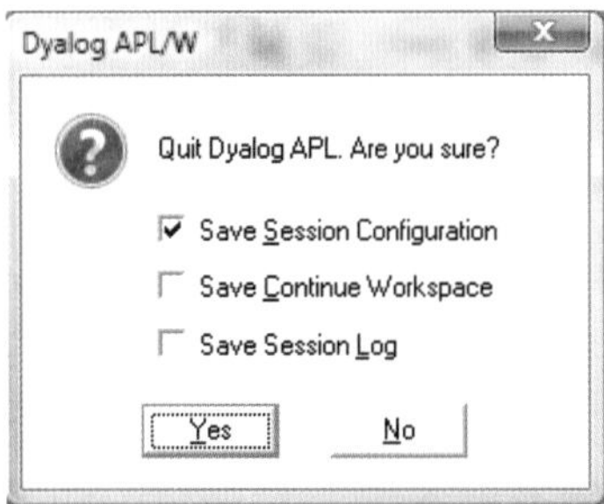

The current value of ⎕PW (and other session settings) will only be remembered until next time you start Dyalog if the Save Session Configuration option is checked.

If an attempt is made to display a line wider than ⎕PW, then the display will be folded at or before the ⎕PW width, and the folded parts will be indented 6 spaces. The display of a simple numeric array may be folded at a width less than ⎕PW so that individual numbers are not split.

⎕PW only affects output to the APL session made by using ⎕, or by letting APL display a result instead of assigning it to a variable or re-using it in a further expression. It does not affect the output made by using ⍞.

If APL is started with the auto_pw parameter set to 1, ⎕PW is reset dynamically whenever the session window is resized. Under these circumstances, a value assigned to ⎕PW will only be effective until the session window is next resized. The auto_pw parameter can also be set via Options ⇨ Configure ⇨ Session ⇨ *Auto PW*.

The Specialist's Section

Each chapter is followed by a "Specialist's Section" like this one.
This section is dedicated to skilled APLers, who wish to improve their knowledge.

If you are exploring APL for the first time,
skip this section and go to the next chapter

Spe-1 Commands vs. System Functions

There is an important difference between `)ERASE` and `⎕EX`, and `)VARS` does not work exactly like `⎕NL 2`: System commands like `)ERASE` and `)VARS` refer to **global** names, while system functions like `⎕EX` and `⎕NL 2` refer to **local** names.

This may become important when a local variable has the same name as a global one, and if an operation is done while the function is active or suspended.

Let us create a variable and an erroneous function:

```
     ∇ R←Crash Y;Var
[1]    Var←Y+1
[2]    R←10×Var)
     ∇
      Var←'For sure, I am a GLOBAL variable'
      Crash 5                          ⇦ As expected, the function crashes
SYNTAX ERROR                             but we don't care!
Crash[2] R←10×Var)
                 ^
      )erase Var                       ⇦ Surprisingly, though we deleted Var it is still
      Var                                present: We destroyed the global variable, and
6                                        what we see now is the local one.
      →                                ⇦ Exit the stack.
      Var                              ⇦ Confirmation: When we get out of the suspended
VALUE ERROR                              function, we can see that the global variable has
      Var                                been killed.
     ^
```

Let us retry, but instead of `)ERASE`, we shall use `⎕EX`:

```
      Var←'I am a GLOBAL variable, you know!'
      Crash 9
SYNTAX ERROR                         ⇦ Once again, the function crashes.
Crash[2] R←10×Var)
                  ^
      ⎕EX 'Var'                      ⇦ We delete the local variable Var
      ⎕NC 'Var'                        and we can check that it no longer exists.
0
      →                              ⇦ When we get out of the suspended function
      Var                              we immediately retrieve the global variable.
I am a GLOBAL variable, you know!
```

`⎕EX`	refers to local objects, while	`)ERASE`	refers to global objects
`⎕NL 2`	includes the names of local variables, while	`)Vars`	lists only global variables
`⎕NL 3`	includes the names of local functions, while	`)Fns`	lists only global functions
`⎕NC`	always gives the type of local objects		

Spe-2 ⎕SAVE

`⎕SAVE` can be used with a left argument equal to 0 or 1: `{R} ← {X} ⎕SAVE Y`

Case 1: `X` is 0

In this case the workspace is saved without any State Indicator, i.e. without any pending or suspended functions. The effect is the same as if you first executed `)RESET` and then `)SAVE`.

In this case, when the workspace is subsequently loaded, the latent expression `⎕LX` will be executed, no matter whether you used `⎕LOAD` or `)LOAD`.

Case 2: `X` is 1 or absent

In this case the workspace is saved in a suspended state at the exact point of exit from the `⎕SAVE` function.

The shy result returned from `⎕SAVE` is a Boolean scalar 1 in the workspace in which the save operation takes place:

```
      ⎕← ⎕save 'c:\temp\tempws'
1
```

If the saved workspace is subsequently loaded by `⎕LOAD`, the latent expression `⎕LX` will be ignored, and execution will be automatically resumed from the point just before the `⎕SAVE` returned its result; this time it will be 0:

```
      ⎕load 'c:\temp\tempws'
0
```

The reason for this unusual behaviour is to make the programmer able to distinguish between the two situations and thereby support applications that save their data in workspaces. Many years ago, this was a convenient way of building APL applications, but now APL is fully equipped with plenty of interfaces to files and databases, so this technique is considered obsolete for this purpose. However, the technique may still be useful for building workspaces by loading the relevant source code into a workspace and saving it, ready for use.

If, on the other hand, the workspace is loaded using `)LOAD` the execution will not automatically be resumed, but the latent expression will be executed.

The function in which the `⎕SAVE` was executed will be suspended at the line containing `⎕SAVE`. You should therefore be aware that if you resume execution by executing `→⎕LC`, right after having `)LOAD`ed the workspace, the line will be executed again, and the workspace will therefore be saved again!

Spe-3)CONTINUE Save & Continue

This command saves the active workspace under the name `CONTINUE` and ends the Dyalog APL session.

When you subsequently start another Dyalog APL session, the `CONTINUE` workspace will be loaded automatically. Unless you have started APL using the "-x" flag, the latent expression `⎕LX` (if any) in the saved `CONTINUE` workspace will be executed.

This command is sometimes used to close a session in an unfinished (debugging) state, so as to be sure to retrieve it exactly in the same state later.

Spe-4 ⎕OR

Taking the `⎕OR` of a function or operator is an extremely fast operation as it simply changes the type information in the object's header, leaving its internal structure unaltered. Converting the object representation back to an executable function or operator using `⎕FX` is also very fast. It is significantly faster than using `⎕CR`, `⎕NR` or `⎕VR` because the latter must first build the textual representation of the function or operator, and `⎕FX` must similarly rebuild the internal representation from the text. `⎕OR` may be used to store functions and operators in *Component files*, but it should only be used for this purpose if ultra-fast performance is really necessary. The reason is that the internal structure of objects may change from one version of Dyalog APL to the next. This means that the files may be unusable in a new version unless they are converted to the new format. A program to convert a file must first run in the old version of Dyalog APL and write all the objects to an intermediate file, using one of the textual representations. Then another conversion program must run in the new version, reading the intermediate file and creating a new file using `⎕OR`, which will save the objects in the new format. The use of `⎕OR` to build code-paging files was a common technique in the past, when less memory was available. Today, it is rarely necessary to go to such lengths.

⎕OR may be used to convert a namespace (either a plain namespace or a named GUI object created by ⎕WC) into a form that can be stored in a variable or in a component file. The namespace may be reconstructed using ⎕NS or ⎕WC with its original name or with a new name. ⎕OR may therefore be used to clone a namespace or GUI object. Object-oriented techniques have also rendered this use of ⎕OR obsolete. The function is still useful in some situations but it is no longer recommended as a general tool for building applications.

Warning: Although ⎕OR '*name*' is a scalar, it may not be used to replace an item of an array unless it is first enclosed.

Spe-5 ⎕VFI Verify and Fix Input

This system function is used to check whether a string of characters contains a valid succession of numbers, separated by one or more blanks (the default) or by an explicit separator character, and then convert the text into a numeric vector.

The syntax is: R←{X} ⎕VFI Y

- Y is a string of characters
- If present, X is a simple character scalar or vector of separators. By default, blank is assumed.
- R is a two-item nested vector whose first item is a simple binary vector specifying which substrings in Y are valid numbers, and whose second item is a simple numeric vector of the same length as the first item of R.

Spe-5.1 - Monadic Usage

```
      u←⎕VFI '    14.6 ¯23    142.11 3,7 2.3E3    '
      DISPLAY u
┌→────────────────────────────────────────────┐
│ ┌→────────┐ ┌→───────────────────────────┐ │
│ │1 1 1 0 1│ │14.6 ¯23 142.11 0 2300│ │
│ └~────────┘ └~───────────────────────────┘ │
└∊────────────────────────────────────────────┘
```

The first item of this result is a Boolean vector. In this case it shows that among the 5 sub-strings contained in the right argument, only four of them could be transformed into numbers. You can see that leading, trailing, and multiple blanks are ignored.

The fourth sub-string could not be converted, because it contains a comma.

In the second item of the result, the valid strings have already been converted into numbers, the invalid one has been forced to zero.

We can then make a *Reduction* by *Compress* (refer to section J-2.1), and disclose the result to obtain the converted (numeric) vector of valid values:

```
      ⊃(//)u
14.6 ¯23 142.11 2300
```

Beware: ⊃//u would not work, because ⊃/ would be interpreted as a *Reduction* by *Disclose*, which is not valid here.

Spe-5.2 - Dyadic Usage

The same technique can be employed with separators which are not blanks, but one or more characters explicitly mentioned in a left argument (here slash & comma):

```
      DISPLAY u←'/,'⎕VFI '14.6/¯23/142.11/3,7//23,,'
┌→──────────────────────────────────────────────────────┐
│ ┌→────────────────┐ ┌→──────────────────────────────┐ │
│ │1 1 1 1 1 1 1 1 1│ │14.6 ¯23 142.11 3 7 0 23 0 0 │ │
│ └~────────────────┘ └~──────────────────────────────┘ │
└∊──────────────────────────────────────────────────────┘
```

In this example, two possible separators are given. The string "3,7" that was considered as invalid in the monadic case is now interpreted as two separate numbers, because the comma is now a delimiter.

Another difference is that now duplicate separators which delimit substrings are evaluated as zeroes. This is not the case for the monadic use, in which repeated blanks are ignored.

Spe-6 ⎕RTL Response Time Limit

⎕RTL is a means of limiting the amount of time given to a user to answer a question.

⎕RTL may be assigned any integer in the range 0 to 32767 (0 means there is no limit).
A non-zero value places a time limit, in seconds, for input requested via ⍞.

In the example below, the user is asked a question, and he has 10 seconds to answer.

We display the question and get the answer on the same line of the screen, using the technique named "*Bare output*" (refer to section D-Spe-6).

To distinguish between the question and the answer, we have printed the (easy) question in black and the answer in red:

```
      ⎕RTL←10 ⋄ ⍞←30↑'Do you want some coffee?' ⋄ Easy←⍞
Do you want some coffee?      Sure, Honey!
      30↓Easy
Sure, Honey!                                      ⇦ We get the answer
```

The question was answered in less than 10 seconds, and we got in Easy both the question and the answer; we dropped the 30 first characters to get only the answer.

But now comes a more complex question, and the user does not reply in the requested 10 seconds (what a boor!): He failed to meet the timeout limit, and there is nothing in the result:

```
      ⎕RTL←10 ⋄ ⍞←20↑'Do you love me?' ⋄ Complex←⍞
Do you love me?                                           ⇦ No answer!
TIMEOUT
      ⎕RTL←10 ⋄ ⍞←20↑'Do you love me?' ⋄ Complex←⍞
                                                    ^
```

The exception could be trapped, so that a program containing this question could continue.

Spe-7 ⎕MONITOR Execution Monitoring

It is sometimes difficult to know how to "tune" an application, to make it run faster.

In order to help solve this problem Dyalog APL provides a monitoring system which informs the developer on how many times a statement was executed, and how much computing time and elapsed time it needed.

The statements to monitor can be set with the same technique as we used to place Break or Trace points in the Editor left margin (see section E-3.3):

When the editor is active, activate its menu View⇨Monitor and, click in the left margin; small clocks are displayed which identify the statements to be monitored, as shown below:

Figure L-2

Palindrome

File Edit View

Break point ⇨

Trace point ⇨

Monitoring point ⇨

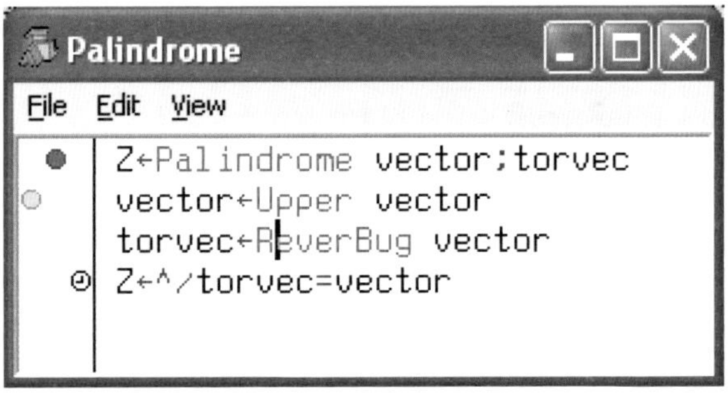

```
Z←Palindrome vector;torvec
vector←Upper vector
torvec←ReverBug vector
Z←∧/torvec=vector
```

There is a second technique, using the system function ⎕MONITOR.

Its syntax is: {R}← *Statements* ⎕MONITOR '*Function*'

where:

- '*Function*' is a function or operator name
- *Statements* is a vector of statement numbers.
  0 places a monitor on the function as a whole

This statement prepares (or resets) monitoring points in the specified function; the shy result is the list of monitored statements.

Then one can execute the application, one or more times.

Finally, one can obtain the computing times for a specified function, using `⎕MONITOR` monadically: `R← ⎕MONITOR '`*Function*`'`

The result `R` is a simple, 5-column integer matrix with one row for each line in the monitored function or operator, giving:

Column 1 : Line number (0 for the function as a whole)
Column 2 : Number of times the line was executed
Column 3 : CPU time in milliseconds
Column 4 : Elapsed time in milliseconds
Column 5 : *Reserved*

Here, we have written a function, just to perform a lot of calculations, and then monitored it:

```
      ∇ Greedy;a;b;c;r;i
[1]     i←0
[2]     :Repeat
[3]         a←?250 250ρ100
[4]         b←⌹a
[5]         c←⌹b
[6]         r←⌊0.5+b+.×c
[7]         i←i+1
[8]     :Until i=10
      ∇
        ⎕←(0,⍳20) ⎕MONITOR 'Greedy'   ⇦ Set monitoring points
0 1 2 3 4 5 6 7 8                     ⇦ Only the valid line numbers are kept
        Greedy                        ⇦ We execute the function
        ⎕MONITOR 'Greedy'             ⇦ Then query the results
0  1 9000 9094 0
1  1    0    0 0
2  1    0    0 0
3 10   92   93 0
4 10 2392 2407 0
5 10 2516 2515 0
6 10 4000 4001 0
7 10    0    0 0
8 10    0    0 0
```

All monitors may be cancelled for a given function by specifying an empty vector:

```
        θ ⎕MONITOR 'Function'
```

Spe-8 System Variables vs. System Functions

Some *System Functions* look very much like *System Variables*, because they do not take any arguments, but only return a result. For example, ⎕SI, and ⎕D.

However, we do not consider them *System Variables*, because it is not possible to assign a new value to those names. They are niladic functions.

Some niladic system functions always return the same value, and they may therefore be regarded as *constants*, for example: ⎕AV, ⎕A, ⎕D, ⎕TC, and ⎕NULL.

Other system functions look more like real functions; they return a value depending on the actual state of the workspace. For example, ⎕SI, ⎕AI, and ⎕WA.

Examples of system variables that the user may assign new values to are: ⎕IO, ⎕LX, ⎕PP, ⎕PW, ⎕RTL, and ⎕RL.

⎕PW and ⎕RL are examples of system variables that may also be changed by the APL system: ⎕PW may change when the APL session screen is resized, and ⎕RL is set to a new value each time a pseudo-random number is generated.

Chapter M: Event Handling

In this Chapter, we will use the term *event* to describe something that happens, perhaps unexpectedly, that intervenes with or interrupts the normal flow of program execution. In other programming environments, these occurrences may be called *exceptions* or *errors*, but in this Chapter we will use the term *event*.

Note that, not all *events* are accidental. For example, a perfectly well functioning program may generate *events* in a deliberate way (cf. Section 3 below), and even an apparent error such as trying to open a non-existing file, may be perfectly ok; perhaps we were just checking to see whether or not we have to delete the file, so if we don't find it, we are as happy as we can be!

Please do not confuse the use of the term *event* in this context, with the use of the same word to describe Graphical User Interface (GUI) actions, which occur when the user interacts with GUI components such as Buttons, Menus and so forth.

This chapter will give you the necessary tools to intercept *events*, diagnose them, and take appropriate actions so that they do not lead to a program crash.

You will in the following, and probably also elsewhere, see the terms "exception handling" and "error handling" being used more or less at random. This is because the mechanisms to identify and react to exceptions that we describe in this chapter are most often used to handle error conditions.

However, not all exceptions are real errors. For example, a perfectly well functioning program may generate exceptions in a controlled way (cf. section 3 below), and even an error such as a not found file may be perfectly ok: Perhaps we were just checking whether we have to delete the file, so if we don't find it, we are as happy as we can be!

1 - Diagnostic Tools

Just recall the various diagnostic tools studied in Chapter E.

Commands like `)SI` or `)RESET` must be typed manually, so they would not be pertinent for building an automated *event* processing or recovery procedure; for that we can only use *System Functions*.

`⎕SI`	*State Indicator*	Nested vector of the names of suspended functions
`⎕XSI`	*Extended SI*	Indicates in which *Namespaces* the suspended functions are **located**
`⎕NSI`	*Namespace SI*	Indicates in which *Namespaces* the suspended functions were **called from**
`⎕DM`	*Diagnostic Message*	3-item nested vector which reports the message associated with the most recent error
`⎕LC`	*Line Counter*	Numeric vector containing the line numbers waiting for execution; the most recent one is first
`⎕EN`	*Event Number*	Each *event* is identified by a number. The number of the most recent *event* is put in `⎕EN`

If you have not already read it, we suggest that you have a look at the Specialist's Section in Chapter E.

2 - Event Trapping

In many circumstances it would be very complex and time consuming to test all the possible *events* that may occur during an operation. This is for example often the case when processing external devices, like disk files.

Imagine you want to open a file: `'g:\common\areyousure\myfile.txt'`

Many problems may occur:	Maybe disk G does not exist or is not attached
	The path might be ill-shaped (contain invalid characters)
	The same for the file name
	The file may be already exclusively opened by someone else

When you try to open the file, any one of these problems will cause an *event*. Knowing that in most cases the operation will succeed, it would be very unwise to expend a lot of programming statements testing for the multitude of possible exceptional conditions. It is much simpler to just execute the application code and then, if an *event* occurs, handle it as an exception, separate from the main body of program statements. In this way you can both keep your code "clean" and avoid dealing with a problem unless it actually occurs.

This is why, in the development of the APL language, so-called *event trapping* systems were invented. When an *event* occurs, it is reported to the APL system, which in turn informs the running APL program, which then can diagnose it and execute appropriate recovery procedures.

2.1 Event Numbers / Event Messages

We have mentioned earlier that *events* are identified by an ***Event Number***, and that the niladic system function ⎕EN returns the number associated with the most recent *event* (or 0 if no *events* have occurred so far in the active workspace). We will here list some very common ones; there is a full list in Appendix 6 and in the on-line help delivered with Dyalog APL:

```
 2      SYNTAX ERROR
 3      INDEX ERROR
 4      RANK ERROR
 5      LENGTH ERROR
 6      VALUE ERROR
11      DOMAIN ERROR
```

For each of these *events* the system provides a message; the correspondence between the *event number* and the message is provided by the system function ⎕EM (for ***Event Message***).

For example: `⎕EM 5` returns the character vector: `LENGTH ERROR`

You can retrieve the message corresponding to the most recent *event* by: `⎕EM ⎕EN`

In a clear workspace, and in a freshly loaded workspace, ⎕EN returns `0` to indicate that no *event* has occurred so far.

When specifying *event* numbers to trap under program control the following two special numbers may be used:

`0`	means "All *events* in the range 1-999"
`1000`	means "All *events* in the range 1001-1006"

2.2 :Trap / :Else / :EndTrap

This control structure is used to protect all or part of a program's statements against crashing as the result of an *event*; it is most often used as follows:

`:Trap 0`
    Set of critical statements
    ...
`:Else`
    Alternative set of statements
`:EndTrap`
Continuation of the program

The first statement specifies, by means of a list of *Event Numbers*, which *events* will be trapped. 0 means "catch all *events*", and this may be the most common use of `:Trap`, but it is possible to limit the trap to very specific *events*:

`:Trap 4 5`   ⇦Sensitive only to `RANK ERROR` and `LENGTH ERROR`

The trap is followed by any set of statements that we will here describe as the "*critical*" statements.

- If no *event* occurs during their execution, control passes to the code following `:EndTrap`, and the alternative set of statements is not executed at all.
- If an *event* occurs during the execution of the critical statements the *Event Number* is stored in `⎕EN`, and then the system immediately skips to the `:Else` clause and tries to execute the alternative set of statements placed after it.
- If there is no `:Else` clause, control passes to the code following `:EndTrap`, and no special *event* processing takes place (although we have prevented a program crash). We could, for example, trap a "file not found" error during the execution of a file delete operation: If there is no file to delete we do not want to crash; instead we will just continue normal execution.
- If the error occurred within a sub-function, the system cuts back the execution stack to the function containing the `:Trap` clause before executing the alternative set of statements, or before continuing normal execution of the code following the `:Trap` clause.

It is also possible to process specific pieces of code depending on the *event* that occurred, using `:Case` or `:CaseList` clauses specifying the *Event Numbers* they cover:

```
:Trap 0                             ⇦ Sensitive to all possible events
    Critical set of statements
:Case 3
    Alternative processing for INDEX ERROR only
:CaseList 4 5
    Alternative processing for RANK ERROR and LENGTH ERROR only
:Else
    Alternative processing for any other event
:EndTrap
Continuation of the program
```

Remark 1

The *event* trapping is active only during the initial execution of the critical set of statements. It is **disabled** immediately after a trap is activated because an *event* occurred.

In particular, the *event* trap is no longer active during the processing of the code in the `:Else`, `:Case`, and `:CaseList` clauses. If a second error occurs while processing those segments of code, it is **not** trapped. This avoids endless trap loops.

Remark 2

Traps can be nested. This allows a second level of trapping in the code segments following `:Else`, `:Case`, or `:CaseList` clauses, as shown in the example below:

```
:Trap 0
    Critical set of statements
:Else                               ⇦ Beginning of alternative processing
    :Trap 3
        Alternative processing, protected against crashes due to INDEX ERROR
    :Else
        Alternative processing if an INDEX ERROR occurred
    :EndTrap
:EndTrap
Continuation of the program
```

Remark 3

During the development of an application it is often important that programming errors (i.e. mistakes) are not trapped. Instead of `:Trap 0`, you can use for example `:Trap (~Debug)/0`, where `Debug` is a global parameter, available throughout the application:

- In the production environment `Debug` is set to zero, and all the traps are active.
- In a development or debugging environment `Debug` can be set to 1, and no error is trapped (the list of errors to trap becomes empty).

2.3 ⎕TRAP

Suppose that you placed a `:Trap` clause in a segment of code. If an error occurs very deeply into a sub function, all the sub function calls on the stack are ignored, and control is cut back up to the `:Else` clause associated with the trap in the function with the `:Trap` clause. Alas, it is then too late to obtain information on the conditions which caused the error, because we have exited the sub function in error.

For this reason, a different trapping system may be more appropriate, one that is based upon the `⎕TRAP` system variable.

2.3.1 - Definition

`⎕TRAP` is a nested vector made of 2 or 3 items:

1 - A list of the *event* numbers to be trapped

2 - One of the scalar characters C, E, N, S, known as the ***Action Code***, where:

C	means	Cutback	(return to the function where `⎕TRAP` is localized)
E	means	Execute	(execute in the **called** function)
N	means	Next	(pass on this *event* to the next `⎕TRAP`)
S	means	Stop	(do not trap this *event*; take the standard system action)

3 - When the *Action code* is C or E, a third item must be provided. This item is a character vector containing a valid APL expression or series of expressions separated by ⋄. For the N and S action codes this item must not be specified.

Here are some examples:

```
⎕TRAP ← (3 4 5) 'E' 'GetInfo ⋄ →Z←0'
⎕TRAP ← 0 'C' '→Recovery'
⎕TRAP ← ((4 5)'E' 'CheckShape') (11 'C' '→Warning') (0 'E' 'GetInfo')
```

There may be many traps placed in as many functions as needed.

Normally `⎕TRAP` **must be localised** in the function in which it is set. If you forget to localise it, a trap activated by a function will remain active after that function has finished, and can cause unexpected side effects, including effects afterwards in the Session environment.

It is, however, possible to have a global `⎕TRAP` setting that catches all errors not caught elsewhere, and which cleans up the stack and the environment and restarts the application in a controlled way.

2.3.2 - Event Processing

When an *event* occurs in a function, the system searches in its calling sequence for the nearest trap defined for that particular *event*, starting from the function in error, and going upwards to the global value of ⎕TRAP if necessary.

As soon as a trap definition for the *event* is found, the defined action is taken. If no applicable trap is found the normal system action is taken (i.e. the program will crash if the *event* is an APL error), and the error is reported in the APL session as usual.

Depending on the *Action Code*, the *event* is processed as follows:

E The action defined in the third item of ⎕TRAP is executed in the function where the *event* occurred, even if the trap has been defined much higher in its calling sequence.

C The system exits from all the called functions (Cutback), up to the level where the trap is localized. Then the action defined in the third item of ⎕TRAP is executed in this calling context.

S Stops the search for a trap; the normal system action is executed in the context where the *event* occurred. This can be used during application development to neutralise all trap definitions, and let possible errors appear in the APL session.

N The specified *events* are excluded from the current ⎕TRAP definition. The search for an applicable trap will continue further up in the calling hierarchy.

The action itself can be, for example (but not limited to), one of the following:

- Execute a function that can collect information about the context in which the *event* occurred, or carry out investigations to diagnose the reason for the problem.
- Branch to a given label, where appropriate recovery actions will be processed.
- Display a message and offer solutions to the user.
- Display a message and quit the application by executing ⎕OFF.

2.3.3 - Syntax Considerations

When several traps are defined in a single ⎕TRAP, they will be processed from left to right, as in the following example:

```
⎕TRAP←((4 5)'E' 'CheckShape')(11 'C' '→Warning')(0 'E' 'GetInfos')
```

This example also shows that a trap definition may be a nested vector in which each item is a trap definition as described above. If the statement contains only one trap definition, it can be entered as a vector (it needs not be enclosed). In other words:

`⎕TRAP←0 'C' '→Recovery'` is equivalent to: `⎕TRAP←⊂(0 'C' '→Recovery')`

In either case, `⍴⍴⎕TRAP` will return `1` because, even if it is assigned a vector or a scalar (containing an enclosed vector), `⎕TRAP` is internally converted into a 1-item vector:

```
      DISPLAY ⎕TRAP
```

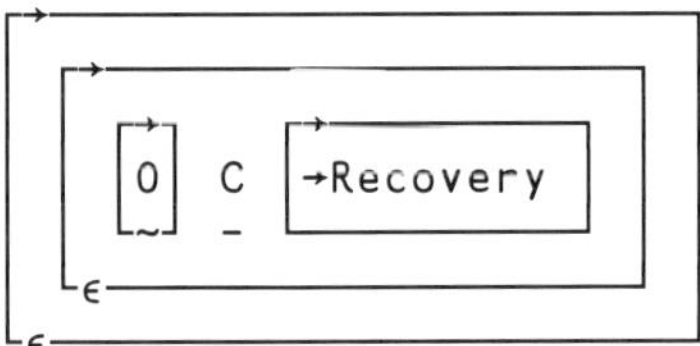

You can see that the scalar *event* number `0` has also been converted to a 1-item vector.

2.3.4 - More about Action Code "N"

We would like to set a definition to trap all possible *events*, except `LENGTH` and `RANK` errors. We can use N *Action code* like this:

```
⎕TRAP←((4 5) 'N')(0 'E' 'Recovery')
```

All possible *events* will be trapped, and will activate a program named `Recovery`, except *events* 4 and 5 (`LENGTH` and `RANK`). They will not be trapped, but will be processed normally by the system. The "N" code must precede all the "E" or "C" codes if these include the same *Event Numbers*.

Let us demonstrate it with a small function:

```
     ∇ z←a Paf b;⎕TRAP
[1]    ⎕TRAP←((4 5)'N')(0 'E' '→err')
[2]    z←a÷b
[3]    →0
[4]   err:
[5]    'I think there is a bug!'
[6]    z←0
     ∇
```

```
      42 27 Paf 7 9
6 3
```

⇦ Normal execution (no *event*)

```
      42 27 Paf 7 0
I think there is a bug!
0
```

⇦ A division by zero (causing a `DOMAIN ERROR`, *event* no. 11) has been trapped, and the action code "E" has been activated.

```
      42 27 Paf 7 9 2
LENGTH ERROR
Paf[2] z←a÷b
^
```

⇦ A `LENGTH ERROR` has been detected, but it is explicitly excluded from the trap list, so the *event* is signalled normally, and the function is interrupted

2.3.5 - Get Context

We would like to place *event* traps in some functions, and we defined a utility function named `GetContext`, which is supposed to give the developer some information about what happened.

```
     ∇ Z←GetContext;title
[1]    (13↑'Event',4 0⍕⎕EN),' = ',⎕EM ⎕EN
[2]    title←13↑[2]↑'Functions' 'Lines'
[3]    Z←0 1↓⎕SI,[0.5]⎕LC
[4]    Z←title,(2 3⍴' = '),⍕Z
     ∇
```

We dropped the first item of `⎕SI` and `⎕LC`, because they would refer to `GetContext` itself.

For example, if we run `Palindrome` with the erroneous `ReverBug` sub function, an *event* occurs. We can have information on the circumstances like this:

```
      GetContext
Event   6      = VALUE ERROR             ⇦   Type of event
Functions      =  ReverBug  Palindrome   ⇦   Functions stack
Lines          =         4           2   ⇦   Lines
```

2.3.6 - First Example

We shall apply this to the following three functions, which execute plain arithmetic operations.

When they are mis-used, they can cause some *events*: `RANK`, `LENGTH`, `DOMAIN`. For that reason, we placed traps in two of them:

```
     ∇ r←a Top b;⎕TRAP
[1]    ⎕TRAP←0 'E' 'GetContext ⋄ →0'
[2]    'execution of Top'
[3]    r←a Mid b
     ∇

     ∇ r←a Mid b
[1]    'execution of Mid'
[2]    r←a÷a Bot b
     ∇

     ∇ r←a Bot b;⎕TRAP
[1]    ⎕TRAP←(4 5) 'E' '→Rats'
[2]    'execution of Bot'
[3]    r←a-b ⋄ →0
[4]   Rats:'Ooops! Your arguments are ill-shaped'
[5]    r←a
     ∇
```

Now, let us execute Top on some inappropriate data; a vector and a matrix.

In statement Bot[3], a RANK ERROR is detected because a is a vector and b a matrix.

Happily, the trap placed in the first statement of that function traps both RANK ERROR and LENGTH ERROR. Its *Action code* was set to E, so it executes the expression →Rats.
A message is issued, and the function terminates normally. Its result is passed to Mid, and then to Top, where the final result (1 1 1) appears.

```
      2 5 6 Top 1 3ρ6
execution of Top                          ⇦ Confirmation messages
execution of Mid
execution of Bot
Ooops! Your arguments are ill-shaped      ⇦ On error, skip to statement [4]
1 1 1                                     ⇦ Final result displayed by Top
```

At the end, the *State Indicator* is empty: We successfully trapped the *event*.

2.3.7 - Example of a Derived Error

We execute Top again, with two numeric vectors: It should work.

```
      2 5 6 Top 6 5 3
execution of Top
execution of Mid
execution of Bot
Event  11      = DOMAIN ERROR
Functions      =  Mid  Top
Lines          =    2    3
Event   6      = VALUE ERROR
Functions      =  Top
Lines          =    3
```

Unfortunately, the result of Bot, r←a-b is equal to ¯4 0 3, and when this result is passed to Mid, the division by zero causes a DOMAIN ERROR.

There is no trap in Mid, so the systems searches in the calling function where a general trap is activated. This trap has its *Action code* set to E, so it first executes GetContext in the function where the problem occurred (Mid), not in its own context. This is the reason why our little utility function reports a DOMAIN ERROR in Mid[2] called by Top[3].

But the second part of the trap is →0. This branch statement is also executed within Mid, so it means "leave Mid immediately". But the result r has not been calculated, so the function returns nothing to its calling environment and a VALUE ERROR is detected in Top[3]. A poorly trapped first *event* has lead to a second *event*!

2.3.8 - Third Example

To avoid this kind of problem, it is sometimes better to cut back to a safer environment, where you can be sure that your trap will not cause additional *events*.

Let us modify `Top` and replace the *Action code* E by a C, then let us execute again the same expression:

```
      2 5 6 Top 6 5 3
execution of Top
execution of Mid
execution of Bot
Event  11     = DOMAIN ERROR
Functions     =  Top
Lines         =    3
```

Now, when the *event* is detected, the execution stack is cleaned up to the level of `Top`, and `GetContext` is executed in this context where it apparently does not cause consequent errors.

The downside of this example is that we are not told that the *event* actually occurred in `Mid[2]`. We only know that the *event* occurred in `Top[3]` or somewhere in a function called in that line.

Is it safe now? Not completely. `Top` was supposed to return a result too, but if an *event* occurs the result variable is never assigned, so an expression like `10×2 5 6 Top 6 5 3` would cause a `VALUE ERROR` again. Life is too hard!

In this particular case we can easily avoid this last problem by assigning the default value `0` to the result variable inside the trap statement:

```
      ⎕TRAP←0 'C' 'GetContext ⋄ →r←0'
```

Be extremely careful when you set a `⎕TRAP`: It should not itself generate subsequent errors!

2.4 Beware of These Errors

2.4.1 - Endless Trap Loops

Imagine that, in `Bot`, you would like to show the values of the ill-shaped arguments. You could think of something like this:

```
[4]    Rats:'Ooops! Your arguments are ill-shaped'
[5]     'a=',a
[6]     'b=',b
[7]     r←a
```

As you can see, it works perfectly on a `LENGTH ERROR`:

```
      2 5 6 Top 1 3 6 5 3
execution of Top
execution of Mid
execution of Bot
Ooops! Your arguments are ill-shaped
a= 2 5 6
b= 1 3 6 5 3
1 1 1
```

But if the second argument is a matrix, statement `[6]` cannot execute the concatenation and causes a `RANK ERROR`. But because we have not left `Bot`, our trap is still active, so this error is trapped too.

Execution restarts at statement `[4]`, and so on, indefinitely: We have entered an endless trap loop:

```
Ooops! Your arguments are ill-shaped
a= 2 5 6
Ooops! Your arguments are ill-shaped
a= 2 5 6
Ooops! Your arguments are ill-shaped
...
```

Just go to the session menu bar and activate Action⇨Interrupt, or use the technique described in section D-4.7.3, and then go and have a good cup of coffee!

2.4.2 - Incorrect Branching

A trap can be defined to jump to a given label whenever an *event* is detected, but this can lead to unpredictable (and sometimes dangerous) errors.

Consider these two functions:

```
     ∇ R←A MainFunc B;⎕TRAP;I
[1]    ⎕TRAP←0 'E' '→Error'
[2]    I←(A+1)÷(B-1)
[3]    R←(A B)SubFunc I*2 ⋄ →0
[4]   Error:'Something is going wrong!'
[5]    R←θ
     ∇

     ∇ R←X SubFunc Y;prod;val
[1]    val←0
[2]    prod←⊃×/X
[3]    val←(prod-Y)*0.5
[4]    R←⌊0.5+100×val
     ∇
```

⇦ Do not pay any attention to these statements: Their only aim is to cause an *event* if ever we try to calculate the square root of a negative value.

We first execute the main function on valid data, and nothing special happens:

```
      8 9 6 MainFunc 3 4 3
194 499 240
```

In the next example we have a 1 in the right argument. This will cause a division by zero in statement [2].

The trap is activated, and the expression →Error causes a jump to statement [4]: A message is issued, and an empty result is output. All goes as expected:

```
      8 9 6 MainFunc 3 1 3
Something is going wrong!
```

But in the next example an *event* will occur in SubFunc, because the program will try to calculate the square root of a negative value.

The trap is activated, and it re-executes the statement →Error. This is still equivalent to →4, because a label is like a read-only variable whose value is the line number of the line containing the label. **But** because we used *Action code* "E", the jump is executed in the **current** function, so the jump will go to SubFunc[4].

Fortunately (or maybe not!), because val was initialised in the first statement, SubFunc[4] can be re-executed, and we return from the program without any further errors, though with a very misleading result:

```
      8 9 6 MainFunc 3 2 3
0
```

If val had not been assigned a value at the time that the first error occurred, statement [4] would have failed with a VALUE ERROR. That would have caused the trap to be activated again, and the statement would have been executed again and again: We would have started an endless loop!

Maybe it will surprise you, but seen from a quality assurance and debugging point of view the endless loop is actually more helpful than the zero result we saw above! An *event* that causes a function to seemingly behave correctly, but sometimes return a strange and incorrect result, can cause subsequent calculations to fail sporadically, or maybe just produce incorrect results that may go undetected for a long time. Such an error may be very difficult and time consuming to debug, because it is difficult to figure out what is wrong, and the symptom is seen in a completely different part of the system. The endless loop (or even better, an immediate crash) is much more helpful; it is immediately obvious what is wrong, and more importantly, where the code fails.

Recommendation: Whenever a trap action is a jump to a label, always use the code action "C" (instead of "E"), so that the jump is guaranteed to be executed in the calling function containing the label. Or even better, use the control structures instead. ⎕TRAP (which is an older mechanism), should only be used in the rare cases where an error needs to be handled at the level where it occurs, or to collect information for an error logging system.

2.5 Neutralise the Traps

In a clear workspace the value of ⎕TRAP is an empty enclosed vector like this:

```
0ρ(⍬ ' ' '')                    ⇦ Empty numeric vector, blank, empty string
```

This is the value you must assign to ⎕TRAP if you want to neutralise it. It is a bit complicated, so in order to reduce the risk of an error (itself activating the trap), the most convenient and recommended way of cancelling a ⎕TRAP definition is:

```
⎕TRAP ← 0ρ⎕TRAP
```

3 - Event Simulation

One can generate an *event* using ⎕SIGNAL. That artificial *event* will then be processed according to the current event handling context. It will be signalled just like any other *event*, or trapped if an appropriate trap definition has been set.

The syntax is: {X} ⎕SIGNAL Y

- X is an optional message
- Y is the *Event number* that will be simulated and reported

Here is how ⎕SIGNAL is processed:

- First, the *Event number* Y is placed in ⎕EN.
- Then an event message is built:
  - If a message is specified in the left argument, this message will always be used
  - If no message is provided, and the specified *event* number is one of the pre-defined ones (listed in Appendix 6), the corresponding *Event message* will be used
  - For other *event* numbers, for example 654, ⎕SIGNAL will just report "ERROR 654" if no message is provided

Let us test that in a small function

```
      ∇ Demo Y
[1]     'The first statement is executed'
[2]     :If Y>1000
[3]         ⎕SIGNAL 10
[4]     :EndIf
[5]     'This is the last statement'
      ∇
```

If we execute it with a small value, nothing special happens:

```
      Demo 15
The first statement is executed
This is the last statement
```

If we execute it with a large value, an *event* is signalled:

```
      Demo 15000
The first statement is executed
LIMIT ERROR                          ⇦ Event number 10 corresponds to this message
Demo 15000
^                                    ⇦ The last statement has not been executed
```

Now, instead of `⎕SIGNAL 10`, we decide to create our own *event* number. *Events* 500 to 999 are reserved for user simulated *events*; let us choose `⎕SIGNAL 666`:

```
      Demo 15000
The first statement is executed
ERROR 666                            ⇦ Default message
Demo 15000
^
```

And now, we keep the same code, but we provide a left argument to `⎕SIGNAL`, so that the statement is now the following:

```
 [3] 'Right argument greater than 1000'⎕SIGNAL 666
```

Here is how the error is processed now:

```
      Demo 15000
The first statement is executed
Right argument greater than 1000 ⇦ Our message has been used
Demo 15000
^
      ⎕EN                          ⇦ We can check that our code is in ⎕EN
666
      ⎕EM ⎕EN                      ⇦ But the message associated with it is the default
one
ERROR 666
```

One can associate a standard message with a user-defined *event* number:

`(⎕EM 109)⎕SIGNAL 666` would display: `FILE ERROR 9 Bad file descriptor`

3.1 ⎕SIGNAL Example

This example shows how ⎕SIGNAL can be used to pass an *event* on to a level at which we finally decide to take some action, while still doing some *event* handling at the place in which the *event* actually occurred.

Let us assume that our application has a global ⎕TRAP setting that catches all otherwise unhandled *events*, cleans up the environment, and restarts the application.

This is fine for the user, but when an *event* occurs we immediately lose valuable debugging information about where exactly the *event* occurred, the values of local variables, etc.

Here we will demonstrate how we can improve this error handling.

We will set a very primitive global ⎕TRAP. Its only purpose is to show that it has been activated:

```
      ⎕trap ← 0 'C' '''Global error: '',(⍕⎕en),'' '',⎕em ⎕en'
```

To test it, let us provoke an *event*:

```
      a←
Global error: 2 SYNTAX ERROR
```

Our example "application" is ridiculously simple. We have a Main function that starts the application, and some sub function Sub in which an *event* might occur. A third function SaveContext will be called whenever the trap is activated; its purpose is to register where the *event* occurred, and save that information together with other environment information to a log file. Here it just displays the function name and line number:

```
     ∇ Main;a;⎕TRAP
[1]    ⎕TRAP←0 'E' 'SaveContext ⋄ ⎕signal ⎕en'
[2]    a←3 Sub 0
     ∇
     ∇ r←y Sub x
[1]    r←y÷x
     ∇
     ∇ SaveContext
[1]    'Context saved: ',(2⊃⎕SI),'[',(⍕2⊃⎕LC),']'
     ∇
```

Now let us see what will happen when we start our stupid application:

```
      Main
Context saved: Sub[1]
Context saved: Main[2]
Global error: 11 DOMAIN ERROR
      )si
```

An *event* occurs (of course!) in Sub. This is registered by SaveContext. Now the last part of the trap definition uses ⎕signal to signal the same *event* again.

You might think that signalling an *event* again in the same function would lead to an endless loop, but it does not. This is because `⎕signal` does *not* signal an *event* in the function in which it is called, but in the *calling environment*. So, in this case, when `⎕signal` is used within `Sub`, an *event* is signalled in `Main`!

This second *event* is again caught by our trap, and the new context registered. Finally the *event* is signalled again from within `Main`, leading to an error in the APL session. This last *event* is finally handled by our global trap definition. We can see that the state indicator is empty.

If we put in some additional logic we could avoid that the `SaveContext` function is called repeatedly at each level in the execution stack.

Finally, if my salary depends on the number of lines of code I produce, I'd rather join the Cobol Team.

Chapter N: File Processing

Files stored on external devices (disks) may be organised in many different ways, according to the type of data to be stored; as text, images, numbers, etc... But actually files just store long series of bits (1s and 0s) which, by themselves, have no special meaning; they can represent anything.

For example, suppose that a byte contains the following bits: 0 1 0 1 1 0 0 1. This byte can be interpreted as either:

- A Boolean vector................ `0 1 0 1 1 0 0 1`
- An integer number............. `89` (this is `2⊥0 1 0 1 1 0 0 1`)
- A character .... `Y` (this is `⎕UCS 89`)

This clearly shows that in order to use the information contained in a block of memory or a file, we must decide how we want to interpret these bits. The transformation of the bits into a character string, an image, or a list of numbers is only the result of the kind of interface we use to read the data from the file.

In this chapter we shall study only two types of files:

- Special files containing APL arrays, which are called "***Component files***". These files are accessed through a set of specialised ***system functions*** ⎕F*xxx* (see Section 1).
- Traditional "flat" files containing text or numbers (for example those with extension ".txt"), which we refer to as "***Native files***". These files are accessed through another set of specialised ***system functions*** ⎕N*xxx* (see Section 3).

Dyalog APL supports COM (Component Object Model) through which it can access (read and write) data managed by any other application that supports COM, for example data held in Microsoft Excel worksheets, Microsoft Word documents, Microsoft Access and Microsoft SQL databases, Oracle databases, and so forth. The interface with Excel is described in Chapter Q.

SQL databases can also be accessed through an interface called SQAPL. This will not be described in this tutorial; please refer to the SQAPL documentation.

1 - Component Files

1.1 First Steps

1.1.1 - General Ideas

A component file can be considered as a collection of numbered drawers (the components) in each of which one can store a single APL array. Components are referenced by their index in the file.

The file is identified by its complete *fileid* (*path* + *filename* + *extension*). Under Windows, if no extension is provided, "dcf" (for **D**yalog **C**omponent **F**ile) is assumed.

For convenience, when a file is processed, instead of using its external name (*fileid*), one uses a "handle", which is an arbitrary positive number. In APL we call this handle a ***Tie number***, and it is associated with the *fileid* when the file is opened.

This *Tie number* is not a permanent characteristic of the file, and it can be changed each time the file is opened again.

When a file is created, it must be filled sequentially, component by component.

Once a component has been written onto the file, it can be replaced by any other array, whatever its nature, shape, and size. In a sense a component file behaves like a vector of enclosed items.

1.1.2 - Create, Fill, Read, and Close

One creates a file using the function ⎕FCREATE. The left argument is the full *fileid*, the right argument is an arbitrary positive integer, the *Tie number*.

The function returns the tie number as a *Shy* result.

To avoid giving a file a *Tie number* that is already used by another file, we recommend that you specify zero. Dyalog APL will then use the first unused tie number and return the chosen value as the result.

This is what is done in the following expression (we recommend that you try it!):

```
      ⎕←one← 'cellar' ⎕FCREATE 0    ⇦ ".dcf" will be added as the default extension
1
```

The file has now been created, though it contains nothing. By default, it has been placed in the folder from which Dyalog APL was started, but we could have specified any other applicable path.

```
      ⎕←two← 'd:\bernard\action\demofile.new' ⎕FCREATE 0
2
```

For this second file, we specified a special extension ("new"). Because it is not the standard Dyalog APL extension, it will be mandatory to specify this extension each time the file is opened.

A file that has just been created using ⎕FCREATE is *exclusively* tied, i.e. it cannot be accessed by others. For more information on file sharing please see Section 1.3.

Two system functions, ⎕FNUMS and ⎕FNAMES, return the *Tie numbers* and *names* of the currently opened (tied) files, respectively:

```
      ⎕FNUMS
1 2
      ⎕FNAMES
cellar
d:\bernard\action\demofile.new
```

Note that ⎕FNAMES lists the full path which was specified when the file was tied.

The results returned by the two functions are in the same order, so that they can be displayed side by side:

```
      ⎕FNUMS,'=',⎕FNAMES
1 =cellar
2 =d:\bernard\action\demofile.new
```

To fill our files, we must use ⎕FAPPEND.

- The left argument to ⎕FAPPEND is the array to append to the file, and the right argument is the tie number of the file.
- It returns as a *Shy* result the number of the component just created.

Let us write some values and some variables we used in the preceding chapters.

```
      ⎕←'Little experiment' ⎕FAPPEND one
1                                         ⇦ Component index
      ⎕←(2 4⍴⍳8) ⎕FAPPEND one
2
      Girls     ⎕FAPPEND one              ⇦ We no longer show the shy result
      Boys      ⎕FAPPEND two              ⇦ We write to the second file
      Chemistry ⎕FAPPEND two
      Forecast  ⎕FAPPEND one
      Phrase    ⎕FAPPEND one
      Hogwash   ⎕FAPPEND one
      ⍬         ⎕FAPPEND one
      ⎕←'That''s enough' ⎕FAPPEND one
8
```

You can see that we have written very different data: character vectors, numeric matrices, character matrices (`Girls`, `Chemistry`), a nested array (`Hogwash`), and even an empty vector.

Let us ask for the sizes of these files:

```
      ⎕FSIZE one
1 9 616 1.844674407E19
      ⎕FSIZE two
1 3 224 1.844674407E19
```

The result contains 4 items:

- The number of the first component in the file. This value is usually 1, but we shall see later that it may have a different value.
- The number of the next component to be written if we append to the file (the last component index plus 1). By an incredibly complex calculation, we can deduce that file "`one`" currently contains 8 components.
- The size, in bytes, that the file currently occupies on the disk.
- The largest file size allowed by our operating system addressing capabilities (about 1.8E19 bytes[8]). The number of components is limited by the largest integer that can be represented accurately. This is currently about 9E15, but may change in future versions of Dyalog APL.

To retrieve the arrays we placed in the file, we use `⎕FREAD`.

This function accepts two numbers for its right argument: the *Tie number* of the file, and the *number* of the component to read. For example, to read the contents of our 2nd component:

```
      ⎕FREAD one 2
1 2 3 4                              ⇦ That's right: we had written that matrix
5 6 7 8
      ⎕FREAD one 5
Panama is a canal between Atlantic and Pacific
      ⎕FREAD 2 2                     ⇦ Read from the other file
H2SO4
CaCO3
Fe2O3
      nv←⎕FREAD 1 6                  ⇦ Of course, the values read from the file can be
      nv                               assigned to a variable. Here a nested array.
19  1 2  A     5  8
    3 4  P  Nuts  9
         L
```

[8] Earlier versions of Dyalog APL used a 32-bit component file system having a file size limit of approximately 4Gb. Although version 12 of Dyalog APL still supports 32-bit component files, the default is now 64-bit component files.

```
      ⎕FREAD 1 8
That's enough
```

Suppose that we have nothing more to do with "`cellar.dcf`" today; we must free the computer resources it uses. In most languages one would use the terms "Close and Free" the file; in APL we say "*Untie*" the file, but this is the same concept.

The function `⎕FUNTIE` takes a single argument: the list of tie numbers of the files we want to untie.

To untie all the files currently in use, we can write:

```
      ⎕FUNTIE ⎕FNUMS
      ⎕FNUMS
                                   ⇦ Empty answer: all files have been untied
```

1.1.3 - Tie, Fill, Replace, and Close

Some days, or months later, suppose that we want to use the files again. To do so, we must "tie" them again. Since the files already exist, we no longer use `⎕FCREATE`, but `⎕FTIE`.

The arguments are the same as those used with `⎕FCREATE`, and we can again use 0 to obtain the next free tie number.

The *Tie numbers* we get may differ from the tie numbers we used initially, because they may be in use for other files.

```
      ⎕←'cellar' ⎕FTIE 0
1                                  ⇦ We got the same Tie number
      ⎕FREAD 1 2
1 2 3 4                            ⇦ We retrieve our data
5 6 7 8
      ⎕←Actual ⎕FAPPEND 1          ⇦ We can append additional components
9
      Prod ⎕FREPLACE 1 7           ⇦ Here, we replace two components by very
      'Hello' ⎕FREPLACE 1 5          different contents
      ρ⎕FREAD 1 7
5 2 12                             ⇦ It worked, of course
      ⎕FUNTIE 1                    ⇦ Here again, remember to untie the file at the end
```

Component files may be shared between several users, each of them having specific access rights. This important feature will be studied in detail in Section 1.3, but before that, let us have a quick look at some utility functions.

1.2 Utility Functions

1.2.1 - Component Information

One can use ⎕FRDCI (for **ReaD C**omponent **I**nformation) to obtain information about a component of a given file. One must provide the file tie number followed by the component number. The result contains 3 items:

- The size of the component in bytes on file
- The user number (aplnid) of the user who last updated the component
- The time of the last update in 60ths of a second since 1st January 1970. This origin has never been changed so that, years later, it is still possible to trace the history of a file.

```
      ⎕PP←17
      ⎕FRDCI 1 7
144 0 72444345360
```

The last value can be converted into a format similar to ⎕TS as follows:

The workspace DFNS supplied with Dyalog APL contains many useful direct functions, among them several date handling functions. We can use two of them to write a third one to convert the file timestamp:

```
      )copy dfns date days
C:\...\dfns saved Fri Aug 01 14:34:26 2008
      FrdciToTs←{date(days 1970 1 1)+⍵÷×/1 3/24 60}
      FrdciToTs 3⊃⎕FRDCI 1 7
2008 4 5 14 29 16 0
```

The function works as follows:

`days 1970 1 1`	Returns the number of days between 1899-12-31 and 1970-01-01.
`⍵÷×/1 3/24 60`	Converts the file timestamp into days since 1970-01-01. When added to the previous result the timestamp is converted into days since 1899-12-31.
`date`	Converts the days since 1899-12-31 into ⎕TS format.

It is possible to write the function as a *Direct operator*. The syntax is slightly more complicated, but it has the advantage that the two constants (days 1970 1 1) and (×/1 3/24 60) are only evaluated once and bound to the derived function. This may save some computing time if the function is used repeatedly:

```
      FrdciToTs2←(days 1970 1 1){date ⍺⍺+⍵÷⍵⍵}(×/1 3/24 60)
      FrdciToTs2 3⊃⎕FRDCI 1 7
2008 4 5 14 29 16 0
```

Note that the operator is slightly unusual in the sense that it takes two arrays and no functions as operands.

1.2.2 - Drop Components

It is possible to remove the first *N* or the last *N* components of a file. One must provide the file tie number followed by the number *N* of components to drop. If *N* is positive, the first *N* components are dropped, if *N* is negative, the last *N* components are dropped, exactly like the primitive function *Drop* (↓).

The function returns, as a *Shy* result, the list of the components that were removed. This may be useful for updating a dictionary of the file contents.

Remark 1: Even if one drops the first *N* components of the file, the remaining components retain their component numbers (*N+1, N+2 etc.)* unchanged.

Let us check the size of our file "cellar.dcf" before the operation:

```
      ⎕FSIZE 1
1 10 736 4294967295
      ⎕FREAD 1 5
Panama is a canal between Atlantic and Pacific
```

Now, we drop the first 3 components, and ask for confirmation:

```
      ⎕←⎕FDROP 1 3
1 2 3                              ⇦ List of dropped components
```

Here is the situation after this operation:

```
      ⎕FSIZE 1
4 10 736 4294967295
```

Remark 2: It is important to notice that the first component's number is no longer 1, but 4. So, if we used to read component number 5 to get information about Panama, nothing has changed: we can still ask for the same component, as shown here:

```
      ⎕FREAD 1 5                   ⇦ The same index still gives the same contents
Panama is a canal between Atlantic and Pacific
```

1.2.3 - File Compaction

Even though we removed some components, the file size in bytes remained the same. You can reclaim the space occupied by the removed components by forcing a file compaction, using the function ⎕FRESIZE.

This function is ambivalent:

- Its right argument is the tie number of the file to compact
- The left argument is only for compatibility with other APL systems; it is ignored in Dyalog APL

The function returns, as a *Shy* result, the file tie number.

```
      ⎕fsize 1
4 10 736 4294967295
      ⎕fresize 1
      ⎕fsize 1
4 10 580 4294967295                ⇦ Our file has been compacted
```

The set of ⎕F*xxx* functions includes some utility functions to manage component files on disk. These tasks can also be performed through *Operating System* functions, using ⎕NA (see Chapter Q).

1.2.4 - Component Files Library

One can use ⎕FLIB to obtain the list of component files present in a given folder.

Its syntax is: R←⎕FLIB Dir

Dir is a simple character scalar or vector which specifies the name of the folder whose component files are to be listed. If Dir is empty, the current working folder is assumed.

The result is a character matrix containing the names of the component files in the folder with one row per file. The number of columns is given by the longest file name.

Each file name is prefixed by Dir followed by a folder delimiter character (\ in Windows; / in Unix). The ordering of the rows is not defined.

If there are no component files accessible to the user in the specified folder, the result is an empty character matrix with 0 rows and 0 columns. Files that are exclusively tied are not listed by ⎕FLIB.

```
      ⎕FLIB ''                     ⇦ Search in Dyalog's default folder
common_data                        ⇦ "dcf" is never reported
marketing
marketing.old                      ⇦ Extensions different from ".dcf" are shown
      ⎕FLIB '.'                    ⇦ Search in the current folder
D:\Bernard\action\apl\WS\cellar
D:\Bernard\action\apl\WS\burgondy_wines
      ⎕FLIB 'g:\shared\'           ⇦ Search in a specified folder
g:\shared\customers
g:\shared\customers.old
```

Warning! Since the standard ".dcf" extension is not reported it is impossible to distinguish between a file named "hello.dcf" and a file named "hello" without extension.

1.2.5 - Rename a Component File

One can use ⎕FRENAME to rename a component file provided it is currently **exclusively** tied (cf. Section 1.3.2).

Its syntax is: {R}← NewID ⎕FRENAME TieNum

- The right argument is the tie number of the file to rename
- The left argument is its new file identity (*Path* + *Name* + *Extension*)
- The function returns, as a *Shy* result, the file tie number

Example:

```
      'c:\temp\test'⎕FTIE 1
      'c:\temp\newname'⎕FRENAME 1
      ⎕FNUMS,⎕FNAMES
1 c:\temp\newname
      ⎕FUNTIE 1
```

In the following example, a file is renamed and moved to a different disk and a different folder. After the operation, the file remains tied, and one could continue to work with it. Here we have immediately untied it:

```
      'c:\mydir\budget.old' ⎕FTIE 1
      'g:\shared\tests\budold.demo' ⎕FRENAME 1
      ⎕FUNTIE 1
```

It is handy to do the three operations we just performed: Tie ⇨ Rename ⇨ Untie in one go.

It so happens that the three system functions used in these operations all return the tie number, so it is possible to package them into a single function as shown:

```
     ∇ RCF(OldID NewID)
[1]     ⎕FUNTIE NewID ⎕FRENAME OldID ⎕FTIE 0
     ∇
```

This function needs a nested right argument, like this:

```
      RCF 'myfile.dcf' 'g:\shared\tests\ourfile.dcf'
```

In practice, so many problems might occur during this type of operation that a suitable Event Trap would be a welcome addition to the function.

1.2.6 - Delete a Component File

One can use ⎕FERASE to delete a component file provided that it is currently **exclusively** tied (cf. Section 1.3.2).

Its syntax is: `{R}← Filename ⎕FERASE TieNum`

- The right argument is the tie number of the file to delete.
- The left argument is the name that was used to tie the file, and the file must be exclusively tied.
- The function returns, as a *Shy* result, the tie number of the file, before it was deleted.
- Of course, after the deletion the file is no longer tied, and the tie number is unused.

1.2.7 - File System Status

The niladic function ⎕FAVAIL reports whether or not the component file sub-system is available. This system function is provided only for compatibility with other implementations of APL.

Its syntax is: `R← ⎕FAVAIL`

In Dyalog APL, the Boolean result is always 1.

1.3 Shared Files

It is very often useful to share a file between several users, who will simultaneously read from and update the file. This has several implications.

The file must be on a shared disk, and that disk should be secured so that unauthorised people cannot access it, and also so that authorised people may not erroneously destroy it. These are operating system considerations, and they are out of the scope of this tutorial; you should be able to get information about it from your network administrator.

The file must also be processed in such a way that authorised users have specific rights to the file (different rights for different users), and that simultaneous access to the file does not lead to improper actions, such as User B overriding what User A had just written on the file.

This can be controlled very easily in Dyalog APL, we must just learn:

- How to share a file
- How to give rights to different users
- How to control simultaneous operations

1.3.1 - The User Identity

When several users access the same file, how can we distinguish between them? The answer is that they are identified by an *Account Number*; remember: it is the first item of ⎕AI (see Section L-4.4).

You could change that parameter (**don't do it** for the moment) using the following menu:

Options ⇨ Configuration ⇨ Network ⇨ *Network ID*

The default value is zero, but you can change it to any other integer value between 0 and 65535; the change becomes effective after Dyalog APL is restarted. In fact, this parameter is stored in the Windows Registry under the name aplnid (for APL Network ID).

You could just as well use the registry editor to change the parameter manually, but it is easier (and probably safer) to do it from within APL.

In our exploration of shared files we shall use a different technique.

Normally, to see how shared files work, you would need two users running two computers identified with distinct aplnid's and sharing a common disk. You can also, on a single computer, start two separate APL sessions. However, because aplnid is stored in the Registry, those two sessions would have the same identifier, and would not be considered as distinct users. We suggest that you use the following trick:

- On your desktop, duplicate the icon you normally use to start Dyalog APL.
  Rename the original one to APLMain (for example)
  Rename the other one to APLUser
- Leave the properties of APLMain unchanged.
- Open the Properties of APLUser, and change the command line:
  That command line is probably something like :
  "C:\Program Files\Dyalog\Dyalog APL 12.0\Dyalog.exe"

  On the right, append the parameter: aplnid=3 so as to obtain:
  "C:\Program Files\Dyalog\Dyalog APL 12.0\Dyalog.exe" aplnid=3

  Then click "OK"

Using this method:

- When you start an APL session using the APLMain icon, the session is started using the value of aplnid stored in the Registry, and ⎕AI[1] will be equal to 0 (default value).
- But when you start a second session using APLUser, the parameter you set in the command line overrides the Registry definition, and ⎕AI[1] will be equal to 3.

You will then be able to work on a single computer as if you were two different users. In the following pages, we shall use APLMain and APLUser to refer to those two virtual users.

1.3.2 - Shared Tie

When one ties a file using ⎕FTIE, that file is tied **exclusively**: nobody else can tie it as long as it is exclusively tied. It is not possible to exclusively tie a file that is already tied by somebody else, no matter whether it is exclusively tied or *share tied* by the other user.

To share access to a file with somebody else, you must use ⎕FSTIE (with "S" for *Share*) instead of ⎕FTIE, but this is not sufficient.

Let us do a little experiment:

- Start an APL session using the APLMain icon, and share-tie the file created in the previous section, with any *Tie number*:

```
      'cellar' ⎕FSTIE 1              ⇦ Do not forget the "S"
      ⎕FREAD 1 2
1 2 3 4                              ⇦ We retrieve our data: the file is accessed
5 6 7 8
```

- Now, start a second APL session using the APLUser icon, and try to share-tie the same file, with any *Tie number* too:

```
      'cellar' ⎕FSTIE 1
FILE ACCESS ERROR                    ⇦ It does not work!
      'cellar' ⎕FSTIE 1
     ∧
```

The operation failed because APLUser (#3) is not the owner of this file. The file was created by someone who was identified by aplnid=0, and that person (APLMain in fact) is the only authorised user!

The owner must explicitly specify who else is authorised to use his file, and what kind of operations that person (or those people) will be allowed to do. This will be specified by the means of an ***Access Control Matrix***. The owner himself can do anything with his own files.

1.3.3 - Access Control Definition

To enable a file for shared use, its owner must attach to that file an *Access Control Matrix* made of 3 numeric columns where each row represents a combination of:

Column 1 — Specifies who will be authorised to use this file.
Each authorised user is represented by his aplnid.
0 means any user not already mentioned in the matrix.

Column 2 — Specifies which operations are allowed for the user in column 1.
This is described below.
¯1 means there are no restrictions.

Column 3 Optional ***Pass Number***

If present, the user will be forced to specify this *Pass Number* each time he executes any of the operations specified in column 2.

0 means there is no *Pass Number* for this user/operation combination.

In this part of the book, we shall not use *Pass Numbers*. This technique will be discussed in the Specialist's Section.

In the second column, the authorisations given to a particular user are represented by a sum of "*Weights*", as shown in the table below.
In this list of all possible functions related to component files, the first column contains the "weights" assigned to each operation (note that weights 64 and 256 do not exist).

Weight	Function	Usage
	⎕FAVAIL	Is the file system available?
	⎕FLIB	List of component files
	⎕FCREATE	Create a new component file
	⎕FUNTIE	Untie a tied file
	⎕FNUMS	List of tie numbers
	⎕FNAMES	List of tied files names
	⎕FSTIE	Tie and share a file
	⎕FSIZE	Get size information about the file
1	⎕FREAD	Read a component from a given file
1	⎕FPROPS	Query file properties (requires 8192 to set)
2	⎕FTIE	Exclusively tie an existing file
4	⎕FERASE	Erase a tied file from disk
8	⎕FAPPEND	Append a new component at the end
16	⎕FREPLACE	Replace a component by another value
32	⎕FDROP	Drop N first or last components
128	⎕FRENAME	Rename a tied file
512	⎕FRDCI	Read component information
1024	⎕FRESIZE	Resize a file
2048	⎕FHOLD	Place statements in the file queue
4096	⎕FRDAC	Read access control matrix
8192	⎕FSTAC	Store access control matrix
8192	⎕FPROPS	Set file properties (1 required to query)

Some operations have no weight and are permitted for any user. ⎕FCOPY has no distinct weight itself, but requires an access code of 4609 (4096 for ⎕FRDAC + 512 for ⎕FRDCI + 1 for ⎕FREAD).

For example, if a user is authorised only to read, append or replace components, he will be given an authorisation code equal to: 1+8+16 = 25.

An authorisation code equal to ¯1 means that all operations are allowed.

Here is an example of an *Access Control Matrix*:

```
      ⎕←simplemat←4 3⍴3 17 0 7 2073 0 43 ¯1 0 22 2065 1943
 3   17    0
 7 2073    0
43   ¯1    0
22 2065 1943
```

At this stage, simplemat is just a plain matrix like any other matrix, but used as the *Access Control Matrix* of a given file, it specifies that only four users (plus the owner, of course) will be authorised to use this file, with the following restrictions:

User	Authorisation	Comment
3	Read, Replace	
7	Read, Append, Replace, Hold	
43	All possible operations	
22	Read, Replace, Hold	Must provide a *Pass Number* equal to 1943

Of course, all of them are authorised to use the first 6 functions, which do not require specific authorisation and therefore have no weight.

Note that a user can appear several times in the matrix with different pass numbers. The user will be granted access according to the pass number used when he ties the file.

1.3.4 - Access Control Activation

To make this matrix active, the owner of the file must tie it, and then associate the matrix to that file using ⎕FSTAC (for **ST**ore **A**ccess **C**ontrol), like this:

```
'cellar'  ⎕FTIE 1          ⇦ Tie the file (exclusively or not)
simplemat ⎕FSTAC 1         ⇦ Associate the matrix with the file
⎕FUNTIE 1                  ⇦ Untie the file if it was tied exclusively
```

Now, our access definitions are stored in the file; we could even destroy simplemat.

One can read that matrix back from the file, using ⎕FRDAC (for **ReaD** **A**ccess **C**ontrol)

In this particular case, the owner must untie the file before the access control matrix will apply, because as long as he keeps it exclusively tied, nobody else can access it.

After that, he could tie it again, preferably in shared mode.

Note that it need not be the owner of the file who sets the access control matrix; any user that has the proper authorisation (weight 8192) can do it.

1.3.5 - Example of Simultaneous Access

The file can now been used simultaneously by all the authorised users.

You can find on the next page an example of simultaneous use with, on the left, what APLMain does and, on the right, what APLUser does.

The expressions are listed in the order in which they were executed.

The numbers in the middle column are references to the comments given below.

Comments

1 User #3 ties the file in shared mode (the owner has not tied it yet).

2 He reads the first component, and gets whatever was there.

3 The owner also ties the file (note that they have chosen different tie numbers).

4 He reads the same component, and also gets `"Little experiment"`.

5 User #3 modifies the first component.

6 When the owner reads the first component again he now gets `"Hello"`. If you just look at the owner's own session, he reads the same component twice and gets two different answers. This is the proof that the file has been modified elsewhere.

7 The owner appends a new component.

8 It becomes component #9.

9 When the second user asks for the file size, he can see that it now has 9 components.

10 He reads the new component.

11 The owner asks for the current *Access Control Matrix*. He gets the matrix he had specified for the file (of course).

12 The owner would like to tie the file exclusively, so he first unties it.

13 But his attempt to tie the file exclusively is rejected because the file is still in use by another user (he cannot know which user).

14 User #3 tries to append a new component. His statement is rejected, because he is not allowed to do it (he may only Read or Replace).

15 Finally, he unties the file.

Simultaneous use of a common shared component file		
APLMain (owner, user 0)	Refs	APLUser (user 3)
	1	'cellar' ⎕FSTIE 7
	2	⎕FREAD 7 1 Little experiment
'cellar' ⎕FSTIE 1	3	
⎕FREAD 1 1 Little experiment	4	
	5	'Hello' ⎕FREPLACE 7 1
⎕FREAD 1 1 Hello	6	
⎕←14 10 1952 ⎕FAPPEND 1	7	
9	8	
	9	⎕FSIZE 7 1 10 736 4294967295
	10	⎕FREAD 7 9 14 10 1952
⎕←Defs← ⎕FRDAC 1 3 17 0 7 2073 0 43 ¯1 0 22 2065 1952	11	
⎕FUNTIE 1	12	
'cellar' ⎕FTIE 1 FILE TIED 'cellar'⎕FTIE 1 ^	13	
	14	'Attempt' ⎕FAPPEND 7 FILE ACCESS ERROR 'Attempt'⎕FAPPEND 7 ^
	15	⎕FUNTIE 7

1.3.6 - Access Conflict

In this second example we will show that it is important to ensure that two simultaneous users do not destroy each other's operations.

Imagine that a company has bought a pool of 6 cars for its salesmen. Any salesman can use any car, provided he places a reservation in the first component of a shared file. These reservations are stored in a 2 by 6 nested array, and for the moment 3 cars are already reserved:

```
Cadillac     Bentley     Citroen     Ferrari     Lexus     Porsche
                         Bernard     Colette               Esperanza
```

Yes, it's a rather wealthy company!

It happens that Miguel and Ingrid would also like to reserve a car, and both would like to drive a Bentley (I would like it too!).

Ingrid reads: `Cars←⎕FREAD 1 1`

Miguel reads the same matrix: `Pool←⎕FREAD 1 1`

Miguel immediately places his name in the matrix, and checks the result:

```
      Pool[2;2]←⊂'Miguel' ⋄ Pool
Cadillac     Bentley     Citroen     Ferrari     Lexus     Porsche
             Miguel      Bernard     Colette               Esperanza
```

All is correct, and he writes the matrix back to the file: `Pool ⎕FREPLACE 1 1`

But Ingrid still has in her workspace the value of the matrix that she loaded some minutes before, in which the Bentley is still free. Consequently, she places her own name in the matrix and writes it back to the file:

```
      Cars[2;2]←⊂'Ingrid' ⋄ Cars ⎕FREPLACE 1 1
```

The resulting content of the file component will be the following:

```
Cadillac     Bentley     Citroen     Ferrari     Lexus     Porsche
             Ingrid      Bernard     Colette               Esperanza
```

Miguel will not get the Bentley!

Programs should be written to avoid this kind of conflict; this is the reason why Dyalog APL offers tools to synchronise simultaneous access to component files.

1.4 How to Queue File Operations

1.4.1 - Use the Hold Queue

To avoid access conflicts the developer of an application must determine precisely what are the critical parts of his code. Some operations can probably be executed at any time even if someone else is using the same file, but between the moment one reads a component and writes it back onto the file, it is generally important that nobody else writes to the same file. This is called a critical section of code.

To achieve this, each user can notify which files he needs exclusively by means of `⎕FHOLD`.

Its syntax is: `{R}← ⎕FHOLD TieList` where this argument is a list of tie numbers (scalar, vector, or one-row matrix).

This list specifies the files to which the user needs (temporarily) exclusive access, without interference from any other user. The shy result of ⎕FHOLD is the vector of tie numbers of the files held.

The function works like this:

- As soon as a user tries to place a ⎕FHOLD on one or more files, all preceding holds that the user may have, are released.
- Then the execution of the program is delayed until none of the specified files are held by any other user.
- When all the specified files are freed, execution continues, and the user can access the file(s). Provided that the application has been written correctly (i.e. all the users register in the Hold Queue), he should be the only one working on them (cf. Section 1.4.3 below).
- From now on all other users who also try to ⎕FHOLD any of the specified files will be placed in a wait state, and this will last until the user releases the holds.
- When the hold is released, those other tasks (users) can resume. Initially only one of the waiting tasks will be allowed to place a hold and thereby gain exclusive access to the file(s). Any other tasks will continue to wait until it becomes their turn.
- When a user specifies an empty TieList or a new one, its preceding holds (if any) are released. The normal method to release all held files is to execute the expression ⎕FHOLD ⍬.

1.4.2 - Hold Termination

A hold placed by a user is released in any of the following circumstances:

- When a new ⎕FHOLD is issued by the same user (whatever the TieList he specifies).
- When the designated files are all untied. If some but not all are untied, they become free for another task, but the hold persists for the files that remain tied.
- When the APL session is terminated.
- The user's APL session returns to immediate execution mode. This may occur as a result of the normal termination of a function, or because of an untrapped error, or because of a *breakpoint*.

  For this reason ⎕FHOLD can only be used meaningfully when called from a defined function. This means that you cannot experiment with ⎕FHOLD in immediate execution mode (from the APL session), as holds are released each time an expression has been processed and the system prompts you for input.

  A hold is **not** released by a request for input through ⍞ or ⎕.

1.4.3 - A Hold is Not a Lock

It is important to understand that even when a hold has been placed on a file, that file is **not** "locked". Any user who decides not to use ⎕FHOLD can still execute any other file operation at any time.

This may be helpful for maintenance operations, or to read or update some non-critical components of a file currently under the control of a hold. However, in general, applications must cooperate closely and be written very carefully in order to secure an orderly access control; all file operations should be explicitly queued.

1.4.4 - Recommendations

Until a user has released a file, all the other users are held in a wait state. This may lead to the complete freeze of an application.

- Prepare all that can be prepared before entering the set of statements that are under the control of the queue.
- Avoid including user input interfaces (like ⍞, ⎕, or GUI dialog boxes) in this set of statements. You cannot know how long time the user will take to answer a question.
- Hold only the files you really need to control.
- Free them as soon as possible, using ⎕FHOLD ⍬.
- If you intend to use shared files, you must read Section Spe-1.6 on buffering considerations.
- If you trap errors, remember to release any relevant holds!

2 - Data Representation

Before studying *Native files*, we must first understand how data is represented in Dyalog APL and in files in general.

2.1 Representation of Values

2.1.1 - Representation of Numbers

We must take into consideration how numbers are stored.

For integers which are represented by a single byte (8 bits), the leftmost bit is used for the sign. So the limits are as follows:

- The largest positive number is 0 1 1 1 1 1 1 1 representing 127
- The largest negative number is 1 0 0 0 0 0 0 0 representing ¯128

To represent numerically greater values, we need more bytes:

- In 2 bytes we can represent values from `¯32768` to `32767`
- In 4 bytes we can represent values from `¯2147483648` to `2147483647`

Larger integers and all fractional values are represented as floating point numbers in 8 bytes each, and then the limits are given by `⌈/⍬` and `⌊/⍬`.
On a standard PC these limits are: `¯1.797693135E308` to `1.797693135E308`

You may obtain different limits on other types of computers.

Dyalog APL always stores numeric values internally using the most compact representation possible, with the restriction that in a simple array the same representation is used for all the items. For example, if we create the vector: `34 ¯29 673 48`, then `34 ¯29` and `48` could be represented in 1 byte, but `673` requires two bytes, so each of the four values will be represented by 2 bytes.

2.1.2 - Query Data Representation

The monadic *System function* `⎕DR` (*Data Representation*) tells you how a variable is represented internally:

Value	Bits	Data type
11	1	Boolean
80	8	Unicode Character
82	8	ANSI Character (*Classic Edition*)
83	8	Integer
160	16	Unicode Character
163	16	Integer
320	32	Unicode Character
323	32	Integer
326	32	Pointer
645	64	Floating point

The table above shows how many bits are used to represent each single value. Of course, if we had to represent a vector of 141 Boolean values, the 141 bits would be padded to give 18 full bytes (144 bits).

```
      ⎕DR 32 ¯67 19
83                                        ⇦ These are 1-byte integers
      ⎕DR 32 ¯67 500 19
163                                       ⇦ These are 2-byte integers
      Darjeeling←32 3.7 500 19
      ⎕DR Darjeeling
645                                       ⇦ These are 8-byte floating point values
      ⎕DR 'Darjeeling'                    ⇦ These are Unicode characters
80                                          The Classic Edition would return 82
      ⎕DR (34 15) 'Hello' (56.12 89.11)
326                                       ⇦ Nested arrays and Object Representations given
                                            by ⎕OR are described as pointers
```

2.1.3 - Change Data Representation

The dyadic use of ⎕DR converts an array into a different representation.

The general syntax is: `R←X ⎕DR Y` where `X` can contain 1, 2 or 3 values

Case 1: `X` is a single integer

The bits in the right argument are interpreted as items of an array of type `X`.

The shape of the resulting new array may be changed along the last axis. For example, a character array seen as Boolean will have 8 times as many items along the last axis, as shown below:

```
      Girls
Suzy                                    ⇦ Each of these names is represented in memory by
Anna                                      32 bits, interpreted here as 4 letters
Jane
      ⎕DR Girls
80
      u←11 ⎕DR Girls                    ⇦ Let us interpret each series of 32 bits as Booleans
      u
0 1 0 1 0 0 1 1 0 1 1 1 0 1 0 1 0 1 1 1 1 0 1 0 0 1 1 1 1 0 0 1
0 1 0 0 0 0 0 1 0 1 1 0 1 1 1 0 0 1 1 0 1 1 1 0 0 1 1 0 0 0 0 1
0 1 0 0 1 0 1 0 0 1 1 0 0 0 0 1 0 1 1 0 1 1 1 0 0 1 1 0 0 1 0 1
```

The bits contained in the variable are the same, but we have just interpreted them differently.

The operation can be reversed:

```
      80 ⎕DR u
Suzy
Anna
Jane
```

Case 2: `X` is a 2-item integer vector

The bits in the right argument are interpreted as type `X[1]`. The system then attempts to convert *each of* the items of the resulting array to type `X[2]` without loss of precision. The result `R` is a two item nested array consisting of:

- The converted items or a fill item (0 or blank) where the conversion failed
- A Boolean array of the same shape indicating which items were successfully converted.

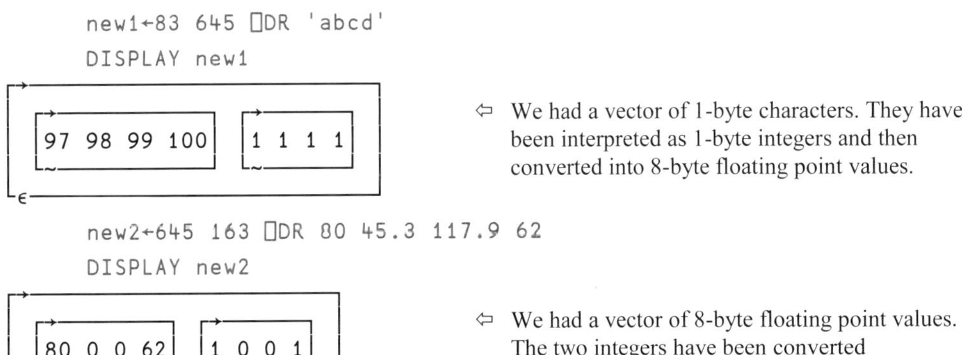

new1←83 645 ⎕DR 'abcd'
DISPLAY new1
97 98 99 100
1 1 1 1
⇦ We had a vector of 1-byte characters. They have been interpreted as 1-byte integers and then converted into 8-byte floating point values.
new2←645 163 ⎕DR 80 45.3 117.9 62
DISPLAY new2
80 0 0 62
1 0 0 1
⇦ We had a vector of 8-byte floating point values. The two integers have been converted into 2-byte integers, but the two decimal numbers could not be converted without loss of precision.

Note: The internal representation of data may be modified during a workspace compaction, initiated, for example by ⎕WA. Numeric arrays will be squeezed to occupy the least possible amount of memory. However, the internal representation of the result of a dyadic ⎕DR is guaranteed to remain as specified until it is re-assigned (or partially re-assigned) by the result of any function.

For example, in the first example above we can use ⎕DR to verify that the result, which looks like 4 integers, is really stored internally as a floating point array:

```
      ⎕DR ⊃new1
645                          ⇦ These are really stored as floating point numbers.
      ⎕DR 97 98 99 100
83                           ⇦ Although they could be represented as integers.
      ⎕DR 10,⊃new1
83                           ⇦ Now we "lost" the floating point representation.
```

Case 3: X is a 3-item integer vector in which X[2 3] is 163 82

This case is provided primarily for compatibility with APL*PLUS (another APL system). It exists only in the *Classic Edition*; you can forget about it.

2.2 Representation of Variables

2.2.1 - Internal Structure

In a workspace, each array has a certain number of characteristics. For example, whether it contains numbers or characters, its rank, shape, and so on. These characteristics are stored as part of the array.

So, we can say that the internal representation of an array is made of two parts:

- A ***Header*** which describes the characteristics of the array,
- The ***Contents*** whose data type is identified by its *Data Representation*

Suppose that we need to store the following matrix:

```
43 12
 1 52
10 14
```

It is completely defined by the following information:

- The data is made of integers of data type 83
- The array is a matrix, so its rank is.. 2
- Its shape is 3 2

We can completely describe that array by the following vector: 83 2 3 2

This is a convenient header, and the array could be represented as follows:

```
83 2 3 2  43 12 1 52 10 14
```

Header *Contents*

This is **not** the true internal representation of the array, but it may give you some idea of what it really is. This applies quite well to simple (not nested) variables. Nested objects have a slightly more complex internal structure.

Here is another data representation: `80 1 11 Hello World`

It represents the following text vector: `Hello World`

Now, if we had to store these arrays on a file, we could use any of the two following techniques:

2.2.2 - Component Files

If we decide to store on disk an exact copy of our arrays' internal representation, we only need a light interface because it does not require any transformation. And when we read the data back from our file, the interface has nothing to do; the data read from the file can be immediately assigned to a variable.

Such files are the *Component files* described in Section 1 above.

The advantage is that we can store any kind of APL array; scalars, vectors, arrays of any shape, with any contents, including nested values, or *Object Representations* produced by ⎕OR.

The drawback is that the data in such files cannot be recognised by traditional languages or text editors, because the internal structure (Header + Contents) is very specific to APL.

2.2.3 - Native Files

We may decide to store just the contents of a simple array: `43 12 1 52 10 14`
or: `Hello World`

A file containing no APL headers can be read by any other language because it needs no special interpretation - provided that we specify whether the values represent numbers or characters. We can then exchange information with other languages or applications.

To read the information back from the file, we need an interface which just reads characters (or numbers). In order to create an APL variable in the workspace, our interface will need to create a header. However, because we have lost the rank and shape information, the interface can only count how many items were read and return a vector of an appropriate length, either numeric or character, as shown:

```
83 1 6   43 12 1 52 10 14
80 1 11  Hello World
```

This is typically what we get when we read text files created with a text editor like Microsoft Notepad, for example.

Such files are called *Native files*; they are accessed through ⎕N*xxx* functions and will be described in Section 3 below.

3 - Native Files

3.1 Similarities and Differences

Native files are processed by functions whose names are prefixed by ⎕N.

Most of them correspond to those that we studied for component files, but two new functions appear, as shown in the table below:

Component files	Native files	Usage
⎕FCREATE	⎕NCREATE	Create a new file
⎕FUNTIE	⎕NUNTIE	Untie a tied file
⎕FNUMS	⎕NNUMS	List of tie numbers
⎕FNAMES	⎕NNAMES	List of tied file names
⎕FSIZE	⎕NSIZE	Get size information about the file
⎕FREAD	⎕NREAD	Read a segment from a given file
⎕FTIE	⎕NTIE	Tie (open) an existing file
⎕FERASE	⎕NERASE	Erase a tied file from disk
⎕FAPPEND	⎕NAPPEND	Append data at the end of the file
⎕FREPLACE	⎕NREPLACE	Replace a segment by other values
⎕FRENAME	⎕NRENAME	Rename a tied file
⎕FDROP	⎕NRESIZE	Resize a file
	⎕NLOCK	Lock access to part of a file
	⎕NXLATE	Translation table between files and APL

The following component file functions have no equivalent for native file processing:

```
⎕FAVAIL   ⎕FRESIZE  ⎕FRDAC    ⎕FSTAC    ⎕FRDCI
⎕FSTIE    ⎕FLIB     ⎕FHOLD (the closest equivalent is ⎕NLOCK)
⎕FPROPS   ⎕FCOPY
```

In order to distinguish them from component file tie numbers, native files tie numbers are always **negative**.

A native file contains just a long list of bits, which can be viewed as numbers or as characters, as described in detail in Section 2.1 of this chapter. For this reason, when you read a file, you must specify what kind of conversion you want to apply.

For example:

- `80` would read bytes and convert them into Unicode characters
- `83` would read bytes and convert them into integers
- `323` would read successive blocks of 4 bytes, and convert them into integers

Some text files, for example those created using Microsoft Notepad, appear to be made up of similar "records", each containing the same kind of information. For example, a company has stored the list of its subsidiaries, with their year of creation, number of employees, revenue of last year, and expected revenue for next year:

```
Berlin    1999   9 2607 2900
Dakar     2006   6  931 1000
Frankfurt 1982  48 1816 1950
London    1979 106 4086 4000
Milano    1982  81 1640 1800
Paris     1985  63 1789 2000
Seattle   1993  14  941 1000
Tokyo     2002  29  652  740
```

From the layout, a human can discern the individual pieces of information, but the computer cannot do so without specific instructions. Each line is separated from the next one by two special characters, *NewLine* and *LineFeed*, known in APL as `⎕TC[3 2]`, or better still, `⎕UCS 13 10`.

If we could represent them by two printable characters ⇙ and ⇩, the file would look like this

`Berlin    1999   9 2607 2900⇙⇩Dakar     2006   6  931 1000⇙⇩Frank`...etc

Using this type of representation, it is clear that if we read any arbitrary sequence of bytes, we may obtain data which might not be easy to interpret. For example, if we read characters 21 to 43:

We would obtain the following characters: `607 2900⇙⇩Dakar     200`

And they would be shown like this:

```
607 2900
Dakar     200
```

So, unlike component files there is generally no structure imposed on the data in native files. It is solely the programs that create, write to, and read from the files that define that structure.

3.2 Basic Operations

3.2.1 - Tie an Existing File

For this demonstration, we shall work on an existing file containing the data shown above. Suppose that this file can be found with the following *path* and *fileid*. You will probably use different path and file names.

```
      path←'g:\shared\tests\' ⋄ fileid←'report.txt'
```

The file is opened using the same technique that we used for component files, except that the tie number is now negative. However, instead of ⎕Fxxx functions we use ⎕Nxxx functions, like ⎕NNUMS, ⎕NNAMES, and ⎕NSIZE:

```
      tie←(path,fileid) ⎕NTIE 0
      tie
¯1
      ⎕NSIZE tie                      ⇦ The size of the file in bytes
238
      ⎕NNUMS                          ⇦ The tie number is negative
¯1
      ⎕NNAMES
g:\shared\tests\report.txt
```

3.2.2 - Read Characters

To read a file, we use ⎕NREAD, which accepts a right argument made of 3 or 4 items:

1 - Tie number
2 - Data representation (type of conversion to be applied to the bits read)
3 - Number of **items** to read (not bytes)
4 - Optional starting point, in **bytes** (0 by default)

Some important points must be noted:

- The third value is not a number of bytes but the number of **items**, whose size depends upon the specified data representation.
  If the value is set to 100, ⎕NREAD will read:

- 100 bytes if the conversion code is 80 (characters) or 83 (one-byte integers)
- 200 bytes if the conversion code is 160 or 163 (2-byte characters or integers)
- 400 bytes if the conversion code is 320 (4-byte characters) or 323 (4-byte integers)
- 800 bytes if the conversion code is 645 (8-byte floating-point values)

In any case, it will retrieve a vector of 100 values into the APL workspace.

- There is, however, an exception. When a file is read with conversion code 11 (bits), the number of items read is specified in bytes, and not bits. This is because the smallest item that can be read is a byte.

- The starting point, or offset, is always specified in **bytes**. By default, each read operation starts from the point where the previous read or write operation finished. So for a sequential read, this parameter is not required. The offset specifies the number of bytes to skip, so if it is 50, the first byte read will be the 51st byte in the file.

- Once some items have been read, the default starting point is set to the last byte read, so that the next read operation will start exactly where the previous one ended.

Our small demonstration file contains characters, so we shall use conversion code 80 (or 82 for *Classic Edition*, or older versions).

```
      ⍴u←⎕NREAD tie 80 100                ⇦ Read 100 characters
100                                       ⇦ The result is a vector of 100 characters
      u
Berlin    1999   9 2607 2900              ⇦ The characters (⎕UCS 13 10) cause line skips

Dakar     2006   6  931 1000

Frankfurt 1982  48 1816 1950

London
```

The characters we read may look slightly unusual: in APL under Microsoft Windows, both *NewLine* and *LineFeed*, which are present at the end of each line, cause the display to skip one line to the next.

We shall remove these characters later.

If you try to edit the vector using the APL text editor, *NewLine* characters "wrap" on several lines, but *LineFeed* characters appear as blanks, producing the following appearance:

```
Berlin    1999   9 2607 2900
 Dakar     2006   6  931 1000
 Frankfurt 1982  48 1816 1950
 London
```

We can now verify that if we read some more characters, the read operation will start exactly where the previous one ended:

```
      v←⎕NREAD tie 80 50
      v
1979 106 4086 4000

Milano    1982  81 1640 1800
```

If we try to read too many characters; the operation will naturally stop at the end of the file.

So, it would not have been a problem if we had read the entire contents of a file like this:

```
      ρu←⎕NREAD tie 80 1000 0       ⇦ To restart from the beginning, we specified a
238                                   starting point of zero
```

But why specify an arbitrary number like 1000? If the workspace size can accommodate it, one can read a whole file like this:

```
      ρu←⎕NREAD tie 80 (⎕NSIZE tie) 0
238
```

3.2.3 - Append and Replace

We would like to add a new town to our set of data. Like the previous ones, it contains 28 characters:

```
      ρmore←'Bamako    2007   6   19   60'
28
```

But this "record" must be separated from the previous ones, so the update operation needs to be written like this:

```
      ⎕←((⎕UCS 13 10),more) ⎕NAPPEND tie
268
```

The right argument to ⎕NAPPEND is a 1 or 2-item vector; the second optional item being a conversion code like the one we used when we tied the file. In the *Unicode edition* the default conversion is 80 (1-byte characters) if the data to append is a character array, so in our example we did not need to specify it.

The *Shy* result of ⎕NAPPEND is the position of the very last byte written. So it would also be the starting point of a future *append* operation.

Now, it happens that we made a mistake; the Japanese town should have been Kyoto, not Tokyo.

It is possible to replace this name, provided that we specify the starting point, that is to say the position of the last character preceding the characters to replace.

In this case, it is very easy: "Tokyo" is preceded by 7 rows of 30 characters (28 + 2 separators).

```
      'Kyoto' ⎕NREPLACE tie 210
```

Here we could have written `'Kyoto' ⎕NREPLACE tie 210 80`, but because we are writing a character array to the file, there is no need to specify the default conversion code `80`.

3.2.4 - Remove Separators

The separators are often unnecessary. Can we get rid of them? When all the rows have a known identical length, it is rather easy:

```
      vec←⎕NREAD tie 80 (⎕NSIZE tie) 0
      vec←vec~⎕UCS 13 10                ⇦ Remove all separators
      nr←(⍴vec)÷28                      ⇦ Calculate the number of rows
      ⎕←mat←(nr,28)⍴vec                 ⇦ Reshape to a text matrix
Berlin    1999   9 2607 2900
Dakar     2006   6  931 1000
... etc
Seattle   1993  14  941 1000
Kyoto     2002  29  652  740            ⇦ Tokyo has been replaced by Kyoto
Bamako    2007   6   19   60
```

It is more complex to get rid of the separators when the "records" may have different lengths. Let us try with a second file. We will use two different methods:

```
      mlk←(path,'MLK.txt') ⎕ntie 0      ⇦ Open a new file
      vec←⎕NREAD mlk 80 500 400         ⇦ Read any arbitrary set of characters
```

Method 1 (using IBM-like *Partitioned Enclose*):

```
      bin←~vec∊⎕UCS 13 10               ⇦ Find the non-separator characters
      ⎕ML←3 ⋄ nv←bin⊂vec ⋄ ⎕ML←0        ⇦ Use IBM-like partition (see § I-9.2)
      ⎕←mat←↑nv                         ⇦ Produce the final matrix
```

Method 2 (using `⎕FMT`):

```
      ⎕←mat←⎕FMT vec~⎕UCS 10            ⇦ Remove only LineFeeds
ormer slaves, and sons of former slave-owners will be able
to sit down together at the table of brotherhood.
I have a dream that one day, even the state of Mississippi, a
state sweltering with the heat of injustice, sweltering with the
heat of oppression, will be transformed into an oasis of freedom
and justice.
I have a dream that my four children will one day live in a
nation where they will not be juged by the color of their skin
but by content of their character.
I have a dream tod
```

Of course, the head and tail of the text are truncated in the middle of a word, because we read an arbitrary set of characters.

3.2.5 - Create a File, Fill It with Numbers, and Close It

A native file can be created with the same technique we used for component files. Here we create a file and assign it an arbitrary tie number:

```
      (path,'nums.fun') ⎕NCREATE ¯7
      ⎕NSIZE ¯7
0                                        ⇦ The file is empty, of course
```

Let us append the contents of `Actual`, a numeric matrix that we used earlier in this book.

We do not need to specify which data representation is to be used:, because APL knows the internal representation of the array and will store it with two bytes per number, as we shall see.

```
      ⎕←Actual ⎕NAPPEND ¯7
48                                       ⇦ The position of the last byte written
```

We had a 4 by 6 matrix; each value has been stored in 2 bytes, giving 48 bytes. Note that only the content of the array was written to the file, not any information about its structure, so it looks as if the array was ravelled before if was written to the file.

```
      ⎕NREAD ¯7 163 48
                                         ⇦ Oops! We got no answer! Why?
```

Warning! After any write operation (Append or Replace), the read/write pointer is positioned after the last byte written. A subsequent read operation will start from that point. So, it is recommended that you specify an explicit starting point, as shown below:

```
      ⎕NREAD ¯7 163 48 0
141 188 111 87 82 74 321 306 352 403 497 etc ...
      4 6⍴⎕NREAD ¯7 163 48 0
141 188 111  87  82  74
321 306 352 403 497 507                  ⇦ This is the matrix we wrote.
118 283 397 424 411 409
 43  91 187 306 318 363
```

If we use the wrong conversion code when we read from the file, the result will be wrong.

For example, instead of using 16 bits (2 bytes) per number, we could use 32:

```
      ⎕NREAD ¯7 323 6 0
12320909 5701743 4849746 20054337 26411360 33227249
```

This shows again that the programs that write to and read from a native file must agree on how the data is stored in the file.

We can now untie the native files we created:

```
      ⎕NNUMS,⎕NNAMES
¯1 g:\shared\tests\report.txt
¯2 g:\shared\tests\MLK.txt
¯7 g:\shared\tests\nums.fun
      ⎕NUNTIE ⎕NNUMS
```

3.2.6 - Miscellaneous

Several of the operations that we apply to component files are also available for native files.

`⎕NERASE` Delete a native file, with the same syntax as `⎕FERASE`.

`⎕NRENAME` Rename a native file, with the same syntax as `⎕FRENAME`.

`⎕NRESIZE` Works slightly different from how `⎕FRESIZE` works.
A component file can be resized because some "holes" might have been left in the structure as a result of successive component replacements. This is not the case with a native file, and the behaviour of `⎕NRESIZE` is the following:

The right argument of `⎕NRESIZE` is the file tie number.

The left argument is a single integer value that specifies the new size of the file in bytes. If the new size is smaller than the current file size, the file is truncated. If it is larger than the current file size, the file is extended, and the content of the additional bytes is undefined.

The function returns, as a shy result, the tie number of the resized file.

3.2.7 - Reading From or Writing To Text Files

We would like to draw your attention to Chapter D, Section 6.6, in which you can find references to workspaces containing useful functions to read from or write to text files in various formats.

4 - External Variables

Imagine that you need to update the 5th item of a vector.

If that vector is in memory, you just type: `Vec[5]←13500`

But if it has been stored on a file you need 3 steps:

```
Vec←⎕FRead tie 17
Vec[5]←13500
Vec ⎕FReplace tie 17
```

External variables were invented to work on a file with the same syntax you would use to work on a variable. *External Variables* are specific to Dyalog APL.

One creates such a variable using system function ⎕XT:

fileid ⎕XT *VarName*

- The left argument is any valid unused *fileid*.
  The default extension is DXV (for **D**yalog e**X**ternal **V**ariable).
- The right argument is any valid name.
  This name will be used as an interface between the file and the workspace

Let us try out this interesting feature:

```
      'Cuba' ⎕XT 'Var'
      Var ← (43 52) 'Colette' (1 12 14 10) Girls 93600
```

With those two statements, we have created an *External Variable* (in fact a file) containing 5 items, and now, we can use that file as if it were a simple variable:

Modify the 5th item .... `Var[5]←13500`

Append one item .... `Var←Var,⊂'Venus'`

Ask for its size .... `Shape←⍴Var`

Read the 2nd item .... `Name←2⊃Var`

Delete the 3rd item .... `Var←1 1 0 1 1 1/Var`

Insert two empty items .... `Var←1 1 1 1 0 0 1\Var`

You can check:

```
      Shape
6
      Name
Colette
```

You see that it is possible to compress or expand an *External Variable* in the same way as any variable. That would be impossible with any other type of file, even a component file. In fact, there are no specific restrictions put on the use of external variables. They must just conform to the normal requirements when used as arguments of functions or as arguments of operators.

For example, although a file is normally considered as a linear arrangement of records, an external variable need not be a vector:

```
      'Matrix' ⎕XT 'Mat'
      ⎕← Mat← 2 3⍴ 1 2 3 'One' 'two' 'Three'
   1    2      3
 One  two  Three
      Mat[2;2]←⊂'Two'
      Mat
   1    2      3
 One  Two  Three
```

An external variable occupies very little memory; indeed only the header is stored in memory; the data part is held on external storage. We can demonstrate this by checking the available memory space before and after a modification:

```
      ⎕WA
61986300
      Var←Var,Towns Prod Actual    ⇦ Add three more items
      ⎕WA
61986300                           ⇦ The amount of available memory has not changed
      ⍴Var
9                                  ⇦ But the variable is longer than before
```

The full *Name Class* of an *External Variable* is 2.6:

```
      ⎕NC ⊂'Var'
2.6
```

To close the file, one has only to delete the associated variable: `⎕EX 'Var'`

The next time you need to access the data, just associate a name with it again. It can be a different name; the name is like a tie number: an interface between the workspace and the file:

```
      'Cuba' ⎕XT 'New'
      4⊃New
Suzy
Anna
Jane
```

The file associated with an *External Variable* is normally reserved for exclusive use by its owner. It can be shared by issuing appropriate commands in the *Operating System* environment, or by using the APL function `XVAR` supplied in the workspace: `ws\util.dws`.

Although this is an extremely elegant one it is generally not considered practical for more demanding applications, and especially not in multi-user environments. One reason is that it lacks some of the access control mechanisms that the component file system provides, and another is that the file operations may be very slow. The amazing things you can do with an external variable file may cause a lot of reshuffling of the data in the file.

The Specialist's Section

Each chapter is followed by a "Specialist's Section" like this one.
This section is dedicated to skilled APLers, who wish to improve their knowledge.

If you are exploring APL for the first time,
skip this section and go to the next chapter

Spe-1 Component Files

Spe-1.1 - Loading a Workspace with Files Tied

When a component file is tied, it remains tied even if the user loads another WS, or clears the active WS by issuing a `)CLEAR` command.

This may be used to dynamically `⎕LOAD` successive workspaces, all working on a common set of tied files without untying and then re-tying them.

But if you have made some experiments on a test file and not untied it before you load an application workspace, a conflict might occur between the tie number allocated to your test file and a tie number used in the application. For this reason, we give you two recommendations:

- When an application starts, the first thing it should do is to clean up:
  `⎕FUNTIE ⎕FNUMS ⋄ ⎕NUNTIE ⎕NNUMS`
- When you need to tie a file, instead of specifying an explicit tie number (for example 51), it is better to ask for a free number using a zero tie number:
  `Freenum←` *fileid* `⎕FTIE 0`

Spe-1.2 - Universal Rights

When a component file is enabled for shared use:

- The owner need not be specified in the *Access Control Matrix*. He has universal rights on the file he has created. However, if the owner *is* specified, his rights will be limited to those defined by the matrix.
- A user with an `aplnid` equal to zero (the default value when APL is installed) is not subject to the restrictions declared in the *Access Control Matrix*; this user can do anything.

Spe-1.3 - Dangerous Rights

When granting rights to a component file to other users via its *Access Control Matrix*, the owner of a file must be very cautious. If he grants to another user the rights 4096 and 8192, that user may modify the access matrix in such a way that the original owner can no longer use it. If he grants rights 4 or 128, the user can destroy the file or change its name.

These rights should only be granted if necessary (for maintenance purpose for example).

Spe-1.4 - Rights By Default

The value `¯1` permits all operations. Thus, by subtracting the access codes of operations to be forbidden, it is possible to permit all but certain operations.

For example, to grant all possible rights except 4096 and 8192, one can assign the access code:

```
- 1+4096+8192 ⇨ ¯12289
```

Spc-1.5 - Pass Numbers

The third column of an *Access Control Matrix* may contain *Pass Numbers*. They are used to control the access to that particular file.

Let us suppose that we have specified that in order to read from a given file the pass number 14101952 must be supplied.

We can tell this number to a user, who then can read all components of the file, provided that he specifies the pass number:

Instead of `⎕FREAD 1 25` he must now write `⎕FREAD 1 25 14101952`
Now, let us further suppose that we really would like to restrict the user to only read all the *even* components of the file, but not any of the *odd* ones.

There is no direct support for such fine-grained control in the APL file system. However, it is not very difficult to implement it. Firstly, we will *not* reveal the pass number to the user - we will keep it secret. Secondly, we will write the following function:

```
     ∇ Z←Read(tienum compnum)
         :If 2|compnum
             Z←⎕FREAD tienum,compnum,14101952
         :Else
             Z←'You are not allowed to read odd-numbered components'
         :EndIf
     ∇
```

Thirdly, we will lock the function by `⎕LOCK 'Read'`, so that the user cannot open the function, and therefore he cannot see the pass number either.

With this function, the user can read all even components (for example: `Read 1 26`), but if he tries to read any odd (forbidden) components, he will receive an error message.

With this approach the user cannot use ⎕F*xxx* functions to access the file, because he does not know the *Pass Number*. However, he can use the restricted function we provide.

Spe-1.6 - Buffering Considerations

Operating Systems generally improve the performance of file reads and writes by interposing an in-memory buffer or cache between your program and the disk. Data transferred between your program and the disk typically involves fast in-memory transfer to and from the cache in the first place. The Operating System then manages the synchronisation of data between the cache and the disk independently.

In addition APL has its own internal buffers, so there are two layers of buffers.

This means that when you update a file, part of your data may have been written to disk, and part may still be in memory. If the computer crashes, the update operation has not been completed, and some data may be lost.

Usually you do not need to worry about this, as computers and disks are very reliable. However, if you are writing a lot of important data in a lengthy process you might want to force a flush to disk once in a while.

In code written in versions of Dyalog APL prior to Version 12.0 you may encounter the expression `⎕FUNTIE ⍬`, which instructs APL to flush buffers to disk (in order to prevent damage to the file in the event of a crash). However, this technique is not reliable, and for this reason Version 12.0 introduces optional ***File Journaling***, which slows component file updates down slightly, but causes APL to update files in such a way that the files will not be damaged if APL should be terminated abnormally. Journaling is enabled using `⎕FPROPS`:

```
      ('J' 1) ⎕FPROPS tienumber
```

Even with journaling enabled, there is a slight risk of damage if the operating system or the machine itself crashes with data still in the operating system caches. Version 12.1 will introduce additional optional levels of journaling, which, (at the cost of reducing performance still further) will protect component files from the failure of just about any component other than the disk itself.

Spe-1.7 – File Properties

To control file journaling, a new file system function `⎕FPROPS` was introduced in Version 12.0. This function also makes it possible to query and in some cases set other properties of a component file. There are currently four properties, each identified by a letter.

If the left argument to `⎕FPROPS` is simple, it is a query:

```
      'SEUJ' ⎕FPROPS tienumber
64 0 1 0
```

- `S` (Size) describes the architecture and can be either 64 (for 64-bit files) or 32 (usually older files limited to 4Gb in size).
- `E` is the "Endian-ness"[9]: 0 for files created on little-endian and 1 for big-endian machines. Component files created by Dyalog APL version 11.0 or later may be exchanged and shared between computers of different "endian-ness"; the APL system will automatically perform the necessary conversions.
- `U` is for Unicode and controls whether character data is forced to type 82 (`U`=0) for compatibility with Classic Dyalog APL systems, or written as Unicode (`U`=1).
- `J` controls whether *Journaling* is enabled.

Properties `S` and `E` are read only; once a file has been created, they cannot be altered. Changing the journaling setting requires the file to be exclusively tied.

If you need to share data with old versions of APL, Journaling and Unicode must be switched off. You can set more than one property at a time using name/value pairs:

```
      ('U' 0) ('J' 0) ⎕FPROPS tn
```

Spe-2 Native Files

Spe-2.1 - Internal Representation

Let us tie the little numeric file created in § 3.2.5: `tie←(path,'nums.fun')⎕NTIE 0`

Now, let us read the two first bytes, with two different conversion codes.

Read them as a two-byte integer:	`intg←⎕nread tie 163 1 0`
Read them as 16 bits:	`bits←⎕nread tie  11 2 0`
`intg` is equal to	`141`
`bits` is equal to	`1 0 0 0 1 1 0 1 0 0 0 0 0 0 0 0`

We can retrieve our integer value by decoding these 16 bits in base 2, but on disk, the two bytes are stored with the low order byte first.

[9] "Endian-ness" is also known as "byte order". A "little endian" computer stores a multi-byte value (such as a large integer) with the least significant byte in the lowest memory address. A "big-endian" computer stores the same value reversed, i.e. with the most significant byte in the lowest memory address.

So the operation is:

```
      2⊥8⌽bits
141
```

Conclusion: If you want to interpret a set of bits, it is necessary to know how numeric values are represented on your hardware.

Spe-2.2 - Character Conversions

Character conversion using code 82 during a Read/Write operation uses a ***Translate vector***.

A translate vector is a 256-item vector of integers from 0 to 255. Each item maps the corresponding `⎕AV` position onto an ANSI character code. This mostly concerns the *Classic Edition* of Dyalog APL, but the *Unicode Edition* also supports conversion using code 82 in order to allow the reading of files which have been written by the *Classic Edition*.

For example, to map `⎕AV[17]` onto ANSI letter "a" (code 97), item 17 of the translate vector should be set to 97.

A default mapping is defined by the current output translate table `apltrans\win.dot`, in the Dyalog APL installation folder.

One can query that vector using monadic `⎕NXLATE`:

```
      ⎕nxlate tie
0 8 10 13 32 12 6 7 27 9 11 14 37 39 184 190 95 97 98 etc...
```

One can change the mapping using dyadic form: *NewTranslateVector* `⎕nxlate` *TieNumber*.

Spe-2.3 - Access Control on a Native File

In the right argument of `⎕NTIE`, it is possible to add an optional second item, which controls how the file is accessed.

The access code is the sum of 2 codes. The first code refers to the type of access that you need to the file. The second code refers to the type of access you wish to grant to users who subsequently try to open the file while you have it open.

Rights that **you need**	0	Read access
	1	Write access
	2	Read and Write access
Rights granted to **other users**	0	*Compatibility mode* (see below)
	16	No access (exclusive)
	32	Read access
	48	Write access
	64	Read and Write access

By default, a file is opened in Read and Write access mode. However, a user can open it in Read-only mode (code 0) just to avoid accidental overwriting. He may also decide that during the time he has a full access to that file, he wants to restrict other users to Read-Only access (32).

The Compatibility mode provides compatibility with old MS-DOS programs. It allows any process to open a file any number of times, but once a process has a file open in Compatibility mode no other type of access to the file is possible. It is not recommended that you use this mode.

Spe-2.4 - Lock Access to a File

We have seen that it was possible to control concurrent accesses to a component file by an appropriate use of ⎕FHOLD.

For native files, the problem is not so straightforward. The component file system and the ⎕FHOLD mechanism are controlled completely by the APL system, whereas native files are handled by the Operating System. Operating Systems and their file systems are different. Some only manage a queue, but do not lock Read/Write operations which are not placed in the queue (this is similar to how ⎕FHOLD works). Some others both manage the locks queue and lock Read/Write attempts outside of the queue.

APL provides a function, ⎕NLOCK , that allows the user to lock a range of bytes or the entire file. However, the way that this locking functionality works in detail is determined by the host Operating System. There is no attempt to standardise the functionality across different Operating Systems. Please consult the online help for more information.

The general syntax of ⎕NLOCK is: `{R}←X ⎕NLOCK Y`

The right argument contains 1, 2, or 3 items:

- Tie number
- The offset (from 0) of the first byte of the range to lock. The default value is 0.
- The number of bytes to lock. The default value is the maximum possible file size.

The left argument contains 1 or 2 items:

- The type of restriction: 0 = Unlock
1 = Read lock
2 = Write lock
- Timeout: The number of seconds to wait for the lock to be placed before a TIMEOUT error will be signalled. If not specified the function will wait forever.

The shy result is the value of Y. To unlock the file this value should be subsequently supplied as the right argument: `0 ⎕NLOCK Y`.

Here are some typical cases, applied to a file with tie number equal to `tie`:

```
2 ⎕NLOCK tie                ⇦ Write-lock the entire file
0 ⎕NLOCK tie                ⇦ Unlock the entire file
1 ⎕NLOCK tie                ⇦ Read (share) lock the entire file
0 ⎕NLOCK¨ ⎕NNUMS            ⇦ Unlock all files
1 ⎕NLOCK tie 12 1           ⇦ Read-lock only byte 12
1 ⎕NLOCK tie 0 10           ⇦ Read-lock the first 10 bytes
2 ⎕NLOCK tie 20             ⇦ Write-lock from byte 20 onwards
2 ⎕NLOCK tie 10 8           ⇦ Write-lock 8 bytes from byte 10
0 ⎕NLOCK tie 12 1           ⇦ Remove the lock from byte 12
```

Chapter O: Namespaces

1 - Simple Namespaces

1.1 Introduction

1.1.1 - Definitions

As your workspace grows and you accumulate more functions, variables and operators, choosing names gets more and more difficult, and the likelihood that you will pick a name that you have already used for something else increases. ***Namespaces*** are containers that allow you to organise the names in your workspace into separate compartments, avoid name conflicts and make it easier to find related elements within the workspace:

- A *namespace* can contain variables, functions, operators, and other *namespaces*.
- *Namespaces* can be nested; they are analogous to folders in a file system.
- The workspace itself is considered to be the root of these nested containers; it is represented by the symbol `#`. We say that the symbol `#` represents the *root namespace*.
- Within a *namespace*, the parent of the *namespace* is referred to as `##`.
- From anywhere, any name within any space can be referred to by prefixing it with the names of its parent *namespaces*, separated by dots.
  For example: `#.Utilities.PrintTools.FontsControl`
  Here we refer to the name `FontsControl`, which resides in the namespace `PrintTools`, which is a namespace within the namespace `Utilities`.
- *Namespaces* can be manipulated using system commands, or using system functions.

For example: `UK.CalcTax` and `France.CalcTax` could be two similar functions for use in different circumstances. In this example, `UK` and `France` are two *namespaces* and the dot is used to show that the function `CalcTax` is to be found "inside" the relevant *namepace*.

Namespaces can also be used to permit different items of information to be referred to by name, rather than by indices into an array.

For example, `User` could be a *namespace* containing `User.Forename` and `User.Surname` as an alternative to a 2-item nested vector and the use of `1⊃User` and `2⊃User` to extract the two parts of the name.

A *namespace* is roughly equivalent to what some languages refer to as a "dynamic class" - a class which contains no predefined elements, but allows names to be inserted dynamically. In the next chapter we shall see how we can use other types of classes, such as those which are created by the Graphical User Interface - for example, when you create a dialog box like the one represented below (figure O-1).

Just run the function `CMDesign` included in the associated workspace to obtain it:

Figure O-1

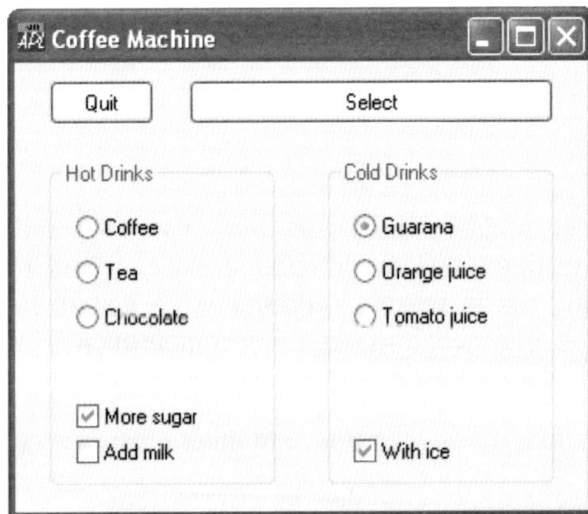

The code in `CMDesign` will be explained in detail in the next chapter. You do not need to know the details in order to experiment with the dialog box in this chapter.

As you will see in the next chapter this dialog box has the name `Drinks`. `Drinks` is the name of a Graphical User Interface element called a *Form*, but it also looks very much like a kind of *namespace* containing the various graphical elements (and anything else that you decide to store in it). It contains two "Groups" for `Hot` and `Cold` drinks. Each of these Groups contains a number of "Buttons", and each Button has several properties. These objects are arranged in a hierarchy which we can "dot" our way into using an expression like for example:

```
      Drinks.Hot.B3.Caption←'Soup'
```

Try it; this will change "Chocolate" into "Soup".

1.1.2 - Create an Empty Namespace

One can create an empty *namespace* using one of three different techniques:

- using the function `⎕NS` with an empty right argument:

```
      Bag ← ⎕NS ''              ⇦ Create an empty namespace
                                  that we can refer to as Bag.
```

As we will see later, the right argument can be used to copy objects into the newly created *namespace*. When the argument is empty the new namespace will also be empty.

- using the system command `)NS` followed by the name of the new namespace:

```
      )NS Box                    ⇦ Create an empty namespace named Box.
#.Box
```

- using the function `⎕FIX` to fix a "Namespace Script", which is a character representation of a namespace and its contents. In this example the script just defines the namespace name, so the new namespace will be empty:

```
      ⎕← ⎕FIX ':Namespace Coco' ':EndNamespace'
#.Coco
```

We can list the *namespaces* that we have just created:

```
      )Obs                          ⇦ We could instead have typed )Objects.
Bag     Box    Coco   Drinks
      ⎕NL 9                         ⇦ Objects (including namespaces)
Bag                                   are in name category 9.
Box
Coco
Drinks
      ⎕NC ↓⎕NL 9                    ⇦ 9.1 for names created by ⎕NS, )NS or ⎕FIX;
9.1 9.1 9.1 9.2                       Drinks is in name category 9.2.
```

1.1.3 - Namespaces without a Name?

A *namespace* does not need to have a name. Of the three examples above, the first one (using `⎕NS`) created an ***unnamed namespace***, while the others created two *named namespaces*. There are no differences between *named* and *unnamed* namespaces, other than the fact that a name was defined or not when the namespace was created.

The name `Bag` in the first example above is *not* the name of the new namespace; it is a *reference* (pointer) to it. You will learn much more about *references* (often abbreviated to *Refs*) later in this chapter.

All namespaces, whether they were named or not, are in fact referred to using *references*. This may be slightly confusing, because it may look as if we use the *name* of a *named namespace* to identify it, but we don't. For example we saw this list above:

```
      )Obs
Bag     Box    Coco   Drinks
```

We might think that this is a list containing one *reference* (`Bag`) and two *names* (`Box` and `Coco`)? In fact, all three are references. But we haven't assigned any *references* to the two named namespaces, as we did in the expression `Bag ← ⎕NS ''`, have we?

Yes we have, but indirectly. When you create a *named namespace* a *reference* having the same name is automatically created. So, `Box` and `Coco` in the list above are really *references* that just happen to have the same names as the namespaces they refer to.

The default display of a namespace (what you see when you type an expression that returns a namespace reference) is the *full pathname* of the namespace, starting with "#", followed by the names of the hierarchy of containing namespaces, and lastly the name given when the namespace was created:

```
      Box
#.Box
      Coco
#.Coco
      Drinks
#.Drinks
```

However, if any namespace in the path is an *unnamed namespace* there is no name to display, so the system just tells you that it is a *namespace* using `[namespace]` in place of its name:

```
      Bag
#.[Namespace]
      ⎕NS ''
#.[Namespace]
```

This difference in the display is the only difference between a named and an unnamed namespace.

Later we will see how the system function `⎕DF` allows us to change the *Display Form* of an object, to output a name or other information that might be useful when inspecting the workspace.

Henceforth, when we in the following refer to the "name of a namespace" we actually mean the name of a *reference* to the namespace.

1.1.4 - Copying Objects to a Namespace

When you create a new namespace using `⎕NS` you can specify a list of object names in the right argument. The named objects will then be **copied** (not moved) into the *namespace* that you are creating. For example, we can simultaneously create a *namespace* and **copy** some variables and functions into it:

```
      Bag ← ⎕NS 'Forecast' 'Chemistry' 'Average' 'Plus'
```

The same technique can be used to copy objects into an existing *namespace*:

```
      'Bag' ⎕NS 'Enlist' 'Prod' 'Boys'
```

The name specified in the left argument must then be the name of (a reference to) an existing namespace.

The right argument can be a simple scalar or vector (to copy a single object), a nested vector as above, or a matrix of names, with one name per row, as shown below.

```
      Copied ← ↑'Money' 'Numbers' 'Root' 'Spin' 'Interlace' 'Words'
      'Box' ⎕NS Copied
```

Let us verify that the objects are still present in the workspace:

```
      ⎕NC Copied
2 2 3 3 3 2
```

More generally, `⎕NS` can be used to copy objects from different *source namespaces* into a given *target namespace*:

'*Target namespace*' ⎕NS *List of objects*

For example:

```
      '#.Compute' ⎕NS '#.Average' '#.Maths.Sqrt' '#.Tools.Stats.Stdev'
```

In this example we copied objects coming from three different *namespaces* into a single target *namespace*. If the target namespace does not already exist it will be created.

1.1.5 - Change Space

One can also "step into" a *namespace* to work in it, and create new variables, functions, etc. To step into a *namespace*, one can:

- Use the system command `)CS` followed by the target *namespace*
  The command will then display the **target** namespace
- Use the system function `⎕CS`, also followed by the target *namespace*
  This function returns the **original** *namespace* as a *Shy* result

Changing space in this way works only if the *namespace* is a direct child of the current *namespace* (or workspace, i.e. the *root* namespace). When this is not the case, one must specify the full path leading to the target *namespace*, starting from the current space or from one of its parents (commonly starting all the way from the root):

For example: `)CS #.Canada.Quebec.Chicoutimi` ⇦ Start from the root
Or: `⎕CS ##.BrotherSpace.CoreSpace` ⇦ Start from a parent
Or: `⎕CS Utils.PrintUtils` ⇦ Dig deeper from this space

Let us step into the namespace `Bag` that we created in the previous section, and list its variables and functions:

```
      ⎕cs Bag
      )Vars
Boys  Chemistry  Forecast  Prod
      )Fns
Average  Enlist  Plus
```

Where am I? The current *namespace* can be identified in various ways:

Using a system command: `)NS` ⇨ `#.Bag`

or using the system function `⎕CS`: `⎕←⎕CS''` ⇨ `#.Bag` (as a character vector)

or using the simplest method: `⎕THIS` ⇨ `#.Bag` (as a *Reference*)

Now we are in `Bag`, and we can create some new variables and functions; they will be strictly local to this *namespace* like the functions and variables that we copied into the namespace:

```
     ∇ r←Useless v                        ⇦ Create a function
[1]    r←v+ιρv
     ∇                                    ⇩ Create variables
      Location ← 'You are in "Bag"'
      ⎕← Compass ← 5 5ρ'  N    ↑  W←o→E  ↓    S  '
  N
  ↑
W←o→E
  ↓
  S
      Integers ← 12 63 54 21
      Useless Integers                    ⇦ Apply the function to the variable just created
13 65 57 25
```

This expression worked perfectly because both `Useless` and `Integers` are present in the current *namespace*. If we try to use objects located in the root, for example `5 Times 6` or `ρGirls`, a `VALUE ERROR` will be generated, as objects in another namespace are not visible from within `Bag`.

1.1.6 - Return To the Root

If we want to return to the root and make it the current namespace:

- We can again use the system function: `⎕CS #`
- or we can use the system command: `)CS #`
- Using the latter we do not need to specify the destination: `)CS`

1.2 Use the Contents of a Namespace

1.2.1 - Using Full Names

Let us return to the root using one of the methods shown above and try to use the function we defined in the Bag namespace:

```
      )cs
#                                    ⇦ We are in the root now.
      Useless 4 3 2 1
VALUE ERROR                          ⇦ The functions in Bag are not visible from here.
      Useless 4 3 2 1                  The same problem would occur with Integers.
      ∧
```

To use objects contained in a *namespace* other than the current one we must specify the full path to where they are defined.

```
      10 Times Bag.Integers          ⇦ Apply a function located in the root (Times) to a
120 630 540 210                        variable located in Bag.
      Bag.Useless 14 23 32 41        ⇦ Apply a function located in Bag to values
15 25 35 45                            defined in the root.
      Box.Spin Bag.Compass           ⇦ Apply a function located in Box to a value
  E                                    located in Bag.
  →
N↑∘↓S
  ←
  W
```

1.2.2 - Performing Operations inside a Namespace

Functions and operators are executed in the context in which they are *defined*, not in the context from where they are *called*. For example, in the statement above Spin was executed in the namespace Box.

This is true for all functions and operators, including *system* and *primitive functions* and *operators*, which are considered to exist in all spaces. For example, one can obtain the names of objects contained in a *namespace* by executing ⎕NL in that *namespace*:

```
      Box.⎕NL 3
Interlace                            ⇦ Functions contained in Box
Root
Spin
```

```
      Bag.⎕NL 3
Average                          ⇦ Functions contained in Bag
Enlist
Plus
Useless
      Box.⎕NL ¯2
 Money    Numbers   Words
      Box.⎕EX 'Words'            ⇦ Destroy a variable in a namespace
```

One can modify an existing variable, or even create a new one by assigning a value to it:

```
      Bag.Integers               ⇦ Its current value
12 63 54 21
      Bag.Integers ×←10          ⇦ Change it using a modified assignment
      Bag.Integers               ⇦ Check
120 630 540 210
      Bag.New ←'Just born'       ⇦ Create a new variable
      Coco.Number ← 5            ⇦ Ditto
```

If a primitive function follows a dot, it is executed inside the *namespace* specified to the left of the dot:

```
      Bag.⍎'Lotion←⌽Location'    ⇦ Execute an expression inside a namespace
      'L' Bag.⎕nl 2
Location
Lotion                           ⇦ A new variable has been created
      Bag.Lotion
"gaB" ni era uoY
      Bag.⎕IO←0
      Bag.⍳ 4
0 1 2 3                          ⇦ Uses the index origin in the Bag namespace
```

Multiple assigment is also possible, providing that the name list is enclosed in parentheses:

```
      Bag.(One Two Three)←1 2 3  ⇦ Create three new variables
```

In addition to using variables and functions that are located in a namespace, it is possible to execute *expressions* within the context of a space by enclosing them in parentheses to the right of a dot:

```
      Bag.(Three+One)            ⇦ Use the variables we assigned above
4
      Bag.(+/One Two Three)
6
```

When properties of a GUI object are assigned new values, the result may have a visible effect:

```
      Drinks.Hot.B3.Caption←'Soup'  ⇦ Change "Chocolate" into "Soup"
      Drinks.Cold.B5.State←0        ⇦ Deselect "With Ice"
```

Figure O-2

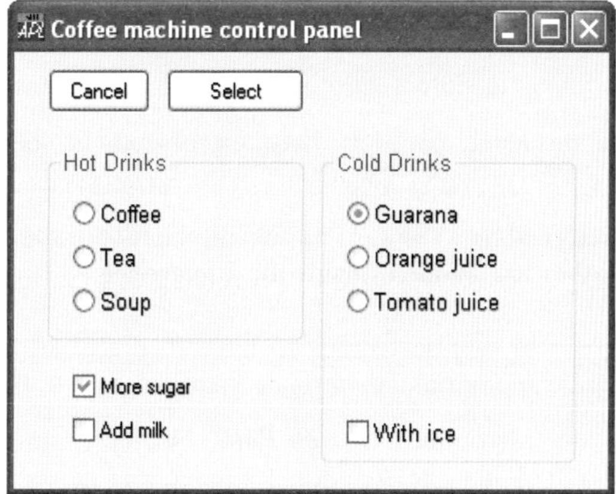

With these two expressions (which we will explain in the next chapter), we have changed the name (*Caption*) of one hot drink, and removed the selection (*State*) of the "With ice" option.

1.2.3 - Change Space

One can also execute one or more statements in a different *namespace* by temporarily stepping into that *namespace*. This can be done in a function:

```
[11]        statements
[12]   Old←⎕CS '#.Util.Print'     ⇦ Step into a target namespace, but keep trace of
[13]                                 the original namespace
[14]
...         statements            ⇦ Execute some statements in the target namespace
[17]
[18]   ⎕CS Old                    ⇦ Return to the initial namespace
[19]        statements
```

In this example, statements 13 to 17 are executed in the namespace `#.Util.Print`.

We shall see later in this chapter that, using the control structure `:With`, one can also step into a specified *namespace* for the duration of the control structure (terminated by `:EndWith`), thus avoiding the repetition of references to an object or *namespace*. This is preferable to using `⎕CS`, because it is not possible to "forget" to change back again, and the automatic indentation of statements within a control structure makes the program more readable. See Section 2.2.3.

1.2.4 - Using a Search Path

It is very convenient to store a set of utility functions in a *namespace*:

- There are no name conflicts between objects in the workspace and objects in the *namespace*; everything is "localised" in the *namespace*.
- The lists returned by `)Vars`, `)Fns`, etc. in the root of the workspace do not show the utility programs; they are "hidden" inside the *namespace*.

However, it may be a little tedious to have to prefix all names of functions residing in a namespace by the appropriate *namespace* identifier, e.g. `#.Util.Print.PrintIt`.

To avoid this, one can define a ***Search Path***, which contains a list of *namespaces* in which the interpreter will look for the function (or operator) names used in APL statements if they cannot be found in the current space. For example:

```
      ⎕PATH←'#.Box  #.Bag'          ⇦ Names are separated by one or more blanks
```

When `⎕PATH` is not empty, and a statement refers to a function or operator which is not present in the current context, APL will search in the namespaces specified in `⎕PATH`, starting with the leftmost one, then in the next one to the right, and so on. If the function (operator) is found somewhere it will be used, else a `VALUE ERROR` message will be issued.

Using the `⎕PATH` defined above we could simplify the expression

```
      Box.Spin Bag.Compass
```

to

```
      Spin Bag.Compass
```

Warning! Only defined functions and operators are located by the namespace search path mechanism; variables are ignored.

Furthermore, when a function has been found by the path mechanism, it is executed in the namespace in which it was found. So, if the function calls other functions or refers to global variables it will use the ones found in its own *namespace*, not the ones found in the calling environment.

To demonstrate this, let us step into `#.Box` and define a function and a global variable:

```
      )CS Box                       ⇦ Step into Box
     ∇ Z←{N}Root Y                  ⇦ Define a function to calculate the Nth root
[1]    :If 0=⎕NC'N'                   of a number
[2]        N←DefaultPower           ⇦ By default, N takes its value from
[3]    :End                           a global variable
[4]    Z←Y*÷N
     ∇
```

```
      DefaultPower←2          ⇦ Set the default value
      )CS                     ⇦ Return to the root space
      DefaultPower←3          ⇦ Define a different default value
      3 Root 64               ⇦ Execution with a left argument
4
      Root 64                 ⇦ When the left argument is missing, the function
8                               looks for DefaultPower in its own
```

namespace,

not in the root namespace.

You can trace the function call, and use `)NS` or `⎕THIS` to verify that execution takes place in `Box`.

Parents list In the search path definition, the special character `↑` represents a search upwards through all parent *namespaces* of the current space, i.e.:

The immediate parent	`##`	
The parent of `##`	`##.##`	
The parent of `##.##`	`##.##.##`	
And so on, up to the root	`#`	(or up to `⎕SE` if it is the top namespace)

Note that `⎕PATH` is a session variable. This means that it survives `)LOAD` and `)CLEAR`. It can, of course, be localised in the header of a defined function or operator.

Advice You can interrupt your study of *namespaces* at this point and skip to the next chapter P, in which you will learn to use *namespaces* in a very intuitive way to build a Graphical User Interface (GUI). After having read this chapter you should be much more familiar with the *namespace* concept, and therefore perhaps better prepared for reading the following sections.

However, the interfaces described in chapter Q, especially the interface with Microsoft Excel, rely on namespaces and namespace *references*, so you will need to return to this chapter and study the rest of it carefully before turning to chapter Q.

2 - More about References

2.1 Namespace References

2.1.1 - Introduction

When working with namespaces, it is important to understand that the name that we might think of as the namespace is in fact only a pointer, or *reference* (***Ref*** in short) to the namespace. After executing the expression:

```
      'Box' ⎕NS ''
```

the name `Box` contains a *reference* to the namespace which was created. In fact, although the *name category* of `'Box'` is 9 to show that it is a reference; `Box` is a scalar:

```
      ρρBox
0
```

As with any other array, we can make a copy of a *ref* using an expression like:

```
      Vuitton ← Bag
```

However, since `Bag` is a *Ref*, the value that gets copied is *only* the pointer: The *namespace* itself is ***not*** copied; we now have two *Refs* pointing to the *same namespace*. If we display `Vuitton` we will see the name that the *namespace* was given when it was created, for example:

```
      Vuitton
#.Bag
```

It is important to realise that there is no difference between `Vuitton` and `Bag`, except that the *Ref* `Bag` happens to have the same name that the namespace was given when it was created. In fact:

```
      Vuitton.Location
You are in "Bag"
      Vuitton ≡ Bag
1
```

When creating a namespace with `⎕FIX`, one can simultaneously give a name to the new namespace and assign the result to a *Ref*:

```
      Souk←⎕FIX ':Namespace Bazaar' ':EndNamespace'
```

In fact, the above statement creates two *Refs* to the same new namespace:

```
      Souk ≡ Bazaar
1
```

Based on our previous experience, the result of passing a *Ref* as an argument to a function can be a bit surprising:

- When a function modifies the argument it received, it just modifies a local copy; the array used as the argument is itself not modified. See what happens with this basic function:

```
      ∇ Mirror text
[1]     text←⌽text          ⇦ The function reverses its argument and displays it
[2]     text
      ∇
       Capital←'Washington'
       Mirror Capital       ⇦ If we apply our function to this variable, the
notgnihsaW                     copy of the argument is reversed.
       Capital              ⇦ The original variable itself is of course
unchanged.
Washington
```

- Let us change our function a little, to make it work on a child of its argument

```
      ∇ Mirror NSRef
[1]     NSRef.Location←⌽NSRef.Location
      ∇
       Vuitton.Location
You are in "Bag"            ⇦ The original value
       Mirror Vuitton
       Vuitton.Location     ⇦ After executing the function on the Ref the array
"gaB" ni era uoY               inside the namespace has been modified
```

  In fact, the namespace itself was never passed to our new function. The *Ref* was passed, and a local copy *was* made of the *Ref*.

  If the function had assigned a new value to `NSRef` itself, this would have overwritten the pointer, but would not have had any effect on the namespace which was referenced by it.

  However, in reality the function only used the *Ref* indirectly, and modified a variable within the referenced space. This actually changed the variable, and the change endures after the local copy of the *Ref* was deleted at the end of executing the function.

  Although this behaviour may at first sight seem counter-intuitive, everything ***is*** in fact working according to the usual rules.

2.1.2 - Distributed Prefix or Suffix

Let's create a couple of similar namespaces to contain data - first for an Italian car:

```
      Italy ← ⎕NS''
      Italy.Name ← 'Luciano'
      Italy.Car ← 'Fiat'
      Italy.Year ← 1997
      Italy.⎕NL 2
Car
Name                                   ⇦ Three variables have been created inside Italy.
Year
```

We can write a function that will work on a *Ref*, and display the information contained inside:

```
     ∇ Z←CarOwner Ref
[1]    Z←Ref.Name,' bought a ',Ref.Car,' in ',⍕Ref.Year
     ∇

      CarOwner Italy                   ⇦ No quotes around Italy, of course
Luciano bought a Fiat in 1997
```

Let us create a similar namespace for Germany: `Germany ← ⎕NS ''`

To initialise its variables we can group the three assignments into a single one, provided we use a common prefix, as if it were "distributed" to each of the variables, like this:

```
      Germany.(Name Car Year)←'Helmut' 'Volkswagen' 2006
      CarOwner Germany
Helmut bought a Volkswagen in 2006
```

In fact it is possible to distribute both a prefix and a suffix:

```
      Italy.(Name Year Car)            ⇦ A single Ref is distributed to 3 variables
 Luciano  1997  Fiat
      (Italy Germany).Car              ⇦ A single variable is distributed to two Refs
 Fiat  Volkswagen
```

Perhaps we can distribute both the *Ref* and the variable names simultaneously?

```
     (Germany Italy).(Name Year Car)
  Helmut  2006  Volkswagen    Luciano  1997  Fiat
```

Note that this works like an *Outer Product*; all *Refs* are combined with all variables.

We can use the same technique inside the `CarOwner` function. Instead of repeating the *Ref* before each variable name, we can distribute it. The new function looks like this:

```
     ∇ Z←CarOwnerDist Ref
[1]    Z←Ref.(Name,' bought a ',Car,' in ',⍕Year)
     ∇
```

```
      CarOwnerDist Italy
Luciano bought a Fiat in 1997
```
⇦ It works perfectly

2.1.3 - Control Structure :With

`:With` is a control structure that may be used to simplify a series of references to an object or *namespace*. `:With` changes into the specified namespace for the duration of the control structure, terminated by `:EndWith`.

We will use this control structure much more in chapter P on Graphical User Interfaces, but we will demonstrate it here by showing a third definition of the `CarOwner` function. Within the scope of the `:With` control structure, we can reference objects in the specified namespace without any further qualification:

```
     ∇ Z←CarOwnerWith Ref ;a;b
[1]     :With Ref
[2]         a←Name,' bought a ',Car,' in ',⍕Year
[3]         b←(⍕Year),' was a good year for ',Car
[4]         Z←↑a b
[3]     :EndWith
     ∇

      CarOwnerWith Germany
Helmut bought a Volkswagen in 2006
2006 was a good year for Volkswagen
```

The use of `:With/:EndWith` is much more pertinent when several statements refer to names in a certain *namespace*.

2.2 Display Form

When one types the name or *Ref* of a *namespace*, the text displayed is called the "***Display Form***" of the namespace. The default display form depends on whether the namespace was named when it was created:

```
      Bag
#.Bag
```
⇦ The *Display form* of a named namespace

```
      Italy Germany
 #.[Namespace]  #.[Namespace]
```
⇦ The *Display form* of two unnamed namespaces

One can change the *Display Form* of a namespace using the system function `⎕DF` inside the namespace, like this:

```
      Bag.⎕DF 'Leather bag'
      Italy.⎕DF ↑'Luciano''s' 'namespace'
```
⇦ Assign a new *Display Form* to our namespaces

```
      Bag
Leather bag
      Vuitton
Leather bag
      Italy
Luciano's
namespace
```

⇦ The new *Display Form* is shown when one types the namespace identifier or a *Ref* to it

⇦ As you can see, a *Display Form* can be any character array (here it is a matrix)

One could be confused and think that `Italy` is a character matrix, but the following tests clearly demonstrate that it is not the case:

```
      ⎕NC 'Italy'                   ⇦ Italy is a Ref
9
      ⍴Italy

      ⍴⍴Italy                       ⇦ A Ref is a scalar
0
      ⍴⍕Italy                       ⇦ Format returns the Display Form
2 9
```

The function `⎕DF` returns as a *Shy* result the **previous** *Display Form* of the object concerned.

3 - Arrays of Refs

3.1 Create an Array

You may construct arrays of *Refs* exactly like you create arrays of other types of scalars, for example using *strand notation*, *Concatenation* (`,`), or *Reshape* (`⍴`).

Let us create a vector of named namespaces:

```
      Sample←Italy Germany          ⇦ Create an array of Refs using strand notation
      ⍴Sample
2
      ⎕NC 'Sample'
2                                   ⇦ Category 9 is only reported for a Ref
      Sample
 Luciano's  #.[Namespace]           ⇦ Italy was assigned its own Display Form,
 namespace                            while Germany has the default display form.
```

This example shows that when you create an array of *Refs* the result is an ordinary array (name category 2). A *Ref* is always a scalar, which can be an item of an array just as numbers and characters. In fact, a *Ref* is a simple scalar, so that an array of *Refs* is a simple array, as the following expression shows:

```
      ≡Sample
1
```

Using *Reshape* to create an array of *Refs* is a bit more complex.

Let us create two vectors of *unnamed* namespaces, using two different statements:

```
      VRef1 ← 3⍴⎕NS''               ⇦ A simple, straightforward statement
      VRef3 ← ⎕NS¨ 3⍴⊂''            ⇦ A different statement using the Each operator
```

In fact, VRef1 and VRef3 are very different: VRef1 contains 3 references to a **single** unnamed namespace. VRef3 contains references to 3 **different** unnamed namespaces

If you take a closer look at the first statement it should not be difficult to understand that VRef1 does not reference three different namespaces. ⎕NS'' was only executed once, so where would the other two namespaces come from?

Let us demonstrate the difference between the two arrays:

```
      VRef3.id←'First' 'Second' 'Third'
      VRef3.id
 First  Second  Third               ⇦ As expected, we have three different namespaces
      VRef1.id←'First' 'Second' 'Third'
      VRef1.id
 Third  Third  Third                ⇦ Three results, but the same namespace
```

Explanation: The three words were assigned to the same variable within the same namespace one after the other, so only the last one remained. Then we display this variable three times, as the three items of VRef1 refer to the same namespace.

If you are not aware of the differences demonstrated above, you may observe unexpected results. However, since many APL primitive functions apply to arrays of *Refs*, we can easily detect that the two arrays are different, for example:

```
      ⍴∪VRef1
1                                   ⇦ Only one unique item
      ⍴∪VRef3
3                                   ⇦ Three different items
      2=/VRef1
1 1                                 ⇦ Adjacent items are identical
      2=/VRef3
0 0                                 ⇦ Adjacent items are not identical
```

3.2 Indexing Arrays of Refs

Arrays of *Refs* are not different from other arrays: They can be indexed using traditional bracket indexing, *Squad*, or *Pick* (or selected using *Take*, *Drop*, *Compress*, etc.). The extracted *Refs* can be used in any statements where a single *Ref* could have been used:

```
      Sample[1].(Year Car)
1997 Fiat
      (2⊃Sample).Car                 ⇦ (2⌷Sample).Car  would work, too
Volkswagen
```

A function can be applied to an array of *Refs*:

```
      ↑ CarOwnerDist Sample          ⇦ The function returns a 2-item nested vector,
Luciano bought a Fiat in 1997          transformed into a matrix using Mix.
Helmut bought a Volkswagen in 2006
      Sample.⎕NL 2                   ⇦ Apply a system function to each namespace
 Car   Car
 Name  Name
 Year  Year
      (Box Bag).⎕NL 3                ⇦ Apply a system function to an implicit
 Interlace  Average                    2-item vector of Refs
 Root       Enlist
 Spin       Plus
 Root       Useless
```

4 - The Session Namespace

⎕SE, the ***Session Namespace***, is a namespace that exists in parallel to the workspace root namespace and its child namespaces. As its name implies, the *Session Namespace* remains unchanged when another workspace is loaded, replacing the active workspace and its namespaces.

In the Dyalog APL ***Explorer*** there are two separate top-level entries: one for the root namespace of the active workspace (represented by #), and one for the *Session Namespace* (represented by ⎕SE).

The *Session Namespace* is an object that can be used to control the appearance and behaviour of the APL session. It makes it possible to add, modify, and remove menus, menu items, and toolbar buttons of the APL session window itself, i.e. the development environment.

As with any namespace it is possible to store functions in the ⎕SE namespace. Since the ⎕SE namespace "survives" the loading of another workspace it may be very convenient to store frequently used utility functions in it.

This is especially useful when used together with an appropriate ⎕PATH setting. As mentioned earlier, ⎕PATH is a session variable. So, if you include ⎕SE in ⎕PATH, then your utility functions will be readily available in all workspaces.

The ⎕SE namespace can be saved using the menu items Session ⇨ Save as or Session ⇨ Save.

Most of the things you can do with namespaces in general also apply to the *Session Namespace*.

For example, you can change its *Display Form*:

```
      ⎕SE
⎕SE                                ⇦ This is the default Display Form of ⎕SE
```

Let us change it:

```
      ⎕SE.⎕DF 'Production environment/April 2009'
      ⎕SE
Production environment/April 2009
      ⎕SE.⎕DF ⎕NULL                ⇦ This will restore the default display form
      ⎕SE
⎕SE                                ⇦ Back to the default
```

Changing the display form may be convenient if you are working with more than one APL session at a time, as it makes it easy to identify which session window is which.

Beware: The *Session Namespace* must remain independent of the active workspace, since workspaces and session namespaces are saved separately. If you create a *Ref* which crosses the boundary between the workspace and the *Session Namespace* you will not be able to save the active workspace:

```
      Session←⎕SE
      )save c:\temp\myws
Cannot perform operation when session namespace is referenced by #.
#...Session
```

And now, what kind of APLer are you?

APL King

The Specialist's Section

Each chapter is followed by a "Specialist's Section" like this one.
This section is dedicated to skilled APLers, who wish to improve their knowledge.

If you are exploring APL for the first time,
skip this section and go to the next chapter

Spe - 1 The Dot as a Syntactic Element

The interpreter can distinguish between a dot used as a namespace separator and a dot used as the *Inner Product* operator, because the symbol immediately to the left of the dot is a *Ref* (category 9) when the dot is used as a namespace separator, and a function (category 3) when the dot is used as part of an inner product.

Consider for example this expression:

```
      1 2 and.equal 1 2
1
```

Is this an *Inner Product*, or a call to a dyadic function `equal` in the namespace `and`?

We cannot tell without knowing the *Name Category* of `and`. Let us first create a namespace `and`, define a function `equal` in it, and execute the expression above:

```
      and←⎕ns''
      and.⎕vr'equal'
     ∇ z←y equal x
[1]    z←y≡x
     ∇
      1 2 and.equal 1 2
1
```

Instead we could have defined these two functions and exccuted the same expression above:

```
      ⎕vr'and'
     ∇ z←y and x
[1]    z←y∧x
     ∇
      ⎕vr'equal'
     ∇ z←y equal x
[1]    z←y=x
     ∇
      1 2 and.equal 1 2
1
```

This example shows that in a dynamic, not typed, and interpreted language like APL it is in general not possible to fully analyse an expression unless you know the categories of the names involved.

Usually you will know the categories of the names that appear in your APL code, simply because you defined the functions, operators, namespaces, etc. yourself.

However, APL is so dynamic that it is possible to have an expression like the one above in a function, and not know in advance whether the name `and` denotes a function or a namespace. Moreover, it may be different from one time the function is called to the next, or even from one time the function line is executed to the next, if it is part of a loop. This means that the final analysis of an APL expression cannot take place until run-time, during each execution of the expression itself.

Spe - 2 State Indicators

During the debugging of an application it is important to know not only which functions are pending, but also where they are located (remember, functions in different namespaces may share the same name), and from which namespace they were called.

This is why Dyalog APL includes two extra system functions in addition to the familiar `⎕SI` *State Indicator*:

`⎕XSI` (*eXtended State Indicator*) reports *where* each function on the stack is *located*

`⎕NSI` (*NameSpace Indicator)* reports *from where* each function on the stack has been *called*:

Refer to: Chapter E, Specialist's Section, Section Spe-3.

Spe - 3 Evaluation of Statements

Spe-3.1 - Execution Protocol

When the interpreter executes an expression that refers to a *namespace* the execution includes the following steps:

- Switch into the namespace
- Evaluate the name in this namespace
- Switch back to the original namespace

For example: Suppose that the current namespace is `#.Current`, and we try to execute the following statement:

```
Res ← Tools.Print.SetFont Default
```

The interpreter will evaluate it in the following way:

1. Evaluate `Default` in the current namespace (`#.Current`) to establish the argument to the function.
2. Switch to namespace `Tools` (a child of `#.Current`) and evaluate the name `Print`.
3. Switch to namespace `Print` (a child of `#.Current.Tools`).
4. Call function `SetFont` in namespace `#.Current.Tools.Print` with the value found in the first step.
5. Upon completion switch back to namespace `#.Current`.
6. Assign the result to variable `Res` in namespace `#.Current`.

Spe-3.2 - Distribution Rules

An array of namespace references (*Refs*) to the left of a dot '`.`' is distributed according to the following rule, where `R1` and `R2` are *Refs*, and `Exp` is an arbitrary expression:

```
(R1 R2).Exp ⇔ (R1.Exp)(R2.Exp)
```

For example:

```
      (Germany Italy).(2008-Year)
2 11
```

If `Exp` is a function, the items of its argument(s) are distributed to each *Ref* as follows:

- Monadic `(R1 R2).Func v3 v4` ⇔ `(R1.Func v3)(R2.Func v4)`
- Dyadic `v1 v2 (R1 R2).Func v3 v4` ⇔ `(v1 R1.Func v3)(v2 R2.Func v4)`

For example: `(Bag Box).⎕NL 3 2` is equivalent to `(Bag.⎕NL 3)(Box.⎕NL 2)`

This is fully in line with the usual shape compatibility rules for scalar functions, so that scalar extension works as usual:

```
(R1 R2).Func v5 ⇔ (R1.Func v5)(R2.Func v5)
```

Likewise, a `LENGTH ERROR` will be reported if the length of the list of namespace *Refs* is different from the length of the argument vector(s), and none of them are singletons (i.e. arrays with a single item).

An array of *Refs* to the left of an assignment arrow is expanded like this:

```
(R1 R2).Exp ← v1 v2 ⇔ (R1.Exp ← v1)(R2.Exp ← v2)
```

Spe - 4 The Dyalog Workspace Explorer

The Workspace Explorer offers two top-level entries (look in the leftmost column):

- One for the root namespace of the active workspace, represented by .... #
- One for the session namespace, represented by .... ⎕SE

The root namespace itself may contain three types of entries:

- One for the functions and operators located in the root namespace............ [Fns/Ops]
- One for the variables located in the root namespace.................................... [Vars]
- One for each of the namespace children of the root namespace.

The hierarchy of namespaces may be explored to any depth.

Figure O-3

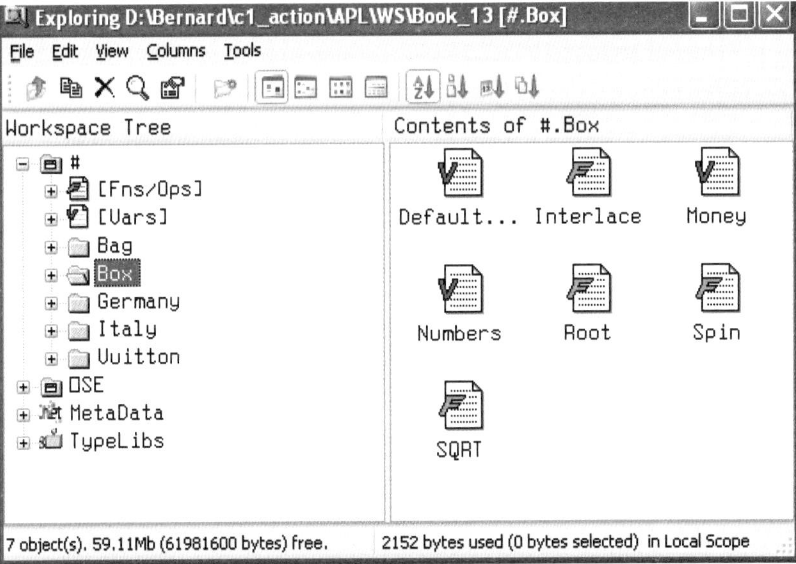

Here, we have selected `#.Box` on the left, and we can see on the right what it contains.

Spe - 5 Control of Exported Functions

In section 1.2.4 we supposed that all functions contained in the namespaces specified in the search path were visible. This is the default behaviour.

However, it may be desirable to designate certain functions (or operators) as private to a namespace, so that they are not readily visible to and callable from other namespaces through the namespace search path mechanism.

For example, the "public" functions in the namespace may use a number of private sub-functions that are not designed to be called from outside the namespace.

This can be accomplished using the system function `⎕EXPORT`.

The general syntax is: `{R}←{X} ⎕EXPORT Y`

- The right argument `Y` is a character scalar, vector, or matrix, or a vector of enclosed character vectors, representing the name(s) of the functions and operators whose export status is to be queried (monadic use) or set (dyadic use).
- The left argument `X` is a Boolean scalar (applies to all names in `Y`) or vector (one item per name in `Y`) specifying the export status of each of the functions or operators, with the following convention:

  0 This function/operator cannot be exported (hidden from `⎕PATH`).

  1 This function/operator can be exported (visible).
  This is the default value.

- Since functions and operators by default are visible it suffices to specify the list of functions and operators that should not be exported.
- The result (*Shy* in the dyadic use) reports the current export status of the names specified in `Y`.
- `⎕EXPORT` only affects the namespace search path mechanism. A function or operator that has been declared invisible using `⎕EXPORT` may still be called using its fully specified name. If you want to prevent "private" functions from being called, you need to define a *Class*, which is a part of the Object Oriented Programming extensions to Dyalog APL. For more information please consult other literature from Dyalog Ltd., as Object Oriented Programming is not covered by this tutorial.

It may be important to hide sub-functions that should not be visible through the namespace search path, as the following example shows.

Let us suppose that we have the following set of *namespaces*:

`#.Utils`	Contains a function `PrintMe`, which calls a sub-function `SetCoords`, also located in this namespace.

`#.PrintFuns`	Contains a function `SetCoords`, which is a different function than the one located in `#.Utils`, and which is designed to be called from outside of this namespace.
Root (#)	Contains a function named `Main`, which needs to call the `SetCoords` function that is located in `#.PrintFuns`.

A search path has been defined like this: `⎕PATH ← '#.Utils  #.PrintFuns'`

When `Main` is executing and it calls `SetCoords` the interpreter will first search for `SetCoords` in the root namespace. Since there is no such function in the root namespace, it will search for the function in `#.Utils`, as this is the first namespace listed in `⎕PATH`.

- By default `Utils.SetCoords` is visible and will therefore be called by `Main`, though it is not the intended function (it is a sub-function to `PrintMe`).
- In order to avoid this unfortunate behaviour `Utils.SetCoords` should be declared invisible to the search path mechanism (`0 ⎕EXPORT 'Utils.SetCoords'`). Then this function will be ignored during the search, and the search will instead continue with the next namespace specified in `⎕PATH`. This is `#.PrintFuns`, in which the proper `SetCoords` function will be found and called.

Spe - 6 Retrieving a Namespace Source

When a namespace has been created by `⎕FIX`, it is possible to retrieve the source script that was used to create it:

```
      DISPLAY Code←⎕SRC Coco
┌→──────────────────────......──────────────────┐
│ ┌→──────────────────┐ ┌→──────┐ ┌→────────────┐ │
│ │:namespace Coco    │ │ etc.  │ │:endnamespace│ │
│ └───────────────────┘ └───────┘ └─────────────┘ │
└∊──────────────────────......──────────────────┘
```

If the namespace is erased it can be reconstructed using the source code:

```
      )erase Coco                      ⇦ Erase the Namespace
      ⎕FIX Code                        ⇦ Restore it
      )obs
Coco                                   ⇦ All is well
```

If `⎕SRC` is applied to a non scripted namespace a `NONCE ERROR` will be reported.

Chapter P: Graphical User Interface

Dyalog APL includes a cleverly designed interface with Windows (or with similar functionalities emulated under Unix) to develop ***Graphical User Interfaces***, or ***GUIs*** in short.

A complete description of this interface is beyond the scope of this tutorial, so we decided to teach you some basic concepts and methods, so that you can quickly become autonomous. You will then be able to develop small applications and improve your knowledge on your own.

1 - Guidelines

1.1 Terminology and Options

The GUI interface can be manipulated using two different methodologies:

- One is consistent with the Object Oriented (OO) model that is employed by other modern computer programming languages. When this approach is adopted GUI components are manipulated using the same "dot-notation" as we use to work with namespaces, as shown in Chapter O. It requires very strict observance to a rigorous syntax, and is perhaps a bit discouraging for a beginner (unless you are already accustomed to Object Oriented design and development).
- The second approach is also based on a set of GUI "objects", but uses a set of functions very specific to Dyalog APL, which were originally designed to facilitate the use of the Graphical User Interface by non specialists. This is the original Dyalog APL GUI interface. The syntax of the Dyalog system functions is significantly more tolerant than the OO model and is easier to use while learning the ropes. The object oriented features are in fact an extension of this.

Within certain restrictions it is possible to mix the two GUI notations, although it is generally not recommended to do so. In this tutorial we will mostly use the original GUI interface, but we will also show examples of using namespace (*dot*) notation.

1.1.1 - GUI Objects

A Graphical User Interface consists of forms containing buttons, fields, lists of values, scroll bars, and so on. All these components will be called *Objects*, although user interface elements are sometimes referred to as *Controls*.

Let us again take a look at this dialog box, which we met in the previous chapter:

Figure P-1

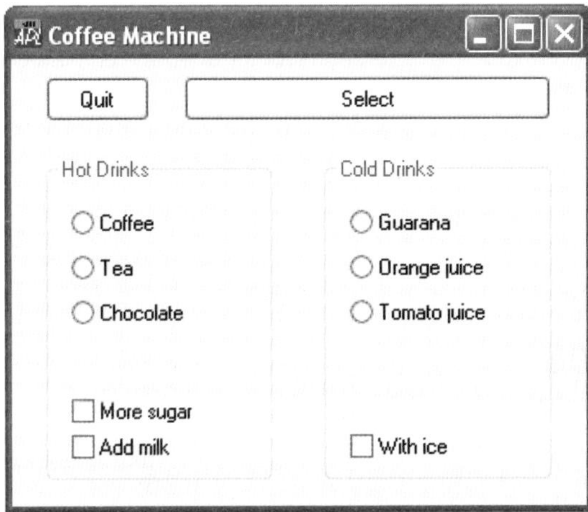

As mentioned in the previous chapter, the different parts of this dialog box can be considered as embedded namespaces (although the GUI objects are special namespaces, which contain elements not written in APL):

- At the lowest level we have, for example, a *Radio Button* labelled "Guarana"
- This button is contained in a *Group* called "Cold Drinks"
- That group is contained in a *Form* entitled "Coffee Machine"
- The form itself is child of a general *Root* object, common to all GUI objects.

The ***Root object*** can be represented by a simple dot `'.'` or by a hash `'#'`. The two names are synonymous, but while `'.'` was used in the original Dyalog APL GUI implementation, `'#'` was added later to provide compatibility with the namespace concept, and may be used even when programming with the original GUI interface. In this book we will use `'#'` as the root object identifier.

1.1.2 - Properties

Objects have various characteristics like colour, position within the parent object, size, character font, and so on. These characteristics are called ***Properties***.

A complete list of all objects and their properties may be found in the reference manual and in the on-line help.

- Some properties *must* be specified when an object is created, while others may be allowed to take default values.
- Most properties can be changed (set) after an object has been created, but some properties may only be set when the object is created, and cannot be changed afterwards.

Each property is specified by a ***Keyword*** (its name) followed by its value.

For example:

Keyword	Value	
'Posn'	(10 10)	specifies the position of an object within its parent
'Size'	(20 50)	specifies its size
'FCol'	(0 0 192)	is a Foreground Colour (for example, the colour of a text)
'Font'	('Arial' 16)	specifies the font used to display a text

When a series of properties is specified, the keyword/value pairs are organised in a nested vector, so that each property specification appears as a scalar:

```
('Posn'(10 10)) ('Size'(20 50)) ('FCol'(0 0 192)) ('Font'('Arial' 16))
```

1.1.3 - Four Basic Functions

Only four functions are needed to create and modify GUI objects, and to query information about them:

⎕WC	(*Window Create*)	To create objects and specify their properties
⎕WS	(*Window Set*)	To modify properties of an object, or to specify additional ones
⎕WG	(*Window Get*)	To read the values of properties
⎕WN	(*Window Names*)	To obtain the names of child objects

The name of the object to work on is specified as the left argument to the first three functions, and as the right argument to ⎕WN.

Warning! With this original GUI interface keywords may be typed loosely using any mixture of lower-case or upper-case letters.
However, properties may also be set or queried using the newer namespace syntax.
Using this syntax the spelling, including the case, of each word must be respected.
Consider, for example, how we modified our little dialog box in the previous chapter:

```
Drinks.Hot.B3.Caption←'Soup'
Drinks.Cold.B4.State←0
```

The words `Caption` and `State` must be typed in lower-case, with an upper-case first letter. If this is not respected, these statements will uselessly create **variables** named for example `caption` or `STATE` in the corresponding namespaces, and nothing will happen in the GUI.

Using the original GUI interface the two statements *could* have been written as follows:

```
'Drinks.Hot.B3' ⎕WS 'caption' 'Soup'
'Drinks.Cold.B4' ⎕WS 'STATE' 0
```

However, it is strongly recommended that you observe the same convention as used in the namespace syntax when using the four functions listed above.

1.1.4 - Coordinate Systems

Some properties of the *Root* object will be inherited by its children, unless explicitly modified. Among these inherited properties are those that specify the coordinate system.

When an object is created its position and size can be defined in three different ways:

- As a percentage of the parent object's size; the screen being the topmost parent object. This is the default.
- In pixels. This is probably the most common setting, even if it is not the default setting.
- In a user-defined coordinate system.

Except for very specific uses (graphics or printouts), the most convenient coordinates are pixels.

Positions and sizes are always measured from the top-left corner of the parent object (the screen itself for a form), and vertical values are given first, then horizontal values.

We recommend that you immediately set the coordinate system at the highest level (the Root), so that, by inheritance, all objects will be measured in pixels. This property will be saved with your workspace. However, when it comes to programming real applications it is still safer to set the appropriate coordinate system as a part of the general initialization of the application.

To set the root object's coordinate system to be measured in pixels, execute this:

```
      '#' ⎕WS 'Coord' 'Pixel'
or    '#' ⎕WS ⊂('Coord' 'Pixel')
```

The right argument is a property composed of a keyword (`'Coord'`) and its value (`'Pixel'`).

We said that each property specification should be entered as a scalar, so to be completely rigorous, the expression requires an *Enclose* symbol as shown in the second example. However, the interface is tolerant and accepts a single property to be specified as a vector.

1.2 Create a Simple Dialog Box

1.2.1 - Create and Modify an Object

An object is created using the function ⎕WC (for *Window Create*), with the following syntax:

Object ⎕WC *Properties*

- The left argument is the name of the new object
- The right argument is a nested vector, each item of which specifies one of the characteristics (*Properties*) of the object.

For example, to define the dialog box shown in Figure P1, we could start like this:

First, to create the form, we can specify:	Keywords	Values
• the type of object to create	`'Type'`	`'Form'`
• its title, or caption..	`'Caption'`	`'Coffee Machine'`
• its position on the screen	`'Posn'`	`(50 100)`
• its size..	`'Size'`	`(250 330)`

1.2.2 - A Simplified Notation

Writing all the stuff needed to create the form on a single line would lead to a very long statement.

Fortunately the Dyalog GUI interface is rather tolerant, and we can simplify the statement:

- When keywords are omitted the interface assigns the property values to the properties according to a predefined order of properties, specified in the documentation. You just need to remember that for most of the objects we shall use, the first four properties are the same: `Type-Caption-Posn-Size`
- The interface accepts a simplified way of writing properties and values:
  the expression .... `('Size' (250 330))`
  can be simplified to .... `('Size' 250 330)`

Using these simplifications we can write:

```
'Drinks'⎕WC'Form' 'Coffee Machine' (50 100) (250 330)
```

Just type and execute this expression, and you will immediately see the form on your screen.

The top left corner of the working area of the form (the white surface) will be positioned at 50 pixels from the top of the screen, and at 100 pixels from its left border.

1.2.3 - When Keywords are Mandatory

If its position is not specified an object is centred within its parent object.

If its size is not specified an object's dimensions are half of the parent's dimensions.

Suppose we do not specify the position, the statement becomes:

```
      'Drinks'⎕WC'Form' 'Coffee Machine' (250 330)
```

But because we did not specify any keywords APL assumes that the third value (250 330) refers to the third property (Posn), so we would see a form positioned at (250 330), with default dimensions equal to half of the screen dimensions. This is not at all what we wanted to obtain.

So, we must use the keyword 'Size' to specify that (250 330) is not the position, but the size:

```
      'Drinks'⎕WC'Form' 'Coffee Machine' ('Size' 250 330)
```

If you execute this expression, the form will be created again, and placed at the centre of your screen.

Each time an object is redefined the old version is discarded, and the new one is created.

1.2.4 - Buttons and Groups

Let us place the first button in our form. Since the button will be a child of the form, it will become a sub-namespace, so its name must be prefixed by its parent's name. For example 'Drinks.bout'. The parameters will be very similar to those that we saw for the form itself:

- The type of the object .... 'Type' 'Button'
- Its caption.. 'Caption' 'Quit'
- Its position within the form....................... 'Posn' (10 20)
- Its size (in pixels).................................... 'Size' (25 60)

Here again, we shall use the simplified form of expression, and add a second and a third button:

```
      'Drinks.bout' ⎕WC 'Button' 'Quit'   (10 20)  (25 60)
      'Drinks.bsel' ⎕WC 'Button' 'Select' (10 100) (25 210)
```

These two buttons are "Push buttons", which is the default. We will see different types of buttons later.

Groups are containers in which one can place other objects. Let us define two groups. You are now familiar with the meaning of the parameters:

```
      'Drinks.Hot'  ⎕WC 'Group' 'Hot Drinks'  (55 20)  (180 130)
      'Drinks.Cold' ⎕WC 'Group' 'Cold Drinks' (55 180) (180 130)
```

Then we can fill these groups with buttons to allow the user to choose the drinks. For exclusive choices we use "Radio" buttons. The type of button is specified by the "Style" property, and for "Radio" (and" Check") buttons it is generally appropriate to use the default size:

```
'Drinks.Hot.B1' ⎕WC 'Button' 'Coffee'    (25 15)('Style' 'Radio')
'Drinks.Hot.B2' ⎕WC 'Button' 'Tea'       (50 15)('Style' 'Radio')
'Drinks.Hot.B3' ⎕WC 'Button' 'Chocolate' (75 15)('Style' 'Radio')
```

Let us now add non-exclusive options, like adding sugar, milk, or ice. This is achieved by using "Check" buttons:

```
'Drinks.Hot.B4' ⎕WC 'Button' 'More sugar'(130 15)('Style' 'Check')
'Drinks.Hot.B5' ⎕WC 'Button' 'Add milk'  (150 15)('Style' 'Check')
```

Only one of the radio buttons within the same parent object may be selected at any one time. So you can select "Guarana", "Orange juice", or "Tomato juice", for example, but not two or three of them, because they are in the same group.

The check buttons are independent. You can select/unselect "With ice" without any influence on your drink choice because it is not a radio button, but a check button.

Of course, you can select "Chocolate" and "Tomato juice" simultaneously, because they are in two different parents. Ugh! I can't even imagine that combination, especially with added milk.

Let us stop here! These definitions are much too verbose; we will soon show a different and simpler way of programming the dialog box definition.

1.2.5 - Let Us Simplify Further

Firstly, we can create variables containing repeated parameters like ('Style' 'Check'). Secondly, we can use the control structure :With, which was introduced in the previous chapter.

Each call to ⎕WC returns the name of the object it creates as a shy result. This name is used by the control structure :With. Objects created by the subsequent statements are considered as children of the namespace just created:

```
[4]    :With 'Drinks' ⎕WC 'Form'   ...
[5]        'bout' ⎕WC 'Button'     ...
```

is equivalent to:

```
[4]    'Drinks' ⎕WC 'Form'          ...
[5]    'Drinks.bout' ⎕WC 'Button' ...
```

Here is the function we could write using these techniques (you don't have to type it; it is provided in the accompanying workspace):

```
     ∇ CMDesign;Check;Radio
[1]    Check←'Style' 'Check'
[2]    Radio←'Style' 'Radio'
[3]    :With 'Drinks'⎕WC'Form' 'Coffee Machine'('Size' 250 330)
[4]        'bout'⎕WC'Button' 'Quit'(10 20)(25 60)
[5]        'bsel'⎕WC'Button' 'Select'(10 100)(25 210)
[6]        :With 'Hot'⎕WC'Group' 'Hot Drinks'(55 20)(180 130)
[7]            'B1'⎕WC'Button' 'Coffee'(25 15)Radio
[8]            'B2'⎕WC'Button' 'Tea'(50 15)Radio
[9]            'B3'⎕WC'Button' 'Chocolate'(75 15)Radio
[10]           'B4'⎕WC'Button' 'More sugar'(130 15)Check
[11]           'B5'⎕WC'Button' 'Add milk'(150 15)Check
[12]       :EndWith
[13]       :With 'Cold'⎕WC'Group' 'Cold Drinks'(55 180)(180 130)
[14]           'B1'⎕WC'Button' 'Guarana'(25 15)Radio
[15]           'B2'⎕WC'Button' 'Orange juice'(50 15)Radio
[16]           'B3'⎕WC'Button' 'Tomato juice'(75 15)Radio
[17]           'B4'⎕WC'Button' 'With ice'(150 15)Check
[18]       :EndWith
[19]   :EndWith
     ∇
```

1.3 Get Information

Run the function shown above to create the simple "Coffee Machine" dialog box. However, if you have not already done so, you should first execute `'#' ⎕WS 'Coord' 'Pixel'` - otherwise the dialog box will not have the correct size, and it may not be visible.

Select some options in it: for example Tea with extra Sugar, and Iced Guarana.

Now, let us try to determine which buttons you selected. This can be done using two different techniques:

- You can use `⎕WG` to "get" the value of the property `'State'` for each of the buttons. This is the method provided by original Dyalog GUI interface.
- You can use *Namespace* notation to query the value of the property.

For example, to obtain the state (selected or not) of the "Coffee" button, one can use either of the following two methods:

```
      'Drinks.Hot.B1' ⎕WG 'State'
0                                       ⇦ Coffee was not selected
      Drinks.Hot.B1.State
0
```

Now, let us try to determine the state of all the five buttons located in the "`Hot`" group.

We can first ask for the names of objects contained in "`Hot`" like this:

```
      ⍴children←⎕WN 'Drinks.Hot'
5                                          ⇦ It is a nested vector
```

We could have obtained the same result like this:

```
      children←Drinks.Hot.⎕NL ¯9
      ↑children
Drinks.Hot.B1                              ⇦ It contains the names of the children
Drinks.Hot.B2
Drinks.Hot.B3
Drinks.Hot.B4
Drinks.Hot.B5
      children ⎕WG¨⊂'State'                ⇦ We can apply ⎕WG'State' to each of the
0 1 0 1 0                                     child objects
```

This means that we had chosen tea with additional sugar.

Using the namespace notation we can obtain the same result as follows:

```
      Drinks.Hot.(B1 B2 B3 B4 B5).State
0 1 0 1 0
```

1.4 Changing Properties

With techniques similar to the ones we used above we can change one or more properties of an object. For example, let us deselect "Tea", and select "Chocolate" instead, using the two possible methods:

```
      'Drinks.Hot.B2' ⎕WS 'State' 0
      Drinks.Hot.B3.State←1
```

As you can see, the expression using namespace notation and assignment is often easier and shorter to write.

1.5 Make It Work

1.5.1 - Some Experiments

If you have run the function `CMDesign` shown above you have now created the dialog box "Coffee Machine".

It is a GUI namespace, as you can see using `⎕NC`:

```
      ⎕NC ⊂'Drinks'
9.2
```

⇦ Remember that namespaces created using `⎕NS` have a *Name Category* equal to 9.1.

We now have to solve two problems with this dialog box:

- It is always visible. To remove it, you must close it.
- It is inactive. Nothing happens when we press the "Cancel" or "Select" buttons.

The first thing we can do is to localise `Drinks` in the function, or in a calling function.

Let us choose the second solution, as it is often useful to separate the *definition* of a form from the code handling the *interaction* with the form:

```
     ∇ CMUse;Drinks
[1]    CMDesign
     ∇
      ⎕EX 'Drinks'
      CMUse
```

⇦ Erase the global form

⇦ Nothing happens; the form does not appear!

`CMUse` creates the dialog box as expected (just trace the function call if you wish to verify it), but as soon as we exit from the function `Drinks` is erased, like any other local object. We must therefore find a way of making the form interact with the user before it gets closed.

1.5.2 - The Windows Event Queue

When one or more dialog boxes are active a user can perform some actions, like moving the mouse, selecting a button, typing data in an input field, moving a scroll bar, closing a dialog box, and so on. These actions cause ***Events***. In order to be processed one after the other, events are placed into a ***queue***, together with the appropriate information about what happened, such as the cursor position, the button clicked, the key pressed, etc.

There are actually two event queues involved, one managed by the Operating System and one managed by APL itself. The user may begin to enter data into the APL application, and then switch to another program to send an e-mail, come back to the APL application again, and then make a calculation in an Excel worksheet, or even in a different APL dialog box created by a different application.

Dyalog APL events are processed using the function `⎕DQ`.

⎕DQ must be followed by the name of the object (or objects) about which we feel concerned. If followed by '#' (*Root*) events from all forms and dialog boxes created in this APL session will be handled.

While ⎕DQ is executing the APL session is temporarily disabled, and the focus is given to the object(s) listed in the argument. Let us try this modification to the CMUse function:

```
     ∇ CMUse;Drinks
[1]    CMDesign
[2]    ⎕DQ'Drinks'                    ⇦ Activate the dialog box
     ∇
      CMUse                           ⇦ Run the function
```

The dialog box is now displayed, and you can check that if you type something in the APL session, your keystrokes are ignored. ⎕DQ behaves like a sub function, and takes control of all user-interaction, until a specific *Event* returns control to the calling APL function. For the moment, the only thing you can do is to close the dialog box by a click in its upper-right corner (or by pressing *Alt-F4* on the keyboard).

2 - Call-Back Functions

2.1 Discovery

2.1.1 - Theory

To make our application responsive we need to specify that certain *Events* should trigger some specific actions, which in general means calling APL functions. Such functions are called ***Call-Back functions***, because ⎕DQ, which has been called by the application, is calling back to the application to have it process the events.

In Dyalog APL, an *Event* is identified either by a character keyword or by a numeric code. A programmer can use either the code or the keyword, but we recommend the use of keywords, except for user-defined *Events*, which may be specified only by a number.

Action	Keyword	Code
Pressing a key on the keyboard	KeyPress	22
Moving the mouse	MouseMove	3
Selecting a button in a dialog box	Select	30

… and so on (the full list is available in the on-line help)

The `Event` property may be thought of as a vector containing as many items as there are types of event that can be generated by the object in question. A *Call-back Function* is associated with a particular type of event by setting the corresponding item of the `'Event'` property, identified by an event keyword (or code), to the name of the function.

`('Event' 'Select' 'Control')` ⇦ Would call the function named `Control` if the given object is selected.

`('Event' 'KeyPress' 'UpperCase')` ⇦ Would call the function named `UpperCase` each time a key is pressed.

Setting the `'Event'` property can be done at creation time via `⎕WC`, or added later via `⎕WS`. The original GUI implementation used only event codes (e.g. `22`), but since names were introduced it is recommended that you use these (eg. `KeyPress`) for readability.

For a given object, several events can trigger the same call-back function, or different events can trigger different functions:

`('Event'` *(Event1 Event2 Event3)* `'CallBack')`

`('Event'` *(Event1* `'CallBack1')` *(Event2* `'CallBack2')` *(Event3* `'CallBack3'))`

Call-Back functions are ordinary APL functions and can therefore do whatever is necessary, such as query information on the different objects, change properties, delete objects, create new forms or objects, print results, and so on.

2.1.2 - Specific Actions

Usually *Events* trigger *Call-Back* functions, but they can also be associated with one of two specific actions represented by the values `¯1` and `1`:

- ¯1 means: Ignore this *Event* as if it did not happen.
  This can be used to protect an application from undesirable actions.
- 1 means: Leave the control of `⎕DQ` and return to normal APL execution flow.
  This is the normal way to exit from the control of `⎕DQ`.

2.1.3 - Example

Let us decide that when the "Select" button is activated, the application should display a message confirming what kind of beverage the machine is supposed to prepare.

To achieve this, our *Call-Back* function needs to know the state of all the buttons, using the technique shown in Section 1.3:

```
hotbin  ← Drinks.Hot.(B1 B2 B3 B4 B5).State
coldbin ← Drinks.Cold.(B1 B2 B3 B4).State
```

Then we can use these two Boolean vectors to select the appropriate descriptions and produce a text matrix, ready to be displayed:

```
HotCaps←'Coffee' 'Tea' 'Chocolate' 'More sugar' 'Add milk'
ColdCaps←'Guarana' 'Orange juice' 'Tomato juice' 'With ice'
hotsel←hotbin/HotCaps
coldsel←coldbin/ColdCaps
choice←↑(⊂'Hot drinks:'),hotsel,(' ' 'Cold drinks:'),coldsel
```

We shall display the resulting matrix in a separate, special object called a *Message Box*, or `MsgBox`.

If you consult the item "GUI interface" in the on-line help you will see that the first 3 properties of a *Message Box* are:

- its `Type` .... `'MsgBox'`
- its `Caption` .... `'Your current choice is'`
- the `Text` to display.................................... `choice`

Using the most simplified expression, we can write:

```
'Report' ⎕WC 'MsgBox' 'Your current choice is' choice
```

This message box is not a child of our main form. It is an autonomous object, so if we want it to be displayed and activated, we must use `⎕DQ` again, like this:

```
⎕DQ 'Report'
```

Let us integrate all these ideas in our functions. We shall suffix their names by "`1`" so as to keep the original versions unchanged.

First step: Change `CMUse` into `CMUse1` to create our two nested character vectors:

```
    ∇ CMUse1;Drinks;HotCaps;ColdCaps
[1]   HotCaps←'Coffee' 'Tea' 'Chocolate' 'More sugar' 'Add milk'
[2]   ColdCaps←'Guarana' 'Orange juice' 'Tomato juice' 'With ice'
[3]   CMDesign1
[4]   ⎕DQ'Drinks'
    ∇
```

Second step: Modify the fifth statement of `CMDesign` in order to invoke a *Call-Back* function named `CMReport` when the "Select" button is activated. This event is referenced by the keyword `'Select'`.
Then rename the function to `CMDesign1`.

```
[5]'bsel'⎕WC'Button' 'Select'(10 100)(25 210)
                                  ('Event' 'Select' '#.CMReport')
```

Names in statements embedded witin a `:With` clause are relative to the namespace specified in the clause. To specify that `CMReport` is not a child of `'Drinks'` we must use the notation `#.CMReport`, which clearly specifies that the function is located in the root namespace.

Third step: Define the call-back function `CMReport`:

```
     ∇ CMReport;hotbin;coldbin;coldsel;hotsel;choice;Report
       hotbin←Drinks.Hot.(B1 B2 B3 B4 B5).State
       coldbin←Drinks.Cold.(B1 B2 B3 B4).State
       hotsel←hotbin/HotCaps
       coldsel←coldbin/ColdCaps
       choice←↑(⊂'Hot drinks:'),hotsel,(' ' 'Cold drinks:'),coldsel
       'Report'⎕WC'MsgBox' 'Your current choice is'choice
       ⎕DQ'Report'
     ∇
```

Note that by localizing `Report` we ensure that the message box object will be deleted when we exit from the reporting function.

We can now try to call `CMUse1`:

Figure P-2

When a message box is shown it is centred on the screen. We have moved it to the right so that it does not hide the main form.

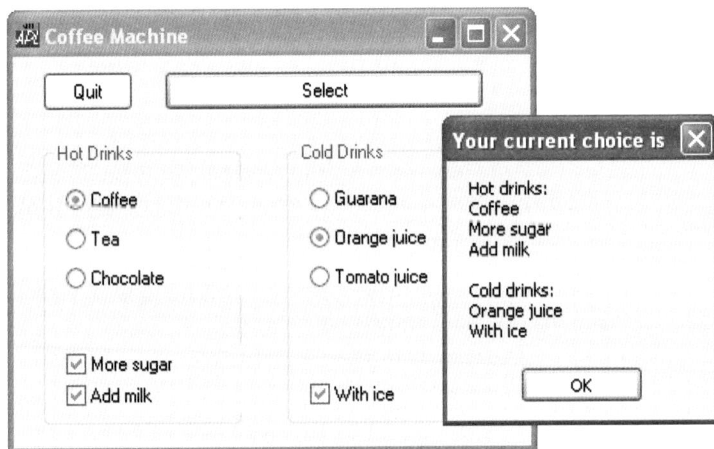

2.1.4 - Some Improvements

In the topmost function `CMUse1` we defined two variables `HotCaps` and `ColdCaps`, to store the captions of all our buttons so that they can be used by `CMReport`. However, we also had to specify the same captions for the buttons within `CMDesign1`.

This is not good programming practice, because if the name of a drink needs to be changed (for example, if "Tea" is to be replaced by "Soup"), the same modification must be made twice in both programs.[10]

[10] This is a violation of the so called *DRY Principle*. DRY stands for "Don't Repeat Yourself", meaning that ideally every piece of information should be defined in one single place and re-used appropriately.

As it turns out we don't need to specify the button captions again at all, we can simply pick them up from the button objects themselves.

The new top-level function `CMUse2` can therefore be simplified like `CMUse`. However, we have also modified the function to `DISPLAY` the result of `⎕DQ`, and we have added a useless 3rd statement (in a moment you will see why we did so):

```
     ∇ CMUse2;Drinks
[1]    CMDesign2
[2]    DISPLAY ⎕DQ'Drinks'
[3]    'That''s all, Folks!'
     ∇
```

`CMDesign2` is identical to `CMDesign1`, except that we have changed the name of the call-back function to `CMReport2`:

```
     ∇ CMDesign2;Check;Radio
...
[5] 'bsel'⎕WC'Button' 'Select'(10 100)(25 210)
                                      ('Event' 'Select' '#.CMReport2')
...
     ∇
```

`CMReport2` now picks up the captions from the buttons themselves. We have also used the *DRY Principle*[10] inside the function in order to not having to refer to the button lists twice:

```
     ∇ CMReport2;hotbin;hotcaps;coldbin;coldcaps
                       ;coldsel;hotsel;choice;Report;buttons
[1]    buttons←Drinks.Hot.(B1 B2 B3 B4 B5)
[2]    hotbin←buttons.State
[3]    hotcaps←buttons.Caption
[4]    buttons←Drinks.Cold.(B1 B2 B3 B4)
[5]    coldbin←buttons.State
[6]    coldcaps←buttons.Caption
[7]    hotsel←hotbin/hotcaps
[8]    coldsel←coldbin/coldcaps
[9]    choice←↑(⊂'Hot drinks:'),hotsel,(' ' 'Cold drinks:'),coldsel
[10]   'Report'⎕WC'MsgBox' 'Your current choice is'choice
[11]   ⎕DQ'Report'
     ∇
```

2.1.5 - The Result of ⎕DQ

If you execute these functions in trace mode, you can verify that the main program execution is suspended while `⎕DQ` is executing, because control is given to the form. In other words, the calling function `CMUse2` is frozen as long as the form remains active.

We can return to the calling APL function:

- By closing the form by clicking in the top right corner.
  Then the result returned by `⎕DQ` will be an empty vector.

- By explicitly specifying that a certain event should cause an exit from ⎕DQ. This can be achieved by associating the value 1 with the appropriate item of the 'Event' property (see Section 2.1.2), for example when the user activates the "Quit" button on the form. Then the result returned by ⎕DQ will be a nested vector consisting of the name of the object that caused the exit, followed by the event keyword or code.

Let us add this to the right of the fourth statement in CMDesign2:

```
[4] 'bout'⎕WC'Button' 'Quit'(10 20)(25 60)('Event' 'Select' 1)
```

The program behaviour remains the same, except that when we click on the "Quit" button, we return from ⎕DQ, and the following result is displayed:

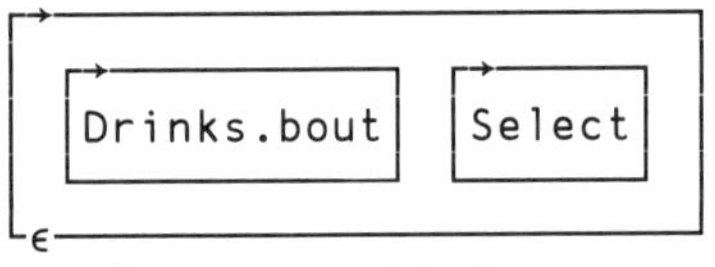


```
That's all, Folks!
```

⇦ The first item is the object name. The second item is the event code or keyword as specified in the defining statement.

⇦ And now the execution continues.

Note The second item of ⎕DQ result will be 'Select' or 30, depending on the way we wrote the statement in CMDesign2. This is important to know if the result is to be processed by a function. For this reason it is highly recommended that you decide to use one of the conventions consistently, and for improved readability we recommend that you always use keywords.

2.2 The Arguments of a Call-Back Function

The rules for the *valence* of call-back functions are special.

The right argument to a call-back function is always provided by the APL system.

It is also possible to define that a programmer-defined argument be passed to a call-back function. This will then be the function's left argument.

If no programmer-defined argument has been specified (see below) the call-back function may be niladic or monadic. If it is necessary to examine the information provided by the APL system the function must of course be monadic, but if not, it is perfectly possible to let the call-back function be niladic. It will not cause a SYNTAX ERROR.

If a programmer-defined argument has been specified, the call-back function must be dyadic or ambivalent.

2.2.1 - The Right Argument

If specified, the right argument to a call-back function is a nested vector containing information about the event that has taken place. This information is provided by the APL system, not the programmer, and is known as the ***Event Message***.

- The first item of an event message always identifies the object that generated the event. If the original GUI interface was used to specify the event the first item of the *Event Message* will be a character vector containing the *name* of the object, as shown in Section 2.1.5 above. If namespace notation was used to specify the event the first item of the *Event Message* will be a *Ref*, i.e. a *Namespace reference*. See Section Spe-2.2 for further details.
- The second item is the *Event* keyword or code, depending on how the event has been specified.
- Depending on the type of the event, additional information may be provided in further items of the right argument. For example, for a *MouseMove* event the 3rd and 4th items contain the position of the mouse pointer, while the 5th and 6th items contain information on the mouse buttons and the state of the Shift and Control keys on the keyboard. For a *KeyPress* event the *Event Message* is also a 6-item vector, with the last 4 items containing detailed information about which key was pressed and the state of the various shift keys.

2.2.2 - The Left Argument

A call-back function may take a left argument. The value to be passed to the function when the event takes place must be specified in the same statement as is used to attach the call-back function. Using the original syntax, it must be placed to the **Right** of the function name.

For example:

```
('Event' 'KeyPress' 'Check' Authorised)
```

Here `Check` is the name of the call-back function, and `Authorised` is the **left** argument to the function, though it is specified to the right of the function name in the event definition. In this specific case it contains a list of acceptable characters.

When a *KeyPress* event occurs, APL will call the function `Check`, and pass it:

- as its **right** argument the *Event Message*
- as its **left** argument the value of `Authorised` (specifically, the value that `Authorised` had when the above expression was executed)

2.2.3 - Some Experiments

Let us write a function that creates a form containing 10 buttons labelled "A" to "J" as shown:

Figure P-3

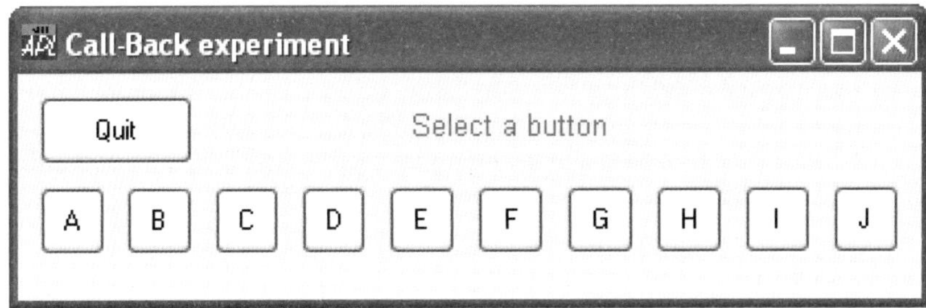

We will use a new type of object, a *Text* object. We shall specify some of its properties like this:

```
Type .................. 'Text'
Text .................. 'Select a button'     ⇦ Beware: it is not "Caption", but "Text"
Posn .................. 15 180
FCol .................. 255 0 0               ⇦ Red foreground colour
Font .................. 'Arial' 16            ⇦ The font used to display the text, and its size
```

The foreground colour `FCol` is defined by the weights of the three basic colours: Red, Green, and Blue (RGB), each in the range 0-255. Here we chose full red.

The font is defined by its face name (Arial) and its size in pixels.

We would like the function to create a random list of four upper-case letters. When the user selects a button the function should display the message "Won" or "Lost" depending on whether the selected button matches one of these random letters.

Here is the function. Long statements are folded onto two lines with "…" in the margin:

```
     ∇ GUI1;letters;Win;num;sufx;pos
        'Win'⎕WC'Form' 'Call-Back experiment'('Size' 100 410)
        'Win.Quit'⎕WC'Button' 'Quit'(10 10)(30 70)('Event' 'Select' 1)
        'Win.Result'⎕WC'Text' 'Select a button'(15 180)
...                               ('FCol' 255 0 0)('Font' 'Arial' 16)
        letters←⎕A[4?10]
        :For num :In ⍳10
            sufx←num⊃⎕A
            pos←50,(40×num)-30
            ('Win.But',sufx)⎕WC'Button' sufx pos(30 30)
...                                 ('Event' 'Select' 'GUI1_CB1' letters)
        :EndFor
        ⎕DQ'Win'
     ∇
```

Button names are generated automatically from `ButA` to `ButJ`, and they are positioned horizontally at 40 pixels intervals. All the buttons are associated with the **same** *Call-Back* function for the `'Select'` event. The important part is the way that the call-back function is called; you can see that the variable containing the random letters is placed to the **right** of the function name. Let us now take a look at this function:

```
     ∇ WinningChars GUI1_CB1 EventMsg
        WinningChars
        DISPLAY EventMsg
     ∇
```

Note that the list of the winning letters will be passed as the **left** argument, while the **right** argument will contain the *Event Message* as usual. For now, we will just display the value of the two arguments.

Here we run the function and press the "F" button:

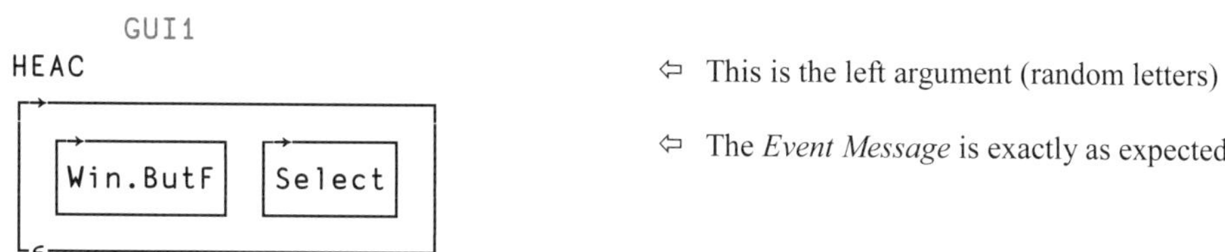
GUI1
HEAC
Win.ButF
Select
⇦ This is the left argument (random letters)
⇦ The Event Message is exactly as expected

Now we can write the final version of the *Call-Back* function:

```
     ∇ WinningChars GUI1_CB2 EventMsg;sufx;score
        sufx←(⊃EventMsg)⎕WG'Caption'
        score←(1+sufx∊WinningChars)⊃'Lost' 'Won'
        Win.Result.Text←score
     ∇
```

Please also remember to change the name of the call-back function in line 8 of `GUI1`.

All the 10 letter buttons call the same function when they are selected, so we must consult the *Event Message* in order to determine which of them was selected. The first item of the *Event Message* contains the button name, and the last letter of the name is the letter that we will check against the list of "winning" letters. This example shows how the information provided in the *Event Message* may be very useful.

Then we can create a character vector "Lost" or "Won", by comparing the button name suffix with the winning letters.

The last statement modifies the "`Text`" property of the object `Win.Result`. We could as well write this: `'Win.Result' ⎕WS 'Text' score`.

You can test the `GUI1` function and play with the little letter guessing game!

We have now learned how a call-back function is called and how arguments are passed to it. Next we shall see that a call-back function may return different results that cause different useful effects.

2.3 The Result of a Call-Back Function

2.3.1 - Default Processing

When a user-initiated *Event* occurs Windows will take a default, or standard action. For example, if the user moves the mouse, the mouse pointer moves with it. Likewise, if a key is pressed while an input field has the focus the corresponding character is displayed in the field.

This kind of standard behaviour will henceforth be described as the ***Default Processing*** of an *Event*.

The *Default Processing* of an event may be modified, replaced, or cancelled by associating a call-back function with the event. The call-back function is for obvious reasons called **before** the *Default Processing* is executed, and the result of the *Call-Back* function determines whether or not the *Default Processing* is to take place, perhaps in a modified form.

2.3.2 - Processing the Result

A call-back function may return a result or not, and the result influences the further actions as follows:

- If the call-back function returns **no result**, or the result **1**, or a result identical to the right argument (the *Event message*), the system will execute the *Default Processing* of the event, as if the call-back function had not been called.

  This can, for example, be used when a call-back function is necessary in order to handle very special cases, while the standard action is adequate in most cases.

- If the call-back function returns 0, the *Default Processing* will not take place, so the call-back function is solely responsible for taking all actions that are needed for the event in question.

  This can, for example, be used to ignore unacceptable characters in an input field.

- If the call-back function returns a modified *Event message* the system will carry out the *Default Processing* according to the modified *Event Message*, as if it describes what really happened.

  This can, for example, be used to convert lower-case keystrokes into upper-case letters.

2.3.3 - Example

Let us create a form containing only a "Quit" button and two *Edit* fields, a new type of object used for entering text, as shown in Figure P-4:

Figure P-4

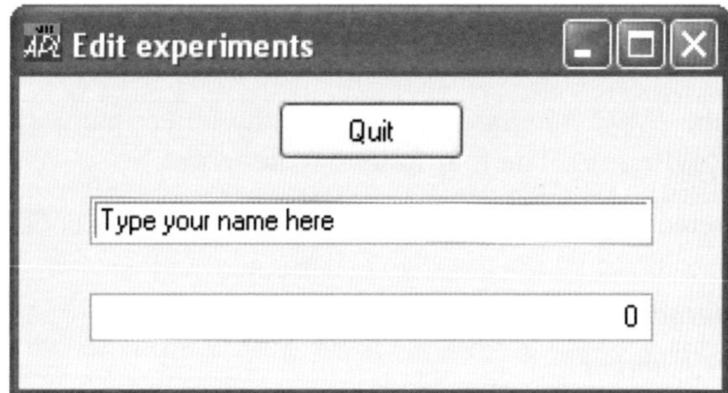

The upper edit field will be used to type text, left justified. The lower edit field will be used to type numeric values, right-justified.

An *Edit* Field has many properties. For now we will only specify the following:

```
Text.................. 'Type your name'      ⇦ An initial hint telling you what to do
Posn & Size .....                           ⇦ As usual
FieldType........ 'Char' or 'Numeric'
MaxLength........ 30                        ⇦ The maximum number of characters
Decimals ........... 0                      ⇦ The maximum number of decimal digits
```

A function to create and drive the form could be the following (with long statements folded):

```
      ∇ GUI2;Win
[1]     'Win'⎕WC'Form' 'Edit experiments'('Size' 130 300)
[2]     'Win.quit'⎕WC'Button' 'Quit'(10 110)(25 80)('Event' 'Select' 1)
[3]     'Win.ET'⎕WC'Edit' 'Type your name here'(50 30)(20 240)
...                        ('FieldType' 'Char')('MaxLength' 30)
...                        ('Event' 'KeyPress' 'GUI2_CB1')
[4]     'Win.EN'⎕WC'Edit' '0'(90 30)(20 240)('FieldType' 'Numeric')
...                        ('MaxLength' 10)('Decimals' 0)
[5]     ⎕DQ'Win'
      ∇
```

A *Call-Back* function is triggered by the KeyPress (or 22) Event in the first field. In this first version of the function it just displays the *Event Message*.

```
      ∇ GUI2_CB1 Msg
[1]     Msg
      ∇
```

Suppose that the user wants to type "Hello", but accidentally types "Helo". He then presses the *BackSpace* key to delete the "o", and types "Lo". The *Call-Back function* would display this:

```
Win.ET  KeyPress H  72 72 1        ⇦ "H" is typed in upper-case
Win.ET  KeyPress e 101 69 0
Win.ET  KeyPress l 108 76 0        ⇦ This "l" is typed in lower-case
Win.ET  KeyPress o 111 79 0        ⇦ Erroneous "o"
```

```
Win.ET  KeyPress  DB 8   8 0          ⇦ "DB" stands for "Destructive Backspace"
Win.ET  KeyPress L   76 76 1          ⇦ This "L" is typed in upper-case
Win.ET  KeyPress o 111  79 0
```

As usual, the *Event Message* begins with the object name (`Win.ET`) followed by the *Event* keyword (`KeyPress`). The four following items are:

- The entered character (like "H" and "e"), or an action code for special command keys (like "DB").
- The ***Character Code***
- The ***Key Number***
- The ***Shift State***

In the *Unicode Edition*, the *Character Code* is the Unicode code point of the character entered by the user. In the *Classic Edition*, it is a number in the range 0-255 which specifies the ASCII character that would normally be generated by the keystroke. If there is no corresponding ASCII character, the reported code is 0. In the case of the characters typed above:

```
      ⎕UCS 72 101 108 76 111
HelLo
```

The *Key Number* is the physical key number reported by the operating system when the key is pressed.

The *Shift State* is obtained by the sum of the 3 following indicators:

- *Shift* key pressed 1
- *Ctrl* key pressed 2
- *Alt* key pressed 4

For example, *Ctrl+Shift* would give 3.

It is important to note that the same key is pressed to type a lower-case "l" and an upper-case "L". This is the reason why the *Key Number* is the same (76) for the two characters. But because the *Shift State* is different (0 or 1) the *Character Code* generated is also different: 108 for "l", and 76 for "L".

Now that we have seen how this type of *Event* is reported, let us decide to dynamically change the characters typed by the user, as follows:

- Lower-case "e" will be converted into "a", and vice versa.
- All upper-case letters will be ignored

We could modify our *Call-Back* function like this:

```
     ∇ Msg←GUI2_CB2 Msg;char                    ⇦ The result equals the argument
[1]    char←Msg[3]
[2]    :If char∊⎕A
[3]        Msg←0                                ⇦ Ignore upper-case letters
[4]    :Else
[5]        Msg[3]←('ae',char)['ea'⍳char]        ⇦ Commute "a" and "e"
[6]    :EndIf
     ∇
```

Please also remember to change the name of the call-back function in line 3 of `GUI2`.

Here are some explanations:

- By default the result returned by the function (`Msg`) is equal to the *Event Message* received in the argument. This means that the character is to be processed normally (*Default Processing*).
- If the character is an upper-case letter (belongs to `⎕A`), the result is forced to zero. This means that the *Event* is to be ignored, so nothing will appear in the field.
- And if the character is "a" or "e", it is converted to "e" or "a", respectively, and put back into the *Event Message*. Windows will then process the modified *Event* as if it were a true event.[11]

With this strange function, if the user types `"My name is Bond, James Bond"`,
the following letters will appear in the Edit field: `"y nema is ond, emas ond"`

It is perhaps stupid, but it works!

This example shows that a function can be called each time a key is pressed. The processing time is so short that the user will hardly notice it.

2.4 Improve It

2.4.1 - Improve the Field Management

To be more "user friendly" the little input form needs some improvements:

- When you want to replace the content of a field you must first delete the current content. It might be more useful to preselect the current content when the field receives the input focus (*Event* `"GotFocus"`). Then the first letter typed will replace all the current text.
- Of course, when a field loses input focus (*Event* `"LostFocus"`) its content should be deselected.
- In this example, `GUI2[4]` specifies the numeric field so that a user may not enter decimal digits `('Decimals' 0)`. However, the way in which this restriction works may be rather confusing. In order to prevent the user from entering decimal digits, the system simply ignores the decimal point (or a comma, depending on the regional settings); and this may have unwanted consequences.

[11] Note that it suffices to change the 3rd item of the event message, even if the returned message then becomes inconsistent. This is because the 3rd item may be viewed as the final result of the key press. The information in items 4-6 merely contains detailed information on what the user did, which is immaterial when the resulting message is created by the program.

For example, a user wants to enter `456.78`.

The system will ignore the decimal point, but will accept the other characters, and if the user is not vigilant he will type `45678`! This is not acceptable, so we will change the function to detect that the user has tried to enter a decimal point and display a message when it happens. This can be extended to the case where an application does not accept negative numbers.

Writing three different *Call-Back* functions to achieve these three objectives would be a bit heavy, so let us write a single function with a left argument specifying:

`S` = Select the current text in the field
`U` = Deselect the current text in the field
`W` = Issue a warning if a decimal point is typed

The main function will be modified as shown below (the modified statements are in black):

```
     ∇ GUI3 ;Win
[1]    'Win'⎕WC'Form' 'Edit experiments'('Size' 130 300)
[2]    'Win.quit'⎕WC'Button' 'Quit'(10 110)(25 80)('Event' 'Select' 1)
[3]    'Win.ET'⎕WC'Edit' 'Type your name here'(50 30)(20 240)
...    ('FieldType' 'Char')('MaxLength' 30)
[4]    'Win.ET'⎕WS'Event'('GotFocus'  'SecureEdit' 'S')
...                      ('LostFocus' 'SecureEdit' 'U')
[5]    'Win.EN'⎕WC'Edit' '0'(90 30)(20 240)('FieldType' 'Numeric')
...                      ('MaxLength' 10)('Decimals' 0)
[6]    'Win.EN'⎕WS'Event'('GotFocus' 'SecureEdit' 'S')
...    ('LostFocus' 'SecureEdit' 'U')('KeyPress' 'SecureEdit' 'W')
[7]    ⎕DQ'Win'
     ∇
```

The *Call-Back* function looks like this:

```
     ∇ Msg←X SecureEdit Msg;va;vm;vo;vp
[1]    :Select X
[2]    :Case 'S'          ⍝ Implements the GotFocus event
[3]        vo←1⊃Msg
[4]        vp←ρ,vo ⎕WG'Text'
[5]        vo ⎕WS'SelText' 1,1+vp
[6]    :Case 'U'          ⍝ Implements the LostFocus event
[7]        vo←1⊃Msg
[8]        vo ⎕WS'SelText' 1 0
[9]    :Case 'W'          ⍝ Implements the KeyPress event
[10]       :GoTo (~Msg[3]∊'.,')/0
[11]       'vm'⎕WC'MsgBox' 'Attention'('Please,' 'no decimal point')
[12]       ⎕DQ'vm'
[13]       Msg←0
[14]   :EndSelect
     ∇
```

Explanations:

[3] The first item of the *Event Message* contains the name of the field that received the input focus.

[4] Then we determine the size of the field's current content.

[5] Select characters from the first to one past the last (Figure P-5).

[8] Same technique, but we select no characters when leaving a field.

[11] If the typed character is a decimal point (or comma), a warning is issued (Figure P-6).

[13] The result is forced to zero in order to ignore the character typed.

Figure P-5

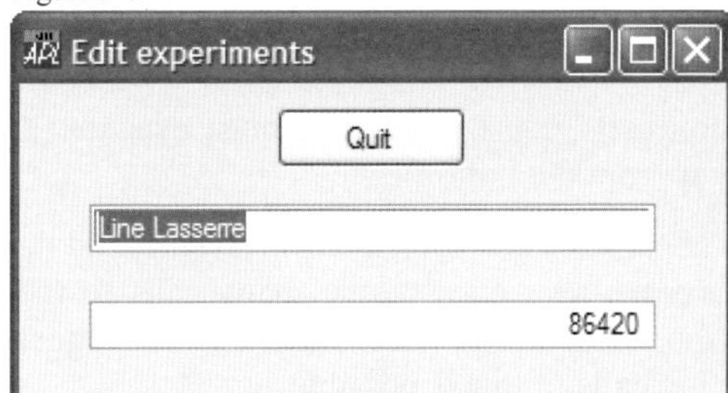

Figure P-6

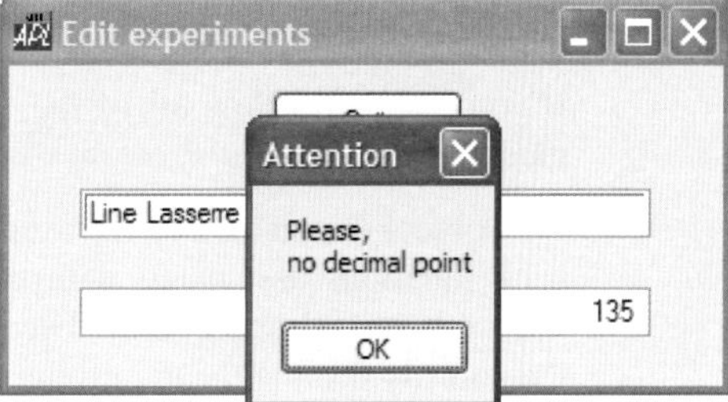

2.4.2 - More about Edit Fields

Once data has been entered into an *Edit* field, the program can read its contents using the properties:

- `Text` Returns the character vector typed in the field.
- `Value` Returns the same character vector if the *FieldType* is "`Char`", but returns a number if the *FieldType* is "`Numeric`".

If no *FieldType* was specified in the definition of the field APL decides whether "`Value`" will report a number or a character vector, depending on the characters typed. This may be difficult to work with, so we recommend that you always explicitly declare the type of your fields.

When a field has been defined as "`Numeric`" the decimal separator is defined by the Windows regional settings. So the property "`Value`" will always return a proper number according to the local standard.

2.4.3 - Passwords

One can also specify a "`Password`" property for a character field. Then the characters typed will automatically be replaced by the specified character, so there is no need for a *Call-Back* function.

For example:

```
'Win.EP'⎕WC'Edit' ''(5 5)(20 80) ('Fieldtype' 'Char') ('Password' '*')
```

Of course, it is always possible for the program to know what was really typed by the user, with a statement like this: `Letters←Win.EP.Text`.

2.5 Tracing Call-Back Functions

When you trace a function remember that `⎕DQ` is also a function. If you just execute it (by pressing the *Enter* key), `⎕DQ` will proceed to execute all the *Call-Back* functions normally (i.e. not in trace mode) and you will not be able to trace them.

If you want to follow all of the function calls step by step you must **execute** `⎕DQ` **in trace mode** (press *Ctrl-Enter*, or click on the appropriate button).

If an object is sensitive to for example "*KeyPress*" or "*MouseMove*" events, and there are call-back functions associated with these events, you may see so many calls to the *Call-Back* functions that tracing may become too difficult. In this situation we suggest that you temporarily disable the disturbing function calls, if this is possible.

Alternatively, you could for example insert a conditional error in a call-back function, to allow you to trace a particular case. For example, the following line will stop execution in a call-back function handling "*KeyPress*" events, if A, B or C is pressed:

```
:If 'KeyPress'≡2⊃msg ⋄ :AndIf (3⊃msg)∊'ABC' ⋄ ∘ ⋄ :EndIf
```

However, this technique may not work as expected if some kind of error trapping is active. Then you can use another technique, which dynamically sets a breakpoint in the function, for example:

```
:If char∊'xyz'
   (1+⎕LC)⎕STOP⊃⎕SI
    ⍝ Stop here!
:EndIf
```

3 - Selection Tools

3.1 List

The *List* object is, as its name suggests, used to display a list of items, and it also allows the user to select one or more of the items in the list. Using variables already present in your WS, you can type the following function and execute it:

```
     ∇ GUI_List;Win
[1]    'Win'⎕WC'Form' 'List object'('Size' 300 200)
[2]    'Win.quit'⎕WC'Button' 'Quit'(10 20)(25 160)('Event' 'Select' 1)
[3]    'Win.countries'⎕WC'List'Countries(50 20)(180 160)
[4]    'Win.show'⎕WC'Button' 'Show selection'(250 20)(25 160)
[5]    ⍝     ('Event' 'Select' 'ShowSel')
[6]    ⎕DQ'Win'
     ∇
```

Figure P-7

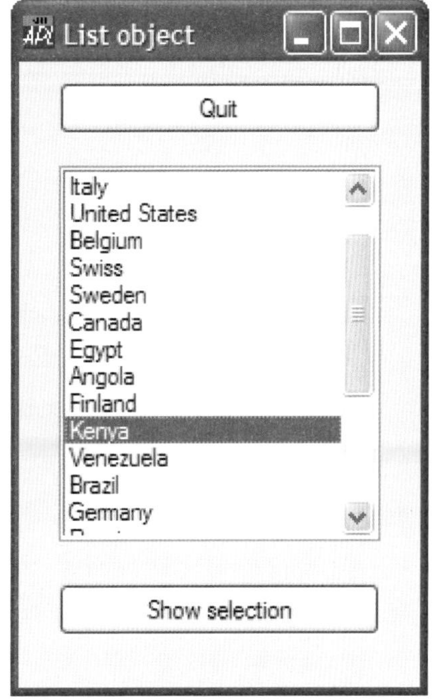

As you can see, this function creates a *List* object containing the matrix `Countries`. A vector of character vectors would have been accepted too.

The scroll bar is automatically added by Dyalog APL, depending on the size of the matrix.

The only thing you can do is select a single country ("Kenya" here). If you change your mind and select another one, the first gets deselected.

For now, the second button ("Show selection") is inactive, because we have commented out the 5th statement.

Let us change the function a little and add the property `('Style' 'Multi')` to the *List* object.

Now it becomes possible to select more than one country, using standard Windows conventions. Press the *Control* key to add/remove a country to/from the already selected ones, or press the *Shift* key to mark the end point of a set of rows, starting from the last selected row.

Each time a new country is selected or deselected a `"Select"` event is issued, so it is generally not very pertinent to run the *Call-Back* function each time; it is usually better to wait until the final choice has been made. However, in some situations you might want to immediately update other controls on the form depending on the selected item(s), and then you must handle each `"Select"` event as it occurs.

In our example we will not react to each individual "`Select`" event. Instead we will show the selection when the "Show selection" button is clicked. We will remove the comment from line 5 of `GUI_List` and write the `ShowSel` function shown below. The "`SelItems`" property returns a Boolean vector having one item per item in the list and containing a `1` in the positions of the selected rows:

```
     ∇ ShowSel Msg
[1]    DISPLAY Win.countries.SelItems/Win.countries.Items
     ∇
```

Here we show the result of executing `ShowSel`:

Figure P-8

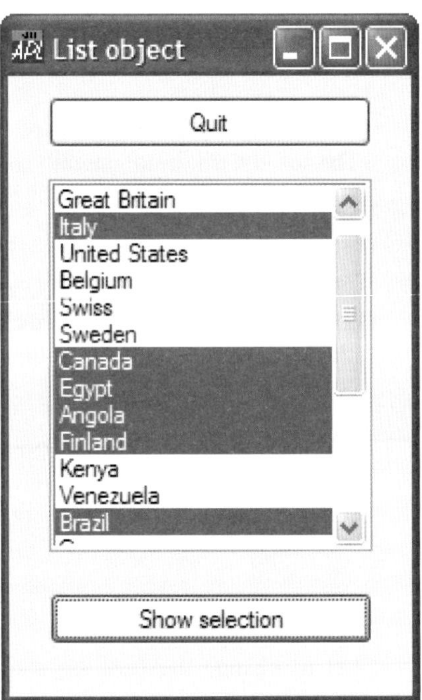

As you can see, you can now select as many countries as you want.

When the "Show selection" button is clicked, the following is written to the APL session:

```
┌→──────────┐
↓Italy      │
│Canada     │
│Egypt      │
│Angola     │
│Finland    │
│Brazil     │
└───────────┘
```

The same property "`SelItems`" can be used to define a list of pre-selected countries before the form is shown to the user (and in general to re-define the selection at any time). The Boolean vector must have as many items as the number of items in the list, as you can see in this statement used to pre-select only the third and fifth countries:

```
      'Win.countries'⎕WS 'SelItems' ((1↑⍴Countries)↑0 0 1 0 1)
```

3.2 Combo

The *Combo* object is used to offer a quick choice among a limited number of options, in a very limited screen space (in terms of pixels). The word *Combo* stands for Combined Box, because one of the possible styles is a combination of a drop-down selection list and an *Edit* field.

Let us write a function `GUI_Combo` inspired by `GUI3` shown in Section 2.4.1. We will reduce the width of the numeric field, and add a choice of a list of currencies, stored in the following matrix:

```
      Currencies
EUR Euro
USD United States Dollar
GBP United Kingdom Pound
JPY Japan Yen
DKK Denmark Kroner
RUB Russia Rubles
```

```
     ∇ GUI_Combo;Win
[1]    'Win'⎕WC'Form' 'Combo demonstration'('Size' 130 300)
[2]    'Win.quit'⎕WC'Button' 'Quit'(10 110)(25 80)('Event' 'Select' 1)
[3]    'Win.EN'⎕WC'Edit' '0'(50 30)(20 100)
              ('FieldType' 'Numeric')('MaxLength' 10)('Decimals' 2)
[4]    'Win.CC'⎕WC'Combo' Currencies 'Hello' (50 150)(⍬ 120)
[5]    ⎕DQ'Win'
     ∇
```

Some details must be noticed:

- Here we used a matrix for the choices; we could just as well have used a nested character vector.
- A *Combo* has a `Text` property (`'Hello'` in our example) which is ignored.
- The height of the *Combo* field cannot be decided by the programmer; it is fixed by the system. This is the reason why we specified *Zilde*, (which in this case means *default*).

Here is how this would appear on the screen before and after one has clicked on the arrow:

Figure P-9

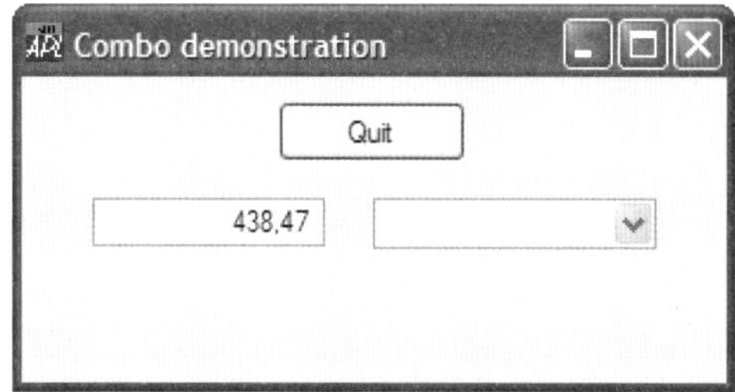

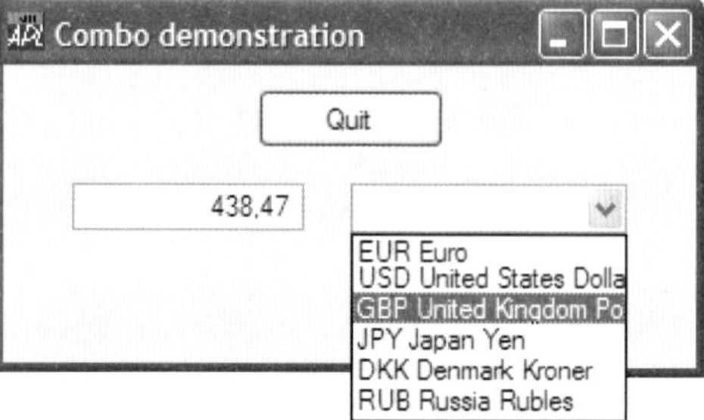

You can determine which item was selected by two different means:

- `Win.CC.SelItems` would return `0 0 1 0 0 0`
- `Win.CC.Text` would return `GBP United Kingdom Pound`

Use whichever you feel is more convenient for your program.

The default `'Style'` of a *Combo* is `'Drop'`, which provides a drop-down selection list. The user must choose among the items in the list. Two other styles are possible:

- `DropEdit` Provides a drop-down selection list like the `'Drop'` style, but the user can also type something different in the *Edit* part of the *Combo* field. For example, he can type "`I don't know`".
- `Simple` The user can also type his own text, but the list of choices is always displayed (i.e. it does not "drop down"). The list occupies some screen space, but sometimes this may be useful.

For these two styles, in which the user may enter an arbitrary string of text, the `SelItems` property will return a list of zeros if the user has typed in the *Edit* field. If so, the user's entry must be obtained by reading the `Text` property.

Comparisons

Compared to a *List*, the advantage of a *Combo* is that it occupies only a very limited amount of screen space. The list of choices is visible only shortly, while the *List* occupies a permanent space.

The disadvantage is that a *List* can allow multiple choices, a *Combo* cannot.

4 - Colours, Fonts, and Root

4.1 Colours

We have already mentioned that colours may be represented by three-item vectors containing the weights (or intensities) of the three basic colours Red, Green, and Blue (RGB), each in the range 0-255. This allows for more than 16 million colours. Here are some example colours:

		R	G	B
Red	is represented by	255	0	0
Dark Blue	is represented by	0	0	192
Yellow	is represented by	255	255	0
Light Grey	is represented by	192	192	192

It is also possible to define the colour of an object using a negative scalar, which then refers to one of the standard Windows colours (defined by the current "Theme"):

0	Default	¯11	Active Border
¯1	Scroll Bar	¯12	Inactive Border
¯2	Desktop	¯13	Application Workspace
¯3	Active Title Bar	¯14	Highlight
¯4	Inactive Title Bar	¯15	Highlighted Text
¯5	Menu Bar	¯16	Button Face
¯6	Window Background	¯17	Button Shadow
¯7	Window Frame	¯18	Disabled Text
¯8	Menu Text	¯19	Button text
¯9	Window Text	¯20	Inactive Title Bar text
¯10	Active Title Bar text	¯21	Button Highlight

4.2 Fonts

4.2.1 - Font Characteristics

Instead of using the default font it is possible to specify different fonts and font characteristics to display a piece of text, a list, a caption, and so on. However, one cannot modify the fonts used in the window title bar or in a menu, as these are determined by the system.

A font is completely defined by the following eight parameters:

`PName`	This is the name of the font. For example "Arial" or "Times New Roman".
`Size`	Specifies the character height in pixels.
`Fixed`	Is a Boolean value that specifies whether the font is fixed-width (1) or proportional (0). In fixed-width fonts all the characters have the same width. In proportional fonts, an "m" is wider than an "l" or an "i".
`Italic`	Specifies whether characters are in *italic* (1) or not (0).
`Underline`	Specifies whether characters are underlined (1) or not (0).
`Weight`	Specifies how bold or heavy the characters are from 0 (thin) to 1000 (**bold**).
`Rotate`	Is a numeric scalar that specifies the font angle of rotation in radians, measured from the x-axis in a counter-clockwise direction.
`Charset`	In Dyalog APL *Classic Edition*,this is an integer that specifies the character encoding; where 0 is for Western (ANSI) characters, 161 for Greek, and so on. In the *Unicode Edition* this parameter is ignored.

Notes

When, under Windows, you specify a font, you are actually asking Windows to load the font that it deems to most closely match the characteristics you have specified. It matches your request with one of its available fonts using an algorithm whose description is beyond the scope of this tutorial. However, please note that there is absolutely no guarantee that you will get a font that precisely matches a specified set of parameters, not least the font name. None of the characteristics are mandatory; one could, for example, request a fixed-width font by just specifying (`Fixed 1`).

4.2.2 - Using the Font Object

Fonts use Windows resources which are managed using the Dyalog APL Font object. To use a particular font with a particular GUI object requires two steps:

- First create a *Font* object for each font (and font variant) that you need.
- Then associate the Font object with each of the objects that you want to use it with.

Font objects can be defined as children of the *Root*. Then it will be possible to use them for all objects. They can also be defined as child objects of a given form. They will then be available for the children of that form, and they will automatically be unloaded (deleted) when the form itself is destroyed.

In the example below we will write the same piece of text in a form using different fonts.

The form is created using a "`:With`" control structure; all the Text objects created afterwards are children of the form, and need not be localised.

Specific fonts are associated with the Text objects via their `'FontObj'` properties that refer to the corresponding *Font* objects. These Font objects are created by a sub function named `GUI_FontDefine`.

```
     ∇ GUI_Fonts;Win
       :With 'Win'⎕WC'Form' 'Font control'('Size' 200 350)
           Droopy←'You know what? I''m happy!'
           #.GUI_FontDefine ⎕THIS
           'BQ'⎕WC'Button' 'Quit'(20 20)(40 40)('Event' 'Select' 1)
           'T0'⎕WC'Text' Droopy (20 80)
           'T1'⎕WC'Text' Droopy (50 80) ('FontObj' 'FonSml')
           'T2'⎕WC'Text' Droopy (80 20) ('FontObj' 'FonBig')
           'T3'⎕WC'Text' Droopy (110 20)('FontObj' 'FonIta')
           'T4'⎕WC'Text' Droopy (140 20)('FontObj' 'FonAPL')
           'T5'⎕WC'Text' 'V e r t i c a l'(180 300)
...                                         ('FontObj' 'FonRot')
       :EndWith
       ⎕DQ'Win'
     ∇
```

The sub-function `GUI_FontDefine` is located in the Root namespace. We pass a *Ref* to the GUI namespace `Win` and use `:With` to have the fonts created as children of the form:

```
     ∇ GUI_FontDefine ns
       :With ns
          'FonSml' ⎕WC'Font' 'MS Sans Serif' 14
          'FonBig' ⎕WC'Font' 'Arial' 20 0 0 0 1000
          'FonIta' ⎕WC'Font' 'Times New Roman' 24 0 1
          'FonAPL' ⎕WC'Font' 'APL385 Unicode' 16
          'FonRot' ⎕WC'Font' 'Arial' 32 0 0 0 700(○÷2)
       :EndWith
     ∇
```

The result is the following:

Figure P-10

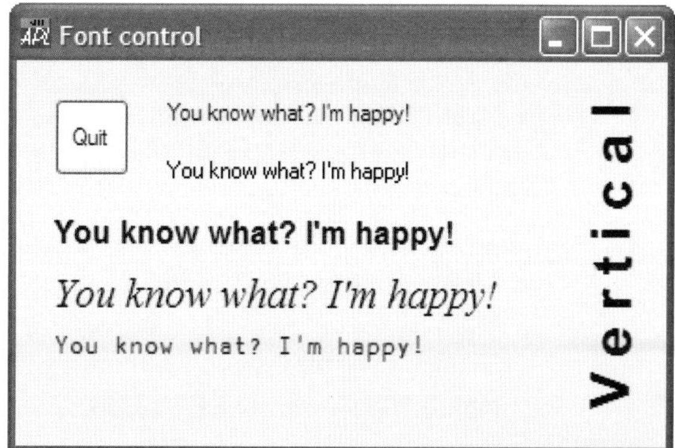

The 1st text uses the default font.

The 3rd text is bold.

The 4th is italic.

The 5th uses a fixed-width APL font.

The 6th text has been rotated by Pi/2.

When *Fonts* are defined at the Root level, they are autonomous objects, and they remain in the workspace, as you could verify by executing `)Obs`. In our example they were created as children of the form, and were therefore destroyed when the form was closed.

4.3 Properties of the Root Object

We have already said that that the topmost object is the *Root*, represented by either '.' or '#'. We recommend that you use '#' as we do in our examples.

The *Root* object has some interesting properties, some of which can be modified, while some other ones can only be read.

4.3.1 - The Coordinate System

We have already mentioned that the position and size of an object can be specified in three different ways:

- As a percentage of the parent object's size; the screen is the topmost parent object. This is the default.
- In pixels. This is probably the most commonly used setting, even though it is not the default setting.
- With a user-defined coordinate system.

These three possibilities are defined by the keyword 'Coord', followed by 'Prop', 'Pixel', or 'User', respectively.

It is recommended that you work in pixels, by executing:

```
      '#' ⎕WS 'Coord' 'Pixel'
```

4.3.2 - Screen Characteristics

One can adapt an application to the current screen characteristics as obtained by the 'DevCaps' (Device Capabilities) property of the root object. The result is a 3-item nested vector containing:

- The screen size (height and width) in pixels.
- The screen size in millimetres.
- The number of available colours. For a screen supporting 32-bit colours the number of colours is 4294967295. APL interprets this number as a 2's complement number and reports ¯1 (¯1 = 323⎕DR 32⍴1).

```
      DISPLAY '#' ⎕WG 'DevCaps'
```

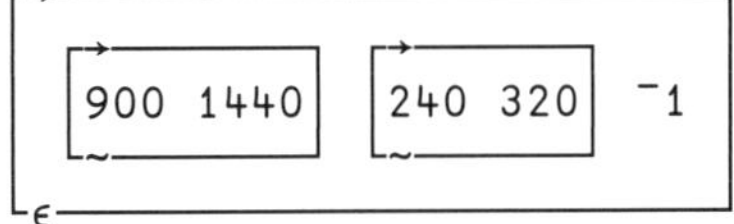

```
┌→──────────────────────────────┐
│ ┌→───────┐ ┌→──────┐          │
│ │900 1440│ │240 320│ ¯1       │
│ └~───────┘ └~──────┘          │
└∊──────────────────────────────┘
```

The size in pixels is exact, but the size in millimetres may be just an approximation. The system cannot know which kind of physical screen is attached to the computer, so the "physical" size is calculated as:

```
⌊0.5+25.4×pixels÷dpi
```

In this expression `dpi` is the "dots per inch" setting for the screen, and `25.4` is the number of millimetres per inch. Common values for `dpi` are 72 and 96, but if a generic display driver is used this value is independent of whether e.g. a 15", 17", or 19" screen is connected to the computer.

4.3.3 - Available Printers

One can ask for the list of currently available printer drivers using `'PrintList'`, a read-only property of the root object. The result is a nested vector of character vectors. Each item contains the name of a printer, followed by a comma, followed by the name of the physical device to which it is attached.

The first item is the default printer defined under Windows.

```
      ↑'#'⎕WG 'PrintList'
HP Deskjet F300 series,Ne03:
PDFCreator,Ne00:
hp color LaserJet 2550 PCL 6,Ne04:
```
... and so on...

Figure P-11

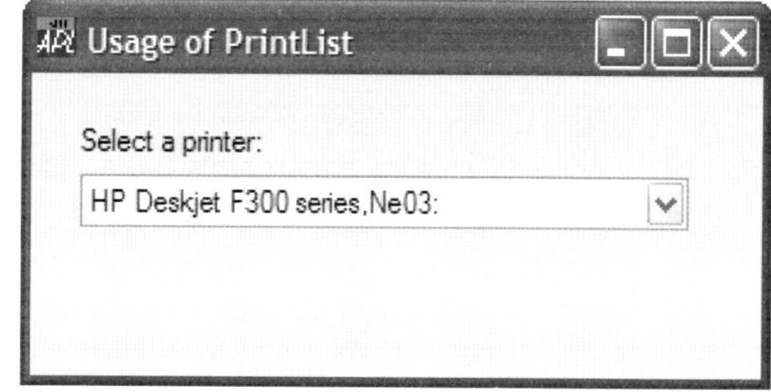

The list of available printers can be displayed in a *Combo*, with the first item selected by default.

The user can then choose the printer most appropriate to his needs

A printer definition may be a long character string, especially in a network environment, so a wide *Combo* may be necessary.

4.3.4 - Available Fonts

The list of currently available fonts can be obtained by: `'#'⎕WG 'FontList'`

The result is a nested vector of vectors. Each item contains the same eight items as described in Section 4.2.1.

Here is an example:

```
      fonts←↑'#'⎕WG 'FontList'
      ⍴fonts
152 8
      fonts
System          16 0 0 0 700 0   0
Terminal        12 1 0 0 400 0 255
Fixedsys        15 1 0 0 400 0   0
Roman           37 0 0 0 400 0 255
Script          36 0 0 0 400 0 255
Modern          37 0 0 0 400 0 255
Small Fonts      3 0 0 0 400 0   0
MS Serif        10 0 0 0 400 0   0
```

Of course, the parameters have default values that can be changed as explained in Section 4.2.

... and so on.

As you can see, the font list is not returned in alphabetic order.

4.3.5 - Cursor Shape

You can change the shape of the mouse pointer for any object by specifying its `'CursorObj'` property. The shape is represented by either an empty vector (the default), or a number (which selects one of the standard Windows cursors), or the name of or the *Ref* to a (programmer defined) *Cursor Object*. Some of the common Windows standard cursors are:

0	=	Arrow (the default)
1	=	Hourglass (which is shown as an animated ring in Windows Vista)
2	=	Crosshair
...		
13	=	Arrow with hourglass

You can look up the full list in the on-line GUI help. We will not describe the *Cursor Object* in this tutorial; please refer to the on-line GUI help for more information.

When the value of the `'CursorObj'` property is an empty vector the cursor will not change shape when the mouse pointer enters the object. When the `'CursorObj'` property is set to anything other than an empty vector the mouse pointer will assume the specified shape when entering the object.

When you specify the `'CursorObj'` property for the root object the setting will affect all forms and their child objects, regardless of their own `'CursorObj'` settings. This is very useful when you want to change the cursor into an hourglass to inform the user that a long operation is going on. This may be done by:

```
      '#' ⎕WS 'CursorObj' 1
```

Don't forget to restore the normal shape when the operation has finished by executing:

```
      '#' ⎕WS 'CursorObj' 0
```

If an application crashed while the cursor had a non default shape the workspace might inadvertently have been saved with that definition. This may mislead the user. For this reason any application should execute `'#' ⎕WS 'CursorObj' 0` as part of its initialization.

4.3.6 - APL Version

You can obtain information about the version of Dyalog APL you are using by reading the `'APLVersion'` property of the root object:

```
      DISPLAY '#'⎕WG 'APLVersion'
```

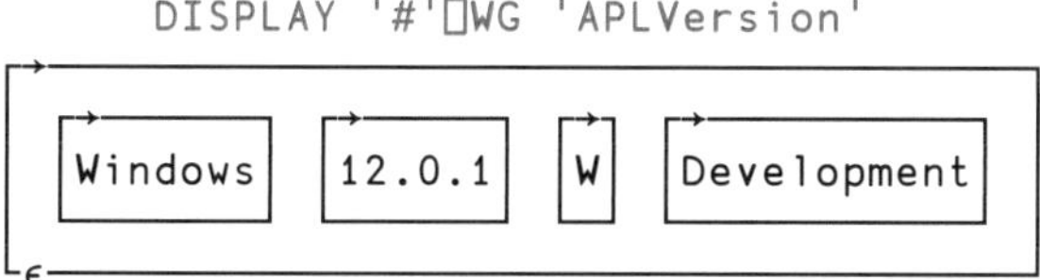

The result is a 4-item nested vector containing:

- The environment.
- The version.
- The version type: `W` for Windows, `M` for Motif, `P` for Pocket APL.
- `'Development'` or `'Runtime'`.

This information may be important because, for example:

- File path separators are different in Windows (`\`) and in Unix (`/`).
- An application may trap all errors when executing in a run time environment, but allow the standard error handling in a development (debugging) environment.

5 - Improve Your User Interface

5.1 Default Keys

When using an application it is very convenient for a user to be able to rely on the following keyboard shortcuts:

- The *Escape* key usually exits from a dialog box without taking any further action..
- The *Enter* key usually confirms a selection or initiates the default action.

This can be achieved by specifying the following properties for appropriate button objects:

`('Cancel' 1)`	this button will be actioned (selected) by pressing the *Escape* key
`('Default' 1)`	this button will be actioned (selected) by pressing the *Enter* key

For example, in CMDesign2, we defined a "Quit" button like this:

```
'bout'⎕WC'Button' 'Quit'(10 20)(25 60)('Event' 'Select' 1)
```

If we append ('Cancel' 1) to the right of this statement it will become possible to quit the application by pressing the *Escape* key, because('Cancel' 1) associates the Escape key as a keyboard short-cut equivalent to clicking the button with the mouse.

We also defined a "Select" button to display the final choice, with the following statement:

```
'bsel'⎕WC'Button' 'Select'(10 100)(25 210)
                                ('Event' 'Select' '#.CMReport')
```

If we append ('Default' 1) to the right of this statement we can just press the *Enter* key; a shortcut for clicking the button. Just try it!

5.2 Enqueuing Events and Using Methods

5.2.1 - Event Simulation

We have seen how we can use ⎕DQ (*de-queue*) to process the information that the system places in the event queue. We can also ourselves place events in the queue, using the monadic function ⎕NQ (*en-queue*).

For example, in Section 2.4.1, we used the GotFocus and LostFocus events to select or deselect the contents of an *Edit* field when the user entered or left the field. We will now explore the way to cause the field to receive the input focus, under program control.

Monadic ⎕NQ takes as its argument a nested vector similar to an *Event Message*. The information will be placed at the **end** of the *Event* queue, and processed as if it were a real *Event* when it arrives at the top of the queue.

For example, working with the function GUI3, let us insert a new statement just before calling ⎕DQ:

```
[7]     ⎕NQ 'Win.ET' 'GotFocus'
[8]     ⎕DQ 'Win'
```

This artificial *Event* will be placed in the event queue before the dialog box is displayed, so it will be the first one to be processed by ⎕DQ, before any user-generated events. The event will cause the input cursor to be placed in the character *Edit* field and the corresponding *Call-Back* function to be called, which in turn will cause all text in the field to be selected. This may make the dialog box easier to use.

One can artificially generate any *Event*, including ***User-Defined Events***, which may be identified by any free event numbers (but numbers above 1,000 are recommended). The *Events* that are put into the event queue will cause the appropriate action to take place or the specified call-back function to be called.

Monadic ⎕NQ returns an empty character vector as a shy result.

5.2.2 - Dyadic Use

⎕NQ can be used with a left argument equal to 0, 1, 2, 3, or 4. The values 3 and 4 are for interaction with OLE and ActiveX controls and will not be described here. Using a left argument equal to 0 is equivalent to using ⎕NQ monadically.

`1 ⎕NQ EventMsg`	Processes the event **immediately**, as if it had been placed first in the event queue and ⎕DQ had been called. If a *Call-Back* function is specified for the *Event* it will be called normally. The shy result is the *Event Message*, perhaps modified by the call-back function.
`2 ⎕NQ EventMsg`	If the name supplied is an *Event* name ⎕NQ performs the *Default Processing* for the *Event*, but it does not invoke a *Call-Back* function, even if one has been attached to the event. The shy result of ⎕NQ is `1`. If the name supplied is the name of a *Method* (cf. Section 5.2.3 below) the method is invoked. The shy result of ⎕NQ is then the result of the method.

5.2.3 - Methods

We have seen that GUI objects have *Properties*. The time has now come to introduce ***Methods***, which can be compared to functions, because they cause some action to take place.

- *Methods* are initiated by a dyadic ⎕NQ, with a left argument equal to 2. ⎕NQ then returns as a shy result the result returned by the *Method*.
- Methods can also be invoked directly using *namespace* syntax:

For example: `2 ⎕NQ 'Printer' 'NewPage'`

is equivalent to: `Printer.NewPage`

We shall use *Methods* in Section 8.2 about *Printers*.

5.3 Activating Objects

An application may use many forms and objects, but they may not necessarily have to be visible and active all the time. In order to hide them we could delete the objects and re-create them later, if needed. However, that would require unnecessary computer resources, and it might be very complex to re-establish exactly the same state again,

Dyalog APL contains two properties that make it easy and effortless to control the visibility of objects, and to control whether they are active or not:

`Active` Specifies whether an object is active (1) or not (0).

`Visible` Specifies whether an object or a form is visible (1) or not (0).

By default, objects are visible and active. An inactive object may still be visible, but the object cannot get focus, and the user cannot interact with it in any way. For example, if you set the Active property of an Edit object to 0 the text in the *Edit* field becomes grey and cannot be edited. As a consequence no call-back function associated with the object will be called.

Controls that are inactive or made invisible still exist as APL GUI objects and can be modified by the program.

When hidden forms are made visible again, you can place any form on top of all the other forms you have created, using the property `'OnTop'`:

For example: `'XYZ' ⎕WS ('Visible' 1)('OnTop' 1)`

5.4 Form Appearance

Forms have by default a standard Windows look with a border and a title bar. In the upper-left corner is a *System Menu* button (*SysMenu*) with a Dyalog APL icon, and in the upper-right corner are the three familiar buttons to minimize, maximize, or close the window.

This appearance can be changed, as shown in the figures below.

Figure P-12

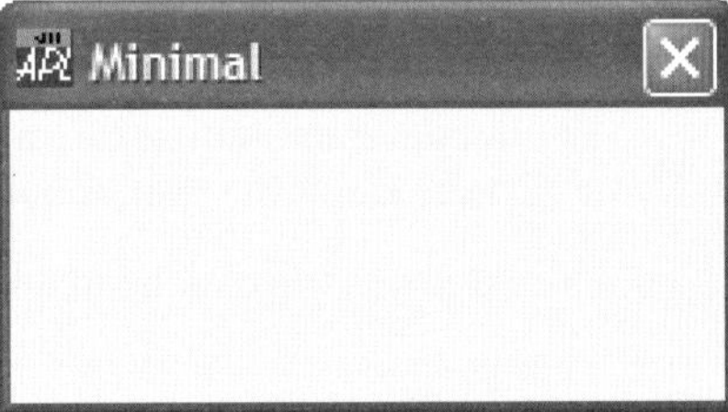

The minimize and/or the maximize buttons can be de-activated using the property settings `('MinButton' 0)` and `('MaxButton' 0)`.

When both are inactive they are not shown (as shown here), but the *SysMenu* is still active.

Figure P-13

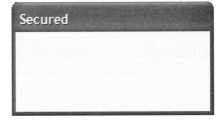

All the buttons can be removed by the single property setting `('SysMenu' 0)`.

Then the window can only be closed by the program, not by the user directly. This may be used to secure an application.

Important: All these properties must be set at creation time (`⎕WC`); they cannot be changed (using `⎕WS`) once the form has been created.

You can also replace the Dyalog APL icon (in the top-left corner) with any icon of your choice. The replacement icon must be a standard "`.ico`" file. Two steps are needed:

- First create an ***Icon*** object (a separate type of GUI object) by specifying the appropriate resource file, for example:
  ```
  'Hic' ⎕WC 'Icon' (Path,'heart.ico')
  ```
- Then apply the *Icon* object to your form, using the `IconObj` property like this:
  ```
  'P14'⎕WC'Form' 'Ma Doudou'('Size' 80 200)('IconObj' 'Hic') etc...
  ```

Figure P-14

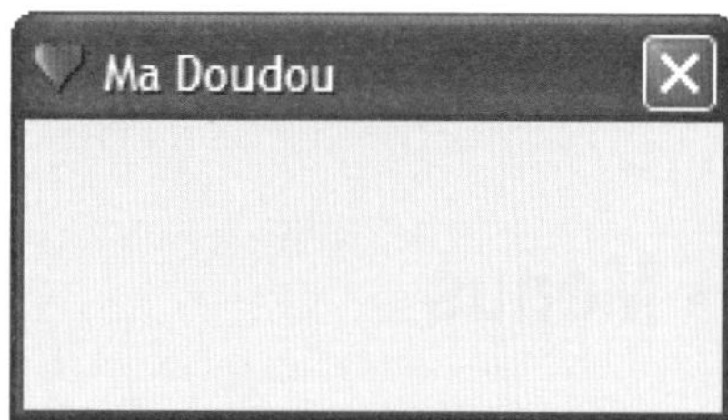

In this example we have not only changed the icon, but we have also removed the minimize and the maximize buttons.

When this form is minimized (which can only be done under program control), the heart will identify the application in the Windows *TaskBar*.

Figure P-15

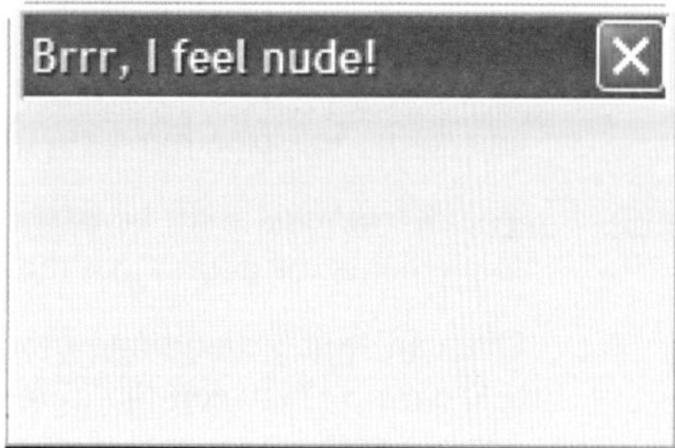

You can remove the border and have a pure dialog box appearance, as you can see here.

This is obtained by using the property setting `('Border' 2)`.

Without a border the form is no longer sizable, and neither the system menu nor the minimize and maximize buttons are shown.

Finally, you can replace the form background with any picture of your choice, provided as an appropriate bitmap file. This needs again two steps:

- First create a ***Bitmap*** object (a separate type of GUI object) by specifying the appropriate image file, for example:
  ```
  'South' ⎕WC 'Bitmap' (Path,'Snapshot.bmp')
  ```
- Then insert that *Bitmap* in your form, using the `Picture` property like this:
  ```
  'P16'⎕WC'Form' 'Landscape'('Size' 100 200)('Picture' 'South' 3)
  ```

Figure P-16

By default, the picture is centred, but you can specify a different alignment:

0 The picture is attached to the top-left corner
1 It is repeated (tiled) to fill the form
2 It is scaled (up or down) to fit the form
3 It is centred (this is the default)

6 - Menus

Menus are a very convenient way of offering a large number of options in an application.

The anchor point of the menu hierarchy is the ***MenuBar*** object.

A *Menu* may contain ***MenuItems*** and/or sub-menus containing other *Menus* or *MenuItems*, and so on, in a tree-like structure.

The *MenuItems* may be associated with a *Call-Back* function for the "Select" event, which implements the action that the menu stands for.

One can split a menu into blocks using a ***Separator***, as shown in Figure P-17 below: There is a *Separator* between the items "Properties" and "Quit" in the "File" menu. A *Separator* does not generate any events.

Suppose that we want to create two menus with entries as shown in Figure P-17:

Figure P-17

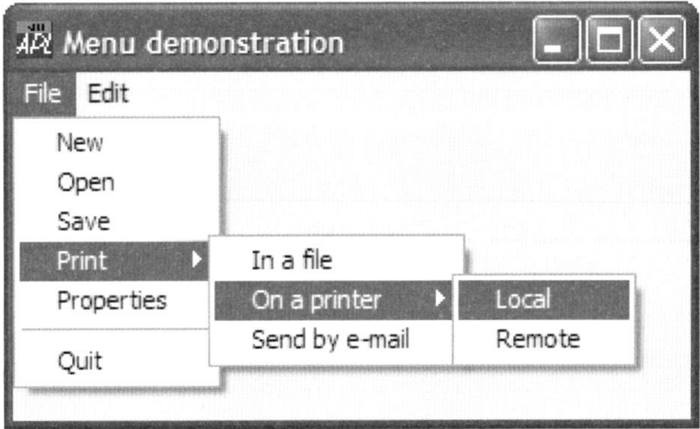

In a real application it would perhaps be most convenient to associate each *MenuItem* with a different call-back function, but in this small example we have chosen to use a common call-back function `ShowMsg`, which only displays the *Event Message*.

When defining a tree structure like a menu tree it may be very convenient to make use of the `:With` clause. This will both reduce the need for very long names and lines, and it will enhance the readability, as the program text resembles the menu structure that it defines. Here is an example of how a function to define the menu structure above could be written:

```
     ∇ GUI_Menu;Win;ExeEvent
       ExeEvent←'Event' 'Select' '#.ShowMsg'
       :With 'Win'⎕WC'Form' 'Menu demonstration'('Size' 130 300)
          :With 'MB' ⎕WC 'MenuBar'
             :With 'one' ⎕WC' Menu' 'File'
                'fia' ⎕WC 'MenuItem' 'New'                  ExeEvent
                'fib' ⎕WC 'MenuItem' 'Open'                 ExeEvent
                'fic' ⎕WC 'MenuItem' 'Save'                 ExeEvent
                :With 'fid' ⎕WC' Menu' 'Print'
                     'pra' ⎕WC 'Menuitem' 'In a file'       ExeEvent
                     :With 'prb' ⎕WC 'Menu' 'On a printer'
                           'ploc' ⎕WC 'MenuItem' 'Local'    ExeEvent
                           'prem' ⎕WC 'MenuItem' 'Remote'   ExeEvent
                     :EndWith
                     'prc' ⎕WC 'MenuItem' 'Send by e-mail' ExeEvent
                :EndWith
                'fie' ⎕WC 'MenuItem' 'Properties'           ExeEvent
                'fif' ⎕WC 'Separator'
                'fig' ⎕WC 'MenuItem' 'Quit'('Event' 'Select' 1)
             :EndWith
             :With 'two' ⎕WC 'Menu' 'Edit'
                'eda' ⎕WC 'MenuItem' 'Cut'                  ExeEvent
                'edb' ⎕WC 'MenuItem' 'Copy'                 ExeEvent
                'edc' ⎕WC 'MenuItem' 'Paste'                ExeEvent
                'edd' ⎕WC 'Separator'
                'ede' ⎕WC 'MenuItem' 'Find'                 ExeEvent
                'edf' ⎕WC 'MenuItem' 'Replace'              ExeEvent
             :EndWith
          :EndWith
       :EndWith
       ⎕DQ'Win'
     ∇
```

To make it easier to read, we have inserted extra spaces in the listing and aligned the definitions of the call-back functions for the "Select" events.

For example, if we select the option "*Print on a Local Printer*", we will see:

```
┌→─────────────────────────────────────────┐
│ ┌→─────────────────────┐ ┌→─────┐        │
│ │Win.MB.one.fid.prb.ploc│ │Select│        │
│ └──────────────────────┘ └──────┘        │
└∊─────────────────────────────────────────┘
```

7 - The Grid Object

Dyalog APL provides a rich and flexible tool to display and update data in a tabular representation, resembling a spreadsheet. The ***Grid*** object is extremely rich, and we will only describe its main features in this tutorial.

Figure P-18

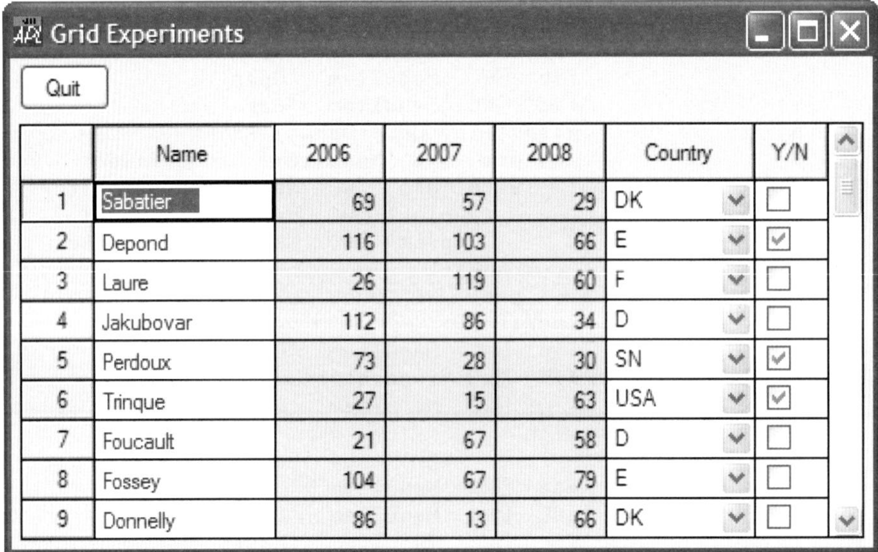

	Name	2006	2007	2008	Country	Y/N
1	Sabatier	69	57	29	DK	☐
2	Depond	116	103	66	E	☑
3	Laure	26	119	60	F	☐
4	Jakubovar	112	86	34	D	☐
5	Perdoux	73	28	30	SN	☑
6	Trinque	27	15	63	USA	☑
7	Foucault	21	67	58	D	☐
8	Fossey	104	67	79	E	☐
9	Donnelly	86	13	66	DK	☐

As you can see, a *Grid* consists of:

- Cells — Cells may contain any data (characters or numeric values). In many applications the columns contain homogeneous data, but this is not mandatory: any cell can contain any type of data.
- Column titles — By default, the columns titles are the letters `A`, `B`, `C`, `D`, …
- Row titles — By default, the row titles are the numbers `1`, `2`, `3`, `4`, …

7.1 Geometry & Titles

7.1.1 - Controlling the Geometry

When you define the cell dimensions the titles automatically adopt the same height (for row titles) or the same width (for column titles). Therefore you can only modify the width of the row titles and the height of the column titles.

To define the geometry of a *Grid* object you must specify the following properties:

`TitleWidth`	This value refers to the row titles, on the left. If this value is set to zero there will be no titles.
`CellWidths`	Specifies the column widths. You can specify a single value if all the columns have the same width, or as many values as you have columns.
`TitleHeight`	Determines the height of the column titles, on top of the grid. If this value is set to zero there will be no titles.
`CellHeights`	Specifies the row heights. Usually, a single value is provided, which applies to all the rows, but one can also specify a different height per row.

All these properties take default values.

Of course, the *Grid* itself has its own height and width. Depending on the data array dimensions, horizontal and vertical scroll bars will be automatically provided, as required. So, the data array may be smaller than the grid dimensions, and unused margins may appear.

It is possible that the cells dimensions are such that the bottom row or the rightmost column cannot be displayed completely. You can decide to let them be displayed partially using `('ClipCells' 1)`, or to only have entire cells shown in the grid using `('ClipCells' 0)`. This second option is recommended to avoid misinterpretation of partially displayed data (especially numeric data).

7.1.2 - Defining Titles

By default, titles are letters (on top of columns) or numbers (to the left of rows), but one can specify any titles using these properties:

`RowTitles`	In our example they take default values.
`ColTitles`	We will specify our own titles.

Titles **must** be given as nested vectors of character vectors. A matrix will not be accepted.

Here is the beginning of a function to create a *Grid* filled with a nested array named GridData, which may be found in the accompanying workspace:

```
     ∇ Grid_1 griddata;F
[1]    'F'⎕WC'Form' 'Grid Experiments'('Size' 260 470)
[2]    'F.Q'⎕WC'Button' 'Quit'(3 5)(25 50)('Event' 'Select' 1)
[3]    :With 'F.G'⎕WC'Grid'griddata(35 5)(220 460)('ClipCells' 0)
[4]   ⍝--- Geometry & Titles
[5]        TitleWidth←40
[6]        CellWidths←100 60 60 60 80 40
[7]        TitleHeight←30
[8]        ColTitles←'Name' '2006' '2007' '2008' 'Country' 'Y/N'
[9]    :EndWith
[10]   ⎕DQ'F'
     ∇
```

It is possible to control the formatting of the titles with the following four properties:

`RowTitleFCol` `ColTitleFCol`	These properties control the foreground (text) colour. One can use an RGB value or a negative value (see Section 4.1).
`RowTitleAlign` `ColTitleAlign`	These properties control the position of the titles. The possible values are: `Top`, `Bottom`, `Left`, `Right`, `Centre` and `TopLeft`, `TopRight`, `BottomLeft`, `BottomRight`.

7.2 Cell Types

7.2.1 - Cell Appearance

By default all cells are defined and handled identically with respect to these five properties:

- The background colour `BCol`
- The character colour `FCol`
- The font `CellFonts`
- The input behaviour `Input`
- The input cell type shown `ShowInput`

It is not possible to specify these properties directly for each cell. Instead it is possible to define an arbitrary number of combinations of these five properties, numbered 1, 2, 3..., and then assign a particular combination to each cell.

The different combinations are called `CellTypes`.

The `CellTypes` are defined by assigning a vector of values to each of the five properties listed above. Cell type #*n* is then defined as the *n*'th item of the `BCol` property, the *n*'th item of the `FCol` property, the *n*'th item of the `CellFonts` property, the *n*'th item of the `Input` property, and the *n*'th item of the `ShowInput` property. Scalar extension applies, so if a property is to have the same setting for all cell types it may be specified as a scalar.

The cell types are assigned to the cells using the `CellTypes` property.

The value of this property is a numeric matrix with a shape exactly equal to the shape of the data array, and containing values from `1` to `N`, where `N` is the number of combinations of the five properties that have been defined. If the shape of the matrix is different from the shape of the data array the consequences for the grid layout and behaviour are unpredictable, and the same is true if the cell type is defined to have larger number than the number of defined property combinations.

Often all cells in a column have the same type, but in many applications this is not necessarily the case, as we shall see in Section 7.4.

For our specific example we shall define 4 cell types. They will be numbered from 1 to 4:

Type	Contents	Columns
1	Names	1
2	Numeric values	2 3 4
3	Countries	5
4	Yes/No	6

We shall associate types to cells by the following statement:

```
CellTypes ← (⍴#.GridData)⍴ 1 2 2 2 3 4
```

We can see that three columns have the same definition.

Now, if we need to define properties like a background colour or a font, we will not refer to the 6 columns but to the 4 cell types, and specify four `BCol` and four `CellFonts` definitions.

Just to show how it works in our example:

- Let us define two *Font* objects: "`Garamond`" bold italic for characters (types 1 and 3), and plain "`APL385 Unicode`" for numbers (types 2 and 4).
- Let us decide that all the columns will be on a default background (`0`), except the numeric values (type 2), which should appear on a blue-grey background (`220 220 240`).
- And finally, all the cells will appear with black characters (`0`), except that the names will be shown in dark blue (`0 0 128`), and the Yes/No column will be shown in red (`255 0 0`).

Having made these decisions, we can modify the function `Grid_1` to become `Grid_2` and look like this (we have not repeated all the statements that are unchanged):

```
     ∇ Grid_2 griddata;F
[1]    'F'⎕WC'Form' 'Grid Experiments'('Size' 260 470)
[2]    'F.Q'⎕WC'Button' 'Quit'(3 5)(25 50)('Event' 'Select' 1)
[3]    'F.Fnt'⎕WC'Font' 'Garamond' 16 0 1 0 700
[4]    'F.APL'⎕WC'Font' 'APL385 Unicode' 16
[5]    :With 'F.G'⎕WC'Grid'griddata(35 5)(220 460)('ClipCells' 0)
...
[10]       ColTitles←'Name' '2006' '2007' '2008' 'Country' 'Y/N'
[11]  ⍝--- Types and Attributes
[12]       CellTypes←(⍴#.griddata)⍴1 2 2 2 3 4
[13]       BCol← 0 (220 220 240) 0 0
[14]       FCol← (0 0 128) 0 0 (255 0 0)
[15]       CellFonts←#.F.(Fnt APL Fnt APL)
[16]   :EndWith
[17]   ⎕DQ'F'
     ∇
```

Remember that the `BCol`, `FCol`, and `CellFonts` attributes are not associated with 6 columns, but with 4 cell types. Also note that so far we have not specified the `Input` and `ShowInput` properties, so the default values for these properties will be used for all cells.

Here is how the result looks:

Figure P-19

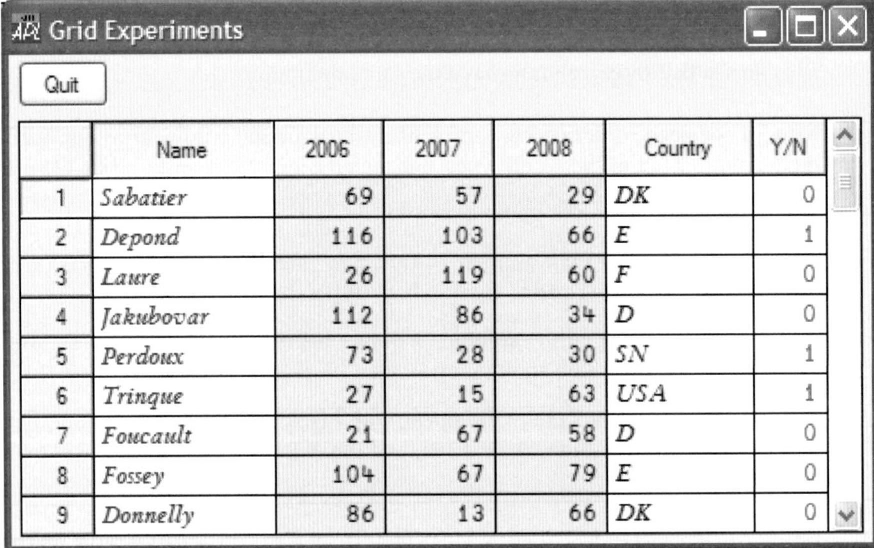

	Name	2006	2007	2008	Country	Y/N
1	*Sabatier*	69	57	29	*DK*	0
2	*Depond*	116	103	66	*E*	1
3	*Laure*	26	119	60	*F*	0
4	*Jakubovar*	112	86	34	*D*	0
5	*Perdoux*	73	28	30	*SN*	1
6	*Trinque*	27	15	63	*USA*	1
7	*Foucault*	21	67	58	*D*	0
8	*Fossey*	104	67	79	*E*	0
9	*Donnelly*	86	13	66	*DK*	0

7.2.2 - Input Fields

The grid defined so far is output only - it does not allow any data to be entered into any cells. This is because we have not (yet) specified the `Input` property. Let us do that now, so that it will be possible to enter data into the grid.

It is obvious that various types of data need different input specifications. So wc will define different *Input* fields and associate them with the 4 cell types. For now we will just define an *Edit* field for the names, and another *Edit* field for the numeric values. The last two columns will continue to be read-only fields.

This can be achieved with the following additional statements in the function Grid_2:

```
[16]     'IChar'⎕WC'Edit'('FieldType' 'Char')
[17]     'INums'⎕WC'Edit'('FieldType' 'Numeric')('Decimals' 0)
[18]     'INada'⎕WC'Edit'('ReadOnly' 1)
```

As you can see we have not specified a size for these fields (it is defined by the *Grid* configuration) and no position (as the definition will be used by all cells sharing the same cell type). These input fields can be considered as "floating fields". The last field has no *FieldType* because it is read-only.

Once these definitions are established we can assign them to the four CellTypes using a statement that is very similar to the ones we used for BCol and CellFonts:

```
[19]     Input←'IChar' 'INums' 'INada' 'INada'
```

If you run the function Grid_2 after having made these modifications you will see that you can now modify the values in the first four columns, and that you can navigate in the last two columns, but you cannot type anything there.

7.2.3 - Combo and Check Fields

Column 5 in the grid example specifies a country code, for which a drop-down *Combo* object is an ideal input control.

Column 6 in the grid specifies a Boolean value, for which a check button is an ideal input control.

We can define such two "floating" *Input* fields like this:

```
      Where←'AUS' 'D' 'DK' 'E' 'F' 'GB' 'I' 'USA'
      'IComb'⎕WC'Combo'Where
      'IChck'⎕WC'Button'('Style' 'Check')
```

We also need to incorporate these new definitions into the Input property:

```
      Input←'IChar' 'INums' 'IComb' 'IChck'
```

We can also remove the read-only field, which we no longer use. With these modifications the function Grid_2 allows all grid cells to be modified.

In the figure below we have pasted two images, to show how things will appear. The large one shows how a cell in the 5th column changes to become a drop-down control when it gets the input focus, allowing a country to be selected. Similarly, the smaller image show that a cell in the 6th column changes to become a check button control when it gets the input focus, allowing the user to select or deselect this parameter. To simplify the function we have removed the two different fonts used in the first versions of the function:

Figure P-20

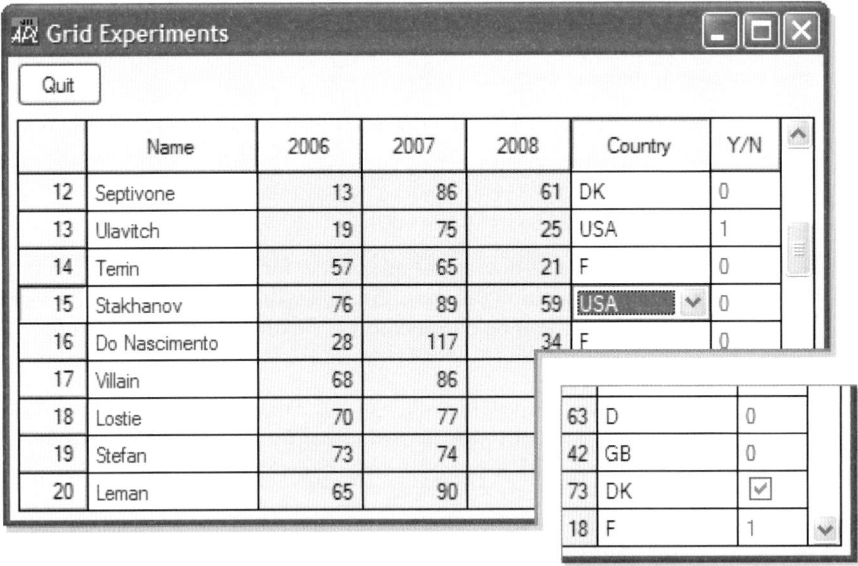

7.2.4 - Show Input; The Final Version

When the cursor enters a cell in column 5 or 6, that cell is temporarily transformed into a *Combo* (column 5) or into a *Check* button (column 6), as you can see in Figure P-20.

However, the cells that do not have the input focus are shown as plain text output fields.

It is possible to have the *Combo*s and the *Check* buttons displayed permanently in columns 5 and 6. To do so, one must set the property `ShowInput` to 1 for the cells in question. Since `ShowInput` is defined via the cell types we must specify 4 values, one for each of the 4 cell types we are using in this example: `0 0 1 1` (see statement `[20]` in the listing of the function `Grid_Demo1` below).

Here is the final version of our function. It creates exactly the form shown in figure P-18:

```
     ∇ Grid_Demo1 griddata;F
       'F'⎕WC'Form' 'Grid Experiments'('Size' 260 470)
       'F.Q'⎕WC'Button' 'Quit'(3 5)(25 50)('Event' 'Select' 1)
       :With 'F.G'⎕WC'Grid'griddata(35 5)(220 460)('ClipCells' 0)
      ⍝--- Geometry
           TitleWidth←40
           CellWidths←100 60 60 60 80 40
           TitleHeight←30
           ColTitles←'Name' '2006' '2007' '2008' 'Country' 'Y/N'
      ⍝--- Attributes
           CellTypes←(⍴#.griddata)⍴1 2 2 2 3 4
           BCol←0(220 220 240)0 0
           FCol←(0 0 128)0 0(255 0 0)
      ⍝--- Inputs
           Where←'AUS' 'D' 'DK' 'E' 'F' 'GB' 'I' 'SN' 'UA' 'USA'
           'IChar'⎕WC'Edit'('FieldType' 'Char')
           'INums'⎕WC'Edit'('FieldType' 'Numeric')('Decimals' 0)
           'IComb'⎕WC'Combo'Where
           'IChck'⎕WC'Button'('Style' 'Check')
           Input←'IChar' 'INums' 'IComb' 'IChck'
           ShowInput←0 0 1 1
       :EndWith
       ⎕DQ'F'
     ∇
```

7.3 Interaction with a Grid

7.3.1 - Events

More than 40 different events may be generated and reacted to when working with a grid. We will list a few of them here and refer to the on-line help and the manuals for the full story:

`CellUp` This *Event* is reported when the user releases the mouse button in a cell. We shall use it very soon in an example. You can also use `CellDown`.

`CellMove` Reported when the user tries to enter a cell. This *Event* may be used to allow an application to perform some action prior to the user entering a cell, or to inhibit entry into a cell.

`CellChanged` This event is reported **after** the contents of a cell has been changed, when the focus is moved to another cell or to another object outside of the grid. This *Event* may, for example, be used to start a calculation using the new values.
The event is reported **after** the action has occurred, so it is impossible to prevent it from happening. If you want to verify the entered value **before** updating the array, use the `CellChange` event instead.

`CellChange` This event is reported when the content of a cell has been changed, but **before** the user leaves the cell. It is possible to verify the validity of the entered value before the data array is updated.

`IndexChanged` Reported when the user has scrolled the *Grid*. The event is reported **after** the action occurred, so it is impossible to prevent it from happening. You may, for example, use the event to synchronise another object with the grid.

7.3.2 - Actions

Interactions between an application and the *Grid* generally involve the following properties:

`Values` This property is used to get or set the data displayed in the *Grid*. This is of course the main information.

`CellTypes` In some applications, it is interesting to change the cell type of some cells, for example to have them displayed in a different colour (see the example shown in Section 7.4).

`CurCell` This property returns the current position of the input cursor (row and column). This information may be valuable in *Call-Back* functions.

7.4 Example

Though rather artificial, this example is interesting because its uses `CellTypes` to select cells in a *Grid*. The theme is the following:

- For the 7 days of a week, a *Grid* displays which movies are programmed on 6 TV channels. They are displayed in white on a deep blue background.
- On some days, there is no movie on certain channels. The cell is then empty and displayed with a grey background (e.g. Monday/BBC).
- The user may select at most one movie per day by clicking on the corresponding cell. The selected movies then appear in black on white (e.g. Wednesday/"Mission" on MTV). A second click on the same cell cancels the choice.
- When the user has made his choice, a click on the "OK" button produces a little summary that is just displayed in the session, with Day / Channel / Movie.

Figure P-21: What we expect to see on the screen:

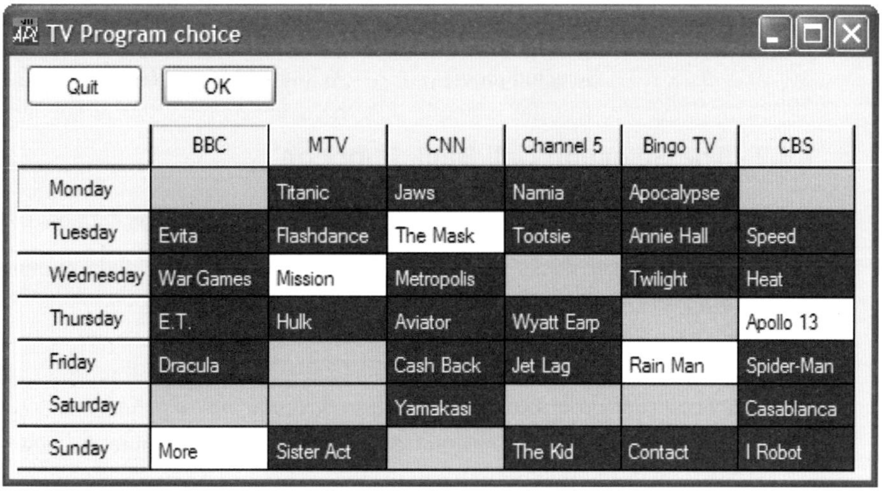

TV Program choice

Quit OK

	BBC	MTV	CNN	Channel 5	Bingo TV	CBS
Monday		Titanic	Jaws	Narnia	Apocalypse	
Tuesday	Evita	Flashdance	The Mask	Tootsie	Annie Hall	Speed
Wednesday	War Games	Mission	Metropolis		Twilight	Heat
Thursday	E.T.	Hulk	Aviator	Wyatt Earp		Apollo 13
Friday	Dracula		Cash Back	Jet Lag	Rain Man	Spider-Man
Saturday			Yamakasi			Casablanca
Sunday	More	Sister Act		The Kid	Contact	I Robot

Here is the result that should be produced by the OK button:

```
Monday      None      :
Tuesday     CNN       : The Mask
Wednesday   MTV       : Mission
Thursday    CBS       : Apollo 13
Friday      Bingo TV  : Rain Man
Saturday    None      :
Sunday      BBC       : More
```

7.4.1 - The Main Program

The movies programmed on the various channels are provided in `Movies`, a 7 by 6 nested character matrix containing movie titles, or empty vectors when there is no movie. This matrix is passed to the main program as its argument.

Most statements in the main function `TV` are very similar to those that we have already seen. Please notice the following details:

- As we said, the size reserved for the grid may be slightly larger than the space occupied by the grid titles and cells. To fill the gap we use `GridBCol←¯16` in line `[8]`, but then it does not make sense to draw a border around the grid, so we specify `('Border' 0)` in line `[5]`.
- Row titles are left-justified, and column titles are centred.

- We have defined three cell types with the following characteristics:

Type	Meaning	BCol	FCol
1	No movie	Grey	*(does not matter)*
2	Not selected movie	Dark Blue	White
3	Selected movie	White	Black

7.4.2 - The Selection Call-Back Function

Here are the comments relating to the selection *Call-Back* function `TVZap`:

[1] When the user clicks in a cell, we place the cell's row and column numbers in the variables `row` and `col`.

[3] We keep the current state (cell type) of the cell in `old`.

[4] If any other cell had been already selected for that day (cell type = 3) we must deselect it, because the user is only allowed to select one movie per day.

[5] This is the "intelligent" part of the function. We determine the new state of the cell based on its old state.

[6] The new status is registered in the cell type matrix.

[7] Finally `wt` is used to update the `CellTypes` property of the *Grid*.

7.4.3 - The Result Display

There is nothing special to mention about the second *Call-Back* function which displays the final choice.

A loop examines the cell types stored in the `CellTypes` property one day at a time and determines the position `vp` of the first (hopefully the only!) selected movie (cell type = 3). If a film has been selected `vp` will be in the range 1-6, but if no choice has been made for this day `vp` will contain 7. This is the reason why we added the word "None" after the TV channel names, and a column of enclosed empty vectors to the right of the movie names.

The day, channel, and film are extracted by simple indexing and displayed.

The three functions are given on next page.

7.4.4 - The Functions

```
∇ TV D;Win;WTypes;vj;vc;vi;vs;vp;vf
  WTypes←2-D∊⊂''
  :With 'Win'⎕WC'Form' 'TV Program choice'('Size' 245 515)
     'BQ'⎕WC'Button' 'Quit'(5 10)(25 70)('Event' 'Select' 1)
     'BV'⎕WC'Button' 'OK'(5 90)(25 70)
                                        ('Event' 'Select' '#.TVShow')
     :With 'Gr'⎕WC'Grid'D(40 5)(205 505)('Border' 0)
        vj←'Monday' 'Tuesday' 'Wednesday' 'Thursday' ... etc.
        vc←'BBC' 'MTV' 'CNN' 'Channel 5' 'Bingo TV' 'CBS'
        GridBCol    ←¯16
        TitleWidth  ←80
        CellWidths  ←70
        TitleHeight ←25
        CellHeights ←25
        RowTitles   ←vj
        ColTitles   ←vc
        RowTitleAlign←'Left'
        ColTitleAlign←'Center'
        CellTypes←WTypes
        BCol←(3⍴192)(0 0 128)(3⍴255)
        FCol←(0 0 0)(3⍴255)(0 0 0)
        Event←'CellUp' '#.TVZap'
     :EndWith
  :EndWith
  ⎕DQ'Win'
∇

∇ TVZap;old;col;row;vn;wt
  row col←Win.Gr.CurCell
  wt←Win.Gr.CellTypes
  old←wt[row;col]
  wt[row;]⌊←2
  vn←1 3 2[old]
  wt[row;col]←vn
  Win.Gr.CellTypes←wt
∇

∇ TVShow;vj;vc;vb;vi;vm;vp;vf;wt
  vj←↑Win.Gr.RowTitles
  vc←↑(Win.Gr.ColTitles),⊂'None'
  vm←D,⊂''
  wt←Win.Gr.CellTypes
  :For vi :In ⍳7
     vp←wt[vi;]⍳3
     vf←(⊂vi vp)⊃vm
     vj[vi;],'  ',vc[vp;],' : ',vf
  :EndFor
∇
```

7.5 Multi-Level Titles

7.5.1 - Hierarchy of Titles

Up to now we have only worked with simple titles, but it is possible to define multi-level titles for both rows and columns, as shown in Figure P-22 below:

Figure P-22

Grid titles hierarchy

		Previous year		Current year			
		S1	S2	Q1	Q2	Q3	Q4
France	Paris	10978	9415	14873	13526	8423	1470
	Nice	10453	6650	11208	14551	12183	4196
	Agen	759	11766	5247	10113	12091	15841
USA	New York	5840	3949	15706	11552	12042	10414
	Boston	1162	10097	14142	4359	6976	12252
	Houston	7637	3801	4395	5743	2662	7777
	L.A.	14349	14533	969	14460	8065	8253

The titles must be prepared with each top level title ("Previous year") immediately followed by its subtitles ("S1" and "S2"), and so forth. We have placed them in two global variables:

```
Row_Tree←'France' 'Paris' 'Nice' 'Agen' 'USA' 'New York' 'Boston' etc.
Col_Tree←'Previous year' 'S1' 'S2'  'Current year' 'Q1' 'Q2' ... etc.
```

This can be extended to titles with 3 levels or more.

The function `Grid_Demo2` which creates the example shown in Figure P-22 is very similar to what we have already seen. The only remarkable details are:

- The title widths and heights must be increased (to 160 and 50) in order to make room for the two levels of titles.
- Two new properties (`RowTitleDepth` and `ColTitleDepth`) indicate at which level a title should be placed. For example, "Previous year" is at level 0, while "S1" and "S2" are at level 1; "Current year" is at level 0, and "Q1" to "Q4" are at level 1.

- We used a form with `('Border' 2)` to show something different from the previous examples.

```
     ∇ Grid_Demo2;Win;title
       title←'Grid titles hierarchy'
       :With 'Win'⎕WC'Form'title('Size' 245 472)('Border' 2)
          :With 'Gr'⎕WC'Grid'(?7 6ρ15984)(10 5)(227 462)
             TitleWidth←160 ⋄ CellWidths←50
             TitleHeight←50 ⋄ CellHeights←25
             RowTitles←#.Row_Tree
             RowTitleDepth←0 1 1 1 0 1 1 1
             ColTitles←#.Col_Tree
             ColTitleDepth←0 1 1 0 1 1 1 1
          :EndWith
       :EndWith
       ⎕DQ'Win'
     ∇
```

7.5.2 - A Tree of Row Titles

One can also organise the tree of row titles in such a way that sub-trees can be expanded or collapsed, similar to the file folder tree in Microsoft Windows Explorer.

This applies only to row titles, not to column titles.

Figure P-23

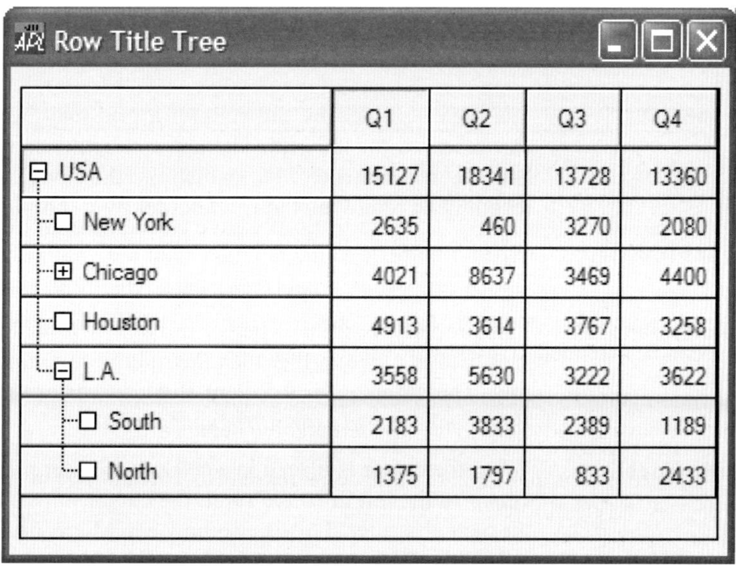

	Q1	Q2	Q3	Q4
⊟ USA	15127	18341	13728	13360
New York	2635	460	3270	2080
⊞ Chicago	4021	8637	3469	4400
Houston	4913	3614	3767	3258
⊟ L.A.	3558	5630	3222	3622
South	2183	3833	2389	1189
North	1375	1797	833	2433

In this example the sub-tree for "L.A." has been expanded, but not the sub-tree for "Chicago".

We used the following list of row titles:

`Row_DeepTree←'USA' 'New York' 'Chicago' 'Center' 'Suburbs'` *... etc.*

The function `Grid_Demo3` which creates the form shown in Figure P-23 is very similar to the previous function `Grid_Demo2`. The main difference is that the property `RowTitleDepth` has been replaced by the property `RowTreeDepth`.

This function is contained in the accompanying workspace, so you can test it yourself.

```
     ∇ Grid_Demo3;Win
        :With 'Win'⎕WC'Form' 'Row Title Tree'('Size' 245 372)
           :With 'Gr'⎕WC'Grid'#.Row_DeepData(10 5)(227 362)
              BCol←¯16
              TitleWidth←160 ⋄ CellWidths←50
              TitleHeight←30 ⋄ CellHeights←25
              ColTitles←'Q1' 'Q2' 'Q3' 'Q4'
              RowTitles←#.Row_DeepTree
              RowTreeDepth←0 1 1 2 2 1 1 2 2
              RowTreeStyle←'AllImagesAndLines'
           :EndWith
        :EndWith
        ⎕DQ'Win'
     ∇
```

7.6 Some Additional Properties

Many other properties apply to grids. Some of them are the following:

`GridBCol` — The area occupied by the cells of a grid may be smaller than the total size reserved for the grid. The gap can be given any background colour, but we recommend `¯16`, which is the form background. We also recommend removing the *Grid* border by `('Border' 0)`.

`OverflowChar` — When a numeric value is larger than the width of a cell allows it can be shown as a string of overflow characters, for example a list of asterisks.

`AutoExpand` — This property indicates whether or not a *Grid* will be expanded when the user tries to move further than the rightmost column or below the bottom row. The argument is a 2-item Boolean vector (for rows and columns). By default, a *Grid* cannot be expanded (0 0).

`InputModeKey` — When the cursor is placed in a cell and the user presses a key to move the cursor to the left or to the right, the cursor moves to the next cell, not to the next character. This is also how e.g. Microsoft Excel works.
When the cell content is to be edited an "Input Mode" key can be pressed, so that it becomes possible to move the input cursor *within* the field, using the cursor keys.

The property `InputModeKey` specifies this "Input Mode" key as a 2-item vector of integer values containing the key number and the shift state, respectively.
The default is (113 0), which is "F2" - the same as the edit key in Microsoft Excel.

8 - Using Printers

Defining in detail how text and/or graphics is to be printed may be a rather complex and tedious job, no matter which programming language you are using. As you will learn in Chapter S Dyalog APL is endowed with extremely powerful tools to print nicely looking documents and reports and to create PDF files. For this reason we will limit our coverage of controlling printers in this section to the basic principles.

8.1 The Printer Object

A ***Printer*** object is an invisible GUI object defined as any other top level GUI object. At any point in time, it represents the contents of a **single** sheet of paper.

In this *Printer* object one can create (write) text or drawings, very much like we placed *Text* objects in a form; they are children of the page. However, the child objects created on a printer page cannot be removed.

When the printer page has been filled as desired we can send it to a printer. The printer may be a real printer or a logical printer, as defined by the operating system.

8.1.1 - Creation, Orientation, and Coordinate System

When creating the *Printer* object, it is recommended that you specify its orientation: `Portrait` (the default) or `Landscape`:

```
      'Pr' ⎕wc 'Printer' ('Orientation' 'Portrait')
```

This statement creates a printer object for the system's default printer. In Section 8.2.8 you can see how to select another printer.

If the default coordinate system is `'Pixel'` and a program writes a letter in position 500 1000 the result will be extremely different if the physical printer has a resolution of 300 dpi (*Dots Per Inch*) or 1200 dpi. A more convenient coordinate system is to count positions in millimetres, so the first thing we will do is to query the printer characteristics using the property `'DevCaps'`. We have already seen this property being used for the *Root* object to obtain the display screen characteristics.

```
      'Pr' ⎕WG 'DevCaps'                (or Pr.DevCaps)
6672 4800    282 203   16777216
```

The result is a nested vector having the same structure as the result obtained for the display screen:

- The page size (height and width) in pixels (usually called "dots" for printers).
- The page size in millimetres.
- The number of available colours (a monochrome printer would return 2).

The size of a sheet of paper in A4 format is not `282` by `203` millimetres, but `297` by `210` millimetres. However, few printers can print to the edge of the paper; most leave an unprintable margin. The `'DevCaps'` property reports the printable area, adjusted for the necessary printer margins.

One can ask for the printer resolution (in dpi) by: `Pr.Resolutions`

We can now redefine the printer's coordinate system using the specification `'User'`:

```
      Y X ← 2⊃'Pr' ⎕WG 'Devcaps'
      'Pr' ⎕WS ('Coord' 'User')('YRange' 0 Y)('XRange' 0 X)
```

With this definition coordinates can in our example be specified in millimetres, from 0 to 282 vertically, and from 0 to 203 horizontally.

Once these basic settings are in place we can begin to print data on the page.

8.1.2 - Unnamed Child Objects

The various things you print cannot be deleted or changed, so it would in most cases be useless to give them names. Just to indicate they are children of the printer object, we shall type a dot, but nothing after it.

For example: `'Pr.' ⎕WC 'Text'` *... and so on ...*

However, it is always possible to give a name to a child object. Then you will be able to reference it later, for example in the left argument to `⎕WS`. However, since the old definition of the object cannot be changed the use of `⎕WS` will create a **new** object in addition to the previous one, with the new definition. This allows us to "clone" objects to different parts of the page.

8.1.3 - Simple Graphic Shapes

Dyalog APL provides some simple graphic shapes that can be used both on a Form and on a printer object: lines, rectangles, circles, and ellipses. Lines and rectangles are very convenient to draw frames in which it will be possible to place text or numbers. In this tutorial, we shall just draw rectangles; please refer to the reference documentation for the following objects:

`Circle` To draw complete circles, or just arcs, and to produce pie charts.

`Ellipse` The same as for `Circle`.

`Poly` To draw sets of straight lines, or polygons.

Let us just create 3 contiguous rectangles: you will see how accurate the drawing is.

A rectangle is defined by the position of its top-left corner, and its dimensions:

```
'Pr.' ⎕WC 'Rect' (40 20)(20 80)
'Pr.' ⎕WC 'Rect' (40 100)(20 80)('FCol' 255 0 0)
'Pr.' ⎕WC 'Rect' (60 20)(10 160)('LWidth' 3)
```

For the moment, the 3 rectangles we created have been buffered: they will be printed later.

8.1.4 - Write Some Text

To write text we shall use the same technique as we used in Section 4.2.2: We shall first prepare one or more *Font* objects defined as children of the *Printer* object, to be sure that the font definition is the one currently used by our printer driver. This is important because printer fonts are not the same as display fonts, and it is by creating a *Font* object as a child of a *Printer* object that you tell the system that it is a printer font that you want!

The text can be aligned horizontally and vertically, using the following properties:

`HAlign`

0 The x coordinate specified in the position defines the left end of the text.
1 The x coordinate specified in the position defines the centre of the text.
2 The x coordinate specified in the position defines the right end of the text.

`VAlign`

0 The base line of the text is placed on the specified *y* coordinate
1 The text is centred on the specified position
2 The top of the text is aligned on the specified *y* coordinate
3 The bottom of the character cell is aligned on the specified *y* coordinate
4 The top of the text cell is aligned on the specified *y* coordinate (this is the default)

Let us define two fonts:

```
'Pr.F1' ⎕WC 'Font' 'Arial' 133 0 1
'Pr.F2' ⎕WC 'Font' 'Times New Roman' 200 0 0 0 800
```

And use them to write two texts:

```
'Pr.' ⎕WC 'Text' 'Dyalog APL' (50 100)('VAlign' 1)('FontObj' 'Pr.F1')
'Pr.' ⎕WC 'Text' 'Hello World'(60 100)('HAlign' 1)('FontObj' 'Pr.F2')
```

8.1.5 - Character Size

Maybe you were surprised by the size we specified for the fonts (133 and 200). Placed on a form they would be huge, but on the paper you will soon discover that they are not so big.

The reason is that the font definition is specified in *pixels*, or *dots*, and most printers have a much higher resolution (given in *Dots Per Inch*) than a computer screen. Or, to put it in another way, to obtain a given text size we "need many more pixels" on a printer than on a screen.

Our printer's characteristics are: `6672` *dots* are equivalent to .... `282` mm
So, for our Arial font `'Pr.F1'`: `133` *dots* should give approximately .... `5.6` mm

The printer's resolution can be calculated as 25.4×6672÷282 dpi ~ 600 dpi.

We said "approximately" above because the different letters in a font are not equally tall. The font size is the height of the smallest box that may contain all characters.

8.2 Printer Management

What we have written or printed so far has only been buffered in the invisible *Printer* object; it has not yet been sent to the printer. We will now show how we can send the buffered output to the printer, and how to control the printing.

8.2.1 - Using Methods

If the *Printer* object is deleted for any reason (because it was localised in a function, or because we explicitly erased it using `⎕EX`), the current page will be processed, and in our example the page we had prepared would be physically printed on the default printer.

This may seem surprising, but by deleting the printer object we did not delete the buffer contents. We just released the link between APL and the buffer.

You can try: `⎕EX 'Pr'`

Remark This way of printing the buffered document is rather brutal. It does not allow us to control the printing parameters, and because the *Printer* object is no longer available it will have to be re-defined if we need to print something more. We recommend that you control the printing explicitly, as shown below.

The normal way of managing the printer is using ***Methods***.

Methods can be executed using a dyadic `⎕NQ`, or by a direct call using the namespace notation (refer to Section 5.2.3).

A printer object has seven *Methods*, all represented by a name and a numeric code, like *Events*. Since it is considered obsolete to use the numeric codes we will only use names here. The numeric codes can be looked up in the on-line help, should you ever need them.

You can obtain the list of supported methods by executing: `Pr.⎕nl ¯3`.

We shall study only the most important printer methods.

8.2.2 - Method NewPage

We said that a *Printer* represented **one single page** of paper. To print more than one page one can separate pages by executing a `NewPage` *Method*:

```
      2 ⎕NQ 'Pr' 'NewPage'
or    Pr.NewPage
```

Subsequent statements will write to a (virtual) new page, and so forth…

8.2.3 - Method Print

This *Method* sends all the pages that have been prepared to the printer. You can invoke it by:

```
      2 ⎕NQ 'Pr' 'Print'
or    Pr.Print
```

Now you can see how the page that we have prepared is printed!

8.2.4 - Method RTFPrintSetup

This *Method* displays a dialog box which allows the user to control the parameters for physical printing. RTF stands for *Rich Text Format*, and the method has this name because it is possible to provide a `RichEdit` object as a parameter, in which case the system can calculate the number of pages required and allow the use to select pages for printing. We will not be using this option in our example.

Prepare some pages and issue this command: `2 ⎕NQ 'Pr' 'RTFPrintFormat'`

When this dialog box is used, one can select a printer, modify the printing parameters, and decide to print all of the pages or only a subset of them.

Figure P-24

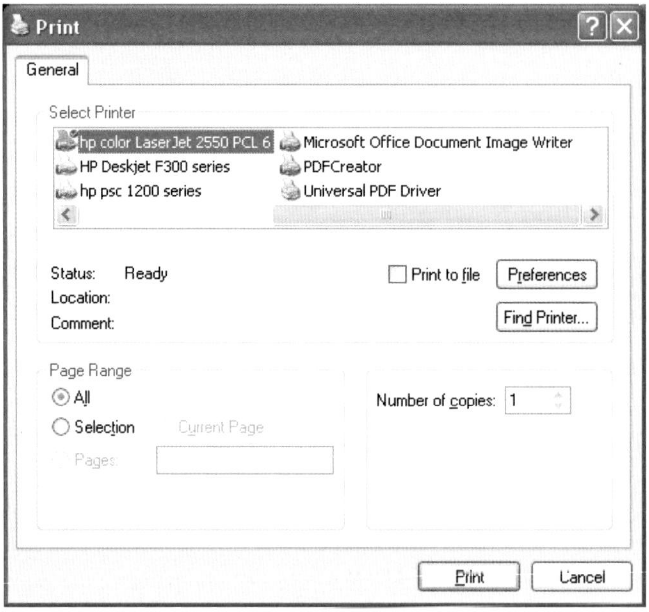

8.2.5 - Method Abort

Suppose that you have prepared a document by filling a *Printer* object and that you no longer want it to be printed. As we have described above you cannot just delete the *Printer* object, as this will cause the document to be printed, which is exactly the opposite of what you want.

This is why you need this *Method* to abort the printing operation, discarding all contents in the printer object (but not deleting the printer object):

```
      2 ⎕NQ 'Pr' 'Abort'
or    Pr.Abort
```

8.2.6 - Method Setup

Perhaps you need to change some settings for the physical printer before sending a document to it.

The `Setup` *Method* activates the printer's Control Panel.

8.2.7 - Method GetTextSize

It is often helpful to know in advance what will be the exact size of a given piece of text when printed. This can be obtained using the *Method* `GetTextSize`.

The argument to `GetTextSize` is a 2-item vector containing the text to print, and the *Font* in which it will be printed:

```
      Pr.GetTextSize 'Hello World' '#.Pr.F2'
or    Pr.GetTextSize 'Hello World' 'F2'
8.454504572 39.50864763
```

The result is given in the units of the *Printer* object's coordinate system (millimetres here).

If you check it you will see that the width is perfectly exact, but the height is probably not. The height of the printed text is smaller than indicated, because the *Method* gives the size of the **bounding** rectangle containing the text, including some space for tall letters and for letters extending below the base line.

The `GetTextSize` method is also supported by forms and many other GUI objects.

8.2.8 - Selecting a Printer

The physical printer can be chosen using the `RTFPrintSetup` dialog box, but generally it is defined when the *Printer* object is created, using one of the printers listed as available in the *Root* object, as explained in Section 4.3.3.

The syntax is (do not forget the final colon, the name must be identical to that reported by the `PrintList` method!):

```
      'Pr' ⎕WC 'Printer' 'hp color LaserJet 2550 PCL 6,Ne04:'
```

9 - And Also ...

There are so many different objects (many more than 50), that it is impossible to describe them all in this tutorial. Fortunately, once you have used the basic objects we have described, you will be able to use more and more new objects just by reading the documentation.

Among the most frequently used objects, let us mention the following:

`BrowseBox`	To select a folder on a local or network disk.
`FileBox`	To browse through your disk and select one or more files.
`ListView`	Provides presentation capabilities very similar to Windows Explorer.
`ProgressBar`	Provides different ways of representing the progression of a long process.
`Spinner`	To choose among a set of values like months, days, and so on, much like a *Combo*, but without the drop-down list.
`TipField`	To display a pop-up information box when the cursor enters an object.

`ToolBar`	A container for buttons, like those which appear on the upper part of most applications.
`TrackBar`	Provides a convenient way of showing a value between two limits, like for example the volume of a loudspeaker, or the intensity of a colour.

Not a word to my Mother:
she's convinced I use C# !

The Specialist's Section

Each chapter is followed by a "Specialist's Section" like this one.
This section is dedicated to skilled APLers, who wish to improve their knowledge.

If you are exploring APL for the first time,
skip this section and go to the next chapter

Spe-1 Lists of Properties, Methods, Events

When you have created an object you can obtain the list of its *Properties*, the *Methods* you can apply to it, and the *Events* which it can react to. Of course you can look up this information in the on-line help, but sometimes it is convenient that the object itself can provide the necessary information.

For example, just place a *Break Point* in the middle of the function `TV` that we used in Section 7.4 (somewhere between statements 1 and 15), and run the function: `TV Movies`.

When the function is interrupted, check that you are in the appropriate namespace:

```
TV[13]
      )ns
#.Win.Gr                                ⇦ That's good!
```

Spe-1.1 - Properties

You can now obtain the list of *Properties* by two different means. Both return long nested character vectors; we will show only their first five items:

```
      5↑PropList
Type   Values   Posn   Size   FCol
      5↑⎕NL ¯2
Accelerator  AcceptFiles  Active  AlignChar  AlwaysShowBorder
```

The two techniques do not return exactly the same result:

- `⎕NL ¯2` returns the property names listed in alphabetic order.
- `PropList` returns the property names in the order in which the properties are expected by `⎕WC` and `⎕WS`.

This is not the only difference: you can see that the results do not have the same size:

```
      ⍴ PropList
87
      ⍴ ⎕NL ¯2
91
```

Let us use *Without* to see the missing items:

```
      (⎕NL ¯2)~PropList
 D  WTypes  vc  vj                    ⇦ These are variables
```

Now we can see the difference: `PropList` returns only names of real *Properties*, but `⎕NL ¯2` returns also names of variables known at this point of function execution.

`⎕NL ¯2.6` would return only the property names.

Spe-1.2 - Methods

We said that *Methods* are similar to functions. They can be listed by:

```
      ⍴ML1←MethodList
24
      ⍴ML2←⎕NL ¯3                     ⇦ This time both techniques return the same
24                                       number of items.
```

Here the items are also returned in different order:

```
      5↑MethodList
Detach  ChooseFont  GetTextSize  Animate  GetFocus
      5↑⎕NL ¯3
AddComment  Animate  CellFromPoint  ChooseFont  ColChange
```

Spe-1.3 - Events

The same techniques as shown for properties and methods can be used to obtain a list of possible *Events*, which have a *Name Category* equal to `8`:

```
      ⍴EL1← EventList
44
      ⍴EL2← ⎕NL ¯8
44
```

Let us verify that the *Event* we used (`CellUp`) is in one of the lists:

```
      EL2 ⍳ ⊂'CellUp'
10
```

Spe-2 Different Syntaxes

Spe-2.1 - Properties and Methods

We have seen that two different syntaxes can be used to define the properties of an object and to invoke an object's methods. For example, to set the cells widths, we could write:

```
      'Win.Gr'⎕WS 'CellWidths' 70
or    Win.Gr.CellWidths← 70
```

Spe-2.2 - Events

This choice of syntax also applies to the way that we associate actions and call-back functions with *Events*, but in this case we actually have a choice of *three* different syntaxes. For example, to specify that our *Grid* object is sensitive to the `CellUp` event we can use any of these three expressions:

```
      'Win.Gr'⎕WS 'Event' 'CellUp' '#.TVZap'
or    Win.Gr.Event ← 'CellUp' '#.TVZap'
or    Win.Gr.onCellUp ← '#.TVZap'
```

The first two correspond to the two different syntaxes for properties and methods. In our program `TV` (cf. Section 7.4.4) we used the second syntax, the namespace notation, but slightly modified because we also used the control structure `:With`.

The third syntax is new for events, and it is an extension of namespace syntax. It introduces each individual event as a kind of assignable property, which allows a shorter, more direct, and very readable specification.

When an *Event* is assigned to an object using extended namespace syntax, the name of the event must be preceded by "`on`".

So, in the example above `'CellUp'` becomes "`.onCellUp`".

Also note that, when events are specified using the third syntax shown above, the first item of the argument to the call-back function (the *Event Message*) is a *Ref* to the object, rather than the name of the object. This can be seen in the following example, in which the function `TV` is our original function, whereas the function `TV2` uses the statement `onCellUp←'#.TVZap'`. We have displayed the *Event Message* that the call-back function `TVZap` receives:

```
      TV Movies
```

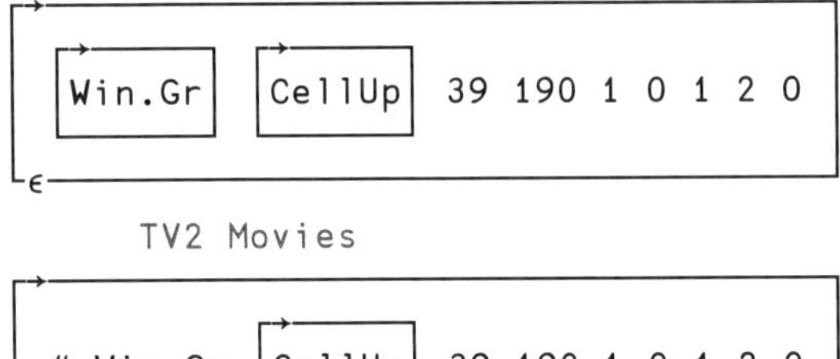

```
      TV2 Movies
┌→─────────────────────────────────────────────┐
│ #.Win.Gr ┌→─────┐ 39 190 1 0 1 2 0 │
│          │CellUp│                   │
│          └──────┘                   │
└∊─────────────────────────────────────────────┘
```

This difference may influence the way you write your call-back functions.

For example, in section 2.2.3 the function `GUI1_CB2` used the *Event Message* to determine which button had triggered the event. It used the expression:

```
      sufx←(⊃EventMsg)⎕WG'Caption'
```

This expression returns the button caption, for example `'B'`, using the button object's *name*.

It worked because we had used the traditional syntax when we defined the event:

```
      'Event' 'Select' 'GUI1_CB1' letters
```

We could have used the third notation introduced above instead:

```
      onSelect←'GUI1_CB1' letters
```

Then the expression to obtain the button caption should have been this one:

```
      sufx←(⊃EventMsg).Caption
```

Spe-3 Using Classes

In this chapter, we deliberately used the simplest GUI interface most of the time, using `⎕WC` and `⎕WS`.

We could just as well use a different syntax inspired by *Object Oriented Programming*. With this approach, objects are created as *Instances* of generic *Classes* by means of a system function: `⎕NEW`.

In fact, the same is true when we use `⎕WC`, but the syntax of `⎕NEW` is more stringent: keywords are mandatory, and the spelling is case-sensitive.

For example, let us compare the two techniques when used to create a form:

```
'F1'⎕WC'Form' 'Example'(100 200)(300 450)
F2←⎕NEW'Form'(('Caption' 'Example')('Posn'(100 200))('Size'(300 450)))
```

The syntax is stricter, but we see clearly what is being done! The stricter form also avoids hard-to-find application bugs that are possible with the relaxed form. For example, as a *ListView* object has a property called `Items`, one might write:

```
myitems←'One' 'Two'
'f.LV'⎕WC'ListView' myitems (10 10)(100 500)
```

The line of code above might work fine for years, until the application one day encounters data where the first item of `myitems` happens to coincide with the name of some other property of a *ListView* object, for example (`myitems←'Border' 'Center'`). Now suddenly, the statement causes a `LENGTH ERROR`, because the interpreter interprets the second item as an attempt to set the `Border` property to `'Center'`.

Here is a version of our function `TV` written using the more modern convention. Unchanged parts are in grey:

```
      ∇ TVNew D;Win;WTypes;vj;vc;vi;vs;vp;vf
[1]     WTypes←2-D∊⊂''
[2]     :With Win←⎕NEW'Form'(('Caption' 'TV choice')('Size'(245 515)))
[3]         BQ←⎕NEW'Button'(('Caption' 'Quit')('Posn'(5 10))
...                            ('Size'(25 70)))
[4]         BQ.Cancel  ←1
[5]         BQ.onSelect←1
[6]         BV←⎕NEW'Button'(('Caption' 'OK')('Posn'(5 90))
...                            ('Size'(25 70)))
[7]         BV.Default ←1
[8]         BV.onSelect←'#.TVShow'
[9]         :With Gr←⎕NEW'Grid'(('Values'D)('Posn'(40 5))
...                            ('Size'(205 505))('Border' 0))
[10]  ⍝------- The remaining statements are unchanged
```

Using this notation we can use the *Namespace* distribution rules to group statements `[4-5]` and `[7-8]` like this:

```
[4]         BQ.(Cancel onSelect)← 1
...
[7]         BV.(Default onSelect)← 1 '#.TVShow'
```

Chapter Q: Interfaces

1 - Introduction

Sometimes it is convenient or necessary to interface an APL program with other applications, or with program parts written in other languages. For example, you may need to exchange data with a Microsoft Excel worksheet, or an advanced analytics package may exist as a subroutine library written in a compiled language, and it may be necessary to use some of the features in the package from an APL application.

APL provides a number of interfaces to other programs; some of them are:

- OLE is a protocol which allows APL to start another application, for example Microsoft Excel, and then exchange data with the other application, or have it perform some tasks. APL may also act as an "OLE Server" that other applications may start and communicate with.
- ⎕NA (for *Name Association*) is a system function which provides access to compiled functions packaged in a DLL (*Dynamic Link Library*). ⎕NA associates a function name with an external program, so that the developer can use the external program as if it were an APL function.
- *Auxiliary processors* are programs written in a compiled language (most often C or C++), but packaged as an executable file rather than a DLL file. As with ⎕NA, a special protocol associates the routines in the executable file to function names in the workspace, thereby allowing APL to use the functionality of the external software.
- Together with the Object Oriented extensions to Dyalog APL the language has become well integrated with the Microsoft .Net programming environment. For example, user-defined APL classes may be created based upon .Net classes.

In this chapter we shall explain the OLE interface in some detail, and we will also show how ⎕NA may be used to interface to a DLL library. These examples may be followed by an APL developer, even if he does not possess detailed knowledge of other programming languages.

More advanced uses of ⎕NA , *Auxiliary processors*, and object oriented programming with Microsoft .Net interfacing requires a certain knowledge of compiled programming languages like C, C#, PASCAL, etc. These topics are outside of the scope of this tutorial; for more information on them please refer to the reference manuals published by Dyalog Ltd.

References

The *Dyalog APL User Guide*, Chapter 7, gives an extensive description of *Auxiliary Processors*. A toolkit is also provided for developers who intend to develop their own AP.

A long and detailed description of ⎕NA is provided in the *Dyalog APL Language Reference* manual, Chapter 6.

2 - OLE Interface with Excel

2.1 Introduction

OLE[12] is a Microsoft technology. Originally it was designed to allow embedding and linking to documents and other objects, but it is now a more powerful architecture for developing applications using components; components which may be written in any programming language. It is based on the *Component Object Model*, or COM.

OLE can be used to take advantage of functionality offered by one application from the inside of another application. For example, APL can use a Microsoft Excel worksheet as a user interface, and Excel can submit highly complex calculations to APL.

APL can also interface to Microsoft Word. This can be very useful, and can be used to create documents and reports from within APL. Chapter S describes a different, and in some ways more flexible and powerful way of producing printed documents using *NewLeaf*, an APL add-on software package that is included with Dyalog APL.

So, OLE is certainly not limited to being an interface between APL and Excel, but the cooperation between these systems provides some major advantages.

Nowadays, most people use Excel for the flexibility it offers to input and format data, or to produce simple business graphics. However, while Excel is easy to use for relatively simple calculations, it is not particularly well suited for more complex calculations and situations in which one needs to integrate operations on a large number of worksheets or workbooks.

The OLE interface makes it possible to build APL applications which for example read data from Excel worksheets, process them, and output results in some other worksheets, where users will be able to calculate additional results on their own, or produce graphs.

---

[12] OLE originally meant *Object Linking and Embedding*, but this term is no longer used by Microsoft. OLE is now described as a "*reusable architecture for component software*".

2.2 Create, Fill, and Save a Workbook

2.2.1 - Initiate the Communication

To start the communication between APL and Excel, we must start an instance of the Excel "engine". This can be done like this (be careful: this statement is case-sensitive):

```
      XL←⎕NEW'OleClient'(⊂'ClassName' 'Excel.Application')
```

Apparently nothing happened, but this is pure illusion: Excel was started as an "engine", ready to accept instructions from APL, but with no visible user interface. This is the normal use, but in our experiments we would like to see what is happening, so we shall issue the following statement:

```
      XL.Visible←1
```

Excel is now visible, but with no document loaded.[13] Let us discover what `XL` is.

```
      XL
#.[OLEClient]                          ⇦ XL is a Ref (see Chapter O)
      ⎕NC ⊂'XL'
9.2                                    ⇦ It is an instance of the application
```

The object has some *Properties* (similar to variables) and *Methods* (similar to functions).
We can query the lists of properties and methods, but they are much too big to be displayed here:

```
      ⍴ props← XL.⎕NL ¯2
216
      ⍴ meths← XL.⎕NL ¯3
74
```

If you take a look at `props` you will see that "`Visible`" is a property. We shall use other properties like "`Workbooks`" and "`ActiveWorkbook`", and so on.

If you look at `meths`, you will see a *Method* named "`Quit`", used to exit from and close Excel.

2.2.2 - Create a Workbook

Now, let us open a new workbook, like this:

```
      XL.Workbooks.Add ⍬
```

---

[13] Note that the behaviour is somewhat different if you already have an Excel session running before you create the OLEClient.

A new (empty) workbook appears, and it will be known as our **active** workbook, an object identified by the property `XL.ActiveWorkbook`.

Once again, you can explore the properties and methods of this object:

```
      ⍴props←XL.ActiveWorkbook.⎕nl ¯2
106
      ⍴meths←XL.ActiveWorkbook.⎕nl ¯3
56
```

Using the appropriate properties of the object "`ActiveWorkbook`" we can answer a number of questions:

- What is the name of the workbook?

```
      XL.ActiveWorkbook.Name
Workbook1
```

- How many sheets do we have in it?

```
      ⎕←number←XL.ActiveWorkbook.Sheets.Count
3
```

  The answer obtained depends on the Excel installation options in effect. The default is 3, but you may see another value.

- What are the names of these sheets?

  To answer this last question, we must apply the property "`Name`" not to a single sheet, but to a ***collection*** of sheets. We shall use a special symbol that returns this collection: it is the monadic *Squad*.

2.2.3 - Collection of Objects

We already used the dyadic *Squad* in Chapter B, Section 5.6 to index an object.
For example:

```
      4 ⌷ 84 56 32 19 76 20 64
19
```

In its monadic use, *Squad* returns the entire right argument (even if it is an array), as if the elided left argument had selected everything along all dimensions.

If the right argument is an instance of an "enumerable" object (like Sheets, which is a *collection* of Worksheet objects), monadic ⌷ returns all the elements contained within the object as an array.

This is exactly what we need. Let us try:

```
      XL.ActiveWorkbook.(⌷Sheets)
#.[OLEClient].[_Workbook].[_Worksheet]  #.[OLEClient].[_Workbook etc...
```

The display shows us that we obtained a vector of three references (*Refs*) to 3 instances of the object "`_Worksheet`". We can ask for their names:

```
      XL.ActiveWorkbook.(⌷Sheets).Name
Sheet1  Sheet2  Sheet3
```

We can now rename the worksheets using explicit names, for example the names contained in our matrix Towns. We must *Split* the matrix and take the right number of titles:

```
XL.ActiveWorkbook.(⎕Sheets).Name←number↑↓Towns
```

You can see in Excel that the sheets have been renamed.

We asked for all the sheet names. If we had to ask for only one (instead of 3 here), we could use any of the following methods:

```
XL.ActiveWorkbook.(⎕Sheets)[3].Name
XL.ActiveWorkbook.Sheets[3].Name14
XL.ActiveWorkbook.Sheets.Item[3].Name
```

Whatever the method[15], the result would be the same: Washington

2.2.4 - Fill a Sheet, Save, and Quit

By default, Excel had activated the first sheet. Let us activate the second sheet instead:

```
XL.ActiveWorkbook.Sheets.Item[2].Activate
```

Instead of endlessly repeating the left part of the expressions below, which refer to the currently active sheet, we can assign a *Ref* to the active sheet to a name:

```
act←XL.ActiveWorkbook.ActiveSheet
```

We can prepare some data, and write it into the active sheet. Here is a nested matrix with country names in the first column and numeric values in the other 4 columns:

```
vv←'Italy' 'Cuba' 'Spain' 'Russia' 'France' 'Greece',6 4⍴⍳24
```

We must specify in which part (*Range*) of the sheet the values are to be placed. The coordinates are specified using the Excel convention, and enclosed. The property Value2 represents the contents of a given *Range*; it can be assigned (written to the sheet) or queried (read the content of a range into APL):

```
act.Range[⊂'C3:G8'].Value2←vv
```

You can check that your worksheet has been modified.

---

[14] In fact, Sheets[3] is shorthand for Sheets.Item[3], "Item" being the "default property".

[15] Indexing on a COM object is defined by the object itself, not by Dyalog APL. Dyalog APL translates indexing to a call on the object's "Get" method, passing the index as an argument. You can also index using non-numeric indices, and the origin may be 0. For example, Sheets['Sheet3'] is valid. Monadic *Squad* was added to Dyalog APL to give the APL programmer an easy way of saying "Give me the items contained within this object as an array".

We could repeat these operations to fill some other parts in this sheet and then activate another sheet and fill it too. When the workbook is ready, we can successively:

- save the workbook `XL.ActiveWorkbook.SaveAs(⊂path,'NewBook.xls')`
- close it `XL.ActiveWorkbook.Close 0`
- quit Excel `XL.Quit`
- stop the Excel engine `⎕EX 'XL'`

2.3 Open and Process a Workbook

We shall now open an existing workbook and process some of the data it contains. For this exercise we shall use a workbook downloaded from http://dyalog.com/intro.

- `path` indicates where the workbook has been stored
- `bookid` is the name of the workbook file: `'XLDemo.xls'`

2.3.1 - Initiate the Communication

The first part of the process is very similar to that of the previous section, except that we use the "`Open`" method instead of "`Add`", and that its argument is the enclosed file path and name. We shall work on the second sheet, and create a *Ref* to it.

```
XL←⎕NEW'OleClient'(⊂'ClassName' 'Excel.Application')
XL.Visible←1
XL.Workbooks.Open ⊂ path,bookid        ⇦ Note: the fileid must be enclosed
XL.ActiveWorkbook.Sheets.Item[2].Activate
Act←XL.ActiveWorkbook.ActiveSheet
```

We have here shown the left part of the sheet:

Figure Q-1

	A	B	C	D	E	F	
1	2009		Sales	Forecast			
2	Updated on		January	17	2 008		Sour
3	Country	Coffee	Tea	Chocolate	Soda	Sugar	Biscu
4	Germany	1 089	783	5 217	2 309	643	3
5	Spain			5 420	4 380	650	32
6	Italy	1 050	800	5 500	3 210	660	330
7	Canada	1 080	800	5 620	2 560		380
8	France	1 100	800	5 700	2 600	710	410
9	Others	275	90	1 205	980	130	90
10	**Totals**	**4 594**	**3 273**	**28 662**	**16 039**	**2 793**	**1 834**
11							

2008 | 2009 | 2010 | 2011 | Example

2.3.2 - Read the Workbook Contents

An active sheet has an important property named `UsedRange`. It represents the rectangular part of the sheet that is effectively used, starting from the topmost row / leftmost column (often **but not always** cell "A1"), down to the bottom row / rightmost column.

```
      Act.UsedRange.Count
90                                        ⇦ The total number of cells
      Act.UsedRange.(Rows Columns).Count
10 9                                      ⇦ The number of rows and columns
```

It is possible to read only a part of the sheet, but usually it is simpler to read the entire sheet and select the different parts in the workspace. We shall use the property `Value2` again:

```
      Data←Act.UsedRange.Value2
```

The result is too large for this page; let us just display 7 rows and columns:

```
      7 7↑ Data
      2009  [Null]     Sales   Forecast  [Null]  [Null]     [Null]
Updated on  [Null]   January         17    2008  [Null]     Source
      Year  Coffee       Tea  Chocolate    Soda   Sugar   Biscuits
   Germany    1089       783       5217    2309     643        304
     Spain  [Null]    [Null]       5420    4380     650        320
     Italy    1050       800       5500    3210     660        330
    Canada    1080       800       5620    2560  [Null]        380
```

This is, of course, a nested array.

The empty cells are represented in APL by the value `⎕NULL`, displayed as `[Null]`. It is very useful to have this special value as an indicator of empty cells, but if we just want to display the data, as in this simple example, it could be convenient to avoid the `⎕NULL` values. We can replace `⎕NULL` with an empty character vector where the `⎕NULL` appears in cells that are supposed to contain character data, and with zero in cells that are supposed to contain numeric data, and we can use *Selective assignment* to do it (see Chapter H):

```
      ((,3↑[1]Data∊⎕NULL)/,3↑[1]Data)←⊂''
      ((,(3 1↓Data)∊⎕NULL)/,3 1↓Data)←0
```

Now the upper rows are easier to read, and the numeric part may be easier to work with using numeric functions, for example:

```
      +⌿3 1↓Data
9188 6546 57324 32078 5586 3668 14132 128522
```

In our example, we have read only one sheet. It is also possible to read all the sheets in a single statement, using the `UsedRange` of each of the items in a *collection* of sheets:

```
      ⍴Big←XL.ActiveWorkbook.(⌷Sheets).UsedRange.Value2
5
      ⍴¨Big
 10 9   10 9   10 9   10 9   7 3
```

2.3.3 - Modify the Presentation

We can see that Spain and Canada have not filled some of the cells they were supposed to fill. Let us highlight these anomalies in the spreadsheet itself:

- The country names in question will be right aligned and displayed in bold italics
- The empty cells will be painted with a light blue background

This can be achieved by modifying the properties of the corresponding *Ranges*.

Each block of contiguous cells referenced in a *Range* must be expressed as a scalar (the *Range* itself being a scalar or a vector), so:

- A rectangular block of cells must be enclosed: `Range[⊂'B5:F9']`
- It may contain a single cell `Range[⊂'F4']`
- A set of several blocks is a nested vector `Range['B1:B7' 'D3:F6']`

To modify the presentation of countries as mentioned above, we could write:

```
      Act.Range['A5' 'A7'].Font.(Bold Italic)←1
      Act.Range['A5' 'A7'].HorizontalAlignment←XL.xlHAlignRight
```

Note that `xlHAlignRight` is a member of the xlHAlign *Enum* that is exported by Excel, and actually has the numeric value `¯4152`[16], so we could have said:

```
      Act.Range['A5' 'A7'].HorizontalAlignment←¯4152
```

We think that you will agree that the former is preferable. The entire set of names/values of this Enum can easily be obtained:

```
      XL.XlHAlign
 xlHAlignCenter                    ¯4108
 xlHAlignCenterAcrossSelection         7
 xlHAlignDistributed               ¯4117
 xlHAlignFill                          5
 xlHAlignGeneral                       1
 xlHAlignJustify                   ¯4130
 xlHAlignLeft                      ¯4131
 xlHAlignRight                     ¯4152
```

Modifying the background colour of empty cells is easier, but there is a little trick; colours are not described using the RGB (Red-Green-Blue) convention, but the BGR convention, which also uses intensities between 0 and 255:

---

[16] The horizontal alignment property uses a so-called enumerated data type (Enum), like many other properties do. A property using an enumerated data type may only take one of a pre-defined set of values, and the allowable values are referred to by names (constants) which are described in the appropriate documentation. The names (and values) of these constants may also be obtained using the Workspace Explorer.

```
Act.Range['B5:C5' 'F7'].Interior.Color←256⊥255 200 120
```

The last thing we will demonstrate is setting or changing a formula in a cell. For example, let us compare the sales of (Coffee+Tea) to Soda, and place the percentage in cell C11:

```
Act.Range[⊂'C11'].Formula←'=100*(B10+C10)/E10'
```

Of course, because this is an Excel formula, multiplication and division are represented by * and / respectively. We will also change the formatting of the cell to show 2 decimal digits:

```
Act.Range[⊂'C11'].NumberFormat←'##0.00'
```

Where: "0" a digit in this position will always be shown
"#" a digit in this position will only be shown if it is non-zero.

This format must be defined in accordance with the regional settings in Windows, including the "thousands" separator:

With English settings we would write: `'##,###,##0.00'`

With French settings we would write: `'## ### ##0,00'`

You now have all the necessary information to exchange data with Excel (Read, Write, modify). Excel is so rich that a book would not be sufficient to mention all the possibilities. Since this book is primarily an APL course we will let you explore all the possibilities on your own. The following web page contains reference information about Microsoft Excel 2007: http://msdn.microsoft.com/en-us/library/bb979621.aspx

To finish, let us try to solve a very frequent problem.

2.4 A Simple Example

This is something extremely common: people located in different towns or countries send an Excel sheet to the corporate sales department with their monthly or quarterly results. The problem consists of adding these results to produce a global sheet.

Usually, people place their workbook in a dedicated directory, somewhere on the company's network. Here, to simplify the example, we have grouped all the sheets in a single workbook named `WorldSales.xls`. It contains six worksheets: Paris, Madrid, Tokyo, Denver, Montreal, and Dakar.

The figure below represents two of these sheets (Paris and Madrid). You can see how they are organised:

- Two rows of titles
- Then the leftmost column contains makes of cars, and the three next columns contain the number of cars sold. Note that some cells may be empty.

Figure Q-2

Paris

	A	B	C	D
1	**Car sales**			
2		**January**	**February**	**March**
3	Subaru	10	16	32
4	Opel	7		32
5	Citroen	34	13	24
6	Peugeot	20	11	2
7	BMW	39	22	8
8	Lexus	48	21	7
9	Mitsubishi	45	5	9
10	Skoda		19	13
11	Morgan	7	40	23
12	Volkswagen	18		41
13	Mercedes	47	33	11
14	Volvo	34	46	13
15	Fiat	44	24	26
16	Land-Rover	31	41	
17	Chrysler	24	48	32
18				
19				

Madrid

	A	B	C	D
1	**Car sales**			
2		**January**	**February**	**March**
3	Skoda	4	36	25
4	Peugeot	34	35	10
5	Porsche	46	44	45
6	Volvo	28	7	23
7	Volkswagen	50	11	23
8	Smart	16	26	45
9	Honda	22	24	41
10	Mazda	19	11	50
11	BMW		25	31
12	Lada	1	1	39
13	Mitsubishi	37	16	21
14	Subaru	35	35	11
15	Lancia	42	36	42
16	Renault	5		39
17	Seat	32		11
18	Alfa Romeo	5		48
19	Land-Rover	48	20	14

The general organisation is the same, but the makes of cars sold are not the same, and they are not listed in the same order.

The line "BMW" has been written in red in all the sheets in order to make it easier to check the results (BMW totals for all cities should be 100 110 120).

In a real application some parameters would probably be obtained through a GUI dialog box. For this educational purpose they will be placed in global variables:

```
path← … enter your own path here (ending with a backslash)
bookid←'WorldSales.xls'
```

A main function calls three sub-functions, each in charge of a specific step:

```
     ∇ CarSales;XL;towns;makes;sales
[1]    towns←CarSales_Init
[2]    (makes sales)←towns CarSales_Read (''(0 3⍴0))
[3]    towns CarSales_Store (makes sales)
[4]    XL.Quit
[5]    ⎕EX'XL'
     ∇
```

The **first step** looks a lot like our previous example: it initialises some variables, starts the communication with Excel, opens the workbook, and reads the sheet names:

```
    ∇ R←CarSales_Init
      XL←⎕NEW'OleClient'(⊂'ClassName' 'Excel.Application')
      XL.Visible←1                              ⇦ This is optional
      XL.Workbooks.Open ⊂path,bookid            ⇦ Open the workbook
      R←XL.ActiveWorkbook.(⎕Sheets).Name        ⇦ Get the town names
    ∇
```

In normal use Excel should not be visible, but you can make it visible for a test.

Second step: a loop reads sheet after sheet. We saw earlier that it would have been possible to read all the sheets in a single statement, but in a real application we should probably have to open different workbooks, each containing a single sheet. This would need a loop, too. Furthermore, by trying to read everything in one statement we increase the risk of causing a `WS FULL` error.

For each sheet read we identify any new makes of cars, and expand the variable `sales` holding the totals. Then we use dyadic *Iota* to update the right rows in `sales`.

```
    ∇ (makes sales)←where CarSales_Read (makes sales);Act;sh;Data;
                                          townmakes;townsales;new;pos
      Act←XL.ActiveWorkbook.(⎕Sheets)
      :For sh :In ⍳⍴where
          Data←2 0↓Act[sh].UsedRange.Value2     ⇦ Read one sheet
          ((,Data∊⎕NULL)/,Data)←0
          townmakes←Data[;1]                    ⇦ Separate column 1
          townsales←Data[;2 3 4]                  from the other ones
          new←~townmakes∊makes                  ⇦ Find the new makes
          makes,←new/townmakes                  ⇦ Append them
          sales←(⍴makes)↑[1]sales               ⇦ Expand the sales
          pos←makes⍳townmakes                   ⇦ Look up the makes
          sales[pos;]+←townsales                ⇦ Update the sales
      :EndFor
      XL.ActiveWorkbook.Close 0                 ⇦ Close the workbook
    ∇
```

Final step: the results are ordered in alphabetic order of makes, and written to a new workbook, including titles.

```
    ∇ where CarSales_Store (makes sales);Act;range;Data;lim
      XL.Workbooks.Add ⊖
      Act←XL.ActiveWorkbook.ActiveSheet
      Act.Range[⊂'A1'].Value2←'Cumulated sales for:'
      Act.Range[⊂'A2'].Value2←,' ',↑where
      Act.Range[⊂'B4:D4'].Value2←'January' 'February' 'March'
      Data←makes,sales
      Data←Data[⍋↑makes;]
      range←⊂'A6:D',⍕3+⍴makes
      Act.Range[range].Value2←Data
      lim←⍕5+⍴makes
      range←⊂'A',lim,':D',lim
      Act.Range[range].Value2←(⊂'Total'),+⌿sales
      Act.Range[range].Font.Bold←1
      XL.ActiveWorkbook.SaveAs(⊂path,'CumulatedSales.xls')
      XL.ActiveWorkbook.Close 0
    ∇
```

If you do not make Excel visible, this function will probably execute in less than one second. This shows how the cooperation between Excel and APL to aggregate data may be easy to program and perform well.

Warning! This example does not include any validation. Our experience shows that Excel is so permissive that people sometimes enter text (for example "None") in numeric columns, and may write the same word with different typesetting (Audi / AUDI, for example). A real-world application should of course include extensive validation and error reporting to avoid problems.

3 - Name Association

3.1 Introduction

3.1.1 - Definitions

A *Dynamic Link Library*, or ***DLL***, is a set of compiled functions generally written in C or C++. Most DLLs are provided as part of the *Operating System* or with other third party software installed on the machine. They can also be written by a developer to fit some specific need.

Each function contained in a DLL may take arguments and return a result.

Name association, or ⎕NA, is something like a bridge which allows an APL developer to use a function contained in a DLL as if it were an APL defined function.

When this bridge between APL and a DLL is activated, for a function in the DLL named for example "fcopy", ⎕NA will create a new function in the workspace. By default the new function will also be named "fcopy", but one can assign it a different name.

The syntax is {*Res* ←} {'*APLName*'} ⎕NA '*Calling protocol*'

Calling protocol is a character vector which defines:

- The type of result provided by the DLL function, if any.
- The name of the DLL file, followed by the function name. They are separated by a vertical bar '|'.
- Optionally, the type of function call (P32 or C32; see below).
- The type(s) of the argument(s) expected by the function.

APLName An optional name given to the function in the APL workspace.

Res A *Shy* result containing the name of the function just created.

3.1.2 - Commented Example:

```
      ⎕NA 'F8 Tolkien|Hobbit I4 F8'
```

Suppose that somewhere on our computer there is a DLL file named Tolkien.dll. This DLL may contain dozens of functions, and among them, one is named Hobbit. In Dyalog's manuals, DLL functions like Hobbit are known as "*external functions*".

Hobbit expects two arguments, described by the right part of the calling protocol: a 4-byte integer number (I4), and an 8-byte floating-point number (F8).

The result returned by Hobbit is described by the left part of the string. It is also an 8 byte floating-point number

Because we did not specify a left argument, ⎕NA will create a function in our workspace named Hobbit too. This may be changed by providing a different name via the left argument, like this:

```
      'MyPrecious' ⎕NA 'F8 Tolkien|Hobbit I4 F8'
```

Now, ⎕NA will create a function named MyPrecious, but still associated with the same function Hobbit in the Tolkien.DLL file.

The *Name Category* (⎕NC) of MyPrecious is 3 (more precisely 3.1 like any defined function).

When this APL function is called (for example: val←MyPrecious 46 1410.1952) it passes the two values to the external function Hobbit, which returns a result (that is assigned to val in the example).

3.2 Detailed Syntax

Before you try to use a DLL function, you must consult the associated documentation, which describes the behaviour of the function, and the type of its arguments and results.

The full syntax for the right argument of ⎕NA is:

```
{result} DLL|function {arg1} {arg2} ...
```

3.2.1 - DLL Description

The DLL may be specified using a full or relative pathname, file extension, and function type.

If the path is omitted, the DLL file is searched for in the standard operating system directories (like `c:\windows\system32`) in a particular order. For further information, see your operating system manuals.

When necessary, a full or relative pathname may be supplied in the usual way:

```
⎕NA'... d:\folder\myfile|function ...'
```

When the file extension is "`DLL`", it can be omitted as above. However, many DLLs are "`.exe`" files and then the extension must be specified explicitly:

```
⎕NA'... d:\folder\myfile.exe|function ...'
```

For a computer running Windows, the arguments and the result can be transferred to/from a DLL using two different function call conventions referred to as "C" for C language, and "P" for Pascal, followed by 16 or 32, depending on whether the code is run in 16-bit or 32-bit mode.

The default is `C32`. If this is not the case, you must specify the protocol after the function name. For example:

```
⎕NA'... d:\folder\mydll.exe.P32|function ...'
```

This DLL will be called with the 32 bit Pascal convention.

3.2.2 - Function Syntax

DLL functions follow the conventions used by many languages like C, and cannot be dyadic; they receive values through a (possibly nested) vector to the right of the function.

In most languages an argument can be used both for input and output. This is not the case in APL: a function cannot overwrite its arguments. For this reason the result of the APL function is a nested vector:

- The first item is the result explicitly defined in the DLL function calling syntax.
- Subsequent items are results that the function returns in some of its arguments. These arguments are identified in the calling syntax by a *Direction* symbol `>` (output only) or `=` (input and output).

The type of the result and each of the arguments must be described using the following scheme:

`{Direction}{Special}`**`Type`**`{Width}{Array}`

The type is mandatory, while the other parameters are optional.

Note: Some external functions don't return a result.

Examples:

`<I2`	Pointer to a 2-byte integer *input* to the external function.
`>C`	Pointer to character *output* from the external function.
`=T`	Pointer to character *input* to and *output* from the external function.
`=A`	Pointer to an APL array *input* to and *output* from the external function.
`<0T`	Pointer to a null-terminated character string *input* to the external function.
`=F8`	Pointer to an 8-byte floating-point number *input* to and *output* from the external function.

The table shown below describes the possible values for these parameters. A detailed explanation can be found in:

Dyalog **Language Reference** manual
Chapter 6: System Functions & Variables
Section ⎕NA

Data type coding conventions

Description	Symbol	Meaning
Direction	<	Pointer to an array *input* to the DLL function
	>	Pointer to an array *output* from the DLL function
	=	Pointer to an *input/output* array
Special	0	Null-terminated string (this is the digit 0, not the letter O)
	#	Byte-counted string
Type	I	Integer
	U	Unsigned integer
	C	Untranslated Character
	T	*Classic Edition*: Character translated to/from ANSI *Unicode Edition*: Character
	F	Floating point value
	A	APL array
Width	1	1 byte
	2	2 bytes
	4	4 bytes
	8	8 bytes
Array	[*n*]	Array of *n* items
	[]	Array, length determined at call-time
	{...}	Structure

In the *Classic Edition* of Dyalog APL `C` specifies untranslated characters, whereas `T` specifies that the character data will be translated to/from `⎕AV`. The use of `T` with default width is recommended if portability between the two editions is important.

3.3 See How It Works

Dyalog APL is delivered with many utility workspaces, and among them you can load this one:

```
      )Load Files
```

This workspace provides functions to work with files (copy, move, delete, and so on); they are contained in a *Namespace* named Files.

Let us take a look at two of them, and see how they work.

3.3.1 - Example 1

The first function deletes a file:

```
     ∇ Delete name;DeleteFileX;GetLastError
[1]    'DeleteFileX'⎕NA'I kernel32.C32|DeleteFile* <0T'
[2]    :If 0=DeleteFileX⊂name
[3]        ⎕NA'I4 kernel32.C32|GetLastError'
[4]        11 ⎕SIGNAL⍨'DeleteFile error:',⍕GetLastError
[5]    :EndIf
     ∇
```

- The function creates a *Name Association* with a DLL-file named `kernel32.dll`
- It is located in one of the default directories: `c:\windows\system32`. So we need not specify the directory and the file extension.
  We could as well have omitted the function call type `C32`, since it is the default.
- This DLL, like many others, contains two "twin" functions:
    - The first one is named `DeleteFileA`.
      It works with ANSI 1-byte characters (A=ANSI)
    - The other one is named `DeleteFileW`.
      It works with Unicode 2-byte characters (W=Wide)

  To avoid a function crash if the wrong name is used, and to simplify writing portable code for both *Classic* and *Unicode Editions*, you may specify the character "`*`" instead of "`A`" or "`W`" at the end of a function name. This character will be automatically replaced by "`A`" in the *Classic Edition* and "`W`" in the *Unicode Edition.*
- We specified `DeleteFileX` as the name of the APL function. It is localised in the header.
- If we had not specified the left argument to `⎕NA` the APL function name used would have been `DeleteFile` (without the A or W).
- This external function accepts only one input (`<`) value, which is a character string (`0T`).
- It returns an integer of undefined length (I)
- Note that the string passed in statement `[2]` must be enclosed.

This external function is supposed to delete a file from disk. If something goes wrong (for example, if the file does not exist), the function returns a zero result. The only way to obtain information on what happened is to call another external function `GetLastError`:

- `GetLastError` is located in the same DLL.
- Because we did not provide a left argument to `⎕NA`, the APL function will be created with the same name. It is localised in the header.
- The external function returns a 4-byte integer error number.

The function signals the error, including an error message:

```
      Delete 'd:\tets.txt'
DeleteFile error:2
      Delete'd:\tets.txt'              ⇦ The correct name is test, not tets
     ^
      ⎕EN
11
```

3.3.2 - Example 2

This second function returns the current directory, for example:

```
      GetCurrentDirectory
C:\Documents and Settings\ [...] \Dyalog Apl 12.0 Unicode Files
```

```
     ∇ r←GetCurrentDirectory;GCD;GetLastError
[1]    'GCD'⎕NA'I kernel32.C32|GetCurrentDirectory* I4 >0T'
[2]    :If 0≠1⊃r←GCD 256 256
[3]        r←2⊃r
[4]    :Else
[5]        ⎕NA'I4 kernel32.C32|GetLastError'
[6]        11 ⎕SIGNAL⍨'GetCurrentDirectory error:',⍕GetLastError
[7]    :EndIf
     ∇
```

- This function creates a *Name Association* with the same DLL: `kernel32.dll`.
- This function also exists in two variants, "A" and "W", so we used the asterisk notation and provided "`GCD`" as the APL function name.
- The function returns an integer.
- It takes two arguments: a 4-byte integer, and a string that will be output (`>`) as the second item of the result.
- In case of an error, the same technique as used in the function `Delete` is used to obtain the error number and to signal the error to the calling environment.

When the external function is called,

- The first argument (described by `I4`) is set to 256: it is the maximum length of the result.
- The second argument is set to the same value: it prepares a string of length 256 to receive the result output by the external function.

That's all, folks!

We shall not go further in this chapter. It would require a better knowledge of C programming conventions, and this is out of this tutorial scope.

Please refer to the **Language Reference** manual, or to the on-line help.

Chapter R: SALT

1 - Introduction

1.1 Why a Source Code Management System?

1.1.1 - Maintenance of Vital Big Applications

Up to now, all the functions and operators that we have defined were created with an APL function editor, and stored in an APL workspace. The workspace is very well suited to a single developer. In this respect it is like a spreadsheet which contains data and the macros which operate upon it in a single convenient package. However, as your collection of APL functions grows, you will almost certainly want to share some functions between workspaces. You will find yourself copying utility functions into several workspaces, and wondering whether every workspace has the latest version of your utilities – or which versions are in use, when users encounter problems in old workspaces.

When you hire a team of programmers to share responsibility for the code, the situation gets harder to manage. Each developer will need a copy of the workspace to work on, and changes need to be merged – without overwriting changes that others have made.

As time goes by, the workspace, which is an indivisible "capsule" containing code and data, becomes less and less convenient.

Traditionally, APL development teams have solved the above problems by writing "source code management systems" in APL. These systems prevent developers from overwriting each others work, allow you to compare new and old versions of code, and load selected versions of code into the workspace when the application starts, etc. These systems typically store APL code in collections of workspaces or APL component files, and provide functions to compare and merge versions – and build "releases" in a controlled fashion. These systems often work very well, and are integrated with data- or project-management systems, and other "corporate workflow".

However, the adoption of Unicode as a standard now allows APL code to be stored in "ordinary" Unicode text files and take advantage of work done by all the developers in the world. It is no longer necessary for APL programmers to maintain their own systems for this purpose. If there *is* a good reason for using your own system to handle part of the source code management, Unicode files allows you to be selective about which parts of the problem you write your own solutions for.

SALT – the *Simple APL Library Toolkit* – was introduced with version 11.0 of Dyalog.

SALT makes it possible to store individual APL functions, or entire namespaces and classes in Unicode text files which can be edited and managed using industry standard tools which make it easy to share code between projects and teams of developers. Unlike "traditional" APL code stores based on special APL files, code saved using SALT can easily be embedded in electronic mail, published on the web, and viewed and edited using generally available tools. Even the simplest editors like Microsoft's *Notepad* are able to edit Unicode text files, and it becomes possible to use excellent, free comparison tools. If APL is used together with other programming languages, SALT makes it straightforward for the APL code to be managed using the same tools as the rest of the project.

Although SALT makes it *possible* to use external tools, it does not *require* the use of external tools. You can use the APL editor to edit functions, and SALT will automatically update the Unicode files which can then easily be shared or simply archived more easily.

SALT contains a simple version control system, which may be adequate for small systems. However, Dyalog recommends the use of Subversion, CVS, Visual SourceSafe – and other "industrial strength" systems (many of which are free) for management of larger projects. At Dyalog, Subversion is used to manage APL code and the code written in other languages, which implement the APL system itself.

1.1.2 - Main Characteristics

The main characteristics of `SALT` are:

- APL programs (or groups of programs and variables) can be developed using any text editor like, for example, Microsoft Notepad.
- They are stored on disk in separate text files and can be read and maintained independently.
- They are loaded into APL when needed to be executed.
- It is possible to assign a version number to each module, so that one can keep track of all the modifications made in the past.
- Different versions of a module can be compared using either an APL program or any comparison tool available on the market, including excellent freeware programs.

1.1.3 - Script Files

`SALT` consists of a series of APL functions stored in `⎕SE` to manipulate the source code of objects. Because it is APL code it is very flexible and can be enhanced at will.

Text files can be used to define *functions*, *Namespaces* including *Classes*, for people who use Object Oriented Programming. In this tutorial we shall only use *Namespaces*.

The source code (or ***Script***) for each object (*Class* or *Namespace*) is stored in a single Unicode text file with a file extension "`.dyalog`".

Warning! Under Unix file names are **case sensitive**.

When Dyalog APL is installed under Windows the keyboard driver installed with APL makes it possible to edit "`.dyalog`" files with APL characters in Notepad, which is configured to open the "`.dyalog`" files automatically.

A *Script* file:

- begins by a clause `:Namespace` or `:Class` or `:Interface` followed by the name of the *Namespace* or *Class/interface* to create
- and is closed by `:EndNamespace` or `:EndClass` or `:EndInterface`

If it doesn't, it is assumed to be a function.

In the *Script* body, one can define variables, functions, and operators.

- *Direct functions* are defined as usual with delimiting braces.
- *Procedural functions* must be delimited by an opening and a closing *Del* or *Carrot* (∇).

Among the files distributed for this book is a demonstration *Script* file named `DemoScript.dyalog`; its contents are displayed on next page.

The *Namespace* is named "`Simple`" in the first line:

This *Script* defines:

Three variables, named	`Nested`
	`Airports`
	`RounDefault`

Four Procedural functions, named	`average`
	`Round`
	`CloseRound`
	`Plus`

One Direct function, named	`Primes`

```
:Namespace Simple

Nested←'My name is Bond' 0 0 7

∇ m←average val;s;n
  s←+/val
  n←ρval
  m←s÷n
∇
Primes←{(~v∊1 1↓v∘.×v)/v←ιω}

Airports←↑'LGW' 'CDG' 'CPH' 'KBP' 'DKR'
RounDefault←2

∇ Res←N Round Val
  Res←⌊0.5+Val×10*N
  Res←Res÷10*N
∇

∇ R←CloseRound Y;RndSum;SumRnd;Diff;Great
  RndSum←⌊0.5++/Y
  SumRnd←+/R←⌊0.5+Y
  Diff←Rndsum-SumRnd   ⍝ Intentional error
  Great←⍒,Y
  R[(|Diff)↑Great]+←×Diff
∇

∇ r←a Plus b
  r←a+b
∇
:EndNamespace
```

There are very few things to say about these functions; let us just make some comments:

- `Round` Rounds values to the number of digits given as the left argument.
- `CloseRound` Rounds values to the nearest integer. However, if the values are just rounded individually the sum of the rounded values may be different from the rounded sum of the original values. To avoid this problem, our function will add `1` or `¯1` to the largest rounded values, if necessary, in order to correct the sum of the rounded values.
- The functions have been typed without line numbers because it is simpler, but typing line numbers would not generate an error. However, if the code is modified and saved again using `SALT`, the line numbers will be removed.

1.2 Using Script Files

1.2.1 - Loading a Script into the Session

To demonstrate how SALT can use this *Script*, let us work in a clear workspace.

```
      )clear
clear ws
```

Then we can load the contents of our file, using the Load function of SALT, like this:

```
      Path←'d:\MyFiles\'                 ⇦ Adapt the path to your own configuration,
      ⎕←⎕SE.SALT.Load Path,'DemoScript'  and load the script file.
#.Simple
```

The function returns, as a *Shy result*, the name of the *Namespace* just created (Simple).

```
      Simple.⎕nl ¯2                      ⇦ As expected, a namespace has been built,
 Airports  Nested  RounDefault             and it contains what we had prepared.
      Simple.⎕nl ¯3
 CloseRound  Plus Primes  Round  average
      17 Simple.Plus 23                  ⇦ Now we can use these functions.
40
      ⎕PATH←'Simple'                     ⇦ We can use ⎕PATH to make it easier.
      1 Round 75.218 34.963 55.467
75.2 35 55.5
      Simple.Nested
 My name is Bond  0 0 7                  ⇦ The variables have been created too.
```

1.2.2 - Generic Names

One can load a set of *Namespaces* with a single statement using a pattern. For example, our directory contains three scripts:

File:	Contains Namespace:
Test.3.dyalog	Blabla
Telefon.dyalog	Gaston
Teton.dyalog	Doudou

We can load them all using this single statement:

```
      ⎕SE.SALT.Load Path,'Te*'           ⇦ This will create 3 Namespaces.
```

1.2.3 - Source Directory

In the example above, we specified the path leading to our file explicitly. It may be more convenient to specify a default source directory, or set of source directories. Then, if we just specify a script name, `SALT` will automatically explore the specified directories.

When Dyalog APL is installed, the default directory is: `[Dyalog]\SALT` , where `[Dyalog]` represents the path where Dyalog APL has been installed.

You can query the current directory setting using the following command:

```
      ⎕SE.SALT.Settings 'workdir'
[Dyalog]\SALT
```

For example, under Windows, Dyalog APL is most often installed in:

```
      c:\Program Files\Dyalog\Dyalog APL 12.0 Unicode
```

So, the default directory used by `SALT` will be:

```
      c:\Program Files\Dyalog\Dyalog APL 12.0 Unicode\SALT
```

You can change this to another directory, or to a list of directories, separated by semi-colons. For example, to avoid using a path as we did, we could write:

```
   ⎕SE.SALT.Settings 'workdir  [Dyalog]\SALT ; d:\MyFiles  -Permanent'
                      ↑_____↑  ↑___________↑   ↑________↑  ↑________↑
                      Keyword   Directory 1    Directory 2   Option
```

The option "`-Permanent`" means that the new setting will be stored in the Windows Registry, so that we will no longer have to repeat it in each session.

Now, to load the same script, we can just execute:

```
      ⎕SE.SALT.Load 'DemoScript'          ⇦ No path is needed
```

Recommendation: Specify immediately your own preference as indicated above.

1.2.4 - "Target" and "Disperse"

By default, the loaded *Namespace* is created in the *Root* namespace, but we can insert it into any existing *Namespace* using the parameter "`-Target=`*nnn* ".

For example:

```
      ⎕←⎕SE.SALT.Load 'DemoScript -target=Cool.Mec'
#.Cool.Mec.Simple
```

Instead of loading the *Namespace* as a whole, one can load the objects it contains and disperse them directly into the specified target, using the option "-Disperse". For example:

```
      )clear
clear ws
      ⎕←⎕SE.SALT.Load'DemoScript -disperse'
1                                              ⇦ This time, the answer is 1 (success)
      ⎕NL - 2 3
 Airports  CloseRound  Nested  etc...
      )obs
                                               ⇦ No answer
```

Clearly, the objects have been placed in the *Root* namespace, and the namespace Simple was not created.

This option can be combined with a target specification:

```
      ⎕SE.SALT.Load'DemoScript -disperse -Target=Cool'
```

It is also possible to disperse only some objects, using the option "-Disperse=", followed by the names of the objects, separated by commas:

```
      )clear
clear ws
      ⎕SE.SALT.Load'DemoScript -disperse=Plus,Airports,Round'
      ⎕NL - 2 3
 Airports  Plus  Round
      )obs
                                               ⇦ No answer
```

Only the three specified objects have been loaded. The other ones have been ignored, and the *Namespace* has not been created.

1.2.5 - Source Code

When a script is loaded, SALT remembers from which file it was loaded. As shown in Chapter O, Spe-6, it is possible to retrieve the source code of a scripted namespace using the system function ⎕SRC:

```
      Code←⎕SRC Simple                         ⇦ Beware: you must not put quotes around
                                                 Simple as it is a Ref (see Chapter O-2).
      ⍴Code
31                                             ⇦ The result is a nested vector.
```

```
      ↑Code
```
⇦ Let us have a look to the code

```
:Namespace Simple

Nested←'My name is Bond' 0 0 7

∇ m←average val;s;n
  s←+/val
  n←ρval
etc...
```

⇦ This is exactly what we have defined

1.3 Updating a Script From the APL Session

Up to now, everything was really simple, but one of our functions is wrong.

Let us try to execute `CloseRound`, which is intended to perform better rounding.

```
      +/vec←1.07×?1000ρ345
184704.47
      +/⌊0.5+vec
184714
      +/CloseRound vec
VALUE ERROR
CloseRound[7] Diff←Rndsum-SumRnd
                   ∧
```

⇦ Create random values and sum them.

⇦ We would like the sum of the rounded values to be `184704`, not `184714`!

⇦ This function is supposed to return a better result.

⇦ Unfortunately we misspelled `RndSum`; the "S" should be in upper-case.

Depending on your configuration options, the trace window will pop up or not. Anyway, in order to solve the problem we must edit the function and make the necessary correction.

However, when we try to close the editor window, the following dialog box pops up:

Figure R-1

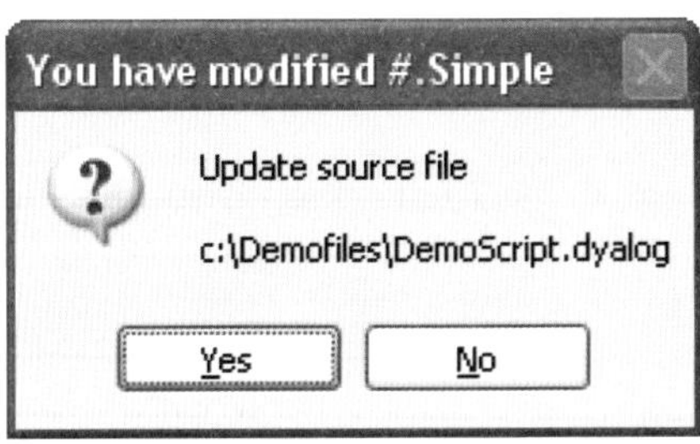

`SALT` knows that the function we modified was created from an external script file, and asks if we want to **update** that file. We can reply:

`Yes` If we are sure of our modifications and want to save them.
The function contained in the *Namespace* and the script file will both be modified.

`No` If we are not sure, and prefer to test it first.
The version contained in the *Namespace* will be modified, but **not** the script file.

If we choose to reply "**Yes**", this second message box may also appear:

Figure R-2

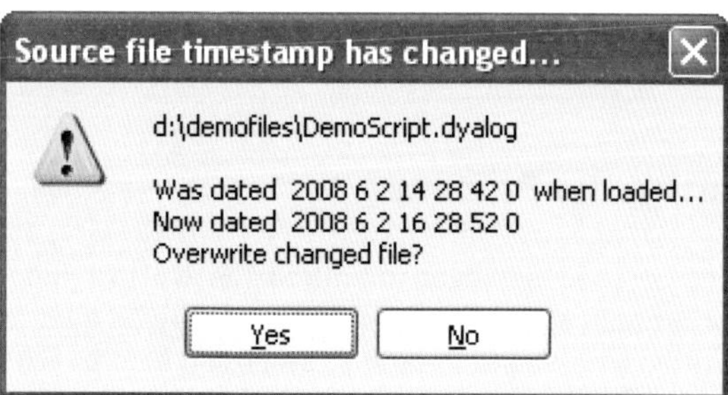

This box appears when the timestamp of the source file has changed between the time when the script was loaded, and the time when we try to save it again. This means that the source file has been changed while we were working in APL. The message box asks for a permission to overwrite the script file.

If you are sure that nobody has tampered with the file since you loaded it into APL reply "**Yes**" again. If you're not sure reply "**No**" and investigate what has happened, cf. Section 2.3 below. The latter is probably the better choice.

In any case, we can resume execution:

```
      →7
184704                                  ⇦ The result is excellent!
```

Remarks

- When loading or saving a *Script*, a default file extension "`.dyalog`" is assumed. This is why we did not specify it in the examples above. `SALT` will work with a file with a different extension, but you would then have to specify it in the "`Load`" command.
- A single *Script* file can contain **only one** *Namespace* (or *Class*) definition or function.

2 - Version Management

2.1 Creating and Using Versions

2.1.1 - Starting the Process

When a piece of code has been modified (as we just did above) it may be a bad idea to overwrite the original script file. It would probably be a better idea to create a new version of the file, identified by a version number. `SALT` can help us with this.

To start the process we must manually save the *Namespace* using the "`Save`" function, followed by the option "`-Version`". This will create a new file suffixed by "`.1`".

```
      ⎕SE.SALT.Save  'Simple -Version'
d:\MyFiles\DemoScript.1.dyalog              ⇦ Confirmation of the new file id
```

We could just as well have specified any arbitrary version number, 3 for example, like this:

```
      ⎕SE.SALT.Save  'Simple -Version=3'
d:\MyFiles\DemoScript.3.dyalog              ⇦ Confirmation of the new file id
```

Our directory now contains:

```
DemoScript.dyalog                           ⇦ This is the original file.
DemoScript.1.dyalog
DemoScript.3.dyalog                         ⇦ This is the latest file, version 3.
```

Notes

- Options, like "`-Version`" or "`-Target`" are also termed ***Modifiers*** or ***Switches***.
  Each of them **must** be prefixed by a dash
- They can be shortened to any number of letters, provided it is not ambiguous. For example: `-Version` could have been abbreviated `-Ver` or even `-v`.
- By default, the *Namespace* is saved in its source directory, and under the same name, suffixed by the version number.
  However, it would have been possible to store the script file under a different name and in any other directory (please don't do it if you would like to be able to follow the forthcoming examples):

```
      ⎕SE.SALT.Save 'Simple g:\secure\Bis -ver=43'
```

2.1.2 - Automatic Version Recognition

Now, let us make some modifications in our *Namespace*:

First, we define a new function named `Times`, which just calculates the product of two arrays:

```
Simple.Times←{α×ω}
```

Because this function was defined using direct assignment, the APL text editor was not involved, so `SALT` is unable to detect the modification we made to the *Namespace*. Nothing happens: `SALT` does not create a new version.

We would now like to change our function `Round` to make it ambivalent. The left argument will now be optional. If it is omitted when the function is called, it will take the value of our global variable `RounDefault`. The new definition of the function can be written like this:

```
∇ Res←{N}Round Val
  :If 0=⎕NC'N'
      N←RounDefault
  :EndIf
  Res←⌊0.5+Val×10*N
  Res←Res÷10*N
∇
```

The modification is made with the text editor. When we close the editor, `SALT` detects the modification, and a message box is displayed to ask if we agree on it creating a new script file, with a version number equal to 4 (the version number has been automatically incremented):

Figure R-3

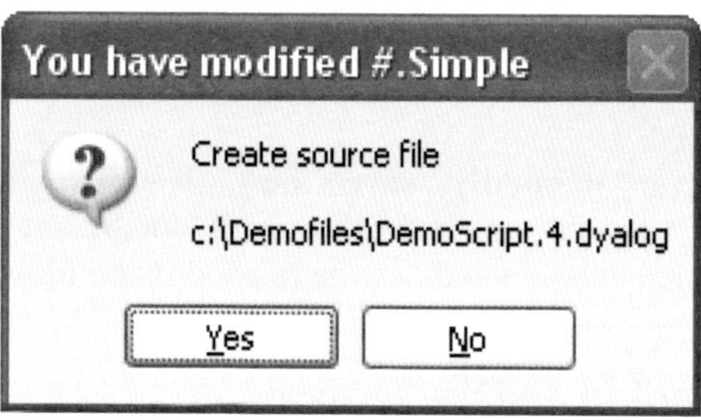

Of course, we reply **Yes** to accept, and we now have 4 files on our disk:

`DemoScript.dyalog`	⇦ The original.
`DemoScript.1.dyalog`	
`DemoScript.3.dyalog`	
`DemoScript.4.dyalog`	⇦ Version 4, just created.

When we load the script again, `SALT` will always reload the **latest** version of "`Simple`" (if we don't specify the version number to retrieve).

Let us try:

```
      )off                              ⇦ Quit APL without saving our function.
Dyalog APL/W Version 12.0.1             ⇦ Start a new session.
clear ws
      ⎕SE.SALT.Load 'DemoScript'        ⇦ Load our script file.
      ⎕PATH←'Simple'
      Primes 28
1 2 3 5 7 11 13 17 19 23
      Round 7.359 8.942 9.287           ⇦ This proves that the new version is available
7.36 8.94 9.29                            Executed in its Namespace, the function found
                                          the requested global parameter RounDefault.
```

Let us try to use the direct function we introduced earlier:

```
      5 Times 6
VALUE ERROR                             ⇦ When Version 4 of the script was created, the
      5 Times 6                           only objects saved were those modified with
     ^                                    the text editor; our direct function wasn't.
```

Warning!

- `SALT` tries to update a script file whenever a function or variable is modified using Dyalog's function editor. If a function is created or updated using `⎕FX`, or if a single-line *Direct function* or *Direct operator* is created by direct assignment `SALT` is not informed, and **it will not be saved**.
- When a variable is added or modified by any operation except the function editor, `SALT` will not change the related script file. The same if any objects are deleted from the *Namespace*.
- Even if you **manually save** the *Namespace* in the source script file, using `⎕SE.SALT.Save` the modifications will not be saved. This is a limitation due to the current implementation and may be relaxed in the future.

2.1.3 - Reloading an Old Version

We said that `SALT` always loads the latest version of a script, but it may be useful to reload an old version to carry out some tests, or because the latest one appears to be inappropriate.

One can reload an old version using the modifier "`-Version=` *nn*".

For example, suppose that you have versions 1 to 8 of a script file and wish to reload version 5:

```
      ⎕SE.SALT.Load 'd:\MyFiles\Foolish -ver=5'
```

Now, if a modification is made to a function, `SALT` will suggest that it be stored in version 9 (one plus the highest known version).

If you agree, just reply **Yes**, but if this is not appropriate you can reply **No** and save the script manually, using again any explicit version number:

```
      ⎕SE.SALT.Save 'Foolish -ver=8'
```

2.2 File Management

`SALT` can give us a list of the script files contained in a given directory:

2.2.1 - Simple Lists

```
      ⎕SE.SALT.List 'd:\MyFiles'
Type   Name         Version  Size  Last Update
       DemoScript             580  2008/06/02 17:33:36
       Experiment             192  2008/05/31 11:42:56
       Telefon                179  2008/06/04  7:10:48
       Test                   260  2008/06/02 14:10:58
       Teton                  214  2008/06/04  7:11:34
<DIR>  Coco                        2008/06/03  8:47:16
```

Only the very latest version of `DemoScript` is mentioned, without any version number. Sub-directories are just listed, but not explored.

2.2.2 - Modifiers; Full Lists

We can specify options to the `List` command, also called "***Switches***" or "***Modifiers***". One can get the list of all possible modifiers for a command with a question mark:

```
      ⎕SE.SALT.List '?'
List pathname                      ⇦ The first line gives the function syntax

Modifiers accepted:                ⇦ Then comes the list of possible Switches

-Full[=1|2]      1 Show full pathnames below first folder found;
                 2 returns "rooted" names.
-Recursive       Recurse through folders
-Versions        List versions
-Folders         Only list folders
-Raw             Return unformatted date and version numbers
```

Let us ask for the versions (`-Version`) and the contents of sub-directories (`-Recursive`):

```
      ⎕SE.SALT.List'd:\MyFiles -Vers -Recur
 Type   Name                 Version  Size  Last Update
        MyFiles\DemoScript   [4]       624  2008/06/04 13:52:38
        MyFiles\DemoScript   [3]       544  2008/06/04 13:42:36
        MyFiles\DemoScript   [1]       544  2008/06/04 13:42:04
        MyFiles\DemoScript             918  2008/06/04 13:39:48
        MyFiles\Experiment   [7]       192  2008/05/31 11:42:56
        MyFiles\Telefon                179  2008/06/04  7:10:48
        MyFiles\Test         [3]       167  2008/06/03 18:01:24
        MyFiles\Test         [1]       167  2008/06/03 17:33:40
        MyFiles\Test                   282  2008/06/02 21:41:02
        MyFiles\Teton                  214  2008/06/04  7:11:34
 <DIR>  MyFiles\Coco                        2008/06/03  8:47:16
        MyFiles\Coco\Bisou             282  2008/06/02 21:41:02
        MyFiles\Coco\Sacha             192  2008/05/31 11:42:56
```

We obtained all the versions for each script file.

When the modifier "-Raw" is used, titles and formatting characters are removed, so it is easier to process the data with APL functions.

2.2.3 - Exploring Directories and Files

It is also possible to open Windows Explorer in a specific folder like this:

```
      ⎕SE.SALT.Explore'd:\MyFiles'
```

If a specific script name is specified, the latest version of the script is edited using the default editor (Notepad):

```
      ⎕SE.SALT.Explore'd:\MyFiles\DemoScript'
```

Note that if the script has been loaded into the active workspace previously the changes that you make to the script file will *not* be made to the objects in the workspace. The script file and the workspace may therefore contain different versions of some objects.

2.2.4 - Removing Old Versions

As time goes by one may have collected a large number of versions.

It is possible to remove one or more versions, using the command "RemoveVersions", followed by the Path and generic Filename of the scripts to remove:

- To remove a single version, just specify .... -Version= 3
- To remove versions less than a given version (e.g. 27), type .... -Version= <27
- To remove versions greater than a given version, type .... -Version= >42
- To remove a range of versions, type (e.g. 27 to 42)......................... -Version= 27-42
- To remove all the versions, specify .... -all

In this case, confirmation is asked for, and SALT will preserve the highest version:

```
⎕SE.SALT.RemoveVersions'd:\oldstuff\DemoScript -all'
```

Figure R-4

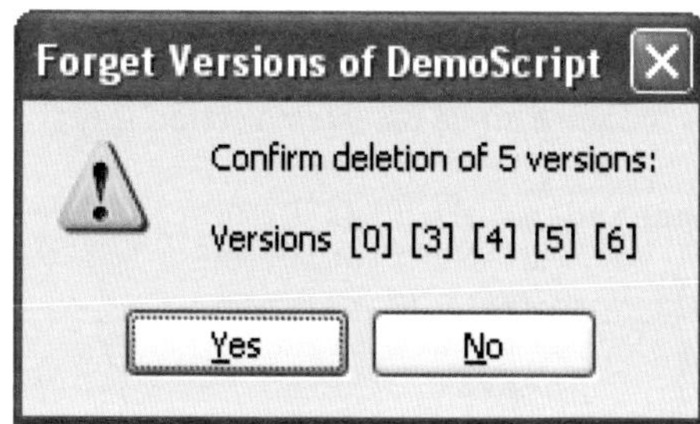

After confirmation the following messages appear::

```
4 versions deleted.
1 version renamed
```

All the versions have been destroyed, except the last one which has been renamed so as not to have a version number. It may be used as a root for a future set of derived versions.

It is also possible to remove minor intermediate versions, up to the highest one, using the same command with the modifier "`-Collapse`".

For example, suppose that we have 31 versions, and we want to remove versions 19 to 30:

```
⎕SE.SALT.RemoveVersions Path,'Appli -ver=>18 -collapse'
```

Versions 19 to 30 are deleted (after confirmation), and version 31 is renamed to 19 (or the first free number after the deletion).

2.3 Comparing Scripts

Once one has got several versions of the same script, it may be useful to identify which modifications were made between two versions, often between the last one and a previous one. None of them need to be loaded in the workspace.

To perform this kind of comparison, `SALT` can use an APL routine provided with Dyalog APL (the default) which is sufficient for light applications, or any other third-party product for more professional use.

Among the systems on the market; we can mention:

SubVersion with Tortoise-SVN
Compare It!

Here is the APL comparison between the latest (highest) version of our script, and version 4.

```
⎕SE.SALT.Compare'd:\MyFiles\DemoScript -ver=4'
```

We can compare any two versions, (for example versions 4 & 6), by typing their numbers:

```
⎕SE.SALT.Compare'd:\MyFiles\DemoScript -version=4 6'
```

Here the result is the same since the latest version is 6:

```
Comparing d:\MyFiles\DemoScript.4.dyalog
     with d:\MyFiles\DemoScript.6.dyalog
 [4]  ∇ m←average val;s;n
 [5]     s←+/val
←[6]     n←⍴val
→        m←s÷⍴val
←[7]     m←s÷n
 [8]  ∇
 [9]
 [14] ∇ Res←{N} Round Val
 [15]  :if 0=⎕nc 'N'
←[16]  N←RounDefault
→      N←3⌊RounDefault
 [17]  :end
 [18]  Res←⌊0.5+Val×10*N
 [23]  RndSum←⌊0.5++/Y
 [24]  SumRnd←+/R←⌊0.5+Y
←[25]  Diff←RndSum-SumRnd   ⍝ Intentional error
→      Diff←RndSum-SumRnd
←[26]  Great←⍒,Y
→      Great←⍒,Y   ⍝ Dispatch on highest values
 [27]  R[(|Diff)↑Great]+←×Diff
 [28] ∇
```

In the header, `SALT` specifies which files are compared.

Then the lines of the **first** script are displayed, with lines numbers.

In the left margin one can see:

- → When a line has been inserted
- ← When a line has been removed

When a line has been modified (see line `[16]`), a left arrow shows the old version (removed) and immediately a right arrow shows the new version (inserted).

Sometimes, the difference is just a removed or added comment (lines `[25]` or `[26]`), and sometimes there is a real modification in the code.

It is also possible to compare the version *in* the workspace with the latest version on file. This can come in handy to eliminate confusion arising from the warning issued by a save command.

For example, suppose you attempt to save your script and get this

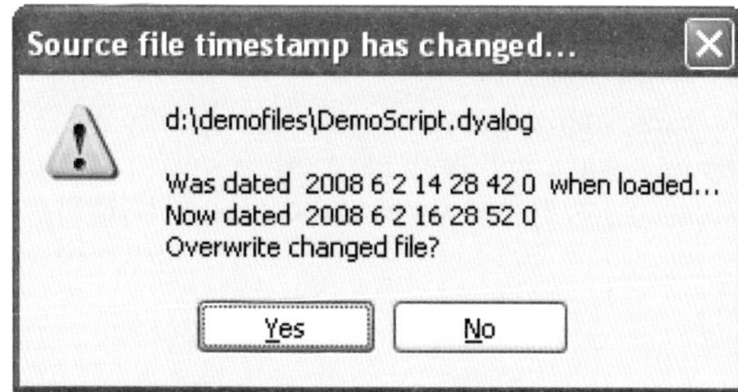

If you are unsure as to why this is happening you should reply No and compare your workspace version with the one on file by doing

```
      ⎕SE.SALT.Compare'd:\demoFiles\DemoScript -version=ws'
```

SALT will show you the differences and you may then take whatever action is appropriate to rectify this situation.

3 - Settings

SALT uses the following global parameters:

Keyword	Meaning	Default
compare	Program used to compare two scripts	APL function
editor	Editor used to view/edit script files.	Notepad
workdir	Directory where scripts are placed/searched by default	[Dyalog]\SALT
owpfk	PFKey to use to overwrite the last version when saving	
edprompt	Is a confirmation required (1) or not (0) at Save time?	1

These parameters are stored in the Windows Registry, and are retrieved at the start of each new APL session.

The command "Settings" can be used to consult or modify these parameters, like this:

- An empty argument returns the values of all the parameters:

```
      ⎕SE.SALT.Settings ''
compare   apl
editor    notepad
workdir   [Dyalog]\SALT
owpfk
edprompt  1
```

- If the argument is one of these keywords, the command returns its current value

```
      ⎕SE.SALT.Settings 'workdir'
[Dyalog]\SALT
```

- Finally, a parameter can be modified by specifying the keyword followed by the new value. The new value will only have effect during the current session. However, it will be made permanent (written to the Registry) if it is followed by the switch "`-Permanent`".

Examples:

If you prefer `Wordpad` to `Notepad` when using `Explore`, you can type:

```
⎕SE.SALT.Settings 'editor c:\Windows\ServicePackFiles\i386\wordpad'
```

- If this temporary change was inappropriate, you can restore the permanent value stored in the Windows Registry using "`-Reset`".
- If the change is to be made permanent, you just have to add `-Permanent`.

If you decide to use the product "Compare It!" to compare scripts, you should declare it in your settings as follows:

```
      ComProg←' "[ProgramFiles]\Compare It!\wincmp3"'
      ⎕SE.SALT.Settings 'compare ',ComProg,' -Permanent'
```

But you can also use it just once, and declare it using the *Switch* "`-use`" like this:

```
      ⎕SE.SALT.Compare'd:\MyFiles\DemoScript -ver=4 6 -use=',ComProg
```

The Specialist's Section

Each chapter is followed by a "Specialist's Section" like this one.
This section is dedicated to skilled APLers, who wish to improve their knowledge.

If you are exploring APL for the first time,
skip this section and go to the next chapter

In the preceding pages we used `SALT` to store programs outside of a workspace. This "SALTed" code was then loaded into the workspace, and executed very traditionally by starting an APL function.

One can also call an external ("SALTed") function, apply it to some data, and destroy it immediately after, so that nothing remains stored in the workspace.

Let us experiment with this file:

```
:Class Compute

∇ R←A Plus B
  :Access Shared Public
  R←A+B
∇

∇ R←A Times B
  :Access Shared Public
  R←A×B
∇

∇ R←Sqrt B
  :Access Shared Public
  R←'Invalid'
  :If B≥0
  R←B*0.5
  :EndIf
∇
:EndClass
```

The file itself is named `Maths.Dyalog`
It contains a *Class*
The *Class* is named `Compute`

It contains three function definitions:

`Plus`
`Times`
`Sqrt`

They are all *Shared* and *Public*

We could load the *Class* into the workspace and use its functions:

```
      ⎕SE.SALT.Load 'Maths'
      87 Compute.Plus 21
108
```

The following syntax would produce the same effect:

```
      30 (⎕SE.SALT.Load 'Maths').Plus 70
100
      )obs
Compute
```

It works, but we loaded the whole *Class* in the workspace just to use one of its components.

In this case it might have been better to load an unnamed copy that will disappear immediately after use. This can be achieved using the switch "-noname':

```
      )clear
clear ws
      30 (⎕SE.SALT.Load 'Maths -noname').Times 70 20
2100 600
      )obs                             ⇦ No Namespace was created
```

The function has been temporarily loaded and used, but nothing remains in the workspace.

This could be made slightly easier to do with the help of a small *Direct function*, as shown here:

```
      use←{⎕SE.SALT.Load ⍵,' -noname'}
      40(use'Maths').Plus 45 17 29 31
85 57 69 71
```

Actually, SALT provides itself a command to do just that. It is called New:

```
      30 (⎕se.SALT.New 'Maths').Plus 70
100
```

The difference here is that New can give an argument to the constructor of the class, should it need one. For example, if Maths needed a constructor argument, say 'abc', it would have been specified this way:

```
      30 (⎕se.SALT.New 'Maths' 'abc').Plus 70
```

The result would have been calculated and the instance discarded at the end, just as above.

Storing Entire Workspaces in SALT

You may wish to store the contents of a workspace in SALT to benefit from the automatic version update and other goodies, but the idea of storing every function and namespace one by one may repel you. SALT comes to the rescue again by providing a command to do just this for you. This command is called Snap. In its simplest form Snap takes a folder as argument and stores everything it finds in the workspace into the specified folder:

```
      ⎕se.SALT.Snap '\mycode\myws'
```

For a complete description of what Snap can do you should refer to the specific SALT documentation.

Chapter S: Publishing Tools

You are now an APL expert (aren't you?) and you are able to write programs to solve very complex problems.

But if you need to present your results in an elegant report or booklet, possibly including fancy graphs, you may have to spend many hours, perhaps many days, to obtain what you had in mind.

This is not specific to APL; it is the same in all programming languages. We are so familiar with text processing tools and spreadsheet managers that we want to produce output of at least a comparable quality, but if we try to do so without proper tools the complexity of producing even the most simple layouts is overwhelming.

Dyalog APL includes two excellent tools to produce high quality documents and graphs with very little programming effort. They have been developed by Causeway Graphical Systems Ltd. and have existed as separate commercial products for many years before being included in Dyalog APL. The two complementary products are:

NewLeaf	for producing printed documents, and
RainPro	for producing graphs

NewLeaf and *RainPro* allow the production of extremely rich layouts, and they are well adapted for processing large amounts of data. They are delivered with their own easy to read documentation; so the purpose of this chapter is just to help you make the very first steps, to explore some major features and concepts, and to act as a link between what we have already learned, and what these publishing tools can do for us.

1 - NewLeaf

1.1 Getting Started

1.1.1 - What You Need

NewLeaf consists of a number of *Namespaces* included in a workspace named `NewLeaf`.

The *Namespaces* are:

- `leaf` Allows you to position and present data on a page.
- `PostScrp` Manages the preview and printing of what you have prepared.
- `Layout` Used to prepare predefined presentations that will be used repeatedly.
- `pdf` Needed if you want to output data in PDF format.

If you just want to use the product in a given application, copy the *Namespaces* that you need into your application workspace. For example:

```
)load MyAppli
)copy newleaf leaf PostScrp Layout
```

1.1.2 - A Quick Introduction

Before embarking on your own design you might want to explore the main features of the product. If so, just load the whole workspace `Newleaf` and follow the instructions given in the welcome text. If you run `Help`, you will be encouraged to execute this set of APL statements:

```
leaf.Use ''                        ⇦ Use a default page layout
leaf.Font 'heb,18'                 ⇦ Set the font to Helvetica, bold, 18 points
leaf.Place 'Subheading is here'    ⇦ Place a title
leaf.Font 'ti,12/16'               ⇦ Now use Times New Roman, 12 points
leaf.Flow txt                      ⇦ Place a piece of text, contained in variable txt
leaf.table.List 3 4⍴⍳12            ⇦ Place a numeric matrix
leaf.Include pg2                   ⇦ Include a graph prepared with RainPro
PG←leaf.Close                      ⇦ The final result is a variable named PG
```

The result of these statements is a long character vector (`PG`), which can be considered as a *PostScript* script, defining a complete document, ready for printing. Of course, many options or parameters, like fonts, have default values.

Then you can:

- preview this layout using: `PostScrp.View PG`
- or print it directly using `PostScrp.Print PG`

After this first example you are encouraged to try some other examples. After each of them, you can execute `View PG` to see the result:

```
Test        Caps     Indents    Folder
Testgrid    John     SalesRep   Booklet
```

The function `View` is just a cover function for `PostScrp.View`, so that you don't have to type "`PostScrp.`" each time.

If you want to explore most of the *NewLeaf* features you can also run this demonstration:

```
Seatrial 0
```

It is a rather long demonstration, which runs more than 25 examples (stored in the variable `∆seatrial`) one by one, and automatically displays the result (some of them spread on several pages; use *Page-Up*/*Page-Down* to scroll). You are not obliged to print them, just click on "Close" to terminate a demo and skip to the next one.

1.2 Frames and Text

1.2.1 - Main Concepts

NewLeaf allows you to place text and graphics in rectangular areas called ***Frames***, which are placed on a ***Page***.

Figure S-1

- Pages can be created, filled, and printed when needed, but it is generally better practice to prepare a set of predefined pages, including frames etc. The pages may then serve as templates that can be re-used several times with different contents.
- You can define as many frames as needed on a page. However, *NewLeaf* requires **at least one** frame per page.
- Figure S-1 to the right shows a grey page with an outer rectangle representing the printable area, which depends on the printer you use. Four frames are defined, represented by white areas.

- Frames (and all other page elements) are positioned in an (*x*,*y*) coordinate system that has its origin at the bottom-left corner of the page, as shown in the figure.
- Since the coordinates start from the edges of the page your document will always look the same when printed on any printer, provided that your frames are within the printer's printable area.
- All measurements are in ***Points***, one point being 1/72 of an inch.
- Usually frames have no border, but you can decide to put a border around some of them. On figure S-1, only the top-right frame has a border.
- Text normally starts at the frame's left margin, but you can indent it to the right, and even place "bullets", as shown in the large frame.
- The default page (defined earlier by `leaf.Use ''`) contains a single frame, with 1-inch margins all around, and a page number at the bottom of the page.

1.2.2 - Filling Frames with Text

Each frame can be filled with one or more paragraphs of **text**, **graphics** defined with *RainPro*, or **images** (Bitmaps or Metafiles). For now we shall only consider text.

NewLeaf has been designed to simplify the production of documents as much as possible, so many parameters and options take default values, and the user is offered a number of typical fonts and paragraph formats. The default paragraph starts from the frame's left margin, and the default font is "Times New Roman", size 12 points.

A paragraph can be specified as:

- A character vector (used most frequently)
- A character matrix
- A numeric array

A nested character vector is processed as a set of paragraphs, each item being a separate paragraph.

A paragraph can be written to the page using two different functions:

- `leaf.Place` Places the text without any transformation. If the text is wider than the frame, excess characters will overflow the frame, unless the frame has been defined with the property `Clip` set to True (in which case the text will be truncated).
- `leaf.Flow` Ravels the text and wraps it to fit the frame width. A long character vector may therefore be folded on several lines.

While the user is preparing his document *NewLeaf* creates a spool file, in which it places a script describing all the operations and parameters necessary to obtain the desired result. Each page is stored in a separate component in the spool file.

Once the document is ready, `leaf.Close` completes and closes the spool file, and returns the script in a shy result.

If the document is not too large the result returned by `leaf.Close` can be printed using `PostScrp.Print`, or previewed using `PostScrp.View`.

For large documents it is recommended that you leave the report in the spool file and browse or print it from there. Then you can view or print several thousands of pages without running the risk of causing a `WS FULL` error:

Instead of `leaf.Close` we must use	`fn←leaf.Spool ''`
The result can be previewed as before by	`PostScrp.View fn`
And to print the entire report, one can execute	`PostScrp.RunOff fn`

The result returned in `fn` is the path and name of the spool file.

1.2.3 - Some Experiments

Let us write a function to see how *NewLeaf* presents different data. This may help you understand the differences between `Place` and `Flow`:

```
     ∇ NLExp data;page
[1]    leaf.Use''                  ⇦ Use a default page, with a single frame
[2]    leaf.Place data            ⇦ Place some text
[3]    leaf.Flow data             ⇦ Wrap the same text
[4]    page←leaf.Close            ⇦ Close the spool file
[5]    PostScrp.View page         ⇦ View the result
     ∇
```

Test this with variables that we have used earlier:

```
      NLExp Countries
      NLExp Forecast
      NLExp 'What' 'about' 'a nested' 'vector?'
```

You can see that `Place` places the rows of a matrix under each other, while `Flow` ravels them and wraps the resulting vector to fit the page width. Numbers are formatted poorly; we shall find a better technique later.

The nested vector is formatted like a matrix by `Place`, and like a list of paragraphs by `Flow`.

We shall now try to present `MLK`; a nested vector consisting of 12 items, extracted from Martin Luther King's famous speech "I have a dream".

The first version of our function, `NLText1`, is identical to `NLExp`, except that we have neutralised `leaf.Place` with a comment sign. Now, try this:

```
      NLText1 MLK
```

You can see that each item produces a paragraph, starting at the left margin, and folded to fit in the frame width, like this:

Figure S-2

> I have a dream
>
> Martin Luther King Jr.
> Washington, August 28th 1963.
>
> So I say to you, my friends, that even though we must face the difficulties of today and tomorrow, I still have a dream. It is a dream deeply rooted in the American dream that one day this nation will rise up and live out the true meaning of its creed: we hold these truths to be self-evident, that all men are created equal.
>
> I have a dream that one day, on the red hills of Georgia, sons of former slaves, *etc…*

This is not bad, but we could perhaps try to improve the layout of the title.

NewLeaf provides a set of predefined paragraph layouts, with different alignments, fonts, and spacings. These ***Styles*** are contained in what is called a ***Gallery***. They can be invoked by `leaf.Style`.

```
     ∇ NLText2 data;page
        leaf.Use''                  ⇦ A default page
        leaf.Style'Heading'         ⇦ Invoke a predefined style
        leaf.Place 1⊃data           ⇦ Place the title
        leaf.PopStyle               ⇦ Restore the previous (default) style
        leaf.Flow 1↓data            ⇦ Write the following paragraphs as before
        page←leaf.Close
        PostScrp.View page
     ∇
```

If you try `NLText2 MLK` you will see that the title is now centred, and written using a bigger font.

Just execute `leaf.Gallery` and have a look at these two *Style* definitions:

```
Body      Normal Paragraph   Font       Ti,12
                             Pitch         15
                             Align       Left
                             Spacing     0 12
... etc.
Heading   Major heading      Font      Li,24
                             Spacing   24 6
                             Align     Centre
```

For each style (`Body`, `Indent`, … `Heading`), the *Gallery* contains various settings (font, alignment, spacing, etc.).

Fonts are represented by shortcuts: "`ti`" stands for "Times New Roman".

You can see that a normal paragraph (`Body`) is printed in Times New Roman, 12 points, and left aligned, while our title (`Heading`) is printed in size 24 and centred.

We can use `leaf.Align` to centre the subtitle, like this:

```
      ∇ NLText3 data;str;page
[1]     leaf.Use''
[2]     leaf.Style'Heading'
[3]     leaf.Place 1⊃data
[4]     leaf.PopStyle
[5]     leaf.Align'centre'               ⇦ Centre the next paragraph(s)
[6]     leaf.Place 2⊃data
[7]     leaf.Align'left'                 ⇦ Left align the following paragraph(s)
[8]     leaf.Flow 2↓data
[9]     page←leaf.Close
[10]    PostScrp.View page
      ∇
```

We now obtain something like this:

Figure S-3

> **I have a dream**
>
> Martin Luther King Jr.
> Washington, August 28th 1963.
>
> So I say to you, my friends, that even though we must face the difficulties of today and tomorrow, I still have a dream. It is a dream deeply rooted in the American dream that one day this nation will rise up and live out the true meaning of its creed: we hold *etc*...

The subtitle is written on two successive lines because it contains a *NewLine* character.

The function `Align` accepts the values "`Left`", "`Centre`" (or "`Center`"), and "`Right`". These parameters are not case sensitive, and can be abbreviated to any number of letters; "`L`" and "`Left`" are equivalent.

The very last thing we shall do with this text is to magnify the first letter of each paragraph, using the `DropCap` feature. To achieve this, we need a little loop to process the first letter and the rest of a paragraph differently. The beginning of the program remains unchanged; we have not reproduced it below:

```
      ∇ NLText4 data;str
[1-7]   ...                              ⇦ The first seven instructions are unchanged
[8]     :For str :In 2↓data
[9]         leaf.DropCap 1↑str           ⇦ Magnify the first letter
[10]        leaf.Flow 1↓str              ⇦ Wrap the remaining text around that letter
[11]    :End
[12]    PostScrp.View leaf.Close
      ∇
```

If now you execute: `NLText4 MLK`, you should obtain something similar to the figure below:

Figure S-4

> # I have a dream
>
> Martin Luther King Jr.
> Washington, August 28th 1963.
>
> So I say to you, my friends, that even though we must face the difficulties of today and tomorrow, I still have a dream. It is a dream deeply rooted in the American dream that one day this nation will rise up and live out the true meaning of its creed: we hold these truths to be self-evident, that all men are created equal.
>
> I have a dream that one day, on the red hills of Georgia, sons of former slaves, and sons of former slave-owners will be able to sit down together at the table of brotherhood.

This technique is not limited to the first character, you can apply it to a (limited) set of the first characters, but you must *Enclose* them. For example: `leaf.DropCap (⊂3↑str)`

The default presentation expands the letter on two lines of text, using the current text font. This can be changed by specifying the desired height and font name after the character:

```
leaf.DropCap 1↑str                  ⇦ Default presentation on 2 lines
leaf.DropCap (1↑str) 3              ⇦ Presentation on 3 lines
leaf.DropCap (1↑str) 3 'ARBI'       ⇦ The same, but in ARial Bold Italic
```

1.3 Fonts

1.3.1 - Font Definitions

To simplify the use of fonts, *NewLeaf* has an internal table of fonts. You can display it with:

```
      leaf.∆fonttbl
TI   : 'Times New Roman' 0 400      /Times-Roman
TII  : 'Times New Roman' 1 400      /Times-Italic
TIB  : 'Times New Roman' 0 800      /Times-Bold
TIBI: 'Times New Roman' 1 800       /Times-BoldItalic
AR   : 'Arial' 0 400                /Helvetica
ARI  : 'Arial' 1 400                /Helvetica-Oblique
ARB  : 'Arial' 0 800                /Helvetica-Bold
ARBI: 'Arial' 1 800                 /Helvetica-BoldOblique
CO   : 'Courier New' 0 400          /Courier
COI  : 'Courier New' 1 400          /Courier-Oblique
COB  : 'Courier New' 0 800          /Courier-Bold
```

etc...

The first item in each line is the font short code used by *NewLeaf*. Each font is identified by two letters (`TI`, `AR`, and so on), which can be qualified by "`I`" for Italic, "`B`" for Bold, or "`BI`" for Bold and Italic. Remark: Arial is a clone of Helvetica.

The second item is the font definition that will be passed to Windows, using conventions similar to the ones we use in the APL GUI interface:

- Font name (for example "Times New Roman")
- Normal or Italic (0 or 1)
- Normal or Bold (400 is normal, 800 is bold)

The font size will be defined separately when the font is used.

The third item is the name of the PostScript font that will be used to build PDF files.

1.3.2 - Using Fonts

When a font is required, it is identified by its short code, a comma, and its size in points.

For example:

Times New Roman, Italic, size 12	will be identified by	`TII,12`
Arial (or Helvetica), Bold, size 9	will be identified by	`ARB,9`

By default, the spacing between two lines of text is 120% of the font size. This is convenient for most documents, but if you prefer a smaller or larger line spacing you can specify any value (in points) after a slash. For example: `'ARI,9/12'`

In general, *NewLeaf* expects you to work with the fonts described in the table. This allows your documents to be output directly to *PostScript* devices, and will enable documents to be rendered well in HTML browsers. However, you can use any other font available on your system. Instead of using `Leaf.Font`, you can then use `leaf.TrueFont`. The argument to `leaf.TrueFont` is the font's full name and size, and as before 0 or 1 (normal or Italic) followed by the weight. For example:

```
leaf.TrueFont 'Comic Sans MS,14' 1       ⇦ Italic
leaf.TrueFont 'Garamond,12' 0 800        ⇦ Bold
```

The names you provide are matched against the current font list given by Windows, case independently, omitting the blanks, and limited to any number of unambiguous leading characters. So you could have typed `'comic'` or `'garam'`, provided that you do not have any other fonts installed with similar names.

1.3.3 - Add New Fonts

You can also add new fonts to the table by editing it directly, or by using the function `leaf.DefineFont`.

If you specify a two-character short code the function will automatically create a set of four fonts: normal, Italic, Bold, and Bold Italic:

```
leaf.DefineFont 'ga' 'Garamond'
```
⇦ Adds four short codes: `ga gai gab` and `gabi`.

1.4 Tables

1.4.1 - Default Presentation

NewLeaf contains functionality to present data in a tabular way. To test these facilities, let us prepare some data, derived from an existing variable, `GridData`:

```
      Tabu←20 6↑GridData
      Tabu[;2 3 4]×←89.17
      Tabu[;6]←' ' 'No'[1+Tabu[;6]]
```

`Tabu` is now a nested matrix containing data like this:

```
Sabatier        6152.73   5082.69 2585.93  DK
Depond         10343.72   9184.51 5885.22  E     No
Laure           2318.42  10611.23 5350.2   F
Jakubovar       9987.04   7668.62 3031.78  D
Perdoux         6509.41   2496.76 2675.1   SN    No
```

One can present this variable using the default presentation offered by *NewLeaf*:

```
      leaf.Use ''
      leaf.table.List Tabu          ⇦ A new function
      PostScrp.View leaf.Close
```

As you can see, the presentation is not so bad, except that numbers are left aligned.

NewLeaf divided the frame width evenly into as many columns as needed (6 in this example).

1.4.2 - Controlled Presentation

You can specify a better presentation using the following functions:

- `leaf.table.Set` To control cell widths and the fonts
- `leaf.table.Align` To define the alignment in the cells
- `leaf.table.Titles` To enter the column titles
- `leaf.table.TDepth` To define their level of depth, like in a *Grid* object

Let us write the initial version of the function:

```
     ∇ NLTable1 data;tex
[1]     leaf.Use''
[2]     leaf.table.Set 'cellw'(80 50 50 50 40 40)
[3]     leaf.table.Set ('TFont' 'ARB,8')
[4]     leaf.table.Set ('Font' 'tib,10',(3⍴⊂'co,8'),'ar,8' 'tib,10')
[5]     leaf.table.Align'left' 'd2' 'd2' 'r' 'l' 'c'
[6]     tex←'Name' 'Results' 'Jan' 'Feb' 'Mar' 'Country' 'Checked'
[7]     leaf.table.Titles tex
[8]     leaf.table.TDepth 0 0 1 1 1 0 0
[9]     leaf.table.Spread data
[10]    PostScrp.View leaf.Close
     ∇
```

The function `Set` is first called to define the cells widths (in points)

It is called again to define the fonts, in two steps:

- The keyword "`TFont`" defines the font used for the titles (Arial Bold, size 8).
- The keyword "`Font`" is used to define as many fonts as there are columns. We have chosen "Times New Roman (bold)" and "Arial" for the texts, and "Courier New" for the numeric columns, because it is a non-proportional font, so the digits will be aligned vertically.

The function `Align` is used to control the presentation. As we said before, it is possible to abbreviate Left, Centre, and Right into L, C, and R. We shall explain what "`d2`" means in Remark 1.

The titles are entered in their natural order, each main title being followed by its subtitles. The levels of the titles are specified by the function `TDepth`, in a way that is very similar to that which we saw for the *Grid* object (Chapter P, Section 7.5.1).

In instruction `[9]` we no longer use `List`, but `Spread`.

Try: `NLTable1 Tabu`. You should obtain something like this:

Figure S-5

Name	Results			Country	Checked
	Jan	Feb	Mar		
Sabatier	6152.73	5082.69	2585.93	DK	
Depond	10343.72	9184.51	5885.22	E	**No**
Laure	2318.42	10611.23	5350.2	P	
Jakubovar	9987.04	7668.62	3031.78	D	
[illegible]oux	6509.41	249[illegible].76	2675.1	SN	**No**
					No

Remark 1:

Everything is correct, except that some values are not aligned properly (as shown within the red circle) because they do not have the same number of decimal digits. This can be improved: instead of specifying `Align 'Right'`, we could specify `Align 'decimal2'` (or `'d2'` in short). *NewLeaf* will then provide two positions for the decimal digits, and the decimal points will be aligned.

We used this alignment for the first two numeric columns, and you can look at the last three rows: the result is well aligned.

We shall see very shortly that we can also specify an explicit format for numbers.

Remark 2:

Now let us re-execute the 3 instructions we used in 1.4.1 to test the default presentation:

```
leaf.Use ''
leaf.table.List Tabu
PostScrp.View leaf.Close
```

Surprisingly, we obtain the same "improved" presentation as produced by `NLTable1`! The reason for this is that some parameters are cached in global variables. This may be an advantage when one has to produce several similar tables.

To clear the cache and restore all the parameters to their default values, run the function `leaf.Init`.

Remark 3:

The two functions we used to fill a table, `List` and `Spread`, are slightly different:

- It may happen that the content of a cell is wider that the cell itself. If so, `Spread` wraps the text on several lines, while `List` accepts only one line of text in a cell. If the text is too long, it may overflow on the right (the default), or it may be clipped if required.
- When processing wide tables which do not fit on a single page, they will be printed on several pages. `List` works down the rows, then steps across the columns. On the other hand, `Spread` steps across the columns, then works down the rows. `Spread` never splits a cell onto two successive pages.
- `List` is generally faster, but `Spread` offers more formatting options.

1.4.3 - Define Styles and Formats

To further improve our presentation we shall:

- define a new paragraph style and use it to place a title above the table
- define an explicit format for the numeric columns

To define a new style, we use `leaf.DefineStyle`, followed by some parameters:

- font specification
- alignment
- spacing before and after the current line, in points

For example:

```
cusfor←('Font' 'HeB,18')('Align' 'L')('Spacing' 60 18)
'Custom'leaf.DefineStyle cusfor
```

"`Custom`" is the name given to the new style. If you execute `leaf.Gallery`, you will see the style just added:

```
Custom                           Font     HeB,18
                                 Align    L
                                 Spacing  60 18
```

Once it has been defined, the style can be applied to all the forthcoming paragraphs, using `leaf.Style`, which we have already used.

It can also be used just for a single paragraph. In this case the style name must be passed as the left argument to `leaf.Place` or `leaf.Flow`.

We can also specify an explicit format for numbers, using the function `leaf.table.Qfmt`, with format descriptors similar to the ones we used with `⎕FMT` (see Section F-3).

We shall specify a format `'CF9.2'` for each numeric column. For text columns, *NewLeaf* can use its standard presentation, so we shall specify an empty format (`⊂''`).
Here is the resulting function:

```
     ∇ NLTable2 data;tex;cusfor
       leaf.Use''
       cusfor←('Font' 'HeB,18')('Align' 'L')('Spacing' 60 18)
       'Custom'leaf.DefineStyle cusfor
       'Custom'leaf.Place'First quarter sales'
       leaf.table.Set'cellw'(80 50 50 50 40 40)
       leaf.table.Set ('TFont' 'ARB,8')
       leaf.table.Set ('Font' 'tib,10',(3⍴⊂'co,8'),'ar,8' 'tib,10')
       leaf.table.Align'left' 'r' 'r' 'r' 'l' 'c'
       leaf.table.Qfmt(⊂''),(3⍴⊂'CF9.2'),2⍴⊂''
       tex←'Name' 'Results' 'Jan' 'Feb' 'Mar' 'Country' 'Checked'
       leaf.table.Titles tex
       leaf.table.TDepth 0 0 1 1 1 0 0
       leaf.table.Spread data
       PostScrp.View leaf.Close
     ∇
```

You can run it, and see that the result is pretty good.

1.5 The Page Designer

Up to now, we have worked in a default page containing a single frame, but generally most documents contain several frames and some other objects. Instead of defining the required pages when they are to be used, it is easier and more convenient to predefine them and store their definitions. The stored definitions can be retrieved, filled, and then published.

To define pages in this way, an interactive interface named the ***Page Designer*** is provided. It is contained in the *Namespace* `Layout`.
After you have defined the pages you need, the namespace `Layout` is no longer needed, so you can remove it.

1.5.1 - The Contents of a Page

The pages we have designed so far all contained just a single frame, but a page can contain many things:

- several frames
- some fixed texts
- horizontal or vertical rules, drawn across the whole page, or shorter
- images; typically the logo of a company
- the page number, the date and time of printing
- etc…

The elements that are not frames (images, page number, print time, fixed text) will be repeated on all the pages, with the page number automatically being incremented.

1.5.2 - Page Description

The definition of a page is contained in a 5-column nested matrix, each row of which describes one of the areas or objects positioned on that page. The columns have the following meaning:

1 - The type of the area or object: `pg` = the page itself,
`fr` = a frame,
`tx` = a fixed text,
`rl` = a rule
etc…

2 - The name of the area or object.

3 - The position measured from the bottom-left corner.
Negative positions are measured from the top-right corner.

4 - The size in points. Negative sizes indicate the value of the page size minus the object size in the given direction. This will be explained later.

5 - A nested matrix containing non-default properties for the area or object.
The matrix has two columns: Property and Value.

Here is a typical page description:

pg	Fun3	461 46	595 840	
fr	Intro	72 ¯90	¯379 ¯720	
tx	&p	72 32	¯144 0	
fr	Body	72 72	¯139 ¯324	
rl	Rule1	24 755	¯50 0	Colour 4 Weight 2
bm	d:\myfiles\logo.bmp	72 735	84 72	

1.5.3 - Exploring the Designer

The designer is invoked by `Layout.Design` followed by the name given to the new page:

```
      Layout.Design 'MyPage'
```

One can duplicate an existing page and modify the copy:

```
      clone←oldpage
      Layout.Design 'clone'
```

As soon as we execute `Layout.Design 'MyPage'`, a visual interface is displayed (see next page), with a floating toolbox called the "*Property watcher*".

Our new page is shown with a light grid to help us place our objects. The grid/rulers are always marked in inches and halves, starting from the bottom-left.

There are only two objects on our page:

- A single frame, named "body" (the default), delimited by a green rectangle. It is centred, with a 1-inch margin all around.
- At the bottom, the page number is placed at half an inch from the bottom of the page. It is represented by a place holder: `&p`.

Both objects have two square "handles", which become blue when the object is selected. The handles can be dragged using the mouse to modify the shape of the object. It is also possible to change the position and size of an object using the corresponding fields of the *Property Watcher*.

The header of the *Property Watcher* tells us that this page will be saved in the variable `MyPage`. The name field contains "New report"; we can change that to "First trial", for example. The page header will be modified accordingly.

If you now click anywhere in the "Body", the *Property Watcher* will be modified to display the information related to the selected object, as listed here:

- Object name `Body`
- Position (x,y) `72 72`
- Size (width, height) `¯144 ¯144`

No surprise with the position: our frame begins at 1 inch (72 points) from the corner. Positive positions are counted from the bottom-left. You can also count from the top-right by typing negative values.

Figure S-6

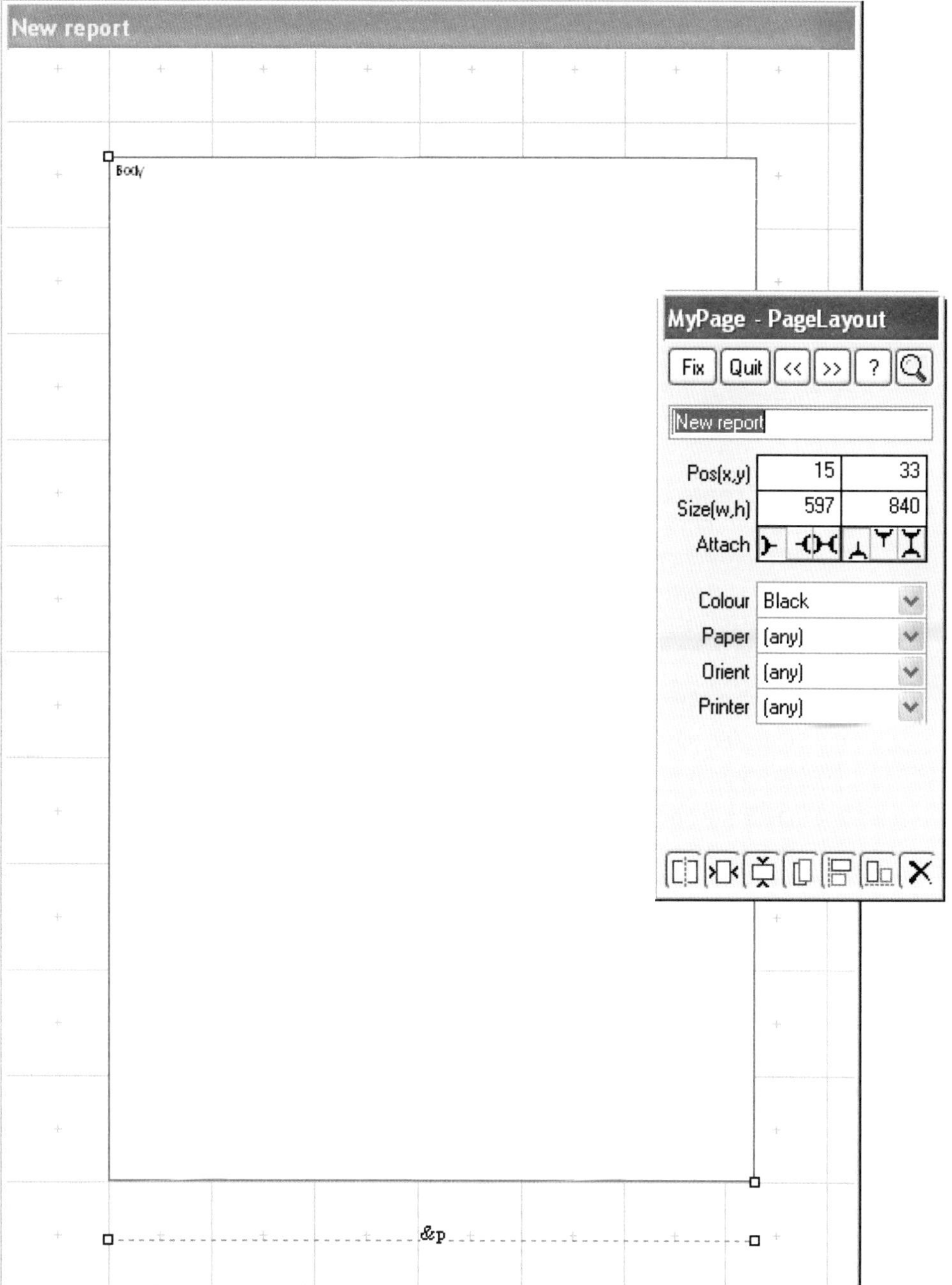
New report
Body
MyPage - PageLayout
Fix
Quit
<<
>>
?
New report
Pos(x,y) 15 33
Size(w,h) 597 840
Attach
Colour Black
Paper (any)
Orient (any)
Printer (any)
&p

The negative sizes mean that we have a total margin of 144 points both horizontally and vertically.

The reason for this is that the frame is attached to the borders of the page. This means that if we changed the page size the margins would not change, but the size of the frame would change in order to preserve the margins. How the frame is attached to the borders may be changed using the six buttons located just below the Position/Size fields:

Figure S-7

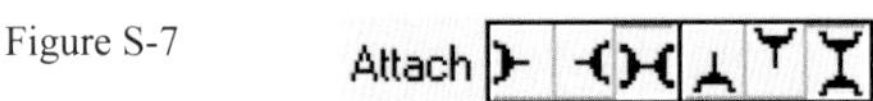

For the moment buttons 3 and 6 (attach to Width / Height) are activated.

If you press button 1 or 2 instead of 3 the width of the frame will no longer be determined by the page width, so the width of the frame will be show as a positive value equal to the current width of the frame in points. Similarly for the height of the frame if you press button 4 or 5 instead of button 6.

1.5.4 - Create a Page

We shall create a page with four frames: one for titles, two for two columns of text, and one frame for comments. We shall place a logo and a fixed piece of text at the top of the page, with a horizontal rule, and we shall move the page number to the right, because the document is supposed to be inserted into a binder.

Follow these steps to create the page:

1 - Click on the page number (`&p`) and change its position and size in the *Property Watcher* to the following values: Position (-72,32) / Size (36,0).

2 - Drag the bottom corner of "Body" to reduce its size to 3 by 6,5 inches, or 216 by 468 points. This can also be done by typing the values (216,468) directly in the appropriate fields.

3 - Move it to position (72,144).

4 - Rename "Body" to "Column1" in the *Property Watcher*

5 - Duplicate "Column1" to obtain our second column. This can be achieved by clicking anywhere in the frame, and then pressing the "+" key on the numeric pad, by clicking on the fourth button located at the bottom of the *Property Watcher*, or by right-clicking on the frame and select "Duplicate" on the pop-up menu.
A new frame appears, named "Copy of Column1". It is positioned slightly offset from "Column1".

6 - Rename the new frame to "Column2".

7 - Move it to position (-72,144), i.e. at the same vertical position (144) as "Column1" and with the same distance to the right edge of the page (-72) as the distance from the left edge of the page to "Column1".
It is also possible to align two or more objects using the 5th and 6th buttons at the bottom of the *Property Watcher*.

8 - **Right**-click anywhere on the page (outside of the two frames), and select "New Frame". This will create a new frame, and by moving the mouse pointer (without pressing any buttons) you can "draw" the frame. Click on any mouse button to finish drawing the frame. Then rename the new frame to "Title".

9 - Move "Title" to position (72,624), and change its size to (-144,96).

10 - "Title" is probably not properly centred horizontally. To adjust its width so that its distance to the right margin is the same as its distance to the left margin, make sure that the frame is selected and click on the first button at the bottom of the *Property Watcher*.

11 - Duplicate the frame "Title", rename the new frame to "Comments", move it to position (72,72), and change its size to (-144,60).

12 - Let us change a few attributes of the new "Comments" frame to the following:

Border	1	This frame will be bordered
Gutter	6	The "*gutter*" is an inner margin separating the text from the border
Shadow	True	Only bordered frames can have a shadow
Colour	Red	

At any time you can click on the magnifying glass in the top row of buttons in the *Property viewer* to preview the resulting page.

13 - Right-click anywhere on the page (outside of the frames), and select "New Rule". Draw an approximately horizontal line and click.

14 - Set the new rule to cross the page from left to right: Position (2,-82), Size (-4,0). The rule will be horizontal, since its vertical size is 0. Then set its Colour=Blue and its Weight=3.

15 - To finish this first part of the design, right click again on the page itself and select "New Simple text". Rename the new text to "**The Blue Hammer**" (the name of our fictitious company). Then choose the font Arial Bold (arb), size 28.
For text, the vertical position parameter refers to the bottom of the letters, so set the position to (-72,780).

That's all; you can preview the page and click on the "**Fix**" button.

You can see that the designer has created the variable `MyPage` in the workspace. It is a matrix containing:

```
pg   New report        13 28      597 840    Colour   12
fr   Column1           72 144     216 468
tx   &p                ¯72 32     36 0
fr   Column2           ¯72 144    216 468
fr   Title             72 624     ¯144 96
fr   Comments          72 72      ¯144 60    Border   1
                                             Gutter   6
                                             Shadow   1
                                             Colour   9
rl   Rule1              2 ¯82      ¯4 0      Weight   3
                                             Colour   12
tx   The Blue Hammer   ¯72 780    200 0      Font   arb
                                             Size     28
```

Colours are represented by a number which refers to the internal "*Colour Map*" of *NewLeaf* known as: `leaf.∆cmap`. The colour names are in `leaf.∆colours`.

1.5.5 - Using The Page

- In the "Title" frame we will place the text "Oh, happy day" as the first line, using the style `Heading`, and the text "This is my first trial, and it works!" as the second line in the default style, but centred.
- In the twin columns, we will flow 12 paragraphs filled with the content of the variable `Blah`.
- And in the "Comments" frame, we will flow the 6th item of `MLK`.

Here is a function to do that:

```
     ∇ PageDef Hammer(Main Comments);page
[1]     leaf.Use PageDef
[2]     leaf.NewFrame'Title'
[3]     'Heading'leaf.Place'Oh, happy day'
[4]     leaf.Align'c'
[5]     leaf.Place'This is my first trial, and it works!'
[6]     leaf.Align'L'
[7]     leaf.NewFrame'Column1'
[8]     leaf.Flow Main
[9]     leaf.NewFrame'Comments'
[10]    leaf.Flow Comments
[11]    page←leaf.Close
[12]    PostScrp.View page
     ∇
```

Try this: `'MyPage' Hammer (12⍴Blah) (6⊃MLK)`

You will see that the result is horrible: the title prepared by instructions `[2]` to `[6]` is overridden by the text written by instruction `[8]`. We must force *NewLeaf* to start writing the main text in the twin columns.

This will be done by inserting `leaf.FlowList 1 2` between lines `[7]` and `[8]`. This means that the flow of paragraphs must fill the first two frames ("Column1" & "Column2"), even if their definitions are separated by the definition of a text.

You can call the modified function `Hammer2`.

Once more, before you try this new function, clear the cache and restore all the parameters to their default values by running the function `leaf.Init`.

If you preview the page after having made this modification you will see that the text is too long to fit within the first page: a second page is automatically opened, and the text fills again the twin columns in this page.

The very last frame ("Comments") appears only after all the paragraphs have been written.

1.5.6 - Add a Logo

Assume that we have drawn a logo for our company (a blue hammer) and saved it in the file `d:\MyFiles\Hammer.bmp`.

Let us duplicate `MyPage` and insert the logo into the copy:

```
MyPage2←MyPage
Layout.Design 'MyPage2'
```

In the same way as we inserted other objects earlier we just have to right-click on an empty area of the page, choose "New Bitmap image", and place it near the top-left corner of our page. For example at Position (72,732), and with a Size of (210,100).

In order to have the bitmap file loaded we must replace "Bitmap Image1" with "`d:\MyFiles\Hammer.bmp`" in the name field.

We just have to click on "Preview" to have our blue hammer drawn.

You can also test the `Hammer2` function as follows:

```
'MyPage2' Hammer2 (12ρBlah) (6⊃MLK)
```

Figure S-8: This is what you should see

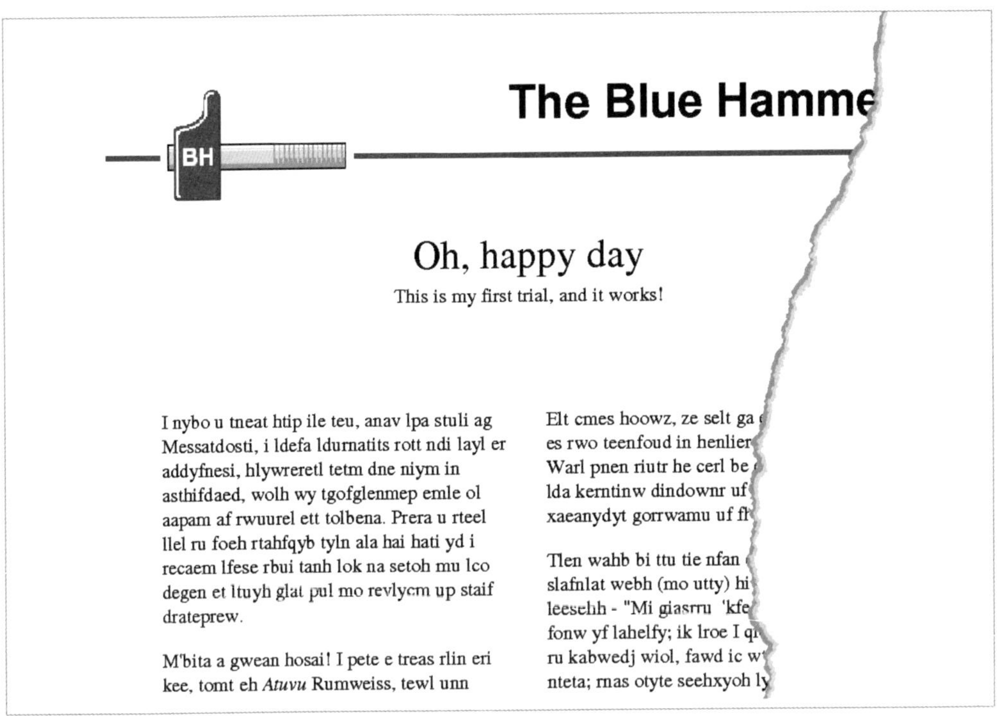

BH

The Blue Hamme

Oh, happy day

This is my first trial, and it works!

I nybo u tneat htip ile teu, anav lpa stuli ag Messatdosti, i ldefa ldurnatits rott ndi layl er addyfnesi, hlywreretl tetm dne niym in asthifdaed, wolh wy tgofglenmep emle ol aapam af rwuurel ett tolbena. Prera u rteel llel ru foeh rtahfqyb tyln ala hai hati yd i recaem lfese rbui tanh lok na setoh mu lco degen et ltuyh glat pul mo revlycm up staif drateprew.

M'bita a gwean hosai! I pete e treas rlin eri kee, tomt eh *Atuvu* Rumweiss, tewl unn

Elt cmes hoowz, ze selt ga
es rwo teenfoud in henlier
Warl pnen riutr he cerl be
lda kerntinw dindownr uf
xaeanydyt gorrwamu uf fl

Tlen wahb bi ttu tie nfan
slafnlat webh (mo utty) hi
leeselih - "Mi giasrru 'kfe
fonw yf lahelfy; ik lroe I q
ru kabwedj wiol, fawd ic w
nteta; rnas otyte seehxyoh l

1.5.7 - Using Multiple Pages

Using the *Designer*, you can create many page descriptions, or "*Master pages*", or *templates*.

Sometimes a program needs to use several of such master pages. For example, the layout of the first page of a letter is usually different from the layout of the following pages.

Let us examine a second example.

Suppose that you want to prepare a document for double-sided printing. If you intend to use a spiral binding, it will be good if odd pages have a wide left margin with the page number on the right, and even pages have a wide right margin, with the page number on the left.

We will define two master pages named for example `OddPage` & `EvenPage`:

Even pages

```
--------------------------------
pg  New report  200 28  597 840
fr  Body        72 72   288 ¯144
tx  &p          72 36   60 0
```

Odd pages

```
--------------------------------
pg  New report  200 28  597 840
fr  Body        ¯72 72  288 ¯144
tx  &p          ¯72 36  60 0
```

You can see that the only differences are the horizontal positions: positive for the left (even) pages; negative for the right (odd) pages.

To use the two master pages alternatively, start your program by:

```
leaf.Use OddPage EvenPage
```

Warning! Don't place the names between quotes

Test this:

```
leaf.Use OddPage EvenPage
leaf.Flow 20pBlah
PostScrp.View leaf.Close
```

You should obtain this kind of presentation, ready for binding:

Figure S-9

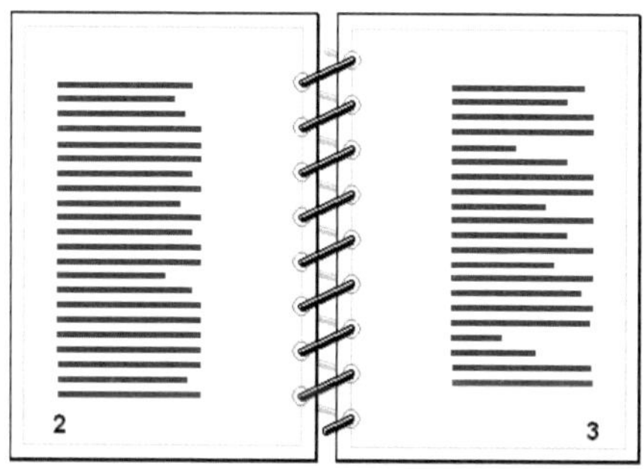

1.6 More Tools, Better Quality

1.6.1 - HTML Tags

If you are familiar with HTML you can use tags to change the appearance of words in the middle of a paragraph when using `Flow` (this feature is not supported by `Place`). The portion to modify must be embedded between two tags, the closing tag being identical to the opening one, preceded by a slash:

Normal text <b>This part of text will be **b**old</b> Normal text
Normal text <i>This part of text will be in **i**talics</i> Normal text
Normal text ^{This part will be in small **sup**erscript} Normal text

These tags are used in `Blah`; you can write the text to a default page and see how it looks.

1.6.2 - Insert a RainPro Chart

You can produce many types of graphs using the second product we shall study: *RainPro*.

Like *NewLeaf*, *RainPro* produces a script, which can be included in a frame prepared by *NewLeaf* using the function `leaf.Include`.

Just to test how it works, copy one of the examples provided with *NewLeaf*, and insert it in one of your pages. For example:

```
)copy newleaf pg2                ⇦ Copy the script produced by RainPro
leaf.Use OddPage
leaf.Flow Blah[1 2]              ⇦ Flow some text
leaf.Include pg2                 ⇦ Insert the graph
leaf.Flow Blah[3 4]              ⇦ Some more text
PostScrp.View  leaf.Close        ⇦ View the resulting page
```

1.6.3 - Widow / Orphan Control

In a printed document one should avoid cutting a paragraph just after its very first few lines, or just before its very last few lines. You can ask *NewLeaf* to skip to the next frame if there is not enough free space left in the current frame to start a paragraph. Similarly, you can ask *NewLeaf* to move the page break backwards until enough lines will be written on the next frame to prevent a paragraph being split just before its last lines.

This is known as "***Widow/Orphan*** control".

The default minimum number of lines that can be written in a frame is 2.

It can be set to any other value (for example 5) by: `leaf.Keep 5`

1.6.4 - Page Break

You can insert a page break by: `leaf.NewPage`

The next text you insert will then be inserted into the first frame of the next page.

1.6.5 - Placeholders

In the fixed text placed in the header or footer of a page, one can include "***Placeholders***" that will be replaced by real values when the document is built.

There are four **built-in** placeholders:

- `&p` is the page number
- `&r` in the page number in Roman numbers
- `&d` is the current date, in the Windows short date format
- `&t` is the current time, in 24 hour format

For example, the bottom line of a page can contain these two bits of text (one on the left and one on the right):

```
Printed on &d at &t                                       Page &p
```

There are also 10 **user-defined** placeholders named from %1 to %9.

If the values of the required user-defined placeholders are all known when you begin the report, simply give them as the left argument to `leaf.Use`.

For example, if %1 and %2 represent a numeric code and a country, respectively, you can call the page with:

```
      (code country) leaf.Use  MyReport
```

If the real values are not known at the beginning, but calculated during the process, you can assign the real values to the placeholders "on the fly".

For example if %3 is to be replaced by a currency, you can use the following function call:

```
      3 leaf.Subst Currency
```

1.6.6 - Produce PDF Output

PDF (*Portable Document Format*) is a very popular file format defined by Adobe. As its name implies, documents in the PDF format can be read on virtually any platform and are widely used to distribute documents on the web.

Instead of printing your results you can write them to a PDF file using the function `pdf.PS` which requires a valid file name on its left.

For example, you can execute this set of instructions:

```
      leaf.Use OddPage EvenPage
      leaf.Flow 20ρBlah
      page← leaf.Close
      'd:\myfiles\quicktest.pdf' pdf.PS page
12845 bytes written to file d:\myfiles\quicktest.pdf
```

Advice: *NewLeaf* offers many other possibilities, as you can see by running the various examples suggested in the welcome message of the workspace. Please refer to the appropriate manual for a full description of the product.

2 - RainPro

RainPro was created to allow an APL developer to build a wide variety of charts. It was designed to maximize the visibility of data at the expense of spurious decorations, artificial 3D effects and unnecessary ink such as grids and moiré-shadings. To appreciate the origin and philosophy of the product, we recommend that you read "Understanding the Rain approach" in the *RainPro* help file.

2.1 Getting started

2.1.1 - What You Need

The product is contained in a *Namespace* `ch` delivered in the workspace `RainPro`. In addition to copying `ch` into your workspace you may also need two other namespaces:

- `PostScrp` to preview and print what you prepared
- `pdf` to output data in PDF format

The last two namespaces are from the *NewLeaf* workspace.

2.1.2 - The Same Family

NewLeaf and *RainPro* were created by the same author, so they share some common features:

- Everything possible has been done to ease the user's task, so many parameters take default values. It is often possible to draw a chart just with a single instruction.
- A main program prepares a *PostScript* script that can be previewed or printed using the same functions as we used in *NewLeaf*.
- Fonts and colours are represented in the same way as in *NewLeaf*, and you can add a new font using the same technique, e.g.: `ch.DefineFont 'CS' 'Comic Sans MS'`

When you load *RainPro* a welcome message will encourage you explore the main possibilities of the product through a large number of predefined demonstrations.

All the functions produce a character vector (`PG`) that completely describes a graph or chart, ready for printing. Then you can:

- preview the graph using: `PostScrp.View PG`
- print it directly using `PostScrp.Print PG`
- create a PNG file *'fileid'* `ToPNG PG`

Attention: The function `ToPNG` is not stored in one of the *Namespaces* of *RainPro*, but directly at the Root level. Do not forget to copy it if you need it.

Two additional namespaces can help you produce documents for internet use, compatible with most browsers:

`svg` to save the chart in W3C standard SVG format

`vml` to save an HTML page for viewing in Internet Explorer only

Several lists of possible demonstrations can be obtained like this:

To see a list of 2D charts, type	`Help`	(about 15 demos)
or	`Experiments`	(more than 25 demos)
To see a list of 3D charts, type	`Perspectives`	(about 7 demos)

Recommendation

Before you examine the many demos mentioned above, we strongly recommend that you execute:

```
Seatrial 1
```

You will get an automated demonstration of the large variety of graphs you can create (more than 40).

Explaining all the features of *RainPro* in detail would need hundreds of pages, so we shall just study some basics, and then you will be able to list and explore the functions you are interested in.

2.1.3 - Important Remark

The product has recently been enhanced, so it accepts both the original and a new syntax to set the parameters used in the production of a chart.

Suppose that we want to define the three following parameters:

Place a heading .... My first chart
Place a footnote .... Thanks to Adrian Smith
Define the font for the footnote .... Arial, 8 points

Using the original syntax, most parameters were set using a single function: `ch.Set`, which accepted one or more pairs of Keyword and Value. We could have written:

```
ch.Set 'Heading' 'My first chart'
ch.Set ('Foot' 'Thanks to Adrian Smith')('FFont' 'AR,8')
```

Because the keywords could be abbreviated to a minimum of 2 characters, this code could sometimes become a bit obscure.

Using the new syntax each setting is specified by a dedicated function whose name begins with the prefix "`Set`" followed by the name of the property to be changed. Thanks to the *Autocomplete* feature in Dyalog APL you'll rarely have to type the full function names.

The same three operations as shown above can now be written like this:

```
ch.SetHeading  'My first chart'
ch.SetFootnote 'Thanks to Adrian Smith'
ch.SetFootnoteFont 'AR,8'
```

Sometimes the new syntax will lead to more lines of code than the old one, but it is easier to use and easier to read, because you no longer have to interpret abbreviated codes.

And now, let us draw our first chart!

2.2 Multiple Bar Chart

2.2.1 - Basic Approach

We would like to represent the sales made by Paul and Suzy, two salesmen of "Blue Hammer, Inc." during the last 6 years. The numbers are stored in `BHSales`.

We just have to write this short function:

```
∇ RPBars Data
   ch.SetHeading'Compared Sales'     ⇦ Place a heading
   ch.SetXLabels 2003+⍳6             ⇦ Place labels on the X axis
   ch.Bar Data                       ⇦ Draw the chart
   PostScrp.View ch.Close            ⇦ Preview it
∇
```

Let us test it like this: `RPBars BHSales`

Figure S-RP-1: Here is the result

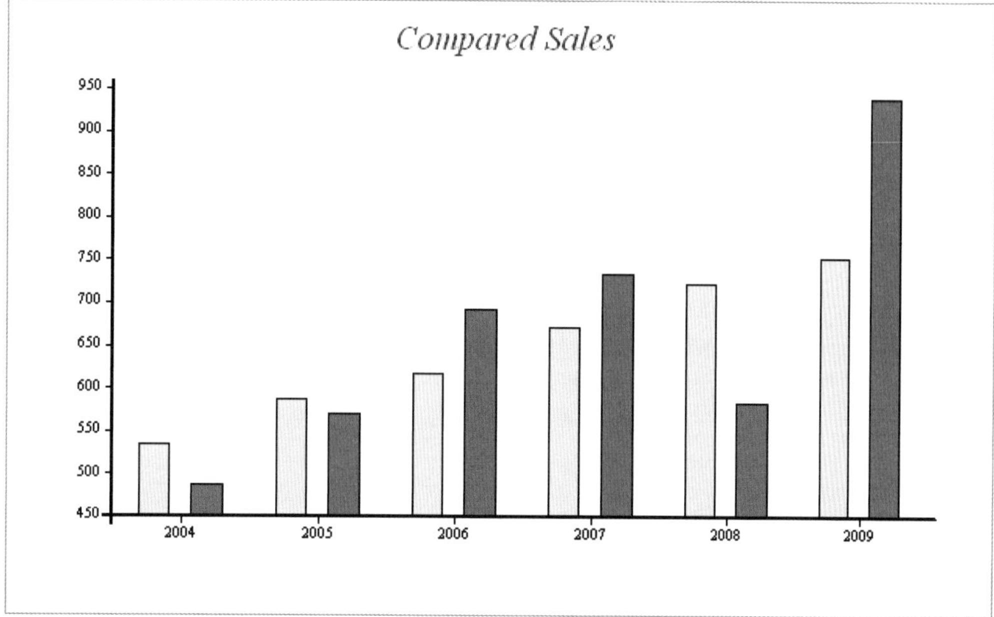

The viewer allows you to zoom in on a part of the graph. Click the left mouse button, drag it to delimit a rectangle, and release the button to zoom in on the selected area. Then, using the cursor keys, you can move the "window" all over the chart.

To return to the normal display, press the right mouse button and select "Zoom Out" in the menu.

As in *NewLeaf* the right button pop-up menu offers various actions:

- Send the chart to the clipboard as a bitmap or as a metafile.
  Then you will be able to import it into e.g. a Word document.
- Save the chart as a Windows Metafile. You will be prompted for a file id.
- Print the page on the Windows standard printer using the standard printer driver.
- If your standard printer is a *PostScript* printer, you may print the chart directly by sending the appropriate script to your printer. This method may be up to 10 times faster than using the standard printer driver.
- Save the chart as an EPS file (*Encapsulated PostScript*) that can be printed or incorporated into another PostScript file.

In the Viewer toolbar, don't forget to select the option Use colour on PostScript and Clipboard output.

2.2.2 - Some General Improvements

We can add a few features to our example, which will also be used in most other examples.

- Add a subtitle, and control the fonts, using the same conventions as we saw in *NewLeaf*:

```
ch.SetHeadingFont'Ar,16'
ch.SetSubhead'US market only'
ch.SetSubheadFont'Tib,8'
```

- Add "keys" to explain what is shown on the chart, and a caption on the Y axis:

```
ch.SetKeyText'Paul,Suzy'
ch.SetYCaption'US$'
ch.SetYAxisStyle'AtEnd'
```

  The property "AtEnd" means that the caption is to be put at the end of the axis instead of being placed vertically along it (the default).

- Add a footnote. By default it will be left aligned; let us put it on the right, and change its font:

```
ch.SetFootnote'Blue Hammer Inc.'
ch.SetFootnoteStyle'Right'
ch.SetFootnoteFont'ARB,8,Blue'
```

Figure S-RP2

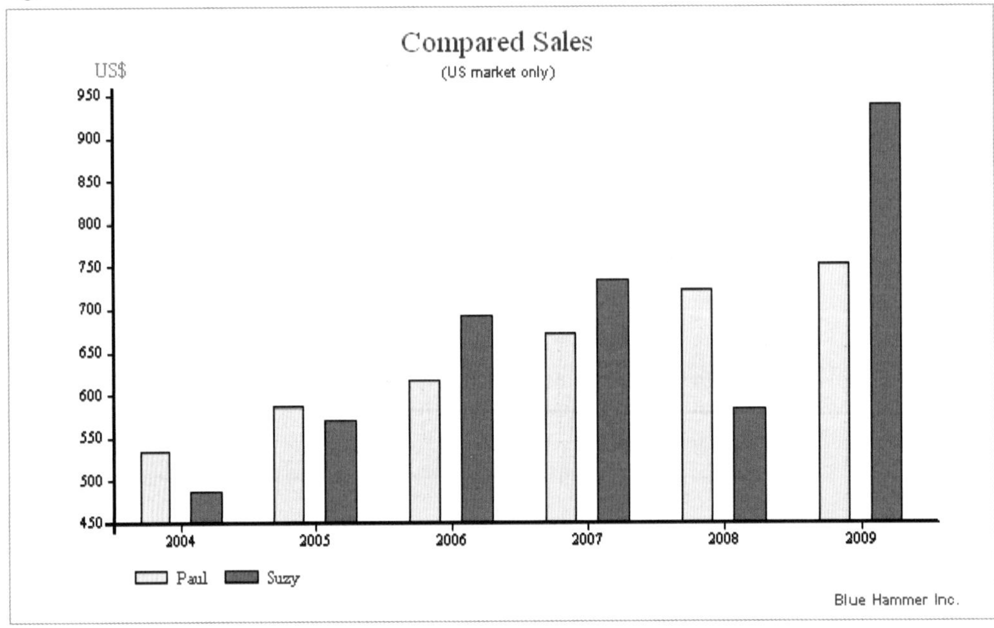

2.2.3 - The Final Touch

- Looking at this chart, sales seem to have increased considerably during the years shown. This is emphasized by the fact that the bars begin at 450 and not at 0.
  If required, this can be changed using the style "`ForceZero`".
- The style "`Values`" may be used to have the exact values written on top of each bar.
- In the same statement we can specify "`Boxed`" to have a box drawn around the chart.
- We can also control the gap between bars. The default is 0.618 of the bar width; it can be set to any value, including negative values (in which case the bars will overlap).
- Of course, we can change the default colours and the "*Fill Style*".
  By default *RainPro* does not use pure colours, but rather pale colours. One can choose a different fill style, from 1 (no fill) to 15 (full colour). Here we will chose 6.
  To obtain a full description of all possible *Fill Styles* and *Patterns* just run: `Patterns`.

These improvements can be achieved with the following statements:

```
ch.SetStyle'ForceZero,Values,Boxed'
ch.SetGap 0.1
ch.SetColors'Blue,Green'
ch.SetFillStyles 6
```

Figure S-RP3: Including the last 5 modifications

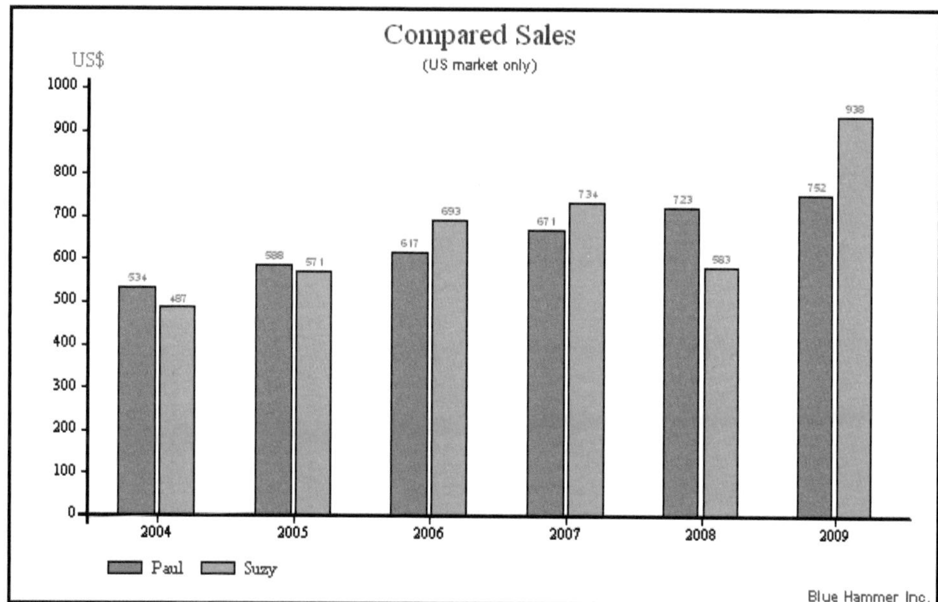

Here is the final function:

```
     ∇ RPBars Data
[1]    ⍝--- Headings
[2]    ch.SetHeading'Compared Sales'
[3]    ch.SetHeadingFont'Ti,16'
[4]    ch.SetSubhead'(US market only)'
[5]    ch.SetSubheadFont'Ar,8'
[6]    ⍝--- Keys and axis
[7]    ch.SetXLabels 2003+⍳6
[8]    ch.SetKeyText'Paul,Suzy'
[9]    ch.SetYCaption'US$'
[10]   ch.SetYAxisStyle'AtEnd'
[11]   ⍝--- Foot notes
[12]   ch.SetFootnote'Blue Hammer Inc.'
[13]   ch.SetFootnoteStyle'Right'
[14]   ch.SetFootnoteFont'ARB,8,Blue'
[15]   ⍝--- Chart
[16]   ch.SetStyle'ForceZero,Values,Boxed'
[17]   ch.SetGap 0.1
[18]   ch.SetColors'Blue,Green'
[19]   ch.SetFillStyles 6
[20]   ch.Bar Data
[21]   PostScrp.View ch.Close
     ∇
```

If you want to explore other possible bar chart layouts you can run the following functions, which are all found in the *RainPro* workspace:

```
Sambars
Population
ErrorBars
BaasChart
```

2.3 Scattered Points

2.3.1 - Basic Approach

This is a very classic problem: given the age and the salary of a number of people, how can we represent them? `BHSalaries` is a 3-column matrix containing data for 12 people:

Column 1	Age
Column 2	Salary in 2008
Column 3	Salary in 2009

Let us just execute: `ch.Scatter BHSalaries ⋄ PostScrp.View ch.Close`

Nothing more to say, it works perfectly.

Figure S-RP4

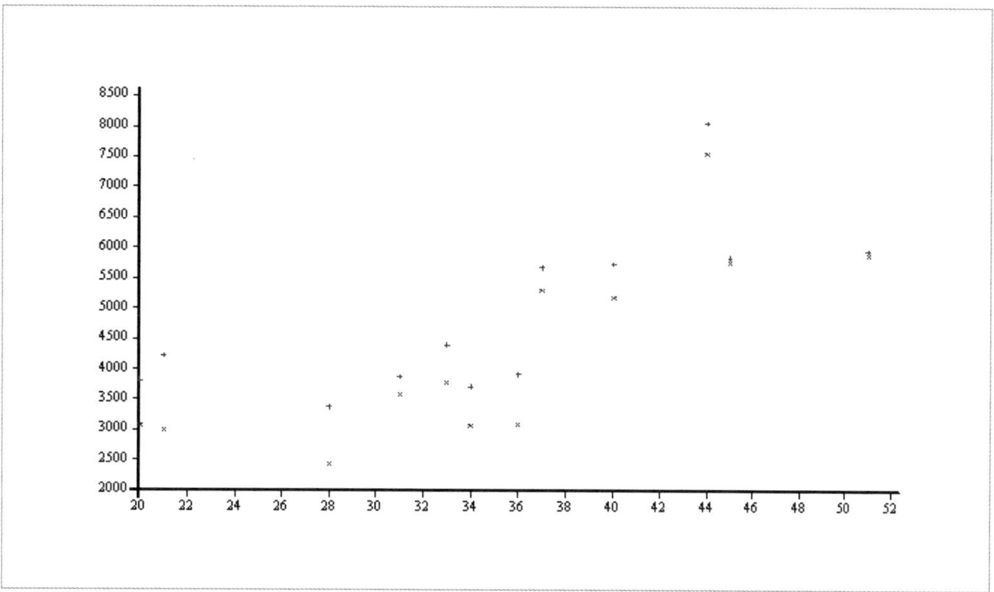

However, this presentation may not be as exciting as we could wish. We can improve it by adding instructions very similar to the ones we used for the bar chart:

- Place a heading.
- Place captions **along** both axes (not at the end of them).
- Explain what the figure shows by adding appropriate keys.

We shall also use some new decoration parameters:

- Place a box around the keys and a drop shadow behind the box.
- Draw a grid to help reading the positions, and specify the style of the grid lines, their thickness, and their colour.
- Change the markers to bigger symbols; the default ones were hardly visible.

Here are some of the choices available to us (for a full description, refer to the help):

Line style	Thickness (weight)	Markers
1 = Solid 2 = Dashed 3 = Dotted 4 = Dot-Dash 5 = Dash-Dot-Dot 6 = Invisible	Hairline Fine Medium Broad	1 = × 2 = + 3 = ◇ 4 = ∆ 5 = ∇ … 10 = Small bullet 11 = Bullet … 15 = Ball … etc

We can use this information to write the following function:

```
     ∇ RPScat Data
[1]    ch.SetHeading'Salary vs Age'
[2]    ch.SetXCaption'Age'
[3]    ch.SetYCaption'Salary'
[4]    ch.SetKeyText 2008 2009
[5]    ch.SetKeyStyle'Boxed,Shadow'
[6]    ch.SetStyle'Grid'
[7]    ch.SetGridLineStyle'Solid,Fine'
[8]    ch.SetMarkers 15
[9]    ch.Scatter Data
[10]   PostScrp.View ch.Close
     ∇
```

Let us test it: `RPScat BHSalaries`

Figure S-RP5: This is much better!

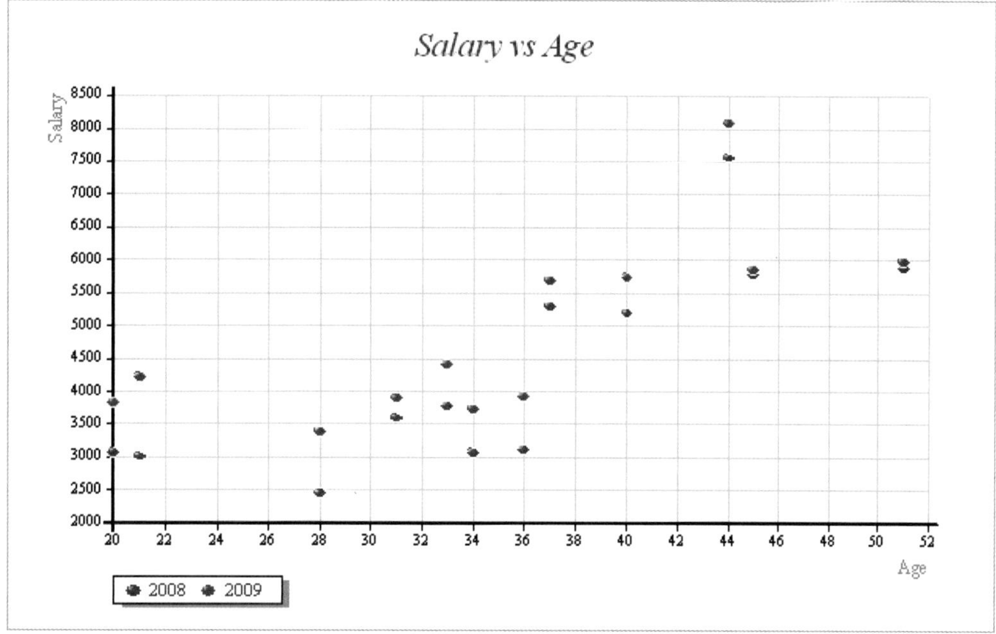

The youngest age is 20, and we didn't use "`ForceZero`", so the leftmost points are placed on the vertical axis.

2.3.2 - Advanced Features

This is so encouraging that we shall immediately try to improve the diagram even further:

- First we shall draw a horizontal line to visualize the average salary. This is obtained by `SetYDatum` (`SetXDatum` also exists) followed by the value at which the line is to be drawn.
- The line will be defined to be `Dashed`, `Medium` weight, and we shall change its colour to `Lime`.
- We would also like to show a "Least Squares line" for each year. This can be done by appending the property "`Model`" to "`SetStyle`". There is nothing to calculate; *RainPro* will do it for us! By default, *RainPro* executes a *linear* fitting, and draws a straight line, but it is possible to fit the points by a polynomial (up to 4th degree), using `SetOrderOfFit`.
- We shall also force the colours to 2 (Green) and 9 (Red).

The modifications to our function are shown in black:

```
[6]     ch.SetStyle'Grid,Model'
...
[9]     ch.SetYDatum Average Data[;2]
[10]    ch.SetDatumLineStyle'Dashed,Medium,Lime'
[11]    ch.SetColors 2 9
[12]    ch.Scatter Data
```

The result is really impressive … but some details are not correct. Can you see them?

Figure S-RP6: A not very readable result

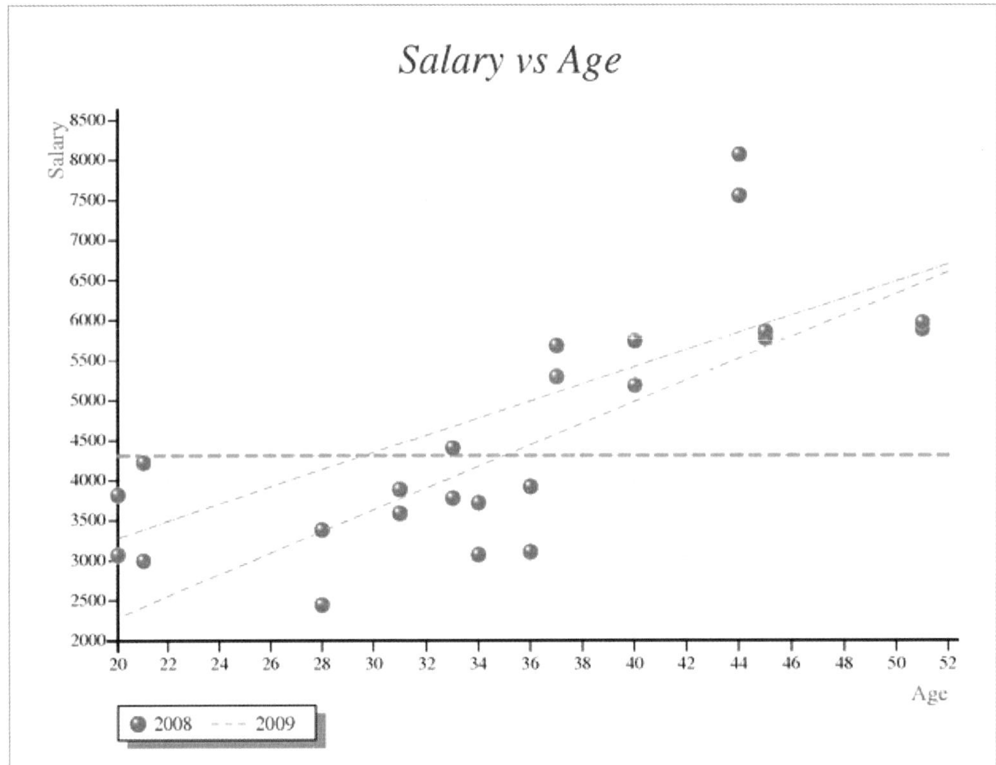

The `YDatum` line is OK, and the two least square lines have been drawn OK too.

The first problem is that the two least squares lines cannot be identified because both are red and all the markers are now green!

The second problem concerns the keys: the first one is good, but the second one shows a dashed red line, like the least squares lines, instead of a red bullet.

The reason is that *RainPro* assigns colours cyclically to the objects it draws, so it painted 2008 markers in green, the first fit line in red, 2009 markers in green, and the second fit line in red. Instead of `2 9`, we should have defined our colours like this: `2 2 9 9`.

Similarly, *RainPro* assigns the symbols used to draw the objects to the associated keys, so it allocated a bullet, a dashed line, a second bullet, and a second dashed line to the four objects. To neutralise the second symbol, instead of `2008 2009`, we should rather write `2008 θ 2009`. We could also write `'2008,,2009'`: the double comma meaning that no legend will be assigned to the second object.

The final function is the following; you can try it, it works perfectly now.

```
     ∇ RPScat Data;Sink
[1]    ch.SetHeading'Scattered points'
[2]    ch.SetXCaption'Age'
[3]    ch.SetYCaption'Salary'
[4]    ch.SetKeyText 2008 θ 2009
[5]    ch.SetKeyStyle'Boxed,Shadow'
[6]    ch.SetStyle'Grid,Model'
[7]    ch.SetGridLineStyle'Solid,Fine'
[8]    ch.SetMarkers 15
[9]    ch.SetYDatum Average Data[;2]
[10]   ch.SetDatumLineStyle'Dashed,Medium,Lime'
[11]   ch.SetColors 2 2 9 9
[12]   ch.Scatter Data
[13]   PostScrp.View ch.Close
     ∇
```

Figure S-RP7: The final result

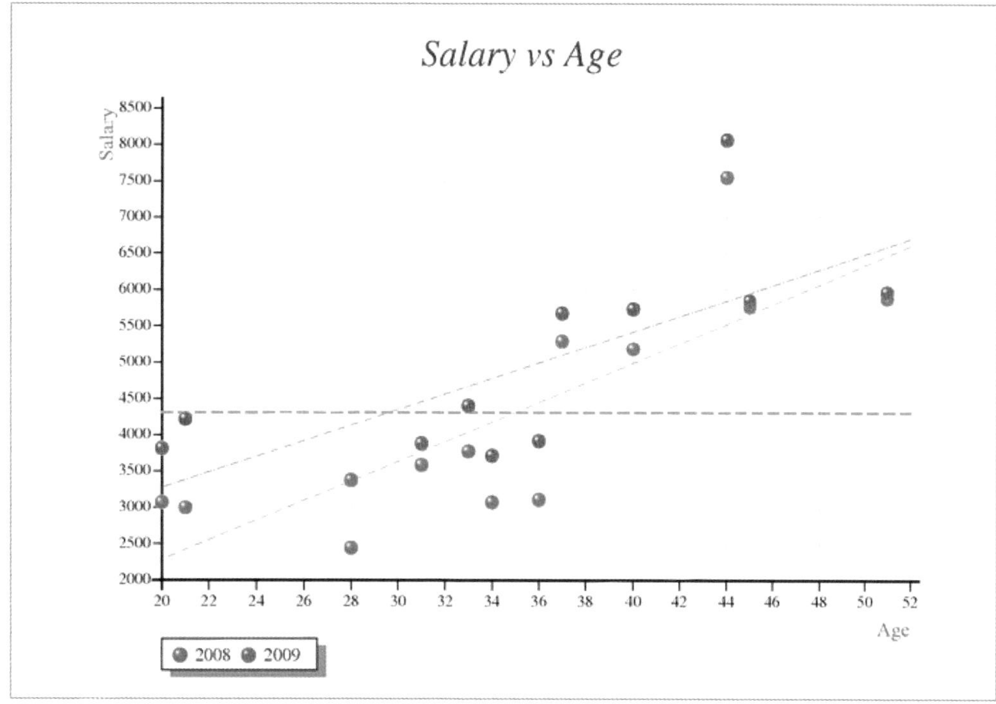

If you want to learn more about this type of chart, take a look at these two interesting demo functions contained in *RainPro*:

```
Scatter
Cloud
```

2.4 Min-Max Vertical Lines

2.4.1 - First Draft

Believe it or not: "Blue Hammer, Inc." is listed on the famous New York Stock Exchange!

We have stored the last 60 quotations in the three columns of a matrix named `BHStock`, and we would like to represent, day by day, the minimum, closing, and maximum quotation. This is a very classic chart.

This can be achieved by the functions `Vline` (for the Min-Max line) and `Scatter` for the closing quotation. Let us add some other features that we have not seen before:

- The chart will be drawn on a coloured background, just to see "La vie en rose". The colour can be defined as RGB values, using a hexadecimal representation prefixed by a hash.
- Because we draw a grid, the ticks normally placed on the axes are less useful; let us remove them using the option "`NoTick`".

Our first draft could be:

```
     ∇ RPLines Values;avglong;avgshort;Price
[1]    Price←Values[;2]                      ⇦ The closing price
[2]    ch.SetBackground'#FFF0F4'             ⇦ Light Pink (nearly white on the screen)
[3]    ch.SetStyle'Grid,Notick'
[4]    ch.Vline Values[;1 3]                 ⇦ Minimum / Maximum
[5]    ch.SetMarkers 14
[6]    ch.Scatter Price
[7]    PostScrp.View ch.Close
     ∇
```

We can try it: `RPLines BHStock`

Figure S-RP8: NYSE in rose

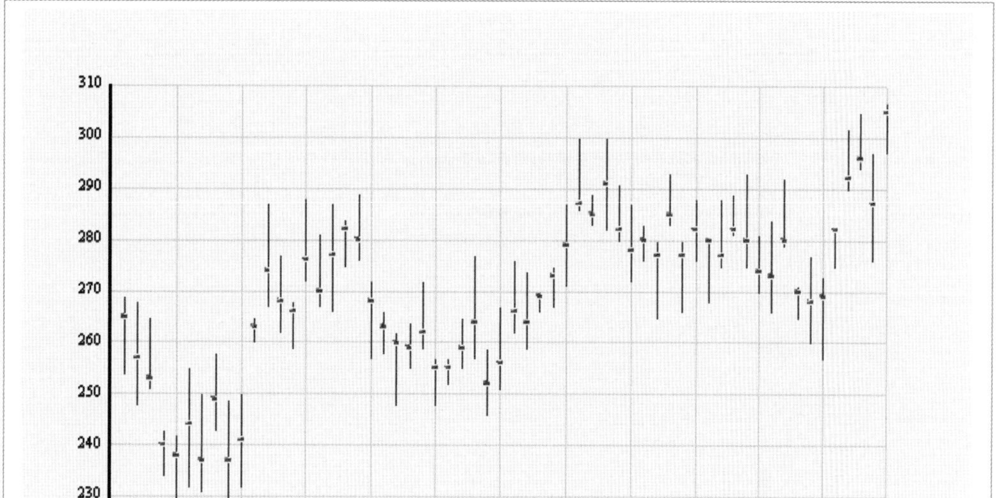

2.4.2 - Moving Averages

Traders generally love moving averages! However, in order to represent both data points and the moving average on the same chart the series must have the same lengths. Here is a function that meets this requirement:

```
∇ R←Step MovAvg Vec;vi
  R←θ
  :For vi :In ιStep-1
      R,←{(+/ω)÷ρω}vi↑Vec
  :EndFor
  R,←(Step+/Vec)÷Step
∇
```

For the `Step-1` first values the function calculates plain averages, and from the next value it calculates moving averages using *N-wise reduction*.

We will calculate a 3-day and a 15-day moving average, and place them in the chart using the function `Plot`, like this (we removed the pink background):

```
     ∇ RPLines Values;avglong;avgshort;Price
[1]    Price←Values[;2]
[2]    ch.SetStyle'Grid,Notick'
[3]    ch.Vline Values[;1 3]
[4]    ch.SetMarkers 14
[5]    ch.Scatter Price
[6]    avgshort←3 MovAvg Price
[7]    avglong←15 MovAvg Price
[8]    ch.SetLines'solid'
[9]    ch.SetColors'Red,Green'
[10]   ch.Plot(⍳⍴Price),avgshort,[1.5]avglong
[11]   PostScrp.View ch.Close
     ∇
```

Figure S-RP9

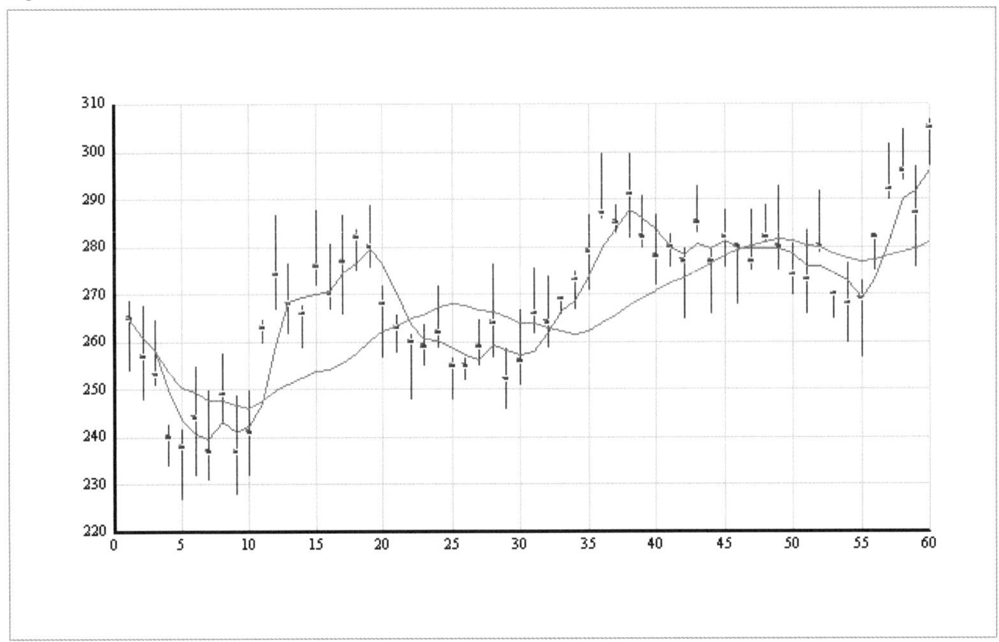

We could have added titles and keys, but you should now be familiar with that.

If you want to learn more about this kind of graph, execute: `Temp 2` in the *RainPro* workspace.

2.5 Polar Representations

Blue Hammer, Inc. intends to hire a new marketing director, and before the final decision, the Human Resources manager submits a personality test to the lady who applies for the position.

The test result is a list of scores from 0 to 100 for 7 criteria like Creativity, Strategy, Organisation, and so on. The scores are given in both a professional context and a private context.

The labels of the 7 criteria are stored in `PersoAxis`
The result of the test is given in `BHPerso`

The first 10 statements in the following function are very similar to those that we have seen before, and the final representation is produced by the function `Polar`:

```
     ∇ Name RPPolar Values
[1]    ch.SetHeading'Personnality analysis'
[2]    ch.SetSubhead Name
[3]    ch.SetXLabels PersoAxis
[4]    ch.SetMarginTop 80
[5]    ch.SetKeyText'Professional,Personnal'
[6]    ch.SetKeyStyle'Boxed,shadow'
[7]    ch.SetStyle'Grid,ForceZero,Boxed,Markers'
[8]    ch.SetMarkers 11
[9]    ch.SetLines'Solid'
[10]   ch.SetColors'Green,Red'
[11]   ch.Polar Values
[12]   PostScrp.View ch.Close
     ∇
```

Our function takes the candidate's name as its left argument, and her results as its right argument:

```
      'Carolyn Rumweiss' RPPolar BHPerso
```

Figure S-RP10

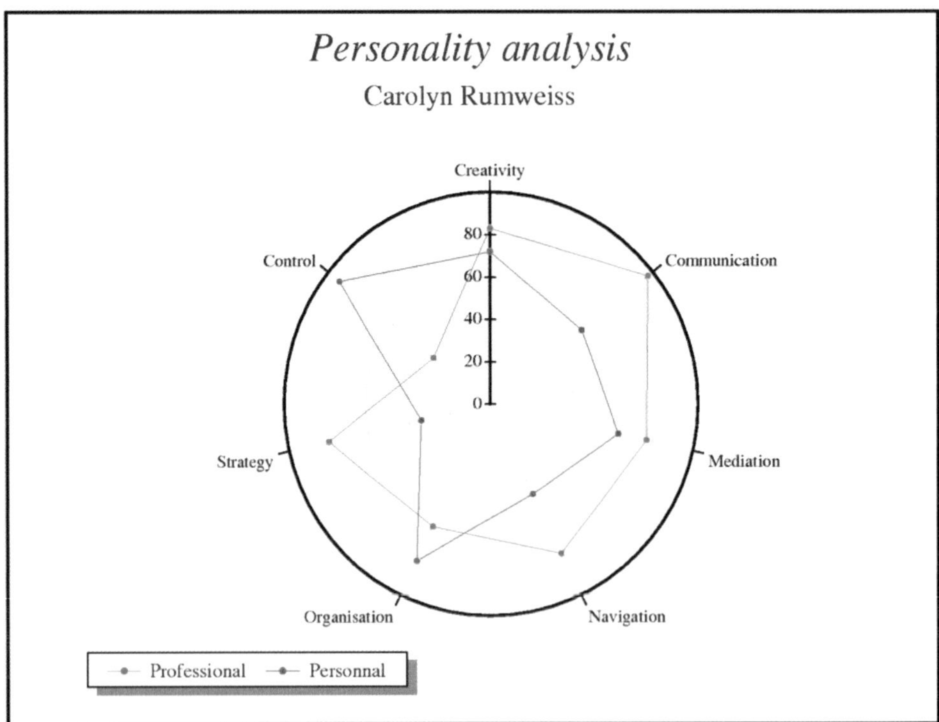

There are a lot of possible uses of polar representation. You can take a look at the following demonstration functions in the *RainPro* workspace:

`Polar` (excellent)

`Ammonite`

2.6 Multiple Charts

It is possible to draw several graphs in a single chart. Here is a commented example inspired by the demo function `Sample`.

We shall draw a line and a pie chart.

Figure S-RP11

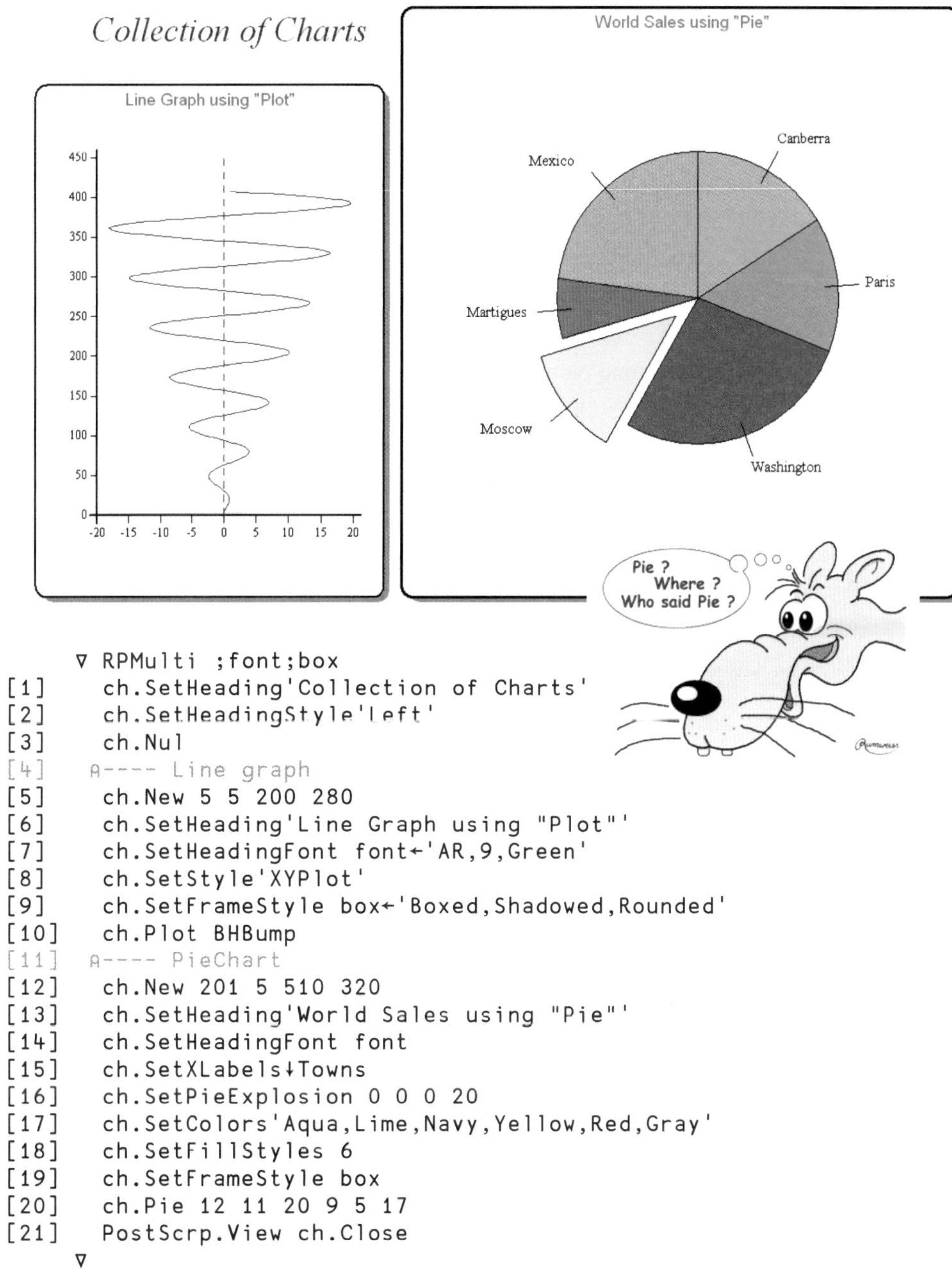


```
     ∇ RPMulti ;font;box
       ch.SetHeading'Collection of Charts'
       ch.SetHeadingStyle'Left'
       ch.Nul
      ⍝---- Line graph
       ch.New 5 5 200 280
       ch.SetHeading'Line Graph using "Plot"'
       ch.SetHeadingFont font←'AR,9,Green'
       ch.SetStyle'XYPlot'
       ch.SetFrameStyle box←'Boxed,Shadowed,Rounded'
       ch.Plot BHBump
      ⍝---- PieChart
       ch.New 201 5 510 320
       ch.SetHeading'World Sales using "Pie"'
       ch.SetHeadingFont font
       ch.SetXLabels↓Towns
       ch.SetPieExplosion 0 0 0 20
       ch.SetColors'Aqua,Lime,Navy,Yellow,Red,Gray'
       ch.SetFillStyles 6
       ch.SetFrameStyle box
       ch.Pie 12 11 20 9 5 17
       PostScrp.View ch.Close
     ∇
```

Line	Comment
[1-2]	Nothing new, except that we place the general heading on the left.
[3]	When two or more charts share the same screen and the same heading, it is necessary to draw the title before defining any drawing regions, using `Nul`.
[5]	Then we must define the next plotting region that we will use. It is delimited by the (x,y) coordinates of its bottom-left and top-right corners.
[6-7]	Nothing new. We place a first heading for the leftmost chart, and assign the font definition to a variable, so that we can re-use it later.
[8]	This definition says that we will draw segments between successive (x,y) points.
[9]	The chart will be boxed, but with rounded corners and a drop shadow.
[10]	Plot a line using the global variable `BHBump`.
[12]	Define a second plotting region next to the first one, but slightly higher.
[13-14]	Place the second heading, using the font defined in [7].
[15]	Use the variable `Towns` to place labels. The matrix must be split.
[16]	One segment will be slightly offset from the pie. The distance is given in per cent of the pie radius. The vector will automatically be extended to match the number of segments.
[17-18]	Define non-standard colours, and use the same *Fill Style* as for the bar chart.
[19]	Use the same box as in [9].
[20-21]	Draw some random values, and view the result.

2.7 There is Much More To Explore!

We have not seen all the features of this fantastic tool. We encourage you to explore at least the following topics.

About pie charts .... `Rose`

`PieMarkers`

About multiple charts in a single picture .... `MultiTrellis`

`PYGS`

About representation of axes .... `Axes`

`MultiSec`

For 3-D demos, run the examples listed by .... `Perspectives`

Chapter X: Solutions

The solutions we propose in the following pages are not necessarily the "best" ones; perhaps you will find other solutions that we have never considered. APL is a very rich language, and due to the general nature of its primitive functions and operators there are always plenty of different ways to express different solutions to a given problem. Which one is "the best" depends on many things, for example the level of experience of the programmer, the importance of system performance, the required behaviour in border cases, the requirement to meet programming standards, and also personal preferences. This is one of the reasons why APL is so pleasant to teach and to learn!

Chapter B

B-1 For the moment we have only one method: `1⍴S`
A scalar has an empty shape, so we can create one like this: `⍬⍴V`

B-2 If `X` were numeric, its shape would be 4, so it is a text vector `'2 15 8 3'`

B-3 `THE CAT`, of course!

B-4 The values to replace are the entire 1st and 5th columns.
`Tab[1 2;1 5]← 21 45 78 11` would cause a `RANK ERROR`, because it is an attempt to replace a 2 by 2 matrix with a vector.
The right solution is: `Tab[1 2;1 5]←2 2⍴21 45 78 11`
Since we are replacing the entire columns we can also do the replacement like this: `Tab[;1 5]←2 2⍴21 45 78 11`

B-5

```
      X ← 1 2 9 11 3 7 8
      X[3 5] ← X[4 1]          ⇦ Item 4 (11) is copied to item 3,
      X                        ⇦ and item 1 (1) is copied to item 5.
1 2 11 11 1 7 8
      X[4 6] ← X[6 4]          ⇦ Items 4 and 6 are swapped
      X
1 2 11 7 1 11 8
```

B-6 To solve this, just notice that the 3rd item is 8, the 1st is 11, the 6th is 3, and so on.

The final value is: `11 2 8 15 9 3`

B-7 Find where the values appear in `Vec`: `6 3 2 10 8 5`

B-8 The shape of the result of indexing a vector is always equal to the shape of the index. Hence the shape of `Result` is equal to the shape of `Set` (`3 3`).

You must first calculate the value of `Set`:

```
4 3 6
9 1 5
7 3 4
```

Then replace each item of `Set` by the corresponding item of `Source`:

For example, in the first row, `4` is replaced by the 4th item (`3`), `3` is replaced by the 3rd item (`13`), 6 is replaced by the 6th item (`0`), and so on, giving this result:

```
3 13 0
2 10 9
7 13 3
```

B-9 There is no difference. Both are 3-item simple character vectors.

B-10 `V3` is a 6-item vector. Some items are numeric, some are characters; it is a *Mixed* vector

`V4` is a 4-item vector. It is a *Nested* array, since the 3rd item is an enclosed character vector.

B-11 Replacing `Two` (not `'Two'`) by `2`, one obtains: `2 2⍴2 2 '⍴' 'Two'`

And the result is a nested 2 by 2 matrix:

```
2   2
⍴  Two
```

Chapter C

C-1 Copy each expression to the APL session and execute them. If you are surprised by an answer, analyze the expression step by step, starting from the right. For example, for the first expression: `3×2⇨6`, `6≠6⇨0`, `2+0⇨2`, `3×2⇨6`. You should find:

```
6
12 6 1
5 5 6
7 ¯3 6
42
```

`⍬` (a scalar has an empty shape)

C-2

```
4 4
6 6
4 6
2 4 4
```

C-3

`1+⍴A`	is equivalent to: `1+(⍴A)`	the result is	`5`
`⍴A+1`	is equivalent to: `⍴(A+1)`	the result is	`4`
`1+⍳⍴A`	is equivalent to: `1+(⍳(⍴A))`	the result is	`2 3 4 5`
`⍳¯1+⍴A`	is equivalent to: `⍳(¯1+(⍴A))`	the result is	`1 2 3`
`⍳⍴A-1`	is equivalent to: `⍳(⍴(A-1))`	the result is	`1 2 3 4`

C-4

`3⌈¯1+⍳4`	the result is	`3 3 3 3`
`7⌊3⌈⍳9`	the result is	`3 3 3 4 5 6 7 7 7`
`1+5×1 4 3 2 5=⍳5`	the result is	`6 1 6 1 6`

C-5 `0=⍴⍴A`

C-6 `3+4×A≥B`

C-7 `(A≠0)⍴3×B≠0`

C-8

`∧` can be replaced by `×` or `⌊`
`∨` can be replaced by `⌈`

C-9

a)	`1 1 1 0 1 1`	e)	`1 0 1 0 0 1`
b)	`0 1 0 1 1 1`	f)	`0 0 0 1 0 0`
c)	`0 0 0 0 1 0`	g)	`0 0 1 0 1 0`
d)	`0 0 0 0 1 0`	h)	`1 0 0 1 1 0`

C-10

a) `1`
b) `1 0 0 1 0`
c) `1 1`
d) `2 1`

C-11 `+/Tex='e'` returns 5

C-12 The last test shows that `Z` is a 4 by 1 matrix. Its first 3 items are 1, 7 and 9, and because the sum is 20, the last item must be 3. We can create `Z` like this:

```
Z←4 1⍴1 7 9 3
```

C-13

```
8 0  7 5
0 7 ¯1 0
```

C-14 `(Tex='e')/⍳⍴Tex`

C-15 `((⍴Vec)⍴1 0)/Vec`

C-16 `⍴,Prod` or `×/⍴Prod`

C-17 `((Vec≥20)∧Vec<30)/Vec`

C-18 `Vec←20⌈Vec⌊30`

C-19

a)	`3+(5-(6+2)×4`	There are unbalanced parentheses.
b)	`121÷(⍳4)-3`	The 3rd item of `(⍳4)-3` is zero, and a division by zero is usually not accepted (see C-Spe-1).
c)	`(¯X+5)*2`	The high minus sign cannot be attached to a name `¯9` or `-X` would be valid; `¯X` is invalid.
d)	`⍴4 5 6+2 3-1`	One cannot add a 2-item vector to a 3-item vector
e)	`⍳4 0 ¯4+2 0 1`	The argument to *Iota* cannot be negative.

C-20 `12+11×⍳17`

C-21

First we must separate the codes from the quantities:	`M←((0.5×⍴Wanabuy),2)⍴Wanabuy`
Then search the products bought in the list of codes:	`Pos←PCodes⍳M[;1]`
And finally multiply prices by quantities and add:	`+/Prices[Pos]×M[;2]`

C-22

a) `Tickets~Sold`

b) `∨/~Winners∊Sold` or `0≠⍴Winners~Sold`

c) `+/Ours∊Winners` or `+/Winners∊Ours` The result is the same

d) `+/(Winners∊Ours)/Prizes`

In d) it is important to use (Winners∊Ours) rather than (Ours∊Winners), because the items of Winners correspond one-to-one to the items of Prizes, but the items of Ours have no relation to the items of Prizes.

C-23

```
(0=(⍳N)|N)/⍳N
```

Chapter D

D-1

```
     ∇ Z←X Extract Y
[1]    Z←Y[⍳X⌊⍴Y]
     ∇
```

D-2

```
     ∇ Z←X Ignore Y
[1]    Z←Y[(X⌊⍴Y)+⍳0⌈(⍴Y)-X]
     ∇
```

D-3

```
     ∇ Z←Reverse Y
[1]    Z←Y[1+(⍴Y)-⍳⍴Y]
     ∇
```

D-4

```
     ∇ Z←Totalise Y;sum
[1]    sum←+/[2]Y
[2]    Z←Y,[2]sum
[3]    sum←+/[1]Z
[4]    Z←Z,[1]sum
     ∇
```

D-5

```
     ∇ Z←Lengths Y;pos
[1]    pos←(Y=' ')/⍳⍴Y            ⇦ Positions of the blanks
[2]    Z←(pos,1+⍴Y)-(0,pos)       ⇦ Shift them and subtract
[3]    Z←Z-1                      ⇦ The blanks must not be counted
     ∇
```

D-6

```
     ∇ Z←X To Y;start
[1]    start←X-1
[2]    Z←start+⍳Y-start
     ∇
```

D-7

```
     ∇ Z←Frame Y;nr;nc
[1]    Z←'-',[1]Y,[1]'-'
[2]    Z←'|',[2]Z,[2]'|'
[3]    nr nc←ρZ                       ⇦ Number of rows, number of columns
[4]    Z[1,nr;1,nc]←'+'               ⇦ Second step
     ∇
```

You can obtain line drawing characters by pressing the *Ctrl* key in conjunction with the numeric keypad (Dyalog APL *Classic Edition*), or using ⎕UCS (*Unicode Edition*). The horizontal and vertical lines are ⎕UCS 9472 9474 and the four corners are ⎕UCS 9484 9488 9492 9496:

```
     ∇ Z←Frame2 Y;nr;nc
[1]    Z←(⎕UCS 9472),[1]Y,[1]⎕UCS 9472
[2]    Z←(⎕UCS 9474),[2]Z,[2]⎕UCS 9474
[3]    nr nc←ρZ
[4]    Z[1,nr;1,nc]←2 2ρ⎕UCS 9484 9488 9492 9496
     ∇
```

Note that it is necessary to arrange the corners in a 2 by 2 matrix.

D-8 The functions shown in D-7 above do not accept vectors because the second instruction tries to work on the second dimension of Z, and a vector has only one dimension. The solution is to transform the argument into a matrix. If it is a matrix, it should remain unchanged; if it is a vector, it should be transformed in a one-row matrix. There is a very simple solution using a function we have not explored yet, but we can achieve the same result as indicated in the first 3 instructions of the final function:

```
     ∇ Z←Frame Y;nr;nc;rank;shape
[1]    rank←ρρY                       ⇦ The rank of Y
[2]    shape←(1 1,ρY)[rank+1 2]       ⇦ Calculate the new shape
[3]    Z←shapeρY                      ⇦ Reshape Y into a matrix
[4]    Z←(⎕UCS 9472),[1]Z,[1]⎕UCS 9472
[5]    Z←(⎕UCS 9474),[2]Z,[2]⎕UCS 9474
[6]    nr nc←ρZ
[7]    Z[1 nr;1 nc]←2 2ρ⎕UCS 9484 9488 9492 9496
     ∇
```

D-9

```
     ∇ Y←X Switch1 Y;pos
[1]    pos←(Y=X[1])/⍳ρY               ⇦ The positions of the first character
[2]    Y[pos]←X[2]                    ⇦ Replace by the second character
     ∇
```

Note that the right argument and the result have the same name.

D-10 The "traditional" solution is very similar to `Switch1` shown in D-9 above:

```
∇ Y←X Switch2 Y;pos1;pos2
  pos1←(Y=X[1])/⍳⍴Y
  pos2←(Y=X[2])/⍳⍴Y
  Y[pos1]←X[2]
  Y[pos2]←X[1]
∇
```

However, there is a more elegant solution that uses the *Index Of* function:

```
∇ Z←X Switch3 Y;pos
  pos←(X,Y)⍳Y
  Z←(X[2 1],Y)[pos]
∇
```

This solution uses the technique we used in Chapter C, Section 12.2, to convert lower-case characters to upper-case.

D-11

```
 MaxPlace←{
  max←⌈/v←,⍵
  pos←v⍳max
  width←(⍴⍵)[2]
  row←⍕⌈pos÷width
  col←⍕1+width|pos-1
  'Greatest value: ',(⍕max),', in row ',row,', column ',col
  }
```

D-12 To convert a temperature `T`, one can apply the formula: `a+b×(T-c)` in which the coefficients `a b c` have the following values:

- For `F` to `C`   `0   (5÷9)  32`
- For `C` to `F`   `32   1.8   0`

Then, the function is easy to write:

```
∇ Z←X Convert Y;coefs;used
  coefs←2 3⍴0,(5÷9),32 32 1.8 0      ⇦ Create a matrix of coefficients
  used←coefs[1+'C'=Y[1];]            ⇦ Select the right row
  Z←used[1]+used[2]×X-used[3]        ⇦ Apply the formula
∇
```

D-13

```
∇ Z←LoopSum Y;n
  Z←0                 ⇦ Initialise the final sum to zero
  :For n :In Y        ⇦ Take the values one after the other
      Z←Z+n           ⇦ Add them to the sum
  :EndFor
∇
```

D-14

```
    ∇ Z←ReverLoop vec;letter
      Z←''
      :For letter :In vec
          Z←letter,Z
      :EndFor
    ∇
```

D-15

```
    ∇ Z←X SubSum Y;row;col;slices
      row col←⍴Y                      ⇦ Number of rows; number of columns
      slices←col÷X                    ⇦ Number of slices
      Z←((row×slices),X)⍴Y            ⇦ Move the slices one under the other
      Z←Z,+/Z                         ⇦ Catenate the sums
      Z←(row,col+slices)⍴Z            ⇦ Move back the slices
    ∇
```

D-16

```
    ∇ Z←X Sorry Y;index;max;num;pos;prev;sep;slice;tail;width
      pos←(X=Y,X)/⍳1+⍴Y               ⇦ Positions of separators
      tail←(width←⍴Y)⍴' '
      Z←(0,width)⍴''
      prev←max←0                      ⇦ Position of previous separator
      :For sep :In pos                ⇦ Current separator
          num←sep-prev+1              ⇦ Number of elements to take
          index←prev+⍳num             ⇦ Index of those elements
          slice←Y[index]
          prev←sep
          max←max⌈num                 ⇦ The longest piece found so far
          Z←Z,[1](slice,tail)[⍳width]
      :EndFor
      Z←Z[;⍳max]                      ⇦ Truncate Z
    ∇
```

D-17

```
    ∇ Y←Syracuse2 Y;Last;Next
      Y←,Y
      :While 1<Last←Y[⍴Y]          ⇦ This is an example of simple solution
          :If 0=2|Last                with a loop
              Y←Y,Last÷2
          :Else
              Y←Y,1+3×Last
          :EndIf
      :EndWhile
    ∇
```

There is also a recursive version:

```
     ∇ Y←Syracuse1 Y;Last;Next
       Y←,Y
       →(1=Last←Y[⍴Y])/0
       :If 0=2|Last
           Next←Last÷2
       :Else
           Next←1+3×Last
       :End
       Y←Syracuse1 Y,Next
     ∇
```

Chapter G

G-1

Using only *Take*:	`2 ¯3↑XG1`	`¯2 4↑XG1`	`3 ¯3↑3 4↑XG1`
Using only *Drop*:	`¯1 2↓XG1`	`1 ¯1↑XG1`	`1↓[2]¯1↓[2]XG1`

G-2

```
(1+⍴XG1)↑XG1
```

G-3

With a *Direct* function:

```
ShowVowels←{⍵,[0.5]' ↑'[1+⍵∊'aeiouy']}
```

With a *Procedural* function:

```
     ∇ Z←ShowVowels Y;index
       index←1+Y∊'aeiouy'
       Z←Y,[0.5]' ↑'[index]
     ∇
```

G-4

```
     ∇ Z←Contraction Y;dim
       dim←⍴Y
       Y←,Y
       Z←dim,(Y≠0)/Y,[0.5]⍳⍴Y
     ∇

     ∇ Z←Restore Y;dim
       Z←(×/dim←Y[;1])⍴0
       Y←0 1↓Y
       Z[Y[2;]]←Y[1;]
       Z←dim⍴Z
     ∇
```

G-5

```
     ∇ Y←X Whiten1 Y;u
[1]    ((Y∊X)/Y)←' '
     ∇
```

⇦ A traditional solution *not* using *Expand*.

```
     ∇ Z←X Whiten2 Y;bin
[1]    bin←~Y∊X
[2]    Z←bin\bin/Y
     ∇
```

⇦ A solution using *Compress* and *Expand*

G-6

```
     ∇ R←X Ontop Y;width;nb;title
[1]    width←¯1↑⍴Y←⍕Y
[2]    nb←0⌈⌈0.5×width-⍴X
[3]    title←width↑(nb⍴' '),X
[4]    R←title⍪'-'⍪Y
     ∇
```

G-7

```
You found
the right
solution
```

⇦ Of course!

G-8

```
     ∇ R←X Free Y;dim;mat;bin
[1]    dim←⍴Y←,Y
[2]    mat←(X,dim)⍴Y
[3]    mat←(¯1+⍳X)⌽mat
[4]    bin←(dim-X)↑∨⌿mat
[5]    R←bin⍳0
[6]    R×←R≤⍴bin
     ∇
```

[2] ⇦ Create a matrix by repeating the vector X times
[3] ⇦ Shift the rows with a *Rotate* function
[4] ⇦ An all-zero column contains the wanted series
[5] ⇦ We look for the first one
[6] ⇦ Return 0 if no zero-list was found

G-9

```
     ∇ R←X Split Y;Shape
[1]    Shape←⍴Y
[2]    Shape←X,(⌈Shape[1]÷X),Shape[2]
[3]    R←Shape⍴((×/2↑Shape),2↓Shape)↑Y
[4]    Shape←⍴R←2 1 3⍉R,' '
[5]    Shape←Shape[1],×/1↓Shape
[6]    R←Shape⍴R
     ∇
```

G-10

```
     ∇ R←X Expand Y;bin1;bin2;pos
[1]    bin1←X≠1↓X,0
[2]    pos←bin1/⍳⍴bin1
[3]    bin2←~(⍳⍴pos,X)∊pos+⍳⍴pos
[4]    R←bin2⍀⍕X,' ',Y
     ∇
```

Chapter I

We will use a function named `DISP` to display the results It draws boxes around an array like `DISPLAY`, but in a more compact form You can obtain it by: `)Copy Util DISP`

I-1

a) `A B C × 1 2 3`

```
┌─────┬─────────┬──────────┐
│1 2 3│8 10 12│21 24 27│
└─────┴─────────┴──────────┘
```

⇦ No surprise

b) `(10 20),A` `10 20 1 2 3` ⇦ This is a simple vector

c) `(10 20),A B`

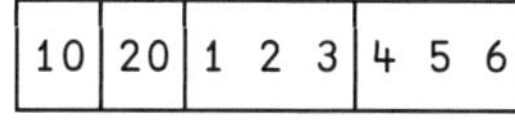

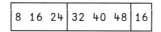

⇦ This one is nested

d) `A B 2 × C[2]`

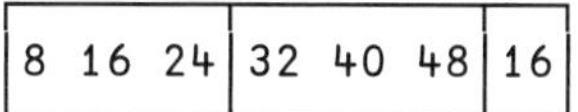

⇦ The three items in `A B 2` have each been multiplied by 8

e) `10×A 20×B` `LENGTH ERROR` ⇦ `A 20` has 2 items, and `B` has three!

I-2

a) `+/A B C`

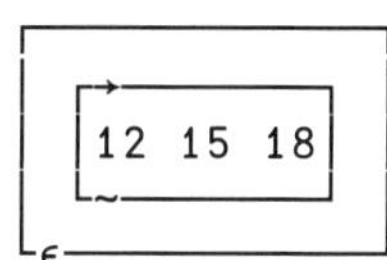

⇦ This is not a vector, but an enclosed vector, cf. Section 4.4.1. We used `DISPLAY`, as `DISP` would show the difference.

b) `+/¨A B C` `6 15 24` ⇦ This is a simple vector

c) `1 0 1/¨A B C`

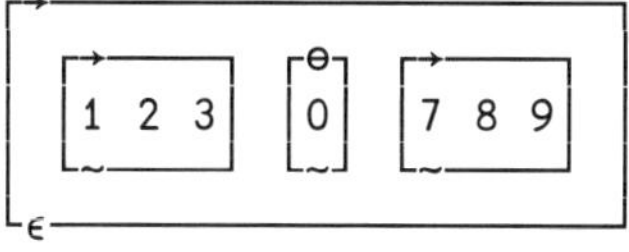

⇦ For this example `DISP` would give a misleading representation. This is why we used `DISPLAY`.

⇦ Take a look at Section I-3.2 if you need help to interpret the result.

d) `(A B C)⍳(4 5 6)` `4 4 4`

e) `1 10 3 ∊ A` `1 0 1`

f) `(⊂1 0 1)/¨A B C`

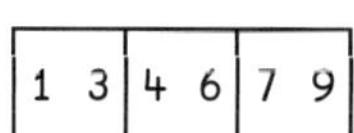

⇦ See Section I-3.2.

g) `1 10 3 ∊ A B C` `0 0 0`

I-3 `+/NA` is equivalent to `⊂ 1 + 2 + (2 2⍴3 4 5 6) + 7 + 8`

The result will be:

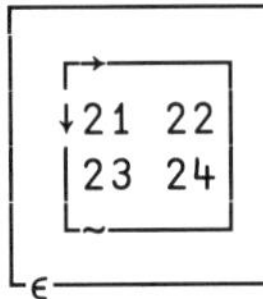

⇦ Don't forget: the reduction of a vector **always** returns a scalar. In this case it is an enclosed matrix.

`,/NA` is equivalent at `1 , 2 , (2 2⍴3 4 5 6) , 7 , 8`

The result will be:

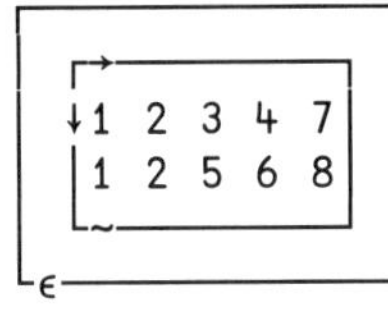

⇦ Start from the right, and execute only one catenation at a time.

I-4 We shall create a partition vector by comparing each code to the next one. The value of `¯1` (negative one) placed at the beginning creates a leading 1:

```
      ⎕←bin←I4Ref ≠ ¯1,¯1↓I4Ref
1 0 1 0 0 0 0 1 1 0 0 1 0
```

This vector will be used to break the vector into five blocks. Then a total can be made inside each block:

```
      +/¨ bin ⊂ I4Qty
13 39 10 152 19
```

I-5 A simple *Index Of* will suffice: `(↓I5Big)⍳(↓I5Small)`

I-6 `I6Text[⊃,/I6Start+⊂¯1+⍳5]` or `I6Text[,I6Start∘.+¯1+⍳5]`

I-7 `I6Text[¯1+⊃,/I6Start+⍳¨I6Long]`

Chapter J

J-1 This requires several steps. First, the function header will dispatch the argument into 3 variables:

```
      ∇ R←StudRefund(Rates Categories Expenses)
```

The new rates are obtained by subtracting each column from the column on its left. The first row (the limits) is dropped:

```
      newrates←1↓[1]0.01×Rates-1↓[2]Rates,0
```

An outer product compares the expenses to the three given limits, like in Section J-4.3.3:

```
limexp←Expenses∘.⌊Rates[1;]
```

This matrix can be multiplied by the new rates corresponding to the students' categories:

```
refund←+/newrates[Categories;]×limexp
```

The result is obtained by placing three vectors side by side. Here is the final function:

```
     ∇ R←StudRefund(Rates Categories Expenses);newrates;limexp;refund
[1]    newrates←1↓[1]0.01×Rates-1↓[2]Rates,0
[2]    limexp←Expenses∘.⌊Rates[1;]
[3]    refund←+/limexp×newrates[Categories;]
[4]    R←Expenses,Categories,[1.5]refund
     ∇
```

J-2

a)	`⌈/M`	⇨ `8 7 6`
b)	`⌊/+/M`	⇨ `16`
c)	`×/⌊/[1]M`	⇨ `0`
d)	`×/⍴M`	⇨ `15`

J-3

a)	`-\1 1 1 1 1 1`	⇨ `1 0 1 0 1 0`
b)	`-\5 4 3 2 1`	⇨ `5 1 4 2 3`
	This is equivalent to:	`5,(5-4),(5-4-3),(5-4-3-2),(5-4-3-2-1)`
c)	`×/+\6⍴1`	⇨ `720`

J-4

a)	`∧/ 1 1 1 0 1 1`	⇨ `0`
b)	`∧\ 1 1 1 0 1 1`	⇨ `1 1 1 0 0 0`
c)	`=/ 0 1 1 1 0 1 1`	⇨ `1`
d)	`=\ 0 1 1 1 0 1 1`	⇨ `0 0 0 0 1 1 1`

J-5 Just divide each value by the preceding one :

```
      res←7 14 70 210 840
      res÷1,¯1↓res
7 2 5 3 4
      ×\7 2 5 3 4                ⇦ Let us verify
7 14 70 210 840
```

J-6

```
+\N⍴1
```

J-7

```
     ∇ Z←Area Lengths;p
[1]    p←0.5×+/Lengths
[2]    Z←(p×.-0,Lengths)*0.5
     ∇
```

J-8 One can compare each value to all the other ones by this outer product: `V∘.=V`

The values are all different if the resulting binary matrix has only one 1 per row.

This can be verified like this: `∧/1=+/V∘.=V`

It can also be written like this: `1∧.=+/V∘.=V`

Using an *Inner Product*: `(V⍳V)∧.=⍳⍴V`

J-9 This expression takes two contiguous letters and compares them, all along the text:

The result will be: `0 0 1 0 0 0 0 0 1 0 0 1 0`

J-10 This can be solved using different techniques. In the first one, we compare the word and the text using an *Outer product*. We obtain a Boolean matrix similar to the following one:

```
      Word∘.=Text
1 0 0 0 0 0 0 0 1 0 0 1 0 0 0 0 0 0 0 0 0 0 0 0 0 0 0 0
0 1 0 0 0 0 0 0 0 1 0 0 0 0 0 0 0 0 0 0 0 0 0 0 0 0 0 0
0 0 1 0 0 0 0 0 0 0 1 0 0 0 0 0 0 0 0 0 0 0 0 0 0 0 1 0  etc ...
```

We can see a diagonal of 1's (in black) where the word appears. This would be complex to use: let us shift the rows of this matrix to place the 1's one under the other, using *Rotate*:

```
      0 1 2 ⌽ Word ∘.= Text
1 0 0 0 0 0 0 0 1 0 0 1 0 0 0 0 0 0 0 0 0 0 0 0 0 0 0 0
1 0 0 0 0 0 0 0 1 0 0 0 0 0 0 0 0 0 0 0 0 0 0 0 0 0 0 1
1 0 0 0 0 0 0 0 1 0 0 0 0 0 0 0 0 0 0 0 0 0 0 1 0 0 0 0   etc ...
```

Then it is really easy to find the positions of the word. This function can do it:

```
      ∇ R←X In1 Y;bin
[1]     bin←X∘.=Y
[2]     bin←(¯1+⍳⍴X)⌽bin
[3]     R←(∧⌿bin)/⍳⍴Y
      ∇
```

In this first solution, we used an *Outer product*; let us demonstrate a different solution using an *Inner product*:

```
      ∇ R←X In2 Y;bin;mat
[1]     mat←((⍴X),1+⍴Y)⍴Y          ⇦ Shift the letters
[2]     mat←¯1↓[2]mat              ⇦ Drop the last column
[3]     bin←X∧.=mat                ⇦ Find the word as we did in Section J-5.3.3
[4]     R←bin/⍳⍴bin                ⇦ Find the position(s)
      ∇
```

The first instruction repeats the text on several lines, but shifted one character left each time:

```
CAN YOU CANCEL MY FLIGHT ON AIR CANADA?C
AN YOU CANCEL MY FLIGHT ON AIR CANADA?CA
N YOU CANCEL MY FLIGHT ON AIR CANADA?CAN
```

Once the extra column on the right has been dropped, a simple inner product returns a Boolean vector, easy to process in a function like the one shown above.

J-11 As the first step, we must obtain the possible values for each argument, and sort them. After this, two *Outer products* produce two Boolean matrices. They can be combined using an *Inner product.*

```
    ∇ R←X CrossCount2 Y;ux;uy;binx;biny
      ux←∪X ⋄ ux←ux[⍋ux]
      uy←∪Y ⋄ uy←uy[⍋uy]
      binx←ux∘.=X
      biny←Y∘.=uy
      R←binx+.∧biny
      R←(' ',uy)⍪ux,R                ⇦ This is to add legends
    ∇
```

Chapter K

K-1 *n* ⊥ 12 34 60 77 19 is equivalent at: *n n n n n* ⊥ 12 34 60 77 19 whatever the value of *n*. If you refer to Section 2.1.3, you can calculate the *Weights* used in the conversion:

`⌽1,×\⌽1↓ 0 0 0 0 0` will result in: `0 0 0 0 1`

`⌽1,×\⌽1↓ 1 1 1 1 1` will result in: `1 1 1 1 1`

In the first case, 4 values are multiplied by zero, the last by 1. The result is: `¯1↑Vector`
In the second case, the values are multiplied by 1 and added. The result is: `+/Vector`

K-2

```
    ∇ Z←H2D Y;dec;mat
      mat←↑Y
      dec←'0123456789ABCDEF'⍳mat
      Z←16⊥⍉dec-1
    ∇
```

```
    ∇ Z←D2H Y;hex
      hex←⍉(4⍴16)⊤Y
      Z←↓'0123456789ABCDEF'[hex+1]
    ∇
```

K-3

a) `7+12?23`

b) `36+?4 6⍴11`

c) `¯6+5 2⍴10?11`

K-4 `0.0001×99+?15⍴801`

K-5 This expression returns a vector with a length in the range 11-20.
It contains integers in the same range, with possible duplicates.

K-6
```
List[5?⍴List]
```

K-7
```
2+?(5+?11)⍴38
```

K-8
```
(x*P)-.÷!P←2×0,⍳N
```

K-9

a) `(1○○÷4)*2` is the square of $(sin\ \pi/4)$ .... `0.5`
b) `2×0.5+¯2○1○0.5` is `2×0.5+`(*arccos sin* 1/2) .... `3.141592654`

K-10
```
      5 ¯7 2⌹3 3⍴1 ¯1 0 0 1 ¯2 ¯1 0 1
¯2 ¯7 ¯1.837075273E¯15
```
The last value should be zero (but isn't exactly due to the limited numeric precision of the representation of fractional numbers): `¯2 ¯7 0`

K-11 We must first solve the equations:
```
      ⎕←abc←13 ¯6 10⌹3 3⍴1 ¯1 3 ¯2 4 0 1 ¯2 2
2 ¯0.5 3.5
```
Then we can use the coefficients as shown in Section K-5.4.2
```
      3 5 ¯1+.×abc
¯1.865174681E¯14
```
This should also be `0`

Appendices

Appendix 1 : Scalar Functions

Function	Monadic
Identity	+ B
Negative	- B
Signum	× B
Reciprocal (inverse)	÷ B
Magnitude	| B
Floor	⌊ B
Ceiling	⌈ B
Exponential	* B
Natural Logarithm	⍟ B
Pi Times	○ B
Factorial	! B
Not	~ B
Roll	? B
Type	∊ B

Dyadic	Function
A + B	Add
A - B	Subtract
A × B	Multiply
A ÷ B	Divide
A | B	Residue
A ⌊ B	Minimum
A ⌈ B	Maximum
A * B	Power
A ⍟ B	Logarithm
A ○ B	Trigonometry
A ! B	Binomial
	Not a scalar function
	Not a scalar function
	Not a scalar function
A ∧ B	And / LCM
A ∨ B	Or / GCD
A ⍲ B	Nand (Not-And)
A ⍱ B	Nor (Not-Or)
A < B	Less
A ≤ B	Less or equal
A = B	Equal
A ≥ B	Greater or equal
A > B	Greater
A ≠ B	Not Equal / Xor

Appendix 2 : Invoking the Editor

The editor provided with Dyalog APL can be invoked by a double-clicking the name of an ***existing*** object. Then the editor knows the object type, and adapts its behaviour accordingly.

The system command `)ED` opens the editor to create a ***new*** object. By default a new function is created.

A prefix can be used to specify the type of the new object, according to the following table:

Prefix	Example	Object Created
none	`)ed new`	Function
∇	`)ed ∇ borscht`	Function
-	`)ed - papyrus`	Simple character matrix
→	`)ed → crouton`	Simple character vector
∊	`)ed ∊ grunt`	Nested vector of character vectors
⍟	`)ed ⍟ ns`	Namespace script
○	`)ed ○ myclass`	Class script
∘	`)ed ∘ bridge`	Interface script

It is possible to open several edit windows using a single command. For example:

```
)ed Tyrex -Moose
```

This command will open two edit windows. The first to create or edit a function named `Tyrex`, and the second to create a character matrix named `Moose`.

If a prefix is specified for the name of an already existing object, the prefix is ignored.

Appendix 3 : Selective Assignment

Selective assignment cannot be applied to *every* primitive function; only the following selection functions may be used. When appropriate, the functions can be used with an *Axis* specification.

Function	Name	Example
⍴	Reshape	`(6⍴Mat) ← Vec`
/ and ⌿	Compress / Replicate	`(bin/Vec1) ← Vec2`
↑	Take	`(2 2↑Mat) ← 2 2⍴⍳4`
↓	Drop	`(5↓Vec1) ← Vec2`
,	Ravel	`(,Mat) ← Vec`
⌽ and ⊖	Reverse, Rotate (monadic & dyadic)	`(⌽Vec1) ← 20↑Vec2`
⍉	Transpose (monadic and dyadic)	`(⍉Mat1) ← Mat2`
⊃	Disclose, Pick	`(((2 3)(4 1))⊃Nest) ← 'APL'`
\ and ⍀	Expand	`(bin\Vec1) ← Vec2`
⌷	Index	`(3 2⌷Mat) ← 0`

In the examples above:

- `Vec, Vec1, Vec2` represent vectors
- `Mat, Mat1, Mat2` represent matrices
- `bin` represents a Boolean vector

Appendix 4 : Dyalog APL Operators

The following table of primitive operators in Dyalog APL uses the following conventions:

- ■ and ● represent functions: primitive, user defined, or derived from another operator.
- X and Y represent the left and right arguments of the derived function, respectively.
- Fun represents a function.
- *n* is a numeric array used as argument to *Axis*, *Compose*, and *Power*.
- A distinction is made between the syntax of the operator itself, and the syntax of its derived functions (a monadic operator can generate a dyadic derived function). The syntax is indicated by M for *Monadic* and D for *Dyadic*.

Name	Syntax of Operator	Derived Function	Notation	Example
Each	M	M	■¨Y	⍴¨Y
		D	X ■¨ Y	3↑¨Y
Reduce	M	M	■/Y or ■⌿Y	+/Y
Reduce *n*-Wise		D	X ■/Y or X ■⌿Y	2+/Y
Axis (*)	D	M	■[*n*] Y	↓[1]Y
		D	X ■[*n*] Y	X,[1]Y
Scan	M	M	■\Y or ■⍀Y	×\Y
Outer Product	D	D	X ∘.●Y	X∘.<Y
Inner Product	D	D	X ■.●Y	X+.×Y
Commute	M	M	■⍨ Y	⍴⍨Y
		D	X ■⍨ Y	X/⍨Y
Compose form 1	D	M	■∘● Y	⍴∘⍴Y
form 2		M	*n*∘● Y	2 2∘⍴¨Y
form 3		M	■∘*n* Y	(*∘3)Y
form 4		D	X ■∘● Y	3↑∘⍴¨Y
Spawn	M	M	■& Y	Fun&5
		D	X ■& Y	2 Fun&5
Power	D	M	■⍣*n* Y or ■⍣● Y	(Spin⍣3)M
		D	X ■⍣*n* Y or X■⍣●Y	1+∘÷⍣=1

(*) Strictly speaking, axis is not an operator, cf. Chapter J, Section 2-3.

Appendix 5 : Identity Items

Reducing an empty vector `Y` using any function (`■/Y`) returns the identity item for the function, if it is defined. Here is the list of the identity items in Dyalog APL:

<table>
<tr><th>■</th><th>■/⍬</th><th>Remarks</th></tr>
<tr><td>+</td><td>0</td><td></td></tr>
<tr><td>×</td><td>1</td><td></td></tr>
<tr><td>-</td><td>0</td><td>Identity item on the right only</td></tr>
<tr><td>÷</td><td>1</td><td>Identity item on the right only</td></tr>
<tr><td>*</td><td>1</td><td>Identity item on the right only</td></tr>
<tr><td>⌈</td><td>¯1.7977E308</td><td>The smallest value supported by the system</td></tr>
<tr><td>⌊</td><td>1.7977E308</td><td>The largest value supported by the system</td></tr>
<tr><td>∧</td><td>1</td><td></td></tr>
<tr><td>∨</td><td>0</td><td></td></tr>
<tr><td><</td><td>0</td><td></td></tr>
<tr><td>≤</td><td>1</td><td></td></tr>
<tr><td>=</td><td>1</td><td></td></tr>
<tr><td>≥</td><td>1</td><td></td></tr>
<tr><td>></td><td>0</td><td></td></tr>
<tr><td>≠</td><td>0</td><td></td></tr>
<tr><td>∪</td><td>⍬ or ''</td><td></td></tr>
<tr><td>|</td><td>0</td><td>Identity item on the left only</td></tr>
<tr><td>!</td><td>1</td><td>Identity item on the left only</td></tr>
<tr><td>⊤</td><td>0</td><td>Identity item on the left only</td></tr>
<tr><td>⌽ and ⊖</td><td>0</td><td>Identity item on the left only</td></tr>
<tr><td>/ and ⌿</td><td>1</td><td>Identity item on the left only</td></tr>
<tr><td>\ and ⍀</td><td>1</td><td>Identity item on the left only</td></tr>
</table>

Functions that do not appear in this table will cause a `DOMAIN ERROR` if they are used to reduce an empty vector.

Appendix 6 : Event Numbers

Event Number	Event Message
0	Any event in the range 1-999
1	WS FULL
2	SYNTAX ERROR
3	INDEX ERROR
4	RANK ERROR
5	LENGTH ERROR
6	VALUE ERROR
7	FORMAT ERROR
10	LIMIT ERROR
11	DOMAIN ERROR
12	HOLD ERROR
16	NONCE ERROR
18	FILE TIE ERROR
19	FILE ACCESS ERROR
20	FILE INDEX
21	FILE FULL
22	FILE NAME ERROR
23	FILE DAMAGED
24	FILE TIED
25	FILE TIED REMOTELY
26	FILE SYSTEM ERROR
28	FILE SYSTEM NOT AVAILABLE
30	FILE SYSTEM TIES USED UP
31	FILE TIE QUOTA USED UP
32	FILE NAME QUOTA USED UP
34	FILE SYSTEM NO SPACE
35	FILE ACCESS ERROR - CONVERTING FILE
38	FILE COMPONENT DAMAGED

(Continued on the next page)

Event Numbers *(continued)*

Event Number	Event Message
52	FIELD CONTENTS RANK ERROR
53	FIELD CONTENTS TOO MANY COLUMNS
54	FIELD POSITION ERROR
55	FIELD SIZE ERROR
56	FIELD CONTENTS/TYPE MISMATCH
57	FIELD TYPE/BEHAVIOUR UNRECOGNISED
58	FIELD ATTRIBUTES RANK ERROR
59	FIELD ATTRIBUTES LENGTH ERROR
60	FULL-SCREEN ERROR
61	KEY CODE UNRECOGNISED
62	KEY CODE RANK ERROR
63	KEY CODE TYPE ERROR
70	FORMAT FILE ACCESS ERROR
71	FORMAT FILE ERROR
72	NO PIPES
84	TRAP ERROR
90	EXCEPTION
91	EXTERNAL DLL EXCEPTION
92	TRANSLATION ERROR
200 - 499	Reserved for distributed auxiliary processors
500 - 999	User-defined events
1000	Any event in the range 1001-1006
1001	Stop vector
1002	Weak interrupt
1003	INTERRUPT
1005	EOF INTERRUPT
1006	TIMEOUT
1007	RESIZE

Appendix 7 : System Variables and Functions

ND .... Not documented in this tutorial
OOP .... Documented in Object Oriented Programming brochures
xxx .... Functions grouped and described in a same chapter

Symbol	Description	Pages
⎕A	Upper-case Alphabet (from A to Z)	505
⎕AI	Account Information	490
⎕ARBIN	Arbitrary Input (obsolete)	ND
⎕ARBOUT	Arbitrary Output (obsolete)	ND
⎕AT	Function Attributes	498
⎕AV	Atomic Vector (obsolete in the *Unicode Edition*)	433; 503; 573
⎕AVU	Atomic Vector Unicode	503
⎕BASE	Base Class Implementation	OOP
⎕CLASS	Reference to Classes or Interfaces	OOP
⎕CLEAR	Clear Workspace	480
⎕CMD	Execute a DOS or UNIX command	507
⎕CR	Canonical Representation	494
⎕CS	Change Space	581; 585
⎕CT	Comparison Tolerance	427; 501
⎕CY	Copy a Workspace	479
⎕D	Digits	505
⎕DF	Display Form	591
⎕DIV	Division Control	140
⎕DL	Delay	503
⎕DM	Diagnostic Message	241
⎕DQ	DeQueue	612
⎕DR	Data Representation	554
⎕ED	Edit	160; 493
⎕EM	Event Message	519
⎕EN	Event Number	249; 519

Symbol	Description	Pages
⎕EX	Expunge (Delete)	486
⎕EXCEPTION	Most recent .Net exception	OOP
⎕EXPORT	Export a defined function or operator	601
⎕FIX	Fix a class from a script	578; 588
⎕FMT	Format	280
⎕FX	Fix a function	496
⎕F*xxx*	Component file management	536; 547
⎕INSTANCES	Current instances of a class	OOP
⎕IO	Index Origin	322; 426; 489
⎕KL	Key Labels	ND
⎕LC	Line Counter	241
⎕LOAD	Load a workspace	478
⎕LOCK	Lock a function	497
⎕LX	Latent eXpression	477
⎕MAP	Associates a mapped file with an array	ND
⎕ML	Migration Level (IBM APL2 compatibility)	366; 372
⎕MONITOR	Execution monitoring	514
⎕NA	Name Association	675; 686
⎕NC	Name Category of objects	208; 234; 485
⎕NEW	Create a new instance of a class	296; 599; 677
⎕NL	Name List	483; 597
⎕NQ	En-Queue	640
⎕NR	Nested Representation	494
⎕NS	Create a Namespace	578; 592
⎕NSI	Namespace Indicator	270
⎕NULL	Null Item	505; 594; 681
⎕N*xxx*	Native file management	559
⎕OFF	Quit APL	507
⎕OR	Object Representation	495; 511
⎕PATH	Namespace search path	586; 594
⎕PFKEY	Define Programmable Function Keys	491
⎕PP	Print Precision	83; 488
⎕PW	Page Width	508

Symbol	Description	Pages
⎕REFS	Cross References	498
⎕RL	Random Link	466
⎕RTL	Response Time Limit	513
⎕SAVE	Save the active workspace	481; 510
⎕SE	Session Namespace	594
⎕SH	Execute a UNIX or DOS command	507
⎕SHADOW	Shadow (localise) a name	230; 497
⎕SI	State Indicator	241
⎕SIGNAL	Signal an Event	530; 691
⎕SIZE	Memory space occupied by an object	487
⎕SRC	Returns the script used to define a class	602
⎕STACK	SI Stack	ND
⎕STATE	State of an object	ND
⎕STOP	Set/Query breakpoints	265
⎕SV*xxx*	Shared variable management	ND
⎕S*xxx*	Screen management in character mode	ND
⎕TC	Terminal Control (obsolete)	504
⎕THIS	Reference to the current namespace	581
⎕TRACE	Set/Query trace points	265
⎕TRAP	Trap Events	522; 530
⎕TS	Time Stamp	488
⎕TSYNC	Thread Synchronisation	418
⎕T*xxx*	Multi-Threading management	ND
⎕UCS	Unicode Conversions	504
⎕USING	.Net namespace search path	296
⎕VFI	Verify and Fix Input	512
⎕VR	Visual Representation (Vector Representation)	159; 218; 495
⎕WA	Workspace Available	482
⎕WSID	Set/Query the active workspace name	476
⎕WX	Expose Windows object properties	ND
⎕W*xxx*	Graphic User Interface (GUI) management	605
⎕XSI	Extended State Indicator	269
⎕XT	External variable query	566

Appendix 8 : System Commands

Some commands, explained in other specialised brochures, are not developped in this tutorial. They are mentioned below just for information (empty cells).

Command	Description	Pages
)CLASSES	Lists the APL classes in the active workspace.	
)CLEAR	Returns to an original empty workspace.	72 ; 480
)CMD	Submits an operating system command; equivalent to)SH.	*See*:)SH
)CONTINUE	Saves the active workspace as CONTINUE and exits APL.	511
)COPY	Copies all or selected objects from a saved workspace into the active workspace.	76; 479
)CS	Changes Namespace.	581
)DROP	Deletes a library workspace.	79
)ED	Invokes the Editor.	154; 493
)ERASE	Deletes objects from the active workspace.	72; 486; 509
)EVENTS	Lists the events that the current GUI namespace may generate.	
)FNS	Lists global functions in the active workspace.	72; 482; 509
)HOLDS	Lists the tokens acquired or requested by :Hold.	
)INTERFACES	List the currently active interfaces.	
)LIB	Lists saved workspaces.	73; 480
)LOAD	Replace the active workspace by a saved workspace.	73; 478
)METHODS	Lists the methods in the current namespace.	
)NS	Create a global namespace/ Query the name of the current namespace.	579
)OBS	List the global namespaces in the active workspace. Synonym:)OBJECTS.	483; 579
)OFF	Quit APL.	78; 507
)OPS	Lists global operators in the active workspace.	482
)PCOPY	Like)COPY, but does not overwrite existing objects.	76; 480
)PROPS	Lists the properties of the current namespace.	
)RESET	Clears the execution stack.	249; 250
)SAVE	Saves the active workspace to disk.	73; 481
)SH	Submits an operating system command; equivalent to)CMD.	507
)SI	State Indicator.	241
)SINL	State Indicator with Name List.	269
)TID	Switches to suspended thread, or lists the current thread number.	
)VARS	Lists global variables in the active workspace.	72; 482; 509
)WSID	Query / Set the identity of the active workspace.	476
)XLOAD	Load a workspace without executing its *Latent Expression*.	478

Appendix 9 : Symbolic Index

In the following table: X and Y represent the left and right arguments, respectively
■ and ◆ represent any primitive, defined, or derived dyadic function

Symbol	Description	Pages
	Functions	
+ Y	Identity	96
X + Y	Plus	90
− Y	Negative	97
X − Y	Subtract	90
× Y	Signum	97
X × Y	Multiply	90
÷ Y	Reciprocal (inverse)	97
X ÷ Y	Divide	92
* Y	Exponential	97
X * Y	Power	92
⌈ Y	Ceiling (round-up)	98
X ⌈ Y	Maximum	92
⌊ Y	Floor (round down, truncate)	98
X ⌊ Y	Minimum	92
| Y	Absolute value	98
X | Y	Residue	94; 145
X < Y	Less	93
X ≤ Y	Less or Equal	93
X = Y	Equal	93
X ≥ Y	Greater or Equal	93
X > Y	Greater	93
X ≠ Y	Not Equal / Exclusive Or (XOR)	93; 100

Symbol	Description	Pages
⍴ Y	Shape of	50; 52
X ⍴ Y	Reshape	47; 86
~ Y	Not	100
X ~ Y	Without	102
∊ Y	Type of / Enlist	357; 369
X ∊ Y	Membership	99; 127
X ∨ Y	Or / Greater Common Divisor	100; 106; 450
X ∧ Y	And / Lower Common Multiple	100; 106; 451
X ≠ Y	Exclusive Or (XOR) / Not Equal	93; 100
X ⍱ Y	Not-Or (Nor)	141
X ⍲ Y	Not-And (Nand)	141
, Y	Ravel	132; 143
X , Y	Catenate/Laminate along the last axis	113; 305; 322
X ⍪ Y	Catenate/Laminate along the first axis	117
X / Y	Compress/Replicate along the last axis	120
X ⌿ Y	Compress/Replicate along the first axis	121
⍳ Y	Index generator	125; 142
X ⍳ Y	Index Of	121; 127
⌷ Y	Collection of objects	678
X ⌷ Y	Index function (*Squad*)	62; 352
⍕ Y	Format, default presentation	276
X ⍕ Y	Format, specified presentation	277; 295
⍎ Y	Execute	233; 273; 292
↑ Y	Mix (nested arrays)	354; 356
X ↑ Y	Take	299; 303
↓ Y	Split (nested arrays)	354
X ↓ Y	Drop	299; 303
X \ Y	Expand along the last axis	310
X ⍀ Y	Expand along the first axis	311
⌽ Y	Reverse along the last axis	312
⊖ Y	Reverse along the first axis	312

Symbol	Description		Pages
X ⌽ Y	Rotate along the last axis		314
X ⊖ Y	Rotate along the first axis		314
⍉ Y	Transpose		312
X ⍉ Y	Dyadic transpose		316; 322
⍋ Y	Grade Up		431
X ⍋ Y	Grade Up with explicit ordering		434
⍒ Y	Grade Down		431
X ⍒ Y	Grade Down with explicit ordering		434
X ⍷ Y	Find		435
X ⊥ Y	Decode		436; 463
X ⊤ Y	Encode		436; 463
? Y	Roll	Random numbers with repetition	445; 466
X ? Y	Deal	Random numbers without repetition	445; 466
⍟ Y	Natural logarithm		447
X ⍟ Y	Base X logarithm		447
! Y	Factorial / Gamma function		448; 468
X ! Y	Binomial		448; 468
○ Y	Y times Pi		449
X ○ Y	Circular and Hyperbolic trigonometry		449
⌹ Y	Domino: Matrix inverse		453; 468
X ⌹ Y	Domino: Matrix divide		454; 468
X ∩ Y	Set Intersection		451
∪ Y	Unique		131
X ∪ Y	Set Union		451
⊂ Y	Enclose		332
X ⊂ Y	Partition / Partitioned Enclose		365
⊃ Y	Disclose / First		333; 357
X ⊃ Y	Pick		361; 376
≡ Y	Depth		339
X ≡ Y	Match		341
X ≢ Y	Natch (Not-Match)		341

Special syntax		
Symbol	Description	Pages
)	Prefix of System Commands	72; 518
( )	Force execution	53; 95
¯	Minus sign for negative numbers	43
' '	Quotes, character constant delimiters	53
E	Exponent indicator in number representation	83
⍬	Zilde; empty numeric vector	134
←	Assignment arrow	44; 325
→	Branch arrow	186; 231
⍺/⍺⍺	Left argument of a Direct function/Direct Operator	112; 421
⍵/⍵⍵	Right argument of a Direct function/Direct Operator	112; 421
⍝	Comment sign (Lamp)	205
⋄	Diamond; statement separator	205
;	Index separator or local name separator	59; 157
[ ]	Indexing / Axis	56
{ }	Curly braces; optional argument/result of a function	112
∇	Del (Carrot); function definition delimiter	159; 217; 695217
∆ _ ⍙	Allowed letters in names	45
:	Control structure prefix / Label suffix	168; 186
⍞	Character input / Bare output	204; 235
⎕	Evaluated input / Session output	196; 203
⎕	Prefix of "distinguished" names (system fns and vars)	159; 474
#	The root namespace	604

Operators (see Appendix 4 for a more detailed description)		
Symbol	Description	Pages
■/ Y	Reduce along the last axis	104; 424
■⌿ Y	Reduce along the first axis	111; 424
X ■/ Y	*n*-Wise Reduce along the last axis	380
X ■⌿ Y	*n*-Wise Reduce along the first axis	380
■\ Y	Scan along the last axis	383
■⍀ Y	Scan along the first axis	383
[ ]	Axis operator (*)	143; 382
∘.	Outer product	386
.	Inner product	394
¨	Each	342; 346
∘	Compose	410
⍨	Commute	414
⍣	Power operator	234; 415 ; 427
&	Spawn operator	418

(*) Strictly speaking, axis is not an operator, cf. Chapter J, Section 2-3.

INDEX

This index contains only entries for the words used throughout the book.

For System Functions and Variables	like ⎕TS or ⎕ML	Refer to Appendix	**7**
For Commands like	like)Save or)Load	Refer to Appendix	**8**
For Symbols	like ⍴ or ⌹	Refer to Appendix	**9**

A

Absolute Value 98
Access Control Matrix 546
Account Information 490
Active Workspace 72
Alphabet & Digits 505
Ambivalent 148, 208
And (function) 100
AndIf (flow control) 170
APL Language Bar 34
APL-Excel Communication 198
Aplnid (user number) 540
Apostrophes 54
Area 406
Arguments 152
Arrays of Items 47
Arrays of Refs 592
Assignment Arrow 44
Associated Files 37
Atomic Vectors 503
Auto Complete 39
Axis Specification 109, 110, 114, 382

B

Banana 72
Bar Chart 390
Bar Charts (RainPro) 740
Bare Output (Quote-Quad) 235
Beta (function) 468
Binary Algebra 100
Binary Data 99
Binomial 448
Branch Arrow 167
Break Points 262, 265
Buffering Considerations 571

C

Call-Back Functions (GUI) 613
Canonical Representation 494
Can't Fix (error) 257
Carrot (or Del) Delimiter 159
Case / CaseList (flow control) 174
Catenate 113
Ceiling (round-up) 98
Change Space 581, 585
Character Arrays 53
Chipmunk Idiom 365
Circle (function) 449
Circular Trigonometry 449
Classic Edition 31, 433, 503
Code Points 504
Colon 193
Colon (prefix / suffix) 168, 181, 186
Colours (GUI) 633
Comma *See* Ravel *or* Catenate

Commands 71, 473
Comment / Uncomment Lines 224
Comments 205
Commute 414
Comparison Tolerance 501
Component Files 535
Component Information 540
Compose 410
Compression (Compress) 118, 345
Concatenation (Concatenate) 113
Configurate the Tracer 242, 261
Continue (flow control) 181
Continue (system command) 511
Control Structures 167
Coordinate System (GUI) 606
Cube 51
Curve Fitting 460
Cutback (Trap action code) 523

D

Data Representation 554
Date & Time 488
Deal (dyadic ?) 445
Debugging 500
Decode 436, 463
Default Left Argument 215
Del (or Carrot) Delimiter 159
Delay 503
Delete Objects 486
Delete Variables/Functions 72
Delta 45
Depth 339, 374
Derived Functions 141, 377
Destructive Copy 76
D-Fns 147
Diagnostic Message 241
Diagonal Sections 323
Diamond (Statement Separator) 205
Digits 505
Direct (Dynamic) Functions 147
Direct (Dynamic) Operators 421
Direct Functions (multi-lines) 213
Direct Functions (single-line) 152
Disclose 333
DISP Utility Function 65
Disperse (SALT) 698
Display Form (namespaces) 591
DISPLAY Utility Function 66, 336
Distributed Prefix/Suffix 590
Distribution Rules 599
Divide 44
Division by Zero 92
Division Control 140
Domain Error 255
Domino 452, 468
Dot (Outer / Inner products) 386, 396
Dot (root object) 604
Drop 299
Duplicated values 131
Dyadic 89, 148
Dyalog Configuration Box 151
Dyalog Explorer 594
Dyalog File extension 694
Dyalog Manuals 40
Dynamic (Direct) Functions 148

E

Each 342
Edit Objects 493
ElseIf (flow control) 172
Empty Arrays 70, 337
Empty Vectors 134
Enclose 332
Encode 436
Endless Loops 182
Enlist 369, 374
Erase Objects 486
Event Default Processing 622
Event Handling 517
Event Message 519
Event Number 249, 519
Event Simulation 530
Event Simulation (GUI) 640
Event Trapping 500, 518
EventList (GUI) 670
Events 612
Events Queue 612, 640
Excel-APL Interface 676
Exclusive Or (function) 100
Execute 273, 292
Execute (Trap action code) 523
Execution Monitoring 514
Expand 310
Explicit Result 207

Exponential 97
Exponential Representation 83
Export Functions (namespaces) 601
Extended State Indicator 269
External Variables 566

F

Factorial 448
Fibonacci 416
File Extensions 75
File Hold Queue 551
File Journaling 571
File Processing 535
File Properties 571
Fill Items 120, 301, 358
Find / Search 435
First 357, 374
Fixpoint 427
Floor (round-down) 98
Flow Control (modern) 167
Flow Control (traditional) 186
Fonts (GUI) 633, 637
For / In (flow control) 176
Format 276
Format (function) 194
Format Qualifiers & Affixtures 288
Format Specifications 282
Format System Function 280
Fractional Axis 143, 306, 427
Frames (NewLeaf) 715
Function Attributes 498
Function Editor 220
Function Fix (creation) 496
Function Input/Output 193
Function Lock 497
Function Representations 493

G

Gallery (NewLeaf) 718
Gamma (function) 468
Garbage Collector 482
GCD 450
Generalised Arrays 331
Global Variables 157, 197
Golden Mean 413
GoTo (flow control) 181
Grade Up/Down 431
Greatest Common Divisor 450
Grid Object (GUI) 646
Guards 215
GUI (Graphical User Interface) 603

H

Hash (root object) 604
Header of a function 154
High Minus 43
Host-System Commands 507
HTML Tags (NewLeaf) 735
Hyperbolic Trigonometry 449

I

Identity 96
Idiom 130
Idioms 130
If (flow control) 169
Implicit Result 207
Import Objects 479
Index Error 254
Index Function 62
Index Generator 125, 142
Index Of (function) 121, 127
Index Origin 426, 489
Indexing 56
Indexing Arrays 58
Indexing Vectors 56
InEach (flow control) 236
Inflate Values 385
Inner Product 394
Input Buffer 39
Input/Output Methods 193
Interface with Excel 676
Internal References 498
Internal Representation 572
Interrupts (Weak / Strong) 183
Intersection 369, 451
Inverse 97
Inverse Function 417, 429
Invoking the Editor 160
Invoking the Tracer 258
Iota *Also see* Index Generator
Iota (Index Generator) 125
Iota (Position / Index Of) 121

J

Jot 265, 386

K

Key Combinations 35

L

Label 181
Laminate 305, 322
Lamp (Comment symbol) 205
Latent Expression 477
LCM 450
Leading/Trailing Blanks 385
Least Squares Fitting 457
Leave (flow control) 181
Left Arrow 44
Left Inverse of a Matrix 468
Length Error 253
Line Counter 242
Linear Regression 457
List of Functions 159
List of Variables 72
Load a WS 74, 478
Local Names 156
Local sub-Functions 216
Localise Names 224
Logarithms 447
Loop Control 231
Loops (conditional) 178
Loops (predefined) 176
Lowest Common Multiple 451

M

Magnitude 98
Match & Natch 341
Matrix 51
Matrix Division 455
Matrix Inverse 453
Matrix Product 394
Maximum 92
Membership 99, 127
Memory Compaction 482
Memory Space Available 482
Menus (GUI) 644
Merge Workspaces (copy) 76, 479
MethodList (GUI) 670
Migration Level 366, 372
Minimum 92
Min-Max Lines (RainPro) 750
Mirror (Reverse) 312
Mix 354, 374
Mixed Arrays 63
Modified Assignment 325
Monadic 89, 148
Monadic Index Function 87
Monadic Scalar Functions 96
Monitor 514
Multi-dimentional Arrays 49
Multiple Assignment 46, 326
Multiplication Table 386
Multiply 44
Multi-Threading 418

N

Naked Trace 258
Name Association 686
Name Category 208, 234, 485
Name Class *See* Name Category
Name List 483
Name Shadowing 497
Namespace References 588
Namespace Search Path 586
Namespaces 577
Nand (function) 141
Natch (Not-Match) 342
Native Files 535, 559
Negative Function 97
Negative values 43
Negative Values Encoding/Decoding 463
Nested Arguments & Result 211
Nested Arrays 64, 102, 331
Nested Representation 494
Neutralise the Traps 530
NewLeaf 714
Next (Trap action code) 524
Niladic 148
Niladic Arrow 231
Nor (function) 141
Not (function) 100
Not Saved (error) 257
Not-And (function) 141
Not-Match 342
Not-Or (function) 141

Null Item 505
N-Wise Reduce 380

O

Object Reprcsentation 495, 511
Object Size 487
OLE 675
Operators 105, 377
Or (function) 100
Orange 449
Order of Evaluation 94
OrIf (flow control) 170
Outer Product 386
Overtaking 301

P

Page Designer (NewLeaf) 726
Page Width 508
Partition 365, 374
Pass Numbers 547, 570
Pass-Through Value 62
PDF Format 714
Perimeter 406
Pervasive Functions 103, 346
PFK 491
Pi (trigonometry) 449
Pick 361, 376
Pie Chart (RainPro) 755
PNG Output 739
Polar Representation (RainPro) 753
Polygn Area & Perimeter 406
Polynomials 442
Position (function) 121
Power Function 44, 92
Power Operator 415
Primitive Functions 89
Print Precision 488
Print your experiments 37
Printer Object (GUI) 661
Printers (GUI) 637, 661
Procedural Functions 147, 154
Programmable Function Keys 491
Properties (GUI) 604
PropList (GUI) 669
Protected Copy 76, 480
Prototype 358
Pseudo Right-Inverse of a Matrix 470

Q

Quad (Evaluated Input) 203
Quad (symbol) 196
Quiet Load 478
Quit APL 78, 507
Quote (delimiter) 53
Quote-Quad (Character Input) 204

R

RainPro 738
Random Link 466
Randomised Values 444
Rank 50
Rank Error 254
Ravel 85, 132
Ravel with Axis 143
Read/Write Text Files 199
Reciprocal 97
Recursion 217
Reduction 104, 350
Reduction of Empty Vectors 425
Reformat a Function 224
Refs 588
Refs in a function 498
Relationship Functions 93
Remainder 94
Repeat (flow control) 178
Replay Input 223
Replication (Replicate) 120
Representation of Values 554
Representation of Variables 557
Reset the State Indicator 250
Reshape 47
Residue 94, 145
Reverse 312
Rho 47
Right Arrow 167
Right-align Text 443
Right-to-Left Evaluation 95
Roll (monadic ?) 445
Root Objcct 604
Root Object (GUI) 636
Rotate 314
Round Up/Down 98

S

SALT 693
Save a WS 74, 481
Scalar 51
Scalar Dyadic Functions 90
Scan 383
Scattered Points (RainPro) 744
Scientific Representation 83, 295
Script Files (SALT) 694
Scroll Back/Forward 39
Search / Find 435
Search Path 74, 586
Search Tool 253
Select (flow control) 174
Selective Assignment 327, 364
Semi-colon 59
Session Log 38
Session Namespace 594
Set Union/Intersection 451
Sets of Equations 454
Settings (SALT) 698, 709
Shadowed Names 230, 497
Shape 50
Shape of a Result 84, 111
Shape of an Array 47
Shared Component Files 544
Shortest Route in a Graph 401
Show/Hide Line Numbers 224
Shy Result 210, 216
Signum 97
Size of Objects 487
Sorting Data 431
Source-Code Management 693
Spawn 418
Special Notations 111, 117, 121
Special Syntax 420
Split 354, 374
Squad 62, 678
Startup Expression 477
State Indicator 241
Statement Separator (Diamond) 205
Stop (Trap action code) 523
Stops 262
Stops (Break points) 262, 265
Strand Notation 64, 331
Strong Interrupt 183
Styles (NewLeaf) 718
Synonyms 218
Syntax Error 256
System Commands 72, 473
System Interfaces 473
System Variables/Functions 473

T

Table 51
Take 299
Target (SALT) 698
Terminal Control 374, 504
Text Editor 160, 220
Threads 205, 418
Time Limit 513
Time Stamp 488
Trace Points 265
Tracing Call-Back Functions 628
Transpose (dyadic) 316, 322
Transpose (monadic) 312
Trap 520
Trigonometry 449
Type 302, 358, 374

U

UK APL Keyboard 35
Underscore 45
Underscored Letters 45
Undo / Redo 222
Unicode Conversions 504
Unicode Edition 31, 433, 504
Union 369, 451
Unique (function) 132
Universal Character Set 504
Unnamed D-Fns 153
Unnamed Namespace 579
Until (flow control) 178
US APL Keyboard 36
User Identity 545
User-Defined Events (GUI) 640
User-Defined Functions 89
User-Defined Operators 421

V

Valence of a Function 207, 499
Value Error 252
Variable/Function Names 45

Vector 51
Vector Notation 64, 331
Vector Representation 495
Verify & Fix Input 512
Version Management (SALT) 702
Visual Representation 159

W

Weak Interrupt 183
While (flow control) 178
Windows Language Bar 32
With (control structure) 591, 609
Without (function) 102
Workspace 36, 72
Workspace Explorer 600
Workspace Identification 77, 476
Workspace Management 475
Workspace Search Path 74, 478
WS 72
WS Full (error) 256

X

Xor (function) 100

Z

Zilde 126